E G L I

ANTHROPOLOGICAL ESSAYS

Books by Oscar Lewis

THE EFFECTS OF WHITE CONTACT UPON BLACKFOOT CULTURE

ON THE EDGE OF THE BLACK WAXY

LIFE IN A MEXICAN VILLAGE: TEPOZTLÁN RESTUDIED

VILLAGE LIFE IN NORTHERN INDIA

FIVE FAMILIES: MEXICAN CASE STUDIES IN THE CULTURE OF POVERTY

TEPOZTLÁN, VILLAGE IN MEXICO

THE CHILDREN OF SÁNCHEZ: AUTOBIOGRAPHY OF A MEXICAN FAMILY

PEDRO MARTÍNEZ: A MEXICAN PEASANT AND HIS FAMILY

LA VIDA: A PUERTO RICAN FAMILY IN THE CULTURE OF POVERTY—
SAN JUAN AND NEW YORK

A STUDY OF SLUM CULTURE: BACKGROUNDS FOR LA VIDA

A DEATH IN THE SÁNCHEZ FAMILY

ANTHROPOLOGICAL ESSAYS

ANTHROPOLOGICAL ESSAYS

· Oscar Lewis ·

Random House

NEW YORK

For my wife, Ruth, my son Gene and my daughter Judy

PREFACE

I want to thank my friend and publisher, Jason Epstein, for his suggestion that I bring together in a single volume some of my anthropological papers which were scattered in various journals and books and therefore not readily accessible to the general reader. The twenty-four essays in this volume were written over a period of twenty-five years, from 1941 to 1966, and reflect the range and variety of subject matter, methods, style, and sense of problem in my professional work.

Twenty-one of the essays are based upon my own field work experience and three upon an analysis of anthropological literature and historical documents. These essays deal with problems of technology, economics, social organization factionalism, family dynamics, culture and personality, and the urbanization process. Two papers deal with the Blackfoot Indians in the United States and Canada, nine with peasant communities in Mexico and India, two with American farmers, one with a Puerto Rican townsman, and seven with the urban scene in Mexico City, New York, and San Juan, Puerto Rico. The transition in my work from the study of tribal societies to the study of peasants and urban societies reflects a major trend in contemporary anthropology, and one to which I have contributed in my own way.

In rereading these essays it now seems clear to me that as a young graduate student in the late 1930's, I was deeply skeptical of the authentic explanatory power of theories then current in anthropology, with their heavy commitment to some form of an equilibrium model of society and the strong element of what Marvin Harris has recently called "cultural idealism." As a student of Ruth Benedict, I admired her writing and her conceptual powers, especially her search for some larger patterns and themes which would organize and explain the mass of detail, of custom and belief, which appeared in the monographs of anthropologists. At the same time I had reservations about the accuracy of her cultural configurations which played down the role of economic factors and which stressed homogeneity at the expense of the range of variation of behavior and values found in even the simplest tribe.

I suspect that both the choice of problem and the methods I have developed in my field work represent a reaction against some of these trends. My skepticism, which persisted through the fifties and to the present time, led me to formulate a cautious, eclectic and empirical strategy for the recording and analysis of socio-cultural phenomena, a strategy which gave considerable attention to the material conditions of life, economics, poverty, conflict, exploitation and social injustice. On the whole, I found conflict theory more productive of insight and understanding than consensus theory. Moreover, my theoretical position in anthropology has a good deal in common with Harris's cultural materialism. My major disagreement with Harris is that there is very little room for the human element in his system of environmental and techno-economic determinism. I think of myself rather as an eclectic materialist.

Throughout my career as an anthropologist I have sought to integrate approaches to the study of man and society which too often have been viewed as contradictory, but which have always seemed to me to be complementary. For example, I have tried to combine both the scientific and the humanistic approaches in my work as well as the historical or diachronic and the functional or synchronic. A good deal of the discussion in the literature as to the difference between the approaches of science and history strikes me as trivial. Any science of society worth its name must be a historical science.

I have organized the essays in this volume into five parts. The articles in Part I deal with problems of field methods and anthropological theory which have been among my major interests, both in my many years of teaching and in my research. Two of the papers in Part I, "Controls and Experiments in Field Work" (Essay 1) and "Comparisons in Cultural Anthropology" (Essay 6) were written in response to requests from editors of anthropological handbooks and are based upon a review of anthropological literature and upon insights from my own field experience. The major issues dealt with in the first article, written in 1953, are still central concerns of anthropology today. Many of the developments and trends in anthropology since 1953, such as ethnoscience, family studies and urban anthropology are elaborations of themes and problems discussed in this early paper.

Some of the innovative trends which I reviewed and helped initiate include: an emphasis upon the study of the range of variation in behavior and custom as against the older emphasis on ideal patterns; more quantification in field data; a more exacting concern for economic aspects of societies; the heuristic value of the family as a unit of analysis and study; the testing of the reliability of anthropological reporting by independent restudies; and the need to order research designs so that villages, slums, and other smaller units studied by anthropologists can be seen within the context of larger regional and national frameworks. I also reviewed the use of photography and tape recorders in anthropology and the effectiveness of group field parties and cross-disciplinary research.

Two of the articles in Part I, "Tepoztlán Restudied" (Essay 2), and "Further Observations on the Folk-Urban Continuum" (Essay 3), as well as Essay 18, "Urbanization without Breakdown," show in many ways the empirical roots of my methodological and theoretical dissent from the anthropology of cultural idealism. On the basis of my experience in the restudy of Tepoztlán it seems clear that when an anthropologist goes into the field with a specific hypothesis there is always the danger that the selective implications of the hypothesis may obscure the larger reality of the village culture. In this connection, I took issue with Robert Redfield for his failure to describe the conditions of poverty and landlessness of the peasants and the effects of these conditions upon their lives and their character. This early critique eventually led to my own effort to formulate the theory of the subculture of poverty.

Essay 4 presents my current thinking about the culture of poverty. It is now more than ten years since I conceived of the idea of a subculture of poverty. I first presented the concept at the Americanist Congress in Costa Rica in 1958 in a paper entitled "The Culture of the *Vecindad*." I mentioned it again in the Introduction to my book *Five Families* (1959) and developed it more fully in 1961 in the Introduction to *The Children of Sánchez*. The version presented in this volume is taken from the Introduction to *La Vida* (1966). However, it includes a few new ideas which appeared in the Introduction to *A Study of Slum Culture: Backgrounds for La Vida* (1968).

Because most of my discussion of the culture of poverty has appeared in the introductions to my various family studies, some misunderstanding has arisen concerning the relationship between the conceptual model and the autobiographical materials. The idea of the model of the subculture of poverty did not grow out of my study of the Sánchez family alone. Rather, it developed out of my study of 171 families from two Mexico City *vecindades*. In reviewing the findings on these families and in comparing them with data on slums published by social scientists (and also with data from novels), I noted certain persistent patterned associations of traits among families with the lowest income level and the least education. It was the configuration of these traits which, for lack of a better term, I called the subculture of poverty. From a theoretical point of view the crucial thing about the subculture of poverty is that it represents both a reaction and an adaptation of the poor to their marginality and helplessness in the larger society.

It should be clear to anyone who has read the Introduction to *La Vida* that the Ríos family, like the Sánchez family, is not an ideal representative of the culture of poverty model. In view of this, it is pointless to seek a one-to-one correspondence between the model and all of the characters in these two books. It would be more helpful to think of the subculture of poverty as the zero point on a continuum which leads to the working class and the middle class. The various characters in *The Children of Sánchez* and *La Vida* would then fall at different points on the continuum.

Some of my colleagues have criticized me for using the term "culture of poverty" instead of "subculture of poverty." I had hoped it would be evident to any careful reader that I was describing a model of a subculture and not of a culture. I made this clear in all of my writings. However, I decided to use the shorter term "culture of poverty" because my books were intended for a wide audience. I believed that the concept of a subculture, difficult even for social scientists, would confuse the average reader and, like the term "subhuman," might suggest inferiority. I hoped that the term "culture" would convey a sense of worth, dignity, and the existence of pattern in the lives of the very poor.

Some people have erroneously applied the idea of a subculture of poverty to entire slum populations. In my experience, the people who live in slums, even in small ones, may show considerable heterogeneity in income, literacy, education, political sentiment and life style. The subculture of poverty may therefore apply to only one sector of a slum population.

"An Anthropological Approach to Family Studies" (Essay 5), published in 1950, was my first statement outlining a methodology for family studies. Since that time I have developed a number of new approaches and methods for family studies, including multiple autobiographies, reconstructed days and observed days. These methods are described in the introductions to my books *Five Families* (1959), *The Children of Sánchez* (1961) and *La Vida* (1966). It seems to me that the data on families obtained by these methods are on the whole more precise, more valid, and more reliable, than a good deal of the generalizations about culture patterns found in traditional monographs. I have done my best to achieve a balanced view of the lives of my subjects by using a broad approach which gives equal attention to ecological, social, economic, religious, psychological, moral, and historical factors. In short, family studies demand a multi-disciplinary approach.

"The Effects of White Contact Upon Blackfoot Culture" in Part II was my doctoral dissertation. It is a historical study which reflects my training as a historian before I became an anthropologist. However, the idea for the thesis—namely, the effect of trade and an expanding economy upon all aspects of Blackfoot Indian culture—grew out of my field work with the Blackfoot Indians in 1939. Most studies of acculturation and culture change document the destructive effects of the intruding civilization upon the native culture. The case of the Blackfoot is unusually interesting because it shows that in the early phase of indirect contact with the whites the native culture expanded and flourished. The breakdown occurred much later. Essay 8, "Manly-Hearted Women among the North Piegan," my very first publication, was based upon field work in Canada and marks my early interest in culture and personality problems. This interest eventually led me to develop the family study approach.

The articles in Part III are based on my work during 1946–1947 as a "Social Scientist" in the Division of Farm Population and Rural Life, Bureau of Agricultural Economics, U.S. Department of Agriculture. These articles reflect my continued interest in combining theoretical concerns with practical issues. While I consider myself a cultural anthropologist rather than an applied anthropologist, I have always been interested in practical applications of my research. One advantage of middle-range theory building of the type that I have occasionally attempted is the potential use of the theories to administrators and other laymen in situations where anthropological research is relevant.

The first four papers of Part IV deal with the Mexican village of Tepoztlán. In my research in Tepoztlán I combined a number of approaches to community studies, the historical, the functional, the statistical, and the psychological, into a unified and holistic research design.

In the article on "Plow Culture and Hoe Culture" (Essay 11) I attempted to go beyond the descriptive level of technology and demonstrate how contrasting technologies bring about and are associated with important social and cultural differences in the community.

"Wealth Differences in a Mexican Village" (Essay 12) reflects my early interest in problems of poverty. This essay introduced for the first time in Latin American anthropological research a scale for rating the wealth of peasant families. The results showed significant economic stratification in an otherwise rather homogeneous village. In August, 1947, the same month that the article was published, the Negro historian, W. E. B. Du Bois, wrote an editorial on my article in the *Chicago Defender*. I would like to cite some of his statements because they are still pertinent today.

> It is characteristic of our modern scientific civilization, that while we want exact facts when we study stones and trees and even animals, we are nevertheless content to talk about human beings without knowing the facts. For instance, we talk about Poverty. Everybody knows that Poverty not only is, but always has been, the great human problem. Now what we ought to know, first of all, is just how poor people are and how many people are poor. This unfortunately we only know indirectly and more or less by guess-work. . . ."
>
> Here then ["Wealth Differences in a Mexican Village"] in micro-cosm is a picture of the poverty of the world; it is not the worst poverty imaginable. These people get food to eat; they have something of clothing and shelter; but three-fourths of them do not get enough to be healthy or send their children to school. We ought to know more facts like this for the great majority of the people of the world, accurately and in detail. Then we would have a firm starting point at which we could say: What is wrong with this civilization: With our work, with our technique, our distribution of wealth. Why is it that the great majority of the people of the world in this heyday of civilization, in this day of mounting wealth, luxury and power, why is it, that the vast majority of the people of the world are desperately, and it seems to most of us inexcusably, poor?

Indeed, it seems that the proper and precise recording of the social facts of poverty and inequality in peasant villages and in the urban slums, and their destructive effects on human beings, is in itself a revolutionary act!

"Medicine and Politics in a Mexican Village" (Essay 14) may be of special interest to readers because it is one of the few examples in the literature in which an anthropologist provides a detailed report of a serious crisis in field work. Anthropologists, like politicians, are reluctant to air their mistakes or failures. I wrote this article in 1943 when I was employed by the U.S. Office of Indian Affairs, then under the leadership of John Collier, who refused permission for its publication at that time. It finally appeared in 1955.

I did the field research for the articles on India almost inadvertently in 1952–1953 while I was a consulting anthropologist for the

Ford Foundation in India. My original assignment was to work with the Program Evaluation Organization of the Planning Commission to help develop a scheme for the objective evaluation of the rural reconstruction program which was going on in fifty-five pilot community projects in India. Although I had had some experience in the study of peasant cultures in Mexico, Cuba, and Spain, I felt at a great disadvantage in acting as adviser to my Indian colleagues without first-hand knowledge of Indian village life. Fortunately, I was invited by Professor D. G. Karve, then head of the Program Evaluation Organization, to direct a pilot research project in a village of my choice. Indeed, my work in village Rampur stands out as the highlight of my year in India. Although I traveled the length and breadth of India, visiting villages as well as cities and universities, and consulting with Indians in all walks of life, it was not until I studied one village intensively that I began to learn something in depth about Indian culture.

"Group Dynamics: A Study of Factions Within Castes" (Essay 15), first published by the National Planning Commission of the Government of India in 1954, created a stir because it challenged the stereotype of Indian villages as little democratic republics. In the article on "Caste and the *Jajmani* System in a North Indian Village" (Essay 16) I demonstrated the economic underpinning of a system that had formerly been explained largely in terms of ritual exchanges of goods and services between different castes. Moreover, I tried to show that the *jajmani* system was not an entirely benevolent one which provided social justice, peace and contentment to the villagers but rather an exploitative system geared to favor the landowners and the higher castes.

My article "Peasant Culture in India and Mexico" (Essay 17) was one of the very few examples in anthropology of first-hand, comparative field research by the same investigator in peasant societies in widely separated parts of the world.

In Part V I have brought together some of my articles on urban life. Urban anthropology is now recognized as a legitimate sub-field of our discipline, but when I began my studies of urban slums and non-slum settlements in 1951 there were very few anthropologists doing this kind of research. My investigation of Tepoztecan migrants living in Mexico City helped to dispel some of the traditional notions about the effects of the city upon rural migrants. In Essay 18, "Urbanization without Breakdown," I recommend a new methodology for studying rural-urban migrants, beginning with careful studies of individuals and families before they migrate, and then following these same families to the city for comparative study.

"The Possessions of the Poor" (Essay 20), published in *Scientific*

American, October, 1969, is an exercise in micro-ethnography and suggests some novel dimensions for the definition of poverty.

The four articles in Part VI are based upon my tape-recorded interviews and reflect a new direction in my work which began in 1959 with the publication of *Five Families.* One of the major objectives of my recent work has been to give a voice to people who are rarely heard and to provide readers with an inside view of a style of life which is common in many of the deprived and marginal groups in our society. The article "Reminiscences of an Aging Puerto Rican" (Essay 24) is published here for the first time and is taken from a larger volume now in preparation on the life history of a Puerto Rican townsman.

CONTENTS

Part Three: RURAL U.S.A.

Part Four: PEASANTRY

A. *Introductory Remarks*

B. *Mexico*

C. *India*

D. *India and Mexico*

Part Five: URBAN STUDIES

Part Six: SELECTIONS FROM LIFE HISTORIES

Contents   [xvii]

Part One:

THEORY AND METHOD

1

Controls and Experiments in Field Work[*]

Anthropologists have for a long time been concerned with problems of method and field techniques.[1] However, the interest in the specific subject of control and experiment in field work is relatively recent, and most of the work in this area remains to be done in the future. The preparation of a "background" paper of this kind therefore presents some difficulty because of the relative scarcity of literature which deals directly and explicitly with this subject. This is not to say that anthropologists have not used controls and even experiments—that is, if we do not define these terms too narrowly. However, there has been little discussion of field work and methodology in just these terms, and the use of controls has not been systematic.

[*] This essay was first published in 1953 in *Anthropology Today* (prepared under the chairmanship of A. L. Kroeber), Copyright 1953, University of Chicago Press, pp. 452–75.

[1] Many of our leading anthropologists have written on the subject at one time or another. For some examples see (under "References" at the end of this essay) Herskovits (1948, chap. vi; 1950); Kluckhohn has dealt with the problem of method and field techniques in many articles (see, e.g., 1938, 1939, 1951*b*; Gottschalk, Kluckhohn, and Angell, 1945, pp. 79–176); F. R. Kluckhohn (1940); Malinowski (1922, see the Introduction); Mead (1933, 1939; also see her rather full discussion of field methods in 1940, pp. 325–38, and 1949, pp. 293–302); S. F. Nadel has an excellent general discussion in his recent book (1951); Weakland (1951). See also the regular feature on "Field Methods and Techniques" in *Human Organization* published by the Society for Applied Anthropology.

In the absence of a clear-cut body of data that might be summarized, I have had to delve into the ethnographic literature to pick out examples of controls implicit in the work or in the formulation of the problem and to survey some of the work in progress which is oriented in an experimental direction.

Before getting into the details of this paper, I would like to point out that the terms "controls" and "experiments" at once suggest a relationship with the physical and biological sciences and to this extent imply a definite value orientation concerning the nature of anthropology and the usefulness of controls and experiments. That there is some divergence of opinion about this was impressed upon me by the differences in the responses of a number of anthropologists whom I interviewed in the preparation of this paper.[2] Some thought that the question of controls and experiments was an important subject which should be explored to the full because of its potential contribution toward making anthropology more scientific. Others tended to dismiss the subject as having little import for cultural studies.

This difference in attitude toward the value and possibilities of controls and experiments reflects a more basic divergence in interests and approaches among anthropologists concerning methodology. On the one hand, there are those who would underscore the kinship of anthropology with the natural sciences, would stress the need for quantification, objective tests, experiments, and a general development and improvement of techniques which might lead to greater precision and objectivity in the gathering, reporting, and interpreting of field data. On the other hand, there are those who, though not denying for a moment the kinship of anthropology with the sciences, believe that what needs to be stressed at this time is the kinship of anthropology with the humanities, and, accordingly, they would emphasize the need for insight, empathy, intuition, and the element of

[2] I want to take this opportunity to thank the following anthropologists for their kindness in discussing this subject with me in interviews or correspondence: Helen Codere, Dorothy and Fred Eggan, Meyer Fortes, A. Irving Hallowell, Melville J. Herskovits, Clyde Kluckhohn, Margaret Mead, George P. Murdock, Ralph Linton, Morris Opler, Hortense Powdermaker, Julian Steward, and Sol Tax. I would recommend the interviewing of anthropologists as a good field technique and would agree with Veblen, who wrote many years ago: "It is no less requisite to come into close personal contact with the men engaged than it is to make first-hand acquaintance with the available materials; for it is a common trait of scientists, particularly when occupied with matter that is in any degree novel and growing, that they know and are willing to impart many things that are not primarily involved in the direct line of their own inquiry and many things, too, to which they may not be ready to commit themselves in print" (Dorfman, 1933).

art. Moreover, they are much less sanguine about the contribution to anthropology which can come from quantification, control, and experiment, and they point out that some of our most adequate and insightful anthropological monographs were written by missionaries who had had no technical training.[3]

This difference in emphasis is not limited to anthropology, where it is perhaps the weakest. It cuts across most of the social sciences. In sociology it is represented by the differences between George A. Lundberg and F. Stuart Chapin (or one of the small-group experimentalists like Robert F. Bales), on the one hand, and Florian Znaniecki and Howard S. Becker, on the other. In psychology it is the difference between Ray B. Cattell and L. L. Thurstone as over against Kurt Lewin, Wolfgang Köhler, and Gordon W. Allport. In anthropology it can perhaps best be represented by the differences in approach to culture by the trait-list enthusiasts as over against the configurationalists. However, there is considerably more overlapping in anthropology, and this is one of our strengths. In anthropology our differences in emphases have not yet become institutionalized in terms of different subject matter, as in psychology. We suffer less from hardening of the categories. For example, we have no division as clear-cut as that between experimental and clinical psychology. Moreover, unlike psychologists—and, I might add, fortunately so—few of us have devoted our lives to the development and refinement of research techniques to the point where we have lost sight of what it was we are studying.[4]

From a cross-disciplinary point of view, the refreshing thing about anthropologists is their eclecticism, their readiness to invent, borrow, or steal whatever techniques or concepts are available at a given time and jump in to do the field job. But it must be admitted that this basically healthy attitude is also partly responsible for the paucity of contributions to methodology and theory. Kluckhohn's

---

[3] For examples of these divergent emphases compare the editorials on "Field Methods and Techniques" in *Human Organization* with Benedict (1948) and Redfield (1948). Another aspect of the divergence mentioned above is the often-discussed question of whether anthropology is a scientific or a historical discipline. For a brief and convenient summary of the highlights of this controversy see M. J. Herskovits (1949), pp. 608–12.

[4] As Dr. Redfield has written: "In places the invention and the teaching of special procedures have gone ahead of the possibility of finding out anything very significant with their aid. It is certainly desirable to be precise, but it is quite as needful to be precise about something worth knowing. It is good to teach men and women who are to be social scientists how to use the instruments of observation and analysis that have been developed in their disciplines. But it is not good to neglect that other equally important side of the social sciences" (Redfield, 1948, pp. 188–89).

observation that American anthropologists were "devoting an over-whelming proportion of their energies to the accumulation of facts" (1939, p. 329) is certainly much less true today than it was in 1939, but it still carries some weight.

It seems to me that there is no necessary contradiction between the two points of view briefly outlined above. Each supplements the other, and students should be familiar with both. In a sense we have here a division of labor. From one we can perhaps expect broader and more meaningful hypotheses and from the other the development of procedures by which these hypotheses may be checked. Both approaches represent significant contributions to anthropology.

Whether one emphasizes quantitative or qualitative analysis is to some extent related to individual differences in temperament and background. But it may also be a function of the state of knowledge at a given time, the particular nature of the problem, and the level of abstraction one is working with. Indeed, it has been asserted that quantification and measurement and the categories of time, space, number, etc., are categories which have been derived from and for the study of nature but are not adequate for the interpretation of culture or value systems. Elija Jordan (see 1952, p. 5), an American philosopher of growing reputation, has suggested that the job of the philosopher is to develop systematically a new set of categories with which the anthropologist and other social scientists can study culture.

A somewhat similar position is taken by the anthropologist and linguist, B. L. Whorf, who writes (1940):

> Measuring, weighing, and pointer-reading devices are seldom needed in linguistics, for quantity and number play little part in the realm of patterning, where there are no variables, but instead, abrupt alterations from one configuration to another. The mathematical sciences require exact measurement, but what linguistics requires is, rather, "patternment"—an exactness of relation irrespective of dimensions. Quantity, dimension, magnitude are metaphors since they do not properly belong in this spaceless, relational world.

Julian Steward (1950, p. 45) has also written that "cultural patterns cannot be described mathematically," and Ruth Benedict made very much the same point when she said that just as soon as you begin to quantify, you are no longer studying culture.[5]

Despite these reservations, it must be noted that the increased use of quantification has been one of the most significant developments

[5] This statement was made in conversation with me shortly before Dr. Benedict's death.

in anthropological field work in recent years. This development is closely related to some of the major trends in anthropology in the last twenty years. The most important of these trends are: (1) an increasing emphasis upon the study of range of variation in behavior and custom as over against the older emphasis upon ideal patterns;[6]

[6] That the traditional derivation of culture patterns neglects range of variation is made clear by R. Linton in an excellent statement on anthropological methodology. Linton explains that, in order to describe and manipulate the variety of behavior found in any society, the anthropologist uses the "culture-pattern construct," which he defines as "the mode of the finite series of variations which are included within each of the real culture patterns." The following example is given: "Thus, if the investigator finds that members of a particular society are in the habit of going to bed sometime between eight and ten o'clock but that the mode for his series of cases falls at a quarter past nine, he will say that going to bed at quarter past nine is one of the culture patterns of their culture" (1945, pp. 45–46). It could be argued that Linton has touched upon a fundamental weakness in most anthropological field studies. From Linton's use of the word "mode" the reader might infer that the anthropologist studied quantitatively the range of each or any particular behavior and then arrived at the mode, which he reports as the culture pattern. However, it is well known that anthropologists rarely use statistical procedures systematically and by no means arrive at the mode in the traditional statistical manner. Furthermore, the "series of cases" is very often only a small number of all the cases. When the average monograph reports that children are nursed for about two years, there is a high probability that this conclusion was arrived at after talking with a few mothers and making some casual and uncontrolled observations in the community. It would probably not occur to most anthropologists, *or seem important,* to seek out and observe all the children being weaned at the time of the study and to determine their exact ages. *Thus, by calling the culture pattern the mode, Linton is giving statistical dignity to what in most cases is probably no more than the anthropologist's guess.* When Linton explains that "the total culture pattern construct is developed by combining all the culture construct patterns which have been developed," what he is saying is that we are adding up our guesses and arriving at a total guess, namely, the total culture-pattern construct. That anthropologists sometimes guess brilliantly is to their everlasting credit and is a tribute to the element of art in the social sciences. But this is still a far cry from the more exact methods of the natural sciences. And perhaps this is as it should be.

The limitations in anthropological derivations of systematic or total culture patterns are clearly recognized by Kroeber, who seems to accept these limitations as being in the nature of things, hardly to be remedied by more informants or other improved field techniques. He writes: "In proportion as the expression of such a large pattern tends to be abstract it becomes arid and lifeless; in proportion as it remains attached to concrete facts it lacks generalization. Perhaps the most vivid and impressive generalizations have been made by frank intuition deployed on a rich body of knowledge and put into skillful words" (1948, p. 317).

(2) the shift from preoccupation with the salvaging and reconstruction of rapidly disappearing cultures to the study of functioning societies; (3) greater awareness of methodological problems resulting in part from closer liaison with other disciplines, particularly with philosophy, sociology, and psychology; (4) the increasing use of anthropological data by other disciplines and, in particular, the pressure from psychologists for more data on individual differences; (5) some modification of our earlier role as a one-man expedition of all the social sciences toward greater specialization and limitation of problem; (6) longitudinal studies in which more time is devoted to the study of a single people, for example, Kluckhohn's intensive work with the Navaho over many years; (7) an increase in cooperative research, in which specialists study a particular aspect of a culture;[7] (8) the development of the field of applied or action anthropology. The cumulative effect of these broad developments upon field-work techniques will be discussed in more detail later.

Because applied and action anthropology are problem-centered, they would seem to be a "natural" for the increased use of controls and experiments. This is ironical in a sense, for a common charge against applied anthropology has been that it is "unscientific." In working for administrators the question of "How many?" becomes particularly pertinent. How many families own land, how many have adopted new practices, how many need medical care? Applied anthropology literally demands quantification.

Anyone who has read the articles on field methods and techniques in *Human Organization* cannot help being impressed by the perceptible straining for objectivity. Indeed, it is here that we find suggestions for a radical departure from traditional ethnographic techniques. Not content with the mere incorporation of quantification and added controls within the old framework of observational methods, a writer in this journal suggests that the process of observation itself be set upon a strict operational basis:

> Throughout the field [these] currents of intuition are still strong today, even when stored up or concealed from superficial view by imposing edifices of statistical ingenuity, made possible, although not valid, by assigning number to the intuitions themselves. Much of the energy that might have been turned profitably to improve the quality of observation, in accordance with procedures used in the biological sciences and in chemistry and physics, has been directed toward the

[7] The more intensive study which comes with specialization naturally leads to more knowledge of range of variation. One might raise the question to what extent the picture of cultural homogeneity of so-called "primitive" societies is a function of the anthropologist's lack of expertness in different aspects of culture.

minute taxonomic dissections of verbalized intuition, which can be quantified.[8]

The highest degree of objectivity in observing and recording data is the goal. In the absence of the sound motion picture, which is considered the ideal instrument, the field worker must attain the accuracy of the camera: "The goal of the well-conducted interview is to secure material similar to what would be obtained if the interviewer had been able to follow his subject about with a notebook, recording everything he did and said as accurately as possible." [9]

There is a strong emphasis upon the problems of semantics and the elimination of all intuitive and subjective statements and interpretative judgments. Statements must be "based upon cultural and physical evidence." Thus: "Membership in a group or occupation should be stated in precise terms: 'He was dressed as a Blackfoot,' not 'He is a Blackfoot.'" [10]

At the basis of their operational approach is the "realization that any given sequence of behavior can be broken up into multitudes of actions that are capable of description and differentiation." [11] The "time when" and "place where," as well as the who, what, and how, in relations between people must be recorded in precise detail. "We would like to know that the particular situation being observed began at 3:05 P.M., March 26, and lasted until 5:17 P.M., and that the two persons involved then went away and were not observed together again until three days later, March 29, at 7 P.M." [12]

This type of "value-free," atomistic material readily lends itself to objective, graphic recording. Thus workers in this field have been utilizing all types of mapping, particularly spot mapping, flow charts, recording sheets, contact questionnaires, extensionalized interviews, and recording of movements (such as dancing, facial expressions, gestures). These suggested techniques apparently have been helpful in concrete, narrowly defined problems such as might arise in the study of a shoe factory. Whether they are practicable and useful in the study of larger groups such as communities remains to be seen.

In the discussion that follows we will consider, first, controls in field work and, second, experiments in field work. This separate treatment of controls and experiments will facilitate the organization of materials because controls and experiments have not always gone

[8] *Human Organization,* Vol. 10, No. 3 (Fall, 1951), p. 40.

[9] *Ibid.,* Vol. 9, No. 1 (Spring, 1950), p. 29.

[10] *Ibid.,* Vol. 9, No. 3 (Fall, 1950), p. 29.

[11] *Ibid.,* Vol. 10, No. 1 (Spring, 1951), p. 36.

[12] *Ibid.,* Vol. 9, No. 4 (Winter, 1950), p. 30.

hand in hand. Under "Controls" we shall deal with the personal equation, group field work, and field techniques (quantification, sampling, etc.), tape recording, photography, etc. Under "Experiments" we shall consider research designs and research problems and restudies.

· CONTROLS ·

For purposes of this paper the term "control" is defined rather broadly to include any technique or method that decreases the probability of error in the observation, collection, and interpretation of field data. Different methods may therefore offer different degrees of control. In this sense one can have control without the controlled group of the laboratory experiment. Indeed, the laboratory experiment is only one type of control. In short, anything that increases the chances of getting more objective, meaningful, and reliable data is a control.

· THE PERSONAL EQUATION ·

Since most field work is done by a single individual, the first question to consider is the problem of control of the personal equation. Nadel (1951, p. 48) has put the question clearly:

> Where the human being is the only instrument of observation, the observer's personal equation must be all pervading; and where the data observed are once more human data, the observer's personality might easily override the best intentions of objectivity. In the final interpretation of the data some such bias is probably inevitable. It might be argued that, as long as interpretative and descriptive statements are kept distinct, no harm is done; on the contrary, the personal viewpoints and the varying philosophies which different students of society may bring to their material would all enrich the science of man. Yet in so far as it is also true that even the observation of facts already entails omission, selection, and emphasis, that is, a first, inevitable interpretation, the observer's personality cannot be permitted such latitude.

One of the first steps in the development of some control over the personal equation is the training of students. We assume that by familiarizing the student with the history of the discipline, with the principles of scientific method, with the broad comparative knowledge of cultures the world over, and with a knowledge of the mistakes which have been made in the past, we automatically reduce the probability of error.

In addition, it has been pointed out that to achieve a high degree of objectivity the student must know himself well and must be aware of his biases, his value systems, his weaknesses, and his strengths (Lombard, 1950).[13] Presumably, self-awareness is something that develops in most of us with maturity. However, it has also been recommended in some quarters that field workers be psychoanalyzed before going out to the field, on the assumption that this would lead to greater self-awareness. A number of anthropologists have been analyzed with this in mind (and some perhaps for other reasons), and I have been told by at least two anthropologists that they believed their field work improved considerably thereafter. But this is one of those uncontrolled controls in which it is difficult to measure or evaluate the supposed improvement. Perhaps a more convincing case could be made for analysis if the analysis were published, so that we could read the analysis and the monograph hand in hand!

Nadel's suggestions of how to deal with the subjective factor are to the point. He writes (1951, p. 49):

> If subjectivity is unavoidable, it can at least be brought out into the open. . . . The reasoning underlying observation and description must be clearly formulated, its premises exactly stated, and its operations shown step by step. . . . The greatest risk of mishandling scientific problems lies not in the different viewpoints and philosophies or perhaps in the divergent personalities of the scientists, but in the inexplicit statement of the assumptions and concepts with which they operate.

• GROUP FIELD PARTIES •

So far, we have been discussing the individual field worker. However, an additional measure of control in field work may be obtained, at least theoretically, whenever the field party consists of more than one person. Such types of field parties may range from a husband-wife team, to a teacher-student expedition, to a co-operative field group with specialists from many disciplines.

The husband-wife field-work team has been a common occurrence. The advantages of a husband-wife team for establishing rapport in the field and for guarding against getting only a male's point of view of a culture have often been noted. Less frequently has it been noted that such a team also offers us a check on the reliability of reporting. The fact that husbands and wives have sometimes

[13] M. Mead (1949) writes in this connection: "There is no such thing as an unbiased report on any social situation. . . . All of our recent endeavor in the social sciences have been to remove bias. . . . Actually, in the matter of ethos, the surest and most perfect instrument of understanding is our own emotional response, provided that we can make a disciplined use of it" (pp. 299–300).

given us different interpretations is in itself a contribution to methodology, in that it raises questions about the factors involved in such differences.[14] I suppose that the usefulness, for methodological purposes, of a husband-wife team is directly proportional to their differences in personality, cultural background, value systems, training, and the quality of their interpersonal relations at the time of the field work or publication.[15]

The frequent practice in the United States of sending out summer field-research groups with students recruited from different departments of anthropology would seem to provide a system of checks and balances of points of view, since each department tends to train its students with some major emphasis. It is, of course, difficult to evaluate the extent of this potential control as it works out in practice, for so much depends upon how the field party is organized. However, it would seem that the element of control might be considerably increased on these field trips if the research were consciously organized around this point.

A field party consisting of professional anthropologists from different national cultures sent out to study a single community might serve as an experiment in checking the role of cultural backgrounds of anthropologists. It would be interesting to know what reports we would get on the Hopi from a field party consisting of an American, English, Mexican, Russian, Chinese, and Panamanian anthropologist. In Mexico, American anthropologists (Ralph Beals, Foster, Lewis, Redfield, Tax) have had field parties which included students from various Latin American countries. However, the leadership of Americans and the teacher-student relationship have reduced the element of control.

Research teams consisting of specialists from more than one discipline also provide some measure of control of the personal equation, in that each specialist brings to the problem a new point of view, a different tradition, and different techniques, all of which, in theory, act as a cross-check upon bias. How much of a control is difficult to say and again depends upon the way in which the research team and the research problem are organized.

There have been numerous examples of group research in which anthropologists have been represented. In the Bureau of Agricultural Economics, anthropologists, sociologists, and psychologists, under the direction of Dr. Carl C. Taylor, worked together in both the planning and the field-work phases in the study of seventy-one

[14] For a striking example see the differences in interpretation of Arapesh temperament by Mead (1935) and Fortune (1939).

[15] For this last item I am indebted to Dr. M. Mead.

sample counties in the United States.[16] The avowed purpose of this team approach was to combine the anthropologist's emphasis upon intensive, qualitative analysis with the rural sociologist's reliance upon the quantification of data based largely upon schedules and surveys. It should be noted that the sampling procedures used in this research design, in order to select counties typical of the major types of farming regions and culture regions in rural United States, were of the highest caliber and might well serve as a model for future studies.

The Harvard comparative study of values in five cultures (see Kluckhohn, 1951*a*) and the earlier studies of the Navaho under Kluckhohn's direction employed many persons from different disciplines and from different institutions. One of the most significant methodological aspects of these projects is that they are longitudinal studies and involve work in the same communities over many years. The value of returning again and again to the same community cannot be overemphasized in any consideration of controls.

The Indian Education Research Project, undertaken jointly by the Committee on Human Development of the University of Chicago and the United States Bureau of Indian Affairs, was begun in 1941 and has involved co-operation among anthropologists, sociologists, psychologists, psychiatrists, medical doctors, geographers, and others. The project has been quite productive (Thompson and Joseph, 1944; Macgregor, 1945; Leighton and Kluckhohn, 1946, 1947; Joseph, Spicer, and Chesky, 1949; Thompson, 1950, 1951).

Fortes (1949) worked in collaboration with an economist and a geographer in his survey of the Ashanti; Foster (1948) worked with a geographer (Donald Brand) on some aspects of the Tarascan project; and I worked with medical doctors, agronomists, and a psychologist in my study of Tepoztlán (Lewis, 1951). Other interesting examples of multidisciplinary research still in progress can be cited. At the University of Michigan, psychologists, sociologists, and anthropologists are co-operating in a study to discover what social resources and typical role adaptations enable persons to function effectively under the pressure of social stress and cultural conflict. The study of Japanese-Americans in Chicago, by Charlotte Babcock, William Caudill, and others, includes scholars from the fields of psy-

[16] For a few examples of publications resulting from this project see Miner (1949) and Lewis (1948). For a discussion of an earlier BAE interdisciplinary study of rural communities see Steward (1950), who cites other examples of multidiscipline research: The long-range study of the Maya by Carnegie Institution of Washington begun under Kidder's direction in 1920, and the Virú Valley Project, Peru, under the sponsorship of the Institute of Andean Research.

chology, sociology, and anthropology.[17] The Columbia University Research in Contemporary Cultures under the direction of Margaret Mead includes anthropologists, clinical psychologists, psychoanalysts, historians, political scientists, sociologists, linguists, specialists in literature and the fine arts, and regional specialists. The University of Michigan Center for Japanese Studies, studying culture change in the inland sea region of Japan, includes representatives from geography, political science, and anthropology.

An evaluation of these group projects in terms of the amount of control which derives from the fact that they are multidisciplinary or interdisciplinary is beyond the scope of this paper but is something that deserves attention.[18] As Caudill (Caudill and Roberts, 1951, p. 12) cautions in a paper on interdisciplinary research, "There is an increasing realization that mere meetings . . . do not produce a unified product; indeed, the product frequently amounts to little more than a diluted version of one of the components." A maximum control would result from working on a common problem, understanding the technical jargon and the basic theoretical formulations of the other disciplines, and working in an atmosphere of smooth interpersonal relations. Some of the pitfalls noted are the pressure of publicity, the low common denominator of common knowledge, the representatives of each discipline being forced into the role of expert, the increased conservatism of participants as their positions are challenged, and the differential status positions of the participants (Caudill and Roberts, 1951).

· FIELD TECHNIQUES AND THE PROBLEM OF CONTROL ·

The time-honored procedures of anthropological field work, such as observation, participation, the use of informants, census-taking, mapping, the recording of genealogies, case studies, and autobiographies—all provide a degree of control in the observation of data. The relatively few innovations in field-research techniques during the past twenty years is striking. Between 1930 and 1953 only seven articles dealing directly with field methods appeared in the *American Anthropologist*, and four of these were concerned with learning native languages.

[17] See William Caudill, *Japanese–American Personality and Acculturation*, Genetic Psychology Monographs, Vol. 45 (Provincetown, Mass.: Journal Press, 1952).

[18] For a brief evaluation of the Tarascan project see Steward (1950), pp. 57–60.

Perhaps the most significant developments in the last twenty years have been the greater attention paid to sampling; the increased use of schedules and questionnaires; the use of more informants in order to cover the major socioeconomic, status, and age groupings; the specialization of research (we now get separate volumes on economics, social organization, magic, and other aspects of culture which were formerly dealt with in a single monograph); the intensive use of photography and the tape recording of interviews; and the use of family studies. We shall comment on a few of these trends.

The greatest amount of quantification in ethnographic field work has been in the study of economics. This is particularly evident in the analysis of work patterns. A few scattered examples may be in order. Titiev (1944, p. 196) recorded the daily work schedules of five Hopi men over a period of three months; time devoted to work was recorded by Foster (1948, pp. 153–50) in Tzintzuntzan, by Redfield and Villa (1934, p. 80) in Chan Kom, and by myself (Lewis, 1951, pp. 145–46) in the analysis of hoe and plow agriculture in Tepoztlán.* I also published (Lewis, 1951, pp. 62–72) a synchronic record of the activities of each member of a Tepoztecan household for a period of four days. The number of occupations and the number of people engaged in each occupation have been reported by several anthropologists. Firth's book, *Malay Fishermen* (1946), includes an extensive use of quantification in his study of occupations, economic activities, and production. Studies of the amount of land under cultivation and the size of yields, as well as budget and dietary studies, have been published by a number of field workers.[19]

I devised a scale for the measurement of the distribution of wealth for use in Tepoztlán (Lewis, 1951, pp. 173–78). Point values were assigned to the different forms of wealth, and a survey of the property owned by each household head made it possible to give each family in the village a point score. The study revealed a much greater range in distribution of wealth than had been expected in this relatively homogeneous village. Quantified in this way, the real economic status of each family was readily correlated with other economic and cultural phenomena. Application of similar scales in other societies might make cross-cultural comparisons more feasible.

Examples of quantification in studies of social organization are

---

* See Essay 11, below.

[19] For land and yield studies see Redfield and Villa (1934, p. 53), Wagley and Galvao (1949), Lewis (1951, pp. 143 and 147); for diet and budget studies see Harris (1944), Redfield and Villa (1934, p. 57), Richards and Widdowson (1936), Lewis (1951, pp. 191–93), Rosemary Firth (1943); for detailed quantitative data on many aspects of economic life see Tax (1952); for an unusually meticulous study suggestive for its method see Henry (1951).

much more scarce in ethnographic literature. Clyde Kluckhohn's study in 1938 of the range of variation in ceremonial participation is a landmark. To my knowledge, Kluckhohn's lead has hardly been followed. In general, there have been few, if any, sociometric studies of social participation among preliterate peoples.

Some examples of rather detailed quantitative studies of certain aspects of social organization are Titiev's study (1944) of Old Oraibi, Fortes' study (1949) of the kinship composition of households in an Ashanti community, and my own study (Lewis, 1951, pp. 77–78) of residence and of barrio intermarriage in Tepoztlán.

Studies of culture and personality have given impetus to the use of controls, primarily in the form of tests, such as the Rorschach, T.A.T., and doll play. However, it should be noted that, while the application of a similar instrument produces an element of control, there is nevertheless increasing concern among psychologists themselves as to the validity of some of these instruments even when used within our own society. In the light of this, one must have some reservations about anthropological field studies which rely heavily upon the Rorschach, or similar tests, to get at the personality picture (Thurstone, 1948; Cronbach, 1949; Schneider, 1950; McFarlane and Tuddenham, 1951; Palmer, 1951; Rabin, 1951).

In most ethnographic monographs, the sections dealing with the life-cycle are still very weak, particularly as regards systematic or controlled observation, quantitative data, and the use of sampling. Most sections on the life-cycle still read as if they were reconstructed from accounts of one or a few informants. This is doubly unfortunate, because detail and exactitude may be crucial in culture and personality studies. If, for example, it is reported that infants are swaddled in a certain tribe and then we go on to suggest some relationship between swaddling and character formation, as some do, it would be good to know at least: (1) how many children are not swaddled; (2) the range in swaddling practices and beliefs; (3) the range in duration of swaddling, i.e., how many children were swaddled two months, four months, etc.; and (4) finally, some comparison of two groups of children within the same society which were subject to different degrees and types of swaddling. Only in this way might one test the hypothesis as to the effects of swaddling. In other words, for some problems the range rather than the mode may be the crucial datum.

Of course, there have been exceptions, but generally these exceptions have been special studies of some one problem or stage of the life-cycle rather than a part of a complete life-cycle picture. Kluckhohn's study on "Some Aspects of Navaho Infancy and Early Childhood" (1947) is noteworthy for its relatively controlled observations, its emphasis upon the range of child-training practices, and the use of some sampling procedures.

Another example of a careful study of one aspect of the life-cycle is the Henrys' study (1944) of Pilagá children, in which all the children in the community were studied, and systematic, direct observations were recorded. Still another example is *The Hopi Child* by Wayne Dennis (1940).

The description of interpersonal relations is another area of weakness in terms of quantification and controlled observation. Many anthropologists are still seeking to isolate and identify the significant variables in this field and are not yet ready for measurement. Moreover, some variables seem less amenable to quantification than others. We have not yet devised accurate measures of such traits as hostility, aggression, dominance, and submission for use even within our own society. How much more difficult must it be to derive measures for these variables for cross-cultural purposes! Then, too, some would argue that the *amount* of aggression or dominance is not nearly so significant as its quality and its context.

The use of photography as a method for the objective recording and portrayal of field data is now widely recognized, but its use is limited and uneven. Most anthropologists still use it in the old-fashioned way to illustrate physical types, landscape, and material culture. A major innovation was Bateson and Mead's photographic study of *Balinese Character* (1942; see also Mead and Macgregor, 1951), or what might be called the "Leica approach" to personality. This is undoubtedly the fullest use to date of the photographic approach. Its major methodological contribution is "objective" data, especially desirable in the description of psychological phenomena because of the absence of a precise scientific vocabulary. Excellent recent examples of ethnographic possibilities of good photography are the study of Peguche by Collier and Buitrón (1949) and *Navaho Means People*, by McCombe, Vogt, and Kluckhohn (1951).

Recording of music in field work has a long history and does not concern us here. More recently there have been examples of the recording of interviews and the direct recording of life stories. I can speak about some of the pros and cons from personal experience with these techniques.

It is difficult to generalize about the effect of the recording machine upon the interview situation. Some informants are very much inhibited by the machine, even after excellent rapport is established. In other cases informants respond positively, and the fact that they are being recorded seems to stimulate and release them. In still other cases the presence of the machine has no apparent effect upon the interview.

The most obvious advantage of recording interviews is the accurate, verbatim record which can be repeated at will for purposes of analysis. The recorded interview also acts as a check upon the role of the anthropologist. A comparative study of the recordings of a number of anthropologists might enable us to develop some criteria for good interviewing. Another advantage in having recorded interview materials is for the training of students. It is almost the equivalent of bringing the informant into the classroom. The usefulness of verbatim records for the linguist is obvious. My own recorded material is now being used by the Spanish Department of the University of Illinois for the study of rural Mexican Spanish.

The drawbacks are the high cost of copying data and the inevitable mechanical troubles, particularly when one is working in villages with no electric power and must depend upon batteries. It seems to me that a more practical alternative (and sometimes more pleasant) is to have a good stenographer as a field assistant.[20]

I have heard anthropologists speculate about the possibility of "planting" secret recording apparatus, but I am unable to report examples of this practice—if it has been used. Similarly, to my knowledge the use of one-way screens has not yet been adopted in anthropological field work.

· CONTROLS AND EXPERIMENTS IN RESEARCH DESIGN AND RESEARCH PROBLEMS ·

The comparative method is the nearest approach we have in cultural anthropology to the experiment. It is significant that Nadel (1951) titled the chapters dealing with the comparative method "Experimental Anthropology."[21] The experiment was defined by Talcott Parsons (1937, p. 743) as "nothing but the comparative method where the cases to be compared are produced to order and under controlled conditions."[22] Since, in the study of culture, we cannot as

[20] Since I wrote this, there has been great improvement in tape recorders, and battery-operated recorders no longer present any serious problems.

[21] See Nadel's chaps. ix and x for a competent and detailed discussion of the comparative method in anthropology.

[22] It is, of course, understood that the experiment involves not only controlled comparisons but also a hypothesis which is being tested. Anthropologists have often referred to primitive societies and history as their laboratory, and they have suggested that the mere study of human beings in different societies is an experiment. This loose use of the term "experiment" should be differentiated from the experimental method.

a rule produce the artificial induction of variations under controlled conditions, we do the next-best thing and study variations as they occur over time, and then compare and correlate. This is the method of co-variation, sometimes also referred to as the "ex post facto experiment." [23]

The comparative method or the method of co-variation can be applied in many situations and on many levels. For example, we can compare institutions or modes of behavior (1) within a single community at a given time; (2) within different communities of a single culture at the same time; (3) within a single community or single culture at different times; (4) in different cultures; and (5) finally, we can compare entire cultures.

All these applications offer some measure of control. However, for the purposes of our paper we are concerned only with the comparative method as it is used in design of field work and the selection of field-work problems. We must therefore put aside many excellent comparative studies done on the basis of library work with secondary sources—for example, Bernard Mishkin's study of the differential effect of the horse upon three Plains Indian societies, L. Spier's study of the Sun Dance, Ruth Benedict's study of the guardian spirit, and E. C. Parsons' study of Pueblo religion.

It should be noted that by far the greater proportion of anthropological field work has been designed in terms of the study of a single community or a single culture. Research designs for field work on a cross-cultural or even multicommunity, comparative basis are strikingly few. We might also observe that the degree of control over data in ethnographic monographs is also a function of the size of the community or society studied. All other things being equal, one can expect a much greater degree of control and coverage of range of variation in a study of a small community than a large one. Compare, for example, the quality of coverage of Foster's monograph (1948) on Tzintzuntzan, a community of about 1,200, or of Redfield and Villa's *Chan Kom* (1934), a community of about 250, with the Herskovits (1938) description of Dahomey, with a population of well over a million. Moreover, I would hazard the guess that there is a direct relationship between the degree to which a monograph concentrates upon the range of variation of one or more aspects of the culture and the extent to which it is experimental or useful for comparative purposes.

Much of the research done within single communities, particularly for modern studies, utilizes the comparative method to some

[23] See Greenwood (1945) for a careful exposition of the ex post facto experiment in sociology.

extent when the researchers study the interrelationships between different aspects of the culture or when they investigate problems or hypotheses. For example, when one studies the relationship between leadership in political life and leadership in religious and ceremonial life, or the relationship between wealth and standard of living, or wealth and the ages of the heads of households, one is using a comparative method. Generally, these kinds of problems are treated as part of a larger descriptive and interpretative study and are not labeled "experimental" or "comparative."

Instances of field studies within a single community which are explicitly labeled experimental or in which there is a clear experimental design are probably very few.[24] The only examples which occur to me are the following: 1. Brown and Hutt (1935). This was described as an "experiment" to determine how useful an anthropologist and an administrator can be to each other in working on a common problem. Its purpose was "to discover what fields of knowledge were of use to the administrator" and "to evolve a simple method of securing and presenting such knowledge in a way that would serve practical ends." An interesting feature of this report is the inclusion (in the Appendix) of a list of the questions asked by the administrator during the course of the experiment and the answers to some of these questions.   2. Spindler and Goldschmidt, "Experimental Design in the Study of Culture Change" (1952). In this study of the Menominee Indians of Wisconsin the authors attempt to relate changes in individual personality with degree of acculturation. The research design is basically similar to that of Hallowell's study (1951), except that the different acculturation groups, which also represent different socioeconomic levels, live within a single Indian reservation. Also, more refined techniques for measuring the level of acculturation were employed. The introduction of a "control group" of whites living on the reservation was meant to serve as a standard against which the Menominee are measured. As the authors point out, this particular "control group," consisting of twelve men, most of whom were married to Menominee women, has severe limitations. However, it completes the "experimental design" nicely.   3. The study by John J. Adair, Dorothea C. Leighton, and others, of the factors in the acceptance or rejection of improved farming practices in the Fruitland Navaho community. "Predictions will be made on the basis of present knowledge of community structure as to which farmers will take up some of the practices shown and which will resist." A central hypothesis to be tested here is "that technological change is more readily accepted if the technological assistants can

---

[24] Time pressure has prevented a survey of the literature from this point of view.

work through informal leaders of the population to be helped." [25]

There are very few multiple, full biographies from the same community, done by the same field worker or by many workers as part of a comparative research design. Only Barton's (1938) three Ifugao biographies come to mind.[26]

The recent interest in intensive family studies exemplifies the use of the comparative method in the design of field research and may in the future lead to experimental studies. Here the problem is to determine how different families in a relatively homogeneous culture react to and reinterpret the local culture, and then to analyze the variables related to these differences. Roberts' study of *Three Navaho Households* is the first publication in this field. His emphasis was upon a detailed comparison of material culture and "some of the more obvious habit relationships" of the three similar groups. He writes (1951, p. 6): "If, despite this presumption of similarity, the three small group cultures were then found to be significantly different from each other in some respects, the hypothesis that every small group defines an independent and unique group-ordered culture would be supported." His survey demonstrates the feasibility of employing small-group cultures as comparative units.

In my study of two Mexican peasant families of different socioeconomic levels in Tepoztlán,[27] the emphasis is upon a comparison of the economic, social, and religious life of the families *as a whole* and the quality of interpersonal relations. Whole-family studies are particularly suitable for the study of problems in culture and personality. The anthropological approach to family studies (Lewis, 1950)* ties in with the currently popular small-group research movement and may lead to a new field of specialization within anthropology.

There are numerous research designs involving more than a single community or culture and employing some experimental or problem approach. A few examples will suffice. A comparative study of the Blackfoot Indians of Canada and the United States was designed by Ruth Benedict to test the effect of differences in government administration and policy upon a people of a common cultural back-

---

[25] *Clearing House Bulletin,* I, No. 1 (Summer, 1951), 11.

[26] Since this article was written, I have published a number of full biographies. See *The Children of Sánchez: Autobiography of a Mexican Family* (New York: Random House, 1961), *Pedro Martínez: A Mexican Peasant and His Family* (New York: Random House, 1964), and *La Vida* (New York: Random House, 1966).

[27] Only one of these studies has been published to date. See *Pedro Martínez: A Mexican Peasant and His Family* (New York: Random House, 1964). My study of a wealthy peasant family will be published at a later date. See also Essay 14.

* See Essay 5, below.

ground. The design was excellent, but unfortunately the project did not materialize as planned. In the course of this study it became clear that it was very difficult to isolate or weigh in the balance the role of a single variable. It turned out that the tribes were put on reservations at different dates, that the pressure of white settlers against the American Blackfoot began much earlier than against the Canadian group, that the land base on the Canadian side differed, and, finally, that a Blackfoot tribe in Canada had the unusual good fortune of getting about a two-million-dollar trust fund from the sale of land to a railroad and of discovering a coal mine, which became a new source of income.

A comparison of the Oklahoma and Mexican Kickapoo has often been suggested, again with the idea of testing the role of a single variable, namely, different government administration. Africa would seem to be an ideal locale for comparative studies of the effects of differences in colonial policy (French, British, Belgian) upon peoples of common culture.

Lystad's comparative study of the Ahafo-Ashanti, in British territory, and the Indenie-Agni, in French territory, is a case in point. Lystad describes the problem as "a laboratory situation for the analysis of the processes by which a culture originally shared by two populations now exhibits differences in two regions in which it has been in contact with two differing ways of life" (1951, p. 1).

Hallowell's study of the relationship between psychological characteristics and degree of acculturation among the Ojibwa is an example of an "experimental" research design based upon the comparative method. Using the Rorschach test (validated by comparison with T.A.T.'s, drawings, direct observation, life histories, ethnographic data, and historical information) to get at "a model personality picture," Hallowell studied and tested three different groups of Ojibwa, each representing a different level of acculturation. Hallowell also utilized the technique of historical reconstruction from the accounts of early observers who had had direct contact with the Indian of the Eastern Woodlands in the seventeenth and eighteenth centuries, to arrive at an approximate psychological picture of the aboriginal Ojibwa. He used this as a base line against which to judge the direction of psychological change among contemporary Ojibwa (1951).[28]

History has been used often and to good effect as a control in the design of field research. It has been basic to the work of Herskovits

[28] A similar study which might be used as a base line for judging Mexican Indian personality was done by one of my students. See Elaine Raasch, "The Character of the Mexican Indians as Described by Some Sixteenth Century Spanish Writers" (Master's thesis, in Spanish), University of Illinois, 1951.

and his students in the Afro-American field. Using West Africa as a base line, Herskovits has traced the degree, direction, and type of culture change in the New World under varying conditions. Some of the questions he asks are "What differences, for example, are to be found in the linguistic adaptation of the Negroes to English, to French, to Spanish, to Portuguese, to Dutch? What are the similarities and differences to be found between the ways of life of Negroes of the same socio-economic classes in these different settings? How has living under Catholicism influenced the development of present-day religious patterns of these Negro groups as against exposure to Protestant tradition? In which aspects of culture, over the whole New World, have African ways proved to be most tenacious?" (1949, p. 613).

Much of the work so far has been limited to the study of survivals of Africanisms. Perhaps at some time in the future it will be possible to take a single West African culture and see what happened to it in various parts of the New World. The publication of Bascom's materials on Yoruban cults in Cuba and Herskovits' materials on the Yoruban cults in Brazil will be a step in this direction.[29]

A field research design which approached an experimental control was reported in my paper on "Urbanization without Breakdown: A Case Study" (Lewis, 1952).* The problem was to test the hypothesis that disorganization and family breakdown result from urbanization. I studied approximately one hundred Tepoztecan families who had moved to Mexico City between 1900 and 1949. The data were obtained by a schedule supplemented with interviews, psychological testing, and living with a few selected families. The methodological innovation was the fact that it was a follow-up study of families from a specific community that had been previously studied.

The application of the experimental small-group research techniques developed by Robert F. Bales and others has not made very much headway in anthropological field work. To my knowledge, these techniques have been used by Strodtbeck (1951) in his comparative study of Navaho, Mormon, and Texan couples in the Southwest and by Roberts in a study of Zuni, Mormon, Navaho, and Spanish-American individuals.[30] These narrow-focus, specialized studies are a far cry from the older ethnographic methods and broad objectives. Just where these newer approaches are going it is still too early to say.

[29] Personal communication from Dr. Herskovits.

* See Essay 18, below.

[30] Personal communication from J. M. Roberts about an unpublished paper.

· RESTUDIES ·

It seems to me that one type of control in field work has to do with the broad problem of testing the reliability of anthropological reporting. One way of getting at this difficult problem is through independent restudies of the same community by different observers, preferably at the same time, but conceivably at different times.

The need for restudies as methodological checks* has been felt by many anthropologists. And yet, to my knowledge there is not a single published case of a restudy in which the express purpose was the interest in methodology, the interest in testing an earlier report.[31] My restudy of Tepoztlán perhaps comes closest to this type, but even here it was not originally planned with this as the central purpose. The differences between Redfield's findings and mine ranged from matters of small factual detail to those of broad interpretations and total impressions of village life. Except for a few glaring exceptions, most of Redfield's descriptive data were confirmed by my findings.

* For a fuller discussion of restudies, see Essay 2, below.

[31] The only example known to me is the case of San Pedro la Laguna, in Guatemala, which was studied by Juan Rosales and later by Benjamin Paul. This case is particularly interesting because it was consciously planned as a methodological check. The problem was to compare the independent report of a native villager with only a minimum of training with that of a professionally trained anthropologist.

Juan Rosales, a native from the nearby village of Panajachel, had worked for Sol Tax as an assistant in gathering field data and filling out questionnaires. He was a schoolteacher and spoke the native Indian language well. Tax sent him to study the village of San Pedro, and later Benjamin Paul studied the same village without having access to the field data of Rosales. The plan was to publish both reports independently. However, after much patient waiting for Rosales to write up his data, the plan was abandoned, and Dr. Paul was given access to the Rosales materials. However, Paul wrote his paper on "Symbolic Sibling Rivalry in a Guatemalan Village" (1950b) before reading the Rosales materials. Dr. Paul tells of how gratifying it was for him to find that Rosales had independently recorded the rather esoteric belief upon which Paul's article was based.

It should be noted that, although this experimental design was well conceived as a check of the factor of professional training, it might have been a more crucial experiment of reliability if both field workers had not been given the same orientation. Both Tax and Paul were from the same department at the University of Chicago, and Rosales was also brought to Chicago for a while. It should be noted, too, that Julio de la Fuente, who has undertaken the heroic task of writing up the Rosales materials, was also trained at Chicago and uses the folk-urban conception as his major theoretical frame of reference (see, e.g., Fuente, 1949, pp. 358–65).

The major divergences resulted from differences in research methodology, in interests, and in theoretical orientation, all of which influenced the selection, coverage, and organization of materials. My study had the advantage of Redfield's pioneer work to start with, more than twice the amount of time for field work, more field assistance, and the development, during a period of almost twenty years, of new approaches and methods, especially in the field of culture and personality. I studied intensively many aspects of the culture only touched upon in the earlier work, with much more emphasis upon quantification and the study of range of variation. Finally, a fundamental difference in approach in the restudy was the emphasis upon ethnohistory and the effort to see the village not as an isolated society but as part of a larger regional and national framework.[32]

Restudies of the same community for the purpose of studying social change would seem to be one of the most important functions of a restudy approach. The restudy approach provides us with a partial solution to one of the traditional problems in the study of culture change among nonliterate peoples, namely, the difficulty of establishing an accurate base line from which change can be measured. All of us have struggled to piece together such a base line from historical data or comparative materials and are aware of the very unsatisfactory and unequal coverage on various aspects of the culture. Having a base line established by an anthropological study is a boon, even admitting the limitations which come from changing interests and techniques in anthropology itself.

A restudy of the same community by the same investigator can also make a contribution to the problem of controls, particularly if the investigator is sufficiently aware of the problem of methodology to make explicit the changes in his outlook and approach which may have occurred in the interval between the two studies.

Examples of full restudies of this type are relatively few: Lynd's *Middletown in Transition*, Redfield's *A Village that Chose Progress*, my *Life in a Mexican Village: Tepoztlán Restudied*. Restudies of larger units include, among other works, three separate and independent restudies of the Ashanti: M. Fortes (1949), R. A. Lystad (1951), and K. A. Busia (1951), respectively; Mair's (1934) restudy of the Baganda, and Powell's[33] restudy of the Trobrianders. A few restudies are now in progress or are being planned. Firth is re-

[32] For a full discussion of some limitations of the community-study approach see Steward (1950).

[33] I understand from Dr. Fortes that Mr. H. A. Powell, Department of Anthropology, University College, London, has just returned from a restudy of the Trobrianders.

studying Tikopia and Margaret Mead plans to restudy Manus in 1953.[34]

By far the largest number of restudies are of the third and fourth types or the purely additive type. Instances of these types are so numerous it would be impossible to mention them within the confines of a short paper.[35] Some peoples have been visited so frequently, particularly by summer laboratories, that they now have professional informants who depend upon the returning anthropologist for their living and who may be kept busy the rest of the year answering questionnaires.

The striking thing about most of these studies (and this applies to many in the third type) is the failure on the part of their authors to evaluate systematically the work of their predecessors and to offer some explanation of differences in findings.[36] Rather, each new worker goes on to study something new with but passing reference to earlier work. This may mean many things. It may in itself be a testimonial to the reliability of previous reports, that is, by silent affirmation; it may mean that the later investigators went in with the same biases as the former and the lack of difference merely reflects

[34] Since I wrote this article Mead's restudy of Manus was published as *New Lives for Old: Cultural Transformation-Manus, 1928–1953* (New York: William Morrow, 1956). Raymond Firth published *Social Change in Tikopia* (New York: Humanities Press, 1959). A number of restudies have appeared since 1953. Redfield went back to Chan Kom, Yucatan, and published *A Village that Chose Progress* (Chicago: University of Chicago Press, 1957). Victor Goldkind then did an independent restudy of Chan Kom, "Class Conflict and Cacique in Chan Kom," *Southwest Journal of Anthropology*, Vol. 22, pp. 325–45, 1966. Charles Leslie returned to Mitla and published *Now We Are Civilized* (Detroit: Wayne University Press, 1960). David Maybury-Lewis revisited the Timbira of eastern Brazil which had been described earlier in Curt Nimuendaju's *The Eastern Timbira* (Berkeley and Los Angeles: University of California Press, 1946). The Maybury-Lewis study is *Akwe-Shavante Society* (New York: Oxford University Press, 1967). Finally, Art Gallagher, Jr., returned to James West's Plainville and published *Plainville Fifteen Years Later* (New York: Columbia University Press, 1961).

[35] A few examples may be cited. For the Kwakiutl there are Boas, Forde, Codere, and Hawthorne; for the Hopi, Cushing, Fewkes, Stephen, Voth, Parsons, Lowie, the Eggans, Beaglehole, Bunzel, Dennis, Forde, Titiev, Simmons and Thompson; for the Blackfoot, Grinnell, McLean, McClintock, Wissler, Schultz, Michelson, Richardson and Hanks, Benedict, Goldfrank, Maslow and Lewis.

[36] Sol Tax tells of how difficult it is to get students to check up on the reliability of earlier work. In a study of the Fox, which has been going on for about three years under his direction, he has been unable to have any of the field workers check up on a prediction he made many years ago concerning some development in the kinship system.

the absence of a critical or fresh outlook; or it may reflect a lack of sensitivity to methodological questions. I suspect that all these factors have been at work to some extent.

Kroeber's six-day restudy of the Seri (1931, p. 3; McGee, 1895–96) is notable as one of the few instances in which a later investigator has troubled to evaluate the earlier findings in some detail and to attempt to explain the differences. Speaking of McGee's work, Kroeber says that "It is easy to read between the lines of this description that McGee leaned toward a romantic and imaginative interpretation of the Seri. Also, his actual contacts with the people themselves were brief, and hampered by imperfect communication" (1931, p. 3). Speaking of how he confined himself to the social and religious sides of Seri life, he states: "There was the more reason for this since it is in dealing with these latter aspects, where verbal communications are as important as observation, that McGee's monograph is most tenuous and dubious" (1931, p. 4). However, his criticism is not completely negative, as we can see when he says, referring to McGee again, that "his work impresses me as that of an extraordinarily good observer, keen in seeing significant evidence, but of uncontrolled imagination and unconscious of his preconceptions. It is only fair to state that where he founds an interpretation on slender or uncertain data, he generally indicates the fact to a careful reader" (1931, p. 18).

Emeneau's eight-month restudy of the Todas (1935) was intended primarily for linguistic purposes. Emeneau writes:

> I had no intention of reinvestigating W. H. R. Rivers' ethnological account when I went to them. However, I found that field work in linguistics is impossible if one does not understand what people are talking about. It proved necessary to check every item of text material by Rivers' account of the ethnology of the tribe, and in the end I found myself with numerous corrections of Rivers' detail, as well as with a few important corrections of the general outline of Toda institutions.[37]

Emeneau has added much new data on the Todas. His major corrections were his findings on the dual descent system and his reinterpretation of the nature of Toda religion (1935, 1937, 1941).

Mair's restudy of the Baganda provides us with a rather balanced and thorough re-evaluation, which challenges many of the earlier findings. Only a sample of the many divergences in findings can be noted here.

After stating many of the positive aspects of John Roscoe's earlier work, she writes (1934, pp. xii–xiv):

[37] Personal Communication, February, 1952.

Nevertheless, it is not altogether satisfactory to the modern anthropologist, for it does not include many data which are now thought indispensable for a sociological study. It does not envisage Baganda society as a mechanism of co-operation, and the links which should connect the structure of kindred and clan, of political and religious authorities, with the normal organization of daily life, are missing. It describes, for example, very fully the ceremonial connected with marriage but does not analyze the system of co-operation within the household. It does not connect the kinship terms with the obligations recognized between relatives, nor the technical processes with the organization through which they were carried out. It is most inadequate at those points at which the student of economic contact most requires accurate and detailed information—in such questions as the system of economic co-operation, or of land tenure, or the relations between people and chiefs.

Moreover, the disadvantage of working largely on the basis of native statements detached from their context is apparent in certain serious distortions of fact. The political organization, for example, is represented as no more than a system whereby a few tyrannical chiefs preyed on the common people and were in turn preyed on by the king. The summary nature of justice and the arbitrary exercise of power by the king and the most important chiefs are exclusively emphasized, while their obligations towards their people, their place in the maintenance of order, and the checks upon abuse are overlooked.

Again, a highly sensational colour is given to the description of the indigenous religion by the overemphasis of human sacrifice, which is made to seem its central feature. Not only is the aspect of religion as a means of recourse in times of danger or difficulty barely considered, but offerings of human victims to the gods are confused with murders for magical purposes, with political executions for crime, and with the wanton slaughter which was indulged in by some of the kings, so that their total is made to appear enormous.

For these reasons the attempt to make a new reconstruction of the past of Baganda seemed to me necessary. In the event I felt it to be justified beyond my expectations, for the number of old men who remember the days before the influence of Christianity and British administration had effectively penetrated the country, and whose accounts, given at places many miles apart, corroborate one another, is surprisingly large. I have indicated in the text the points at which my informants differed positively from Roscoe's, those in which they simply denied knowledge of customs which he describes, and those in which I differ from him for reasons of evidence other than that of native statements which contradict those made in his book. In some cases these differences may be due to the falling into disuse of old customs; in others, for the reasons which I give in each context, I think they cannot be.

Fortes' restudy of the Ashanti points to a few important differences from Rattray, particularly as to the nature of the local matrilineal group and the difference between the part played by matrilineal descent and that played by kinship on the father's side in the total social structure.[38] However, there is no attempt at a systematic re-evaluation.

A recent translation from the Russian of G. F. Debets' study of the Chukchee and of T. Semushkin's Chukotka provides us with another example of a restudy for the purpose of studying social change. An unexpected and highly interesting aspect of these studies is the fact that the investigators disagree strongly with Vladimir Bogoras' description of the physical characteristics of the people, such as head and facial measurements, beard developments, and hair texture. Debets concludes: "It is clearly indicated that the existing descriptions of racial characteristics of this people must be basically altered." [39]

Elsie Clews Parsons, with typical historical interest, has given us an incisive characterization of the role of the personal equation in explaining differences in findings on the Zuni. Because her statement (1939, pp. 939–40) illustrates several of the problems discussed in the foregoing pages, I shall quote it by way of conclusion:

> Some of the interpueblo variation now familiar to us may be put down to differences between observers or historians as well as to unequal opportunities for observation. Observation differs within a single pueblo. [For example, Frank Hamilton] Cushing, the poet and craftsman, did not see the same facts at Zuni as the museum collectors who were there at the same time. Thirty years later Kroeber visited Zuni and devoted himself to those aspects of culture which in the interval had become more significant to the trained observer of Indian life, to language and social organization. Cushing, [Matilda Cox] Stevenson, and Kroeber—to these three would any culture look alike! Familiar with the medicine bundle-complex of Plains Indians, Kroeber could see homologues in the cane or corn-ear fetishes of Zuni and appreciate the significance of their ceremonial life. But the actual use of these fetishistic bundles or of other ritual objects, Kroeber unfortunately had no opportunity to see, as had Stevenson or, among Hopi, [Henry R.] Voth and [A. M.] Stephen. These scrupulous observers of Hopi ritual were allowed to be present at kiva altar ritual. . . . Is Zuni ritual less intricate than Hopi, or is it merely that part of its complexity has not been recorded? Matilda Stevenson,

[38] See Fortes (1949). I am also grateful for a personal communication on this from Dr. Fortes.

[39] Sonia Bleeker, "Maritime Chukchee Acculturation" (unpublished essay prepared under the direction of Ruth Benedict).

who usually failed to distinguish between what she saw and what she heard about, was far from being an accurate recorder, nor did she have any facility for interpretation or evaluation. . . . Fortunately, more comparable reports may be expected of recent students who have had more or less the same training, who go over one another's work, and who are learning the tribal languages.

· REFERENCES ·

BARTON, R. F. 1938. *Philippine Pagans.* London: Routledge.

BATESON, G., and MEAD, M. 1942. *Balinese Character: A Photographic Analysis.* ("Special Publications of the New York Academy of Sciences," Vol. II.)

BENEDICT, R. 1948. "Anthropology and the Humanities," *American Anthropologist,* Vol. 50, No. 4, pp. 585–93.

BROWN, G. G., and HUTT, A. M. B. 1935. *Anthropology in Action.* London: Oxford University Press.

BUSIA, K. A. 1951. *Position of the Chief in the Modern Political System of the Ashanti.* London and New York: Oxford University Press; published for the International African Institute.

CAUDILL, W., and ROBERTS, B. H. 1951. "Pitfalls in the Organization of Interdisciplinary Research," *Human Organization,* Vol. 10, No. 4, pp. 12–15.

COLLIER, J., JR., and BUITRÓN, A. 1949. *The Awakening Valley.* Chicago: University of Chicago Press.

CRONBACH, L. 1949. "Statistical Methods Applied to Rorschach Scores: A Review," *Psychological Bulletin,* Vol. 46, No. 5, pp. 393–429.

DENNIS, W. 1940. *The Hopi Child.* ("Monographs of the Virginia University Institute for Research in Social Sciences," No. 26.) New York: Appleton-Century.

DORFMAN, J. 1933. "An Unpublished Project by Thorstein Veblen for an Ethnological Inquiry," *American Journal of Sociology,* Vol. 39, pp. 237–41.

EMENEAU, M. B. 1935. "Toda Culture Thirty-five Years After: An Acculturation Study," *Annals of the Bhandarkar Oriental Research Institute,* Vol. 19, pp. 101–21.

———. 1937. "Toda Marriage Regulations and Taboos," *American Anthropologist,* Vol. 39, pp. 103–12.

———. 1941. "Language and Social Forms: A Study of Toda Kinship Terms and Dual Descent," pp. 158–79, in Hallowell, A. I.; Newman, S. S.; and Spier, L. (eds.), *Language, Culture, and Personality.* Menasha, Wis.: Sapir Memorial Publication Fund.

FIRTH, RAYMOND. 1946. *Malay Fishermen: Their Peasant Economy.* London: Kegan Paul.

FIRTH, ROSEMARY. 1943. *Housekeeping among Malay Peasants.* ("London School of Economics Monographs on Social Anthropology," No. 7.) London.

FORTES, MEYER. 1949. "Time and Social Structure: An Ashanti Case Study," pp. 54–84, in Fortes, Meyer (ed.), *Studies Presented to A. R. Radcliffe-Brown.* Oxford: Clarendon Press.

FORTUNE, R. F. 1939. "Arapesh Warfare," *American Anthropologist,* Vol. 41, No. 1, pp. 22–41.

FOSTER, G. 1948. *Empire's Children: The People of Tzintzuntzan.* ("Publications of the Institute of Social Anthropology, Smithsonian Institution," No. 6.) Washington, D.C.

FUENTE, JULIO DE LA. 1949. *Yalalag, una villa zapoteca serrana.* ("Serie científica, Museo Nacional de Antropología." Mexico, D.F.)

GOTTSCHALK, L.; KLUCKHOHN, C.; and ANGELL, R. 1945. *The Use of Personal Documents in History, Anthropology, and Sociology.* (Social Science Research Council Bulletin 53.) New York.

GREENWOOD, E. 1945. *Experimental Sociology: A Study in Method.* New York: King's Crown Press.

HALLOWELL, A. I. 1951. "The Use of Projective Techniques in the Study of the Socio-psychological Aspects of Acculturation," *Journal of Projective Techniques,* Vol. 15, No. 1, pp. 27–44.

HARRIS, J. S. 1944. "Some Aspects of the Economics of Sixteen Ibo Individuals," *Africa,* Vol. 14, pp. 302–35.

HENRY, J. 1951. "The Economics of Pilagá Food Distribution," *American Anthropologist,* Vol. 53, No. 2, pp. 187–219.

HENRY, J. and Z. 1944. *Doll-Play of Pilagá Indian Children.* ("American Orthopsychiatric Association Monograph Series," No. 4.) New York.

HERSKOVITS, M. J. 1938. *Dahomey, An Ancient West African Kingdom.* 2 vols., New York: J. J. Augustin, Inc.

————. 1948. *Man and His Works.* New York: Knopf.

————. 1950. "The Hypothetical Situation: A Technique of Field Research," *Southwestern Journal of Anthropology,* Vol. 6, No. 1, pp. 32–40.

JORDAN, E. 1952. *Essays in Criticism.* Chicago: University of Chicago Press.

JOSEPH, A.; SPICER, R.; and CHESKY, J. 1949. *The Desert People: A Study of the Papago Indians of Southern Arizona.* Chicago: University of Chicago Press.

KLUCKHOHN, C. 1938. "Participation in Ceremonials in a Navaho Community," *American Anthropologist,* Vol. 40, pp. 359–69.

————. 1939. "The Place of Theory in Anthropological Studies," *Philosophy of Science,* Vol. 6, No. 3, pp. 328–44.

————. 1947. "Some Aspects of Navaho Infancy and Early Childhood." In ROHEIM, G. (ed.), *Psychoanalysis and the Social Sciences,* I, 37–86. New York: International Universities Press.

————. 1951a. "A Comparative Study of Values in Five Cultures," in Vogt, E., *Navaho Veterans: A Study of Changing Values.* ("Papers of the Peabody Museum of American Archaeology and Ethnology, Harvard University," Vol. 41, No. 1.) Cambridge, Mass.

————. 1951b. "The Study of Culture," pp. 86–101, in Lerner, D., and Lasswell, H. D. (eds.), *The Policy Sciences: Recent Developments in Scope and Method.* Stanford: Stanford University Press.

KLUCKHOHN, F. R. 1940. "The Participant Observer Technique in Small Communities," *American Journal of Sociology,* Vol. 46, No. 3, pp. 331–43.

KROEBER, A. L. 1931. *Report on the Seri.* ("Los Angeles Southwest Museum Papers," Vol. 6.) Los Angeles.

————. 1948. *Anthropology.* New York: Harcourt, Brace.

LEIGHTON, D. C., and KLUCKHOHN, C. 1946. *The Navaho.* Cambridge, Mass.: Harvard University Press.

————. 1947. *Children of the People.* Cambridge, Mass.: Harvard University Press.

LEWIS, O. 1948. *On Edge of the Black Waxy: A Cultural Survey of Bell County, Texas*. ("Washington University Studies in Social and Philosophical Sciences," No. 7.) St. Louis.

——. 1950. "Anthropological Approach to Family Studies," *American Journal of Sociology*, Vol. 55, No. 5, pp. 468–75.

——. 1951. *Life in a Mexican Village: Tepoztlán Restudied*. Urbana, Ill.: University of Illinois Press.

——. 1952. "Urbanization without Breakdown: A Case Study" (paper read at annual meeting of the American Anthropological Association, Chicago), *Scientific Monthly*, Vol. 75, No. 1, pp. 31–41.

LINTON, R. 1945. *The Cultural Backgrounds of Personality*. New York: Appleton-Century.

LOMBARD, G. F. F. 1950. "Self-awareness and Scientific Method," *Science*, Vol. 112, pp. 289–93.

LYSTAD, R. A. 1951. "Differential Acculturation of the Ahafo-Ashanti of the Gold Coast and the Indenie-Agni of the Ivory Coast" (Doctoral dissertation). Northwestern University.

McCOMBE, L.; VOGT, E.; and KLUCKHOHN, C. 1951. *Navaho Means People*. Cambridge, Mass.: Harvard University Press.

McFARLANE, JEAN W., and TUDDENHAM, R. D. 1951. "Problems in Validating of Projective Techniques," chap. ii, in Anderson, H. H. and G. M. L., *Introduction to Projective Techniques*. New York: Prentice-Hall.

McGEE, W. S. 1895–96. *The Seri Indians*. ("Publications of the U.S. Bureau of Ethnology," Vol. 57, Part I.)

MACGREGOR, G. 1945. *Warriors without Weapons: A Study of the Society and Personality Development of the Pine Ridge Sioux*. Chicago: University of Chicago Press.

MAIR, L. P. 1934. *An African People in the Twentieth Century*. London: Routledge.

MALINOWSKI, B. 1922. *The Argonauts of the Western Pacific*. London: Routledge.

MEAD, M. 1933. "More Comprehensive Field Methods," *American Anthropologist*, Vol. 35, No. 1, pp. 1–15.

——. 1935. *Sex and Temperament in Three Primitive Societies*. New York: William Morrow.

——. 1939. "Native Languages as Field-Work Tools," *American Anthropologist*, Vol. 41, No. 2, pp. 189–205.

——. 1940. *The Mountain Arapesh. II. Supernaturalism*. ("Anthropological Papers of the American Museum of Natural History," Vol. 37, Part 3.) New York.

——. 1949. *The Mountain Arapesh. V. The Record of Unabelin with Rorschach Analysis*. ("Anthropological Papers of the American Museum of Natural History," Vol. 41, Part 3.) New York.

MEAD, M., and MACGREGOR, G. 1951. *Growth and Culture: A Photographic Study of Balinese Childhood*. New York: Putnam.

MINER, H. 1949. *Culture and Agriculture: An Anthropological Study of a Corn Belt County*. ("Occasional Contributions from the Museum of Anthropology of the University of Michigan," No. 14.) Ann Arbor: University of Michigan Press.

NADEL, S. F. 1951. *The Foundations of Social Anthropology.* Glencoe, Ill.: Free Press.

PALMER, J. O. 1951. *A Dual Approach to Rorschach Validation: A Methodological Study.* ("Psychological Monographs," ed. HERBERT S. CONRAD, Vol. 65, No. 8 [whole No. 325].) Washington, D.C.: Psychological Association of America.

PARSONS, E. C. 1939. *Pueblo Indian Religion.* Chicago: University of Chicago Press.

PARSONS, T. 1937. *The Structure of Social Action.* New York: McGraw-Hill.

PAUL, BENJAMIN. 1950*a.* "Life in a Guatemala Indian Village." Reprinted from *Patterns for Modern Living.* Chicago: Delphian Society.

————. 1950*b.* "Symbolic Sibling Rivalry in a Guatemalan Indian Village," *American Anthropologist,* 52, No. 2, pp. 205–18.

RABIN, A. I. 1951. "Validating and Experimental Studies with Rorschach Method," chap 5, in Anderson, H. H. and G. M. L., *Introduction to Projective Techniques.* New York: Prentice-Hall.

RADIN, P. 1933. *The Method and Theory of Ethnology.* New York: McGraw-Hill.

REDFIELD, R. 1948. "The Art of Social Science," *American Journal of Sociology,* Vol. 54, No. 3, pp. 181–90.

REDFIELD, R., and VILLA, A. 1934. *Chan Kom, a Maya Village.* Washington, D.C.: Carnegie Institution of Washington.

RICHARDS, A., and WIDDOWSON, E. M. 1936. "A Dietary Study in North-eastern Rhodesia," *Africa,* Vol. 9, pp. 166–96.

ROBERTS, J. M. 1951. *Three Navaho Households.* ("Papers of the Peabody Museum of American Archaeology and Ethnology, Harvard University," Vol. 11, No. 3.) Cambridge, Mass.

SCHNEIDER, L. I. 1950. "Rorschach Validation: Some Methodological Aspects," *Psychological Bulletin,* Vol. 47, No. 6, pp. 493–508.

SPINDLER, G., and GOLDSCHMIDT, W. 1952. "Experimental Design in the Study of Culture Change," *Southwestern Journal of Anthropology,* Vol. 8, No. 1, pp. 68–83.

STEWARD, J. H. 1950. *Area Research, Theory and Practice.* (Social Science Research Council Bulletin 63.) New York.

STRODTBECK, F. L. 1951. "Husband-Wife Interaction over Revealed Differences," *American Sociological Review,* Vol. 16, No. 4, pp. 468–73.

TAX, S. 1952. *Penny Capitalism: A Guatemalan Indian Economy.* ("Smithsonian Institution Publications in Social Anthropology.") Washington, D.C.

THOMPSON, L. 1950. *Culture in Crisis: A Study of the Hopi Indians.* New York: Harper.

————. 1951. *Personality and Government.* Mexico City: Inter-American Indian Institute.

THOMPSON, L., and JOSEPH, A. 1944. *The Hopi Way.* ("Indian Education Research Series," No. 1.) Chicago: University of Chicago Press.

THURSTONE, L. L. 1948. "The Rorschach in Psychological Science," *Journal of Abnormal and Social Psychology,* Vol. 43, pp. 471–75.

TITIEV, G. 1944. *Old Oraibi.* ("Papers of the Peabody Museum of American Archaeology and Ethnology, Harvard University," Vol. 22, No. 1.) Cambridge, Mass.

WAGLEY, C., and GALVAO, E. 1949. *The Tenetehara Indians of Brazil*. New York: Columbia University Press.

WEAKLAND, J. H. 1951. "Method in Cultural Anthropology," *Philosophy of Science*, Vol. 18, No. 1, pp. 55–69.

WHORF, B. L. 1940. "Linguistics as an Exact Science," *Technology Review*, Vol. 43, No. 2, pp. 61–63, 80–83.

2

Tepoztlán Restudied:

A Critique of the Folk-Urban
Conceptualization of Social Change*

Anthropologists who like to think that there is an element of science in the social sciences, including anthropology, have often called primitive societies the "laboratory" of the social scientists, where hypotheses about the nature of man and society can be tested. Although the experiments and observations of the natural scientist are generally repeated and checked independently by different observers, the reports of the anthropologists have to be accepted on their face value, and their reliability has to be judged in terms of the respect for and confidence in the author's integrity, the inner consistency of his work, and the extent to which it agrees with one's own preconceptions. If the analogy with the natural sciences is to be taken seriously, we must develop methods for checking the reliability of our observations and the validity of interpretation. Restudy is one such method. This point has been recognized by a number of anthropologists, but to date there have been very few restudies. The reasons for this are many. Perhaps most important have been the limited funds for field research, the time pressure to study tribes that were rapidly becoming extinct, the shortage of field workers, the

* This paper was read in September, 1951, at the annual meeting of the American Sociological Society in Chicago, and was published in June, 1953, *Rural Sociology*, Vol. 18, No. 2, pp. 121–36. Much of it has also appeared in the author's book, *Life in a Mexican Village: Tepoztlán Restudied* (Urbana: University of Illinois Press, 1951).

greater appeal in studying a community never before studied, and finally, the lack of emphasis upon methodology.

Of course, there is some difference of opinion in regard to the value of restudies. Those who would emphasize the subjective element, the element of art in field work, tend to be skeptical about the methodological value of restudies. On the other hand, those who have greater faith in objective methods, in operational procedures for observation, are inclined to be more favorable toward restudies. The former would argue that all human beings make errors, that this can be taken for granted, and that we can learn more by going ahead with new studies than by concerning ourselves with past mistakes. The latter would argue that it is important to learn what kinds of errors have been made, particularly if the scientific aspect of anthropology is to grow stronger. The former would argue that we do not need to have a restudy to know that there is something wrong with a report. This can be determined in terms of our wider comparative knowledge, in terms of internal consistency, or in terms of whether it agrees with a particular school of thought. The latter would perhaps agree but add that this is not enough, that we need empirical evidence as to just what the facts are. Finally, some would suggest that there may be a further dichotomy involved—namely, the difference between those who hold that truth is relative and subjective and that each field worker is probably correct within the limits of the problem set and the materials selected for study, and those who hold that truth is absolute and objective and can be approximated more nearly by some methods than by others.

It must be emphasized that the aim and value of restudies is not to prove one man right and another wrong. It is not a matter of listing another's errors, in itself a distasteful and painful task, but rather of finding out what kinds of errors tend to be made by what kinds of people under what kinds of conditions. Given a sufficiently large number of restudies, it might be possible to develop a theory of error of observation which would help to evaluate the role of the personal equation, personality, and ideological or cultural variables. If we could eventually arrive at generalizations in which we could say, given an anthropologist from such and such a cultural background, we can expect that his account of tribe X will be slanted in such and such a way, then we would have made some progress.

It may be useful to distinguish four types of restudies: (1) those restudies in which a second or third investigator goes to a community with the express design of re-evaluating the work of his predecessor; (2) those in which the same or an independent investigator goes to a community studied earlier, this time to study cultural change, and utilizing the first report as a baseline against which to measure and evaluate change; (3) those in which one returns to study some aspect of the culture not studied earlier; and (4) those in which one studies more intensively, and perhaps from a new point of view, some aspect of the culture studied earlier. There is, of course, some overlapping between these types. All restudies are additive in a sense. However, it is a matter of emphasis in research design.

From the point of view of testing reliability, the first type would seem to be the most suitable, though not without its methodological difficulties. Communities change, and it is sometimes difficult to know to what extent differences in findings reflect changes in the culture. Much depends upon the area and community being restudied. In cases where many years have elapsed between the first and second study and where change has been rapid and profound, it may well be impossible to reconstruct the earlier condition with sufficient accuracy to make it useful for reliability purposes. On the other hand, there are many areas where change is relatively slow and superficial. Moreover, when not too many years have elapsed, it may be possible to interview the same informants as in the earlier study. Also, the use of village records and archive records can act as a control. Finally, much depends upon the amount of quantitative data in the first report. Where the amount is large, restudies have a more solid base for comparisons. Indeed, this is perhaps the major positive function of quantification.

To my knowledge, there is not a single published case of a restudy of the first type—i.e., where the express purpose was the interest in methodology, the interest in testing an earlier report. My recent restudy of Tepoztlán perhaps comes closest to this type, and in the following pages some aspects of this restudy will be discussed.

In 1926, Robert Redfield first studied the village of Tepoztlán and gave us his pioneer work, *Tepoztlán—A Mexican Village.*[1] This book has since become a standard reference and a classic in the field of community studies. It is of particular importance in the history of community studies in that it contains Redfield's first statement on the nature of the folk society, and, at least implicitly, the concept of the folk-urban continuum, a hypothesis of societal change later made explicit in *The Folk Culture of Yucatan.*[2] The folk-urban conceptualization of culture change now enjoys great prestige among sociologists and anthropologists and has served as the theoretical

[1] Chicago: University of Chicago Press, 1930.

[2] Robert Redfield, *The Folk Culture of Yucatan* (Chicago: University of Chicago Press, 1941).

frame of reference for many of the community studies done by Redfield's students.

Seventeen years after Redfield's study, I went to Tepoztlán to take another look, with the specific objective of studying the social, economic, political, and religious life of the community, with special emphasis upon an analysis of the changes which had occurred in the village since 1926. This involved a restudy of the village and a comparison of findings. Special attention, however, was given to those aspects of village life that Redfield had merely touched upon, such as demography, the land problem, systems of agriculture, the distribution of wealth, standards of living, politics and local government, the life cycle of the individual, and interpersonal relations.

Readers who are familiar with the earlier study of Tepoztlán by Redfield will want to know how the findings compare. Such a comparison is made here, not only for a better understanding of Tepoztlán, but also because of its broader implications for anthropological method and theory. The questions are these: To what extent and in what ways do the results obtained from the independent study of the same society by two anthropologists differ? What are the implications of such differences concerning the reliability and validity of anthropological reporting?

The differences in findings range from discrepancies in factual details to differences in the over-all view of Tepoztecan society and its people. The impression given by Redfield's study of Tepoztlán is that of a relatively homogeneous, isolated, smoothly functioning, and well-integrated society made up of a contented and well-adjusted people. His picture of the village has a Rousseauan quality which glosses lightly over evidence of violence, disruption, cruelty, disease, suffering, and maladjustment. We are told little of poverty, economic problems, or political schisms. Throughout his study we find an emphasis upon the co-operative and unifying factors in Tepoztecan society. My findings, on the other hand, would emphasize the underlying individualism of Tepoztecan institutions and character, the lack of co-operation, the tensions between villages within the *municipio*, the schisms within the village, the pervading quality of fear, envy, and distrust in interpersonal relations.

Now let us consider some of these differences in more detail. Redfield's account of Tepoztlán stresses the role of communal lands as a unifying factor within the village and the *municipio*. Although this is certainly true, it is only part of the story. With the single exception of church lands, communal lands were and are individually operated, and the ideal of every Tepoztecan is to own his private plot of land. Furthermore, the communal lands have been a source of intervillage quarrels, and during the year that Redfield was in Tepoztlán these quarrels resulted in violence. Similarly, Redfield gives the impression that the *cuatequitl* (a traditional form of collective labor) was part and parcel of village life. He described a *cuatequitl*, which occurred during his stay, as if it were a common and regular occurrence. As a matter of fact, it was the first village *cuatequitl* of importance since the Revolution of 1910–1920, and there have been very few subsequent ones. The particular *cuatequitl* that Redfield observed was due to the curious circumstance whereby a local socialistically oriented political faction, directed from Mexico City by a group of Tepoztecans who were members of the Regional Confederation of Mexican Workers (Confederación Regional de Obreros Mexicanos), locally known as "the Bolsheviki," revived the traditional *cuatequitl*. Before the Revolution, the village *cuatequitl* was not viewed simply as a voluntary, co-operative endeavor but was also associated with forced labor and imposition by the local *cacique* groups that ruled the village during the Díaz regime. In the Colonial period, the Spaniards similarly utilized the traditional *cuatequitl* as a source of labor. In short, Redfield's account of the co-operative aspects of village life needs to be modified somewhat in the light of other data.

Redfield portrayed Tepoztlán as a community of landowners and did not mention a land problem. But in the restudy it was found that over half of the villagers did not own private land, and that there was an acute shortage of good land and considerable population pressure in the face of dwindling agricultural resources. Redfield gave a rather glowing picture of Tepoztlán during the Díaz regime as having reached a period of great cultural florescence, but he failed to point out that this was limited to only a few Tepoztecans, and that the vast majority of Tepoztecans were illiterate, desperately poor, landless, and living under an oppressive political regime which forbade them to utilize their own communal resources. In this connection it is interesting to note that Tepoztlán was one of the first villages in the state of Morelos to join the Zapatista revolt against the Díaz regime. Redfield apparently viewed the Mexican Revolution as having had the effect of halting the tendency toward the merging of social-class differences; but I found that the Revolution had a marked leveling influence, economically, socially, and culturally.

Redfield presented only the positive and formal aspects of interpersonal relations, such as forms of greeting and the respect-relations of *compadres;* he failed to deal with some of the negative and disruptive aspects of village life, such as the fairly high incidence of stealing, quarrels, and physical violence. An examination of the local records revealed that, in the year that Redfield lived in the village, there were 175 reported cases of crimes and misdemeanors in the local court. Most of these cases were offenses against person and property. Since not all cases reach the local authorities, this number is indicative of considerable conflict.

Redfield described local politics as a game, but it appears that politics was a very serious affair which frequently led to violence. The year Redfield was there, the political schisms culminated in open violence bordering on civil war, and it was this situation that finally resulted in Redfield's leaving the village.

Another important difference between the findings concerns Redfield's delineation of the social structure of the village in terms of what he called the *tontos,* or representatives of folk culture, and the *correctos,* or representatives of city ways. It should be pointed out that Tepoztecans do not conceive of these terms as designations of social classes, in the sense used by Redfield, nor did they twenty years ago. Tepoztecans use the words as descriptive adjectives, with *tonto* meaning stupid, backward, foolish, or ignorant, and with *correcto* meaning well mannered, well bred, proper, or correct. The poorest, least-educated, and most conservative man may be *correcto* to a Tepoztecan if he is polite and behaves in the accepted manner. Similarly, a well-educated, acculturated man may be called *tonto* if he permits himself to be fooled by others or dominated by his wife. Within any one family, some of the members may be considered *tonto* and others *correcto,* depending almost entirely upon personality traits and manners.

But, granting that the degree of exposure to and influence of city ways is an important criterion in making for status differences in Tepoztlán, it is by no means the only one, and certainly not the most significant one in terms of the actual operation of the many status distinctions in the village. Among status distinctions which were then, and are today, more meaningful to Tepoztecans are those of rich and poor, landowners and landless, owners of private lands and holders of *ejidos, ejidatarios* and *comuneros,* farmers in hoe culture and farmers in plow culture, sons of *caciques* and sons of ex-Zapatistas, to mention but a few.

Furthermore, Redfield's concept of *tontos* and *correctos* as social classes representing different cultural levels, led to his misunderstanding of the local political situation. The opposing political factions in the village during Redfield's stay were not composed of *tontos* on the one side and *correctos* on the other. The leaders on both sides included highly acculturated and little acculturated individuals, as did the members at large. A study of the personnel of each of the local government administrations (*ayuntamientos*) from 1926 to 1947 gives no support to Redfield's statement that politics, like the religious fiestas, is in the hands of the *tontos*.

The use of the terms *tonto* and *correcto* to designate social groups which did not and do not exist and operate as such, makes much of Redfield's analysis of Tepoztecan society oversimplified, schematic, and unreal. There is a much wider range of custom and belief among the so-called *tontos* than was reported by Redfield; and by the same token there was less of a gap between the *tontos* and *correctos*. Whereas Redfield's concept would tend to make for two cultures, I see Tepoztlán as a single culture, with more and less acculturated individuals in close and frequent contact, each influencing the other, as they have for the past four hundred years.

More important than the differences in findings is the question of how to explain these differences. In a sense, it is inevitable that different students studying the same society will arrive at different conclusions. Certainly the personal factor, and what Redfield has recently referred to as the element of art in social science, cannot be overlooked. Nevertheless the differences in findings on Tepoztlán are of such magnitude as to demand some further and more detailed explanation.

Some of the differences in the two sets of data can be explained by changes in the village in the interim of nearly twenty years between the studies. Other differences result from the difference in the general scope of the two studies. My study had the advantage of having Redfield's pioneer work to start with, the assistance of Mexican personnel, more than twice the amount of time for field work, and the new approaches and methods, especially in the field of culture and personality, developed during the past twenty years. The much greater emphasis upon economic analysis in my study also reflects a fairly recent trend in anthropology. In addition, this study was based on the testimony of well over one hundred informants, as compared with about a half-dozen used by Redfield. This revealed a wide range of individual differences and enabled more thorough checking of data.

Still other differences, such as those summarized, must be attributed for the most part to differences in theoretical orientation and methodology, which in turn influenced the selection and coverage of facts and the way in which these facts were organized. A re-examination of Redfield's book, in the light of the more recent field observations in the village, suggests that the concept of the folk culture and folk-urban continuum was Redfield's organizing principle in the research. Perhaps this helps to explain his emphasis on the formal and ritualistic aspects of life rather than the everyday life of the people and their problems, on evidence of homogeneity rather than heterogeneity and the range of custom, on the weight of tradition rather than deviation and innovation, on unity and integration rather than tensions and conflict.

Redfield's interest was primarily in the study of a single cultural process: the evolution from folk to urban, rather than a well-rounded ethnographic account. He only incidentally considered Tepoztlán in its historical, geographical, and cultural context in Morelos and Mexico, and attempted rather to place Tepoztlán within the broader, more abstract context of the folk-urban continuum.

The questions he asked of his data were quite different from those asked in this study. For example, he was not concerned with determining just what Tepoztlán is typical of, in relation to rural Mexico; nor was he concerned with determining how a study of Tepoztlán might reveal some of the underlying characteristics and problems of Mexico as a whole. Thus, the Revolution in Tepoztlán is not analyzed in terms of its social, economic, and political effects upon the village, nor in terms of what light it might throw upon the nature of the Revolution as a whole, but rather in regard to the more limited question of the emergence of Zapata as a "folk hero."

To what extent does the trend of change found in the present study of Tepoztlán fall within the categories suggested by Redfield in his study, *The Folk Culture of Yucatan?* He postulates that with increased urban influences there are greater disorganization, secularization, and individualization. Taking each separately, we shall consider the family first, as an example of disorganization. Redfield summarized the broad trends of change in family organization as follows:

> As one goes from Tusik [peasant village] toward Merida [urban community] there is to be noted a reduction in the stability of the elementary family; a decline in the manifestation of patriarchal or matriarchal authority; a disappearance of institutions expressing cohesion in the great family; a reduction in the strength and importance of respect relationships, especially for elder brothers and for elder people generally; an increasing vagueness of the conventional outlines of appropriate behavior toward relatives; and a shrinkage in the applicability of kinship terms primarily denoting members of the elementary family toward more distant relatives or toward persons not relatives.[3]

The first generalization that can be made in the case of Tepoztlán is that, despite the increased city influences in the last seventeen years, the stability of the nuclear family has not been seriously mod-

[3] Redfield, *The Folk Culture of Yucatan*, p. 211.

ified.* The family remains strong and cohesive, separations have not
noticeably increased, and divorce is all but nonexistent. The extended family is relatively weak but continues to serve in cases of
emergency. This weakness, however, is not a recent phenomenon.
Quarrels between husband and wife and wife-beating occur with
some frequency; but this, too, seems to be an old pattern. The tensions and quarrels within families reflect a type of family organization, as well as Tepoztecan personality, but are not necessarily
symptoms of disorganization.

Parental authority remains strong in Tepoztlán despite the elimination of arranged marriages and the increase in elopements. Parents continue to have control over their children, in many cases even
after marriage. On about a sixth of the house sites there are joint
families, and about half of these are extended families in which married sons are treated as children subject to the authority of the parents (*hijos de familia*).

Although about half of the marriages now begin as elopements,
which flout the authority of the parents, the old form of asking for
the girl's hand by the boy's parents continues. In any case, elopements do not lead to disorganization, for most elopements end in
marriage, and the couples make peace with their parents. Assuming
that elopements are an old pattern, as seems to be indicated, here we
have a case in which urban influence has intensified an old pattern
rather than caused its breakdown. Moreover, because Redfield
found practically no elopements in Tusik and many elopements in
Merida, he associated elopements with urbanism and disorganization. But this assumes what has still to be proved. In Tepoztlán,
which, by Redfield's own standards, is much less urban than Merida,
we find a much higher proportion of elopements than in Merida.
Furthermore, in Tzintzuntzan, an even more isolated village, George
M. Foster found that 90 per cent of the marriages began as elopements. And he cites documentary evidence for the antiquity of this
pattern.[4] Beals, in another connection, has also called attention to a
pattern of change different from that reported by Redfield. Beals
writes:

> Cherán, like many Indian communities of Mexico, is increasingly
> influenced by the town and the city. Nevertheless, the process again
> seems significantly different from those hitherto described by Red-
> field. In Cherán there is no distinction of *los tontos* and *los correctos*,
> *mestizo* and *indio*, or *ladino* and *indio*, although such may exist in

---

* See also Essays 13 and 18, below.

[4] *Empire's Children: The People of Tzintzuntzan* (México: Imprenta Nuevo
Mundo, 1948), p. 429.

some Tarascan towns with an appreciable *mestizo* population. Nor does the neat diminishing-order of city, town and village hold in this area. Cherán is probably more influenced by Gary (Indiana), Mexico City, and Morelia (possibly in diminishing order) than it is by Uruapan and Patzcuaro. Indeed, it is quite probable that fundamentally Cherán is more progressive, more in touch with the modern world, than is *mestizo* Patzcuaro with its conscious idealization of a Colonial past.[5]

The desire of young couples to become independent of their parents and to set up their own homes reflects a greater individualism but does not necessarily imply a breakdown in family life. On the contrary, the lesser role of the in-laws and the greater dependence of the husband and wife upon each other, plus the fact that they are each of their own choice, may make for better marriage relations and greater family stability.

Although it is true that some outer forms of respect have been discarded, the fundamental respect status of elders remains. Perhaps the single exception has been the decline in the respect accorded to elder brothers. But it is questionable whether the elder brother in Tepoztlán ever enjoyed the special position that he had in Maya society.

There seems to be no evidence of any marked change in the reciprocal behavior of relatives, perhaps because such changes have occurred so far back in history that informants have no memory of them today. As stated previously, the extended family is weak, and seems to have been so for many generations. The same may be said for the use of kinship terms, which have not changed in recent history. In surrounding villages, which generally conserve older culture elements, kinship terms are used in substantially the same way as in Tepoztlán.

In the examples cited, it is clear that changes have occurred in the village, but these changes do not necessarily imply disorganization. Rather, they involve a new kind of organization or reorganization.

The second conclusion of the study in Yucatan showed a clear trend toward secularization:

> The conclusion has been reached that the city and town exhibit greater secularization than do the villages. The principal facts offered in support of this conclusion are . . . the separation of maize from the context of religion and its treatment simply as a means of getting food or money; the increase in the number of specialists who carry

[5] Ralph L. Beals, *Cherán: A Sierra Tarascan Village*, Institute of Social Anthropology, Pub. No. 2 (Washington, D. C.: Smithsonian Institution, 1946), pp. 211–12.

on their activities for a practical livelihood relative to those that carry on traditional activities which are regarded as prerogatives and even moral duties to the community; the change in the character of the institution of guardia whereby from being an obligation, religiously supported, to protect a shrine and a god it becomes a mere job in the town hall; the (almost complete) disappearance of family worship; the decline in the sacramental character of baptism and marriage; the conversion of the pagan cult from what is truly religious worship to mere magic or even superstition; the decline in the veneration accorded the santos; the change in the novena in which from being a traditional form expressive of appeal to deity, it becomes a party for the fun of the participants; the alteration in the festival of the patron saint in which it loses its predominant character as worship and becomes play and an opportunity for profit; the separation of ideas as to the cause and cure of sickness from conceptions as to moral or religious obligation.[6]

The data from Tepoztlán do not enable a careful comparison on each of the cited points. However, many of the data are comparable and show the trend toward secularization noted. The attitude toward corn in Tepoztlán combines the secular and the religious. Certainly corn is viewed as the basic crop, both for subsistence and for trade. But the religious aspects have not been entirely lopped off. The corn is still blessed in the church on San Isidro's Day, and some families still burn incense in the home and address a prayer to the corn before planting. Some also make the sign of the cross when planting the first seed. Moreover, on San Miguel's Day, crosses are still placed at the four corners of the *milpa* to ward off the winds. From informants' accounts, it appears that these customs were more widespread before the Revolution. It is difficult to say how much change has occurred since 1926, for Redfield did not report on this subject.

The study of occupational changes and division of labor in Tepoztlán showed that most of the old "folk specialists" have continued and even increased in number, side by side with the increase in the number of new specialists. There were more *curanderos, chirimiteros,* fireworks-makers, and maskmakers in 1944 than in 1926, and there seemed to be every indication that these occupations would continue. The only exceptions are the *huehuechiques,* who must be able to speak Nahuatl, and the *chirimiteros,* who are being displaced by the modern band. However, the rate of increase in what Redfield would call the secular specialists has been much greater than that of the "folk specialists." To this extent, the independent findings for Yucatan and Tepoztlán agree. But it should be noted that before the

[6] Redfield, *The Folk Culture of Yucatan,* p. 352.

Revolution there were more shoemakers, carpenters, saddle-makers, and other artisans than in 1926 or 1944. Were it not for the specific historical information to explain this phenomenon, one might conclude that with increasing urban contacts there is a decrease in the number of specialists. The reason for this decrease has been, rather, the destruction of many neighboring haciendas which were formerly supplied by labor from Tepoztlán, and the abolition of the *cacique* class, which had offered a market for the products of the artisans.

In Tepoztlán there does not appear to have been any appreciable decline in the sacramental character of baptism and marriage. At any rate, both are considered important and are standard practices. Despite the legalization of secular marriage, church marriage is still considered the best marriage by most Tepoztecans.

Similarly, there is no evidence of any decline in the veneration of the *santos;* the *novena* continues to be an appeal to the deity rather than a party for fun; the patron saints of the *barrios* are still regarded as protectors and are worshipped as such. Nor have *barrio* fiestas become primarily an occasion for profit. In fact, Tepoztecans do not show the marked commercial spirit reported in Mitla by Parsons,[7] and in communities of the Guatemalan highlands by Sol Tax.[8] Unlike Parsons in Mitla, the researchers in Tepoztlán were never besieged by questions about the cost of things, nor did they ever witness Tepoztecans haggling among themselves or with strangers.

The third conclusion of the Yucatan study pertains to the trend toward individualization, or individualism, as one goes from folk to urban. The specific facts found in the study of the four Yucatan communities are listed as follows:

> . . . the relative decrease in importance of specialized functions which are performed on behalf of the community and the relative increase of specialties discharged for the individual's own benefit; the development of individual rights in land and in family estates; the diminution or disappearance of collective labor and of the exchange of services in connection with civic enterprises and religious worship; the decreasing concern of the family or of the local community in the making and the maintaining of marriages; the becoming less common of the extended domestic family; the lessening of emphasis and of conventional definition of the respect relationships among kin; the decline in family worship and the disappearance of religious symbols expressive of the great family; the decrease in the tendency to

[7] Elsie Clews Parsons, *Mitla, Town of the Souls* (Chicago: University of Chicago Press, 1936).

[8] Sol Tax, *Penny Capitalism: A Guatemalan Indian Economy* (Washington, D.C.: Smithsonian Institution, 1953).

extend kinship terms with primary significance for members of the elementary family to more remote relatives or to persons unrelated genealogically; the increasing vagueness of the conventional outlines of appropriate behavior towards relatives; the change in the nature of marriage and baptism rites so as less to express the linkage of the families and more to concern the immediately involved individuals only; the decline in relative importance of the santo patron of the local community; the suggested relation of the increase in sorcery to the separation of individuals, especially of women, from the security of familial groups.[9]

Some of the items listed above were also listed under the categories of disorganization and secularization and have been treated earlier. The development of individual rights in land may date back to before the Spanish Conquest. Cortes and his heirs owned land in Tepoztlán and rented it out to Tepoztecans as early as 1580. In the past twenty or thirty years there have been no changes in the direction of the private ownership of the communal resources. The persistence of the communal land, which still accounts for over four-fifths of all the area of the *municipio,* is impressive.

The trend toward the breakdown of collective labor is seen clearly in Tepoztlán, particularly in connection with the difficulty in getting *barrio* members to turn out for the plowing and planting of the *barrio* fields. In 1947, three of the *barrios* had rented out the land and used the rental for the *barrio.* On the whole, many of our findings for Tepoztlán might be interpreted as confirming Redfield's more general finding for Yucatan, particularly with regard to the trend toward secularization and individualization, perhaps less so with regard to disorganization.

Since the concept of the folk society as an ideal type is, after all, a matter of definition, there can be no quarrel with it as such, provided that it can be shown to have heuristic value. On the basis of the restudy of Tepoztlán, however, it seems necessary to point out a number of limitations found in the conceptual framework of the folk-urban continuum, both as a scheme for the study of culture change, and for cultural analysis. These criticisms can be discussed under seven related points.

1. The folk-urban conceptualization of social change focuses attention primarily on the city as the source of change, to the exclusion or neglect of other factors of an internal or external nature. So-called folk societies have been influencing each other for hundreds of years and out of such interaction has come cultural change. The archaeological record in Tepoztlán, as well as in other parts of Mexico, indicates quite clearly a great mingling of people and cultures, which

[9] Redfield, *The Folk Culture of Yucatan,* p. 355.

dates back at least a thousand years before the Spanish Conquest. Tepoztlán itself was first conquered by the Toltecs and later by the Aztecs, and with each conquest came new influences, new religious ideas, and new customs.

Another example of nonurban factors in culture change can be seen in the case of Tepoztlán and other parts of Latin America, where the introduction of rural culture elements was at least as far-reaching in effect as any changes brought about by later urban influences. Similarly, we find that the Mexican Agrarian Revolution (particularly in its Zapatista phase) was a profound influence for change, but can hardly be classified as an urban influence. It is evident that the folk-urban continuum concept covers only one of a wide variety of situations which may lead to culture change. In the case of Tepoztlán, to study the urban factors alone would give us only a partial picture of culture change.

2. It follows that in many instances culture change may not be a matter of a folk-urban progression, but rather an increasing or decreasing heterogeneity of culture elements.* For example, the incorporation of Spanish rural elements—such as the plow, oxen, plants, and many folk beliefs—did not make Tepoztlán more urban but instead gave it a more varied rural culture. The introduction of plow culture in Tepoztlán did not eliminate the older system of hoe culture but gave the Tepoztecans an alternative and, in some ways, a more efficient method of farming, making for greater heterogeneity in the economic life and in the forms of social relationships.

3. Some of the criteria used in the definition of the folk society are treated by Redfield as linked or interdependent variables, but might better be treated as independent variables. Sol Tax, in his study of Guatemalan societies, has shown that societies can be both culturally well organized and homogeneous and, at the same time, highly secular, individualistic, and commercialistic. He has also shown that interpersonal relations in a small and homogeneous society can be characterized by formalism and impersonality. His findings are supported by the present study. Moreover, this study shows other possible combinations of variables. Thus, whereas Tax found family disorganization as a concomitant of commercialism, in Tepoztlán the family remains strong, and there is little evidence of family disorganization. Moreover, collective forms of land tenure exist side by side with private landownership and individual working of the land.

4. The typology involved in the folk-urban classification of societies tends to obscure one of the most significant findings of modern cultural anthropology, namely, the wide range in the ways of life

* See also Essays 3 and 11, below.

and in the value systems among so-called primitive peoples. The "folk society," as used by Redfield, would group together food-gathering, hunting, pastoral, and agricultural peoples, without distinction. To apply the term "folk society" to high cultures like that of the Aztecs (Tepoztlán was part of this high-culture area) and at the same time to apply it to simple food-gathering peoples like the Shoshone robs the term of its discriminatory value. Also, to write of a "folk element" in Tepoztlán in 1926 (the so-called *tontos*) as if it were identical with the folk element of the pre-Hispanic days neglects all the cultural influences to which this element has been subjected in the intervening four hundred years and blurs many distinctions which have to be made. Similarly, it would put into one category societies which are as different culturally and psychologically as the Arunta and the Eskimo, the Dobu and the Ba Thonga, the Zuni and the Alorese, the Dahomey and the Navaho. Indeed, one might argue that the folk-urban classification is not a cultural classification at all, since it rides roughshod over fundamental cultural differences—i.e., differences in the ethos of a people. The point is that in attitudes and value systems, folk societies may resemble some urban societies much more than they resemble other folk societies. For example, the individualism and competitiveness of the Blackfoot Indians* remind one much more of American urban value systems than of Zuni values. This suggests that the criteria used in the folk-urban classification are concerned with the purely formal aspects of society and are not necessarily the most crucial for cultural analysis.

What has been said of the folk end of the folk-urban formula applies also to the urban end. Focusing only on the formal aspects of urban society reduces all urban societies to a common denominator and treats them as if they all had the same culture. Thus, Greek, Egyptian, Roman, Medieval, and twentieth-century American and Russian cities would all be put into the same class. To take but one example, there are obvious and significant differences between American and Russian urban culture, and in all probability these two "urban influences" would have a very different effect upon a preliterate society exposed to them.

It should be clear that the concept "urban" is too much of a catchall to be useful for cultural analysis. Moreover, it is suggested here that the question posed by Redfield—What happens to an isolated homogeneous society when it comes into contact with an urbanized society?—cannot possibly be answered in a scientific way because the question is too general and the terms used do not give us the necessary data. What we need to know is what kind of an urban

---

* See also Essays 7 and 8, below.

society, under what conditions of contact, and a host of other specific historical data.

5. The folk-urban classification has serious limitations in guiding field research because of the highly selective implications of the categories themselves and the rather narrow focus of problem. The emphasis upon essentially formal aspects of culture leads to neglect of psychological data and, as a rule, does not give insight into the character of the people. We have already seen how this approach has influenced the selection, interpretation, and organization of the data in Redfield's study of Tepoztlán.

6. The folk-urban conceptualization of social change as developed by Redfield assumes a uniform, simultaneous, and unilateral change in all institutions, which is reminiscent of early evolutionary theory. Moreover, it tells us nothing about the rate of change.

7. Finally, underlying the folk-urban dichotomy as used by Redfield is a system of value judgments which contains the old Rousseauan notion of primitive peoples as noble savages, and the corollary that with civilization has come the fall of man. This type of value system is particularly prone to influence the interpretation of a given cultural change as to whether it shall be called disorganization or simply reorganization. Since the concept of disorganization is one of the three key concepts in Redfield's folk-urban hypothesis, it can be seen how directly this value system may affect the interpretation. This is not, of course, an objection to the fact of values *per se*, but rather to the failure to make them explicit, as well as to this particular value system. Redfield's values suggest what Lovejoy and Boas have called "cultural primitivism," which they define as "the discontent of the civilized with civilization, or with some conspicuous and characteristic feature of it." [10]

These authors show that primitivism has existed in various forms throughout the recorded history of mankind.

> Of direct, or even indirect, influence of the classical primitivistic tradition there is probably little. But since the beginning of the present century, Western man has become increasingly skeptical concerning the nineteenth-century "myth of progress," increasingly troubled with the misgivings about the value of the outcome of civilization thus far, about the future to which it tends, and about himself as the author of it all; and similar doubts and apprehensions found expression two millennia or more ago. In spite of the more complex and sophisticated general ideology of the contemporary exponents of these moods, there are striking parallels to be observed between certain of the texts that follow (i.e., Greek, Roman, and Indian) and

[10] Arthur A. Lovejoy and George Boas, *Primitivism and Related Ideas in Antiquity* (Baltimore: Johns Hopkins Press, 1935), p. 7.

some passages in such writings as Freud's *Civilization and Its Discontents* and Spengler's *Man and Technics.*[11]

Again and again in Redfield's writings there emerges the value judgment that folk societies are good and urban societies bad. It is assumed that all folk societies are integrated whereas urban societies are the great disorganizing force. In his introduction to Miner's study of St. Denis,[12] Redfield suggests that the usual view of peasant life "as something to be escaped, an ignominy to be shunned" may be wrong. He finds that the habitant of St. Denis has order, security, faith, and confidence "because he has culture." In another essay, "The Folk Society and Culture" in *Eleven Twenty-Six,* he contrasts the "organization and consistency which gives a group moral solidarity" with the "impaired" moral organization of the urban society.[13] Even in his most recent study, which in my view represents a great departure from his earlier thinking, in that he is less concerned with formalism and categories and more concerned with people, we find the old values reappearing. "Progress" and urbanization now are seen as inevitable, but they are still evil.[14]

The limitations in the folk-urban conceptualization of social change stand out even more clearly when we compare the results of this type of analysis with the results obtained by another method—namely, a combined historical-functional approach, in which the categories for analysis of change grow out of the historical data from a given situation. From this point of view, the history of culture change in Tepoztlán may be divided into three major periods: (1) from the Spanish Conquest to about 1910; (2) from 1910 to about 1930; (3) from 1930 to the present. No single formula will explain the whole range of phenomena embraced by these periods. Indeed, it appears that each period is characterized by a different rate of change and by varying degrees of change within different institutions. In some periods we find both destructive and constructive aspects, disorganization and reorganization. In one period, the technological changes affect primarily the lives of women; in another, primarily the lives of men.

[11] Lovejoy and Boas, p. 10.

[12] Horace Miner, *St. Denis: A French-Canadian Parish* (Chicago: University of Chicago Press, 1939).

[13] Robert Redfield, "The Folk Society and Culture," in *Eleven Twenty-Six: A Decade of Social Science Research* (Chicago: University of Chicago Press, 1940), p. 50.

[14] Robert Redfield, *A Village That Chose Progress, Chan Kom Revisited* (Chicago: University of Chicago Press, 1950), p. 178.

During the first period, change was on the whole gradual but far-reaching, touching all aspects of life from material culture and technology to social organization, economics, and religion. The changes during this period were the result of outside influence and consisted of the transformation of the culture by the superimposition of Spanish culture—consisting of both urban and rural elements—on the native culture, with a resultant fusion of the two. During the second period, the changes were caused by a combination of external and internal factors, and changes were more rapid and violent, affecting primarily the social and political organization. The third period was in a sense a continuation of the second, with the changes primarily in the fields of communication, literacy, education, consumption patterns, and values, and with economics, social organization, and religion remaining quite stable. In all periods, particularly in the field of material culture, the new culture elements tended not to supplant the old but to be added to them, thus making for a richer and more heterogeneous culture.

This discussion can be summarized in three general conclusions: (1) There is a need for more independent restudies in anthropology and, if possible, simultaneous studies of the same community or region by different investigators. (I would welcome an independent restudy of Tepoztlán twenty years hence.) (2) The approach to community and regional studies must be of the broadest possible type, in which the community is seen in its geographical and historical contacts rather than as an independent isolate. (3) The checking of a specific hypothesis in the course of a community study is certainly worthwhile, but one must be aware of the highly selective role of the hypothesis itself in directing the gathering of data. It may be that what is left out, because of the limiting needs of the hypothesis, is *all-important* for an understanding of the total cultural situation.

3

Further Observations on the Folk-Urban Continuum and Urbanization, with Special Reference to Mexico City*

My interest in studies of urbanism and the urbanization process in Mexico City has been a direct outgrowth of my earlier study of Te-poztlán.† In that work I suggested that the folk-urban continuum was an inadequate theoretical model for the study of culture change and needed drastic revision.[1] Later, in my follow-up study of Tepoz-tecans who had migrated to Mexico City I found evidence that strengthened this conviction, this time viewing the problem from the urban pole.[2]

* First published in 1965 in Philip M. Hauser and Leo F. Schnore, eds., *The Study of Urbanization* (New York: John Wiley & Sons).

† See Essay 2, above.

[1] Oscar Lewis, *Life in a Mexican Village: Tepoztlán Restudied* (Urbana, Ill.: University of Illinois Press, 1951).

[2] There has been a growing literature of criticism of the folk-urban and rural-urban dichotomies by urban sociologists. See, for example, Theodore Caplow, "The Social Ecology of Guatemala City," *Social Forces*, Vol. 28 (December, 1949), pp. 113–33; Philip M. Hauser, "The Urban-Folk and Urban Rural Dichotomies as Forms of Western Ethnocentrism," mimeographed paper for the SSRC Committee on Urbanization, 1959; William L. Kolb, "The Social Structure and Function of Cities," *Economic Development and Culture Change*, Vol. 3 (October, 1954), pp. 30–46; Otis Dudley Duncan and Albert J. Reiss, Jr., *Social Characteristics of Urban and Rural Communities, 1950* (New York: John Wiley, 1956), Part IV; Gideon Sjoberg, "Comparative Urban Sociology," in *Sociology Today* (New York: Basic Books, 1959), pp. 334–59. Horace Miner has attempted to defend the Redfield position in what seems to me to be a

Each of the terms "folk," "rural," and "urban" encompasses a wide range of phenomena, with multiple variables which have to be carefully sorted out, ordered, dissected, and perhaps redefined, if we are to establish meaningful, causal relationships among them. Each of these terms imply relatively high-level abstractions intended for the characterization of whole societies or large segments thereof. While such characterizations are attractive because of their simplicity and may be useful in distinguishing gross stages or types in societal evolution, they confuse issues in the study of short-run changes, and their heuristic value as research tools has never been proven.

Hauser has put this criticism admirably. He writes:

> There is evidence, by no means conclusive as yet, that both parts of these dichotomies (i.e., folk-urban and rural-urban) represent confounded variables and, in fact, complex systems of variables which have yet to be unscrambled. The dichotomizations perhaps represent all too hasty efforts to synthesize and integrate what little knowledge has been acquired in empirical research. The widespread acceptance of these ideal type constructs as generalizations, without benefit of adequate research, well illustrates the dangers of catchy neologisms which often get confused with knowledge.[3]

In his elaboration of the folk-urban continuum, Robert Redfield sought to achieve greater sophistication than earlier societal typologies by utilizing traits or variables which were of a general, more abstract nature. For example, whereas Hobhouse, Wheeler, and Ginsberg[4] distinguished between food-gathering, hunting and fishing, agricultural, and pastoral economies, and sought to establish their social and juridical correlates, Redfield's definition of the folk society as an ideal type never specified a type of technology or economy beyond stating that it was simple, subsistence motivated, without money, familial, etc.

In his later work Redfield showed some important but subtle changes in his thinking which have not been given sufficient emphasis by his followers and disciples, many of whom suffer from fixation or culture lag. Here I should like to mention two such changes. First, he seemed to be less sanguine about the possibility of deriving sound

---

rather apologetic article. A careful reading will show that he accepts most of the criticism although he swallows hard. See his "The Folk-Urban Continuum" in *Cities and Society,* ed. Hatt and Reiss (Glencoe, Ill.: Free Press, 1957), pp. 22–34.

[3] Hauser (above, note 2), p. 14.

[4] L. T. Hobhouse, J. C. Wheeler, and M. Ginsberg, *The Material Culture and Social Institutions of the Simpler Peoples: An Essay in Correlation* (London, 1915).

general propositions concerning social and cultural change and gave more stress to descriptive integration, "understanding," and the element of art in the social sciences. Compare for example his *Folk Culture of Yucatan*[5] with *A Village That Chose Progress, Chan Kom Restudied.*[6] In the former, he was still optimistic about finding regularities in culture change. In the latter, he gave us a brilliant description of changes in Chan Kom but made no attempt to relate these changes to the theoretical framework of the folk-urban continuum.

A second change is to be seen in *The Primitive World and Its Transformation,*[7] in which Redfield no longer conceives of the folk society exclusively as an ideal type. Rather, he treats it as a type of real society. In this book, Redfield takes a frank neo-evolutionary stance, identifying the folk society with the preagricultural or pre-Neolithic period and with the tribal (and I would add pretribal) level. In an effort to find common elements he paints with a big brush, lumping together all the peoples of the world prior to the Neolithic, irrespective of whether they were food-gatherers, fishers or hunters, whether they had rich or poor resources, whether they were starving or produced some surplus. In the very nature of the case, this approach glosses over the more refined archeological distinctions between the Lower and Upper Paleolithic, each with subdivisions based upon new technologies and inventions

True, we have little evidence about societal types for the prehistoric periods. However, a theoretical scheme must somehow take into account many levels and types of societal development prior to the rise of cities. Otherwise, there are unexplained and sudden breaks in the postulated evolutionary sequence from folk to urban. Indeed, if one had to choose between evolutionary schemes, there is still a good deal to be said in favor of Morgan's *Ancient Society*[8] despite its many factual errors and crude technological determinism. Fortunately, we have other and more sophisticated alternatives, such as the multilinear evolution of Julian Steward [9] and the recent work of Irving Goldman.[10]

The identification of the folk society with the pre-Neolithic seems to me to invalidate or, at least, to raise serious questions about Redfield's work in *The Folk Culture of Yucatan*, since all of the Yuca-

[5] Chicago: University of Chicago Press, 1941.

[6] Chicago: University of Chicago Press, 1950.

[7] Ithaca, N.Y.: Cornell University Press, 1953.

[8] L. H. Morgan, *Ancient Society* (New York, 1877).

[9] *Theory of Culture Change* (Urbana, Ill.: University of Illinois Press, 1963).

[10] "Status Rivalry and Cultural Evolution in Polynesia," *American Anthropologist*, Vol. 57, 1955, pp. 680–697. See also his book *Ancient Polynesian Society*, University of Chicago Press, 1970.

tan communities were agricultural peasant societies, which, by his own definition, are part societies subject in varying degree to urban influences. Even his most "folk-like" community of Quintana Roo was producing chicle for the world market!

Similarly, some of my own criticism of Redfield's Tepoztlán work, as well as Sol Tax's criticism based upon the Guatemalan studies,[11] would seem to be beside the point since both Tax and I were dealing with communities which had left the folk stage (if they were ever in it), for at least a few thousand years. To this extent, Ralph Beals' comment that Tepoztlán was not a crucial case for evaluating the transition from folk to peasant to urban has considerable merit, because Tepoztlán was already a well-advanced peasant society in pre-Hispanic days. But by the same token, I know of no other contemporary community study in Meso-America which would serve this purpose any better. Actually, Redfield had assumed a survival of folk, that is Paleolithic, elements in Tepoztlán, a period for which we have no evidence in that village.

The traditional contrast between societies based on kinship versus those based on nonkinship or contract, is not only inaccurate but of so broad and general a nature as to be of little help in the analysis of the process of change. To say of a society that it is organized on a kinship basis doesn't tell us enough for purposes of comparative analysis. It may be a nuclear family system, as among the Shoshone Indians; a lineage system, as in Tikopea; or a clan system, as among the Zuni Indians. We still have a lot to learn about the more modest problem of how and under what conditions in a given society, a simple nuclear, bilateral system turns into a unilateral clan system, and the social, economic, and psychological concomitants thereof. As a general proposition I would like to suggest that we may learn more about the processes of change by studying relatively short-run sequential modifications in particular aspects of institutions in both the so-called folk and urban societies, than by global comparisons between folk and urban.

Preurban and preindustrial societies have been capable of developing class stratification, elaborate priesthoods, status rivalry, and many other phenomena which are implicitly and unilaterally attributed to the growth of cities, according to the folk-urban conception of social change. Tonga, the Maori, and native Hawaii are good examples of this. Even among a fishing and hunting people like the Kwakiutl Indians, we find class stratification, slavery, and war. The Kwakiutl case illustrates the importance of including natural re-

---

[11] Sol Tax, "Culture and Civilization in Guatemalan Societies," *Scientific Monthly*, Vol. 43 (1941), pp. 22–42.

sources as a significant variable in evolutionary schemes. I find no such variable in the folk-urban continuum.

In place of, or in addition to, the handy designations, "folk society," "peasant society," "urban society," we need a large number of subtypes based upon better-defined variables and perhaps the addition of new ones.[12] Hauser's observations on the Western ethnocentrism implicit in the folk-urban and rural-urban dichotomies are well taken. Redfield's first-hand research experience in Mexican communities, which were essentially endogamous, tended to confirm his preconception of the folk society as "inward-looking." The thinking of Simmel, Tönnies, Durkheim, and others, which influenced Redfield, was also based on experience with the endogamous peasant communities of Europe. Had these men done field work with the Nuer of Africa, with the Australian aborigines, or with the north Indian peasants, it is quite possible that Redfield's ideal type model of the folk society might have been somewhat different.

Before turning to an examination of some of the assumptions of the Simmel-Wirth-Redfield axis regarding urbanism, I would like to present in brief some of my own research findings in Mexico which can serve as a starting point for the discussion. The relevant findings of my first Mexico City study of 1951 can be summarized as follows: (1) Peasants in Mexico City adapted to city life with far greater ease than one would have expected judging from comparable studies in the United States and from folk-urban theory. (2) Family life remained quite stable and extended family ties increased rather than decreased. (3) Religious life became more Catholic and disciplined, indicating the reverse of the anticipated secularization process. (4) The system of *compadrazgo* continued to be strong, albeit with some modifications. (5) The use of village remedies and beliefs persisted.

In the light of these findings I wrote at the time, "This study provides evidence that urbanization is not a single, unitary, universally similar process but assumes different forms and meanings, depending upon the prevailing historic, economic, social, and cultural conditions."[13]

[12] I have made this point in an earlier paper, "Peasant Culture in India and Mexico," in *Village India* (ed. McKim Marriott), *American Anthropologist*, Vol. 57, No. 3, Part 2. Memoir No. 83, June, 1955: "For both applied and theoretical anthropology we need typologies of peasantry for the major culture areas of the world. . . . Moreover, within each area we need more refined subclassifications. Only after such studies are available will we be in a position to formulate broad generalizations about the dynamics of peasant culture as a whole," p. 165. [See Essay 17, below.]

[13] Oscar Lewis, "Urbanization without Breakdown: A Case Study," *Scientific Monthly*, Vol. 75, No. 1 (July, 1952). In this article I have suggested a num-

Because of the unusual nature of my findings, I decided to test them in 1956–57 against a much wider sample of non-Tepoztecan city families. I selected two lower-class housing settlements or *vecindades*, both located in the same neighborhood within a few blocks of the Tepito market and only a short walk from the central square of Mexico City. In contrast to the Tepoztecan city families who represented a wide range of socioeconomic levels and were scattered in twenty-two *colonias* throughout the city, my new sample was limited to two settlements whose residents came from over twenty-four of the thirty-two states and territories of the Mexican nation.[14]

On the whole, our research findings tended to support those of the earlier study. The findings suggested that the lower-class residents of Mexico City showed little of the personal anonymity and isolation of the individual which had been postulated by Louis Wirth as characteristic of urbanism as a way of life. The *vecindad* and the neighborhood tended to break up the city into small communities which act as cohesive and personalizing factors. It was found that many people spend most of their lives within a single *colonia* or district, and even when there were frequent changes of residence they were usually within a restricted geographical area determined by low rentals. Lifetime friendships and daily face-to-face relations with the same people were common, and in this way resembled a village situation. Most marriages also occurred within the *colonia* or adjoining *colonias*. Again, we found that extended family ties were quite strong, as measured by visiting, especially in times of emergency, and that a relatively high proportion of the residents of the *vecindades* were related by kinship and *compadrazgo* ties.

In spite of the cult of *machismo* and the over-all cultural emphasis upon male superiority and dominance, we found a strong tendency toward matri-centered families, in which the mother plays a crucial role in parent-child relations even after the children are married. In genealogical studies we found that most people recalled a much larger number of relatives on the mother's side than on the father's side.

We also found that the *vecindad* acted as a shock absorber for the

---

ber of specific Mexican conditions which might explain the special findings. More recently Joseph A. Kahl has restated and elaborated upon some of these points in his article "Some Social Concomitants of Industrialization and Urbanization: A Research Review," *Human Organization*, Vol. 18 (Summer, 1959), pp. 53–74. [See Essay 18, below.]

[14] Oscar Lewis, "The Culture of the *Vecindad* in Mexico City: Two Case Studies," *Actas del III Congreso Internacional de Americanistas*, Tomo I (San José, Costa Rica, 1959), pp. 387–402. [See Essay 19, below.]

rural migrants to the city because of the similarity between its culture and that of rural communities. Both shared many of the traits which I have elsewhere designated as the culture of poverty.* Indeed, we found no sharp differences in family structure, diet, dress, and belief systems of the *vecindad* tenants according to their rural-urban origins. The use of herbs for curing, the raising of animals, the belief in sorcery and spiritualism, the celebration of the Day of the Dead, illiteracy and low level of education, political apathy and cynicism about government, and the very limited membership and participation in both formal and informal associations, were just as common among persons who had been in the city for over thirty years as among recent arrivals. Indeed, we found that *vecindad* residents of peasant background who came from small landholding families showed more middle-class aspirations in their desire for a higher standard of living, home ownership, and education for their children, than did city-born residents of the lower-income group.

These findings suggest the need for a re-examination of some aspects of urban theory and for modifications which would help explain the findings from Mexico City and other cities in underdeveloped countries, as well as those from Chicago.

Wirth defines a city as "a relatively large, dense, and permanent settlement of socially heterogeneous individuals." By "socially heterogeneous" he meant primarily distinctive ethnic groups rather than class differences. Wirth defines urbanism as the mode of life of people who live in cities or who are subject to their influence. Because Wirth thinks of the city as a whole, as a community (and here, I believe, is one of his errors), he assumes that all people who live in cities are affected by this experience in profound and similar ways, namely, the weakening of kinship bonds, family life and neighborliness, and the development of impersonality, superficiality, anonymity, and transitoriness in personal relations. For Wirth, the process of urbanization is essentially a process of disorganization.[15]

This approach leads to some difficulties. For one thing, as Sjoberg has pointed out, "their interpretations [i.e., those of Park, Wirth and Redfield] involving ecology have not articulated well with their efforts to explain social activities." [16] Wirth himself showed some of the contradictory aspects of city life without relating them to his theory of urbanism. He writes of the city as the historic center of progress, of learning, of higher standards of living and all that is

* For a fuller discussion of the culture of poverty, see Essay 4, below.

[15] Louis Wirth, "Urbanism as a Way of Life," *American Journal of Sociology,* Vol. 44 (July, 1938), pp. 1–24.

[16] Sjoberg, (above, note 2), p. 340.

hopeful for the future of mankind, but he also points to the city as the locus of slums, poverty, crime, and disorganization. According to Wirth's theory, both the carriers of knowledge and progress (the elite and the intellectuals) and the ignorant slum dwellers have similar urban personalities, since presumably they share in the postulated urban anonymity.

It is in the evaluation of the personality of the urban dweller that urban theory has gone furthest afield. It leaps from the analysis of the social system to conjecture about individual personality; it is based not upon solid psychological theory but upon personal values, analogies, and outmoded physio-psychological concepts. Some of the description of the modern urbanite reads like another version of the fall of man. The delineation of the urbanite as blasé, indifferent, calculating, utilitarian, and rational (presumably as a defensive reaction, to preserve his nervous system from the excessive shocks and stimuli of city life), suffering from anonymity and anomie, being more conscious and intellectual than his country brother yet feeling less deeply, remains a mere statement of faith.[17]

Besides the lack of an adequate personality theory, it seems to me that some of the difficulty stems from the attempt to make individual psychological deductions from conditions prevailing in the city as a whole. The city is not the proper unit of comparison or discussion for the study of social life because the variables of number, density, and heterogeneity as used by Wirth are not the crucial determinants of social life or of personality.[18] There are many intervening variables. Social life is not a mass phenomenon. It occurs for the most part in small groups, within the family, within households, within neighborhoods, within the Church, in both formal and informal groups.

Any generalizations about the nature of social life in the city must be based upon careful studies of these smaller universes rather than upon *a priori* statements about the city as a whole. Similarly, generalizations about urban personality must be based on careful personality studies. The delineation of social areas within cities and a careful analysis of their characteristics would take us a long way beyond the overgeneralized formulations of "urbanism as a way of life."

Basic to this Simmel-Wirth-Redfield approach are the supposed consequences of the predominance of primary relations in small

[17] Wirth, "Urbanism as a Way of Life," in *Community Life and Social Policy*, pp. 119–20.

[18] Sjoberg has correctly criticized the logic of comparison inherent in the writings of Redfield and Wirth on folk-urban theory on the ground that they were comparing a whole society with a part society. Here my criticism is that Wirth treated the city as a whole society for purposes of social relations and personality.

rural communities versus the predominance of secondary relations in large cities. It seems to me that the psychological and social consequences of primary versus secondary relations have been misunderstood and exaggerated for both the country and the city. I know of no experimental or other good evidence to indicate that exposure to large numbers of people *per se*, makes for anxiety and nervous strain or that the existence of secondary relations diminishes the strength and importance of primary ones. Primary group relations are just as important psychologically for city people as they are for country people, and sometimes they are more satisfying and of a more profound nature. And although the sheer number of secondary relations in the city is much greater than in the country, these relations can be said to be secondary also in the sense that their psychological consequences are minor.

The number of profound warm and understanding human relationships or attachments is probably limited in any society, rural or urban, modern or backward. Such attachments are not necessarily or exclusively a function of frequency of contact and fewness of numbers. They are influenced by cultural traditions which may demand reserve, a mind-your-own-business attitude, a distrust of neighbors, fear of sorcery and gossip, and the absence of a psychology of introspection.

George Foster's comparative analysis of the quality of interpersonal relations in small peasant societies, based upon anthropological monographs, shows that they are characterized by distrust, suspicion, envy, violence, reserve, and withdrawal.[19] His paper confirms my earlier findings on Tepoztlán.

In some villages, peasants can live out their lives without any deep knowledge or understanding of the people whom they "know" in face-to-face relationships. By contrast, in modern Western cities, there may be more give and take about one's private, intimate life at a single "sophisticated" cocktail party than would occur in years in a peasant village. I suspect that there are deeper, more mature human relationships among sympathetic, highly educated, cosmopolitan individuals who have chosen each other in friendship, than are possible among sorcery-ridden, superstitious, ignorant peasants, who are daily thrown together because of kinship or residential proximity.

It is a common assumption in social science literature that the process of urbanization for both tribal and peasant peoples is accompanied by a change in the structure of the family, from an extended

---

[19] George M. Foster, "The Personality of the Peasant." Paper read at the 68th Annual Meeting of the American Anthropological Association, Mexico City, 1959. Later published as "Inter-personal Relations in Peasant Society," *Human Organization*, Vol. 19 (Winter, 1960–61), pp. 174–78, 183–84.

to a nuclear family. It is assumed that the rural family is extended and that the urban family is nuclear. It must be pointed out that not even all primitive or preliterate people are characterized by a preponderance of the extended family as the residential unit. The Eskimo is a good example. Among peasantry, also, one finds a wide range of conditions in this regard. In most highland Mexican villages the nuclear family predominates as the residence unit. Very often, and without any evidence, this fact is interpreted as a symptom of change from an earlier condition. In India, one finds a remarkable difference in family composition by castes within a single village. For example, in Rampur village in the State of Delhi, the Jats and Brahmans, both of whom own and work the land, have large extended families, whereas the lower-caste sweepers and leatherworkers have small nuclear families. *

I suggest that we must distinguish much more carefully between the extended family as a residence unit and as a social group. In Mexico, the extended family is important as a social group in both rural and urban areas where the nuclear family predominates as the residence unit. In Mexico, the persistence of extended family bonds seems compatible with urban life and increased industrialization. Moreover, the *compadre* system, with its extension of adoptive kinship ties, is operative, though in somewhat distinctive ways, on all class levels. I suspect that increased communication facilities in Mexico, especially the telephone and the car, may strengthen rather than weaken extended family ties.

One of the most distinctive characteristics of cities, whether in the industrial or the preindustrial age, is that they provide, at least potentially, a wider range of alternatives for individuals in most aspects of living than is provided by the nonurban areas of the nation or total society at a given time. Urbanism and urbanization can be defined as the availability of a wide range of services and alternatives in types of work, housing, food, clothing, educational facilities, medical facilities, modes of travel, voluntary organizations, and types of people.

If we were to accept these criteria we could then develop indices of the degree of urbanization of different sectors of the population within cities. For example, if the population of any subsector of a city had fewer alternatives in such things as types of clothing or foods, because of traditional ethnic sanctions or for lack of economic resources, we could designate this population sector as showing a lower degree of urbanization than other sectors. This does not apply to the city alone; the scale of urbanization can also be ap-

* For additional discussion of the points raised in this paragraph, see also Essays 2, 15, 16, 18, and 19.

plied to villages and towns, and to their respective populations.

As I see it, therefore, there are two sides to the urbanization coin: one, the number and variety of services and material goods to be found in any city, and two, the extent to which different sectors of the city residents can partake of these services. From this distinction it follows that two cities may show the same urbanization index in terms of the number and variety of services per capita but may be very different in terms of the degree of urbanization (cosmopolitanism) of the various sectors of its inhabitants.

It also follows that there are many ways of life which coexist within a single city. This is particularly evident in the underdeveloped countries where class or caste differences are sharp. In Mexico City, for example, there are approximately a million and a half people who live in one-room *vecindades* or in primitive *jacales*, with little opportunity to partake of the great variety of housing facilities available for the tourists and the native bourgeoisie. Most people in this large mass still have a low level of education and literacy, do not belong to labor unions, do not participate in the benefits of the social security system, and make very little use of the city's museums, art galleries, banks, hospitals, department stores, concerts, and airports. These people live in cities—indeed, a considerable number were born in the city—but they are not highly urbanized. From this point of view, then, the poor in all cities of the world are less urbanized—that is, less cosmopolitan—than the wealthy.

The culture or subculture of poverty is a provincial, locally oriented culture, both in the city and in the country. In Mexico City, it is characterized by a relatively higher death rate, a higher proportion of the population in the younger age groups (less than fifteen years), a higher proportion of gainfully employed in the total population, including child labor and working women. Some of these indices for poor *colonias* of Mexico City are much higher than for rural Mexico as a whole.

On another level the culture of poverty in Mexico, cutting across the rural and the urban, is characterized by the absence of food reserves in the home, the pattern of frequent buying of small quantities of food many times a day as the need occurs, the borrowing of money from money lenders at usurious interest rates, the pawning of goods, spontaneous informal credit devices among neighbors, the use of second-hand clothing and furniture, particularly in the city which has the largest second-hand market in Mexico, a higher incidence of free unions or consensual marriages, a strong present-time orientation, and a higher proportion of pre-Hispanic folk beliefs and practices.

In the preoccupation with the study of rural-urban differences there has been a tendency to overlook or neglect basic similarities of people everywhere. Bruner[20] has illustrated this point for Indonesia where he found that the urban and rural Toba Batak are essentially part of a single social and economic ceremonial system.

Contrasts between Mexico and India also illustrate his point.[*] In Mexico, Catholicism gives a similar stamp to many aspects of life in both rural and urban areas. The nucleated-settlement pattern of most Mexican villages, with the central church and plaza and the *barrio* subdivisions, each with its own chapel, makes for a distinctive design which is in marked contrast to the north Indian villages, where Hinduism and the caste system have made for a much more segmented and heterogeneously organized type of settlement pattern. It is my impression that a similar contrast is to be seen in some of the cities of these two countries, and I believe this merits further study. Taking another example from India, we find that the way of life of the urban and rural lower castes, such as washermen and sweepers, have much more in common with each other than with the higher-caste Brahmans in their respective urban and rural contexts.

Although I agree that number, density, permanence of settlement and heterogeneity of population constitute a workable definition of a city, I believe we need an additional, more elementary, set of variables, with a narrower focus, to explain what goes on within cities. The sheer physical conditions of living have a considerable influence on social life, and I would include, among the variables, such factors as stability of residence, the settlement pattern, types of housing, the number of rooms to a family, property concepts, etc.

A type of housing settlement such as the *vecindad,* which brings people into daily face-to-face contact, in which people do most of their work in a common patio and share a common toilet and a common washstand, encourages intensive interaction, not all of which is necessarily friendly. It makes little difference whether this housing and settlement pattern is in the city or the country; indeed, whether it occurs among the tribal peoples of Borneo or the Iroquois Indians. In all cases it produces intense interaction, problems of privacy, of quarrels among children and among their parents.

Stability of residence too has many similar, social consequences wherever it occurs. As I have already shown, in Mexico City the *vecindades* make for a kind of community life which has greater re-

[20] Edward M. Bruner, "Urbanization and Culture Change: Indonesia." Paper read at the 58th Annual Meeting of the American Anthropological Association in Mexico City, December 28, 1959. Later published as "Urbanization and Ethnic Identity in North Sumatra," *American Anthropologist*, Vol. 63 (June, 1961), pp. 508–21.

[*] See also Essay 17, below.

semblance to our stereotyped notions of village life than to Wirth's description of urbanism. Stability of residence may result from a wide variety of factors, in both rural and urban areas. Nor can we assume that it is a necessary concomitant of nonurban societies, witness the nomadism of the Plains Indians or of agricultural workers in parts of the Caribbean.

Certain aspects of the division of labor stand up well as an elementary narrow-focus variable. When the family is the unit of production, and the home and the work place are one, certain similar consequences follow for family life, in both the country and the city. I have in mind similarities in family life of small artisans in Mexico City and rural villages. In both, husband and wife spend most of the day together, children are early recruited into useful work, and there is much interaction between family members. Thus, in terms of the amount of time husbands spend away from home, there is much more similarity between a peasant and a factory worker than between either of these and an artisan.

What we need in comparative urban studies as well as in rural-urban comparisons, within a single culture and cross-culturally, are carefully controlled, narrow-focus comparisons of subunits. Here I will list what seem to me to be priorities in research, with special reference to the underdeveloped countries.

1. The delineation of distinctive regions within cities in terms of their demographic, ecological, economic, and social characteristics, with the objective of developing measures of urbanization for distinctive population sectors as well as for the city as a whole.

2. Cross-cultural studies of comparable population sectors within cities. For example, we might compare lower-class areas in cities of Japan, India, England, and Mexico, utilizing a common research methodology, so that we could check the role of distinctive cultural factors on comparable urban sectors.

3. Comparisons of the economic, social, and psychological aspects of an equal number of families with the same full-time nonagricultural occupations in a village and in the city within a single country. One objective would be to test the influence of rural versus urban milieu and the many theories associated with same.

4. Studies of the socioeconomic and psychological consequences of the introduction of factories in villages and towns in predominantly peasant countries. A crucial methodological point in such studies would be to select communities prior to the introduction of the factory so that we could have a solid baseline against which changes could be measured.

One of the weaknesses of practically all studies to date is that they have had to reconstruct the prefactory conditions of the community.

For example, the otherwise excellent study of a Guatemalan community by Manning Nash[21] had to reconstruct the village culture as it was seventy years before, when the factory was first introduced. Similarly, the study now being done by Noel D. Burleson in Zacapu, Michoacan, Mexico, on the effects of a Celanese rayon factory, has to reconstruct the town conditions as they were fourteen years ago. Since the population has risen from about 6,000 to 25,000 in the interim, he is finding it difficult to do.

5. Most studies of the influence of factories have dealt with light industries such as textiles or rayons. It would be good to have studies on the effects of heavy industries such as steel, or mining, or chemical plants which demand more skilled labor and continuous operation.

6. Intensive case studies of individuals and families who have moved from tribal communities to urban centers, focusing on the problems of adjustment and the process of acculturation. In terms of method, it would be important to select families from communities that have been carefully studied.

7. Similar studies should be done for peasants and plantation workers who move to the city. The objective of studying subjects from different backgrounds is to learn what differences, if any, their backgrounds will have upon the urbanization process. I suspect that the greater disorganization reported by Kahl in his review of African materials as compared to Mexican data[22] can be explained by the fact that the African studies reported on tribal peoples moving to the city whereas in Mexico we are dealing with peasants. On purely theoretical grounds I would expect that culture shock would be greater for tribal peoples.

[21] *Machine Age Maya: The Industrialization of a Guatemalan Community,* American Anthropological Association, Memoir 87, 1958.

[22] Kahl (see note 13, above).

4

The Culture of Poverty[*]

Although a great deal has been written about poverty and the poor, the concept of a culture of poverty is relatively new. I first suggested it in 1959 in my book *Five Families: Mexican Case Studies in the Culture of Poverty*. The phrase is a catchy one and has become widely used and misused.[1] Michael Harrington used it extensively in his book *The Other America*,[2] which played an important role in sparking the national antipoverty program in the United States. However, he used it in a somewhat broader and less technical sense than I had intended. I shall try to define it more precisely as a conceptual model, with special emphasis upon the distinction between poverty and the culture of poverty. The absence of intensive anthropological studies of poor families from a wide variety of national and cultural contexts, and especially from the socialist countries, is a serious handicap in formulating valid cross-cultural regularities. The model presented here is therefore provisional and subject to modification as new studies become available.

Throughout recorded history, in literature, in proverbs, and in

[*] This appeared in 1966, in my book *La Vida* (New York: Random House).
[1] There has been relatively little discussion of the culture of poverty concept in the professional journals, however. Two articles deal with the problem in some detail: Elizabeth Herzog, "Some Assumptions About the Poor," *The Social Service Review* (December, 1963), pp. 389–402; and Lloyd Ohlin, *Inherited Poverty*, Paris, Organization for Economic Cooperation and Development, n.d.
[2] New York: Macmillan, 1962.

popular sayings, we find two opposite evaluations of the nature of the poor. Some characterize the poor as blessed, virtuous, upright, serene, independent, honest, kind, and happy. Others characterize them as evil, mean, violent, sordid, and criminal. These contradictory and confusing evaluations are also reflected in the in-fighting that is going on in the current war against poverty. Some stress the great potential of the poor for self-help, leadership, and community organization, while others point to the sometimes irreversible destructive effect of poverty upon individual character, and therefore emphasize the need for guidance and control to remain in the hands of the middle class, which presumably has better mental health.

These opposing views reflect a political power struggle between competing groups. However, some of the confusion results from the failure to distinguish between poverty *per se* and the culture of poverty, and from the tendency to focus upon the individual personality rather than upon the group—that is, the family and the slum community.

As an anthropologist I have tried to understand poverty and its associated traits as a culture or, more accurately, as a subculture[3] with its own structure and rationale, as a way of life which is passed down from generation to generation along family lines. This view directs attention to the fact that the culture of poverty in modern nations is not only a matter of economic deprivation, of disorganization, or of the absence of something. It is also something positive and provides some rewards without which the poor could hardly carry on.

Elsewhere I have suggested that the culture of poverty transcends regional, rural-urban, and national differences and shows remarkable similarities in family structure, interpersonal relations, time orientation, value systems, and spending patterns.[4] These cross-national similarities are examples of independent invention and convergence. They are common adaptations to common problems.

The culture of poverty can come into being in a variety of historical contexts. However, it tends to grow and flourish in societies with the following set of conditions: (1) a cash economy, wage labor, and production for profit; (2) a persistently high rate of unemployment and underemployment for unskilled labor; (3) low wages; (4) the failure to provide social, political, and economic organization, either on a voluntary basis or by government imposition, for the low-income population; (5) the existence of a bilateral kinship system

[3] Although the term "subculture of poverty" is technically more accurate, I sometimes use "culture of poverty" as a shorter form.

[4] Oscar Lewis, *Five Families: Mexican Case Studies in the Culture of Poverty* (New York: Basic Books, 1959).

rather than a unilateral one; and finally, (6) the existence of a set of values in the dominant class which stresses the accumulation of wealth and property, the possibility of upward mobility, and thrift, and explains low economic status as the result of personal inadequacy or inferiority.

The way of life which develops among some of the poor under these conditions is the culture of poverty. It can best be studied in urban or rural slums and can be described in terms of some seventy interrelated social, economic, and psychological traits. However, the number of traits and the relationships between them may vary from society to society and from family to family. For example, in a highly literate society, illiteracy may be more diagnostic of the culture of poverty than in a society where illiteracy is widespread and where even the well-to-do may be illiterate, as in some Mexican peasant villages before the Revolution

The culture of poverty is both an adaptation and a reaction of the poor to their marginal position in a class-stratified, highly individuated, capitalistic society. It represents an effort to cope with feelings of hopelessness and despair which develop from the realization of the improbability of achieving success in terms of the values and goals of the larger society. Indeed, many of the traits of the culture of poverty can be viewed as attempts at local solutions for problems not met by existing institutions and agencies because the people are not eligible for them, cannot afford them, or are ignorant or suspicious of them. For example, unable to obtain credit from banks, they are thrown upon their own resources and organize informal credit devices without interest.

The culture of poverty, however, is not only an adaptation to a set of objective conditions of the larger society. Once it comes into existence, it tends to perpetuate itself from generation to generation because of its effect on the children. By the time slum children are six or seven years old, they usually have absorbed the basic values and attitudes of their subculture and are not psychologically geared to take full advantage of changing conditions or increased opportunities which may occur in their lifetime.

Most frequently the culture of poverty develops when a stratified social and economic system is breaking down or is being replaced by another as in the case of the transition from feudalism to capitalism or during periods of rapid technological change. Often it results from imperial conquest in which the native social and economic structure is smashed and the natives are maintained in a servile colonial status, sometimes for many generations. It can also occur in the process of detribalization such as that now going on in Africa.

The most likely candidates for the culture of poverty are the people who come from the lower strata of a rapidly changing society and are already partially alienated from it. Thus, landless rural workers who migrate to the cities can be expected to develop a culture of poverty much more readily than migrants from stable peasant villages with a well-organized traditional culture. In this connection there is a striking contrast between Latin America, where the rural population long ago made the transition from a tribal to a peasant society, and Africa, which is still close to its tribal heritage. The more corporate nature of many of the African tribal societies, in contrast to Latin American rural communities, and the persistence of village ties tend to inhibit or delay the formation of a full-blown culture of poverty in many of the African towns and cities. The special conditions of apartheid in South Africa, where the migrants are segregated into separate "locations" and do not enjoy freedom of movement, create special problems. Here, the institutionalization of repression and discrimination tends to develop a greater sense of identity and group consciousness.

The culture of poverty can be studied from various points of view: the relationship between the subculture and the larger society; the nature of the slum community; the nature of the family; and the attitudes, values, and character structure of the individual.

1. The lack of effective participation and integration of the poor in the major institutions of the larger society is one of the crucial characteristics of the culture of poverty. This is a complex matter and results from a variety of factors which may include lack of economic resources, segregation and discrimination, fear, suspicion, or apathy, and the development of local solutions for problems. However, participation in some of the institutions of the larger society—for example, in the jails, the army, and the public relief system—does not *per se* eliminate the traits of the culture of poverty. In the case of a relief system which barely keeps people alive, both the basic poverty and the sense of hopelessness are perpetuated rather than eliminated.

Low wages, chronic unemployment, and underemployment lead to low income, lack of property ownership, absence of savings, absence of food reserves in the home, and a chronic shortage of cash. These conditions reduce the possibility of effective participation in the larger economic system. And as a response to these conditions, we find in the culture of poverty a high incidence of pawning of personal goods, borrowing from local money lenders at usurious rates of interest, spontaneous informal credit devices organized by neighbors, the use of second-hand clothing and furniture, and the pattern of frequent buying of small quantities of food many times a day as the need arises.

People with a culture of poverty produce very little wealth and receive very little in return. They have a low level of literacy and education, do not belong to labor unions, are not members of political parties, generally do not participate in the national welfare agencies, and make very little use of banks, hospitals, department stores, museums, or art galleries. They have a critical attitude toward some of the basic institutions of the dominant classes, hatred of the police, mistrust of government and those in high position, and a cynicism which extends even to the church. This gives the culture of poverty a high potential for protest and for being used in political movements aimed against the existing social order.

People with a culture of poverty are aware of middle-class values, talk about them, and even claim some of them as their own; but on the whole, they do not live by them.[5] Thus it is important to distinguish between what they say and what they do. For example, many will tell you that marriage by law, by the church, or by both, is the ideal form of marriage; but few will marry. For men who have no steady jobs or other source of income, who do not own property and have no wealth to pass on to their children, who are present-time oriented and who want to avoid the expense and legal difficulties involved in formal marriage and divorce, free union or consensual marriage makes a lot of sense. Women will often turn down offers of marriage because they feel that marriage ties them down to men who are immature, punishing, and generally unreliable. Women feel that consensual union gives them a better break; it gives them some of the freedom and flexibility that men have. By not giving the fathers of their children legal status as husbands, the women have a stronger claim on their children if they decide to leave their men. It also gives women exclusive rights to a house or any other property they may own.

2. In describing the culture of poverty on the local community level, we find poor housing conditions, crowding, gregariousness, but above all, a minimum of organization beyond the level of the nuclear and extended family. Occasionally there are informal temporary groupings or voluntary associations within slums. The existence of neighborhood gangs which cut across slum settlements represents a considerable advance beyond the zero point of the continuum that I have in mind. Indeed, it is the low level of organization which gives the culture of poverty its marginal and anachronistic quality in our highly complex, specialized, organized society.

[5] In terms of Hyman Rodman's concept of "The Lower-Class Value Stretch" (*Social Forces*, Vol. 42, No. 2 [December, 1963], pp. 205–15), I would say that the culture of poverty exists where this value stretch is at a minimum, that is, where the belief in middle-class values is at a minimum.

Most primitive peoples have achieved a higher level of socio-cultural organization than our modern urban slum dwellers.

In spite of the generally low level of organization, there may be a sense of community and *esprit de corps* in urban slums and in slum neighborhoods. This can vary within a single city, or from region to region or country to country. The major factors which influence this variation are the size of the slum, its location and physical characteristics, length of residence, incidence of home and landownership (versus squatter rights), rentals, ethnicity, kinship ties, and freedom or lack of freedom of movement. When slums are separated from the surrounding area by enclosing walls or other physical barriers, when rents are low and fixed and stability of residence is great (twenty or thirty years), when the population constitutes a distinct ethnic, racial, or language group, is bound by ties of kinship or *compadrazgo*, and when there are some internal voluntary associations, then the sense of local community approaches that of a village community. In many cases this combination of favorable conditions does not exist. However, even where internal organization and esprit de corps are at a bare minimum and people move around a great deal, a sense of territoriality develops which sets off the slum neighborhoods from the rest of the city. In Mexico City and San Juan this sense of territoriality results from the unavailability of low-income housing outside of the slum areas. In South Africa the sense of territoriality grows out of the segregation enforced by the government, which confines the rural migrants to specific locations.

3. On the family level the major traits of the culture of poverty are the absence of childhood as a specially prolonged and protected stage in the life cycle, early initiation into sex, free unions or consensual marriages, a relatively high incidence of the abandonment of wives and children, a trend toward female- or mother-centered families and consequently a much greater knowledge of maternal relatives, a strong predisposition to authoritarianism, lack of privacy, verbal emphasis upon family solidarity, which is only rarely achieved because of sibling rivalry, and competition for limited goods and maternal affection.

4. On the level of the individual, the major characteristics are a strong feeling of marginality, of helplessness, of dependence, and of inferiority. I found this to be true of slum dwellers in Mexico City and San Juan among families that do not constitute a distinct ethnic or racial group and that do not suffer from racial discrimination. In the United States, of course, the culture of poverty of the Negroes has the additional disadvantage of racial discrimination; but as I have already suggested, this additional disadvantage contains a great potential for revolutionary protest and organization which

seems to be absent in the slums of Mexico City or among the poor whites in the South.

Other traits include a high incidence of maternal deprivation, orality, weak ego structure, confusion of sexual identification, a lack of impulse control, a strong present-time orientation with relatively little ability to defer gratification and to plan for the future, a sense of resignation and fatalism, a widespread belief in male superiority, and a high tolerance for psychological pathology of all sorts.

People with a culture of poverty are provincial and locally oriented and have very little sense of history. They know only their own troubles, their own local conditions, their own neighborhood, their own way of life. Usually they do not have the knowledge, the vision, or the ideology to see the similarities between their problems and those of their counterparts elsewhere in the world. They are not class conscious although they are very sensitive indeed to status distinctions.

In considering the traits discussed above, the following propositions must be kept in mind. (1) The traits fall into a number of clusters and are functionally related within each cluster. (2) Many, but not all, of the traits of different clusters are also functionally related. For example, men who have low wages and suffer chronic unemployment develop a poor self-image, become irresponsible, abandon their wives and children, and take up with other women more frequently than do men with high incomes and steady jobs. (3) None of the traits, taken individually, is distinctive *per se* of the subculture of poverty. It is their conjunction, their function, and their patterning that define the subculture. (4) The subculture of poverty, as defined by these traits, is a statistical profile; that is, the frequency of distribution of the traits both singly and in clusters will be greater than in the rest of the population. In other words, more of the traits will occur in combination in families with a subculture of poverty than in stable working-class, middle-class, or upper-class families. Even within a single slum there will probably be a gradient from culture of poverty families to families without a culture of poverty. (5) The profiles of the subculture of poverty will probably differ in systematic ways with the difference in the national cultural contexts of which they are a part. It is expected that some new traits will become apparent with research in different nations.

I have not yet worked out a system of weighing each of the traits, but this could probably be done and a scale could be set up for many of the traits. Traits that reflect lack of participation in the institutions of the larger society or an outright rejection—in practice, if not in theory—would be the crucial traits; for example, illiteracy, provincialism, free unions, abandonment of women and children, lack of membership in voluntary associations beyond the extended family. When the poor become class conscious or active members of trade-union organizations or when they adopt an internationalist outlook on the world, they are no longer part of the culture of poverty although they may still be desperately poor. Any movement, be it religious, pacifist, or revolutionary, which organizes and gives hope to the poor and which effectively promotes solidarity and a sense of identification with larger groups, destroys the psychological and social core of the culture of poverty. In this connection, I suspect that the civil-rights movement among the Negroes in the United States has done more to improve their self-image and self-respect than have their economic advances although, without doubt, the two are mutually reinforcing.

The distinction between poverty and the culture of poverty is basic to the model described here. There are degrees of poverty and many kinds of poor people. The culture of poverty refers to one way of life shared by poor people in given historical and social contexts. The economic traits which I have listed for the culture of poverty are necessary but not sufficient to define the phenomena I have in mind. There are a number of historical examples of very poor segments of the population which do not have a way of life that I would describe as a subculture of poverty. Here I should like to give four examples:

a) Many of the primitive or preliterate peoples studied by anthropologists suffer from dire poverty which is the result of poor technology and/or poor natural resources or both, but they do not have the traits of the subculture of poverty. Indeed, they do not constitute a subculture because their societies are not highly stratified. In spite of their poverty, they have a relatively integrated, satisfying, and self-sufficient culture. Even the simplest food-gathering and hunting tribes have a considerable amount of organization—bands and band chiefs, tribal councils, and local self-government—elements which are not found in the culture of poverty.

b) In India the lower castes (the *Camars* or leatherworkers, and the *Bhangis* or sweepers) may be desperately poor both in the villages and in the cities, but most of them are integrated into the larger society and have their own *panchayat* organizations which cut across village lines and give them a considerable amount of power.[6] In addition to the caste system, which gives individuals a sense of identity and belonging, there is still another factor, the clan system. Wherever there are unilateral kinship systems or clans, one

---

[6] It may be that in the slums of Calcutta and Bombay an incipient culture of poverty is developing. It would be highly desirable to do family studies there as a crucial test of the culture-of-poverty hypothesis.

would not expect to find the culture of poverty because a clan system gives people a sense of belonging to a corporate body which has a history and a life of its own and therefore provides a sense of continuity, a sense of a past and of a future.

c) The Jews of Eastern Europe were very poor but they did not have many of the traits of the culture of poverty because of their tradition of literacy, the great value placed upon learning, the organization of the community around the rabbi, the proliferation of local voluntary associations, and their religion, which taught that they were the chosen people.

d) My fourth example is speculative and relates to socialism. On the basis of my limited experience in one socialist country—Cuba—and on the basis of my reading, I am inclined to believe that the culture of poverty does not exist in the socialist countries. I first went to Cuba in 1947 as a visiting professor for the State Department. At that time I began a study of a sugar plantation in Melena del Sur and of a slum in Havana. After the Castro Revolution I made my second trip to Cuba as a correspondent for a major magazine, and I revisited the same slum and some of the same families. The physical aspect of the slum had changed very little, except for a beautiful new nursery school. It was clear that the people were still desperately poor, but I found much less of the feelings of despair, apathy, and hopelessness which are so diagnostic of urban slums in the culture of poverty. They expressed great confidence in their leaders and hope for a better life in the future. The slum itself was now highly organized, with block committees, educational committees, party committees. The people had a new sense of power and importance. They were armed and were given a doctrine which glorified the lower class as the hope of humanity. (I was told by one Cuban official that they had practically eliminated delinquency by giving arms to the delinquents!)

It is my impression that the Castro regime, unlike Marx and Engels, did not write off the so-called lumpen proletariat as an inherently reactionary and anti-revolutionary force, but rather saw their revolutionary potential and tried to utilize it. In this connection, Frantz Fanon makes a similar evaluation of the role of the lumpen proletariat based upon his experience in the Algerian struggle for independence. In *The Wretched of the Earth* he writes:

> It is within this mass of humanity, this people of the shanty towns, at the core of the lumpen proletariat, that the rebellion will find its urban spearhead. For the lumpen-proletariat, that horde of starving men, uprooted from their tribe and from their clan, constitutes one of the most spontaneous and most radically revolutionary forces of a colonized people.[7]

[7] New York: Grove, 1965, p. 103.

My own studies of the urban poor in the slums of San Juan do not support the generalizations of Fanon. I have found very little revolutionary spirit or radical ideology among low-income Puerto Ricans. On the contrary, most of the families I studied were quite conservative politically and about half of them were in favor of the Statehood Republican Party. It seems to me that the revolutionary potential of people with a culture of poverty will vary considerably according to the national context and the particular historical circumstances. In a country like Algeria, which was fighting for its independence, the lumpen proletariat were drawn into the struggle and became a vital force. However, in countries like Puerto Rico, in which the movement for independence has very little mass support, and in countries like Mexico, which have achieved their independence a long time ago and are now in their post-Revolutionary period, the lumpen proletariat is not a leading source of rebellion or of revolutionary spirit.

In effect, we find that in primitive societies, and in caste societies, the culture of poverty does not develop. In socialist, fascist, and highly developed capitalist societies with a welfare state, the culture of poverty tends to decline. I suspect that the culture of poverty flourishes in, and is generic to, the early free enterprise stage of capitalism and that it is also endemic in colonialism.

It is important to distinguish between different profiles in the subculture of poverty depending upon the national context in which these subcultures are found. If we think of the culture of poverty primarily in terms of the factor of integration in the larger society and a sense of identification with the great tradition of that society, or with a new emerging revolutionary tradition, then we will not be surprised that some slum dwellers with a lower per capita income may have moved farther away from the core characteristics of the culture of poverty than others with a higher per capita income. For example, Puerto Rico has a much higher per capita income than Mexico, yet Mexicans have a deeper sense of identity. In Mexico, however, even the poorest slum dweller has a much richer sense of the past and a deeper identification with the great Mexican tradition than do Puerto Ricans with their tradition. In both countries I presented urban slum dwellers with the names of national figures. In Mexico City quite a high percentage of the respondents, including those with little or no formal schooling, knew about Cuauhtémoc, Hidalgo, Father Morelos, Juárez, Díaz, Zapata, Carranza, and Cárdenas. In San Juan the respondents showed an abysmal ignorance of Puerto Rican historical figures. The names of Ramón Power, José de Diego, Baldorioty de Castro, Ramón Betances, Nemesio Canales,

Llorens Torres rang no bell. For the lower-income Puerto Rican slum
dweller, history begins and ends with Muñoz Rivera, his son Muñoz
Marín, and *doña* Felisa Rincon!

I have listed fatalism and a low level of aspiration as among the
key traits for the subculture of poverty. Here too, however, the national context makes a big difference. Certainly the level of aspiration of even the poorest sector of the population in a country like
the United States, with its traditional ideology of upward mobility
and democracy, is much higher than in more backward countries
like Ecuador and Peru, where both the ideology and the actual possibilities of upward mobility are extremely limited and where authoritarian values still persist in both the urban and rural milieu.

Because of the advanced technology, the high level of literacy, the
development of mass media, and the relatively high aspiration level
of all sectors of the population, especially when compared with underdeveloped nations, I believe that although there is still a great
deal of poverty in the United States (estimates range between thirty
and fifty million people) there is relatively little of what I would call
the culture of poverty. My rough guess would be that only about 20
per cent of the population below the poverty line (between six and
ten million people) in the United States have characteristics which
would justify classifying their way of life as that of a culture of poverty. Probably the largest sector within this group would consist of
very low-income Negroes, Mexicans, Puerto Ricans, American Indians, and southern poor whites. The relatively small number of people in the United States with a culture of poverty is a positive factor
because it is much more difficult to eliminate the culture of poverty
than to eliminate poverty *per se*.

Middle-class people, and this would certainly include most social
scientists, tend to concentrate on the negative aspects of the culture
of poverty. They tend to associate negative values with such traits as
present-time orientation and concrete versus abstract orientation. I
do not intend to idealize or romanticize the culture of poverty. As
someone has said, "It is easier to praise poverty than to live in it"; yet
some of the positive aspects of these traits must not be overlooked.
Living in the present may develop a capacity for spontaneity, for the
enjoyment of the sensual, the indulgence of impulse, which is often
blunted in the middle-class, future-oriented man. Perhaps it is this
reality of the moment which the existentialist writers are so desperately trying to recapture but which the culture of poverty experiences as a natural, everyday phenomenon. The frequent use of
violence certainly provides a ready outlet for hostility so that people
in the culture of poverty suffer less from repression than does the
middle class.

In the traditional view of culture, anthropologists have said that it provides human beings with a design for living, with a ready-made set of solutions for human problems so that individuals don't have to begin all over again from scratch each generation. That is, the core of culture is its positive adaptive function. I, too, have called attention to some of the adaptive mechanisms in the culture of poverty— for example, low aspiration level helps to reduce frustration; legitimization of short-range hedonism makes possible spontaneity and enjoyment. However, on the whole it seems to me that it is a thin, relatively superficial culture. There is a great deal of pathos, suffering, and emptiness among those who live in the culture of poverty. It does not provide much support or satisfaction and its encouragement of mistrust tends to magnify helplessness and isolation. Indeed, the poverty of culture is one of the crucial aspects of the culture of poverty.

The concept of the culture of poverty provides a high level of generalization which, hopefully, will unify and explain a number of phenomena which have been viewed as distinctive characteristics of racial, national, or regional groups. For example, matrifocality, a high incidence of consensual unions, and a high percentage of households headed by women, which have been thought to be distinctive of Caribbean family organization or of Negro family life in the U.S.A., turn out to be traits of the culture of poverty and are found among diverse peoples in many parts of the world and among peoples who have had no history of slavery.

The concept of a cross-societal subculture of poverty enables us to see that many of the problems we think of as distinctively our own or distinctively Negro problems (or that of any other special racial or ethnic group) also exist in countries where there are no distinct ethnic minority groups. It suggests, too, that the elimination of physical poverty *per se* may not be enough to eliminate the culture of poverty which is a whole way of life.

What is the future of the culture of poverty? In considering this question, one must distinguish between those countries in which it represents a relatively small segment of the population and those in which it constitutes a very large one. Obviously the solutions will differ in these two situations. In the United States, the major solution proposed by planners and social workers in dealing with multiple-problem families and the so-called "hard core" of poverty has been to attempt slowly to raise their level of living and to incorporate them into the middle class. Wherever possible, there has been some reliance upon psychiatric treatment.

In the underdeveloped countries, however, where great masses of people live in the culture of poverty, a social-work solution does not seem feasible. Because of the magnitude of the problem, psychiatrists can hardly begin to cope with it. They have all they can do to care for their own growing middle class. In these countries the people with a culture of poverty may seek a more revolutionary solution. By creating basic structural changes in society, by redistributing wealth, by organizing the poor and giving them a sense of belonging, of power, and of leadership, revolutions frequently succeed in abolishing some of the basic characteristics of the culture of poverty even when they do not succeed in abolishing poverty itself.

Some of my readers have misunderstood the subculture of poverty model and have failed to grasp the importance of the distinction between poverty and the subculture of poverty. In making this distinction I have tried to document a broader generalization; namely, that it is a serious mistake to lump all poor people together, because the causes, the meaning, and the consequences of poverty vary considerably in different socio-cultural contexts. There is nothing in the concept that puts the onus of poverty on the character of the poor. Nor does the concept in any way play down the exploitation and neglect suffered by the poor. Indeed, the subculture of poverty is part of the larger culture of capitalism, whose social and economic system channels wealth into the hands of a relatively small group and thereby makes for the growth of sharp class distinctions.

I would agree that the main reasons for the persistence of the subculture are no doubt the pressures that the larger society exerts over its members and the structure of the larger society itself. However, this is not the only reason. The subculture develops mechanisms that tend to perpetuate it, especially because of what happens to the world view, aspirations, and character of the children who grow up in it. For this reason, improved economic opportunities, though absolutely essential and of the highest priority, are not sufficient to alter basically or eliminate the subculture of poverty. Moreover, elimination is a process that will take more than a single generation, even under the best of circumstances, including a socialist revolution.

Some readers have thought that I was saying, "Being poor is terrible, but having a culture of poverty is not so bad." On the contrary, I am saying that it is easier to eliminate poverty than the culture of poverty. I am also suggesting that the poor in a precapitalistic caste-ridden society like India had some advantages over modern urban slum dwellers because the people were organized in castes and *panchayats* and this organization gave them some sense of identity and some strength and power. Perhaps Gandhi had the urban slums of the West in mind when he wrote that the caste system was one of the greatest inventions of mankind. Similarly, I have argued that the poor Jews of Eastern Europe, with their strong tradition of literacy and community organization, were better off than people with the culture of poverty. On the other hand, I would argue that people with the culture of poverty, with their strong sense of resignation and fatalism, are less driven and less anxious than the striving lower middle class, who are still trying to make it in the face of the greatest odds.

5

An Anthropological
Approach to Family Studies[*]

The field of family studies is one which has become identified with sociologists rather than anthropologists, and even among sociologists it is sometimes viewed as the highly specialized field of practical problems in applied sociology rather than the more general and theoretical treatment of cultural dynamics. One might ask, therefore, just what can anthropology contribute to this field, since anthropologists have, in fact, neglected the field of family studies. However, on the basis of my own experience with family studies in rural areas in Mexico and Cuba, I believe that anthropology can make a distinctive contribution by utilizing the family approach as a technique for the study of culture and personality. In this paper I describe an anthropological approach to family studies and the contribution of such an approach for at least two important methodological problems in anthropology and other social sciences, namely, how to arrive at a more reliable and objective statement of the culture patterns of a given society and obtain a better understanding of the relationship between culture and the individual.

The field work upon which this paper is based was done in the Mexican village of Tepoztlán, where, in 1943, I undertook a broad ethnographic study of the community.[†]

At the outset there was the problem of method. Tepoztlán is a

* This was first published in 1950, in *The American Journal of Sociology*, Vol. 55, No. 5, pp. 468–75.
† See Essay 2, above.

large and complex village, with seven *barrios* or locality groupings, generation and wealth differences, and a rapidly changing culture. The traditional anthropological reliance upon a few informants to obtain a picture of the culture and the people, though perhaps feasible in a small, primitive, tribal society, was inadequate to this situation. The question of sampling and of securing data and informants representative of all the significant differences in the village was just as pertinent here as in a study of a modern urban community. Sampling and quantitative procedures were therefore employed wherever possible, as were census data, local government records and documents, schedules, and questionnaires.

But how could we best study the individual and understand his relationship to the culture? How might we reveal the great variety of practices and the range of individual differences to be found in such a complex village? How might we understand Tepoztecans in all of their individuality? Again, though we came prepared with the traditional anthropological techniques as well as with some of the psychologist's, such as the Rorschach and other projective tests, something more was needed, and we turned to the study of the family. We hoped that the intensive study of representative families, in which the entire family would be studied as a functioning unit, might give us greater insight into both the culture and the people. Family studies therefore became one of the organizing principles in the entire research.

The first problem was how to select the families to be studied. The first few weeks were spent in analyzing a local population census of the village taken a year before our arrival. The census data were reorganized first on a *barrio* basis. *Barrio* lists were drawn up and each family and household was assigned a number which thereafter was used to identify the family. In addition, alphabetical lists of both sexes were drawn up in each *barrio* with the corresponding number after each name. In this way we were able to identify all individuals in the village in respect to *barrio* and family membership.

As a preliminary to selecting for special study families which would be representative of the various socioeconomic groupings in the village, several informants were asked to rank the families in each *barrio* according to relative wealth and social position. The criteria used in this tentative classification were items which seemed important in this peasant community, namely, the ownership of a house, land, and cattle. Thus we obtained a rough idea of the relative standing of all the families of the village. On this basis three families, representing different socioeconomic levels, were tentatively selected for study in each of the seven *barrios*.

At this point, after I had been in the village for about a month, student assistants from the University of Mexico began to come into the village one at a time. Soon there were six assistants, for each of whom arrangements were made to live with a selected family in a different *barrio*. An effort was made to place these assistants with families representative of the different socioeconomic levels as well as of differences in family size, composition, and degree of acculturation. However, we found that there was a greater willingness among the better-to-do and more acculturated families on our list to have one of the staff live with them. Some of the selected poorer families expressed willingness to accept a student but were unable to do so because of crowded living conditions.

We were now ready to begin to accumulate a great variety of information on every family in the village. Each assistant was made responsible for gathering the data in his *barrio*. In the three smaller *barrios*, none of which had over forty families, it was possible to get a few informants who knew of the families there quite intimately. In these smaller *barrios* practically any male adult knows who does or does not own land or other property. In the larger *barrios* no single informant was well acquainted with more than a small percentage of the families and we therefore had to use many more informants. In effect we were doing a census in each *barrio*, with the number of items investigated progressively increasing as our rapport improved and as we felt free to ask more questions.

Among the items of information which we eventually obtained by survey for each family were (1) ownership of property, such as house, land, cattle and other animals, fruit trees, and sewing machines; (2) occupation and sources of income; (3) marital status, number of marriages, *barrio* of origin or other birthplace of each spouse, kinship relations of all persons living on the same house site; (4) social participation and positions of leadership; (5) educational level and whether or not any of the children had attended school outside the village. These items were supplemented by a number of partial surveys on other items; we also utilized and checked much of the information contained in the population census of 1940.

In addition to this survey of the village as a whole, each assistant studied the individual family with which he was living. The family was treated as if it were the society. We learned that most of the categories traditionally used in describing an entire culture could be used effectively in the study of a single family. Thus, we obtained data on the social, economic, religious, and political life of each of the families observed. We studied the division of labor, sources of income, standard of living, literacy, and education. An area of special concentration was the study of interpersonal relations within the family between husband and wife, parents and children, brothers and sisters, as well as relations with the extended family and with nonrelatives. In addition each member of the family was studied individually.

We applied to the single family all the techniques traditionally used by the anthropologist in the study of an entire culture—living with the family, being a participant-observer, interviewing, collecting autobiographies and case histories, and administering Rorschach and other psychological tests. A long and detailed guide was prepared for the observing and recording of behavior. Seven families were studied in this intensive manner. Each family study runs to about 250 typed pages.

How does this approach compare with other approaches? Certainly the family case study is not in itself a new technique.[1] It has been used by social workers, sociologists, psychologists, psychiatrists, and others; but their studies invariably have centered around some special problem: families in trouble, families in the depression, the problem child in the family, family instability, divorce, and a hundred and one other subjects. These might be characterized on the whole as segmented studies, in which one particular aspect of family life is considered, and generally the methodology has been of a statistical nature, with emphasis upon large numbers of cases, supplemented by interviews and questionnaires. Despite all the emphasis in the textbooks on the family as an integrated whole, there is little published material in which the family is studied as that.[2]

If the sociological studies of the family have tended to be of the segmental, specific-problem type, the work of the anthropologist has been of the opposite kind, that is, generalized description with little or no sense of problem. In most anthropological community studies the family is presented as a stereotype. We are told not about a particular family but about family life in general under headings such as composition, residence rules, descent rules, kinship obligations, parental authority, marriage forms and regulations, and separation. And always the emphasis is upon the presentation of the structural and formal aspects of the family rather than upon the content and variety of actual family life. Anthropologists have developed no spe-

[1] Professor Thomas D. Eliot comments that Le Play used the family as a unit of research. However, the tradition which he began has not been continued by American sociologists. I understand from Professor Florian Znaniecki that he and his students did family studies in Poland somewhat similar to those described here.

[2] Professor Eliot's comment at a meeting of the American Sociological Society in December, 1924, still applies today. He said, "Each feels and interprets only the small part of the problem with which he is in direct contact, and thinks he is describing the whole."

cial methodology for family studies and to my knowledge there is not a single published study in the entire anthropological literature of a family as a unit.[3]

Despite all that has been written and the considerable progress that has been made, I believe that it is still a challenge to anthropology and the other social sciences to devise new and better methods for studying the relationship between the individual and his culture. Most monographs on so-called primitive or folk cultures give an unduly mechanical and static picture of the relationship between the individual and his culture: individuals tend to become insubstantial and passive automatons who carry out expected behavior patterns. For all the pronouncements in theoretical treatises, little of the interaction between culture and the individual emerges in the monographs. Indeed, as theoretical concepts in the study of culture have increased and our level of generalization and abstraction has been raised, we have come to deal more and more with averages and stereotypes rather than with real people in all their individuality. It is a rare monograph which gives the reader the satisfying feeling of knowing the people in the way he knows them after reading a good novel. Malinowski, many years ago in his famous preface to the *Argonauts of the Pacific*, wrote of anthropological monographs as follows: "We are given an excellent skeleton so to speak, of the tribal constitution, but it lacks flesh and blood. We learn much about the framework of their society but within it we cannot conceive or imagine the realities of human life." [4] More recently Elsie Clews Parsons wrote: "In any systematic town survey much detail is necessarily omitted and life appears more standardized than it really is, there is no place for contradiction or exceptions or minor variations; *the classifications more or less preclude* pictures of people living and functioning together." [5] (Italics mine.) Here we have it. Parsons, in her book on Mitla, has attempted to remedy this situation by writing a chapter on gossip, and in other monographs we sometimes get more insight into what the people are like from scattered field-note references or from chance remarks about the nature of the informants in the Foreword of the monograph than from the remainder of the study. These vivid and dynamic materials are too important to be treated in such a haphazard way.

Anthropologists have made some attempt to salvage the individ-

[3] Since this was written, I have published a number of family studies. See the list of Publications at the end of this volume.

[4] Bronislaw Malinowski, *Argonauts of the Pacific* (New York: Dutton, 1932), p. 17.

[5] *Mitla, Town of the Souls* (Chicago: University of Chicago Press, 1936), p. 386.

ual through the use of autobiographies and life histories. Such studies represent a great step forward but they also have their limitations, both practical and theoretical. Autobiographies by their very nature are based upon informants' verbalizations and memory rather than upon direct observation by the trained observer. Furthermore, autobiographies give us a picture of a culture as seen through the eyes of a single person.

Intensive family case studies might help us to bridge the gap between the conceptual extremes of the culture at one pole and the individual at the other. The family would thus become the middle term in the culture-individual equation. It would provide us with another level of description. And because the family unit is small and manageable, it can be described without resort to the abstraction and generalization which one must inevitably use for the culture as a whole. Also, in the description of the various family members we see real individuals as they live and work together in their primary group rather than as averages or stereotypes out of context.

It is in the context of the family that the interrelationships between cultural and individual factors in the formation of personality can best be seen. Family case studies can therefore enable us better to distinguish between and give proper weight to those factors which are cultural and those which are situational or the result of individual idiosyncrasies. Even psychological tests become more meaningful when done on a family basis. For example, on the basis of our family Rorschach tests we can study the extent to which personality differences run along family lines and the range within families, as well as what seems to be common among all families and can therefore be attributed to broader cultural conditioning.

One of the advantages of studying a culture through the medium of specific families is that it enables us to get at the meaning of institutions to individuals. It helps us to get beyond form and structure or, to use Malinowski's terms, it puts flesh and blood on the skeleton. The family is the natural unit for the study of the satisfactions, frustrations, and maladjustments of individuals who live under a specific type of family organization; the reactions of individuals to the expected behavior patterns; the effects of conformity or deviation upon the development of the personality. Certainly those problems can also be studied in other contexts. However, I am assuming that the more data we gather on a small group of people who live and work together in the family, the more meaningful does their behavior become. This is a cumulative process, especially important for understanding the covert aspects of culture.

Family case studies can also make a contribution to the study of culture patterns. The concept of culture and culture patterns is cer-

tainly one of the proud achievements of anthropology and other social sciences. But here again conceptualization has run far ahead of
methodology. Kroeber writes of culture patterns: "In proportion as
the expression of such a large pattern tends to be abstract, it becomes arid and lifeless; in proportion as it remains attached to
concrete facts, it lacks generalization. Perhaps the most vivid and impressive characterizations have been made by frank intuition deployed on a rich body of knowledge and put into skillful words." [6]
The recent writings of anthropologists on national character and national culture patterns are an excellent example of where conceptualization has run far ahead of methodology.[7] One of the results of
these writings has been to make sociologists and others wonder
about the reliability of anthropological reporting even in the case of
so-called primitive or folk societies.

A real methodological weakness in anthropological field work has
been too great a reliance upon a few informants to obtain a picture
of the culture. The traditional justification of this procedure has been
the assumption of the essential homogeneity of primitive or folk societies. But this very presupposition has often affected the methods
used and therefore colored the findings. An account of a culture
based upon a few informants is bound to appear more uniform than
it really is. This became apparent in the restudy of the village of
Tepoztlán, where we found a much wider range in custom and in
individual behavior than we had been led to expect from Redfield's
earlier work on the same village.[8]

One of the virtues of the intensive study of representative families
is that it can give us the range of custom and behavior and can serve
as a more adequate basis from which we can derive culture patterns.
In doing intensive studies of even two or three families, one must use
a larger number of informants than is generally used by anthropologists in monographs on an entire culture. Furthermore, in studying a
family, we get a deeper understanding of our informants than is
otherwise possible. This intimate knowledge of them is extremely
helpful in evaluating what they tell us and in checking the accounts
of family members against one another. By the same token such intimate knowledge of informants can be used in checking the usefulness of Rorschach and other projective techniques developed in our
own society.

[6] Alfred Kroeber, *Anthropology* (New York: Harcourt, Brace, 1948), p. 317.
[7] See, for example, Geoffrey Gorer, *The American People: A Study in National
Character* (New York: Norton, 1948).
[8] Robert Redfield, *Tepoztlán—A Mexican Village* (Chicago: University of Chicago Press, 1930).

In my article "Family Dynamics in a Mexican Village," * I have attempted to convey some idea of the range in custom and family life which can be found in even a relatively homogeneous peasant society like Tepoztlán. The comparison in that article of two similar yet very different families makes it clear that any statement of over-all culture patterns would have to be made in terms of the range of differences rather than in the terms of some abstract, hypothetical norm. The difference in the husband-wife relationship in these two families cannot be explained in terms of class or subcultural differences, since they cut across class lines in Tepoztlán.

A practical advantage of this type of approach to the study of culture and personality is that a reasonably complete family case study can be done within a relatively short time, about two or three months, and might be profitably carried on by anthropologists or sociologists who have only their summer vacations in which to do field work. Several intensive family case studies done in as many summers would be in effect a cumulative study of the culture.

The family case study also presents us with an excellent method of introducing anthropology students to field work. The family, small in size but reflecting at the same time almost all aspects of the culture, is a manageable unit of study well within the comprehension and abilities of the student—certainly much more so than an entire community. The traditional training field party too often spends itself in either a confused, pathetic scramble on the part of the students to gather and understand a large amount of data covering all aspects of the culture or in the limited pursuit by each student of a single problem or institution. From my own experience with groups of students in rural Cuba and Mexico, I have found the family approach to field work an invaluable aid. Furthermore, family case studies are very useful as a teaching aid in communicating a feeling for real people.

There is a need for intensive individual family case studies in cultures all over the world. The publication of such studies would give us a literature on comparative family life not now available and would be of use to many social scientists interested in a variety of problems concerning culture and the individual. Moreover, because individual families can be described without recourse to abstractions and stereotypes, the publication of case studies would provide us with some basis for judging the generalizations made by anthropologists and others concerning the total culture patterns of any community. The implication of the family case study for anthropological research is clear. It means that we have to go more slowly, that we

* See Essay 14, below.

have to spend more time doing careful and detailed studies of units smaller than the entire culture before we can be ready to make valid generalizations for the entire culture. These suggestions for individual family studies may seem excessively cautious at this time, when some anthropologists are writing with such abandon about the character structure of entire nations. Yet it may be necessary to take a few steps backward if we are to forge ahead on surer ground.

6

Comparisons in Cultural Anthropology[*]

It is part of the thesis of this paper that there is no distinctive "comparative method" in anthropology, and that the persistence of this expression has led to unnecessary confusion and artificial dichotomies in much of the theoretical writing on this subject. Thus, we prefer to discuss comparisons in anthropology rather than the comparative method. This simple semantic change makes a difference, for it highlights the fact that the method of a comparison is only one aspect of comparison, other relevant aspects being the aims or objectives, the content, and the location in space of the entities compared. Our subject at once becomes broader than most considerations of "the comparative method" and includes comparisons within a single society as well as cross-cultural comparisons, comparisons over time as well as in space.

The unfortunate tendency to identify "the comparative method" with a particular type of research design or anthropological school of thought dates back to 1896, when Boas identified the comparative method with the early evolutionists. His juxtaposition of his "historical method" and the comparative method of the evolutionists obscured what is fundamental for our purpose, namely, that both used

[*] This paper first appeared in 1955 in William L. Thomas, Jr., ed., *Yearbook of Anthropology* (New York: Copyright 1955, Wenner-Gren Foundation for Anthropological Research), pp. 259–92. I am grateful to the Behavioral Sciences Division of the Ford Foundation for a grant in aid, a portion of which was used for research assistance in the preparation of this study.

comparisons toward the end of arriving at general laws. Of course, Boas was not against comparisons or comparative method. He wanted to improve the comparative method, and specifically referred to his historical method as an improved comparative method. What I should like to emphasize is that the differences in anthropology are not between approaches which use comparisons and those which do not. All approaches—functionalism, diffusionism, Kulturkreis, or evolutionism—make use of comparisons, but in different ways and for different ends.

Comparison is a generic aspect of human thought rather than a special method of anthropology or of any other discipline. Laymen as well as scientists make comparisons. The major difference between common-sense, everyday comparisons by laymen and those by scientists is that scientists, in their systematic study of similarities and differences, strive for a greater degree of control by utilizing the methods of correlation and co-variation.

It does not follow, however, that those studies which use quantification and express co-variation statistically are the only valid, useful, or scientific studies. Nor must all comparisons necessarily be directed toward testing hypotheses or arriving at general principles of societal development, worthwhile as these objectives are. Comparisons may have other values, depending upon the nature of the data and the objectives of the study. And so long as cultural anthropology feels a sense of kinship with the humanities as well as with the natural sciences, comparisons which increase our general understanding will have their rightful place.

Most anthropological writing contains comparisons. Even the monographs which are primarily descriptive generally make comparisons with earlier literature, and many have a final comparative chapter. Textbooks use comparisons as illustrations. Theoretical articles compare methods, points of view, and schools of thought, or review the literature of an area in a comparative manner. There are comparisons between single culture traits, between institutions, between subcultures, between areas, nations, and civilizations. There are synchronic and diachronic comparisons, controlled and uncontrolled, localized and global, formal and functional, statistical and typological. The kinds of comparisons made by anthropologists seem to be of an endless variety.

This paper attempts to classify and analyze comparisons found in the literature for the five-year period 1950–1954 in order to determine the major types of comparisons, their objectives, methods, and research designs, and the location in space and time of the entities compared. References to earlier comparative studies will be made only when necessary for background purposes. The scheme used for the classification of comparisons will be presented later. Here let us first examine some of the highlights of recent theoretical articles on comparative method.

· THEORETICAL WRITINGS* ·

Within the past five years there have appeared an unusually large number of theoretical writings dealing with comparative method in anthropology.[1] In addition, an equally large number of books and articles have touched upon problems of comparative method indirectly or in passing. In all, probably more has been written on this subject within the past five years than within any comparable period since Boas published his famous piece of 1896. It is noteworthy that many of the authors cited here refer back to Boas, accepting, modifying, or rejecting his position. This concentration of interest in comparative method is probably a reflection of the growing maturity of anthropology as a science, the ever-increasing concern of anthropologists with problems of theory and method, and the accumulation of great masses of data which cry out for systematic comparative analysis.

A review of the literature cited here suggests a number of observations. Many of the theoretical discussions still use the phrase "the comparative method" as if it were a unitary and distinctive method of anthropology. For example, Ackerknecht (1954), who uses the expression "the comparative method" over thirty times in his short piece without once defining it, treats it almost as if it were a culture trait. He attempts to trace its introduction into anthropology from the biological and natural sciences and finally concludes that it was probably a case of convergence, if not of independent invention! He writes of the method as being "abandoned" by the functionalists and cites (p. 117) the publication of Murdock's *Social Structure* in 1949 as a sign of "a renaissance of the comparative method." Kroeber (1954, p. 273), in commenting on Ackerknecht's article, quite properly points out that "the comparative method has never gone out, it has only changed its tactic."

The titles of some of the papers on comparative anthropology are in themselves revealing. Thus Radcliff-Brown (1951), like Ackerknecht, follows the old tradition and calls his paper "The Comparative Method in Social Anthropology." He gives two major purposes

* References cited in this section are listed on pp. 120–123.

[1] Murdock, 1950*a*, *b*; Steward, 1950; Evans-Pritchard, 1951; Nadel, 1951; Radcliffe-Brown, 1951; Köbben, 1952; Ackerknecht, 1954; Kluckhohn, 1953, 1954; Lowie, 1953; Schapera, 1953; Eggan, 1954; Herskovits, 1954; and Whiting and colleagues, 1954.

of comparisons: the reconstruction of history, which he identifies with ethnology, and the discovery of regularities in the development of human society, which he identifies with social anthropology. He frankly defines the comparative method as a library method of "armchair anthropologists" and calls for more rather than less armchair anthropology. He writes (1951, p. 15),

> At Cambridge sixty years ago Frazer represented armchair anthropology using the comparative method, while Haddon urged the need of intensive studies of particular societies by systematic field studies of competent observers. The development of field studies has led to a relative neglect of studies making use of the comparative method. This is both understandable and excusable, but it does have some regrettable effects. The student is told that he must consider any feature of social life in its context, in its relation to the other features of the particular social system in which it is found. But he is often not taught to look at it in the wider context of human societies in general.

Singer's summary (1953, p. 362) of the discussion on Schapera's paper, titled "Some Comments on Comparative Method in Social Anthropology," is germane here. He writes,

> Schapera's original paper which was circulated before the conference was entitled "Some Thoughts on the Comparative Method in Social Anthropology." . . . Dropping the "the" from the title of the revised paper is perhaps the most eloquent, if inconspicuous, testimony of the impact of the conference: for Schapera and the other participants agreed that there is no single method of comparison in anthropology, that method is largely determined by problem, and that a method appropriate for the comparison of kinship systems is not necessarily most appropriate for other types of cross-cultural comparisons.

Eggan's excellent paper "Social Anthropology and the Method of Controlled Comparisons" (1954) gets away from "the comparative method" in the title and speaks instead of methods of comparisons. But even Eggan lapses again and again into the older terminology. He writes (p. 747), "In the United States . . . the comparative method has long been in disrepute, and was supplanted by what Boas called the 'historical method.' In England, on the other hand, the comparative method has had a more continuous utilization." Or again, he writes (p. 749) that most of Boas' students were predisposed against "the comparative method" and "hence against any generalizations which require comparisons." The use of the term "the comparative method" makes the above statements confusing. It is doubtful that the Boas students were against all comparisons. Certainly they have contributed their share of comparative studies.

Rather, they objected to what they thought were uncontrolled comparisons, comparisons out of context.

Murdock (1954) and Whiting (1954) think of the comparative method almost exclusively in terms of the testing of hypotheses on a global scale with a heavy reliance upon statistics. Schapera (1953) tends to identify the comparative method with the intensive study of limited areas as a prerequisite to testing regionally derived general propositions in other areas. Eggan recognizes the validity and usefulness of a wide range of comparisons, from those within a single community to global comparisons, but prefers the more limited and controlled comparisons to the more global and less controlled.

Lowie (1953) and Nadel (1951) take exception to the trend toward identifying "the comparative method" with a particular school or approach in anthropology. Lowie challenges the meaningfulness of equating the old dichotomy between historians and generalizers with that between ethnographers and social anthropologists, as suggested by some British anthropologists. He makes the point that comparisons are just as important in an intensive study or descriptive integration of a single community as they are in cross-cultural analysis, and sees the two as part of a single continuum of comparisons. An intensive study of a single community "implies cognizance of correlated phenomena and thereby precludes erroneous inferences due to the currency of the same labels. . . . Complete description involves a *global* survey of correlations because only such a global survey guarantees accurate definition of the cultural phenomenon under discussion in relation to its real or apparent equivalents elsewhere" (p. 532).

Nadel offers us by far the most systematic and comprehensive treatment of comparative method. He defines it in terms of the systematic study of similarities and differences through the use of correlation and co-variation. It is therefore not a distinctive method of anthropology, but one shared by all the sciences. Following Durkheim, Nadel distinguishes (1951, p. 226) three applications of the method of co-variation: (1) in the study of broad variations in particular modes of action or relationships within a single society; (2) in the study of the same society at different periods of time or of several essentially similar societies which differ only in certain respects; (3) in the study of numerous societies of a widely different nature. Nadel does not regard these three applications "as separate and independent lines of inquiry." Moreover, he believes that regularities can be derived from all three applications, the major differences being that the regularities derived from "narrow-range applications," i.e., within a single society, "are themselves of narrow applicability; they would exhibit specific phenomena present in only a limited number of societies" (p. 227).

While Nadel recognizes the value of cross-cultural comparison and its distinctive place in anthropology as compared with other disciplines, he would not define anthropology exclusively in terms of cross-cultural studies. Indeed, he takes exception to a statement of Radcliffe-Brown which suggests that a study of a single society cannot "demonstrate" co-variations but can only lead to hypotheses which have to be tested in other societies. Nadel writes (1951, p. 240),

> Though this conclusion undoubtedly often holds, I do not think it applies invariably. Thus, if we include time perspective and cultural change in our enquiry, the necessary co-variations will be available, too, in societies sufficiently differentiated to exhibit the "broad" variations in the behavior of different group sections we spoke of before. Furthermore, in any society, . . . inasmuch as cultural elements "hang together" in their own institutional setting, they do so by means of co-variations; the standardized, predictable patterns of behavior which are the elements of social existence mean nothing else.

Many of the recent writings on comparative methods and problems in anthropology express the particular theoretical preferences of the authors but they do not provide us with a systematic examination and analysis of contemporary comparative research. In this sense, the theoretical writing has lagged behind the field work. Steward (1950) reviews a good sample of community studies and older ethnographic studies and points to difficulties in comparability due to the uneven coverage, which seems to depend largely upon individual interests. But he does not deal with the vast number of comparative studies in the literature. Similarly, Kluckhohn (1953) raises important theoretical problems in connection with the comparability of anthropological data and reports on the comparability of anthropological monographs based upon the examination of the table of contents of ninety monographs, but he does not deal extensively with comparative studies as such. The single article within the past five years which makes some attempt at an evaluation of comparative research is the excellent piece by Köbben (1952), titled "New Ways of Presenting an Old Idea: The Statistical Method in Social Anthropology," in which he critically reviews *one type* of comparative study. His work will be cited later.

· ANALYSIS AND CLASSIFICATION OF COMPARISONS ·

A total of 248 writings dealing with comparisons, within the period 1950–1954, were examined in the preparation of this paper.[2] These include 52 books, 173 articles, and 23 dissertations. Twenty-eight of these writings deal primarily with theory and method in comparative anthropology and have been summarized earlier. The remaining 220 writings (45 books, 152 articles, and 23 dissertations) are reports of comparative research. The 152 articles with which we will be concerned were found after an examination of 23 scientific journals, including most of the major anthropological journals which are concerned with cultural or social anthropology. While the coverage is not exhaustive, it probably represents about 90 per cent of the comparative writings in the past five years.[3] Only a few of the dissertations cited were available to me. The analysis of most of the dissertations is based primarily upon published abstracts and is therefore partial and tentative.

In the light of recent discussions as to whether British or American anthropologists are more vitally concerned with comparative studies, it is interesting to note that 40, or 17 per cent, of the 220 writings, were British publications. This is a high proportion in view of the relatively small number of British anthropologists. However, it demonstrates that American anthropologists are also active in the field of comparative studies. Our survey of the major French and German anthropological periodicals yielded very few comparative studies for the period covered.

In our analysis and classification of the above writings five broad dimensions of comparisons were considered: (A) the location in space of the entities compared, (B) the content, (C) the aims of the comparisons, (D) methods of obtaining data, and (E) research design. These dimensions were, in turn, subdivided so that each comparative study was judged against a check list of numerous items. (See Table 1.)

The geographical distribution of the comparative studies is shown in Table 2 (note that 1e and 1f have been combined, and 1b divided as between continents or nations or as within one continent). It can

[2] I am grateful to Dr. Ruth Landman for bibliographical research assistance in preparation of this paper.

[3] Unfortunately the two major Indian anthropology journals were not available to me and so articles and books on India are not well covered.

TABLE 1

OUTLINE FOR THE CLASSIFICATION AND ANALYSIS OF
COMPARATIVE STUDIES

1/ Location in space of the entities compared [a]
   - a) comparisons of cultures or aspects thereof selected randomly over the globe, i.e., global comparisons
   - b) comparisons of societies or aspects thereof located in different nations or major civilizations
   - c) comparisons within a nation
   - d) comparisons within a single culture area (for example, the Plains or Southwest in the United States)
   - e) comparisons of local groups within a single culture (for example, different bands within a single tribe, or two Blackfoot Indian tribes)
   - f) comparisons within a single local group (band, village, or other type of localized settlement)

2/ Content of comparisons

a) material culture	l) personality and culture
b) settlement pattern	m) life cycle
c) ecology	n) sex
d) technology	o) disease
e) economics	p) relations with other communities
f) social organization	q) acculturation and culture change
g) political organization	r) race relations
h) religion	s) law
i) mythology	t) values
j) art	u) total culture
k) warfare	

3/ Aims of the comparisons
   - a) to establish general laws or regularities
   - b) to document range of variation in the phenomena studied
   - c) to document distribution of traits or aspects of culture
   - d) to reconstruct culture history
   - e) to test hypotheses derived from Western society
   - f) to test hypotheses derived from non-Western societies

4/ Methods of obtaining data
   - a) library comparisons
   - b) comparisons based upon library data plus field work
   - c) comparisons based primarily upon field work

5/ Research design
   - a) statistical comparisons
   - b) broad typological comparisons
   - c) descriptive, functional analyses of one or more aspects of culture
   - d) descriptive and analytic comparisons of total cultures
   - e) restudies by the same investigator
   - f) restudies by different investigators

[a] Most of the geographical categories under 1 above are self-explanatory. Categories 1c and 1d are intended to distinguish between tribal studies of peasantry, rural, and urban groups. The culture area is taken as the frame of reference of the former, the nation for the latter.

TABLE 2

Location of Studies

	Oceania	Asia	Africa	Europe	Latin America	North America	Total
Random or global comparisons (34)	—	—	—	—	—	—	—
Comparisons between continents or nations (20)	2	9	2	6	8	6	33 (13 repeat)
Comparisons within one continent (31)	1	5	8	0	8	9	31
Comparisons within one nation (31)	0	9	1	3	10	8	31
Comparisons within one culture area (70)	10	2	17	0	14	27	70
Comparisons within one group or culture (34)	7	3	2	0	9	13	34
Total	20	28	30	9	49	63	199

TABLE 3

DISTRIBUTION OF METHODS BY CATEGORY OF COMPARISON

Method	I. Random or global comparisons (34)	II. Comparisons between continents or nations (20)	III. Comparisons within one continent (31)	IV. Comparisons within one nation (31)	V. Comparisons within one culture area (70)	VI. Comparisons within one group or culture (34)	Total number of cases
Library comparison	28	6	20	3	23	0	80
Comparisons based upon field work and library data	6	6	7	6	37	9	71
Comparison based primarily upon field work	0	8	4	22	10	25	69

be seen that the greatest number of studies occur in North America and Latin America, the smallest number in Europe and Oceania; Africa and Asia hold an intermediate position. Although the location of the entities to be compared may seem like a relatively unimportant consideration, I find that it correlates significantly with the other major categories, but especially with methods. Comparative studies within a single culture area seem, by and large, to be interested in controlling the greatest number of variables and in relatively modest and limited goals. Global comparisons generally have more ambitious goals and seek world-wide typologies or evolutionary sequences.

The relationship between methods used and the location of the entities compared can be seen in Table 3.

One of the most striking conclusions to be drawn from the data in Table 3 is that comparative studies in anthropology can no longer be defined as library studies. The three methods—library comparisons, library plus field work, and primarily field work comparisons—are used about equally.

As we move from the global and larger categories to the smaller ones, we find an increasing reliance upon field work. Conversely, as we go from the smaller to the larger categories (Table 4) we find an increasing use of library comparisons.

The inverse relationship is most striking when we compare the two extremes of our geographical categories, i.e., global or random comparisons as over against comparisons within a single local group or culture (Column I versus VI in Table 3). In the former, there is a complete absence of comparisons based primarily upon field work and a predominance of library comparisons. In the latter, there are no library comparisons but there are a large number of studies based on field work. The zero scores in Columns I and VI in Table 3, though understandable in terms of the nature of the research, are by no means inevitable. As comparative field research designs organized on a world-wide basis increase (for example, the Cornell Project on the effects of technological change and the Whiting field study of

TABLE 4

DISTRIBUTION OF METHODS OF THE THREE LARGER CATEGORIES
COMPARED WITH THAT OF THE THREE SMALLER CATEGORIES

Method	Large groups (I, II, III)	Small groups (IV, V, VI)
Library comparisons	63.5%	19.2%
Comparisons based on field work plus library data	22.3%	38.5%
Comparisons based primarily upon field work	14.1%	42.2%

socialization in five cultures, now under way),[4] the zero scores will disappear.[5] Similarly, with the increase of restudies of local communities by the same or different investigators, library comparisons within this category will be possible.

Another interesting aspect of the relationship between method and geographical categories can be seen by comparing the distribution of methods in the one-nation category (peasantry and rural studies) with the culture-area category (tribal studies). (See Columns IV and V, Table 3.) Seventy-one per cent of the studies in the former as compared to only 14 per cent in the latter are based primarily upon field work. Moreover, 29 per cent of the comparisons within a nation which were based primarily upon field work were done co-operatively by research teams rather than by a single investigator, as over against 1 per cent within a single culture area. Since the comparative study of peasantry is a much more recent trend in anthropology than comparative tribal studies, it is here that we find the greatest concentration of field work and co-operative research. However, comparisons based upon tribal studies still outnumber the others by more than two to one.

The distribution of content in the 220 studies examined shows that the bulk of comparative work is being done in six fields: social organization, 68; culture change and acculturation, 65; total culture, 39; economics, 30; religion, 27; culture and personality, 21. Studies of social organization and culture change each constitute approximately 30 per cent of the total number of studies. The relatively high number of total culture comparisons is a tribute to the holistic approach of many anthropologists. The fields in which we find the fewest comparative studies are race relations, 1; law, 2; relations with other communities, 3; sex, 3; life cycle, 4; mythology, 5; warfare, 5; settlement patterns, 7; and art, 8.

It will be seen (Table 3) that 61 per cent of all the studies are within the three smaller categories and 39 per cent in the three larger categories. If we assume that the comparisons within small geographical areas give one greater control than widespread comparisons, we might interpret the above distribution to mean that contemporary comparative anthropology has moved a great distance toward the limited and controlled comparisons which Eggan and others have called for. Studies of social organization and culture

---

[4] This has since been published as *Six Cultures: Studies of Child Rearing*, ed. Beatrice B. Whiting (New York: John Wiley, 1963).

[5] An outstanding and monumental example of this type of research design is the three-volume work produced under the editorship and guidance of Julian H. Steward, *Contemporary Change in Traditional Societies* (Urbana, Ill.: University of Illinois Press, 1967).

change are concentrated in the smaller geographical categories. Thirty-five per cent of all the studies of culture change and acculturation are found concentrated in the category of a single community or culture.

The classification of the writings in terms of the theoretical aims of the comparisons proved extremely difficult because of the lack of any explicit statement in so many of the writings. The categories we have listed in our outline must therefore remain as items for future analysis of comparative studies. However, some general findings can be given here. Approximately 40 per cent of the studies are descriptive, functional, comparative analyses of one or more aspects of culture, which seek to establish the relationship between variables, for the purpose of either establishing typologies or refining existing types. Approximately 30 per cent of the studies deal with acculturation and culture change. The culture-change studies are generally historical reconstructions intended to show the direction of change. Only a few studies explicitly formulate developmental hypotheses. Approximately 18 per cent of the studies are concerned primarily with demonstrating the range of variation in the phenomena studied; another 8 per cent are straight distribution studies, and 3 per cent are attempts to delineate or redefine the nature of culture areas. Let us now examine the studies in more detail.

· GLOBAL OR RANDOM COMPARISONS* ·

Twelve books, 18 articles, and 4 dissertations, making a total of 34 out of 220 writings examined, fall into this category. All have in common the comparison of societies selected either at random or in accord with some special sampling design, but in no case limited to a single culture area, region, nation, or continent. Twenty-seven are library comparisons and ten are library plus field work comparisons.

The content covers a wide range, 17 of our 21 content categories (Table 1). The largest number are studies of social organization (8 cases), followed by economics (4), technology (4), religion (4), socialization (4), and disease (4). Seven studies deal with culture change and/or acculturation.

The objectives of these writings show a wide range from tracing the distribution of a single trait to testing one or more hypotheses or reconstructing stages in the history of human society. However, the writings can be divided into subgroups in terms of a combination of methods and general research design: (A) Statistical Comparisons,

* References cited in this section are listed on pp. 123–124.

10 cases;[6] (B) Broad Typological Comparisons, 6 cases;[7] (C) Functional Cross-cultural Analysis of One or More Aspects of a Culture, 7 cases;[8] (D) Simple Distribution Studies, 3 cases;[9] and (E) Case Books and Texts, 8 cases.[10] The volume edited by Spicer (1952) deserves special mention because many of the cases have come out of the Cornell Project in Applied Anthropology, one of the few centrally organized comparative research projects with field stations in major ethnographic areas of the world.

Here I will discuss only two of the five subcategories above, namely, the statistical and the typological approaches.

• STATISTICAL COMPARISONS •

All ten statistical studies are based in part or in whole upon the Cross-cultural Files and the Human Relations Area Files at New Haven. The strengths and weaknesses of this type of study have received much discussion in the literature. Perhaps the fullest evaluation of this approach is to be found in the lengthy discussion of Murdock and Whiting's paper (1951) on "The Cultural Determination of Parental Attitudes," by a panel which included, among others, Sibylle K. Escalona, Erik H. Erikson, and Dorothy D. Lee. More recently Köbben (1952) has provided a searching analysis in his paper, "New Ways of Presenting an Old Idea: The Statistical Method in Social Anthropology."

The use of the physical sciences as a model, the testing of hypotheses derived primarily from Freudian or Hullian* thinking, faith in quantification and large numbers of cases, optimism about the possibility of arriving at general laws, and the definition of the cross-cultural method as the statistical method are characteristics of some of the writings of members of this group. Whiting (1954, p. 528), for example, in his article on "The Cross-Cultural Method," † generalizes the steps he used in his own study on *Child Training and Personality* (1953) to define *the* cross-cultural method. Murdock re-

[6] For example, Murdock and Whiting, 1951; Ford and Beach, 1951; Charles, 1953; McClelland and Friedman, 1952; Whiting and Child, 1953.

[7] For example, Redfield, 1953; Meggers, 1954; Fried, 1952.

[8] For example, Freedman and Ferguson, 1950; Aberle, 1952; Erickson, 1950; James, 1952.

[9] For example, Anderson and Cutler, 1950; Balfour, 1951.

[10] For example, Spicer (ed.), 1952; Hoebel, 1954; Goode, 1951; Herskovits, 1952.

* Clark L. Hull.

† The full citation appears on p. 123.

peatedly identifies the cross-cultural method with the statistical method based upon the cross-cultural files. He writes, "We believe that the day is past when we can depend upon an analysis of single cases or single societies to give us scientific answers. We feel the hypotheses suggested by the exploratory studies of individual societies should be tested by quantitative methods in a large number of societies" (Murdock and Whiting, 1951, p. 32).

Murdock (1949, p. 183)* believes that "the data of culture and social life are susceptible to exact scientific treatment as are the facts of the physical and biological sciences. It seems clear that the elements of social organization, in their permutations and combinations, conform to natural laws of their own with an exactitude scarcely less striking than that which characterizes the permutations and combinations of atoms in chemistry and of genes in biology." Elsewhere, Murdock (1954, p. 30) optimistically writes that anthropology "if it rises to the occasion, may ultimately become the final arbiter of the universality of social science propositions."

Although Köbben's discussion deals primarily with the cross-cultural studies published prior to our limiting date of 1950 (i.e., Horton, 1943; Ford, 1945; Murdock, 1949), much of his criticism applies also to the studies covered in this review. Köbben notes (1952)† that the "Grand Design" of the cross-cultural files is not novel and lists as direct precursors the works of S. R. Steinmetz, 1898; E. B. Tylor, 1889; L. T. Hobhouse, G. C. Wheeler, and M. Ginsberg, 1930; H. J. Niebohr, 1910; and Unwin, 1934. Köbben finds that in some ways the work of these precursors was methodologically more rigorous than the later studies; it was also more meaningful, in that they attempted to deal with the interrelationships between various institutions or aspects thereof, in contrast to the more limited problems posed by the recent studies. For example, they sought answers to the question: How do systems of social organization vary with economic systems or modes of production? On the other hand, by limiting his problem, Murdock arrived at a useful typology of social structures, albeit largely in terms of kinship systems and residence rules. Moreover, Murdock's broad interest in general laws, his concern with evolutionary problems, and his striving for scientific rigor in comparative studies, constitute a salutary trend in contemporary anthropology.

The questions raised by Köbben and others about the statistical type of study are many and serious, and might be summarized as follows: The units compared are not always truly independent; the

---

* The full citation appears on p. 122.

† The full citation appears on p. 122.

conclusions would be changed considerably if the size of the sample were increased; the items compared are taken out of context and are therefore not truly comparable; the items compared are frequently atomized traits rather than functioning wholes; questions asked of the materials are frequently beyond what the data can answer (this applies better to the culture-personality studies than to Murdock's *Social Structure*). The study of Whiting and Child (1953) raises an additional question by its use of a presumed modal or average custom as the basic unit of comparison. It thereby maximizes one of the weaknesses of anthropological reporting of the past, namely, the assumption of an underlying homogeneity in the customs of so-called primitive peoples. We have here indeed a curious combination of sophisticated statistical techniques applied to poor materials in such a way as to eliminate by definition the possibility of studying the range of behavior or custom within any of the societies examined.

Murdock and Whiting (1951) and Whiting (1954) among others, are not unaware of the problems posed by the criticism, and when pressed, have admitted to some crucial weaknesses. For example, when Erikson (1950, p. 38), in discussing the 1950 paper by Murdock and Whiting (published in 1951), suggested that most anthropological data on parental attitudes and child training were extremely uneven and unsystematic and rarely distinguished among observed behavior, ideal patterns, and projections of the investigators' stereotypes, Murdock replied,

> The points he [Erikson] made raise very serious problems. . . . In justification of our method, we can only say that in our selected societies, in general, what the sources report is what the informants said was supposed to be the case, so that the comparisons are generally between two supposed or ideal patterns. We have to assume, to make these results valid, that the difference between the ideal pattern and the manifest behavior is approximately the same from society to society, which is a very questionable assumption, I grant (Murdock and Whiting, 1951, pp. 40–41).

Granting limitations in the data and the methods used, many social scientists find the hypotheses themselves stimulating and suggestive. In this connection it appears to me that, of all the recent cross-cultural studies of a statistical nature done on the grand scale, Murdock's is the most original and creative in the sense that he is not simply testing Freudian or Hullian hypotheses derived from the data of Western societies, but that he comes up with original general propositions derived from the data of non-Western societies.

To me, one of the contributions of the studies by Whiting is to reveal the serious gaps in anthropological data on culture and personality for cross-cultural comparative purposes and the need for planned comparative field research. Whiting and colleagues are now engaged in such a project, "Field Guide for a Study of Socialization in Five Societies," (1954). The detailed directions and questions to field workers recently prepared by Whiting and colleagues to insure greater comparability of data is evidence of the lessons learned from working with library materials.

• BROAD TYPOLOGICAL COMPARISONS •

The outstanding item is the book by Redfield, *The Primitive World and Its Transformations*, which is a comparison, on a vast scale, of mankind all over the world before "civilization"—i.e., before the growth of cities—with that after the growth of cities. While recognizing the wide range of cultural differences among precivilized (prior to 6000 B.C.) and contemporary primitive peoples, both of whom are treated together, Redfield (1953, p. 1) attempts to go beyond cultural relativism and asks the question, What do these peoples have in common, irrespective of "whether they lived in the arctic or in the tropics, whether they hunted, fished, or farmed," which sets them apart from civilized man? His findings are stated in terms of the now familiar characteristics of the folk society, such as isolation, homogeneity, and the predominance of the moral order. However, Redfield's major concern is with the broad problems of culture change, evolution, and the transformation of the folk societies into other kinds of societies, peasant and urban.

In terms of the global nature of the design, Redfield yields nothing to the statistically oriented studies. But unlike the latter, which suffer from atomism, Redfield, in the great humanist tradition, never loses sight of man as a whole, and maintains the sense of the wholeness of culture by his constructed types. But at the same time the emphasis upon the similarities within the type and the lumping together of prehistoric peoples with contemporary primitive peoples tend to neglect differences. Perhaps this weakness, if it is a weakness, is inevitable when working on such a high level of abstraction without the controls inherent in the more limited kinds of comparisons to be considered later. Moreover, in a recent paper on "The Cultural Role of Cities," Redfield and Singer (1954) take a long step in the direction of correcting the earlier stereotyped urban category by showing the considerable range in the forms and functions of cities in different historical periods in various parts of the world.

Although Steward's recent work on Puerto Rico is in our category of studies within a single nation, his theoretical approach properly belongs here. It too, is a typological approach of a global nature which cuts across culture areas to seek out the phenomena intended for study. It shares some of the strengths and weaknesses of the Redfield approach. It differs from the latter, however, in that it deals with more limited problems, for it strives for empirically derived, rather than ideal, types; it shows greater concern with developmental sequences; it is more selective in the variables treated; and, on the whole, it manifests a materialistic rather than an idealistic philosophical position. The major emphases are upon productive relations, technology, social structure, and ecology. Values and ethics are given much less weight; indeed, some would feel that they are neglected, and perhaps it is this which makes for a somewhat mechanistic approach.

· COMPARISONS BETWEEN CONTINENTS OR NATIONS* ·

Three books, 16 articles, and 1 dissertation, or a total of 20 out of 220 writings examined, fall into this category. This category is defined by the fact that the comparisons are either between nations or major civilizations as such or between societies or aspects thereof located in different nations or continents. Six are library studies, 6 are a combination of library and field work, and 8 are based primarily upon field work.

The range of content of these studies is narrower than that of the global studies. Studies of religion (7), total culture (6), economics (5), and social organization (3) account for over 90 per cent of all the studies.[11] The studies in this category fall into the following groups: (A) Comparisons between Two or More Major Civilizations, 4 cases;[12] (B) Studies of Variants of One Culture, or Aspects Thereof, in Two Continents, 6 cases;[13] (C) Problem-oriented Studies with Examples from Two Continents or Nations, 8 cases;[14] and (D) Distribution Studies, Independent Invention vs. Diffusion, 2 cases.[15]

The studies in this category deal with a variety of interesting theoretical problems. On the whole, the studies are of two contrasting types: first, those which compare historically related peoples and attempt to show the readaptations and reinterpretations of culture

* References cited in this section are listed on pp. 125–126.

[11] Some of these studies cover two or three fields and are therefore listed more than once.

[12] For example, Hsu, 1953; Patai, 1954.

[13] For example, Bascom, 1950; Mintz and Wolf, 1950; Foster, 1953.

[14] For example, Lewis, 1954; Steward and Murphy, 1954; Needham, 1954.

[15] For example, Erasmus, 1950; Hatt, 1951.

traits or institutions in a new setting; second, those which compare historically unrelated peoples. The latter—which predominate in this geographical category—are especially suitable for pointing up contrasts, for testing the applicability of generalizations formulated on the basis of studies in other areas, and for formulating new hypotheses.

Hsu's interesting study (1953) is the fullest total cultural comparison between two nations done by an anthropologist in recent years. He contrasts the American "individual-centered" way of life with the Chinese "situation-centered" way of life and examines the manner in which these key concepts are reflected in such areas as child training, marriage, economics, government, religion, ethics, art, alcoholism, and suicide. The book is based primarily upon library sources, plus insights which have come to Hsu from living in two cultures. Hsu paints with a big brush, combines psychoanalytic and anthropological interpretations, and is often closer to the literary than the scientific tradition.

The studies by Bascom (1950, 1952) and Foster (1951, 1953) share the advantage of first-hand comparative field research in their respective areas. This, combined with the controls inherent in the historical research design, gives their work a fresh quality and lends weight to their findings. Foster's ethnographic research in Spain throws new light on the difficult problem of what is Indian and what is Spanish in Mexico and Latin America. His paper on "Cofradía and Compadrazgo in Spain and Spanish America" illustrates the differential role of a common trait or institution in two or more cultures, as well as the differential solution in two cultures to a basic need of both. Bascom's comparison of Cuban worship of African deities with the Yoruba practice of rituals involving stones, blood, and herbs, shows the reinterpretation of a trait cluster in a new setting. Moreover, it shows how a study of Cuba can throw light on native African institutions which could not be discerned from a contemporary study of Africa alone. In the same sense, it may be possible to learn by a study of contemporary Mexican societies much about sixteenth-century Spain which could not be learned by a direct study of contemporary Spain. The study by Mintz and Wolf (1950), though not based on comparative field work in the regions compared, relies heavily upon historical controls and is of a high caliber of scholarship.

My own detailed comparison between a Mexican and a north Indian village (1954), based upon field work in each village, covers social organization, economics, politics, and other aspects of culture. I found that despite similarities in their economic base, the two villages had strikingly different systems of social organization. This suggests that we need to restudy the whole problem of peasant communities in greater detail, and within nations and regions, before we can venture broader generalizations about peasantry as a whole.

Goldschmidt's fascinating comparisons (1951) between the Protestant ethic of sixteenth-century Europe and the values of the Hurok-Hupa and other California tribes raises important critical questions about our traditional assumptions as to the relationships among economy, social structure, and value systems. Steward and Murphy (1954), concerned more with structure than with culture content, show how the fur-trapping Montaignais and the rubber-tapping Mundurucu develop similar types of social organization in reaction to a market economy.

Needham (1954), drawing upon a field study of the forest Penan of Borneo, offers both confirmatory and contradictory findings on A. R. Holmberg's seventeen hypotheses derived from his study of the Siriono of Bolivia. Holmberg's hypotheses were intended to apply to societies "where conditions of food insecurity and hunger frustration are comparable to those found among the Siriono." Penan meets these conditions admirably. However, Needham was able to confirm only five of seventeen hypotheses; two could not be tested, and ten were patently contradicted. Space permits only two examples of the latter. One of Holmberg's hypotheses is that "aggression will be expressed largely in terms of food: if not, such aggression will be so severely punished that it will be almost entirely repressed." However, Needham writes:

> Aggression in Penan society cannot be expressed in terms of food. They do not fight and quarrel about food, do not manifest a strong reluctance to share food, and do not lie about food. On the contrary, they are extremely punctilious about sharing equally in all circumstances. . . .
>
> Penan are born into a culture lacking these aggressive features, and there are no sure signs that it is only severe disapproval of them which represses the assumed aggressive desires. The reaction of Penan culture to food insecurity is not individualistic aggressiveness but scrupulously exact sharing (p. 230).

Another hypothesis of Holmberg was that "there will be a tendency to kill, neglect, or otherwise dispose of the aged, the deformed young, and the extremely ill. If not, such dependents will occupy a favored status in the society."

Of this Needham writes:

> This is completely false of the Penan, in conception and action. The old, deformed, and extremely ill are cared for in every way known to the Penan. The group changes or postpones its movements for their sake, even to the considerable detriment of its members. No

suggestion so horrifies the Penan as that they might kill, abandon, neglect, or otherwise dispose of such individuals. On the other hand, these are recognized for the burdens they are on the group, and in no way occupy a favored status (p. 232).

· COMPARISONS WITHIN ONE CONTINENT* ·

Three books, 25 articles and 3 dissertations, a total of 31 out of 220 writings, fall in this group, which is defined by the fact that the entities compared, be they single traits, institutions, cultures, or culture areas, are within a single continent.[16] Twenty studies are purely library comparisons, seven combine library and field work, and four are based primarily upon field work. The content covers a wide range, 19 out of 21 content categories. The greatest concentration is in social organization (13 cases), followed by total culture (7), acculturation (4), economics (4), and art (3).

These studies fall into four groups: (A) Culture Area Studies, 5 cases,[17] (B) Typological Studies, 6 cases,[18] (C) Problem-oriented Studies Comparing One or More Aspects of a Culture, 9 cases,[19] and (D) Distribution Studies, 9 cases.[20]

The studies in this category, though preponderantly library comparisons, are, on the whole, of high quality and capitalize upon the controls inherent in the study of continuous geographical areas which, though large, have usually been subject to common historical influences. It should be noted that most of the comparative studies of culture areas are found here. Let us consider briefly three studies.

Lowie's paper (1952), "The Heterogeneity of Marginal Cultures," is critical of the traditional typology which distinguishes sharply between food-collectors and food-producers because, among other reasons, it tends to overlook important differences among the cultures within each type. Lowie stresses the wide range of variation in the culture of food-collectors, in ecological adaptation, social organization, and religion, and emphasizes the creativity of such peoples.

Foster's paper (1952), "Relationships between Theoretical and Applied Anthropology: A Public Health Program Analysis," reports on a study of the operation of a health program in seven Latin American countries, sponsored by the Health and Sanitation Division of

* References cited in this section are listed on pp. 126–127.
[16] Note the inclusion of Latin America in this category.
[17] For example, Naroll, 1950; Murdock, 1951; Lange, 1953.
[18] For example, Smith, 1951; Bacon, 1954; Wolf, 1955.
[19] For example, Flannery, 1952; Goldfrank, 1952; Lowie, 1952; Foster, 1952.
[20] For example, Collins, 1951; Riley, 1952; Spinden, 1952.

the Institute of Inter-American Affairs. It is one of the few comparative analyses in the field of applied anthropology. This cross-cultural study of "folk medicine" and the nature of interpersonal relationships between patients and doctors revealed a number of basic similarities in all the countries and suggested (p. 16) that regularities are of sufficiently wide validity to supply useful guidelines for health programs in other Latin American countries and in other parts of the world where similar culture types exist.

Wolf's paper (1955), "Types of Latin American Peasantry: A Preliminary Discussion," raises the interesting question of the differential effects of the industrial revolution and the growing world market upon peasantry. He distinguishes seven types of peasantry in Latin America. Two of these—the "corporate type" and the "open type"—are treated in detail. The "corporate type" of the highland areas is characterized by location on marginal land, use of a traditional technology, limited production (primarily for subsistence), reliance upon a variety of occupations to supplement income from agriculture, a strong sense of community defined in terms of the politico-religious system, the predominance of the nuclear family, conspicuous consumption geared to religiously oriented communal ends rather than individual maximation, a "cult of poverty" based upon the need to restrict expenditures, and institutionalized envy.

The "open type," located in the tropical humid lowlands, is characterized by production of a cash crop (sugar cane, bananas, coffee) for the world market, dependence upon outside capital, the private ownership of land, an alternating cycle between reliance upon subsistence crops and reliance upon cash crops, a greater emphasis upon individualism, a weaker sense of community solidarity, the accumulation and display of wealth, and greater social and economic mobility.

· **COMPARISONS WITHIN ONE NATION*** ·

Three books, 27 articles, and 1 dissertation, a total of 31 writings out of 220, are in this category, in which we find for the first time that the greatest proportion of the comparative studies are based primarily upon field work. Twenty-two studies are based primarily upon field work, six upon a combination of library work and field work, and only three are purely library comparisons.

Although there is a considerable range in the content of these studies—15 of our 21 content categories—there is a marked cluster-

* References cited in this section are listed on pp. 127–129.

ing: acculturation (10), economics (8), social organization (7), total culture studies (6), personality and culture (3).

The studies can be divided conveniently into three groups: (A) Comparisons of Regions, Subcultures, or Total Communities, 8 cases,[21] (B) The Documentation of Range of Variation, 10 cases,[22] and (C) Culture Change, 14 cases.[23]

Taken as a whole, the category of comparisons within a nation contains some of the most interesting studies, in terms of content, competence, and originality of research design. The study of Puerto Rico by several research teams under the direction of Steward (1955) is a case in point. In line with his concept of socio-cultural levels of integration, Steward stresses the need to distinguish between what is local and what is national in community and regional studies. Viewing Puerto Rico as a socio-cultural whole characterized as a tropical island with a long history of colonial dependency, "part of a capitalistic world," depending upon cash, credit, and an export crop, and importing nearly all of its manufactured goods and about half its food, Steward's teams attempted to formulate and test hypotheses which would hold for Puerto Rico and similar "socio-cultural wholes" anywhere in the world. Critical of national character studies and assuming that no single community was Puerto Rico in microcosm, they organized detailed field studies in four rural communities to sample some of the major crop and community types on the island. In addition, they made a study of prominent upper-class families. Although Steward uses the term "sociocultural," the greatest emphasis is clearly upon economic variables, such as methods of production, technology, crops, cash, credit, and markets. Moreover, the emphasis is upon structural analysis rather than culture content.

Another very interesting study is the comparison of a highland and a lowland Totonac village in Mexico, based upon first-hand field work in each (Viqueira and Palerm, 1954). This is one of the few comparative studies in Mexico since Redfield's *Folk Culture of Yucatan* was published in 1941. Eloxochitlan, the highland community, has an economy of scarcity, population pressure, production primarily for subsistence, strong political controls, community solidarity against the outside, collective labor, monogamy, and the predominance of the nuclear family. The world is viewed as hostile, and sorcery and black magic are all-pervasive. Tajin, the lowland commu-

[21] For example, Ryan, 1950; Fried, 1952; Viqueira and Palerm, 1954; Manners and Steward, 1953.

[22] For example, Wagley, 1952; Wolf, 1952; Sanders, 1953.

[23] For example, Raper, 1951; Du Wors, 1952; Zen Sun, 1952; Caudill, 1952; Van der Kroef, 1954.

nity, has an economy of relative abundance, an important cash crop in vanilla, the predominance of the extended family, polygyny, an almost Apollonian sense of order and restraint, and no sorcery. Against this background the authors contrast the differential role of alcoholism. In the highland village, drinking is frequent, generalized, and socially sanctioned; and drunkenness is common but inoffensive, leading to social cohesion and euphoria. In the lowland village, drinking is infrequent and drunkenness rare, but when it occurs it almost inevitably leads to violence and homicide.

· COMPARISONS WITHIN A SINGLE CULTURE AREA OR REGION* ·

This category is defined in terms of comparisons within a single culture area or attempts to treat the area as a unit. It is by far the largest category, with a total of 70 studies: 12 books, 45 articles, and 13 dissertations. Twenty-three are library comparisons, 37 library plus field work, and 10 primarily field work. The content coverage is extremely broad, including 19 out of our 21 content categories, with only sex and mythology absent. The greatest concentration, however, is in studies of social organization (30 cases), followed by total culture (11), religion (9), economics (5), technology (5), and settlement patterns (4).

The 70 studies of this category can be grouped as follows: (A) Reviews of Research Trends on One or More Aspects of an Area, 4 cases,[24] (B) Definitions and/or Reconstruction of Culture Areas, 6 cases,[25] (C) Detailed, Intensive, Functional Analyses of One or More Aspects of Culture in a Small Number of Societies, 14 cases,[26] (D) Survey Studies of a Single Aspect of Culture among a Larger Number of Societies, 15 cases,[27] (E) Studies Concerned Primarily with Culture Change, Either in Terms of Acculturation or Internal Development (Evolution) or Both, 12 cases,[28] (F) Studies of Rela-

---

* References cited in this section are listed on pp. 129–132.

[24] For example, Evans-Pritchard, 1952; Elkin, 1953; Kluckhohn, 1954; Keesing, 1953.

[25] For example, Kirchhoff, 1952; Smith, 1952; Read, 1954.

[26] For example, Eggan, 1950; Richards, 1950; Nadel, 1950; Nadel, 1952; Smith, 1953.

[27] For example, Paul and Paul, 1952; Fischer, 1950; Hogbin and Wedgewood, 1953; Berndt, 1951; Wisdom, 1952.

[28] For example, Tax, 1952b; Lystad, 1951; Leacock, 1954; Secoy, 1953; Wagley, 1951.

tions between Communities, 3 cases,[29] and (G) Single-trait Distribution Studies, 5 cases.[30]

Before commenting upon some of the exemplary studies of this category, I should like to note that within the past few years a number of anthropologists have reaffirmed the earlier Boasian position on the methodological advantages made possible by careful studies within the context of a single culture area. Kluckhohn (1954) quotes the Boas statement that a primary requirement for valid comparison is that the phenomena compared be derived "psychologically or historically from common causes." Kluckhohn writes:

> One of the main rewards of intensive study of a culture area . . . is that such study eventually frees investigators to raise genuinely scientific questions—problems of process. Once the influences of various cultures upon others in the same area and the effects of a common environment (and its variant forms) have been reasonably well ascertained, one can then operate to a first approximation under an "all other things being equal" hypothesis and intensively examine the question: why are these cultures and these modal personality types still different in spite of similar environmental stimuli . . . and access over long periods to the influence of generalized area culture or cultures? We are ready now, I believe, for such studies, but no one is yet attempting them seriously (p. 693).

Schapera (1953, p. 359)[*] claims at least three advantages for the intensive study of single regions as over against global or random comparisons, namely, it eliminates the need for sampling (since all the peoples of an area should be studied), it solves the problem of what is the proper unit for comparative study, and it eliminates the need to deal with large numbers of societies. Instead, the method relies heavily upon typologies. Once types have been established for a region, they can be tested in adjoining regions and later in distant regions.

Eggan (1954, p. 746),[†] too, prefers "the utilization of the comparative method on a smaller scale and with as much control over the frame of comparison as it is possible to secure. It has seemed natural to utilize regions of relatively homogeneous culture or to work within social or cultural types, and to further control the ecology and the historical factors as far as it is possible to do so."

Goldman has given us a forceful statement (1955) on the value of

[29] For example, Honigmann, 1952; Starr, 1954; Underhill, 1954.

[30] For example, Riesenfeld, 1951; Suttles, 1951; Lemert, 1952.

[*] The full citation appears on p. 122.

[†] The full citation appears on p. 121.

the intensive study of culture areas, especially for arriving at generalizations concerning cultural evolution. He writes:

> Cultural evolution, to rephrase Maitland's classic remark, will be history or nothing. If it is to be history its proper focus is the culture area, or to be more precise, the comparative study of culture areas. A culture area comprises historically related societies each showing significant variations from a common pattern. In these variations— their nature, origin and direction—are revealed the basic processes of cultural development in the area—that is, its cultural evolution. From a comparison of culture areas rather than from the comparative study of historically unrelated societies may emerge the more general and more meaningful laws of development (p. 1).

Despite the recognition of the great potentialities for deriving scientific generalizations by the intensive study of culture areas, there is still a surprising paucity of adequate and well-rounded area studies. Kluckhohn (1954, p. 757) and Eggan (1954, p. 689) independently have pointed this out. This impression is confirmed further by our review of the comparative writings of the past five years. The single attempt at a developmental interpretation of a culture area, seeking broad generalizations, and covering most aspects of the culture, is Goldman's study (1955) on "Status Rivalry and Cultural Evolution in Polynesia"—all the more striking as an example of what can be done by purely library research, given an adequate theoretical frame of reference.

Goldman classifies eighteen Polynesian societies into three types: traditional (10 societies), where social status is based primarily upon seniority of age or lineage and social mobility is limited; open (4 societies), which, "paying lip service to hereditary rank, reserved their honors for outstanding achievement in war and tribal politics. . . . Social mobility was, accordingly, very high and status gradations were uneven"; and stratified (4 societies), where the distinctive feature was "the fundamental cleavage between the landed and the landless." These three types represent stages of social, economic, political, and religious complexity and are due primarily to an evolutionary process of internal development within Polynesia rather than to diffusion, as is evidenced by the fact that single societies seem to recapitulate the development of the entire area. Goldman then summarizes the fundamental changes in the Polynesian status systems in a series of thirty-eight general developmental propositions covering such areas as religion, authority, property, social organization, and warfare. These propositions serve as hypotheses which can be tested in other areas. One of the distinctive aspects of this work is the central role it gives to value systems; in the case of Polynesia it is status rivalry, and the manner in which this rivalry relates changes in value systems to changes in other aspects of culture.

Although most of the studies in a single culture area deal with more limited problems than those considered by Goldman, many are models of controlled comparisons approaching very close to experimental studies. Nadel's study (1952) of witchcraft is a model of this type in which a large number of factors are controlled so that a single variable can be tested. In Nadel's study of witchcraft each of the two pairs of societies shows wide cultural similarities with only a few differences, chief of which is the role of witchcraft or its absence. Nadel demonstrates how the witchcraft beliefs are causally related to specific anxieties in social life, in Nupe owing to marriage relations, in Mesakin owing to relations between mother's brother and sister's son. He stresses the role of adult experiences in addition to infantile experiences in the formation of anxieties in the societies examined, and attempts to test a Freudian hypothesis in terms of his findings.

The research model of Wagley's paper (1951) on differential population trends among two Tupi tribes under the influence of white contact is much the same as Nadel's, although the problem here is culture change. The tribes examined share many cultural similarities as well as a common language but are shown to have differed, even in aboriginal times, in the attitudes toward family size, which in turn was related to other differences between them.

· COMPARISONS WITHIN A SINGLE LOCAL GROUP OR CULTURE[*] ·

Twenty-two articles and 12 books, a total of 34 items, fall into this category. The range of content is fairly wide, touching upon 15 of our 21 content items. However, the greatest concentration is in studies of culture change and acculturation (22), followed by social organization (8), total culture (7), personality and culture (6), values (4), and economics (4). As we noted earlier, 25 studies are based primarily upon field work and 9 upon a combination of field work and library research.

As a group these studies are fresh and reflect some of the most sophisticated methodological trends, in both field work and research design, to be found in contemporary anthropology. Most of the studies are theoretically eclectic, combining a number of interests and approaches, chief of which is the concern with culture change,

[*] References cited in this section are listed on pp. 132–134.

functional and historical analysis, restudies, the use of quantification and the documentation of range of variation within a single community, and, finally, the control of as many variables as possible so as to approach the experimental method.

It is difficult to classify these studies into subgroups without considerable overlapping. However, the following subdivisions may serve for our purpose: (A) Studies Dealing with Research Methods, 4 cases,[31] (B) Restudies by the Same Investigator, 3 cases,[32] (C) Restudies by Different Investigators, 4 cases,[33] (D) Studies Showing Range of Variation in Culture Forms or Personality, 9 cases,[34] (E) Acculturation Studies, 6 cases,[35] and (F) Historical Reconstructions Based upon Library and/or Field Work, 9 cases.[36]

I have discussed elsewhere (Lewis, 1951, 1953)[*] the pros and cons of restudies, both in providing a baseline for the study of culture change and as a test of the reliability of anthropological reporting. However, studies dealing with range of variation, for which Herskovits (1954)[†] has suggested the term "microethnography," deserve further comment.

These studies are a much needed corrective to the tendency of anthropologists in the past to assume the essential homogeneity of the culture of folk societies or little communities. The demonstration by some of the articles cited above of a wide range in personality, in family life, and in ceremonial forms, within relatively simple and homogeneous societies, highlights the difference between real and ideal culture patterns, leads to a search for more refined concepts than the catch-all of basic personality and culture, and focuses upon the role of additional factors—personal, social, situational, environmental, accidental, etc. The studies by Vogt (1951), Roberts (1951), Voget (1952), Hart (1954), and Mandelbaum (1954)[‡] illustrate some of these points.

Despite a presumed Navaho basic personality, Vogt is more impressed by the range of variation in the reactions of twelve Navaho

[31] For example, Barnes, 1951; Goldschmidt and Spindler, 1952; Colson, 1954.

[32] Redfield, 1950; Mead, 1954; and Firth's restudy of Tikopia.

[33] For example, Lewis, 1951; Firth, 1952; Nett, 1952.

[34] For example, Roberts, 1951; Vogt, 1951; Fenton (ed.), 1951; Hart, 1954; Mandelbaum, 1954; Tremblay, Collier, and Sasaki, 1954.

[35] For example, Barnouw, 1950; Hallowell, 1952; Spindler, 1952.

[36] For example, Bascom, 1950; Kaplan, 1951; Hogbin, 1951; Marriott, 1952; Schmidt and Schmidt, 1952.

[*] The full citations appear on pp. 133 and 122.

[†] The full citation appears on p. 121.

[‡] The full citations appear on pp. 133 and 134.

veterans to army life experiences than by the common elements. He relates the differential changes in attitudes and values to specific life experiences before entering the army as well as to army experiences. As a result we get a picture of acculturation in terms of understandable human beings rather than stereotypes and averages.

Mandelbaum's vivid and detailed study of a funeral ceremony and its variations within a single community with a population of 1,200 leads him to suggest a typology of variations in terms of invariant patterns, alternative patterns, contingent patterns, elective patterns, patterns of neutral variation, optative patterns, weighted alternatives, and compulsive alternatives. He then discusses the meaning of the modal statements of anthropologists in the light of these variations.

· CONCLUSIONS ·

One of the distinctive characteristics of cultural or social anthropology has been its simultaneous concern with the intensive and holistic study of small societies and their cultures and with the comparative analysis of these same societies and cultures over the entire world. Traditionally, the former has been based upon field work and comparative analysis, the latter upon library studies, with or without the statistical manipulation of large masses of data.

Our survey of the comparative studies over the past five years reveals an important trend in the relationship between these two aspects of our discipline. Comparative anthropology no longer can be defined as a library method and is becoming increasingly based upon field work. Comparisons based upon library research alone constitute only one-third of all the studies examined. Moreover, most anthropologists have had first-hand experience both in the intensive study of small communities and in comparative cross-cultural analysis.

By the traditional definition of comparative anthropology as cross-cultural comparisons, the many comparisons within a single community or culture which we have cited would have been excluded. However, there is a need to broaden our view of comparative anthropology to include the latter type studies, for our theoretical writing has lagged behind the actual field work. We have included such studies, therefore, as a legitimate part of comparative anthropology because they can make an important contribution in their own right toward the formulation of general principles, and in addition can help establish a more solid basis for cross-cultural comparisons by their careful definition of types and their increasing use of quantification. In short, now that anthropology has achieved its historic task of documenting the wide range of variation in the cultures of the world, we can join our sociological brethren and take a closer and more careful look at individual small societies. The numerous studies and restudies of "microethnography" which we have cited reflect this trend. These studies also reveal a much wider range of variation than might have been expected from our earlier overplaying of homogeneity, and this variation, in turn, serves as a basis for comparative analysis.

The trend toward comparisons based upon first-hand field work in more than one society holds great promise for improving the quality of comparative studies. Field work by the same investigator in the societies compared assures greater comparability of data and leads to more refined insights than is generally possible in working with library data alone. It is important that anthropologists become more aware of the advantages inherent in this kind of comparative study. We suspect that many who have done field work in more than a single society have not given us the benefit of their comparative experience, in terms either of their field problems or of detailed comparative analysis of their data.

On the whole, first-hand field experience in different societies is of greatest value for comparative analysis when the societies compared are on the same general socioeconomic level. For example, my study of the Blackfoot Indians of Canada, a tribal reservation people, was of little help in my later study* of the peasant village of Tepoztlán, Mexico. On the other hand, the study of Tepoztlán was of enormous help in my later studies of peasantry in Spain, Cuba, and India. If this observation is confirmed by the experiences of others, it has some implications for training programs and planning field research for students. For a marked improvement in comparative anthropology, it might be wise to encourage our students to specialize in either tribal, peasant, or rural societies.

Comparative studies in anthropology might be grouped into two broad types: first, comparisons of historically related societies, in which common history, language, and culture serve as controls against which variables may be tested; and second, comparisons of historically unrelated societies in which similarities in form, structure, and process are a basis for establishing typologies or causal relationships between various aspects of culture. These two approaches clearly are reflected in our earlier grouping of studies by the location in space of the entities compared. On the whole, the three smaller spatial categories, i.e., comparisons within a single community or culture, comparisons within a single culture area, and comparisons within a single nation, contain examples of the first ap-

* See Essays 7 and 2.

proach, and the three larger categories, i.e., comparisons within a continent, between nations and continents, and global comparisons, contain examples of the second. The major exceptions are the relatively few studies of Africanisms in the New World and of Spanish influences in Latin America.

Although highly competent and interesting studies are to be found in each approach, it seems that each has its distinctive strengths and weaknesses. Some of the advantages of the former are: (1) a large proportion of the studies are based upon first-hand comparative field research, (2) there is a greater certainty about the comparability of the data, (3) the wholeness of culture is maintained and aspects of culture are seen in context, (4) a larger number of variables can be studied functionally, and (5) the objectives generally are of limited scope and the research designs more closely approximate those of the experimental method. Certainly the bulk of our model, small-scale, comparative studies are found in this approach. Perhaps the single greatest weakness to be noted is the lack of broad developmental hypotheses and the paucity of intensive comparative analyses of culture areas as wholes.

The comparative studies based upon historically unrelated societies are, as a whole, more ambitious, seek broader generalizations on a wider scale, in terms of either universals, world-wide typologies, or evolutionary sequences, and are based primarily upon library studies rather than field work. Here we must distinguish between the statistical studies, which rely upon a large number of cases, control only a few variables, and tend to atomize culture, and the broader typological studies, which seek to maintain the wholeness of culture by establishing types based upon form, structure, content, and process. Though lacking many of the controls inherent in the more limited studies, many of these studies seem more daring and give the satisfaction which comes from painting with a big brush and searching for general laws.

One of the problems of contemporary anthropology is to develop a strategy of research which will combine the strengths of each of the two major approaches outlined above. The quality and reliability of comparative cross-cultural analysis can hardly be better than that of the original field data upon which it is based. As the intensive studies of particular societies improve, they make possible more meaningful comparative studies of higher quality. Similarly, comparative studies point up the weaknesses or lacks in data, confirm or refute favorite hypotheses, and help thereby to guide further field research. Some anthropologists prefer to wait for better data from single societies before attempting world-wide comparisons. Others utilize whatever data is now available on the ground that we cannot afford to lose time. Others would change the research design and employ more limited and controlled comparisons. Finally, still others place their greatest faith in organizing comparative field research projects around specific problems of limited scope.

In conclusion, our survey of the literature of the past five years has revealed a remarkably large number of comparative studies of high quality, a broad coverage of subject matter, a variety of methods and approaches, a wide range of objectives, and a healthy eclecticism which speaks well for anthropology and its future.

· R E F E R E N C E S ·

THEORETICAL WRITINGS

ACKERKNECHT, ERWIN H. 1954. "On the Comparative Method in Anthropology," pp. 117–25, in Spencer, Robert F. (ed.), *Method and Perspective in Anthropology*. Minneapolis: University of Minnesota Press, 323 pp.

BECKER, HOWARD. 1954. "Anthropology and Sociology," pp. 102–59, in Gillin, John (ed.), *For A Science of Social Man*. New York: Macmillan, 289 pp.

BIDNEY, DAVID. 1954. "The Ethnology of Religion and the Problem of Human Evolution," *American Anthropologist*, Vol. 86, No. 1 (Feb.), pp. 1–18.

BRAM, JOSEPH. 1953. "The Application of Psychodrama to Research in Social Anthropology," *Transactions of the New York Academy of Sciences*, Vol. 151, No. 7, pp. 253–57.

EGGAN, FRED. 1954. "Social Anthropology and the Method of Controlled Comparison," *American Anthropologist*, Vol. 56, No. 5, Pt. 1, pp. 743–63.

EVANS-PRITCHARD, E. E. 1951. *Social Anthropology*. London: Cohen and West, 134 pp.

FIRTH, RAYMOND. 1951a. "Contemporary British Social Anthropology," *American Anthropologist*, Vol. 53, No. 4, Pt. 1, pp. 474–89.

———. 1951b. *Elements of Social Organization*. New York: Philosophical Library, 257 pp.

GOLDSCHMIDT, WALTER. 1950. "Social Class in America—A Critical Review," *American Anthropologist*, Vol. 52, No. 4, Pt. 1, pp. 483–98.

HALLOWELL, A. IRVING. 1954. "Psychology and Anthropology," pp. 160–226, in Gillin, John (ed.), *For a Science of Social Man*. New York: Macmillan, 289 pp.

HENRY, JULES. 1953. "Direct Observations and Psychological Tests in Anthropological Field Work," *American Anthropologist*, Vol. 55, No. 4, pp. 461–80.

HERSKOVITS, MELVILLE J. 1954. "Some Problems of Method in Ethnography," pp. 3–24, in Spencer, Robert F. (ed.), *Method and Perspective in Anthropology*. Minneapolis: University of Minnesota Press, 323 pp.

HILGER, SISTER M. INEZ. 1954. "An Ethnographic Field Method," pp. 28–42, in Spencer, Robert F. (ed.), *Method and Perspective in Anthropology*. Minneapolis: University of Minnesota Press, 323 pp.

KLUCKHOHN, CLYDE. 1953. "Universal Categories of Culture," pp. 507–23, in Kroeber, A. L. and others, *Anthropology Today*. Chicago: University of Chicago Press, 966 pp.

————. 1954. "Southwestern Studies of Culture and Personality," *American Anthropologist,* Vol. 56, No. 4, Pt. 1, pp. 685–97.

KÖBBEN, A. J. 1952. "New Ways of Presenting an Old Idea: The Statistical Method in Social Anthropology," *Journal of the Royal Anthropological Institute of Great Britain and Ireland,* Vol. 82, Pt. 2, pp. 129–46.

KROEBER, A. L. 1954. "Critical Summary and Commentary," pp. 273–99, in Spencer, Robert F. (ed.), *Method and Perspective in Anthropology.* Minneapolis: University of Minnesota Press, 323 pp.

KROEBER, A. L. and KLUCKHOHN, CLYDE. 1952. *Culture: A Critical Review of Concepts and Definitions.* (Papers of the Peabody Museum of American Archaeology and Ethnology, Harvard University, Vol. 47, No. 1.) Cambridge, Mass., 223 pp.

LEVY, MARION J., JR. 1952. *The Structure of Society.* Princeton, N.J.: Princeton University Press., 584 pp.

LEWIS, OSCAR. 1953. "Controls and Experiments in Field Work," pp. 452–75, in Kroeber, A. L. and others, *Anthropology Today.* Chicago: University of Chicago Press, 966 pp.

LOWIE, ROBERT H. 1953. "Ethnography, Cultural and Social Anthropology," *American Anthropologist,* Vol. 55, No. 4, Oct., pp. 527–34.

MURDOCK, G. P. 1949. *Social Structure.* New York: Macmillan, 387 pp.

————. 1950a. "Feasibility and Implementation of Comparative Community Research," *American Sociological Review,* Vol. 15, No. 6, pp. 713–20.

————. 1950b. *Outline of Cultural Materials.* 2nd ed. New Haven: Yale University Press, 56 pp.

————. 1954. "Sociology and Anthropology," pp. 14–32, in Gillin, John (ed.), *For A Science of Social Man.* New York: Macmillan, 289 pp.

NADEL, S. F. 1951. *The Foundations of Social Anthropology.* Glencoe, Ill.: Free Press, 426 pp.

RADCLIFFE-BROWN, A. R. 1951. "The Comparative Method in Anthropology," *Journal of the Royal Anthropological Institute of Great Britain and Ireland,* Vol. 81, No. 1, pp. 15–22.

RAY, VERNE F. 1952. "Techniques and Problems in the Study of Human Color Perception," *Southwestern Journal of Anthropology,* Vol. 8, No. 3, pp. 251–59.

SCHAPERA, I. 1953. "Comparative Method in Social Anthropology," *American Anthropologist,* Vol. 55, No. 3, pp. 353–61.

SINGER, MILTON B. 1953. "Summary of Comments and Discussion" (of I. Schapera, "Some Comments on Comparative Method in Social Anthropology"), *American Anthropologist,* Vol. 55, No. 4, pp. 363–66.

SMITH, BREWSTER M. 1954. "Anthropology and Psychology," pp. 32–66, in Gillin, John (ed.), *For A Science of Social Man.* New York: Macmillan, 289 pp.

SMITH, MARIAN W. 1952. "Different Cultural Concepts of Past, Present, and Future, A Study of Ego Extension," *Psychiatry,* Vol. 15, No. 4, pp. 395–400.

STEWARD, JULIAN H. 1936. "The Economic and Social Basis of Primitive Bands," pp. 331–50, in Lowie, R. H. (ed.), *Essays in Anthropology.* Berkeley: University of California Press, 433 pp.

————. 1950. *Area Research: Theory and Practice* (Social Science Research Council Bulletin 63). New York: Social Science Research Council. 164 pp.

————. 1951. "Levels of Sociocultural Integration: An Operational Concept," *Southwestern Journal of Anthropology,* Vol. 7, No. 4, pp. 374–390.

WHITING, JOHN W. M. 1954. "The Cross-Cultural Method," pp. 523–31 in Lindzey, G. (ed.), *Handbook of Social Psychology.* Cambridge, Mass.: Addison-Wesley. 2 vols.

WHITING, JOHN W. M. and colleagues. 1954. "Field Guide for a Study of Socialization in Five Societies" (*manuscript*).

GLOBAL OR RANDOM COMPARISONS

ABERLE, DAVID F. 1952. " 'Arctic Hysteria' and Latah in Mongolia," *Transactions of The New York Academy of Sciences,* Series II, Vol. 14, No. 7, May, pp. 291–97.

ANDERSON, EDGAR and CUTLER, HUGH C. 1950. "Methods of Corn Popping and Their Historical Significance," *Southwestern Journal of Anthropology,* Vol. 6, No. 3, pp. 303–08.

BALFOUR, HENRY. 1951. "Ritual and Secular Uses of Vibrating Membranes as Voice Disguisers," *Journal of the Royal Anthropological Institute of Great Britain and Ireland,* Vol. 78, Pts. 1 & 2, pp. 45–70.

BARNETT, H. G. 1953. *Innovation: The Basis of Cultural Change.* New York: McGraw-Hill, 462 pp.

BOHANNAN, L. M. 1951. "A Comparative Study of Social Differentiation of Primitive Society" (Doctoral dissertation). Oxford University.

BROWN, JULIA S. 1952. "A Comparative Study of Deviation from Sexual Mores," *American Sociological Review,* Vol. 17, No. 2, pp. 135–46.

CHARLES, LUCILLE H. 1951. "Drama in First-Naming Ceremonies," *Journal of American Folklore,* Vol. 64, No. 251, pp. 11–36.

————. 1953. "Drama in Shaman Exorcism," *Journal of American Folklore,* Vol. 66, No. 260, pp. 95–122.

ERIKSON, ERIK H. 1950. *Childhood and Society.* New York: Norton, 397 pp.

FORD, CLELLAN S. and BEACH, FRANK A. 1951. *Patterns of Sexual Behavior.* New York: Harper, 307 pp.

FREEDMAN, LAWRENCE Z. and FERGUSON, VERA M. 1950. "The Question of 'Painless Childbirth' in Primitive Cultures," *American Journal of Orthopsychiatry,* Vol. 20, No. 2, pp. 363–72.

FRIED, MORTON. 1952. "Land Tenure, Geography and Ecology in Contact of Cultures," *American Journal of Economics and Sociology,* Vol. 11, No. 4, July, pp. 391–412.

GOODE, W. J. 1951. *Religion Among the Primitives.* Glencoe, Ill.: Free Press, 321 pp.

HEIZER, ROBERT F. 1953. "Aboriginal Fish Poisons," *Bureau of American Ethnology Bulletin No. 151,* pp. 225–83.

HERSKOVITS, MELVILLE J. 1952. *Economic Anthropology: A Study in Comparative Economics.* New York: Knopf, 551 pp.

HOEBEL, ADAMSON E. 1954. *The Law of Primitive Man: A Study in Comparative Legal Dynamics.* Cambridge, Mass.: Harvard University Press, 357 pp.

JAMES, E. O. 1952. "Religion and Reality," *Journal of the Royal Anthropological Institute of Great Britain and Ireland,* Vol. 80, Pts. 1 & 2, pp. 25–36.

McClelland, D. C. and Friedman, G. A. 1952. "A Cross-Cultural Study of the Relationship between Child-Training Practices and Achievement Motivation Appearing in Folk-Tales," pp. 243–49 in Swanson, G. E.; Newcomb, T. M.; and Hartley, E. L. (eds.), *Readings in Social Psychology*. New York: Holt, 680 pp.

Meggers, Betty J. 1954. "Environmental Limitation on the Development of Culture," *American Anthropologist*, Vol. 56, No. 6, pp. 801–24.

Murdock, George P. 1950. "Family Stability in Non-European Cultures," *Annals of the American Academy of Political and Social Sciences*, Vol. 270, November, pp. 195–201.

Murdock, George P. and Whiting, John W. M. 1951. "Cultural Determination of Parental Attitudes: The Relationship between the Social Structure, Particularly Family Structure and Parental Behavior," pp. 13–34 in Senn, M. J. E. (ed.), *Problems of Infancy and Childhood* (Transactions of the Fourth Conference, March 6–7, 1950). New York: Josiah Macy, Jr., Foundation, 181 pp.

Paul, Benjamin D. (ed.). 1955. (In press) *Medicine and Social Science: A Casebook*. New York: Russell Sage Foundation.

Pitkin, Donald S. 1954. "Land Tenure and Family in an Italian Village" (Doctoral dissertation). Harvard University.

Queen, Stuart A. and Adams, John B. 1952. *The Family in Various Cultures*. Philadelphia: Lippincott, 280 pp.

Radin, Paul. 1953. *The World of Primitive Man*. New York: Schuman, 370 pp.

Redfield, Robert. 1953. *The Primitive World and Its Transformations*. Ithaca: Cornell University Press, 185 pp.

Redfield, Robert and Singer, Milton. 1954. "The Cultural Role of Cities," *Economic Development and Cultural Change*, Vol. 3, No. 1, pp. 53–73.

Spicer, Edward H. (ed.). 1952. *Human Problems in Technological Change: A Casebook*. New York: Russell Sage Foundation, 301 pp.

Stewart, Omer C. 1954. "The Forgotten Side of Ethnography," pp. 221–48 in Spencer, Robert F. (ed.), *Method and Perspective in Anthropology*. Minneapolis: University of Minnesota Press, 323 pp.

Velsen, J. Van. 1951. "Delict in Primitive Law" (Doctoral dissertation). Oxford University.

Whiting, Beatrice B. 1950. "A Cross Cultural Study of Sorcery and Social Control," pp. 82–91 in Whiting, Beatrice B., *Paiute Sorcery* (Viking Fund Publications in Anthropology, No. 15). New York: The Viking Fund, 110 pp.

Whiting, John M. and Child, Irving L. 1953. *Child Training and Personality: A Cross-Cultural Study*. New Haven: Yale University Press, Vol. 1, 353 pp.

Wright, G. O. 1952. "Projection and Displacement: A Cross-Cultural Study of the Expression of Aggression in Myths" (Doctoral dissertation). Harvard University.

Yap, M. A. 1951. "Mental Disease Peculiar to Certain Cultures: A Survey of Comparative Psychiatry," *Journal of Mental Science*, Vol. 97, No. 407, pp. 313–27.

**COMPARISONS BETWEEN
CONTINENTS OR NATIONS**

Bascom, W. R. 1950. "The Focus of Cuban Santeria," *Southwestern Journal of Anthropology*, Vol. 6, No. 1, pp. 64–68.
———. 1952. "Two Forms of Afro-Cuban Divination," pp. 169–79 in Tax, Sol (ed.), *Selected Papers of the XXIXth International Congress of Americanists*, Vol. 2. Chicago: University of Chicago Press, 339 pp.
Bouteiller, Marcelle. 1950. *Chamanisme et Guérison Magique*. Paris: Presses Universitaires, 337 pp.
Comas, Juan. 1954. "Influencia Indígena en la Medicina Hipocrática, en la Nueva España del Siglo XVI," *América Indígena*, Vol. 14, No. 4, October, pp. 328–61.
Drews, R. A. 1952. "The Cultivation of Food Fish in China and Japan: a study disclosing contrasting national patterns for rearing fish consistent with the differing cultural histories of China and Japan" (Doctoral dissertation). University of Michigan.
Erasmus, Charles John. 1950. "Patolli, Pachisi, and the Limitation of Possibilities," *Southwestern Journal of Anthropology*, Vol. 6, No. 4, pp. 369–87.
Firth, Raymond. 1951. "Religious Belief and Personal Adjustment," *Journal of the Royal Anthropological Institute of Great Britain and Ireland*, Vol. 78, Pts. 1 & 2, pp. 25–43
Foster, George M. 1951. "Report on an Ethnological Reconnaissance of Spain," *American Anthropologist*, Vol. 53, No. 3, pp. 311–25.
———. 1953. "*Cofradía* and *Compadrazgo* in Spain and Spanish America," *Southwestern Journal of Anthropology*, Vol. 9, No. 1, pp. 1–28.
Goldschmidt, Walter. 1951. "Ethics and Structure of Society. An Ethnological Contribution to the Sociology of Knowledge," *American Anthropologist*, Vol. 53, No. 4, Pt. 1, pp. 506–24.
Hatt, Gudmund. 1951. "The Corn Mother in America and Indonesia," *Anthropos*, Vol. 46, pp. 853–914.
Hsu, Francis L. K. 1952. *Religion, Science and Human Crises: A Study on China in Transition and Its Implications for the West*. London: Routledge & Kegan Paul, 142 pp.
———. 1953. *Americans and Chinese, Two Ways of Life*. New York: Schuman, 457 pp.
Levy, Marion J., Jr. 1953. "Contrasting Factors in the Modernization of China and Japan," *Economic Development and Cultural Change*, Vol. II, No. 3, pp. 161–97.
Lewis, Oscar. 1954. "Peasant Culture in India and Mexico: A Study in Contrasts," *Transactions of The New York Academy of Sciences*, Series II, Vol. 16, No. 4, pp. 219–23.
Mintz, Sidney W. and Wolf, Eric R. 1950. "An Analysis of Ritual Co-Parenthood (*Compadrazgo*)," *Southwestern Journal of Anthropology*, Vol. 6, No. 4, pp. 341–68.
Needham, Rodney. 1954. "Siriono and Penan: A Test of Some Hypotheses," *Southwestern Journal of Anthropology*, Vol. 10, No. 2, pp. 228–32.
Patai, Raphael. 1954. "Religion in Middle Eastern, Far Eastern and Western

Culture," *Southwestern Journal of Anthropology,* Vol. 10, No. 3, pp. 233–54.

STEWARD, JULIAN H. and MURPHY, ROBERT F. 1954. "The Mundurucu and the Algonkians: A Parallel in Processes of Acculturation," Paper given at Annual Meeting of the American Anthropological Association, December, 1954.

WELTFISH, GENE. 1952. "The Study of American Indian Crafts and Its Implication for Art Theory," pp. 200–09 in Tax, Sol (ed.), *Selected Papers of the XXIXth International Congress of Americanists,* Vol. 3. Chicago: University of Chicago Press, 410 pp.

COMPARISONS WITHIN ONE CONTINENT

ARMSTRONG, ROBERT C. 1952. "State Formation in Negro Africa" (Doctoral dissertation). University of Chicago.

BACON, ELIZABETH E. 1954. "Types of Pastoral Nomadism in Central and Southwest Asia," *Southwestern Journal of Anthropology,* Vol. 10, No. 1, Spring, pp. 44–65.

BARBEAU, MARIUS. 1952. "The Old-World Dragon in America," pp. 115–22, in Tax, Sol (ed.), *Selected Papers of the XXIXth International Congress of Americanists,* Vol. 3. Chicago: University of Chicago Press, 410 pp.

BEALS, RALPH L. 1952. "Social Stratification in Latin America," *American Journal of Sociology,* Vol. 58, No. 4, pp. 327–39.

BEATTIE, J. H. M. 1951. "Checks on the Abuse of Political Power: A Comparative Study of the Social Factors Acting in Restraint of the Abuse of Such Powers by Indigenous Political Authorities in Certain Native Societies of Africa" (Doctoral dissertation). Oxford University.

BEKKER, KONRAD. 1951. "Historical Patterns of Culture Contact in Southern Asia," *Far Eastern Quarterly,* Vol. 11, No. 1, pp. 3–15.

COLLINS, J. L. 1951. "Antiquity of the Pineapple in America," *Southwestern Journal of Anthropology,* Vol. 7, No. 2, pp. 145–55.

EISENSTADT, S. N. 1964. "African Age Groups, A Comparative Study," *Africa,* Vol. 24, No. 2, pp. 100–13.

ELMENDORF, W. W. 1952. "Soul Loss Illness in Western North America," pp. 104–14, in Tax, Sol (ed.), *Selected Papers of the XXIXth International Congress of Americanists,* Vol. 3. Chicago: University of Chicago Press, 410 pp.

FLANNERY, REGINA. 1952. "Two Concepts of Power," pp. 185–89, in Tax, Sol (ed.), *Selected Papers of the XXIXth International Congress of Americanists,* Vol. 3. Chicago: University of Chicago Press, 410 pp.

FOSTER, GEORGE M. 1952. "Relationships between Theoretical and Applied Anthropology: A Public Health Program Analysis," *Human Organization,* Vol. II, No. 3, Fall, pp. 5–16.

GLUCKMAN, MAX. 1950. "Kinship and Marriage among the Lozi of Northern Rhodesia and the Zulu of Natal," pp. 116–206 in Radcliffe-Brown, A. R. and Forde, Daryll (eds.), *African Systems of Kinship and Marriage.* Oxford: Oxford University Press, 399 pp.

GOLDFRANK, ESTHER S. 1952. "The Different Patterns of Blackfoot and Pueblo Adaptation to White Authority," pp. 78–79 in Tax, Sol (ed.), *Selected Papers of the XXIXth International Congress of Americanists,* Vol. 2. Chicago: University of Chicago Press, 339 pp.

KAPLAN, B. 1954. *A Study of Rorschach Responses in Four Cultures* (Papers of the Peabody Museum of American Archaeology and Ethnology, Harvard University, Vol. 42, No. 2). Cambridge, Mass., 44 pp.

LANGE, CHARLES H. 1953. "A Reappraisal of Evidence of Plains Influences among the Rio Grande Pueblos," *Southwestern Journal of Anthropology*, Vol. 9, No. 1, pp. 212–30.

LOWIE, ROBERT H. 1952. "The Heterogeneity of Marginal Cultures," pp. 1–8 in Tax, Sol (ed.), *Selected Papers of the XXIXth International Congress of Americanists*, Vol. 3. Chicago: University of Chicago Press, 410 pp.

MILLER, ROBERT J. 1953. "Areas and Institutions in Eastern Asia," *Southwestern Journal of Anthropology*, Vol. 9, No. 2, pp. 203–11.

MÜLLER, A. R. 1951. "A Study of the Social Organization of Indian Tribes of South America" (Doctoral dissertation). Oxford University.

MURDOCK, GEORGE PETER. 1951. "South American Culture Areas," *Southwestern Journal of Anthropology*, Vol. 7, No. 4, pp. 415–36.

NAROLL, RAOUL S. 1950. "A Draft Map of the Culture Areas of Asia," *Southwestern Journal of Anthropology*, Vol. 6, No. 2, pp. 183–87.

PATAI, RAPHAEL. 1951. "Nomadism: Middle Eastern and Central Asian," *Southwestern Journal of Anthropology*, Vol. 7, No. 4, pp. 401–14.

PHILLIPS, ARTHUR. 1953. *Survey of African Marriage and Family Life*. New York: Oxford University Press, 462 pp.

RADCLIFFE-BROWN, A. R. and FORDE, DARYLL (eds.). 1950. *African Systems of Kinship and Marriage*. New York: Oxford University Press. 399 pp.

RILEY, CARROLL L. 1952. "The Blowgun in the New World," *Southwestern Journal of Anthropology*, Vol. 8, No. 3, pp. 297–319.

RUBIO ORBE, GONZALO. 1953. "Aculturaciones de Indígenas de los Andes," *América Indígena*, Vol. 13, pp. 187–222.

SCHUSTER, CARL. 1952. "V-Shaped Chest-Markings: Distribution of a Design-Motive in and around the Pacific," *Anthropos*, Vol. 47, pp. 99–118.

SELIGMAN, BRENDA Z. 1950. "The Problem of Incest and Exogamy: A Restatement," *American Anthropologist*, Vol. 52, No. 3, pp. 305–16.

SMITH, MARIAN W. 1951. "American Indian Warfare," *Transactions of The New York Academy of Sciences*, Series II, Vol. 13, No. 8, pp. 348–64.

SPINDEN, HERBERT J. 1952. "Power Animals in American Indian Art," pp. 195–99 in Tax, Sol (ed.), *Selected Papers of the XXIXth International Congress of Americanists*, Vol. 3. Chicago: University of Chicago Press, 410 pp.

TEGNAEUS, HARRY. 1952. *Blood Brotherhood: An Ethno-Sociological Study of the Institution of Blood-Brotherhood with Special Reference to Africa*. New York: Philosophical Library, 181 pp.

WOLF, ERIC. 1955. "Types of Latin American Peasantry: A Preliminary Discussion," *American Anthropologist*, Vol. 57, pp. 452–471.

COMPARISONS WITHIN ONE NATION

BELTRAN, GONZALO AGUIRRE. 1952. "El Gobierno Indígena en México y el Proceso de Aculturación," *América Indígena*, Vol. 12, No. 4, October, pp. 271–97.

CARRASCO, PEDRO. 1951. "Las Culturas Indígenas de Oaxaca México," *América Indígena*, Vol. 11, No. 2, April, pp. 99–114.

CAUDILL, WILLIAM. 1952. *Japanese-American Personality and Acculturation* (Genetic Psychology Monographs, Vol. 45). Provincetown, Mass.: Journal Press, 102 pp.

DU WORS, RICHARD E. 1952. "Persistence and Change in Local Values of Two New England Communities," *Rural Sociology,* Vol. 17, No. 3, September, pp. 207–17.

ERASMUS, CHARLES JOHN. 1952. "Changing Folk Beliefs and the Relativity of Empirical Knowledge," *Southwestern Journal of Anthropology,* Vol. 8, No. 4, pp. 411–27.

FRANCIS, E. K. 1952. "The Adjustment of a Peasant Group to a Capitalistic Economy: The Manitoba Mennonites," *Rural Sociology,* Vol. 17, No. 3, September, pp. 218–28.

FRIED, MORTON H. 1952. "Chinese Society: Class as Sub-culture," *Transactions of The New York Academy of Sciences,* Series II, Vol. 14, No. 8, pp. 331–36.

LANDMAN, RUTH. 1954. "Mexican Acculturation, Compared with Jewish and Japanese Immigrant Acculturation." Paper given at the Annual Meeting of the American Anthropological Association, December, 1954.

MANNERS, ROBERT A. and STEWARD, JULIAN H. 1953. "The Cultural Study of Contemporary Societies: Puerto Rico," *American Journal of Sociology,* Vol. 59, No. 2, pp. 123–30.

MUKHERJEE, R. K. and GIRLING, F. K. 1950. "Breton Family and Economic Structure," *Rural Sociology,* Vol. 15, No. 1, March, pp. 49–62.

OLMSTEAD, DAVID L. 1951. "Two Korean Villages: Culture Contact on the 39th Parallel," *Human Organization,* Vol. 10, No. 3, pp. 33–36.

OPLER, MARVIN K. 1950. "Two Japanese Religious Sects," *Southwestern Journal of Anthropology,* Vol. 6, No. 1, pp. 69–78.

OPLER, MORRIS E. and SINGH, RUDRA DOTT. 1952. "Two Villages of Eastern Uttar Pradesh (U.P.), India: An Analysis of Similarities and Differences," *American Anthropologist,* Vol. 54, No. 2, Pt. 1, pp. 179–91.

PAINTER, NORMAN W. and MORRISON, PAUL C. 1952. "Rural Population Stability, Central District of Turrialla Canton, Costa Rica," *Rural Sociology,* Vol. 17, No. 4, December, pp. 356–66.

PATAI, RAPHAEL. 1953. *Israel Between East and West: A Study in Human Relations.* Philadelphia: Jewish Publication Society, 348 pp.

PATERSON, T. T. and WILLET, F. J. 1951. "An Anthropological Experiment in a British Colliery," *Human Organization,* Vol. 10, No. 2, pp. 19–25.

PEDERSEN, HAROLD A. 1951. "Cultural Differences in the Acceptance of Recommended Practises," *Rural Sociology,* Vol. 16, No. 1, March, pp. 37–49.

RAPER, ARTHUR F. 1951. "Some Recent Changes in Japanese Village Life," *Rural Sociology,* Vol. 16, No. 1, March, pp. 3–16.

ROOKSBY, R. L. 1951. "Ritual and Society in Selected South Indian Societies" (Doctoral dissertation). Oxford University.

RYAN, BRUCE. 1950. "Socio-Cultural Regions of Ceylon," *Rural Sociology,* Vol. 15, No. 1, March, pp. 3–18.

———. 1952. "The Ceylonese Village and the New Value System," *Rural Sociology,* Vol. 17, No. 1, March, pp. 9–28.

SANDERS, IRWIN T. 1953. "Village Social Organization in Greece," *Rural Sociology,* Vol. 18, No. 4, December, pp. 366–75.

STEWARD, JULIAN H. and collaborators. 1955. *The People of Puerto Rico.* Urbana: University of Illinois Press.

TAYLOR, GORDON D. 1953. "Some Crop Distributions by Tribes in Upland Southeast Asia," *Southwestern Journal of Anthropology*, Vol. 9, No. 3, pp. 296–308.

VAN DER KROEF, JUSTUS M. 1954. "Disorganization and Social Change in Rural Indonesia," *Rural Sociology*, Vol. 19, No. 2, June, pp. 161–73.

VAZQUEZ-CALCERRADA, P. B. 1953. "A Research Project on Rural Communities in Puerto Rico," *Rural Sociology*, Vol. 18, No. 3, September, pp. 221–33.

VIQUEIRA, CARMEN and PALERM, ANGEL. 1954. "Alcoholismo, Brujeria y Homocidio en dos Comunidades Rurales de México," *América Indígena*, Vol. 14, No. 1, January, pp. 7–36.

VOGT, EVON Z. and O'DEA, THOMAS F. 1953. "A Comparative Study of the Role of Values in Social Action in Two Southwestern Communities," *American Sociological Review*, Vol. 18, No. 6, pp. 645–54.

WAGLEY, CHARLES. 1952. *Race and Class in Rural Brazil*. New York: Columbia University Press, 160 pp.

WOLF, KATHLEEN L. 1952. "Growing Up and Its Price in Three Puerto Rican Subcultures," *Psychiatry*, Vol. 15, No. 4, pp. 401–33.

ZEN SUN, E-TU. 1952. "Results of Culture Contact in Two Mongol-Chinese Communities," *Southwestern Journal of Anthropology*, Vol. 8, No. 2, pp. 182–210.

COMPARISONS WITHIN A SINGLE
CULTURE AREA OR REGION

BAILEY, F. G. 1951. "The Political Organization of the Plains Indians" (Doctoral dissertation). Oxford University.

BELLAH, ROBERT N. 1952. *Apache Kinship Systems*. Cambridge, Mass.: Harvard University Press, 151 pp.

BERNARDI, B. 1952. "The Age-System of the Nilo-Hamitic Peoples," *Africa*, Vol. 22, No. 4, pp. 316–32.

BERNDT, RONALD M. 1951. "Ceremonial Exchange in Western Arnhem Land," *Southwestern Journal of Anthropology*, Vol. 7, No. 2, pp. 156–75.

BROCKENSHA, D. W. 1951. "The Political Institutions of Some Southern Nguni Tribes" (Doctoral dissertation). Oxford University.

BROWN, P. S. 1950. "A Study in Authority in Indigenous West African Societies" (Doctoral dissertation). University of London.

BURRIDGE, K. O. L. 1951. "Aspects of Rank in Melanesia" (Doctoral dissertation). Oxford University.

BUTT, A. J. 1951. "The Social Organization of the Central and Eastern Eskimo" (Doctoral dissertation). Oxford University.

CAMARA, FERNANDO. 1951. "Religious and Political Organization," pp. 142–64, in Tax, Sol (ed.), *Heritage of Conquest*. Glencoe, Ill.: Free Press, 312 pp.

DRUCKER, PHILIP. 1951. *The Northern and Central Nootka Tribes* (Bureau of American Ethnology Bulletin 144). Washington, D.C.: Smithsonian Institution, 480 pp.

EGGAN, FRED. 1950. *Social Organization of the Western Pueblos*. Chicago: University of Chicago Press, 373 pp.

ELKIN, A. P. 1950. "The Complexity of Social Organization in Arnhem Land," *Southwestern Journal of Anthropology*, Vol. 6, No. 1, pp. 1–20.

————. 1953. *Social Anthropology in Melanesia*. London: Oxford University Press, 166 pp.

ELLIS, FLORENCE HAWLEY. 1951. "Patterns of Aggression and the War Cult in Southwestern Pueblos," *Southwestern Journal of Anthropology*, Vol. 7, No. 2, pp. 177–201.

ESTERMANN, C. 1952. "Clans et alliances entre clans dans le sudouest de l'angola," *Anthropos*, Vol. 47, pp. 587–606.

EVANS-PRITCHARD, E. E. 1952. "Nilotic Studies," *Journal of the Royal Anthropological Institute of Great Britain and Ireland*, Vol. 80, Pts. 1 & 2, pp. 1–6.

FALLERS, L. A. 1953. "Bantu Bureaucracy: A Study of Role Conflict and Institutional Change in the Soga Political System" (Doctoral dissertation). University of Chicago.

FISCHER, H. T. 1950. "The Concept of Incest in Sumatra," *American Anthropologist*, Vol. 52, No. 2, pp. 219–24.

FUENTE, JULIO DE LA. 1952. "Ethnic and Communal Relations," pp. 76–94, in Tax, Sol (ed.), *Heritage of Conquest*. Glencoe, Ill.: Free Press, 312 pp.

GARIGUE, PHILIP. 1954. "Changing Political Leadership in West Africa," *Africa*, Vol. 24, No. 3, pp. 220–32.

GIBSON, GORDON D. 1952. "The Social Organization of the Southwestern Bantu" (Doctoral dissertation). University of Chicago.

GILLIN, JOHN. 1952. "Ethos and Cultural Aspects of Personality," pp. 193–212, in Tax, Sol (ed.), *Heritage of Conquest*. Glencoe, Ill.: Free Press, 312 pp.

GOLDMAN, IRVING. 1955. "Status Rivalry and Cultural Evolution in Polynesia," *American Anthropologist*, Vol. 57, pp. 680–697.

GUIART, JEAN. 1951. "Forerunners of Melanesian Nationalism," *Oceania*, Vol. 22, No. 2, pp. 81–90.

GUITERAS HOLMES, CALIXTA. 1952. "Social Organization," pp. 97–108, in Tax, Sol (ed.), *Heritage of Conquest*. Glencoe, Ill.: Free Press, 312 pp.

HAWLEY, FLORENCE. 1950. "Big Kivas, Little Kivas, and Moiety Houses in Historical Reconstruction," *Southwestern Journal of Anthropology*, Vol. 6, No. 3, pp. 286–302.

HOGBIN, H. IAN and WEDGEWOOD, CAMILLA H. 1953. "Local Grouping in Melanesia," *Oceania*, Vol. 23, No. 4, pp. 241–76; Vol. 24, No. 1, pp. 58–76.

HOLAS, B. and DEKEYSER, P. L. 1952. *Mission dans l'est Libérien* (Mémoires de l'Institut Français d'Afrique Noire, No. 14). Dakar. 566 pp.

HONIGMANN, JOHN J. 1952. "Intercultural Relations at Great Whale River," *American Anthropologist*, Vol. 54, No. 4, pp. 510–22.

HOWELL, P. P. 1950. "A Comparative Study of Customary Law Among Cattle-Owning Tribes of the Southern Sudan (Doctoral dissertation). Oxford University.

JAMES, ALICE. 1950. "Village Arrangement and Social Organization Among Some Amazon Tribes" (Doctoral dissertation). Columbia University.

KEESING, FELIX M. 1953. *Social Anthropology in Polynesia; A Review of Research*. London: Oxford University Press, 126 pp.

KIRCHHOFF, PAUL. 1952. "Meso-America," pp. 17–30, in Tax, Sol (ed.), *Heritage of Conquest*. Glencoe, Ill.: Free Press, 312 pp.

————. 1954. "Gatherers and Farmers in the Greater Southwest: A Problem in Classification," *American Anthropologist*, Vol. 56, No. 4, Pt. 1, pp. 529–60.

KLUCKHOHN, CLYDE. 1954. "Southwestern Studies of Culture and Personality," *American Anthropologist*, Vol. 56, No. 4, Pt. 1, pp. 685–97.

KURATH, GERTRUDE P. 1952. "Dance Acculturation," pp. 233–242, in Tax, Sol (ed.), *Heritage of Conquest*. Glencoe, Ill.: Free Press, 312 pp.

LANE, BARBARA S. 1953. "A Comparative and Analytic Study of Some Aspects of Northwest Coast Religion" (Doctoral dissertation). University of Washington.

LEACH, E. R. 1954. *Political Systems of Highland Burma*. Cambridge, Mass.: Harvard University Press, 323 pp.

LEACOCK, ELEANOR. 1954. *The Montagnais Hunting Territory and the Fur Trade* (Memoir 78, American Anthropological Association). 59 pp.

LEMERT, EDWIN M. 1952. "Stuttering Among the North Pacific Coastal Indians," *Southwestern Journal of Anthropology*, Vol. 8, No. 3, pp. 420–41.

————. 1954. *Alcohol and the Northwest Coast Indians* (University of California Publications in Culture and Society, Vol. 2, No. 6). Berkeley: University of California Press, 103 pp.

LÉVI-STRAUSS, CLAUDE. 1952*a*. "Kinship Systems of Three Chittagong Hill Tribes (Pakistan)," *Southwestern Journal of Anthropology*, Vol. 8, No. 1, pp. 40–51.

————. 1952*b*. "Les Structures Sociales dans le Brésil Central et Orientales," pp. 302–10, in Tax, Sol (ed.), *Selected Papers of the XXIXth International Congress of Americanists*, Vol. 3. Chicago: University of Chicago Press, 410 pp.

LYSTAD, R. A. 1951. "Differential Acculturation of the Ahafo-Ashanti of the Gold Coast and the Indenie-Agni of the Ivory Coast" (Doctoral dissertation). Northwestern University.

MASON, J. ALDEN. 1952. "Notes and Observations on the Tepehnan," *América Indígena*, Vol. 12, No. 1, January, pp. 33–53.

McCONNELL, URSULA H. 1950. "Junior Marriage Systems: A Comparative Survey," *Oceania*, Vol. 21, No. 2, pp. 107–143.

NADEL, S. F. 1950. "Dual Descent in the Nuba Hills," pp. 333–59, in Radcliffe-Brown, A. R. and Forde, Daryll (eds.), *African Systems of Kinship and Marriage*. New York: Oxford University Press, 399 pp.

————. 1952. "Witchcraft in Four African Societies. An Essay in Comparison," *American Anthropologist*, Vol. 54, No. 1, pp. 18–29.

NEWCOMB, W. W. 1950. "A Re-examination of the Causes of Plains Warfare," *American Anthropologist*, Vol. 52, No. 3, pp. 317–30.

PAUL, BENJAMIN D. and PAUL, LOIS. 1952. "The Life Cycle," pp. 174–92, in Tax, Sol (ed.), *Heritage of Conquest*. Glencoe, Ill.: Free Press, 312 pp.

PETTERSSON, OLOF. 1953. *Chiefs and Gods: Religious and Social Elements in South Eastern Bantu Kinship* (Studia Theologia Lundensia, No. 3). Lund: C. W. K. Glerrup, 405 pp.

POCOCK, D. F. 1951. "A Comparative Study of Social Organization Among the Nilotic People" (Doctoral dissertation). Oxford University.

READ, K. E. 1954. "Cultures of the Central Highlands, New Guinea," *Southwestern Journal of Anthropology*, Vol. 10, No. 1, pp. 1–43.

RICHARDS, A. I. 1950. "Some Types of Family Structure Amongst the Central Bantu," pp. 207–51, in Radcliffe-Brown, A. R. and Forde, Daryll (eds.), *African Systems of Kinship and Marriage*. New York: Oxford University Press, 399 pp.

RIESENBERG, SAUL H. and GAYTON, A. H. 1952. "Caroline Island Belt Weaving," *Southwestern Journal of Anthropology*, Vol. 8, No. 3, pp. 342–75.

RIESENFELD, A. 1951. "Tobacco in New Guinea and Other Areas of Melanesia," *Journal of the Royal Anthropological Institute of Great Britain and Ireland*, Vol. 81, Pts. 1 & 2, pp. 69–103.

SAUER, JONATHAN D. 1950. "Amaranths as Dye Plants Among the Pueblo Peoples," *Southwestern Journal of Anthropology*, Vol. 6, No. 4, pp. 412–15.

SECOY, FRANK RAYMOND. 1953. *Changing Military Patterns on the Great Plains* (Monographs of the American Ethnological Society, Vol. 21). New York: J. J. Augustin, 112 pp.

SMITH, MARIAN W. 1952. "Culture Area and Culture Depth: With Data from the Northwest Coast," pp. 80–96 in Tax, Sol (ed.), *Selected Papers of the XXIXth International Congress of Americanists*, Vol. 3. Chicago: University of Chicago Press, 410 pp.

SMITH, M. G. 1953. "Secondary Marriage in Northern Nigeria," *Africa*, Vol. 23, No. 4, pp. 298–323.

STARR, BETTY W. 1954. "Levels of Communal Relations," *American Journal of Sociology*, Vol. 60, No. 2, September, pp. 125–35.

STEVENSON, H. N. C. 1951. "Religion and Society Among Some Tribes of Chota-Nagpur (Doctoral dissertation). Oxford University.

SUTTLES, Wayne. 1951. "The Early Distribution of the Potato Among the Coast Salish," *Southwestern Journal of Anthropology*, Vol. 7, No. 3, pp. 272–88.

TAX, SOL. 1952a. "Economy and Technology," pp. 43–75, in Tax, Sol (ed.), *Heritage of Conquest*. Glencoe, Ill.: Free Press, 312 pp.

————. 1952b. "The Sixteenth Century and the Twentieth," pp. 262–81, in Tax, Sol (ed.), *Heritage of Conquest*. Glencoe, Ill.: Free Press, 312 pp.

THOMPSON, LAURA. 1951. *Personality and Government: Findings and Recommendations of the Indian Administration Research*. Mexico, D. F.: Instituto Indigenista Inter-Americano. 229 pp.

UNDERHILL, RUTH. 1954. "Intercultural Relations in the Greater Southwest," *American Anthropologist*, Vol. 56, No. 4, pp. 645–62.

VAN DER KROEF, JUSTUS M. 1952. "Some Head-Hunting Traditions of Southern New Guinea," *American Anthropologist*, Vol. 54, No. 2, Pt. 1, pp. 221–35.

WAGLEY, CHARLES. 1951. "Cultural Influences on Population: A Comparison of Two Tupi Tribes," *Revista do Museu Paulista*, Vol. 5, *n.s.*, pp. 95–104.

WISDOM, CHARLES. 1952. "The Supernatural World and Curing," pp. 119–34, in Tax, Sol (ed.), *Heritage of Conquest*. Glencoe, Ill.: Free Press, 312 pp.

COMPARISONS WITHIN A SINGLE
LOCAL GROUP OR CULTURE

BARNES, J. A. 1951. "Measures of Divorce Frequency in Simple Societies," *Journal of the Royal Anthropological Institute of Great Britain and Ireland*, Vol. 79, Pts. 1 & 2, pp. 37–62.

BARNOUW, VICTOR. 1950. *Acculturation and Personality Among the Wisconsin Chippewa* (Memoir 70, American Anthropological Association). 152 pp.

————. 1954. "The Changing Character of a Hindu Festival," *American Anthropologist*, Vol. 56, No. 1, pp. 74–86.

BASCOM, WILLIAM R. 1950. "Ponape: The Cycle of Empire," *Scientific Monthly*, Vol. 70, No. 3, pp. 141–150.

COLSON, ELIZABETH. 1954. "The Intensive Study of Small Sample Communities," pp. 43–59, in Spencer, Robert F. (ed.), *Method and Perspective in Anthropology*. Minneapolis: University of Minnesota Press, 323 pp.

FENTON, WILLIAM N. (ed.). 1951. *Symposium on Local Diversity in Iroquois Culture* (Bureau of American Ethnology, Bulletin No. 149). Washington, D.C.: Smithsonian Institution, 187 pp.

FIRTH, RAYMOND. 1952. "Notes on the Social Structure of Some South-Eastern New Guinea Communities," *Man*, Vol. 52, No. 5, pp. 65–67; No. 6, pp. 86–89.

FRIED, JACOB. 1953. "The Relation of Ideal Norms to Actual Behavior in Tarahumara Society," *Southwestern Journal of Anthropology*, Vol. 9, No. 3, pp. 286–95.

GOLDSCHMIDT, WALTER, and SPINDLER, GEORGE. 1952. "Experimental Design in the Study of Culture Change," *Southwestern Journal of Anthropology*, Vol. 8, No. 1, pp. 68–83.

HALLOWELL, A. IRVING. 1950. "Values, Acculturation and Mental Health," *American Journal of Orthopsychiatry*, Vol. 20, No. 4, pp. 732–43.

———. 1952. "Ojibway Personality and Acculturation," pp. 106–12, in Tax, Sol (ed.), *Selected Papers of the XXIXth International Congress of Americanists*, Vol. 2. Chicago: University of Chicago Press, 339 pp.

HART, C. W. M. 1954. "The Sons of Turimpi," *American Anthropologist*, Vol. 56, No. 2, Pt. 1, pp. 242–61.

HENRY, JULES. 1951. "The Economics of Pilagá Food Production," *American Anthropologist*, Vol. 53, No. 2, pp. 187–219.

HOGBIN, IAN. 1951. *Transformation Scene: The Changing Culture of a New Guinea Village*. London: Routledge and Kegan Paul, 326 pp.

KAPLAN, BERNICE A. 1951. "Changing Functions of the Huanancha Dance at the Corpus Christi Festival in Paracho, Michoacán, México," *Journal of American Folklore*, Vol. 64, No. 254, pp. 383–96.

LEWIS, OSCAR. 1950. "An Anthropological Approach to Family Studies," *The American Journal of Sociology*, Vol. LV, No. 5, pp. 468–75.

———. 1951. *Life in a Mexican Village: Tepoztlán Restudied*. Urbana: University of Illinois Press, 512 pp.

MANDELBAUM, DAVID G. 1954. "Form, Variation and Meaning of a Ceremony," pp. 60–102, in Spencer, Robert F. (ed.), *Method and Perspective in Anthropology*. Minneapolis, University of Minnesota Press, 323 pp.

MARRIOTT, McKIM. 1952. "Social Change in an Indian Village," *Economic Development and Cultural Change*, No. 2, June, pp. 145–55.

MEAD, MARGARET. 1954. "Manus Restudied: An Interim Report," *Transactions of The New York Academy of Sciences*, Ser. II, Vol. 16, No. 8, pp. 426–32.

NETT, BETTY R. 1952. "Historical Changes in the Osage Kinship System," *Southwestern Journal of Anthropology*, Vol. 8, No. 2, pp. 164–81.

REDFIELD, ROBERT. 1950. *A Village that Chose Progress: Chan Kom Revisited*. Chicago: University of Chicago Press, 187 pp.

REICHEL-DOLMATOFF, GERARDO. 1953. "Actitudes hacia el Trabajo en una Población Mestiza de Colombia," *América Indígena*, Vol. 13, No. 3, July, pp. 165–74.

ROBERTS, JOHN M. 1951. *Three Navaho Households* (Papers of the Peabody Museum of American Archaeology and Ethnology, Vol. 40, No. 3). Cambridge, Mass., 84 pp.

SCHMIDT, KARL and SCHMIDT, OSANAI IVA. 1952. *Wichita Kinship, Past and Present*. Norman, Okla.: University Book Exchange, 72 pp.

SPINDLER, GEORGE D. 1952. "Personality and Peyotism in Menomini Indian Acculturation," *Psychiatry*, Vol. 15, No. 2, pp. 151–59.

STOUT, D. B. 1952. "Persistent Elements in San Blas Cuna Social Organization," pp. 262–65 in Tax, Sol (ed.), *Selected Papers of the XXIXth International Congress of Americanists*, Vol. 3. Chicago: University of Chicago Press, 339 pp.

TREMBLAY, MARC-ADELARD, COLLIER, JOHN, JR., and SASAKI, TOM T. 1954. "Navaho Housing in Transition," *América Indígena*, Vol. 14, No. 3, pp. 187–220.

TUMIN, MELVIN M. 1952. *Caste in a Peasant Society: A Case Study in the Dynamics of Caste*. Princeton, N.J.: Princeton University Press, 300 pp.

WALLACE, ERNEST and HOEBEL, E. ADAMSON. 1952. *The Comanches, Lords of the South Plains* (Civilization of the American Indian Series, No. 34). Norman, Okla.: University of Oklahoma Press, 381 pp.

WATSON, JAMES B. 1952. *Cayuá Culture Change: A Study in Acculturation and Methodology* (Memoir 73, American Anthropological Association), 144 pp.

VOGET, FRED. 1952. "Crow Socio-Cultural Groups," pp. 88–93, in Tax, Sol (ed.), *Selected Papers of the XXIXth International Congress of Americanists*, Vol. 2. Chicago: University of Chicago Press, 339 pp.

VOGT, EVON Z. 1951. *Navaho Veterans, A Study of Changing Values* (Papers of the Peabody Museum of American Archaeology and Ethnology, Vol. 41, No. 1). Cambridge, Mass., 223 pp.

Part Two:

AMERICAN INDIANS

7

The Effects of White Contact Upon Blackfoot Culture[*]

· PREFACE ·

This paper was submitted as a dissertation in partial fulfillment of the requirements for the degree of doctor of philosophy in the Faculty of Philosophy of Columbia University. I am grateful to the American Ethnological Society for having awarded this study publication in their Monograph Series.

I should like to express my gratitude to Professor Ruth Benedict and Professor Wm. Duncan Strong for their guidance and encouragement in writing this study. I am further indebted to Professor Benedict for obtaining financial assistance from the Buell Quain Fund to partially cover the cost of publication.

I also wish to thank Professor Melville Herskovits, Professor F. Keesing, Professor Ralph Linton, Dr. Julian H. Steward, Dr. Clark Wissler and Dr. Gene Weltfish for their kindness in reading the manuscript and for their valuable criticism and suggestions.

This statement of indebtedness would not be complete without paying tribute to the work of that great fur-trader and explorer David Thompson, whose *Narrative of His Explorations in Western America* . . . has become a classic on the early history of the Northwest. His work has been invaluable for this study because of the insight it gives into the changing character of Blackfoot institutions.

[*] This was first published in 1942, in *Monographs of the American Ethnological Society*, A. Irving Hallowell, ed. (New York: J. J. Augustin).

· I. INTRODUCTION ·

· ANTHROPOLOGY AND HISTORY ·

For a period of over a hundred years (1730-1860) the fur trade was the sole medium of contact between Western civilization and the Blackfoot Indians and had a profound effect upon the Blackfoot and other Plains tribes. Despite this, the role of the fur trade in the development of Plains culture has been neglected. Anthropologists interested in the historical problems of this area have centered their attention upon the effects of the horse practically to the exclusion of other factors. There has been little reliance upon documents in reconstructing the history of the Plains. In the case of the Blackfoot, had the documents been studied, the importance of the fur trade would have been inescapable, for the history of the Blackfoot is to be found largely in the records of the fur trade. To some extent the fur trade has been considered by anthropologists for the Woodland area, where the historical documents are more numerous and date back to an earlier period than for the Plains. In general, however, the neglect of available written history for its problems is a characteristic of present-day anthropology.

Anthropology has been designated as an historical science for, like history, it has had as one of its fundamental objectives the reconstruction of the history of human society. But the conventional distinction between history and anthropology is that the historian works with written documents from which he derives objective chronological sequence, whereas the anthropologist works with ethnographic data from which he must infer these time relations. This difference in the evidence used has resulted in an essential difference in method.

Of the two major schools which have been concerned with historical problems in anthropology, the early evolutionists and the diffusionists, neither have used documentary evidence for their interpretations. The former used ethnographic data to formulate crude and sweeping generalizations of unilinear evolution, "built up of subjectively selective evidence torn out of their historical context." The latter, particularly the German school, set up arbitrary culture complexes or strata, essentially artificial constructs, and endeavored to trace the distribution of these complexes throughout the world. The history of anthropology thus presents the paradoxical picture of great preoccupation with historical problems, and no end of historical interpretations from ethnographic data, with only a minimum use of documented history.

The very concept of history and its function in anthropology has been so colored by these nineteenth-century anthropologists that when their speculations fell into disrepute there was a reaction away from historical studies in general. Functionalism, with its emphasis upon the intensive study of cultures on one time level, represented the new trend. Although this interest in the integration and functioning of institutions has contributed to our understanding of individual cultures, it has been unable to formulate any valid generalizations about the processes of social change, which is an ever-present problem.

It is a striking commentary on the present state of anthropology that archeology is the only branch of anthropology which is concerned about the history of culture change. Recent contributions in archeology indicate a new and creative approach, a departure from the interests of early archeologists who were preoccupied with collection of artifacts.[1] Because the ethnologists, with few exceptions, have practically abandoned the study of the evolution of institutions, the archeologists alone have had to cope with the problem.

The failure of anthropologists to deal successfully with these problems can be attributed in part to their systematic neglect of documentary material. Where they have been concerned with social change, the emphasis has generally been on the formulation of a number of refined techniques to infer time perspective. Sapir, for example, in a classic paper,[2] devoted only one page to the importance of documentary evidence; the major portion of his paper enumerated the various methods of inferring time (seriation, association, and geographical distribution), followed in each case by examples of the weakness in method. Sapir visualized a very limited application of documented history for anthropology, that is, "to give the maximal and minimal dates to the appearance of a culture element, or to assign the time limits to a movement of population."[3] To show the more constructive and embracing use to which historical

[1] See, for example, the work of William Duncan Strong, *An Introduction to Nebraska Archeology*, Smithsonian Miscellaneous Collections, Vol. 93, No. 10 (Washington, D.C., 1935), pp. 1–315, and "From History to Prehistory in the Northern Great Plains," in *Essays in Historical Anthropology of North America*, Smithsonian Misc. Col., Vol. 1 (Washington, D.C., 1940), pp. 353–94. For a recent theoretical discussion, see article by Julian H. Steward and Frank M. Setzler, "Function and Configuration in Archeology," *American Antiquity*, Vol. 4 (1939), pp. 4–11.

[2] Edward Sapir, *Time Perspective in Aboriginal American Culture: A Study in Method*, Memoir 90, Geological Survey of Canada, Anthropological Series, No. 13 (Ottawa, 1916).

[3] Sapir, pp. 5–6.

material can be put, we need merely cite Professor Keesing's study, in which he has reconstructed early Menomini institutions from early seventeenth-century documents.[4]

In the stimulating exchange between Kroeber and Boas in their articles, "History and Science in Anthropology," we find documented history relegated again to a minor position.[5] Despite the title neither deals with real history. Both have tacitly assumed that the paucity of historical material makes it negligible for the anthropologist. Nevertheless it is this material, largely taken for granted or overlooked, that can be of great value.

For almost every primitive people available for study today, there is some recorded history of contact with either western or eastern civilization. These records of contact are capable of much greater service than has been generally recognized by the anthropologist. The intensive search for such materials and their exhaustive and critical analysis can help bridge the gap between the disciplines of history and anthropology and thereby establish the latter as an historical science. This would undoubtedly benefit both disciplines. To the anthropologist, primitive society, with its greater homogeneity and simplicity, becomes more valuable as a testing ground for sociological and psychological theories when combined with a knowledge of written history. Conversely, the advantage to the historian is that the anthropologist's interest in process will help rescue the study of history from its preoccupation with the recording of facts for facts' sake.

By its emphasis on the need for documentary history as one of its basic controls, the recent trend toward the study of acculturation is most encouraging. In setting up standards for acculturation studies, Herskovits writes,

> That all actual historical documents bearing on a given situation should be exhaustively analyzed goes without saying. Especially in the case of contact between European and non-European peoples will material of this sort prove important. . . . Information of this character has been neglected to a surprising degree—not only in studies of acculturation but also in studies of the ethnology of relatively undisturbed folk. Yet the light such materials shed on changing custom, the strictly ethnological data that they supply, since the early travelers

[4] Felix M. Keesing, *The Menomini Indians of Wisconsin: A Study of Three Centuries of Cultural Contact and Change*, Memoirs of the American Philosophical Society, Vol. 10 (Philadelphia, 1939).

[5] Alfred L. Kroeber, "History and Science in Anthropology," *American Anthropologist*, n.s., Vol. 37 (Oct., 1935), pp. 539–69, and Franz Boas, "History and Science in Anthropology: A Reply," *American Anthropologist*, n.s., Vol. 38 (Jan., 1936), pp. 137–41.

were far keener observers than the ethnologists generally credit them with having been—and the sense of sureness in time depth afforded, are of the greatest value in the study of any civilization, acculturated or not.[6]

However, most acculturation studies have employed history merely for background purposes.[7]

In areas where documentary material has been voluminous, such as Africa, Mexico and Peru, the anthropologists have literally been forced to recognize and to use these data in their studies. In areas where there is a paucity of historical sources, such as the Plains, it has either been assumed that the material was too scant to warrant intensive study or it has been used as descriptive material for static distribution studies. This has been the procedure in a number of Plains studies. Smith, for example, has used documents covering a time span of about 150 years to construct a "timeless" Plains war complex.[8] Actually there was rich material here to show the changing nature of Plains warfare. This use of historical documents in anthropology has inadvertently scuttled their principal asset—that is, an objective record of development.

The Plains area is particularly suited to studies of culture change because of the rich history of movements of peoples from outlying areas onto the Plains and within the Plains itself. The recency of these movements, many of which coincided with the introduction of the horse and gun, has fortunately placed them within the historic period.

A number of studies, based upon archeological and historical material, have established the value of the historicity of the Plains to our understanding of ethnological problems. Strong has demonstrated, on the basis of archeology, the recency of the seminomadic hunting culture of the northern and central Plains.[9] Another type of study by Mandelbaum presents in great detail the metamorphosis which occurred in Cree institutions when part of the Cree moved from the Woodland onto the Plains.[10] Other studies have emphasized the role of the horse as an agent of culture change on the Plains. Since

[6] Melville J. Herskovits, *Acculturation: A Study in Culture Contact* (New York, 1938), pp. 25–26.

[7] See Ralph Linton (ed.), *Acculturation in Seven American Indian Tribes* (New York, 1940).

[8] Marian W. Smith, "War Complex of the Plains Indians," in *Proceedings of the American Philosophical Society*, Vol. 78, No. 3 (Philadelphia, 1938), pp. 425–64.

[9] Strong, "From History to Prehistory."

[10] David G. Mandelbaum, *The Plains Cree* (New York: The American Museum of Natural History, 1940).

Wissler's well-known essay, this point of view has been developed in the works of Kroeber, Strong, and Mishkin. Strong has shown that the acquisition of the horse was responsible for the transformation of the semisedentary agricultural Crow and Cheyenne to the nomadic hunting peoples of later years. Mishkin, in an intensive study, contended that the horse had an effect more profound and far-reaching than that attributed to it by Wissler, and concluded that it was the most important single factor in the development of the Plains cultures of the nineteenth century.[11]

It follows from these studies that time perspective is essential in a study of Plains institutions. Yet, with but few exceptions, the ethnography of the Plains has been written with little consideration of the history of the institutions described. As an example of what can be learned of the development of institutions from the recorded history of white contact, we have selected for our study the Blackfoot, a "typical" Plains tribe. The historical sources concerning the Blackfoot are not numerous but they are, for the most part, well known. Despite this, Blackfoot ethnography has been treated unhistorically. Here again, the documentary material has been used for descriptive purposes or, at most, for the solution of limited problems such as the verification of the southern range of the Blackfoot.[12]

It is my purpose to present a developmental study of Blackfoot institutions and to show, to the extent that historical material permits, the changes which occurred in Blackfoot economy, social organization, marriage, and warfare, following their contact with western civilization. My method of procedure has, in a sense, paralleled that of the archeologist. It has consisted of "digging" into historical records for information concerning culture change among the Blackfoot. For this purpose, I have examined traders' journals, travelers' reports, records of fur companies, government papers, and a host of secondary sources. I have arranged the ethnography contained in these sources in a chronological framework, thus producing a time schedule of the culture elements in the order in which they appear in the records of observers. It is inevitable that there should be many gaps and some of my conclusions are therefore only tentative.

A few words concerning the organization of the material and the problems dealt with in this study are necessary at this point. Western civilization was brought to the Blackfoot by the fur trade, and the principal source of Blackfoot history for over 130 years is the writ-

[11] Bernard Mishkin, *Rank and Warfare Among the Plains Indians*, Monographs of the American Ethnological Society, No. 3 (New York, 1940).

[12] Clark Wissler, *Material Culture of the Blackfoot Indians*, American Museum of Natural History, Anthropological Papers, Vol. 5, Part 1 (New York, 1910).

ten record of the fur trade in Canada and the United States. The intimate relation between the history of the Blackfoot and that of the fur trade has direct bearing upon this study and offers interesting contrasts with the southern and central Plains, where the fur trade was unimportant.

In the light of the significance of the fur trade, the role usually attributed to the horse as an agent of culture change must be re-examined.[13] Is the expansion of Blackfoot economy in the nineteenth century and the commercialism that became part of Blackfoot values to be explained solely in terms of the horse? Is the horse alone responsible for the rapid spread and uniformity of Plains culture, or did the fur trade also play a part in this process? These and related problems will be treated in this study.

One other aspect of my work, related more directly to problems of acculturation, must be pointed out here. The unique geographical position of the Blackfoot tribes, situated as they were on both sides of the international line, subjected them to two influences, a Canadian and an American. This first presented itself in the differences in policy and character of the Canadian and American fur companies, and it continued in the differences in the pre-reserve treatment of the Indians by the Canadian and American governments. Finally, it manifested itself in the post reserve adjustments in Canada and in the United States.

Although these conditions make a study of Blackfoot acculturation more complicated, they also make it more useful in that we can trace the role of the differential factors in Canada and in the United States and evaluate their effects upon the Blackfoot. In this paper, I shall consider these effects up to the reserve period.

· II. ORIGIN AND EARLY MOVEMENTS [14] ·

The origin of the Blackfoot is one of the puzzling problems in the history of the northern Plains. Unlike the Plains Cree, the Cheyenne, the Gros Ventre, and the Sarsi, who moved out into the Plains from surrounding regions in the historic period, the previous location of the Blackfoot has not been established. Wissler has dealt with this

[13] Mishkin, pp. 5–24.

[14] The Blackfoot, Blood, and Piegan tribes are at the present time located on four reserves, of which three are in Alberta, Canada, and one in Montana. In pre-reserve days they roamed the Plains near the foothills of the mountains from the northern branches of the Missouri to the North Saskatchewan. To avoid confusion I shall use the Blackfoot term *Siksika* to refer to the Northern Blackfoot and the term "Blackfoot" to refer to all three tribes.

subject at various times. Writing in 1905 he stated, "The Blackfoot
. . . presumably came out of the wooded lake area to the east into
the open country of the west, as did their kindred the Arapaho and
Cheyenne, where they gradually adopted the culture of the Sioux
tribes." [15] Again, in 1908, he stated that it seemed certain that the
Blackfoot migrated from the region of the Great Lakes, which he
believed to be the center of dispersion of the Algonkian-speaking
people of the Plains.[16] In 1910, after a detailed examination of some
of the available historical sources, he concluded that "no satisfactory
evidence has come to hand that the Blackfoot ever occupied other
definite territory than their historic habitat, the western Plains." [17]
Although this was written before the publication of *David Thompson's Narrative* (1916) and the *Kelsey Papers* (1929), it remains
true today with but minor modifications.

Hyde, in the most recent study of the subject (1933), supports
Wissler's earlier hypothesis and enlarges upon it. "Early in the 17th
century the Red River country and the lands lying immediately west
of Lake Winnipeg were held by Algonkin and Siouan tribes, most of
whom were partly sedentary, dwelling in earth lodges, making pottery, planting corn and other crops. Among these people we may
include the three Blackfoot tribes." [18] Although we know that the
Blackfoot had pottery[19] and a vague tradition of agriculture,[20] there
is no evidence of earth lodges and nothing that would locate them in
Red River country. Hyde's reconstruction is based upon a purely
speculative identification of the Blackfoot with descriptions of a
people in this area given by the early Jesuit missionaries.

In the absence of archeological evidence, any reconstruction of
early Blackfoot locations and movements must rely upon their lin-

---

[15] Clark Wissler, *The Blackfoot Indians*, Annual Archeological Report, Appendix to the Report of the Minister of Education of Ontario, 1905 (Toronto,
1906), p. 162.

[16] Clark Wissler, "Ethnographic Problems of the Missouri-Saskatchewan Area,"
American Anthropologist, n.s., Vol. 10 (April, 1908), p. 199.

[17] Wissler, *Material Culture*, p. 18.

[18] George E. Hyde, *The Early Blackfoot and Their Neighbors* (Denver, 1933),
p. 6.

[19] Matthew Cocking, "An Adventure from Hudson Bay: Journal of Matthew
Cocking from York Factory to the Blackfoot Country, 1772–1773," in Lawrence
J. Burpee (ed.), *Proceedings and Transactions of the Royal Society of Canada*,
3rd ser., Vol. 2 (Ottawa, 1908), p. 111.

[20] Though Wissler found no tradition of agriculture, there is a statement made
and signed by important chiefs of the Piegan, Blood, and Blackfoot in 1879 to
the effect that their ancestors were tillers of the soil. See U.S., Department of
the Interior, *Annual Report, 1878/79* (Washington, D.C., 1879), Part 3, p. 80.

guistic and cultural affiliations, the tradition of the Blackfoot and that of surrounding tribes, and any available historical material.

· LINGUISTIC CONSIDERATIONS ·

A basic assumption in the studies of Wissler, Hyde, Donaldson, Schultz, and others is that the Blackfoot were the westernmost outpost of the Algonkian-speaking peoples, and it followed quite easily that they came from the east. Although this conclusion may still be true, it can no longer be based upon the above premise, for since Sapir has shown that there is practically a continuous distribution of the Algonkian language to the Pacific coast, the question of direction of movement becomes more complicated.[21] Voegelin recently expressed the opinion that there were some close affinities between the Blackfoot language and the Kutenai to the west of the mountains.[22] As early as 1885, Hale pointed to "non-Algonkian" aspects of the Blackfoot language and suggested that they might have been derived from their early contact with the Kutenai.[23] Michelson and Kroeber have also shown that the Blackfoot language is most differentiated from the typical Algonkian forms. Kroeber writes, "The methods of inflexion and the forms of pronominal affixes resemble those of the Ojibwa, Cree, and more eastern dialects; but etymologically, it seems to differ considerably more from all other Algonkian forms than these vary from each other." [24] This would in itself seem to argue for a long separation from the eastern groups, and is con-

[21] Edward Sapir, "Wiyot and Yurok, Algonkin Languages of California," *Amorican Anthropologist,* n.s., Vol. 15 (Oct., 1913), pp. 617–46.

[22] C. F. Voegelin wrote in a letter to me, "The linguistic evidence which distinguishes the Blackfoot from the two other divergent western Algonquians is that we know of a language, Kutenai, which shares with Blackfoot the Algonquian obviative and some other morphological features, but we know of no language to associate with Arapaho and Cheyenne in any correlative way. Are Blackfoot and Kutenai ultimately related? If so, a point of dispersion near the Rockies is called for. Are Blackfoot and Kutenai not genetically related? If not, they have had contact in proto-historic times which permitted borrowing. Either way, the Blackfoot used to be placed adjacent to the Kutenai to account for the linguistic facts." Voegelin has a paper now in press, in which he shows "the rather paradoxical closeness of Blackfoot to proto-Algonquian despite its lexical divergence." Later published in C. F. Voegelin and E. W. Voegelin, *Map of North American Indian Languages* (New York, 1944).

[23] Horatio Hale, "Report on the Blackfoot Tribes," in *Report of the British Association for the Advancement of Science, 1885* (London, 1886), pp. 696–708.

[24] Alfred L. Kroeber, *The Arapaho,* Bulletin of the American Museum of Natural History, Vol. 18, Parts 1–2 (New York, 1902–04), p. 4.

firmed by historical data which show that the Blackfoot were the earliest Algonkian people to inhabit the northern Plains in the historic period. Kroeber has used the divergence from eastern Algonkian languages to locate the Blackfoot at the foothills of the Rockies and concludes that they were "ancient occupants of the northern Plains." [25]

• CULTURAL AFFILIATIONS •

Distinctly western traits are discernible in items of Blackfoot material culture. Among these are the sinew-backed bow, quilted leather armor, horn utensils, moccasin types, and the hand game. The sinew-backed bow and quilted leather armor were first obtained from the northern Shoshone about 1730, when the latter were still east of the mountains,[26] and as late as 1810 the Blackfoot were still trading pemmican for sinew-backed bows with the tribes west of the mountains.[27]

Of the hand game, Wissler writes, "The particular form of the button used in the Blackfoot hand game seems to belong to the west of the Rocky mountains, to the coast and southward to the plateau. . . . The Blackfoot indifference to seed and button dice tends to class them with the western tribes. Neither the Blackfoot nor the Gros Ventre seem to have used the large hoop and double darts of the Dakota, Omaha, and Arapaho. Thus, in a general way, the Blackfoot fall into an ill-defined group comprising tribes on the headwaters of the Missouri and Columbia Rivers. They seem on the whole to incline more toward the Plateau and Shoshone area, than to the Siouan or Algonkian." [28]

The case of the moccasin suggests the presence of eastern as well as western elements. The structural pattern common to the Thompson, Nez Perce, Sarsi, northern Shoshone, and western Cree was substituted for an eastern type, but the old eastern style of decoration (U pattern), was retained.[29]

[25] Alfred L. Kroeber, *Natural and Cultural Areas of North America* (Berkeley, 1940), p. 82.

[26] David Thompson, *David Thompson's Narrative of His Explorations in Western America, 1784–1812*, ed. Joseph Burr Tyrell, The Champlain Society Publications, No. 12 (Toronto, 1916), pp. 330–32.

[27] Alexander Henry and David Thompson, *New Light on the Early History of the Greater Northwest: The Manuscript Journals of Alexander Henry and of David Thompson . . . 1799–1814*, ed. Elliott Coues, 3 vols. (New York, 1897), Vol. 2, pp. 713–14.

[28] Wissler, *Material Culture*, p. 62.

[29] Clark Wissler, *Structural Basis to the Decoration of Costumes Among the*

Although this material indicates that the Blackfoot were influenced from both the east and the west from the earliest historic times, it tells us little of their location and movements.

• HISTORICAL EVIDENCE •

The introduction of historical material allows for more definite conclusions. A survey of the source material reveals the following data. Henry Kelsey was the first white man to reach the Saskatchewan River from Hudson Bay and to view the Canadian Plains. From his journal (1691–1692) we learn that at that time the Assiniboine and some Cree were on the Plains between the South Saskatchewan and the Carrot and Red Deer Rivers to the east. Under the date of Sept. 6, 1691, he writes of a tribe to the west of the Assiniboine who ". . . knew not ye use of Canoes and were resolved to go to wars. . . ." [30] Mandelbaum [31] and Bell [32] suggest that these were the Blackfoot, whereas Morton identifies them as the Gros Ventre. [33] In any case, since the traditions of the Blackfoot, Assiniboine, and Cree all agree that the Blackfoot were the most westerly group, it seems certain that the Blackfoot were on the Plains west of the South Saskatchewan by 1690 and most probably a good deal earlier.

The next location of the Blackfoot is more definite, for according to the story of an old Piegan chief, Saukamapee, given by David Thompson in his *Narrative*, the Piegan, the frontier tribe of the Blackfoot nation, were on the plains of the Eagle Hills, near the North Saskatchewan River, in 1730, a distance of over four hundred miles east of the Rockies. [34] This would place them on the fringe of a mixed prairie-woodland region, especially in the case of the Blood and Blackfoot, who were probably north and east of the Piegan.

This early location of the Piegan is highly interesting in that it would indicate that they moved into their present location in the historic period and would corroborate the views expressed by Wiss-

Plains Indians, American Museum of Natural History, Anthropological Papers, Vol. 17, Part 3 (New York, 1916), p. 107.

[30] Henry Kelsey, *The Kelsey Papers*, ed. Arthur G. Dougherty and Chester Martin (Ottawa, 1929), p. 16.

[31] Mandelbaum, p. 27.

[32] Charles N. Bell, ed., *The Journal of Henry Kelsey (1691–1692), the First White Man to Reach the Saskatchewan from Hudson Bay*, The Historical and Scientific Society of Manitoba, Transactions No. 4, n.s. (Winnipeg, 1928), p. 28.

[33] Arthur Silver Morton, *A History of the Canadian West to 1870–71* (Toronto, n.d.), p. 16.

[34] Thompson, p. 329.

ler and Kroeber that the western Plains were but little utilized in the prehorse period. But there is the possibility that even at this time the Piegan ranged to the mountains on intertribal visits. Blackfoot origin traditions are singularly contradictory and are therefore of little help. Hayden, Curtis, and Wissler have recorded Piegan tradition to the effect that they originally came from the southwest, beyond the mountains, while Grinnell and others have been told just as positively that they came from the northeast. The latter version, as we shall see, is more in keeping with the picture of Blackfoot movements in the historic period as gleaned from the early literature. However, our problem is further complicated by the evidence from tribes to the west and southwest as given by Teit.[35] This indicates that the Flathead and Kutenai, who lived east of the mountains, carried on trade with the Blackfoot in the prehorse period.[36] As we have seen, early western contact of the Blackfoot has also been suggested by the linguistic similarities to the Kutenai referred to above.

Although the western limits of the Blackfoot are not clearly defined for this early period, a review of the literature enables us to reconstruct a general picture of tribal locations in this area in the prewhite period.

We know that the Piegan were being hard pressed by the Shoshones, who were to the south and west along the Red Deer River.[37] Further to the southwest were the Kutenai, in the valley of the Belly River, and below them were the Pend d'Oreilles and Flathead.[38] David Thompson (1787) writes, from Piegan country near the present Calgary, "All these Plains, which are now the hunting ground of the above Indians (Blackfoot), were formerly in full possession of the Kootenaes, northward; the next the Saleesh and their allies, and the most southern the Snake Indians." [39] This agrees to a remarkable degree with Piegan tradition as recorded by Wissler over 110 years later, and also with that of Teit for the Flathead. To the east and north were the Cree and Assiniboine; the Gros Ventre were south of

[35] James A. Teit, "The Salishan Tribes of the Western Plateaus," *Forty-fifth Annual Report of the Bureau of American Ethnology, 1927–28* (Washington, D.C., 1930), pp. 304, 358.

[36] Harry Holbert Turney-High's material does not fit in with this picture: he contends that the Flathead crossed the mountains for their seasonal buffalo hunts only after they had acquired the horse. See *The Flathead Indians of Montana*, Memoirs of the American Anthropological Association, No. 48 (Menasha, Wis., 1937).

[37] Thompson, p. 330.

[38] Teit, pp. 304–05.

[39] Thompson, p. 328. This agrees with Wissler's information from the Piegan. See Wissler, *Structural Basis*, p. 17.

the main Saskatchewan and east of the South Saskatchewan. (See Map A.)

TRIBAL LOCATIONS BEFORE 1730

MAP A

Within the short period from 1730 to 1745 the old habitat and tribal locations in the northern Plains were changed. The Blackfoot received their first horses from the Shoshone in 1730 and at about the same time obtained firearms and iron from the Cree and Assiniboine. Thus armed with the gun and with iron for their arrows, and aided by a smallpox epidemic among the Shoshone, the Blackfoot, with the aid of the Assiniboine and Cree, defeated the Shoshone about 1733 and initiated a period of great expansion to the west and southwest. Again, Thompson explains a good deal of this:

> In questioning them of their origen and from whence they formerly came they appear to have no tradition beyond the time of their great

grandfathers, that they can depend on, and in their idle time, sometimes this is the subject of their conversation. They have no tradition that they ever made use of canoes, yet their old men always point out the North East as the place they came from, and their progress has always been to the southwest. Since the Traders came to the Saskatchewan River, this has been their course and progress for the distance of four hundred miles from the Eagle Hills to the Mountains near the Missouri but this rapid advance may be mostly attributed to their being armed with guns and iron weapons.[40]

In their push from the North Saskatchewan near the Eagle Hills, southwestward to the waters of the South Saskatchewan, they drove the Snakes and Kutenai west of the mountains. The Piegan, as the frontier tribe, led in this movement. They took possession of the Bow River and the territory south along the foothills. The Blood came to the present Red Deer River, and the Blackfoot proper to the upper waters of the Battle River, south of Edmonton.[41] During this time the Sarsi joined the Blackfoot and were at the North Saskatchewan. The Gros Ventre, driven by the Cree and Assiniboine, occupied the vacancy left by the Blackfoot.[42] The Cree pushed farther west along the wooded country of the North Saskatchewan.[43] (See Map B.)

Still another great movement of the Blackfoot took place. This was the southern movement from the Bow River down to the Missouri and even as far as the mouth of the Yellowstone. This probably occurred about 1750–1770 or earlier. When Thompson met the Piegan in 1787, he said that they were formerly on the Bow River but now extended southward to the Missouri. The reasons for this southern movement were probably to obtain horses from the Flathead and to find better buffalo country. The whole country along the eastern foot of the Rockies north of the Yellowstone was now in possession of the Blackfoot, who extended their war expeditions west of the Divide, penetrating far into Flathead, Nez Perce, and even Kalispel country.[44]

According to Flathead tradition, it was at about this time (1750), that the Crow were first heard of on the Plains, advancing from the east and fighting the Shoshone, whom they drove out of the Yellowstone River country. With this dislocation of tribes, the tribal relationships changed. In 1730, the Blackfoot were the allies of the Assiniboine and Cree, to whom they had applied for aid against the

[40] Thompson, p. 348.

[41] Morton, p. 19.

[42] Morton, p. 19. Also Pierre Margry (ed.), *Découvertes et établissements des français dans l'ouest et dans le sud de l'Amérique Septentrionale (1614–1754)*, Vol. 6 (Paris, 1886), p. 598.

[43] Morton, p. 19.

[44] Teit, p. 318.

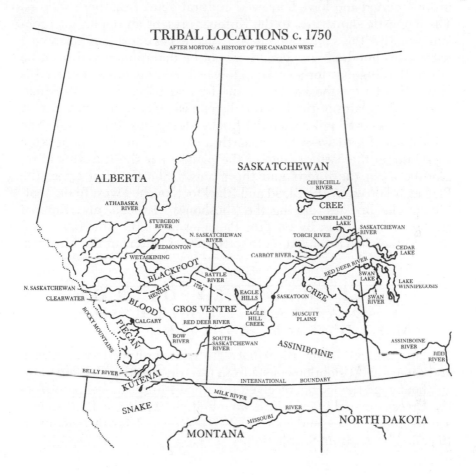

MAP B

Snakes. Again, in 1774, Cocking speaks of the Blackfoot and Assiniboine as being friendly. Until 1800, there is no evidence of Cree hostility. But as the Crees were pushed west with the exhaustion of the woodland food and fur supply, they forged out into the Plains and encroached upon Blackfoot territory. The once peaceful western plains now became a scene of continued bloody warfare that was to last until the reserve period.

• SUMMARY •

My tentative findings can be summed up as follows. The linguistic and cultural affiliations of the Blackfoot do not give us sufficient evidence to determine their early locations. The Blackfoot were in contact with tribes to the east and west for over a hundred years in the historic period and have borrowed cultural items from both sources. The linguistic similarities to the Kutenai present an important problem. Whether this similarity is to be explained as a result of borrowing within this hundred-year period cannot be determined and must be left to the linguists for solution. However, the historical material is clear. About 1730 the Piegan, as the frontier tribe of the Blackfoot, were on the plains of the Eagle Hills in Saskatchewan, a distance of over four hundred miles from the Rocky Mountains. Presumably, the Siksika and Blood were to the north and east. The Blackfoot were therefore on the eastern edge of the plains near the transitional region between the forests and the plains.[45] Shortly after 1730, the Piegan, followed by the Blood and Blackfoot, pushed west to the foothills of the Rockies, driving the Shoshone, Flathead, and Kutenai across the mountains. By 1754 the Piegan were on the Bow River, and by 1787 they had extended south to the upper waters of the Missouri.

· III. HISTORY OF THE CANADIAN FUR TRADE WITH THE BLACKFOOT ·

The first contacts of the Blackfoot with white culture were indirect, and came almost simultaneously from the tribes to the east and west. In about 1728 the Piegan received their first European weapons from the Crees—several guns, a little ammunition, iron-tipped lances and arrows, some knives, and an ax. Only a few years later they acquired their first horses from the Shoshone.

· WESTWARD EXPANSION ·

Direct contact with the whites came about as a result of the expansion of the fur trade to the Canadian Northwest. Beginning with the explorations of La Verendrye in 1738, the French penetrated the hinterland to the west of Hudson Bay and set up trading posts with the purpose of intercepting the Indian trade with the Hudson's Bay Company. The French trading posts were outside Blackfoot territory, for Fort Paskoyac, built in 1750, Fort La Jonquiere (1751), and Fort St. Louis (1753) were all east of the forks of the Saskatchewan.[46]

[45] There is evidence that the Plains between the North Saskatchewan River and the Battle River were at one time a parkland region which was reduced to treeless plains by frequent fires. See Morton, p. 3.

[46] John Blue states that Fort Jonquiere was at either Calgary or Edmonton, in the heart of Blackfoot country. See *Alberta, Past and Present, Historical and*

To counteract these French incursions, which were seriously affecting their trade, the Hudson's Bay Company sent Anthony Henday inland in 1754 to induce the more remote tribes to go down to Fort York on Hudson Bay to trade. Henday was the first white man to meet the Blackfoot (Blood Tribe.)[47] Henday's *Journal* gives some account of this first meeting. After going through the ritual of smoking the peace pipe, he delivered his message, explaining that he had been sent by the great Leader to invite them to bring their beaver and wolf skins, in return for which they would get powder, shot, guns, cloth and the like. A council was held on the following day and the chief gave their reply: "It was far off, and they could not live without Buffalo flesh; and that they could not leave their horses etc.: and many other obstacles, though all might be got over if they were acquainted with a canoe, and could eat fish, which they never do. The chief further said they never wanted food, as they followed the Buffalo and killed them with Bows and Arrows; and he was informed the natives that frequented the Settlements, were oftentimes starved on their journey." [48] At this point in the journal Henday observed, "Such remarks I thought exceedingly true." [49] The Blood evidently were aware of the trading that went on between the neighboring Indians and the whites. Henday reported meeting a party of "Trade Indians," middlemen for the Hudson's Bay Company, in Blackfoot country, making it probable that the Blackfoot carried on trade through them.

Undeterred by Henday's failure to induce the Blackfoot to undertake the hazardous journey east, Hudson's Bay Company men made many voyages into the interior in the years following.[50] The next record of direct contact with the Blackfoot is that of Henry Pressick,

---

Biographical, Vol. 1 (Chicago, 1924), p. 18. More recent authorities have shown that it was below the forks of Saskatchewan. See J. B. Tyrell (ed.), *Journals of Samuel Hearne and Philip Turner* (Toronto: Champlain Society, 1934), pp. 23–24, and Morton, pp. 237–38.

[47] I have followed Lawrence J. Burpee's edition of "York Factory to the Blackfoot Country: The Journal of Anthony Hendry, 1754–55," *Proceedings and Transactions of the Royal Society of Canada,* 3rd ser., Vol. 1 (Ottawa, 1907), p. 316, and Morton, p. 19, in identifying as Blackfoot the "Architinues" natives visited by Hendry and referred to by Cocking. However, I am indebted to Dr. Clark Wissler for pointing out that there is no absolute warrant for this identification, although there is a strong probability in its favor. Morton has shown (p. 244) that the surname appearing in the Company records is *Henday* rather than *Hendry.*

[48] Hendry, p. 338.

[49] Hendry, p. 338.

[50] Morton, p. 272.

1760–61, who was sent into the country of the Blood and Blackfoot.[51] Unfortunately, we know nothing of Pressick's experiences with the Blackfoot.

Beginning with 1763, the Hudson's Bay Company was met by a new threat—independent French and English traders from Montreal who went inland and carried their trade goods to the very doors of the Indians. They were derisively named "Pedlars" by the Hudson's Bay Company servants. To meet this competition, the Company sent Matthew Cocking west in 1772. He visited the Blackfoot in 1773, and again attempted to induce them to trade at Fort York on Hudson Bay, but he received the same reply given to Henday twenty-one years earlier.[52]

• ESTABLISHMENT OF TRADING POSTS •

Faced by the persistent refusal of the Blackfoot to go east and by the increasing competition of the traders from Montreal, the Hudson's Bay Company abandoned its old policy of waiting for the Indians to bring their furs to the posts on the Bay and sent their men inland to build their own trading posts. In 1774, Cumberland House was built on the North Saskatchewan River, and two years later Hudson's House, a little farther up the same river.[53] These posts were still outside the Blackfoot country and we have no records of trade with the Blackfoot.

With the formation of the Northwest Company in 1784, the Hudson's Bay Company renewed its efforts to establish its trade with the Blackfoot. David Thompson with a party of six was sent out for this purpose. In October 1787, Thompson set out to find the Piegan, "to induce them to hunt for furs, and make dried provisions; to get as many as possible to come to the houses to trade, and to trade the furs of those that would not come." [54] Thompson wintered with the Piegan near the present site of Calgary, and although he gathered much valuable ethnographical data, his trading mission was not entirely successful. The trading posts were still too far outside of Blackfoot country; the nearest post at this time was South Branch House built in 1785 on the South Saskatchewan at Gardipuys Crossing on the border of the woods and Plains.

Trading posts were finally established within easy reach of the Blackfoot. In 1794, Fort Augustus was built on the South Saskatch-

[51] Morton, p. 252.
[52] Cocking, p. 92.
[53] Thompson, p. 318.
[54] Thompson, p. 324.

ewan with the object of drawing the Blood and Piegan southward.[55]
Blackfoot country was now surrounded by a ring of posts belonging to
both companies. (See Map C.)

• BLACKFOOT RELATIONS WITH TRADERS •

Until this point the relations between the Blackfoot and whites were
perfectly friendly. Henday, Pressick, Cocking, Thompson, and others
had wintered with the Blackfoot and had returned unharmed and
undespoiled. However, beaver were becoming scarce east of the
mountains and the Northwest Company once more had to expand
westward. The agents of this company began to make overtures to

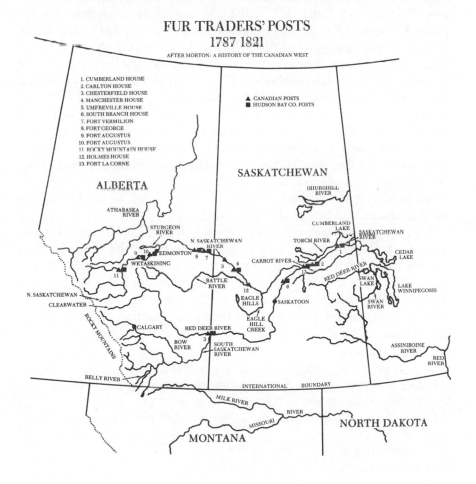

FUR TRADERS' POSTS
1787 1821

AFTER MORTON: A HISTORY OF THE CANADIAN WEST

1. CUMBERLAND HOUSE
2. CARLTON HOUSE
3. CHESTERFIELD HOUSE
4. MANCHESTER HOUSE
5. UMFREVILLE HOUSE
6. SOUTH BRANCH HOUSE
7. FORT VERMILION
8. FORT GEORGE
9. FORT AUGUSTUS
10. FORT AUGUSTUS
11. ROCKY MOUNTAIN HOUSE
12. HOLMES HOUSE
13. FORT LA CORNE

▲ CANADIAN POSTS
■ HUDSON BAY CO. POSTS

MAP C

55 Morton, p. 511.

the Kutenai, the enemies of the Blackfoot. The Piegan, who were the frontier tribe and who would bear the brunt of a strengthened Kutenai, sensed the danger at once.[56] Earlier the Kutenai had made several attempts to reach Fort George on the upper Saskatchewan but were prevented by the Piegan. M'Gillivray's journal of 1795 tells of the Kutenai's trying to force their way through Blackfoot territory and attempting to bribe them with horses, but in vain.[57] The Blackfoot also succeeded in preventing the Salish and Pend d'Oreille from establishing contact with the Canadian posts until 1806 and forced the western tribes to trade in a roundabout way through the Mandan and Hidatsa to the South.[58]

In 1805, Thompson attempted to cross the mountains but was stopped by the Piegan, the same people who had befriended him in 1787.[59] It was not until 1807 that he managed to get across. He explains, "The murder of two Peeagan Indians by Captain Lewis of the U.S. drew the Peeagans to the Missouri to avenge their deaths; and thus gave me an opportunity to cross the mountains by the defiles of the Saskatchewan River which led to the headwaters of the Columbia River." [60] Thompson descended the Columbia and built the first Kutenai trading post. A few months later the Piegan returned from the south and learned of Kutenai House. The civil chief of the Piegan advised the formation of a strong war party to crush the whites and natives to the west of the mountains immediately, before they became too well armed. Said the chief, "They (Kutenai) have always been our slaves, and now they will pretend to equal us—we must destroy them before they become too powerful for us." [61]

A war party of three hundred men was formed to destroy the Kutenai post. Thompson was in serious danger but he succeeded in buying them off by sending large gifts of tobacco and pipes to the leader of the war party.[62] However, the barrier of the Piegan had important historical significance, for it delayed Thompson long enough to allow the Astor party to reach Oregon first and establish a prior claim which won the Columbia valley for the Americans.[63]

[56] Thompson, p. 375.

[57] Duncan M'Gillivray, *The Journal of Duncan M'Gillivray of the Northwest Company at Fort George on the Saskatchewan, 1794–1795*, ed. Arthur S. Morton (Toronto, 1929), p. 56.

[58] Francis Laroque, *Journal*, ed. L. J. Burpee (Ottawa: Canadian Archives, 1911), p. 72.

[59] Thompson, p. 375.

[60] Thompson, p. 375.

[61] Thompson, p. 381.

[62] Thompson, p. 383.

[63] Morton, p. 491.

Within a few years after the expansion of the fur trade across the Rockies, the balance of power among the Indian tribes had shifted. The apprehensions of the Piegan concerning the arming of the tribes to the west were indeed well founded. Formerly, the Kalispel, Spokane, Flathead, and Kutenai were the easy prey of the Blackfoot. Now, supplied with firearms, they had become formidable enemies. In the summer of 1810 the Piegan suffered their first defeat at the hands of the Kutenai and Flathead, who were as well armed as they.[64] This defeat increased the hostility of the Piegan towards the whites. The Piegan would have attempted vengeance but feared that such action would deprive them of further ammunition and supplies, now doubly needed against their newly armed enemies.[65]

The relations of the Blackfoot to the tribes to the east were also affected by the Canadian fur trade. A special grievance against the traders was the belief that they were partial to the Crees, and to all appearances were more liberal in arming them.[66] To understand the seriousness of this from the point of view of the Blackfoot, we must remember that the differences in the rate of arming of the various tribes was crucial in determining the balance of power in this area. Here the Cree, specialists in beaver trapping, had a great advantage over the Plains Indians, whose wolves and foxes were relatively worthless. This was another potent source of hostility against the whites on the part of the Blackfoot tribes, once the Cree began their incursions into Blackfoot territory. However, except for a few instances, peace was maintained at the posts.[67]

Trading at the posts continued but in an atmosphere of greater tension. The journal of Alexander Henry, the younger, under the date of 1810, states, "The natives have become so troublesome that we find it is necessary to keep them at a distance while at our establishment and not allow them to come in numbers inside our principal fort." [68] The cannon in the bastion of the forts were kept ready for action, and men were stationed with loaded muskets in the sentinels gallery that surrounded the palisade when the Blackfoot came to trade. Sometimes strong-arm men were on hand to administer beatings to the Indians who were suspected of making trouble.[69]

[64] Thompson, p. 424.

[65] Henry and Thompson, *Manuscript Journals,* Vol. 2, p. 583.

[66] M'Gillivray, p. 31.

[67] In 1807 a Blood band under Old Swan pillaged and burned Fort Augustus, and in the 1840's Old Fort Bow was destroyed. See Thompson, p. xc, and Katherine Hughes, *Father Lacombe, the Black-Robe Voyageur* (New York, 1897), p. 61.

[68] Henry and Thompson, Vol. 2, p. 545.

[69] M'Gillivray, p. 46.

The rivalry between the Hudson's Bay Company and its competitors led the former to abandon its old policy of keeping intoxicating drink from the Indians, and by the time the posts were in Blackfoot country the Hudson's Bay Company traded liquor as freely as the others. Liquor soon supplanted other goods in desirability and became the most important single item in the trade. It provided the Blackfoot with their greatest incentive to trap. But if the liquor trade was profitable, it was also dangerous. The Blackfoot were a numerous people, conscious of their power and especially violent when drunk. Consequently, the whiskey served to them was more diluted than that traded to the neighboring tribes. Whereas they would mix one part "high wine" to three or four parts of water for the Cree and Assiniboine, they added seven or eight parts of water for the Blackfoot, and the diluted drink became known as "Blackfoot rum." [70]

In 1821 the struggle between the Hudson's Bay Company and the Northwest Company came to an end when both companies united under the name of the former. This had a very wholesome effect upon the Indians. The immediate effect was to cut down the sale of liquor to the Blackfoot to a minimum and to stabilize the fur trade. The relations between the company and the Blackfoot Indians during this period became routine and peaceful. Stanley observed, "Inspired though they may have been by prudence and self-interest, rather than by enlightened motives of native welfare, their dealings with the Indians were marked by a sense of trusteeship and strict integrity." [71]

By 1830 the heyday of the Canadian fur trade was over. The supply of beaver was almost exhausted east of the Rockies and the Hudson's Bay Company was forced to introduce methods of conservation in their attempts to restore the waning beaver supply. The period of expansion with its exploration and independent trappers was also over. We therefore find few journals of travelers or traders in Blackfoot country in Canada for the period from 1830 to 1870, the period when the Canadian fur trade was the sole monopoly of the Hudson's Bay Company. The gap in our descriptive material for this period will be filled only when the complete records of the Hudson's Bay Company, which are now in the London archives, are made available to the public. However, just as our information on the Blackfoot in Canada begins to dwindle, a tremendous expansion in the American fur trade occurred, with the result that our records there are much more complete.

[70] Henry and Thompson, Vol. 2, p. 514.

[71] George Francis Gilman Stanley, *The Birth of Western Canada: A History of the Riel Rebellions* (London, 1936), p. 197.

· IV. HISTORY OF THE AMERICAN FUR TRADE WITH THE BLACKFOOT ·

· HOSTILITY OF BLACKFOOT ·

The first Americans to cross Blackfoot country were the members of the Lewis and Clark expedition in 1806. Through an unfortunate misunderstanding they killed two Piegan Indians. The journals of Lewis and Clark state that two Gros Ventres were killed. However, according to David Thompson, the Piegan went south in 1807 to avenge the deaths of the Piegan killed by Lewis. This was later confirmed by Dr. Clark Wissler, who unequivocally established the fact that it was two Piegan who were killed. It is certain that this episode did not make for friendly feelings toward the whites.

Shortly after the return of the Lewis and Clark expedition, the American fur trade was brought to the southern limits of Blackfoot country by Manuel Lisa, who settled at the junction of the Yellowstone and Big Horn Rivers in 1807–1808.[72] He and his men were unmolested until a member of his party, Coulter, was found in a Crow camp by a Blackfoot war party. Coulter aided the Crow against the attack and killed a number of Blackfoot. The latter now considered the whites as allies of their enemies and treated them accordingly. The next time they met a party of whites, the Blackfoot attacked. In 1810 Lisa built a fort at the mouth of the Big Horn River. It was attacked and destroyed by the Blackfoot and thirty whites were killed.[73]

When the St. Louis–Missouri Fur Company was organized in 1808, it sent out a party of 150 trappers to the rich beaver country at the forks of the Missouri.[74] The Blackfoot considered this an encroachment on their hunting grounds and attacked the party. Again in 1810–1811 trappers were attacked by the Blood and Blackfoot, "who hung about constantly in the neighborhood attacking every party." [75] The trappers now armed themselves and kept up a continual warfare with the Indians. For protection, independent trappers

[72] Hiram M. Chittenden, *The American Fur Trade of the Far West: A History of the Pioneer Trading Posts and Early Fur Companies of the Missouri Valley and the Rocky Mountains, and of the Overland Commerce with Santa Fe,* 3 vols. (New York, 1902), Vol. 1, p. 137. See also *American State Papers,* Vol. 2 (Washington, D.C., 1834), pp. 201–02.

[73] *American State Papers,* Vol. 2, pp. 201–02.

[74] Chittenden, Vol. 1, p. 142.

[75] Chittenden, Vol. 1, p. 330.

traveled with the Nez Perce and Flathead, the traditional enemies of the Blackfoot, thus aggravating the situation.

The Blackfoot found a further powerful incentive to attack the trappers in the promise of rich loot in valuable beaver skins and horses which they speedily and profitably disposed of at the Canadian trading posts. An account of a raid by the Bloods in 1810 near the three forks of the Missouri tells of the variety of goods they carried off: "fine cotton shirts, beaver traps, hats, knives, handkerchiefs, Russia sheeting tents, and a number of bank notes, some signed New York and Trenton Banking Company." [76]

The journals of the Canadian traders reveal that they were aware of the manner in which the Blackfoot had acquired their beaver, for at this time, the Blackfoot still did little beaver trapping of their own. The Missouri River traders attributed much of the Indian hostility to the instigation of the Canadians. However this may be, it is certain that the Blackfoot needed little encouragement, for raiding for loot fitted in well with their own war patterns.

Up to 1831, the Blackfoot successfully prevented the establishment of trading posts in their territory in the United States, and they twice drove out agents of the Missouri Fur Company. It is not clear from the records whether or not the Piegan took part in these raids, but it is probable that they did.[77]

In 1830 Catlin observed, "The Blackfoot are, perhaps, the most powerful tribe on the continent and being sensible of their strength have stubbornly resisted the Traders in their country who have been gradually forming an acquaintance and trying to set up a profitable system of trade. The country abounds with beaver and buffalo and others. The American Fur Co. has established itself and white trappers are rapidly destroying the beaver. The Blackfoot have repeatedly informed the traders of the company that if this persists they will kill the trappers. The company lost 15–20 men. The Blackfoot therefore have been less traded with and less seen by whites and less understood." [78]

[76] Chittenden, Vol. 1, p. 146.

[77] Chittenden, Vol. 1, p. 330.

[78] George Catlin, *Illustrations of the Manners, Customs, and Conditions of the North American Indians* (London, 1842), p. 52. In 1833, John F. A. Sanford, an Indian agent, in a letter to General William Clark, reported several Blackfoot chiefs as saying, "If you will send Traders into our country we will protect them and treat them well; but for your Trappers—never." Quoted in Francis A. Chardon, *Chardon's Journal at Fort Clark*, ed. A. H. Abel (Pierre, S. Dak., 1932), p. 254.

• ESTABLISHMENT OF TRADING POSTS •

In 1831 a group of Piegan Indians, acting as delegates of their people, signed a treaty with Mackenzie, the American trader, who promised them a fort of their own the following year.[79] A fort was finally established in Blackfoot country in 1833 and was called Fort Piegan, for the trade was almost exclusively with the Piegan. This fort was soon burned by a party of Bloods, "who apparently were not aware of the intentions [of the builders]." [80] A year later Fort Mackenzie was built and it continued to operate up to 1844, the longest-lived of the forts.[81]

The setting up of Fort Mackenzie coincided with a great change in the fur trade. Until the 1830's beaver was the most important item in the trade but after that year beaver became scarce. The American Fur Company began an extensive trade in buffalo hides, the most immediate effect of which was to improve their relations with the Blackfoot.

Much of the friendliness which followed was due also to the influence of Alexander Culbertson, agent for the American Fur Company. He had married a Blood woman and had won the complete confidence of the Indians.[82] So long as he was present, there were no hostile incidents, despite the harrowing experience of a deadly smallpox epidemic in 1837. The disease had broken out on the company's steamer when it was about to deliver a load of goods to the fort. About five hundred lodges of Piegan and Blood Indians camped there, awaiting the arrival of the boat. When they were informed by Major Culbertson that the boat must be held up they were displeased and threatened to take it by force. Unable to restrain them, despite warning of the consequences, Culbertson allowed the boat to land its supply.[83] For the next two months no Indian came to trade

[79] Maximilian, Prince of Wied, *Travels in the Interior of North America, 1832–1834*, trans. H. Evans Lloyd, Vols. 22–25, in Reuben Gold Thwaites (ed.), *Early Western Travels, 1746–1846* (New York, 1906), Vol. 24, p. 317.

[80] *Father Point's Journal* (1817), extract reprinted in Chardon, p. 403.

[81] Chardon, p. 403.

[82] James H. Bradley, *Affairs at Fort Benton, 1831–1869*, Contributions of the Montana Historical Society, Vol. 3 (Helena, 1900), p. 233.

[83] Chittenden gives a very different slant on this epidemic. He places the responsibility squarely upon the shoulders of the American Fur Company officials who permitted a Blackfoot Indian to board the steamer at St. Peters at the mouth of the Little Missouri and then go to his people without finding out whether he had the disease. In this way the disease was spread among the Blackfoot. See Chittenden, Vol. 2, p. 626.

and Culbertson went out to locate them. He met a ghastly scene of death; thousands had perished. The disease had spread to Canada and over two-thirds (6,000) of the Blood and Blackfoot had died.[84] "But amid all this misery and depopulation they attached no blame to the whites. They remembered Major Culbertson's remonstrances, and felt they had brought the scourge upon themselves; differing in this respect from the lower Indians who . . . were disposed to sweep the whites out of existence as the authors of their woe." [85]

In 1842 an unfortunate change took place at the fort. Culbertson was called away and the fort was now placed in the hands of Chardon and Harvey, who promptly attacked a band of Bloods. Chardon and Harvey planned to massacre the Indians in revenge for the death of a colored servant. They invited the unsuspecting Blackfoot to trade and fired into them as they arrived, killing and later scalping thirty Indians.[86] In retaliation, the fort was burned and all trading ceased until 1844, when Culbertson was sent back to patch matters up.[87] Culbertson again succeeded in pacifying the Indians and the American Fur Company continued its trade well into the 1870's with but few hostilities.

· V. COMPARISON OF THE FUR TRADE WITH THE BLACKFOOT IN CANADA AND THE UNITED STATES ·

The Canadian fur trade with the Blackfoot had been going on for over sixty years before the first American trading post was built in Blackfoot country. The major part of this period was characterized by an absence of conflict. However, from the start, Blackfoot relations with the whites in the United States were marked by hostility and open conflict. A number of historical factors combined to bring this about.

The first American contact with the Blackfoot came at a most inopportune time. The Blackfoot had just had their first break with the Canadian fur traders in their sixty years of friendly dealings and now looked upon the whites as enemies or allies of enemies. The Piegan

[84] Bradley, p. 225.

[85] Bradley, p. 226.

[86] Accounts differ as to the number of Blackfoot killed. Compare Chittenden, Vol. 1, p. 373, and Vol. 2, pp. 694–95, with Charles Larpenteur, *Forty Years a Fur Trader on the Upper Missouri: The Personal Narrative of Charles Larpenteur, 1833–1872*, ed. Elliott Coues, 2 vols. (New York, 1898), Vol. 1, pp. 144, 216.

[87] Bradley, pp. 233–37.

had warned the traders that all whites found west of the mountains would be treated as enemies in consequence of their arming the Flathead and Kutenai.[88] Undoubtedly they had also meant this to apply to their southern borders. The fact that the first Americans they met were camped with the Crow, who were their enemies, resulted in open hostilities.

More important in explaining the hostility toward the Americans was the policy of the early American fur companies of sending white trappers into Blackfoot country rather than depending upon the Indian supply. The Blackfoot resented this competition of the white trappers and attacked them as trespassers. The Canadian fur companies, on the other hand, established trading posts and encouraged the Indians to trap. Furthermore, a glance at the map will show that without exception the Canadian trading posts were on the outskirts of Blackfoot territory, and therefore the traders never represented a threat in the eyes of the Blackfoot.

The greater harmony in the relations of the Blackfoot with the Canadians, as compared to their relations with the Americans, was due also to the differences in organization, personnel, and administration of the respective trading companies. The American fur trade reflected the rugged individualism and lack of organization of the newly developing capitalist economy of which it was a part. In contrast, the Hudson's Bay Company, with its highly centralized and efficient organization, was part of the long established and smoothly functioning British Empire. The Hudson's Bay Company had years of experience in dealing with Indians and exercised the strictest control over its employees. All Company men were subject to carefully formulated rules governing their personal conduct and their relations with the Indians. The Standing Rules of the Fur Trade summarized the policy of the Company: "40th. That the Indians be treated with kindness and indulgence, and mild and conciliatory means resorted to in order to encourage industry, repress vice, and inculcate morality; that the use of spiritous liquors be gradually discontinued in the very few districts in which it is yet indispensible; and that the Indians be liberally supplied with requisite necessaries, particularly with articles of ammunition, whether they have the means of paying for it or not, and that no gentleman in charge of district or post be at liberty to alter or vary the standards or usual mode of trade with the Indians, except by special permission of the Council." [89]

Although we can discount the tone of altruism in parts of the

[88] Genevieve Murray, *Marias Pass*, Studies in Northwest History, No. 12, State University of Montana (Missoula, 1930), p. 14.

[89] Great Britain, *Parliamentary Papers*, Vol. XV, 1857, Report from the Select Committee on Hudson's Bay Company, Appendix No. 2 (D1), p. 368.

above, nevertheless it contrasts sharply with conditions in the American trade, which had no such clearly formulated policy towards the Indians. The massacre of Blackfoot by irresponsible representatives, such as occurred on the American side under Chardon, could not have happened in Canada.

When the traders came to the Canadian northwest they attempted to deal with the Indians of the Plains in the same manner in which they had dealt with the Indians of the forest. That is, they attempted to turn the Plains Indians to large-scale trapping of beaver and other small game. In this they met with little success. Among the Blackfoot tribes only a few bands of the Piegan responded to the demands of the traders. These were the bands who lived in the foothills of the Rockies and who had always done considerable beaver trapping. The Blood, Siksika, and remaining Piegan refused to turn to beaver trapping. For a long time the fur trade with the Blackfoot therefore consisted only of wolf and fox skins, both of which the Blackfoot had trapped before the coming of the whites. However, with the expansion of the fur trade the Blackfoot tribes were to play an important though different role. The Plains tribes came to be the chief providers of food for the far-flung fur trade, whose numerous posts extended throughout the Woodland area and the Barren Grounds, and along the Churchill, Columbia, and Frazer rivers.[90] The Blackfoot, because of their control of the rich buffalo grounds, became a major source of provisions. The fur traders of the forest regions above the North Saskatchewan depended upon those posts which were supplied with provisions by the Blackfoot and, whenever a shortage of food occurred, sent to them for assistance. The food trade consisted of large quantities of dried and pounded meat, pemmican, backfat, and dried berries.

The Canadian fur trade also provided the Blackfoot with a market for horses, and horses became an important item of trade very early. The fur traders needed horses to transport supplies by land to the outlying posts. Every summer, traders came up the North Saskatchewan from Fort York, their canoes loaded with supplies. They went by water as far as Edmonton, and from this point the supplies were distributed and dispatched by trains of pack horses. For this purpose there were over three hundred horses at Fort Edmonton alone, most of them procured in trade with the Blackfoot.[91] The American fur trade, because it was established at a later period, never provided a

[90] Harold A. Innis, *The Fur Trade in Canada: An Introduction to Canadian Economic History* (New Haven, Conn., 1930), p. 304.

[91] G. M. Grant, *Ocean to Ocean: Sanford Fleming's Expedition Through Canada in 1872* (Toronto, 1873), p. 122.

market for horses or so large a market for food supplies. Their main trade with the Blackfoot was in buffalo robes.

The time difference in the appearance of the Canadian and American fur trade among the Blackfoot had further significance, for the establishment of Fort Piegan in Blackfoot territory coincided roughly with a great change in the fur trade. This was the displacement of the beaver trade by that of buffalo hides, which had its greatest development in the United States. Until the 1830's, beaver was the most important item of trade. The figures for 1805, a typical year, show that the Northwest Fur Company received from all its posts the following:

> 77,500 beaver skins
> 51,250 muskrat
> 40,400 martin
> 1,135 buffalo robes.[92]

The almost complete disappearance of beaver in the early thirties, together with style changes, created a demand for buffalo robes.[93] It is estimated that in the years 1833–1843 the American Fur Company traded 70,000 robes annually, and the Hudson's Bay Company, 10,000. In 1846, Fort Benton was established at the Marias and Missouri rivers to accommodate the large number of buffalo robes offered by the Piegan. This site had been a rendezvous for Indians and traders since 1834, when over 2,000 robes were collected. By 1841 it had risen to 20,000, and from this date until 1870 that was the average number of robes sent annually from Fort Benton.[94] In addition, there was an extensive trade in tongues and tallow. In 1848, the number of buffalo tongues sent to St. Louis had reached 25,000.

The introduction of the steamboat on the Missouri in 1833 gave the American Company a great advantage over its Canadian competitors, who were still relying upon canoes and horses for transportation. Because of the difficulty and expense of transporting the bulky hides, the buffalo trade never reached the proportions in Canada that it did in the United States.

The American Fur Company, because of its advantages in trans-

---

[92] Harold E. Briggs, *Frontiers of the Northwest: A History of the Upper Missouri Valley* (New York, 1910), p. 128.

[93] John Work, *The Journal of John Work, a Chief-Trader of the Hudson's Bay Co., During His Expedition from Vancouver to the Flatheads and Blackfeet of the Pacific Northwest*, ed. William S. Lewis and Paul C. Phillips (Cleveland, 1923), pp. 29–30.

[94] Work, pp. 148–49.

portation, was able to offer higher prices for buffalo skins. The Blackfoot planned their trading practices to fit in with their seasonal movements in such a way as to obtain the maximum prices for their furs. In the summer, they went north to the Saskatchewan, where the returns for their small peltries were highest; in winter they returned to the Marias River, where they traded their buffalo robes with the Americans, who paid better prices.[95]

The differences in the values of the natives and those of the traders were a source of recurring misunderstanding on both the American and Canadian sides. The Blackfoot would not pay for drinks, for they considered this "water" as due them out of ordinary hospitality. Henry wrote, "This is the cause of all our misunderstanding with them. They insist upon our treating them with their favorite liquor."[96] Again, when they gave the trader a horse as a gift, they expected good payment or angrily demanded the return of the horse.[97]

Liquor was sold to the Blackfoot in both Canada and the United States, though at different periods. In Canada, the sale of liquor was greatest from about 1784 to 1821, when the competition between the Hudson's Bay Company and the Northwest Company was fierce. After the amalgamation of the two companies in 1821, liquor was almost entirely eliminated from the trade. It was at this time, however, that the American trading posts were established in Blackfoot country. With their establishment came the liquor trade on a large scale, with its usual disruptive and demoralizing influences.

To recapitulate, a comparison of the American and Canadian fur trade with the Blackfoot shows important differences in policy toward the Indians by the respective trading companies. This resulted in an initial period of hostility toward the American, in contrast to a long period of friendship with the Canadians. The American trade supplied the Blackfoot with a market for buffalo robes, the Canadian trade with a market for provisions, horses, and small pelts. The presence of competing fur companies on both sides of the international line presented the Blackfoot with serious problems of adjustment.

[95] James Doty, "Reports of Mr. James Doty on the Indian Tribes of the Blackfoot Nation," dated Fort Benton, Dec. 28, 1853, in *Reports of Explorations and Surveys to Ascertain the Most Practicable and Economical Route for a Railroad from the Mississippi River to the Pacific Ocean* (Washington, D.C.; U.S. War Department, 1855), pp. 441–45.

[96] Henry and Thompson, Vol. 2, p. 723.

[97] Henry and Thompson, Vol. 2, p. 730.

· COMPARISON OF THE
THREE BLACKFOOT TRIBES ·

In our discussion so far we have not pointed to differences among the three Blackfoot tribes, primarily because the early material does not always mention the specific tribe under discussion. Although little can be found concerning cultural distinctions, the differences in location of the three tribes and their lack of a common history have resulted in some divergences in their relations with other tribes and in their reactions to the whites.

The Blood and Siksika, the two northernmost Blackfoot tribes, were throughout their history more closely united to each other than to the Piegan. This appears to have been true in prewhite times, for the Piegan were the frontier tribe of the westward-moving confederacy, while the Blood and Siksika brought up the rear.

The tribes were united against their common enemies, the Shoshone and the Assiniboine, but each had particular enemies against whom it concentrated its efforts. The Piegan defended the western and southern frontiers from the Kutenai, Flathead, and Nez Perce; the Blood fought the Crow and, together with the Siksika, the Cree.[98] There are accounts of clashes of interest among the three tribes and of separate treaties and alliances.

Such a situation occurred in the early part of the nineteenth century after the hostile western tribes had been armed. The Piegan wished to make peace with the Kutenai, who had become a formidable enemy, but the Blood and Siksika, who were protected by the Piegan territory, which was a buffer between them and the Kutenai, did not agree. The Kutenai refused an agreement with the Piegan because the latter could not speak for the entire nation and could not guarantee against transgression.[99]

Of the three tribes, the Piegan were the most powerful, warlike and numerous. They were held in awe by the others and, according to Thompson, were the leading group. He believed that it would have been more appropriate to speak of the "Piegan Confederacy" than of the "Blackfoot Confederacy." [100]

According to Henry, the Piegan "imagine themselves to be a superior race, braver and more virtuous than their own countrymen whom they always seem to despise for their vicious, treacherous

[98] Bradley, p. 283.
[99] Maximilian, Vol. 24, p. 87.
[100] Thompson, p. 327.

conduct. They are proud and haughty and studiously avoid the company of their allies further than is necessary for their own safety in guarding against their common enemies." [101] This description reflects the esteem which the traders had for the Piegan and is indicative of the manner in which the tribes reacted to the whites. It is worthy of note that the Piegan is the tribe most often mentioned in the journals, again indicating their more intimate relations with the traders. The Blood and Siksika are often described as being insolent, independent, inclined to mischief and murder, and difficult to trade with.[102]

The Canadian trading companies tried to separate the Piegan from the Blood and Siksika by sending them to trade at a different post, fearing that the latter would have an adverse influence upon the Piegan. The American Fur Traders met with the same situation, suffering from the attacks and depredations of the Siksika and Blood while trading peaceably with the Piegan. The traders, therefore, treated the Piegan preferentially, thus encouraging jealousy and discord among the three tribes. This developed to the point of open hostilities on a few occasions, on both sides of the international boundary. Such an incident occurred in the United States in 1830. Mitchell, in charge of Fort Mackenzie, attempted to set an example for the Blood and Siksika by presenting a new uniform and double-barreled gun to a Piegan chief who had been faithful to the "Whites," that is, never traded with the Canadians. The Blood Indians present were offended and spoke loudly of their intentions of killing the Piegan. A few days later the Blood shot a relative of this Piegan chief. The Piegan chiefs immediately used this as an excuse to attack and beat the Bloods. A Piegan sought to win the support of the whites: "Kutonapi . . . stepped forward and made a violent speech, in which he described, in lively colors, the offenses of the Blood Indians against the Whites, and exhorted us to take vengeance for them." [103]

The greater accord of the Piegan with the traders was due to the fact that the Piegan took to large-scale trapping whereas the other two tribes did not. This enabled the Piegan to establish themselves as an important source of beaver for the Americans. The American trader Mackenzie stated, "The Piegan band of the Blackfoot is warmly attached to our interests. They are the beaver hunters of

---

[101] Henry and Thompson, Vol. 2, p. 722.

[102] Henry and Thompson, Vol. 2, p. 530; Chittenden, Vol. 2, p. 853.

[103] Maximilian, Vol. 23, pp. 134–35. In 1810, Henry reported that the Piegan frequently offered to quell the disturbances of the Blood and Siksika. See Henry and Thompson, Vol. 2, p. 530.

their nation. The other bands (tribes) traded robes and provisions principally." [104]

Another difference among the three tribes can be traced to the fur trade. On the American side the trading posts were in the heart of Piegan country. This made for the growth of a half-breed population among the Piegan which has increased up to the present day. In Canada the posts were almost without exception north of Blackfoot country, and the half-breed settlements at Edmonton, for example, consisted mainly of Crees. As a result, the Blackfoot and Blood were less subject to the infiltration of white values and were independent right up to the last.

· VI. EFFECTS OF THE FUR TRADE UPON THE BLACKFOOT ·

If we were to characterize in a word the effects of the fur trade on Blackfoot culture, that word would be "expansion." The key to the understanding of this expansion is the transition from an economy which produced for its own needs to one which produced for an ever-increasing market. Far from breaking down the existing Blackfoot institutions, the fur trade acted as a stimulus to their development. The changes wrought in Blackfoot culture are most discernible in their material culture, social organization, and warfare. Some of the more important points that will be discussed are the increase in the size of tipis, the enlargement of buffalo corrals, the higher standard of living following the introduction of elements of white material culture, the improved means of subsistence, the increase of wealth, the growth of polygyny, and the development of a commercialism which permeated Blackfoot life.

When the fur traders first came to the Blackfoot, the Blackfoot were friendly, but aloof and independent. This was due largely to their economic self-sufficiency. Unlike the Cree, and later the Flathead and Kutenai, who saw in the superior technology of the whites a guarantee against the ever-present threat of starvation and became specialists in trapping, the Blackfoot scorned to turn to trapping. Blackfoot economy, in contrast to that of the tribes to the east and west, never became subservient to that of the whites for its subsistence needs.[105] Duncan M'Gillivray, a clerk of the Northwest Company, put it very well in a passage written in 1794:

[104] Chittenden, Vol. 2, p. 851.

[105] For the contrast with the Plains and Woodland Cree, see Mandelbaum, p. 38.

The inhabitants of the Plains are so advantageously situated that they could live very happily independent of our assistance. They are surrounded with innumerable herds of various kinds of animals, whose flesh affords them excellent nourishment and whose skins defend them from the inclemency of the weather, and they have invented so many means for the destruction of animals that they stand in no need of ammunition to provide a sufficiency for their purposes. It is then our luxuries that attract them to the fort and make us so necessary to their happiness.[106]

With the infiltration of the labor-saving devices of white material culture, and the consequent rise in the standard of living, the "luxuries" soon became necessities, and Blackfoot dependence upon the whites, though on a different level from that of the Cree, was no less real. After a time it was only the poorest households which were without guns, iron axes, kettles, beads, awls, and blankets.

• CHANGES IN MATERIAL CULTURE •

The enlargement of the buffalo corrals and the increase in the size of tipis were a direct result of the fur trade. In order to supply the traders with more buffalo hides, the Blackfoot enlarged the corrals and pounds by adding appendages in the following manner:[107]

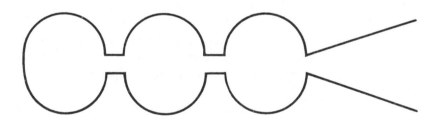

It is possible to discern an increase in the size of tipis at two points in Blackfoot history. The first occurred a short time after the introduction of the horse. Although we have no description of Blackfoot tipis in prehorse days, we can infer the limits of their size from the fact that the maximum load that could be carried by the dog travois was between forty and fifty pounds. Since the weight of a buffalo

[106] Mandelbaum, p. 47.

[107] Jane Richardson, "Blackfoot Field Notes," ms. Later published in L. M. Hanks, Jr., and Jane Richardson, *Observations on Northern Blackfoot Kinship.* Monographs of the American Ethnological Society, Vol. IX (New York, 1945).

hide was well over fifty pounds, a six- to eight-skin tipi would probably tax their transportation facilities to the limit. Such a tipi could accommodate between six and eight persons. However, in the earliest reference to Blackfoot tipis found in Henday (1754) or about twenty years after their acquisition of horses, Henday writes that the "leaders" tent in a camp of two hundred was "large enough to contain 50 persons." [108] From this we can infer that the size of tipis had increased to a point that would have been impossible without the improved means of transportation supplied by the horse. I think we can assume that the tipi mentioned by Henday represented the maximum size for this period and that tipis of this size were constructed only by well-to-do chiefs.

A further increase in the size of tipis occurred in the 1830's, and was related to the expansion of the fur trade and the growth of polygyny among the Blackfoot. The average tipi was made of from six to twelve skins and accommodated from six to ten people. However, in the case of wealthy individuals with large families, tipis were made of eighteen to twenty skins. There were a few made of as many as forty skins which could accommodate close to a hundred persons.[109] These huge tipis contained three to four fireplaces. The skins were sewn together in as many as four strips, and when the lodge was set up, the skins were pinned together.[110] This method of construction enabled the women to set up the tipi and to load it onto pack horses.

Probably the first native item of material culture to fall into disuse following the coming of the whites was pottery. In 1774, Cocking found pottery in use among the Blackfoot and wrote that it was of their own manufacture.[111] It is significant that the Blackfoot were still using pottery at this time, almost fifty years after they had obtained their first horses. Soon after 1774, trading posts were established within easy reach of the Blackfoot, who were now supplied with kettles by the traders. When Thompson visited the Piegan in 1787 and again in 1800, he did not mention the presence of pottery, nor is it ever mentioned in the later literature. The disappearance of pottery must therefore be primarily related to the introduction of a superior substitute by the whites which could be transported without fear of breaking, and only secondarily to the greater mobility consequent to their adoption of the horse. However, for a long time

[108] Hendry, p. 337.

[109] Bradley says that Culbertson saw such a tipi about 1810.

[110] George B. Grinnell, *Blackfoot Lodge Tales: The Story of a Prairie People* (New York, 1912), p. 187.

[111] Cocking, p. 111.

the infiltration of kettles and other items was slow. In 1810 Henry wrote that "kettles are scarce," [112] but by 1833, we learn from Culbertson's journal that there were about "one gun, an axe, a kettle, and ten knives to a lodge" and that "tobacco was extremely precious and eagerly sought for." [113]

Tobacco was another item for which the Blackfoot early became dependent upon the whites. Thompson says, "Until the year 1800 they had always raised tobacco in proportion to their own wants. When they became acquainted with the tobacco . . . brought by the traders which they found so superior to their own, they gradually left off planting it." [114] Woven rabbit-skin robes and basketry are two other items that appear to have been used by the Blackfoot at one time. Reference to the former is made by Teit[115] and is based on Flathead tradition to the effect that the Flathead traded rabbit-skin robes to the Blackfoot in prehorse days. That the Blackfoot used basketry is more certain, for in 1754 Henry tells us that the Blackfoot he visited used "baskets of a species of bent" in which they served buffalo meat.[116]

Native clothing persisted until the reserve period and later, but from the beginning the Blackfoot adopted the clothes of the whites, which they regarded as superior to their own. As early as 1787, Thompson, writing of the Piegan, remarked that in wet weather leather injures the constitution and added, "Of this the natives appear sensible, for all those who have it in their power buy woolen clothing." [117] Culbertson, in about 1833, noted that the women were more conservative in this respect and took to cotton and woolen clothing much later than the men.[118]

Aside from guns, ammunition, powder, awls, iron, beads, and the items mentioned above, the Blackfoot required little from the traders. As late as 1855, accounts show that they were unfamiliar with white man's food and did not know how to prepare even the most common varieties. When the Blackfoot had convened to make a treaty with the American government and were given gifts of foodstuffs, "they threw the flour into the air to watch it drift in slufting streams, men emptied sugar into a stream, and as it dissolved drank of the sweetened water until they could drink no more. And when

---

[112] Henry and Thompson, Vol. 2, p. 721.

[113] Bradley, p. 256.

[114] Thompson, p. 365.

[115] Teit, p. 318.

[116] Hendry, p. 338.

[117] Thompson, p. 353.

[118] Bradley, p. 262.

they cooked the rice as they were accustomed to cook the roots, no camp had kettles enough to hold the startling quantities." [119]

In the mythology that refers to the prehorse days, the food quest looms as a serious problem. The people frequently starve and have difficulty in locating and corraling the buffalo. Yet this probably refers only to periods of abnormal scarcity, for there is reason to believe that even in prehorse times the efficiency of Blackfoot techniques of hunting and food preservation furnished an ample food supply for even large social groups.[120] The supply varied with the season. In the summer, fresh meat was to be had in abundance and the surplus was dried and stored for the winter. The bands were almost completely immobilized in the winter by the snow and storms, and buffalo hunting was well-nigh impossible. Even when snow did not cover the ground, it was difficult to locate and follow the roaming herds of buffalo. The horse became an invaluable aid in scouting, and allowed entire bands to follow the movements of the herds. In addition the horse was used as a pack animal. Formerly, when hunting parties went on foot, they were limited in the amount of meat they could carry back to camp. It was the practice to take only the best cuts and leave the remaining meat to decay. The horse made it possible to transport more meat and hides back to camp. The horse therefore insured a larger and more regular food supply, lessening the contrasts between periods of plenty and periods of scarcity. However, it was the fur trade which allowed the Blackfoot to utilize the productive capacities of the horse to the full, for we have seen that the fur trade provided a market for dried provisions, buffalo hides, and horses.

[119] Murray, p. 34.

[120] Kroeber (*Natural and Cultural Areas*, p. 77) asks, "Could any good sized group live permanently off the bison on the open Plains while they and their dogs were dragging their dwellings, furniture, provisions, and children? . . . How could several thousand people have congregated in one spot to hold a four or eight days' Sun Dance?" To these questions the historical material gives a positive answer. An account of a prehorse war party (Thompson, pp. 328–29) tells of 350 Piegan warriors fighting the Shoshone. At the conservative estimate of one warrior to every five persons, we would have a group of about 1,500 people gathered in one spot for a number of days. This gives a picture differing decidedly from the speculative reconstructions of prehorse Plains conditions with their atomistic social groups, "miserably poor and chronically hungry" (Kroeber, *Natural and Cultural Areas*, pp. 76–77).

• MARRIAGE •

It is well to recall that over 20,000 robes were annually gathered at Fort Benton. Since the Blackfoot, and especially the Piegan, were the principal traders at Fort Benton, we can gauge the effects of this trade on their lives. The increased burden of preparing provisions and tanning put new demands on female labor and increased the economic importance of women. Polygyny grew to an extent unprecedented for the Plains.

From the journals of those who visited the Blackfoot at various intervals in the history of the fur trade, we can piece together a picture of this growth of polygyny. In 1787 Thompson observed that three or four wives were not uncommon, and that the greatest number any man had was six.[121] From his account we conclude that most men had only one or two wives. When Thompson returned in 1800, he reported no change. Alexander Henry, the younger, who was with the Blackfoot in 1810, reported six or seven wives as the greatest number.[122] Maximilian, writing in the 1830's, mentions eight wives in the case of wealthy chiefs.[123] Unfortunately, there is a great gap in the historical information on this subject until about 1870. However, tracing back to 1840 a number of genealogies gathered from informants, we have found further evidence of this steady increase of wives. Grinnell, writing of approximately the same period (1840) stated, "It was a very poor man who did not have three wives. Many had six, eight, and some even more than a dozen; I have heard of one who had sixteen." [124] Denny, a captain in the first contingent of the Northwest Mounted Police in 1874 and later an Indian agent for the Blackfoot, wrote, "I have known Blackfoot with as many as twenty or even thirty women so acquired (by purchase)." [125] These numbers appear to be extreme but they were borne out by information that I gathered in the field. One informant told of her great-grandfather, Chief Many Horses, who in about 1855 had twenty wives. Our material therefore suggests that the sharpest spurt in the increase in wives occurred after 1833, a period which coincides with the increase in the buffalo-hide trade both in Canada and the United States.[126]

[121] Thompson, p. 347.

[122] Henry and Thompson, Vol. 2, p. 526.

[123] Maximilian, Vol. 23, p. 110.

[124] Grinnell, p. 218.

[125] Sir Cecil Edward Denny, *The Law Marches West* (Toronto, 1939), p. 51.
[126] There was a great disproportion in the sex ratio because of the increased casualties in warfare. In 1847 Father Point estimated that between two-thirds

The possession of a large number of wives was a source of wealth and was therefore cherished by the Blackfoot. The missionaries learned this when they attempted to suppress polygyny. A traveler, in his account of the region, quotes a Blackfoot chief, " 'Tell the priest . . . that if he wishes to do anything with my people he must no longer order them to put away their wives. I have eight all of whom I love, and all have children by me—Which am I to keep and which to put away?' " The traveler James Carnegie, Earl of Southesk, continues, "This chief however injured the moral force of his remarks by going on to say that his eight wives could dress a hundred and fifty skins in the year whereas a single wife could only dress ten, supposing that she was always well, and that such a loss was not to be thought of." [127]

Since wives had to be paid for in horses, we must briefly consider the relation of this expansion in polygyny to the accumulation of horses and the growth of herding. We know that the Blackfoot first obtained their horses from the Shoshone in 1730. When Henday visited the Piegan in 1754, he described them as mounted but made no mention of herds.[128] This is also true of Cocking's description of the Blackfoot in 1774.[129] In 1787 Thompson describes Blackfoot horses, and though he does not specifically mention herding, he states that he saw a group of thirty horses and a dozen mules at the camp at which he was staying.[130] In 1800 Thompson was again with the Blackfoot, but he recorded nothing new on this matter. In 1808, however, Alexander Henry, the younger, writes, "Some of the Blackfoot own forty to fifty horses. But the Piegan have by far the greatest numbers. I heard of one man who owns three hundred." [131] By 1833 we find that Maximilian reports as many as four to five thousand horses owned by one wealthy Piegan chief.[132] Although this evidence is scanty, it certainly is suggestive of an increase in the size of herds. What is most significant for our purposes is that by 1833, the time when the large markets for tanned robes in the States first developed, there already existed an accumulation of horses that made

---

and three-quarters of the adult population were women. See *Life, Letters, and Travels of Father Pierre Jean de Smet,* ed. H. M. Chittenden and A. T. Richardson, 4 vols. (New York, 1905), Vol. 3, p. 952.

[127] James Carnegie, Earl of Southesk, *Saskatchewan and the Rocky Mountains* (Edinburgh, 1875), p. 155.

[128] Hendry, pp. 337–38.

[129] Cocking, p. 111.

[130] Thompson, p. 371.

[131] Henry and Thompson, Vol. 1, p. 300.

[132] Maximilian, Vol. 23, p. 121.

possible the ensuing expansion of polygyny. This expansion in turn perpetuated and intensified the social gradations that already existed, for men with large herds were the ones who could purchase many wives and in the exchange could thereby transform idle capital (surplus horses) into productive capital (women).

Following the growth of polygyny and the increasing importance of the bride price in horses, we find that the age at which marriages occurred was also altered. There was a tendency for girls to marry at a younger age and for men to marry at a later age. In 1787 Thompson reported that girls usually married between sixteen and eighteen, and men at twenty-two or somewhat later.[133] In 1885, Rev. Wilson's informants told him that girls normally married at twelve.[134] Our own informants, speaking of the period of the latter half of the nineteenth century, placed the age of marriage for girls between ten and sixteen and that of men rarely at less than thirty-five. It is during this period that we get the first cases of child marriage. Fathers now wished to marry off their daughters as early as possible in order to realize the bride price. On the other hand, men were not chosen as sons-in-law until they had accumulated sufficient property and had acquired good reputations as warriors or hunters.

The increase in the number of wives brought greater friction within the household. The effect of the sororate in eliminating hostilities diminished and at the same time the contrasts between the status of upper and lower wives were intensified. The native term for a wife lower than third or fourth means slave wife, which accurately describes the status of wives in that position. Lower wives performed the most difficult tasks, rarely put up Sun Dances, were most often beaten and most often suspected of adultery.

• SOCIAL ORGANIZATION •

The fur trade stimulated intertribal intercourse. Tribes that had little contact with each other met at trading posts, with the result that much borrowing and spreading of culture elements occurred. A case in point is the borrowing of age grade societies by the Blackfoot from some of the village tribes to the south.

The historical material offers little in the way of positive evidence for the age of these societies among the Blackfoot. If the widespread distribution of such societies in the Plains is taken as a criterion of age, then the existence of a rudimentary system of age grades is very

[133] Thompson, p. 350.

[134] R. N. Wilson, "Report on the Blackfoot Tribes," *Report of the 57th Meeting of the British Association for the Advancement of Science, 1887* (London, 1888), p. 192.

old among the Blackfoot and probably prewhite. The fact that Blackfoot mythology refers to four basic age grades in a tale of the early days may be significant, depending upon the degree of historicity we grant to their mythology. Some Blackfoot tales are remarkable for their historical accuracy. For example, the tales which tell of their obtaining horses from the Shoshone to the west and guns from the Cree to the east are both verified by historical material.

Henday's account of 1754 suggests some policing organization, for he remarks upon the excellent discipline in a camp of two hundred Piegan tipis.[135] Thompson in 1787 is the first specifically to mention a policing group. He writes of "soldiers"—young men, married or about to be married—who keep peace and order in camp and prevent gambling disputes.[136] Thompson knew the Piegan well, and that he said nothing more of societies is significant negative evidence. Our first description of Blackfoot societies as we know them was written by Maximilian in 1833. He describes a fully developed and flourishing system of age grades and their associated rituals.[137] Maximilian remarked that the Blackfoot age grades were almost identical with those of the Siouan tribes to the south.

Kroeber[138] and Lowie[139] have shown that there is greater similarity between certain Blackfoot societies and those of the village tribes, the Mandan and Hidatsa, than between Blackfoot and Crow and Assiniboine. How are we to account for these similarities? There are at least two alternative explanations. Either these similarities are due to borrowing from the south through intermediary tribes, or, as seems more probable, they were borrowed directly. Our knowledge of early tribal locations for our area shows that the Blackfoot had no contact at all with the village tribes. The first contacts in the historical period as shown by the literature and the tradition of the tribes themselves occurred in the 1820's and 1830's, when the American Fur Company established trading posts frequented by both the Mandan and Hidatsa and the Blackfoot. It is therefore suggested that the increase in the number of age societies took place at a relatively late period, probably in the late 1820's or early 1830's. This development would therefore coincide with the period in which the

---

[135] Hendry, p. 337.

[136] Thompson, p. 358.

[137] Maximilian, Vol. 23, pp. 116–17.

[138] Alfred L. Kroeber, *The Ceremonial Organization of the Plains Indians of North America* (Quebec: Congrès International des Américanistes, 1907), p. 57.

[139] Robert H. Lowie, *Plains Indian Age-Societies*, American Museum of Natural History, Anthropological Papers, Vol. 11, Part 13 (New York, 1916), pp. 930, 938.

expansion of polygyny and herding occurred. The borrowing of age grades at this time is understandable in that they were an ideal mechanism for expressing and channeling the vertical mobility which came with the increase in wealth.

Of great significance was the effect of the fur trade on the authority of the chiefs. This varied at different periods in the history of the fur trade, depending upon whether monopoly or competition prevailed. In periods of monopoly the fur trade had a positive effect; that is, it increased the prestige and authority of the chiefs. In periods of competition it had a disruptive effect; that is, it weakened the authority of the chiefs. The Hudson's Bay Company had had a well-established trade with the Blackfoot. It had made it a matter of policy to deal only with the chiefs and headmen and had conferred many honors upon them (medals, chief's coats, etc.) to enhance their authority over their followers. Since all trading with the whites had to be carried on through the chiefs and headmen, it gave the latter a monopoly of white trading goods. With the increase in competition these conditions were altered. In order to gain a foothold, the competitors of the Hudson's Bay Company brought their wares to the very tipi doors of the Indians and made their appeal to the younger men. The result of this policy is stated by Henry, the younger: "It is lamentable that the natives in general, in this country, have lost that respect they formerly had for their chiefs. The principal cause of this is the different petty co-partnerships which of late have invaded this country from Canada; the consequences are now serious to us as the natives have now been taught to despise the council of their elders. . . ." [140]

The competition between the fur companies was accompanied by sharp trading practices which the Blackfoot soon learned themselves. Franklin, writing from Fort Carlton where he met some Blackfoot in 1819, said, "The mode of carrying on the trade (competition) is also productive of an increasing deterioration of the character of the Indians and will probably ultimately prove destructive of the fur trade itself. Indeed, the evil has already in part recoiled upon the traders, for the Indians long deceived have become deceivers in turn, and not infrequently after having incurred a heavy debt at one post, move to another, to play the same game." [141]

Another fur trader remarked that the authority of the elders had diminished to the point where fathers could no longer control the produce of their own sons: "They are all remarkably proud of being great men but still they have little or no influence over the others.

[140] Henry and Thompson, Vol. 2, p. 550.

[141] John Franklin, *Narrative of a Journey to the Shores of the Polar Seas, in the Years 1819–20–21–22,* 2 vols. (London, 1824), Vol. 1, pp. 130–31.

. . . After making the father a chief, you are sometimes obliged to do the same with his son in order to secure his hunt, for the former has not the power to secure it for you." [142]

The above suggests that the instability of bands in the middle of the nineteenth century, pointed out by Collier,[143] may have been, at least in part, related to the competitive fur trade, which undermined the chiefs' monopoly of the highly valued white trade goods. Once the young men did not have to depend upon their chiefs and elders for their liquor, for example, one of the economic bases of the chiefs' authority disappeared. The prestige and authority of a chief were therefore dependent upon his generosity, and Collier considers the lack of generosity on the part of a chief as one of the most important causes for a man's changing his band membership.

• THE BLACKFOOT AS TRADERS •

The Blackfoot were unusually shrewd in their trade with the whites and with other Indian tribes. They took advantage of the competition between the Hudson's Bay Company and the Pedlars, and later between the Hudson's Bay Company and the Northwest Company by demanding higher prices and better liquor. In return for horses and provisions the Blackfoot received arms, ammunition, traps, axes, kettles, awls, strouds, blankets, chiefs' coats, and liquor. The prices paid the Indians for provisions varied with the scarcity or abundance of game near the forts: "Generally they receive 20 balls and powder for all the flesh of a buffalo cow, or even less when the animals are numerous; but as many as 40 charges for a gun are paid them when the buffalo are at a distance." [144] The Blackfoot, with remarkable commercial perspicacity, were quick to take advantage of this and created an artificial scarcity by setting fire to the prairie in the neighborhood of the forts. Duncan M'Gillivray, writing from Fort George on the North Saskatchewan in 1794, stated, "The Plains around us are all on fire—The Indians (Blackfoot) often make use of this method to frighten away the animals in order to enhance the value of their own provisions." [145]

The journals of the traders give us an interesting picture of some other aspects of the trade with the Blackfoot. Of the Indians' behav-

[142] L. R. Masson, *Les bourgeois de la compagnie au Nord Ouest: récits de voyages, lettres et rapports, inédits relatifs au Nord-Ouest,* 2 vols. (Quebec, 1889–90), Vol. 2, p. 273.

[143] John Collier, "Blackfoot Field Notes," ms. Later published in *The Indians of the Americas* (New York, 1947).

[144] Maximilian, Vol. 23, p. 93.

[145] M'Gillivray, p. 46.

ior at the forts, Henry, the younger, wrote (1810): "They are the most arrant beggars I ever saw; refusing them an article is to no purpose; they plague me as long as they can get within hearing. Refuse them an awl, they ask for a gun. . . ." [146] And also: "They are notorious thieves; when we hear of a band coming in every piece of iron or other European article that can be carried off must be shut up." [147] They are also described as great bargainers. M'Gillivray says "I have seen one of this tribe employ ½ hour in bartering a dozen wolves and twice as many Depouilles (fat on the ribs and back) and so unreasonable as to demand a Gun, Pistol, or any other article that attracted his attention for one Skin. . . ." [148] Maximilian notes this in another connection: "The Crows in their visits and negotiations presented the Blackfeet with valuable articles, costly feather caps, shields, horses, etc. but received nothing at all when they came to the latter, by which all the Indian nations are incensed against the Blackfeet." [149]

The unusual shrewdness of the Blackfoot in their trade with the whites, their sharp bargaining, their disregard of tradition in not giving return gifts to the Crow, and the firing of the prairie to raise the price of meat were, according to the fur traders, uniquely Blackfoot and must be attributed, at least in part, to the fact that they were subject to a competitive fur trade which made good businessmen of them.

• RELIGION •

This commercialism of the Blackfoot was not limited to their trading practices but became characteristic of many aspects of their institutions. This was especially apparent in the buying and selling of [ritual] bundles. Religious bundles such as the Medicine Pipe bundle, Beaver bundle, and Sun Dance bundle were bought by an individual, usually in fulfillment of a vow made in time of misfortune. Although the bundle transfer was part of a religious ceremony, the interest of the buyer, the seller, and the community was centered upon the property exchanges involved. To sell at a high price and to buy at a low price was a major objective in most bundle transfers. The buying of bundles was frequently a profitable investment, for the bundle owners received fees for the religious services they rendered to the community. Finally, some individuals bought bundles

[146] Henry and Thompson, Vol. 2, p. 526.
[147] Henry and Thompson, Vol. 2, p. 544.
[148] M'Gillivray, p. 46.
[149] Maximilian, Vol. 23, p. 161.

as an investment for prestige, since such wealth could be displayed.

The above picture of bundle transfers applies only to the latter part of the nineteenth century. Earlier, it appears that the number of bundle transfers was less frequent and the property exchanged much smaller. In a discussion of Blackfoot medicine bundles in 1833, Culbertson says, "They might be transferred but the owners were seldom willing to surrender the dignity they conferred." [150] This suggests a very different condition from the frequent buying and selling during the 1850's–1880's. Culbertson tells us that a bundle was valued at nine horses.[151] This, too, is far below the later bundle prices of thirty to sixty horses.

Judging from our more complete information of the reserve period, there seems to be a direct relation between the fluidity of bundle transfers and the price of bundles on the one hand, and the number of horses on the other. Thus, with the falling off in the number of horses on the North Piegan reserve following the depression of 1929, the bundle transfers practically came to a standstill and there was a sharp fall in the prices paid for them.

Our material therefore suggests that the greater fluidity in bundle transfers is related to the expansion in Blackfoot economy and the increase in wealth that we have already noted. We have seen that the increase in the size of herds and the growth of polygyny occurred in the 1830's and thereafter. It is significant that the first mention in the literature of medicine bundles and the fact that they were sold for horses also occurs in this period (1833).[152]

This raises the question of the age of Blackfoot medicine bundles. When Thompson visited the Piegan in 1787 he made no mention of bundles and specifically observed that medicine bags were absent. It may be assumed that had bundles been present Thompson would have mentioned them because of their resemblance to medicine bags. The following passage from Thompson's journal gives an interesting account of medicine pipes, which were probably the precursors of the medicine pipe bundle.

> The natives of the forest pride themselves on their Medicine bags, which are generally well stocked with a variety of simples which they gather from the woods and banks of the Lakes and Rivers, and with the virtues of which they are somewhat acquainted. The Indians of the Plains had none of these. . . . But these people must also have something to which they can attach somewhat of a supernatural character for religious purposes; and for this purpose they have adopted

[150] Bradley, p. 265.
[151] Bradley, p. 265.
[152] Bradley, p. 265.

the Red Pipe, and Pipe Stem, which seems to have been such from old times. . . . For a medicine pipe there are certain ceremonies to be gone through and a woman is not allowed to touch a medicine pipe . . . and their long pipe stems are equally sacred. These are of three to more than four feet in length, and about three to five inches in girth and well polished. Each respectable man has from three to four of these pipes which are tied together when not in use and hung on a tree; on removing from place to place the owner slings them over his back and at the encampment again hangs them up.[153]

The statement that a woman is not allowed to touch a medicine pipe makes it quite clear that he is not referring to the medicine pipe bundle, for in the case of the latter, husband and wife were the normal ritual unit. Thompson's statement about the absence of medicine bags is significant, for in 1833 Catlin gives a detailed description of Blackfoot otterskin medicine bags.[154]

Although this evidence is not sufficient to determine the age of medicine bundles among the Blackfoot, it at least suggests as one possibility that the bundle complex came in between 1787 and 1833. In any case we believe that the commercialism in bundle transfers which sets the Blackfoot apart from other Plains groups developed in the period after 1830.

• CHANGES IN WARFARE •

Probably there have been no changes in any aspect of aboriginal culture greater than those which have occurred in warfare. These changes were brought about by the introduction of the horse, gun, and fur trade on the northern Plains.

It must be pointed out here that our conclusions about the Blackfoot are at variance with those made in Smith's intensive study of Plains warfare, and suggests that the problem of the effect of the horse and gun on the Plains may profitably be re-examined. Dr. Smith writes, "With due consideration to their cultural importance (horse and gun) there is however, no conclusive evidence that they revolutionized war procedures. Apparently, their effect was not radically to change the existing war complexes, but to accelerate the momentum of warfare."[155]

This conclusion is based on a survey of the distribution and varieties of war honors, methods of counting coup, scalping, and motives of war on the Plains, without due regard to time perspective and diffusion. The author's "war complex," which is a static picture of

[153] Thompson, pp. 365–66.
[154] Catlin, p. 36.
[155] Smith, p. 433.

nineteenth-century Plains warfare, assumes a degree of stability and integration of the above elements which seems unwarranted. In view of the nonhistorical approach, it is not surprising that no "evidence" of vital changes was found. It is our purpose to show on the basis of the historical documents the nature of the changes in the motives, methods, and organization of Blackfoot warfare.

· EARLY WARFARE ·

In one of the most dramatic accounts in the literature, we are treated to a description of a prehorse battle between the Piegan and the Shoshone given to David Thompson in 1787 by an old Piegan chief, Saukamappee. Saukamappee was a Cree by birth, and as a boy of sixteen accompanied a party of twenty men led by his father to aid the Piegan against the Shoshone.

Our weapons was a Lance, mostly pointed with iron, some few of stone, a Bow and a quiver of Arrows; the Bows were of Larch, the length came to the chin; the quiver had about fifty arrows, of which ten had iron points, the others were headed with stone. He carried his knife on his breast and his axe in his belt. Such was my fathers' weapons, and those with him had much the same weapons. I had a Bow and Arrows and a knife, of which I was very proud. We came to the Peeagans and their allies. They were camped in the Plains on the left bank of the River (the north side) and were a great many. We were feasted, a great war tent was made, and a few days passed in speeches, feasting and dancing. A war chief was elected by the chiefs, and got ready to march. Our spies had been out and had seen a large camp of the Snake Indians on the Plains of the Eagle Hill, and we had to cross the river in canoes, and on rafts, which we carefully secured for our retreat. When we had crossed and numbered our men, we were about 350 warriors (this he showed by counting every finger to be ten, and holding up both hands three times and then one hand) they had their scouts out, and came to meet us. Both parties made a great show of their numbers, and I thought that they were more numerous than ourselves.

After some singing and dancing, they sat down on the ground and placed their large shields before them, which covered them. We did the same but our shields were not so many, and some of our shields had to shelter two men. Theirs were all placed touching each other; their Bows were not so long as ours, but of better wood, and the back covered with the sinews of the Bisons which made them very elastic, and their arrows went a long way and whizzed about us as balls do from guns. They were all headed with a sharp smooth black stone (flint) which broke when it struck anything. Our headed arrows did not go through their shield, but stuck in them; on both sides several were wounded, but none lay on the ground; and night put an end to the battle without a scalp being taken on either side, and in those days such was the result, unless one party was more numerous than the other.[156]

We can only speculate on the degree to which this battle was typical of prehorse warfare. The points to be noted here are: (1) The weapons consisted of the lance and bows and arrows, both iron and stone tipped. (2) The shields were effective protection against even iron-tipped arrows and were used to make a temporary wall of shelter between the warriors of the two sides. (3) There were no casualties, largely because of the use of the shield.

After a few years had passed, Piegan messengers again came to the Cree for aid. The account of Saukamappee continues:

> By this time the affairs of both parties had much changed; we had more guns and iron-headed arrows than before; but our enemies the Snake Indians and their allies had Misstutim (Big Dogs, that is, Horses) on which they rode, swift as the Deer, on which they dashed at the Peeagans, and with their stone Pukamoggan knocked them on the head, and they thus lost several of their best men. This news we did not well comprehend and it alarmed us, for we had no idea of horses and could not make out what they were. Only three of us went. . . . When we came to our allies, the great War Tent (was made) with speeches, feasting and dances, as before; and when the War Chief had viewed us all it was found between us and the Stone Indians we had ten guns and each of us about thirty balls, and powder for the war, and we were considered the strength of the battle. After a few days march our scouts brought us word that the enemy was near in a large war party, but had no horses with them, for at that time they had very few of them. When we came to meet each other, as usual, each displayed their numbers, weapons, and shields, in all of which they were superior to us, except our guns which were not shown, but kept in their leathern cases, and if we had shown them, they would have taken them for long clubs. For a long time they held us in suspense; a tall chief was forming a small party to make an attack on our center, and the others to enter into combat with those opposite to them; We prepared for the battle the best we could. Those of us who had guns stood in the front line, and each of us had two balls in his mouth, and a load of powder in his left hand to reload.
>
> We noticed they had a great many short stone clubs for close combat, which is a dangerous weapon, and had they made a bold attack on us, we must have been defeated, as they were more numerous and better armed than we were, for we could have fired our guns no more than twice; and were at a loss what to do on the wide Plain, and each chief encouraged his men to stand firm. Our eyes were all on the

[156] Thompson, pp. 328–29.

tall chief and his motions, which appeared to be contrary to the advice of several old chiefs, all this time we were about the strong flight of an arrow from each other. At length the tall chief retired and they formed their long usual line by placing their shields on the ground to touch each other, the shield having a breadth of full three feet or more. We sat down opposite to them and most of us waited for the night to make a hasty retreat. The War Chief was close to us anxious to see the effect of our guns. The lines were too far asunder for us to make a sure shot, and we requested him to close the lines to about sixty yards, which was gradually done, and lying flat on the ground behind the shields, we watched our opportunity when they drew their bows to shoot at us, their bodies were then exposed, and each of us, as opportunity offered, fired with deadly aim, and either killed, or severely wounded, every one we aimed at.

The War Chief was highly pleased, and the Snake Indians finding so many killed and wounded kept themselves behind their shields; the war chief then desired we should spread ourselves by two's throughout the line, which we did, and our shots caused consternation and dismay along their whole line. The battle had begun about Noon, and the Sun was not yet half down when we perceived that some of them had crawled away from their shields, and were taking to flight. The War Chief seeing this, went along the line and spoke to every Chief, to keep his men ready for a charge of the whole line of the enemy, of which he would give the signal; this was done by himself stepping in front with a spear, and calling on them to follow him as he rushed on their line, and in an instant the whole of us followed him; the greater part of the enemy took to flight, but some fought bravely and we lost more than ten killed and many wounded; Part of us pursued and killed a few, but the chase had soon to be given over, for at the body of every Snake Indian killed, there were five to six of us trying to get his scalp, or part of his clothing, his weapons, or something as a trophy of the battle.[157]

Here we have an account of the Piegan's first view of horses, which was from the unfortunate view of infantry unable to cope with the attacks of Shoshone cavalry. The guns brought by the Cree, however, more than offset the Shoshone advantage. We are also given a detailed picture of the organization of the war party. The large body of over 350 warriors was grouped into small units, probably the band groupings, under the direction of their respective chiefs, who in turn were led by the decisions of the war chief. The selection of a war chief by all the bands is in contrast to later procedure, as is the elaborate feasting, singing, and dancing which took place in the preliminary ceremonies and even on the field of battle. The line-up of fighters on both sides, the large size of the war party, and the bold show of numbers are also to be noted.

[157] Thompson, pp. 330–32.

The great emphasis on numbers in this account brings us to one of the most important differences between aboriginal Blackfoot warfare and Blackfoot warfare of the nineteenth century. Before the gun and horse, a simple difference in numbers might well decide the outcome of the battle. Large war parties were therefore essential. This necessitated band co-operation and made war a tribal affair. At the same time it called for close co-operation between individuals on the battlefield, for their strength in numbers depended upon unified action. With the introduction of the horse and gun, all this changed. As we have seen, the few armed Cree and Assiniboine were now considered "the strength of the battle." It is this new importance of equipment as over against men (numbers) that distinguishes the "primitive" Blackfoot warfare from that of the later period.

• MOTIVES •

Economic motives were not lacking in early Blackfoot warfare but they differed from those of later years. They were, principally, the defense and expansion of tribal hunting grounds and the capture of women. Women were necessary to strengthen the tribe, both by their own numbers and as child-bearers. This was a vital consideration, and had great implications for survival value—a point frequently appearing in the mythology. Captive women were therefore usually married and adopted into the family. The relatively few casualties in warfare must have resulted in a much more even proportion between the sexes. The almost three to one preponderance of women over men which was a "normal" condition in the nineteenth century did not exist in the days before the horse and gun.

After the coming of the whites, the capture of women received a further impetus and took on new significance, as loot—women captives could be sold to the traders. Umfreville (1790) writes: "In these war excursions many female slaves were taken, who are sold to the Canadian traders, and taken down to Canada. . . . None are spared but young girls, who are taken captive and sold to the Canadian traders. . . ." [158] As early as 1774, Cocking mentions the exchange of two young girl captives between the Blackfoot and the trading Indians (Cree), who acted as middlemen for the Hudson's Bay Company.[159] I have not been able to determine the extent of this trade, but the material suggests that it was of some importance.

After 1830, women captives were no longer sold or traded. They were now valued by the Blackfoot as an additional labor supply to

[158] Edward Umfreville, *The Present State of Hudson's Bay* (London, 1790), pp. 177, 188.
[159] Cocking, p. 110.

meet the new needs of tanning hides and preparing provisions for the enormous market provided by the fur trade. Here again, the old importance of women in terms of numbers was overshadowed by their new importance as aids in the acquisition of the new equipment (such as guns and ammunition) that had become so necessary to Blackfoot life.

Loot as an objective of prehorse war was restricted to weapons, leather armor, tools, and other small articles. These objects had usefulness but were of limited economic value, and in a sense fell into the category of war trophies.

Another motive for war was the desire for scalps and the prestige connected with scalp-taking. Early in the eighteenth century an old Piegan chief tells us, "We were fond of war, even our women flattered us to war, and nothing was thought of but scalps for dancing and singing." [160] Warfare had little of the commercialism of later years, but was intimately tied up with religious motives which later almost completely disappeared.

An interesting aspect of this is found in Thompson, in Saukamappee's recounting of a theological discussion concerning questions of scalping and the use of the soul of a slain enemy. A successful war party had returned with over fifty scalps. A war tent was made where all the chiefs, warriors, and mourners assembled.

> All those whose faces were blackened for the loss of relations or friends, now came forward to claim the scalps to be held in their hands for the benefit of their departed relations and friends; this occasioned a long conversation with those who had scalps; at length they came forward to the War Chief. Those who had taken the trophy from the head of an enemy they had killed, said the Souls of the enemy that each of us has slain belongs to us and we have given them to our relations in the other world to be their slaves, and we are contented. Those who had scalps taken from the enemy that were found dead under the shields were at a loss what to say, as not one could say he had actually slain the enemy whose scalp he held, and yet wanted to send their souls to be the slaves of their departed relations. This caused much discussion, and the old chiefs decided it could not be done; and that no one could send the soul of an enemy to be a slave in the other world except the warrior who had actually killed him; the scalps you hold are trophies of the Battle but they give you no right to the soul of the enemy from whom it was taken; he alone who kills an enemy has a right to the soul, and to give it to be a slave to whom he pleases. This decision did not please them, but they were obliged to abide by it.[161]

[160] Thompson, p. 339.
[161] Thompson, pp. 332–33.

This concept is to be found in almost identical form among the Winnebago,[162] but I know of no other Plains tribe for which it was reported. From this it would appear that Blackfoot warfare contained some elements of Woodland ideology in the 1730's,[163] but the methods of fighting differed from the Woodland man-to-man style, and had become well adapted to the conditions of the Plains.[164]

The large-scale warfare described above demanded a good degree of centralized leadership, and Thompson's account of Piegan chieftainship (1787) suggests that there was a clearly differentiated tribal war chief of more or less permanence, with authority limited to war matters and war periods.

> They [Piegan] have a civil and military Chief. The first was called Sakatow, or orator, and the office appeared hereditary in his family as his father had been the civil Chief, and his eldest son was to take his place at his death, and occasionally acted for him . . . , his insignia of office was the backs of two fine otterskins covered with mother of pearl, which from behind his neck hung down his breast to below the belt; When his son acted for him he always had this ornament on him. In every council he presided except one of war. He had couriers which went from camp to camp and brought news . . . of where the great bison herds were feeding, and of the direction they were taking. . . .
>
> The War Chief confined himself to war matters and the care of the camp of which he was, which was generally of fifty to one hundred tents, generally a full day's march nearer to the Snake Indians than any other camp. It was supposed he looked on the Civil chief with indifference as a garrulous old man more fit for talking than for any thing else, and they rarely camped together.[165]

This comparison of the peace chief and war chief seems to attribute an equal degree of permanence to both offices. But the existence of a war chief as over against the temporary leader of small parties is suggested even more strongly from the following description refer-

[162] Paul Radin, The Winnebago Tribe, Thirty-seventh Annual Report of the Bureau of American Ethnology (Washington, D.C., 1923), p. 144. See his description of the four-nights' wake.

[163] The only later reference which I have found to this concept among the Blackfoot is that in Maximilian, Vol. 23, pp. 140–41. A Piegan had been killed by some Bloods and the dead man's brother made this speech to the weeping relatives: "Why do you lament and cry?—see, I do not cry! he is gone into the other country and we cannot awaken him; but at least two Blood Indians must accompany him and wait upon him there."

[164] "War in the open Plains between the natives is very different from war in the woods; in the former they act as a body in concert in all their movements, in the woods it is almost Man to Man." Thompson, p. 552.

[165] Thompson, pp. 346, 347.

ring to an event in about 1750. The Piegan were eighty miles below the Bow River and were undecided whether to go further south because of their fear of the Shoshone. "After consultation it was agreed to send out a war chief with about fifty warriors to examine the country a few days journey. The chief soon collected his warriors and having examined their arms, and having seen that every one had two pairs of shoes, some dried provisions and other necessaries, in the evening *the principal war chief* [my emphasis] addressed the chief at the head of the party; reminding him that the warriors now accompanying him would steadily follow him, that they were sent to destroy their enemies, that he must be wise and cautious and bring back the warriors entrusted to his care." [166]

So long as fighting was regularly carried on by large massed forces, the war chief had a definite function. However, subsequent changes in methods of warfare affected his role. The battle described earlier in this paper, which took place in the 1730's, marked the beginning of a transition period which was explained by Thompson's informant (1787): "The terror of that battle and our guns has prevented more general battles, and our wars have since been carried on by ambuscade and surprise of small camps in which we have greatly the advantage, from our Guns, arrow shods of iron, long knives, flat bayonets and axes from the Traders." [167]

With the increase in smaller war parties so characteristic of the later period, there was a corresponding decline in the position of the war chief, who disappeared entirely by the middle of the nineteenth century when the temporary leader of small war parties became the rule. This explains a discrepancy in the literature whereby some have reported the office of a tribal war chief and others have claimed no knowledge of it. Our last reference to the war chief as described above is found in MacLean's report of 1885.[168] In all later accounts the emphasis is upon the leader of small parties.

It is tempting to draw a further inference from our last quotation, namely, that the small raiding party did not exist in prehorse Blackfoot culture. However, in the face of the widespread distribution of the small war party in North America, more evidence would be necessary for such a conclusion. It is more probable that both the large-scale warfare and the small war party existed side by side earlier, as they did in the nineteenth century. The question is really one of their relative importance. I intend to show that the horse and gun

[166] Thompson, p. 342.

[167] Thompson, p. 336.

[168] Rev. John MacLean, "Social Organization of the Blackfoot Indians," in *Transactions of the Canadian Institute,* Vol. 4, 1892–93 (Toronto, 1895), p. 252.

increased the use of the small raiding party to the point where it became the most characteristic type of Blackfoot warfare.

This change in emphasis occurred gradually. The Blackfoot utilized the large-scale pattern of tribal warfare during the fifty-year period of territorial expansion, beginning in the 1730's, whereby they moved across the western Plains, driving the Shoshone, Kutenai, and Flathead before them. In addition to the horse and gun, we must now attribute a good part of this successful conquest to the military strength made possible by their well-developed political system. The systematic sending out of the small raiding party became important only after they had established their domination of the western Plains, when continued raids for horses superseded disputes over territory.

Large war parties persisted even after the pattern of the raiding party was well established. This occurred mainly when the tribal interests were threatened, as in the attempts of the allied Plateau groups to hunt buffalo on the Plains. In 1787 Thompson wrote, "A party of about 250 warriors under the command of Kutenai Appe went off to war against the Snake Indians." [169] In 1800 the same chief "was utterly adverse to small parties, except for horse stealing. . . . He seldom took the field with less than 200 warriors, but frequently with many more." [170]

In these accounts we find elements similar to those described in Saukamappee's account. In a battle between the Piegan and Kutenai in 1810, in which both sides were armed with guns, the Kutenai formed a rude rampart with their tents, tent poles, and baggage. The Piegan attacked with their cavalry but were three times repulsed. They then resorted to their older practice of infantry fighting. About 170 men drew up a rude line some four hundred yards from the enemy, and at intervals sent forty men forward to dare them to battle. They would approach to about sixty to eighty yards, shouting insults, calling them old women, and dancing and springing in a frantic manner so as to make more difficult targets.[171] These elements are clearly a survival of an old pattern.

• LATER WARFARE •

Changes occurred in the use of weapons following the introduction of the gun. The lance, once so important, was discarded as a useful weapon and became a ceremonial object. The quilted leather shirts

[169] Thompson, p. 347.
[170] Thompson, p. 370.
[171] Thompson, pp. 424–25.

that were worn for protection against arrows were of little use against bullets and gradually disappeared. The shield, though losing most of its utilitarian value, became very important as a medicine object, deriving its power from the symbols painted upon it.[172]

The camp circle is recent among the Blackfoot. When Henday visited the Blackfoot in 1754 he came upon two hundred tents camped in two parallel lines with an open avenue between them.[173] Jenness suggests that this arrangement was "very satisfactory for repelling slow infantry attacks, but not the sudden raids of mobile horsemen." [174] Undoubtedly the adoption of the camp circle was also related to their attempts to protect their newly acquired horses from raiding parties, for Maximilian tells us that horses were kept in corrals within the camp circle.[175] The origin of the camp circle among the Blackfoot may therefore tentatively be attributed to the changes in warfare consequent to the introduction of the horse on the Plains.

More important, warfare had become an integral part of the new Blackfoot economy. To understand this relationship more clearly, we must consider briefly the role of the horse in Blackfoot economy.

The importance of horses can be gauged by the extensive native terminology used to describe them. I have gathered more than twenty terms describing the types and qualities of horses. Horses were classified according to their functions, as race horses, war horses, travois horses, and pack horses, and by their special abilities, as "horses that can go long distances" or "horses that can run in deep snow." It is clear that horses were valued for their aid in hunting, in war, and in transportation. But in addition to their utilitarian and productive values, horses became a medium of exchange and the main form of wealth.

The accumulation of wealth, the manipulation of property, spending, buying, and selling, dominated Blackfoot life. Social position depended upon the liberal use of wealth, ostentatious display, and other forms of social investment. Every step in religious and secular

[172] An attempt on the part of the American Fur Company to introduce polished metal shields was effectively blocked by the medicine men, who, as Bradley tells us, "would have thus been deprived of an important source of revenue." Bradley, p. 282.

[173] Hendry, p. 355. The arrangement of two parallel lines was used in marching, as is described in Stanley's account of 1854: "In less than one hour the whole encampment was drawn out in two parallel lines on the Plains, forming one of the most picturesque scenes I have ever witnessed." U.S., Office of Indian Affairs, *Annual Report, 1854* (Washington, D.C., 1854), p. 200.

[174] Diamond Jenness, *The Sarsi Indians of Alberta,* National Museum of Canada, Bulletin 90, Anthropological Series, No. 23 (Ottawa, 1938), p. 13.

[175] Maximilian, Vol. 23, p. 123.

ritual involved property payments; the number of horses that changed hands in the bundle transfers and the incidence of buying into societies were truly remarkable. The ownership of horses therefore became a major index of social status.

The ownership of horses had still further importance, for horses were used as capital, earning interest for the owner in the form of a "gift" of additional horses or equivalent property from the borrower. When a man had a number of horses over and above the domestic needs of his family, the surplus could be loaned out. With the accumulation of large herds this lending of horses became general. Horses were borrowed for use in hunting and war parties. The borrower had to give in return one-half of the game killed and one-half of the loot captured.[176] In this way, owners of huge herds, who had long given up the war path, could replenish their supply of horses by frequently lending them to poor young men.

A large surplus of horses was not necessary for lending. Men who were too old to hunt and old women who had no relatives upon whom to rely could secure food and clothing for themselves if they owned but two horses. Horses were looked upon as a source of security in one's old age, a point often repeated to young men.

Horses were also in demand at the trading posts and were used by the Blackfoot to pay for goods, ammunition, liquor, tobacco, and other supplies. As we have seen, the Blackfoot never took to the trapping of small game on a large scale. They had few furs for exchange before the 1830's and relied upon horses almost from the start, Blackfoot horse trading was carried on as early as 1774, as shown by Cocking.[177] This need for horses, both for the tribal economy and for trading purposes, gave continual impetus to horse-stealing parties.

The organization of a raiding party was a purely individual affair. A party was organized by the man who wished to be the leader. He notified a number of carefully selected men of his intentions and arranged for a meeting at which the plans would be discussed. Participation in a raiding party was determined by rank, equipment, and the relationship to the leader. The party normally was composed of members of one band; brothers and brothers-in-law were a favorite

[176] The rigidity of the interest concept could not be ascertained, though all informants insisted upon the 50 per cent principle. Probably much depended upon the relationship of the "contracting" parties. A somewhat different arrangement is reported by Jane Richardson for the Northern Blackfoot. Here the hired men under the famous chief, Crowfoot, gave him the entire loot and catch, in return for which they were fed and clothed by the chief and received some horses upon their marriage. See Richardson, ms.

[177] Cocking, p. 110.

raiding unit, for they could thereby keep the horses in the family. The leader never invited a 'man superior to him in war record nor would such a man raid under him. Similarly, a poor man would not attempt to lead a group of wealthier men, even though they were younger.[178] A man of high status, whether in terms of war record, wealth in horses, or the ownership of medicine bundles, would refuse to be led by one of lower standing. Not only were the poor rarely leaders, but they often had difficulty in joining a raiding party, for participation was limited to those who had the necessary equipment—a gun, powder and ammunition, a good supply of moccasins, dried provisions, protective war charms, and, when the party went on horse, a good horse.

With adequate skill, any member of the tribe could produce the equipment necessary for the early type of warfare, but the new equipment—guns and ammunition—could be purchased from the trading posts only by those who had a surplus of horses, dried provisions, or hides. This put the poor at a distinct disadvantage and was a check upon vertical mobility. It also gave a new paternalistic role to the chief as a distributor of valuable goods.

Differences between rich and poor were reflected in their participation in war in still another way. Not owning war bonnets, beautiful headdresses, or medicine pipes, the poor went to the hills to seek supernatural power for a successful war party, whereas those who could afford it bought their charms from renowned medicine men. Despite this handicap, informants relate that the poor were the most daring on horse-stealing parties, for they had the least to lose and the most to gain.

Normally, raiding parties started out in the early spring, the summer, or the fall, rarely the winter; the Blackfoot did not like to go out in cold weather. A wise leader would leave at nightfall, travel until dawn, and then rest during the day in shelters constructed in the foothills.

The function of the leader consisted mainly in enforcing simple precautionary rules, such as prohibiting a fire for cooking, or the shooting of game once in enemy territory. Every party had one or two scouts who reported to the leader. When the party neared the camp of the enemy, the leader decided who was to do the raiding. If the party was small, it would break up, every man for himself, and arrange to meet at an appointed spot. In other cases, the leader ordered some to stay, usually the inexperienced or the poorer ones, while the leader, alone or with a choice few, went for the horses.

[178] A poor man, "kimataps," is one who has not or who never has had any valuable property or religious articles. A man with a good war record would not be called "kimataps" though he might have little or no property.

This rear-guard duty was resented, for there was a possibility that those who were left behind would not be allowed to share the loot. The chief might present them with a horse, a gift which they were expected to acknowledge at the victory dance.[179] Many parties broke up because of this. Those ordered to remain behind often disobeyed and went out for their own horses. In cases where the party was mounted and had ambushed the enemy, this individualism was even more marked. It was every man for himself, with a great deal of snatching and bickering over the loot, even among brothers.

The leader divided the loot, irrespective of whether he himself had obtained the horses or had remained behind, provided of course that the party had not broken up. If a split occurred, every man retained what he had acquired and there were no recriminations. In the division of the spoils, the leader was guided by the relative age and status of the men and by their part in capturing the horses. It is not clear from the material how these considerations were weighed. In no case did the leader return empty-handed. Unlike the Comanche, the Blackfoot were not content with the prestige of leadership alone.[180]

The return of a successful war party was an impressive event and occasioned general rejoicing and feasting. The party stopped a few miles from the camp, painted their faces, put on their war clothing, and rode quietly to the top of a hill overlooking the camp. "There they would begin the war song, whip the horses to a mad run, and firing guns and driving before them animals they had taken, charge swiftly down the hill into the bottom." [181]

If there were only a few casualties, or if the casualties befell men of little importance or those with few relatives, a victory dance would be held, at which there was much exchange of property. Young unmarried men gave most of their captured horses to older relatives. Since one principle of the division of loot was age, distribution of even a few gifts soon exhausted the loot of the young men. Young men had to go to war from six to ten times before they could accumulate enough horses for an impressive bride price. In giving away their loot they were establishing a source of future credit and aid in joining societies or in raising a bride price. Married men retained more for themselves and went to war less frequently than the unmarried. Scalps given to relatives or friends were repaid by a gift

[179] Richardson, ms.

[180] E. Adamson Hoebel, *The Political Ogranization and Law-Ways of the Comanche Indians,* Memoirs of the American Anthropological Association, No. 54 (Menasha, Wis., 1940).

[181] James Willard Schultz, *My Life as an Indian: The Story of a Red Woman and a White Man in the Lodges of the Blackfeet* (New York, 1907), p. 47.

of a buckskin suit or a horse. Modern informants emphasize the trade value of scalps.[182]

The classical view of nineteenth-century Plains warfare is that it was in the nature of a sporting game for honor, prestige, and scalps. If this were true at all, it was, for the Blackfoot, characteristic of the period before the introduction of the horse and gun, and loot in horses as the dominating motive. Coup was largely ruled out in the parties organized for raiding because of the necessity for stealth and the desire to avoid face-to-face encounters. Although it is true that the capture of a picketed horse rated high as a war deed, it did not compare with the taking of a gun and was not a formal requirement for chieftainship. As a matter of fact, the seeking of coup was confined to defensive encounters where the possibility of loot was necessarily ruled out. Defensive battles were the occasion for a show of bravery, for the capture of guns, shields, and bonnets. The prestige derived from this counting of coup and from the ceremonial recitation of war deeds, though present, was in later years overshadowed by the prestige of wealth.

The relative importance of war honors and wealth can be judged from the fact that bravery and war deeds, the usual requirements for chieftainship on the Plains, though important, were here not essential. There were many chiefs who had never been on the warpath but who had achieved their position by their kindness, generosity, good judgment, and wealth.[183] Even a coward, "kopum," one who feared the warpath, could become a chief, provided that he had accumulated sufficient wealth to attract followers. By giving frequent feasts, spreading gifts judiciously, and buying into the beaver and medicine-pipe societies, any man could gain considerable prestige. This is made more striking when we compare the place of war honors and the counting of coup in Crow life with that among the Blackfoot. The Crow had an elaborate and systematic grading of war honors which was absent among the Blackfoot.

We have indicated earlier that large war parties were used to keep the Plateau tribes out of the Plains. Large parties were also occasioned by two other situations: first, in attacks against the trading posts, where the motive was solely loot, and second, in revenge attacks on other tribes, when the people felt the death of a prominent warrior or chief at the hands of an enemy as a tribal loss. In such cases, parties were organized in the spring or summer when the bands came together for the Sun Dance. The revenge parties were composed of members of a few bands, rarely of the whole tribe. It is

182 Richardson, ms.

183 A favored son was not expected to go on the warpath; often he became a chief.

significant that even on these revenge parties, and this applies to both the large and the small, loot was never overlooked.

There were, however, fundamental differences between the organization and motives of the large parties of prehorse days and later ones. The latter were no more than expanded raiding parties. That is, the large party of warriors broke up into small units which acted like small raiding parties intent upon plunder instead of a unified army under centralized control.

The existence of highly organized warfare among the Blackfoot in the prehorse period is of special interest in view of the fact that the coming of the horse has become associated in a general way with the development of a high degree of political organization. This process has been shown for the southern Ute of Colorado, where the advent of the horse consolidated the small family groups into large bands and transformed a peaceful, retiring population into a predatory and dominating people.[184] Much the same process occurred among the Sahaptin people of the southern Plateau and among the Kutenai and Flathead to the east and north. Here, the change was from small village units to large band organizations.[185] In this case, the stimulus for the changes was the horse, plus the necessity of presenting a powerful front against the tribes of the Plains.

The Blackfoot exemplify a very different process, in which the effect of the horse was to bring about a decentralization in political organization and a florescence of individualism. The Blackfoot had already achieved a remarkable degree of political organization in prehorse times, when the activities of the bands, at least for war purposes, were unified under a central leader.

The concerted action of early tribal warfare was a cohesive force in Blackfoot culture. Far from acting as a unifying factor, the introduction of the horse and gun represented a disruptive one. Later warfare carried on by the small raiding parties became essentially a means of individual aggrandizement in which the tribal interests gave way to those of the individual. Differences between rich and poor became more clearly defined and cut across all institutions. Some chiefs owned thousands of horses while the poor owned none. This developed to a point of incipient social stratification on the basis of horse ownership which resulted in internal disunity.

We can now briefly summarize the more important changes that occurred in warfare as a result of the introduction of the horse and gun and fur trade. The prehorse motives of warfare, that is, vengeance and the defense and expansion of the tribal hunting grounds,

[184] Marvin Opler, "The Southern Ute of Colorado," in Ralph Linton (ed.), *Acculturation in Seven American Indian Tribes* (New York, 1940), p. 123.

[185] Teit, pp. 151–52.

persisted but were displaced in importance by raiding for loot. The religious element in scalping dropped out and scalps were sought only as trophies of war. There followed changes in organization and tactics. Large massed forces under central leadership gave way to small raiding parties under temporary leaders; open battles with a great show of numbers became less frequent. Instead, stealth, secrecy, and ambuscade were employed. Equipment as over against mere numbers became a vital factor. Casualties increased and warfare became a serious and deadly affair.

· V I I .   C O N C L U S I O N S ·

The proposition that the contact with Western civilization acted as a stimulus to the development of Plains culture is now well known and generally accepted. Yet we have few detailed studies of this process, and there has been no attempt to solve this essentially historical problem from the historical material. Instead there have been various studies based upon logical and functional analysis of the nature of this process. Although some of these speculations show remarkable insight, they are no substitute for the actual history.

The development of Plains culture has been discussed mainly in terms of the effects of the horse. Thus Kroeber writes:

> Then about 1650 came the horse which could be taken over with immense profit and without serious readjustment by the bison hunting dogtravois tribes. Population, wealth, leisure increased rapidly and there was a florescence of culture. The material side of life acquired a certain sumptuousness; the warfare of the eastern type was made over into a specialized system with refined social values; rituals and societies multiplied and acquired some magnificence or developed elaborations like age gradings.[186]

Wissler, on the other hand, held that posthorse and prehorse Plains culture were similar in most respects.

How do these views of the Plains as a whole compare with our findings for the Blackfoot, a typical Plains tribe? First, the material indicates that the developments so admirably summed up by Kroeber took place, in the case of the Blackfoot, approximately 180 years after the date suggested by him. We have seen that the increase in the size of herds, the expansion of polygyny, the borrowing and elaboration of societies and their rituals, and the development of bundle purchases probably occurred about 1830. Nor did all of this follow automatically after the introduction of the horse, for the

[186] Alfred L. Kroeber, *Native Culture of the Southwest,* University of California Publications in American Archeology and Ethnology, Vol. 23, No. 9 (Berkeley, 1928), p. 395.

Blackfoot obtained their first horses in 1730 and were all mounted by 1754.

It is not enough to think of posthorse Blackfoot culture as representing merely an expansion or florescence of earlier conditions. Our study has shown that in the middle of the eighteenth century the Blackfoot made pottery and baskets and, according to Flathead tradition, wore blankets of woven rabbit skins before the time of the horse. On the other hand, the camp circle, considered so characteristically Plains, did not appear until sometime after 1754. Warfare was carried on in large groups under a war chief and was a tribal affair. The unified action of the bands in time of war indicates a higher degree of political organization than is usually ascribed to prehorse Plains.

The fur trade was the mainspring of Blackfoot culture change. The horse alone cannot explain the florescence of Blackfoot culture which took place in the nineteenth century. Rather, it was the fur trade together with the horse and gun which had a dynamic effect upon Blackfoot institutions. The horse without the fur trade would probably have had only the limited effects attributed to it by Wissler for the Plains as a whole. In this sense, the differences between the interpretations of Wissler and Mishkin may reflect objective regional and historical differences between the northern and southern Plains.

In the past the uniformity of Plains culture has also been attributed to the horse. It was argued that with the greater mobility supplied by the horse there was an increase in intertribal contacts and an ensuing spreading of culture traits. The role of the fur trade in stimulating this increasing tribal intercourse has hitherto been neglected. I have shown that tribes which formerly had little contact with each other met at trading posts, and I have suggested that this was probably the manner in which societies of Mandan and Hidatsa were transmitted to the Blackfoot. Radin has pointed to an analogous process which took place in the Woodlands, whereby the traveling white fur traders were responsible for much of the uniformity which characterizes the Woodland area,[187] and Goldman has suggested that the fur trade was instrumental in the diffusion of Northwest Coast culture elements to the interior. It therefore appears that at least three of our culture areas, the Northwest Coast, the Plains, and the Woodlands, are recent historical products due in large measure to the role of the fur trade as an agent of diffusion.

This study demonstrates both the possibilities and limitations in the use of the recorded history of white contact toward constructing a developmental picture of Blackfoot culture. Although I have been

[187] Radin (above, note 162).

able to show the general direction of development of Blackfoot culture, the specific processes are not always discernible. Nor does the material shed light equally on all Blackfoot institutions. Thus, I have been able to show the process most clearly in the changes in warfare, whereas the material on economics and social organization is only suggestive of the direction of development. Because there is little reference in the literature to other aspects of Blackfoot culture, such as art and religion, it has been impossible to include them in this study.

· A P P E N D I X ·
· P R E-R E S E R V E   B L A C K F O O T   R E L A T I O N S   W I T H   T H E   A M E R I C A N   A N D   C A N A D I A N   G O V E R N M E N T S[1] ·

· UNITED STATES ·

The United States government first concerned itself about its western Indians in order to advance American trading interests on the Upper Missouri. When, in 1824, Indian agents were appointed for the Indian tribes of the Upper Missouri, they were for the first time within reach of Blackfoot country. It was not until 1834 that an official agent of the government met with the Blackfoot.[2] Indian agents at this time were working in the interest, if not in the employ, of the American Fur Company. Until the 1850's, meetings of Indian agents with the Blackfoot were sporadic. The agents limited their activities to the trading posts, where they occasionally distributed goods to the Blackfoot in the name of the Great Father at Washington.[3] There was thus from the beginning an association of the fur companies and the government in the minds of the Indians.

The movement of settlers to the west, which had begun in the thirties, reached great proportions by 1850. The increase in the number of immigrants led to plans for the construction of a transcontinental railroad. Before this could be undertaken, the intertribal warfare among the Blackfoot, Crow, Gros Ventre, Flathead, Nez Perce, and Kutenai had to be stopped. Governor Isaac Stevens, who headed the railroad survey, therefore began a series of peace councils with

---

[1] Since the differential treatment of the Blackfoot by the American and Canadian fur companies was paralleled by their treatment at the hands of the American and Canadian governments, we will trace the relations of the Blackfoot with both governments up to the reserve period.

[2] Chardon, p. 254.

[3] Chardon, p. xxxviii.

the Indians of the northern Plains which led to the signing of the treaty of 1855 with the Blackfoot, otherwise known as the Judith Treaty.[4]

In this treaty Blackfoot territory from the valleys of the Three Forks of the Missouri River east to the upper waters of the Yellowstone, an area of 30,000 square miles, was set aside as a common hunting ground for the Blackfoot and Gros Ventre. The country north of this common hunting ground as far as the Canadian boundary and east and south as far as the Musselshell River and north of the Missouri to its junction with the Milk River was defined as the territory of the Blackfoot nation. The United States government was to guard the Indians against whiskey traders, attacks by white men, and any abrogation of their treaty rights. The United States further agreed to spend $20,000 a year for ten years in goods and provisions for the Piegan, Blood, and Gros Ventre, and $15,000 a year for ten years to establish and instruct them in agriculture and mechanical pursuits, education, and Christianization.[5] This treaty was ratified in 1856.

The Annual Reports of the Indian Bureau indicate that the annuities were peaceably distributed in the years following, but much of the goods received had no relation to the needs of the Indians. One agent wrote, "I would respectfully recommend that the following be dispensed with altogether . . . calico, ½ of the coffee, fish hooks and lines, combs, thread, . . . and that there be substituted . . . shirts, bed-ticking, flour, powder ball. . . ."[6]

These requests were sent in year after year but for the most part went unheeded. There were some feeble attempts to introduce farming and cattle grazing, to which the Indians were definitely not receptive. From 1855 to 1860 there was little change in the conduct of the Indians. The older men tried to abide by the treaty stipulations but the warriors continued on the war path.[7]

Until 1860 the penetration of Blackfoot country by white settlers had been gradual. Routes to the Pacific lay south of the Blackfoot and did not directly affect them. However, the cattle ranching that had existed near Fort Bridger since the 1840's now began to push north into Blackfoot country. The discovery of gold in 1862 at Grass-

[4] Alban W. Hoopes, *Indian Affairs and Their Administration, with Special Reference to the Far West, 1849–1860* (Philadelphia, 1932), p. 101.
[5] Hoopes, p. 115.
[6] U.S., Office of Indian Affairs, *Annual Report, 1857/58* (Washington, D.C., 1858), p. 82.
[7] U.S., Office of Indian Affairs, *Annual Report, 1858/59* (Washington, D.C., 1859), p. 116.

hopper Creek, within the common hunting grounds of the Blackfoot and Gros Ventre, brought still another invasion. Immigrants now came by the thousands and towns sprang up almost overnight. On May 26, 1864, the territory of Montana was created.[8]

There now began a period of bitter conflict between the Blackfoot and the settlers. The low types of American frontiersmen were largely responsible. Of these, General Sully, Superintendent of Indians in the Territory of Montana, said, "There is a white element in this country which from its rowdy and lawless character cannot be excelled in any section."[9]

The liquor trade was still rampant, in open violation of the Indian Intercourse Act of 1832 and the Judith Treaty of 1855. Liquor was taking a great toll of Indian lives. The agent at Fort Benton was helpless, but when he objected he was reminded by the citizens "that as they were the advance guard of civilization in the far northwest, barbarians must succumb to their opinions."[10] Given the popular prejudice against the Indians, it was impossible to get a conviction against the whiskey traders in the local courts. "Rather than have a white man punished for assaulting an Indian, the justice of the peace and the sheriff resigned their offices."[11] Violation of government treaties with the Indians concerned them little. "The people claim superior rights to the Indians—and they are indiscriminately killing an Indian when seen," wrote an agent.[12]

Agent after agent sent annual reports to Washington pleading for a reservation to be set up for the Blackfoot, to avoid the clashes between Indians and settlers. One agent wrote: "If my services are for good, they are being poorly used while I remain at this place (Benton). It has become a city, duly incorporated as such by the territorial legislature, and has its municipal officers who are unfriendly to the Indians and whose sympathies are with the whites in their attacks upon them. If, as I earnestly hope, a reservation will be established for the Blood, Blackfoot and Piegan tribes . . . there may be much good effected throughout this territory. The agent would then be his own master in controlling his agency, without being dictated

[8] Briggs, pp. 161–62, 185–86.

[9] U.S., House of Representatives, "Letter from the Secretary of War," 41st Cong., 2d Sess., H. Ex. Doc. No. 269, 1870, p. 3.

[10] U.S., Department of the Interior, *Annual Report, 1867/68* (Washington, D.C., 1868), p. 256.

[11] U.S., Department of the Interior, *Annual Report, 1862/63* (Washington, D.C., 1863), p. 222.

[12] U.S., Department of the Interior, *Annual Report, 1867/68* (Washington, D.C., 1868), p. 206.

to as he now is by old trading posts, merchants, thieves, and black-guards." [13] These pleadings went unheeded until 1874, when a reservation was finally set aside for the Blackfoot.

In the meantime the friction between the settlers and the Blackfoot increased. In 1865 a treaty was negotiated with the "Blackfoot Nation" in the person of a single Blackfoot chief! The object was to open legally to settlement territory that had already been occupied by the whites. The Blackfoot were to cede all their land lying south of the Missouri.[14]

This treaty was not recognized by the Blackfoot, nor was it ratified by Congress. Immediately after its conclusion the Bloods, Blackfoot, and Piegan started to war against the Gros Ventre and the whites.[15] In April 1866 a party of North Piegan burned the buildings of the government farm on Sun River and continued with an attack on a flourishing cattle ranch nearby.[16] It is significant that the Piegan, until now the most friendly to the whites, took an active part in these raids. It was their tribal lands that were being invaded by the white settlers (the Blood and Blackfoot ranged north of the line) and they were thoroughly aroused to the danger.

The white inhabitants of Montana viewed the situation with alarm. It was reported that the Blackfoot were planning a war of extermination. "The militia were called out, intense excitement prevailed, but history fails to disclose that these wars ever materialized." [17] What is more, from the Indian agents' reports at this time, we learn that the settlers were on the offensive. W. J. Cullen, Special Commissioner, who was sent to the Blackfoot, worked to put down the abuses against the Blackfoot. He wrote, "I am risking my life among a set of desperadoes, who live by their wits off the Indians." [18] He tried to prevent a frontier war "which the majority of the settlers appear to be in favor of." [19] Cullen succeeded in concluding a treaty with the Gros Ventre and Blackfoot in 1868. By this treaty all land south of the Missouri was to be ceded to the government, in return for which a payment was to be made. The Blackfoot were restricted to the land north of the river up to the Canadian line. The treaty was not to be binding on either party until ratified by the United States

[13] *Ibid.*, pp. 207–08.

[14] U.S., Department of the Interior, *Annual Report, 1865/66* (Washington, D.C., 1966), p. 13.

[15] *Ibid.*, p. 202.

[16] *Ibid.*, p. 203.

[17] John Carter, "The Blackfoot Claim," ms., p. 12.

[18] U.S., Department of the Interior, *Annual Report, 1867/68* (Washington, D.C., 1968), p. 222.

[19] *Ibid.*

government. The failure of the government to ratify it created much discontent among the Piegan. Horse-stealing and petty thieving began again and culminated in the so-called Piegan war of 1869–70.

In the summer of 1869, a few wagons of emigrants were attacked near Fort Benton by Indians, later identified as the Crow. Just after this, the brother of Mountain Chief, the head of the Piegan, and a young Blood boy rode into Fort Benton with special orders from Major Alexander Culbertson. They were shot down by the excited settlers. The Piegan were now thoroughly aroused. Major Clark, a former agent of the American Fur Company, who had married the daughter of a Piegan chief, was at this time living among the Piegan. A cousin of Clark's wife took advantage of this feeling against the whites to avenge a personal grudge and killed Clark. Four troops of cavalry and fifty-five mounted infantry under Brevet Colonel Eugene M. Baker, started for the Piegan on January 19, 1870. They came upon a Piegan camp whose lodges were filled with sick women and children. Chief Heavy Runner, a friendly Indian, came toward them unarmed and was shot down. The camp was exterminated; 173 women and children were slaughtered and many more wounded. In the investigation that followed, Baker was exonerated and the killing justified.[20]

This massacre, followed by an outbreak of smallpox, effectively and completely cowed the Piegan. If any resistance on their part had been contemplated, it never materialized. As Curtis wrote: "A study of the Piegan conflict with the white people, either citizens or soldiers, shows that, considering their number and their provocation, they were one of the most harmless tribes." [21]

· CANADA ·

It was not until after 1870 that the Blackfoot felt the force of white expansion in Canada. Blackfoot country had remained free from settlers. The North Saskatchewan, the main highway of traffic to the northwest, was north of Blackfoot country. So long as the Hudson's Bay Company retained its trade monopoly, the Blackfoot were free to continue their old life. But the days of the company were limited. In response to an increasing pressure for a national policy to deal with the growing westward expansion and immigration, Alberta and Saskatchewan were ceded to the Canadian government by the Hudson's Bay Company in 1870.

[20] Robert George Raymer, *Montana: The Land and the People*, 3 vols. (Chicago, 1930), Vol. 1, p. 237.
[21] Edward S. Curtis, *The North American Indian*, Vol. 6 (Cambridge, Mass., 1909), p. 7.

With the passing of the political authority of the Hudson's Bay Company, there came an end to the harmonious relations with the Blackfoot in Canada. A period of free trade now set in. "New and reprehensible practises in trade were introduced. Competition was keen. Trader outbid trader and upset the century old values fixed by the Hudson's Bay Company. Alcoholic spirits, long discontinued by the company . . . for many years now poured in from Red River and from across the border. In southern Alberta, American whiskey runners from Montana introduced the lawless spirit of the American frontier. Contemptuous of Canadian authority, they built forts in Canadian territory, and debauched the Indians with alcohol." [22]

In 1872, Colonel Ross was sent west by the Canadian government to investigate. In his report he recommended that police be sent to put down the liquor trade: "The demoralization of the Indians and injury resulting to the country from this illicit traffic are very great. It is stated upon good authority that during last year (1871) eighty-eight (88) of the Blackfoot Indians were murdered in drunken brawls amongst themselves, produced by the whiskey and other spirits supplied to them by the traders. At Fort Edmonton during the present summer whiskey was openly sold to the Blackfoot . . . by some smugglers from the U.S." [23]

In the same year, John McDougall, a missionary, visited the Blood, promising that the whites would soon bring law and order. He later arranged to meet Crowfoot, head chief of the Siksika, and told him that the mounted police were coming to suppress the liquor trade, horse stealing, and intertribal warfare.[24] When the mounted police arrived they were welcomed by the Blackfoot. The literature contains many speeches of welcome of which the following are typical. "The Great Mother sent Stamixoton (Col. MacLeod) and the Police to put an end to the traffic in fire water. I can sleep now safely. Before the arrival of the Police, when I laid my head down at night, every sound frightened me; my sleep was broken; now I can sleep sound and am not afraid." [25]

"If the Police had not come to this country where would we be all now? Bad men and whiskey were killing us so fast that very few, indeed, of us would have been left today. The Police have protected us as the feathers of the bird protect it from the frosts of winter." [26]

[22] Stanley, p. 199.

[23] Stanley, p. 199.

[24] Rev. John MacLean, *McDougall of Alberta: Life of Rev. John McDougall* (Toronto, 1927), p. 88.

[25] Stanley, p. 203.

[26] A. W. Haydon, *The Riders of the Plains: A Record of the Royal Northwest Mounted Police of Canada, 1873–1910* (Toronto, 1910), p. 16.

In 1877, a treaty was signed with the Blackfoot tribes, including the Sarsi, in which provisions were made for them to confine themselves to one large reserve. However, the government thereafter decided upon a separate reserve for each tribe. The treaty provided a payment of $12 and an annuity of $5 for each man, woman, and child, $25 for each chief, and $15 for each minor chief. An annual allowance was provided for schools, ammunition, cattle, and agricultural implements.

• COMPARISON AND SUMMARY •

The tempo of western development in Montana was more rapid and sudden than in Alberta and accordingly was more devastating in its effects upon the Blackfoot, particularly the Piegan. Long before the disappearance of the buffalo they were hemmed in by cattle ranchers, homesteaders, and miners and were ruthlessly pushed off their land. In the ensuing conflict between the Indians and settlers, the government with its militia was on the side of the whites. The "bluecoats" became a symbol of a partial government and were heartily feared and hated by the Indians. Treaty after treaty was made with the Indians to legalize the inroads of the settlers, pushing the Indians within more and more confining limits. The Indians were bewildered by the rapid succession of treaties which were often not ratified in Washington and remained mere scraps of paper.

In Canada the Blackfoot fared much better. The later settlement of Alberta, the absence of a lawless frontier class, the prompt and efficient action of the few mounted police in suppressing the liquor trade that cropped up after 1870, and the establishment of reserves for the Indians before the influx of white settlers spared the Blackfoot the bitter experiences of their American brethren.

Considering the strength of the Blackfoot tribes and the number of their grievances in nearly two hundred years of white contact, the absence of any organized resistance or war against the whites is truly remarkable. The literature is replete with statements about threatened uprisings which never occurred. Throughout, conflict with the whites was limited to actions of individuals or a few bands.

On at least three occasions the Blackfoot refused to join antiwhite movements. The first was when Sitting Bull fled to Canada after the Custer battle and appealed to the Blackfoot (1877) to join the Sioux in their war against the whites.[27] Later, in 1885, the Blackfoot refused to associate themselves with the rebellion led by Riel, the Cree half-breed.[28] The third was the failure of the Blackfoot to participate

[27] Denny, p. 104.
[28] Stanley, p. 361.

in the Ghost Dance movement of the nineties, with its revolutionary antiwhite ideology, which was eagerly taken up by neighboring tribes.[29]

This nonparticipation in antiwhite movements is to be understood in the light of a number of considerations. The slower and later influx of white settlers in Canada provided a refuge for the Siksika, Blood, and a portion of the Piegan, for a long time, and gave them a sense of security, though ultimately a false one. Had the Blackfoot tribes been pushed to the wall in the States, without the presence of this Canadian safety valve, they might have offered more stubborn resistance. As it was, it seemed pointless for them to fight American troops when they could still retire to their own land north of the line.

The absence of any well-developed political organization prevented the three tribes from presenting a solid front against the whites and made it impossible for them to utilize the strength inherent in their numbers. The so-called Blackfoot confederacy, a concept used by the traders, had little basis in fact. Despite the bonds of a common language, common customs and traditions and intermarriage, the tribes rarely acted in unison. They had no common council and no central leaders. Furthermore, within each tribe the bands were highly unstable units. The frequency with which individuals changed band allegiances was not conducive to successful resistance against the whites, either moral or military.

The days of tribal warfare in defense of hunting grounds were long past. Warfare had become a matter of individual aggrandizement and there appeared to be no motives which would unite the tribes or the bands. In addition to these factors in their social organization and warfare, there was the further disruption of their intertribal unity by the fur trade, as was pointed out in the preceding section.

Of no less importance was the conciliatory role played by the chiefs and headmen, who very often did not consider it to their personal interests to resist the influence of the whites. The early missionaries first commented upon this when they recorded the support they received from the chiefs in their efforts to suppress intertribal warfare and horse stealing. Father Point stated, "Among the Blackfoot, the rich people who undertake to rebuke the wicked who

[29] The Ghost Dance was taken up by the Assiniboine, Gros Ventre, Northern Cheyenne, Arikara, Gros Ventre (Minataree), Shoshone, and Northern Arapaho. See James Mooney, *The Ghost-Dance Religion and the Sioux Outbreak of 1890*, Fourteenth Annual Report of the Bureau of American Ethnology, Part 2 (Washington, D.C., 1896), pp. 641–1136.

possess nothing, have naught to gain and all to lose." [30] Indeed, peace would insure the security of those who had large herds.

Opposition, both to the cessation of the raiding parties and to the signing of treaties with the whites, came from the younger men. However, they were for the most part successfully restrained by the chiefs. Although it is true that Little Dog, head chief of the Piegan, was killed by his own warriors for his council of peace and friendship with the whites in 1860, Crowfoot, who had much more influence, was successful in keeping down hostile movements against the whites. Crowfoot, who was largely responsible for the maintenance of peace, was motivated by personal, and to some extent tribal, interests. He prophesied the extinction of the buffalo and the ensuing dependence of the Indians upon the whites, and looked upon resistance as foolhardy and hopeless. In 1876, he told Denny, a member of the mounted police: "We all see that the day is coming when the buffalo will all be killed, and we shall have nothing more to live on and then you will come into our camp and see the poor Blackfoot starving. I know the heart of the white soldier will be sorry for us, and that they will tell the Great Mother who will not let her children die." [31] In 1877, he won out against those who counseled against the signing of the treaty. In 1882–83, he allayed the resentment of his people incurred by the putting through of the Canadian Pacific railroad. Without the consent of the other chiefs, Crowfoot secretly capitulated to the railroad for a personal annuity of $700.[32] He was able to mollify the embittered chiefs by judiciously distributing horses. Again, in 1885, Crowfoot used his influence to keep the Blackfoot out of the Riel rebellion, but he played upon the fear of the whites to get a promise of larger rations in the future.

· REFERENCES ·

American State Papers, Vol. 2. Washington, D.C., 1834.

BELL, CHARLES N. (ed.). *The Journal of Henry Kelsey (1691–1692), the First White Man to Reach the Saskatchewan from Hudson Bay*. The Historical and Scientific Society of Manitoba, Transactions No. 4, n.s. Winnipeg, 1928.

BLUE, JOHN. *Alberta, Past and Present, Historical and Biographical*. 3 vols. Chicago, 1924.

BOAS, FRANZ. "History and Science in Anthropology: A Reply," *American Anthropologist*, n.s., Vol. 38 (Jan., 1936), pp. 137–41.

[30] Quoted in De Smet, p. 950.

[31] Denny, p. 221.

[32] Richardson, ms.

BRADLEY, JAMES H. *Affairs at Fort Benton, 1831–1869*. Contributions of the Montana Historical Society, vol. 3. Helena, 1900.

BRIGGS, HAROLD E. *Frontiers of the Northwest: A History of the Upper Missouri Valley*. New York, 1910.

CARNEGIE, JAMES, EARL OF SOUTHESK. *Saskatchewan and the Rocky Mountains*. Edinburgh, 1875.

CARTER, JOHN. "The Blackfoot Claim" (unpublished manuscript).

CATLIN, GEORGE. *Illustrations of the Manners, Customs, and Conditions of the North American Indians*. London, 1842.

CHARDON, FRANCIS A. *Chardon's Journal at Fort Clark*, ed. A. H. Abel. Pierre, S. Dak., 1932.

CHITTENDEN, HIRAM M. *The American Fur Trade of the Far West: A History of the Pioneer Trading Posts and Early Fur Companies of the Missouri Valley and the Rocky Mountains, and of the Overland Commerce with Santa Fe*. 2 vols. New York, 1902.

COCKING, MATTHEW. "An Adventurer from Hudson Bay: Journal of Matthew Cocking from York Factory to the Blackfeet Country, 1772–1773," ed. Lawrence J. Burpee, in *Proceedings and Transactions of the Royal Society of Canada*, 3rd ser., Vol. 2, Ottawa, 1908, Section 3, pp. 89–121.

COLLIER, JOHN. "Blackfoot Field Notes," ms. Later published in *The Indians of the Americas* (New York, 1947).

CURTIS, EDWARD S. *The North American Indian*. 20 vols. Cambridge, Mass., 1907–30.

DENNY, SIR CECIL EDWARD. *The Law Marches West*. Toronto, 1939.

DOTY, JAMES. "Reports of Mr. James Doty on the Indian Tribes of the Blackfoot Nation," dated Fort Benton, Dec. 28, 1853, in *Reports of Explorations and Surveys to Ascertain the Most Practicable and Economical Route for a Railroad from the Mississippi River to the Pacific Ocean* (Washington, D. C.; U.S. War Department, 1855), pp. 441–45.

FRANKLIN, JOHN. *Narrative of a Journey to the Shores of the Polar Seas, in the Years 1819–20–21–22*. 2 vols. London, 1824.

GRANT, G. M. *Ocean to Ocean: Sanford Fleming's Expedition Through Canada in 1872*. Toronto, 1873.

Great Britain. *Parliamentary Papers*. Vol. XV. 1857.

GRINNELL, GEORGE B. *Blackfoot Lodge Tales: The Story of a Prairie People*. New York, 1912.

HALE, HORATIO. "Report on the Blackfoot Tribes," in *Report of the British Association for the Advancement of Science, 1885* (London, 1886), pp. 696–708.

HAYDON, A. W. *The Riders of the Plains: A Record of the Royal Northwest Mounted Police of Canada, 1873–1910*. Toronto, 1910.

HENDAY, ANTHONY. See Hendry, Anthony.

HENDRY, ANTHONY. "York Factory to the Blackfoot Country: The Journal of Anthony Hendry, 1745–55," in *Proceedings and Transactions of the Royal Society of Canada*, 3rd ser. Vol. 1 (Ottawa, 1907), pp. 307–54.

HENRY, ALEXANDER, and THOMPSON, DAVID. *New Light on the Early History of the Greater Northwest: The Manuscript Journals of Alexander Henry and David Thompson, 1799–1814*, ed. Elliott Coues. 3 vols. New York, 1897.

HERSKOVITS, MELVILLE J. *Acculturation: A Study in Culture Contact.* New York, 1938.

HOEBEL, E. ADAMSON. *The Political Organization and Law-Ways of the Comanche Indians.* Memoirs of the American Anthropological Association, No. 54, Menasha, Wis., 1940.

HOOPES, ALBAN W. *Indian Affairs and their Administration, with Special Reference to the Far West, 1849–1860.* Philadelphia, 1932.

HUGHES, KATHERINE. *Father Lacombe, the Black-Robe Voyageur.* New York, 1897.

HYDE, GEORGE E. *The Early Blackfoot and Their Neighbors.* Denver, 1933.

INNIS, HAROLD A. *The Fur Trade in Canada: An Introduction to Canadian Economic History.* New Haven, Conn., 1930.

JENNESS, DIAMOND. *The Sarsi Indians of Alberta.* National Museum of Canada, Bulletin 90, Anthropological Series, No. 23, Ottawa, 1938.

KEESING, FELIX M. *The Menomini Indians of Wisconsin: A Study of Three Centuries of Cultural Contact and Change.* Memoirs of the American Philosophical Society, Vol. 10. Philadelphia, 1939.

KELSEY, HENRY. *The Kelsey Papers,* ed. Arthur G. Dougherty and Chester Martin. Ottawa, 1929.

KROEBER, ALFRED L. *The Arapaho,* in *Bulletin of the American Museum of Natural History,* Vol. 18, Parts 1–2 (New York, 1902–1904), pp. 1–229.

———. *The Ceremonial Organization of the Plains Indians of North America.* Quebec: Congrès International des Américanistes, 1907.

———. "History and Science in Anthropology," *American Anthropologist,* n.s., Vol. 37 (Oct., 1935), pp. 539–69.

———. *Native Culture of the Southwest.* University of California Publications in American Archaeology and Ethnology, Vol. 23, No. 9. Berkeley, 1928.

LAROQUE, FRANCIS. *Journal,* ed. L. J. Burpee. Ottawa: Canadian Archives, 1911.

LARPENTEUR, CHARLES. *Forty Years a Fur Trader on the Upper Missouri: The Personal Narrative of Charles Larpenteur, 1833–1872,* ed. Elliott Coues. 2 vols. New York, 1898.

LINTON, RALPH, ed. *Acculturation in Seven American Indian Tribes.* New York, 1940.

LOWIE, ROBERT H. *Plains Indian Age-Societies.* American Museum of Natural History, Anthropological Papers, Vol. 11, Part 13. New York, 1916.

MACLEAN, JOHN (REV.) *McDougall of Alberta: Life of Rev. John McDougall.* Toronto, 1927.

———. "Social Organization of the Blackfoot Indians," in *Transactions of the Canadian Institute,* Vol. 4, 1892–93 (Toronto, 1895), pp. 249–60.

MANDELBAUM, DAVID G. *The Plains Cree.* New York: The American Museum of Natural History, 1940.

MARGRY, PIERRE (ed.). *Découvertes et établissements des français dans l'ouest et dans le sud de l'Amérique Septentrionale (1614–1754).* 6 vols. Paris, 1886.

MASSON, L. R. *Les bourgeois de la compagnie au Nord-Ouest: récits de voyages, lettres et rapports, inédits relatifs au Nord-Ouest.* 2 vols. Quebec, 1889–90.

MAXIMILIAN, PRINCE OF WIED-NEUWIED. *Travels in the Interior of North America, 1832–1834.* Trans. from the German by H. Evans Lloyd in 1843.

Vols. 22–25, in Reuben Gold Thwaites (ed.), *Early Western Travels, 1746–1846*. New York, 1906.

M'GILLIVRAY, DUNCAN. *The Journal of Duncan M'Gillivray of the Northwest Company at Fort George on the Saskatchewan, 1794–1795*, ed. Arthur S. Morton. Toronto, 1929.

MISHKIN, BERNARD. *Rank and Warfare Among the Plains Indians*. Monographs of the American Ethnological Society, No. 3. New York, 1940.

MOONEY, JAMES. *The Ghost-Dance Religion and the Sioux Outbreak of 1890*, in *Fourteenth Annual Report of the Bureau of American Ethnology*, Part 2. (Washington, D.C., 1896), pp. 641–1136.

MORTON, ARTHUR SILVER. *A History of the Canadian West to 1870–71*. Toronto, n.d.

MURRAY, GENEVIEVE. *Marias Pass*. Studies in Northwest History, No. 12, State University of Montana. Missoula, 1930.

OLIVER, E. H. (ed.). *The Canadian Northwest: Its Early Development and Legislative Records*. 2 vols. Ottawa: Government Printing Bureau, 1914–15.

OPLER, MARVIN. "The Southern Ute of Colorado," in Ralph Linton (ed.), *Acculturation in Seven American Indian Tribes* (New York, 1940), pp. 119–206.

RADIN, PAUL. *The Winnebago Tribe*. Thirty-seventh annual *Report of the Bureau of American Ethnology*. Washington, D.C., 1923.

RAY VERNE. *Cultural Relations on the Plateau of Northwestern America*. Publications of the F. W. Hodge Anniversary Publication Fund, Vol. 3. Los Angeles: The Southwest Museum, 1939.

RAYMER, ROBERT GEORGE. *Montana: The Land and the People*. 3 vols. Chicago, 1930.

RICHARDSON, JANE. "Blackfoot Field Notes," ms. Later published in *Observations on Northern Blackfoot Kinship*, by L. M. Hanks, Jr., and Jane Richardson. Monographs of the American Ethnological Society, Vol. 9. New York, 1945.

SAPIR, EDWARD. *Time Perspective in Aboriginal American Culture: A Study in Method*. Memoir 90, Geological Survey of Canada, Anthropological Series, No. 13. Ottawa, 1916.

———. "Wiyot and Yurok, Algonkin Languages of California," *American Anthropologist*, n.s., Vol. 15 (Oct., 1913), pp. 617–46.

SCHULTZ, JAMES WILLARD. *My Life as an Indian: The Story of a Red Woman and a White Man in the Lodges of the Blackfeet*. New York, 1907.

SMET, PIERRE JEAN DE. *Life, Letters, and Travels of Father Pierre Jean de Smet*, ed. H. M. Chittenden and A. T. Richardson. 4 vols. New York, 1905.

SMITH, MARIAN W. "War Complex of the Plains Indians," in *Proceedings of the American Philosophical Society*, Vol. 78, No. 3 (Philadelphia, 1938), pp. 425–64.

STANLEY, GEORGE FRANCIS GILMAN. *The Birth of Western Canada: A History of the Riel Rebellions*. London, 1936.

STEWARD, JULIAN H., and SETZLER, FRANK M. "Function and Configuration in Archaeology," *American Antiquity*, Vol. 4 (1939), pp. 4–11.

STRONG, WILLIAM DUNCAN. "From History to Prehistory in the Northern Great Plains," in *Essays in Historical Anthropology of North America*, Smithsonian Miscellaneous Collections, Vol. 100 (Washington, D.C.), 1940, pp. 353–94.

————. *An Introduction to Nebraska Archeology*. Smithsonian Miscellaneous Collections, Vol. 93, No. 10. Washington, D.C., 1935.

TEIT, JAMES A. "The Salishan Tribes of the Western Plateaus," in *Forty-fifth Annual Report of the Bureau of American Ethnology, 1927–28* (Washington, D.C., 1930), pp. 23–396.

THOMPSON, DAVID. *David Thompson's Narrative of his Explorations in Western America, 1784–1812*, ed. Joseph Burr Tyrell. The Champlain Society Publications, No. 12. Toronto, 1916.

TURNEY-HIGH, HARRY HOLBERT. *The Flathead Indians of Montana*. Memoirs of the American Anthropological Association, No. 48. Menasha, Wis., 1937.

TYRELL, J. B. (ed.). *Journals of Samuel Hearne and Philip Turner*. Toronto: Champlain Society, 1934.

UMFREVILLE, EDWARD. *The Present State of Hudson's Bay*. London, 1790.

U.S. DEPARTMENT OF THE INTERIOR. *Annual Report, 1862/63*. Washington, D.C., 1863.

————. *Annual Report, 1865/66*. Washington, D.C., 1866.

————. *Annual Report, 1867/68*. Washington, D.C., 1868.

————. *Annual Report, 1878/79*. Washington, D.C., 1879.

U.S. HOUSE OF REPRESENTATIVES. "Letter from the Secretary of War," 41st Cong., 2d Sess., H. Ex. Doc. No. 269, 1870.

U.S. OFFICE OF INDIAN AFFAIRS. *Annual Report, 1854*. Washington, D.C., 1854.

————. *Annual Report, 1857/58*. Washington, D.C., 1858.

————. *Annual Report, 1858/59*. Washington, D.C., 1859.

VOORHIS, E. *Historic Forts and Trading Posts of the French Regions and of the English Trading Posts*. Ottawa, 1930.

WALLACE, T. A. *The Passes of the Rocky Mountains along the Alberta Boundary*. Calgary: The Historical Society of Calgary, 1927.

WILSON, R. N. "Report on the Blackfoot Tribes," in *Report of the 57th Meeting of the British Association for the Advancement of Science, 1887* (London, 1888), pp. 183–97.

WISSLER, CLARK. *The Blackfoot Indians*. Annual Archeological Report, Appendix to the Report of the Minister of Education of Ontario, 1905. Toronto, 1906.

————. *Ceremonial Bundles of the Blackfoot Indians*, in *Social Organization and Ritualistic Ceremonies of the Blackfoot Indians*, American Museum of Natural History, Anthropological Papers, Vol. 7, Part 2. New York, 1912.

————. *The Diffusion of Culture in the Plains of North America*. Proceedings of the International Congress of Americanists. Quebec, 1906.

————. "Ethnographic Problems of the Missouri-Saskatchewan Area," *American Anthropologist*, n.s., Vol. 10 (April, 1908), pp. 197–207.

————. "The Influence of the Horse in the Development of Plains Culture," *American Anthropologist*, Vol. 16 (Jan., 1914), pp. 1–25.

————. *Material Culture of the Blackfoot Indians*. American Museum of Natural History, Anthropological Papers, Vol. 5, Part 1. New York, 1910.

————. *Social Life of the Blackfoot Indians*, in *Social Organization and Ritualistic Ceremonies of the Blackfoot Indians*, American Museum of Natural History, Anthropological Papers, Vol. 7, Part I. New York, 1912.

————. *Societies and Dance Associations of the Blackfoot Indians*, in *Societies of the Plains Indians,* ed. Clark Wissler, American Museum of Natural History, Anthropological Papers, Vol. 11, Part IV. New York, 1912–16.

———. *Structural Basis to the Decoration of Costumes Among the Plains Indians.* American Museum of Natural History, Anthropological Papers, Vol. 17, Part 3. New York, 1916.

———, and DUVALL, D. C. *Mythology of the Blackfoot Indians.* American Museum of Natural History, Anthropological Papers, Vol. 2, Part I. New York, 1908.

WORK, JOHN. *The Journal of John Work, a Chief-Trader of the Hudson's Bay Co., During his Expedition from Vancouver to the Flatheads and Blackfeet of the Pacific Northwest,* ed. William S. Lewis and Paul C. Phillips. Cleveland, 1923.

8

Manly-Hearted Women among the North Piegan[*]

It is the purpose of this paper (1) to present new material on North Piegan Indian women, introducing a unique type of female personality known as the manly-hearted woman, and (2) to consider manly-hearted women in terms of Blackfoot institutions, in relation to the broader problem of the effect of institutions on behavior.

The manly-hearted woman, *ninauposkitzipxpe*, represents a behavior pattern that is in striking contrast to the imputed docility of Plains Indian women and indicates a keen appreciation of personality differences among a simple people. The term is applied to a small group of women who do not behave in the restricted manner of the women of this tribe, but who have a freedom and independence more like that of women in our own culture. Manly-heartedness is manifested in a woman's interest in and ownership of property, in her behavior in public, in her domestic and sexual life, and in her participation in religious affairs. These will be discussed under separate headings, although it must be understood that there is considerable overlapping. An understanding of the manly-hearted woman hinges upon a knowledge of Blackfoot institutions and the role generally played by women in this culture.

[*] This study was made with the aid of Ruth Lewis during the summer of 1939, at the Brocket Reserve in Alberta. Funds for the study were provided by Columbia University. The North Piegan are a Canadian Blackfoot tribe. This was first published in the *American Anthropologist*, n.s., April-June, 1941, Vol. 3, No. 2, pp. 173–87.

The Blackfoot were a typical Plains tribe in their dependence upon the buffalo, in the importance of horses, in the war complex, the Sun Dance, medicine bundles, and the vision quest. What set them apart was their emphasis upon the ownership, manipulation, and disposition of property. Horses, medicine pipes, painted tipis, war charms, war bonnets, songs, and ritual knowledge were all private property and could be bought and sold. The ownership of horses was a major index of social status. Bravery and war deeds, the usual requirements for chieftainship, were here not as essential as wealth and generosity. There was a striking commercialism in religion, every step in ritual involving property payments.[1] Even the transfer of a bundle from father to son had to be validated, and visions were bought and sold without loss of prestige. Despite the fluidity of wealth resulting from this and from the ostentatious distribution of property made in the name of the favored child, the contrast between rich and poor was sharp and was intensified by the marked social distinctions which were based on ownership of property and participation in religious affairs. However, concentration of wealth in the same family unit for more than one generation was prevented by the absence of rigid interest mechanisms and primogeniture, the continual depletion of horses by raiding parties, the destruction of property at one's death, and the distribution of property by a system of lateral inheritance.

Women were basic to the functioning of the economic system, both in the domestic household and as producers of wealth. They enjoyed the prerogatives of wealth and could own and inherit property. Women were also accorded a major role in Blackfoot religion, as is evidenced by the part they play in the Sun Dance, the greatest religious and social event of the year.[2] Whereas among other Plains tribes women take part in the Sun Dance in one small capacity or another, here they are the central figures.[3] In addition, husband and wife constitute the normal ritual unit in the transfer of bundles, the

[1] Clark Wissler was the first to point out the extreme individual character of Blackfoot bundle ownership and the "unusual development of the social and investment character of the bundle transfer." See *Ceremonial Bundles of the Blackfoot Indians*, American Museum of Natural History, Anthropological Papers, Vol. 7, Part 2 (New York, 1912), pp. 280, 282.

[2] For a full description of Sun Dance ritual see Clark Wissler, *The Sun Dance of the Blackfoot Indians*, American Museum of Natural History, Anthropological Papers, Vol. 16, Part 3 (New York, 1918).

[3] The contrast is particularly sharp in the case of the "Antler" women, who had no active part in religion. See M. Mead, *The Changing Culture of an Indian Tribe* (New York, 1932), p. 139.

selling of painted tipis, and the joining of age grade societies, both sharing the prestige involved.

The position of women among the North Piegan is further affected by the emphasis placed upon women as sexual objects. Those who are desirable sex partners can attain a freedom, independence, and security denied other women. Such women more often become favorite wives, *ninauake*, which is a position parallel to that of favored children, except that it is even more desirable and envied. All children are well treated by their parents but only few wives are so favored by their husbands; the contrast between a favored child and other children is not as sharp as that between a favorite wife and other wives.

A *ninauake* is an ideal wife, kind, loyal, and deeply attached to her husband. Her greater personal freedom is the result of a feeling of trust in her on the part of her husband. This is based largely upon the fact that a *ninauake* departs considerably from the conventional sex behavior of Piegan women, that of being passive and undemonstrative, and makes a point of satisfying her husband sexually. She undresses for him, is demonstratively affectionate even in the daytime, and allows a great deal of sex play. Today, the younger men place great emphasis upon their sexual activity and they take the term *ninauake* to have reference to a passionate woman.

In pre-reserve days polygyny and the junior levirate were practised. The sororate tended to lessen friction in the polygynous household, but the sharp contrast in status between upper and lower wives remained. The most coveted position was that of the chief or "sit-by" wife. Lower wives were called "slave wives," which was a rather accurate description of their status. A lower wife could achieve the status of a chief wife only, and this was a rare exception, when the upper wives died—and then she was usually charged with having used sorcery. Reversals in the position of wives did occur, but they usually involved women of wealthy families who had become lower wives. Such women might improve their condition by putting up a Sun Dance, getting medicine power, and brazenly dominating the other wives. If a poor, lower wife became troublesome and bossy, she would be beaten unmercifully until cowed or she would be sent away, while a lower wife who was the daughter of a well-to-do family, if persistent, often succeeded in becoming the chief wife and sometimes became known as a manly-hearted woman.

Despite the important social, economic, and religious role of women, the Piegan culture puts a premium upon masculinity and encourages male dominance. The bride price, preferred patrilocal residence, the double standard and wife beating, the formal age grades and institutionalized friendship relationships which exist only for men, the exclusive participation of men in the tribal government, and the general channeling of prestige to the men are sufficient evidence for this. The presence of manly-hearted women in such a milieu is therefore particularly striking.

An analysis of manly-hearted women may be approached from two points of view, that is, the manly-hearted woman as a personality type and manly-heartedness as a socially recognized though deviant status. The former may be described in terms of character traits, the latter in terms of the culturally dictated requisites for status membership.[4] Since the material gathered for this study is not complete enough for an intense psychological study, we will confine ourselves mainly to a consideration of the institutional and status aspects of manly-heartedness.

A complex of traits go to make up manly-heartedness: aggressiveness, independence, ambition, boldness, and sexuality. This configuration of traits is not a stable entity, nor do all manly-hearted women share in them equally. Although certain character traits are associated with manly-heartedness, it is only when a woman of a definite status manifests them in a particular social situation that she is considered manly-hearted. The manly-hearted designation is applied only to married women. Unmarried girls who exhibit similar characteristics are not called by that term. Secondly, the term manly-hearted woman is applied only to women of wealth and high social position. There are poor women among the Piegan today who are aggressive and bold, but they are considered presumptuous upstarts rather than manly-hearted women. Such behavior, to be called manly-hearted, must be validated by wealth.

The behavior considered ideal in Piegan women is submissiveness, reserve, faithfulness, and kindness. However, in this culture with its groupings of rich and poor, we find there are different standards of behavior, which cut across sex lines, sanctioned for members of each group. Poor men and women generally exhibit more humility and shame in public situations, in keeping with their low social position. Thus, although all women, considered as a group in contrast to men, are expected to be submissive and retiring, there is a qualitative difference in their behavior according to their position on the social and economic scale.

Manly-heartedness is a definite classification recognized by all in the community. Of 109 married women on the reserve, 14 are manly-hearted. The following chart gives the range of ages of these women:

---

[4] See Ralph Linton, *The Study of Man* (New York, 1936), chap. 26.

Name	Age	Name	Age
Widow G.	80	Mrs. L. G.	60
Widow S. L.	75	Mrs. J. O.	59
Widow N. G.	75	Mrs. J. E.	53
Mrs. M. W. S.	66	Mrs. M. G.	52
Widow E.	63	Mrs. S. A.	49
Mrs. C. W.	63	Mrs. C. P.	45
Widow S.	63	Mrs. L. M.	32

From the chart we see that there are no manly-hearted women below the age of 32, while the majority are above 50. We have here, then, maturity as a third criterion of manly-heartedness. The percentage of manly-hearted women in each of the age groups in which they are found is as follows:

Age Group	No. of Women	Percentage of Manly-Hearted Women
30–40	21	5%
40–50	10	20%
50–60	14	21%
60–70	14	36%
70–80	6	33%
80–90	2	50%

Of the two women over 80, one is manly-hearted. Thirty percent of the women on the reserve over 50 and 36 percent of those over 60 are manly-hearted. The increased proportion of manly-hearted women in each ascending age group indicates that age is not a negligible factor.

The percentages, however, are low enough to show that age is by no means the sole determinant of manly-heartedness and that, clearly, other factors are involved.

We have classified as manly-hearted only those women about whom there was unanimity of opinion on the part of informants. Lack of agreement occurred only in connection with a few younger women who were designated as manly-hearted by some and as almost manly-hearted by others. This disagreement reflects the indecisiveness and lack of consistency in the behavior of these younger women, whose position becomes more clearly defined as they grow older.

The Piegan make a clear distinction between the real and the would-be manly-hearted women, and they differentiate between the manly-hearted women of the old days and the mere boldness of the modern, younger women. It is considered easier to be bold today, for the white-man's law protects wives from their husband's severe discipline, and the older women look with disdain upon some of the would-be manly-hearts. It is important to note that the group given above are probably the last representatives of the old type of manly-hearted women.

· P R O P E R T Y ·

There is complete agreement among informants that property ownership is one of the main factors in the development of "manly" traits in women. Informants laughed at our question, "Are any manly-hearted women poor?" The answer invariably was that a poor woman would not have the nerve to do the things that are considered manly-hearted.

Investigation of property ownership on the reserve today among the 109 married women revealed that the 14 manly-hearted women own more property than all the others combined. Twelve non-manly-hearted women own property in their own right; 7 of these fall into the almost-manly-hearted category. There are 83 women who own no property. Some in this group had horses which were taken over by their husbands upon marriage. In contrast, manly-hearted women insist upon having their own horse and cattle brands, despite pressure from the agency, which is striving to have husband and wife use the same brand. The difference in attitude toward husband-wife property relations is made clear by the fact that in conversation most women, in speaking of their own horses, say "my husband's horses," whereas the manly-hearted woman will speak of her own and her husband's as "my horses."

The acquisition of property by women is dependent upon three sources: their own work, inheritance, and gifts. In all three of these, manly-hearted women, largely as a result of their native ability and interest and their background and social position, are more fortunate than the average Piegan woman.

Manly-hearted women excel in both men's and women's work. Their efficiency and drive enable them to get more work done in a shorter time. For example, it takes most women six days to tan a hide which a manly-hearted woman can do in four or five days. A manly-hearted woman can bead a dress or a man's suit in a week of hard work, while it takes most women a month. An average worker makes a pair of moccasins in a week, while a manly-hearted woman can make it in little over a day. These excellent workers are able to produce over and above the personal needs of the household, creating a surplus that could be traded for horses. A manly-hearted woman is therefore an economic asset, which is the only justification the Piegan give for a woman's dominating her husband. There are many men who, in the past as well as today, owe their wealth and standing

in the community to the encouragement, hard work, and perseverance of their manly-hearted wives.

The ability of these women to take on the economic role of men
makes them self-sufficient and gives them an added source of independence. This is invaluable in the present depressed condition of
reserve economy. Most women who are left stranded with their families, either by the death or desertion of their husbands, are forced to
accept the first offer of marriage because of the need of support.
However, Mrs. C. P., a manly-hearted woman who was deserted by
her husband for four years, supported herself and her three children
by hiring herself out as a farm laborer, stacking hay and breaking
horses. She was also able to raise money by making and selling bead-
work and ceremonial outfits. Another manly-hearted woman who
was left a childless widow at the age of twenty-eight maintained
herself alone on her small farm for ten years before she decided to
remarry.

The practice of medicine is another source of income for women.
Manly-hearted women are very active in this field, for the six most
important medicine women on the reserve are all in the manly-
hearted group.

Inheritance is another major source of property. Women can inherit from their grandparents, parents, siblings, and friends. Wissler
and Grinnell report that a wife does not inherit her dead husband's
property, except those horses or other property that he may have
presented to her during his lifetime. This has probably been the conventional procedure, but my case material leads me to believe that
there are numerous exceptions. An examination of fifty wills voluntarily written and deposited with the agency since 1900 shows that
wives have consistently received a good portion of the property.
Both the wills and the case histories show that horses, medicine
bundles, and the ceremonial clothing and regalia of age-grade societies have been bequeathed to wives. The earliest cases of this go
back to 1900 and 1903, making it difficult to determine whether this
was due exclusively to white influence or was a continuation of an
old pattern.[5]

Women who outlive several husbands often gain a goodly fortune
from this type of inheritance. The effect of this can most clearly be
seen in cases where women do not become manly-hearted until after
several marriages. Mrs. M. had three husbands. She put up a Sun

[5] Gittel Poznanski Steed, who worked with the South Piegan, told me of a number of cases going back to the early 1880's in which wives inherited property
from dead husbands. One of the techniques used was for the husband's best
friend, *taka,* to step in and safeguard the widow from her husband's family by
putting aside his property for her.

Dance during her first marriage but was not considered manly-hearted. Her husband was a hard man and she was docile. When he died, she inherited a good deal of his property and remarried. She began to change. People made remarks about it. When guests came to visit, she was no longer a quiet, timid woman, but contradicted her new husband and asserted her own opinions. When he died, she married Mr. M., a much older man, known for his brutality and severe discipline of his other wives. It was after her third marriage that Mrs. M. became an out-and-out "manly-heart," dominating the "poor old man." Here, then, her experience in dealing with men, the personalities of her husbands, and the property inherited from each, seem to be among the contributing factors.

The case of Mrs. C., a manly-hearted woman and the favorite wife of a chief, is another illustration of the importance of inheritance from a dead husband. When Chief C. died, One Owl married Widow C. because she had inherited a major portion of C.'s estate. She became One Owl's third wife, but after a year with the other two wives, who quarreled incessantly, she left their tipi and moved into another, taking One Owl with her. She thereby reversed the former status arrangements and became his chief or "sit-by" wife. She began to reform One Owl, who had been a drunkard and a gambler. She forced him to give up drinking and interested him in buying holy things. She became more dominating than ever, taking advantage of her high rank and of her greater wealth.

Widows with property are sought out as wives, with the result that they are often able to marry men much younger than themselves. The discrepancy in ages in ten such marriages ranges from five to twenty-six years, the median age difference between man and wife being thirteen years.

Finally, we must consider gift-giving as a source of income for women. This is related to the institution of the favored child, whereby parents returned twofold any gifts given in honor of their favorite. This stimulated gift-giving has proved a reliable source of income for favored children. A favored daughter has usually a considerable amount of her own property by the time she is to marry. Widow G. at the age of fifteen owned fifteen head of horses, a shield bundle, and a medicine bonnet, aside from the tipi furnishings given to her as a marriage gift. Mrs. C. P., another favored child, owned over thirty horses when she married. A wife may occasionally give her husband a gift of a horse or buy a medicine pipe for him, but more often will merely allow him the use of her horses, retaining her right of ownership.

· B E H A V I O R   I N   P U B L I C ·

Manly-hearted women were most easily distinguished from other women by their behavior and appearance. They dressed better than the rest; they wore well-tanned skins, expensive buckskin dresses decorated with elk-teeth, and fine leggings embroidered with porcupine quills. At dances and other public occasions their clothes and those of their husbands were the finest, testifying to their skill in tanning, sewing, and beading. Today they wear neat cloth dresses, always scrupulously clean, and evidently take more than usual interest in their appearance.

In the old days a modest woman never went out without her blanket and shawl. A manly-hearted woman, especially if she were well formed, discarded her shawl and sometimes her blanket. Her husband was proud to have her admired, which is quite contrary to the usual situation in which husbands are intensely jealous. Today, in mixed social gatherings, when other women sit with lowered eyes, their shawls tightly clasped about them, rarely contributing a word to the conversation, a "manly-heart" is at ease, removes her shawl, and talks as freely to the men as do women in our own culture. Manly-hearts do not hesitate to make speeches in crowds; they joke and tease and express opinions and disagreements "just as though they were men." They are often avoided because of their sharp tongues and readiness to defend themselves from criticism by exposing others to ridicule and humiliation. We heard repeatedly that a manly-hearted woman "takes no lip," and our observation fully confirmed this.

Their behavior at dances is in sharp contrast to that of other women. Many women are too shy to choose male partners when it is their turn to do so. Manly-hearted women and older women usually jump up first and select their partners without hesitation. There is no shyness in their manner of dancing and they speak loudly and tease their partners so that all may hear. A proud chief who insults the other women by dancing only with his wife is often embarrassed by the manly-hearted women present who shout out against him and tell him to dance with someone else. No one but an aggressive, daring person would speak to a chief in this manner. It is this boldness which often leads to quarrels and to physical violence.

These women use "dirty" words in conversation and vituperative terms in argument, as do men. One of our manly-hearted informants made a pun based on the similarity of the words "it is mine" and "vagina." The same woman, who is eighty years old, is the only person on the reserve who urinates in public.

In song most women have little freedom of expression. They fear to sing alone lest their husbands become jealous and beat them, interpreting it as a secret love song. Only manly-hearted women are ever heard to sing alone or in the presence of their husbands. Religious songs are sung by women only in chorus, and even manly-hearted women were too embarrassed to sing alone and refused our request. However, Widow G., a very manly-hearted woman, did not wait to be asked but took out her bag of one hundred sticks and sang a song for each of them. She is the only woman who sings men's songs during religious ceremonies.

· DOMESTIC AND SEXUAL BEHAVIOR ·

In almost every domestic situation manly-hearted women behave in a more independent, assured, aggressive manner than others. They are more respected by their husbands and in many cases conduct their lives without interference. In the opinion of most people they dominate their husbands and control their business affairs.[6] When a man marries such a woman his friends say, "He will be bossed by his wife from now on." As an old informant put it, "It's easy to spot a manly-hearted woman; the husband simply has nothing to say." When he wishes to give a gift, sell a horse, or make a purchase, he must consult his wife and get her consent. When visitors, including anthropologists, come, the man will call his wife to take part in the conversation. However, in many of the homes we visited, wives were not permitted or were too shy to come into the room for the duration of our visit.

A manly-hearted woman won't "take as much" from her husband as other women. If things cannot be changed to suit her, she will leave the tipi and marry again. The successive marriages of Mrs. N. illustrate this. She left her first husband because he wanted a second wife, which she would not tolerate. Her next husband was hard to get along with. If she made a pair of moccasins that did not fit precisely, he would become angry and beat her. She fought back and resisted him for two years; when she could bear it no longer, she left him and married Mr. N.

A different reaction to mistreatment may be seen in the case of Widow G., who was much abused by her first and second husbands

[6] This was aptly put by a trader as early as 1794, who wrote, "But notwithstanding the boundless authority of the men,—a few of the other sex wear the Breeches." *The Journal of Duncan M'Gillivray* . . . , *1794–1795*, ed. Arthur S. Morton (Toronto, 1929), pp. 33–34.

during the first few months of both marriages. She never took her beatings without fighting back, which is rare for Piegan women. Once, after receiving a severe beating and threats of being killed because she refused to go to a dance, Widow G. took her knife and said to her husband, "Your body is not made of iron and I can kill you too." He was so frightened he ran away. Another time, in order to humiliate him for mistreating her, she tore off all her clothes and ran out of the tipi saying she was going back to her people that way. He was embarrassed and carried her back in a blanket. This type of resistance is found only in manly-hearted women and usually results in an improvement of their situation.

If a manly-hearted woman was not a chief wife, she always tried to become one. When Mrs. N., cited above, married Mr. N., she became a fourth wife and had to live in one tipi with his three other wives. Mrs. N. became troublesome and even cruel to the three higher wives and before long took the bed of the "sit by" wife. Her behavior caused the other wives to leave, one by one. She was an excellent worker and shrewd in business transactions, thus redeeming herself in the eyes of her husband, who soon became well-to-do through her efforts. Widow G., an even more striking case, became a third wife at the age of seventeen. This was unusual because she was the favored child of a wealthy family and the daughter of a chief. She worked hard at first under the supervision of the other wives, who were much older. Soon, however, this young girl began to order them about and caused trouble in the tipi. She looked after the personal needs of her husband, which was the duty of the "sit-by" wife. At eighteen she put up a Sun Dance and used that as a reason to move her bed to the chief wife's place. She mistreated the other wives and caused so many arguments that they moved into another tipi.

The secure position of manly-hearted women in the tipi is largely a result of their active sexuality. All manly-hearted women today are reputedly *ikitaki* (passionate women), and their sexual unconventionalities are the subject of much gossip. They are known to be more demonstrative, to take the male position in sexual intercourse and allow their husbands to play *motsini* (pulling the labia). Manly-hearted women speak with scorn of women "whose husbands are always complaining, and reminding them to like it more."

Widow G. was famous on the reserve as a passionate woman. When her husband died she almost went mad with grief. She spent four days and nights alone in his death tipi. Once her husband's sister came to the tipi to pray and saw her lying on the corpse as though having intercourse with it! For a time the young widow "went wild," chasing men and boys and going to the bush with them.

She fell in love with a medicine man and rode for miles each day to see him. She would call out at the door of his tipi and ask him to come and teach her songs. They would go to the bush together to "learn songs." Interestingly, the usual pattern is that of medicine men seducing women by promising to teach them ritual songs. In this case the role of seducer was reversed.

Manly-hearted women, although not necessarily more virtuous than others, claim to be so. They prove themselves virtuous and make themselves feared by publicly shaming men who dare to flirt with them. If these bold women have broken their marriage vows, they do not fear contradiction or exposure, for they are quick to defend themselves and are believed to take vengeance by sorcery. That they can protect themselves from gossip is seen in the case of Widow G., who, despite general knowledge of her early wantonness, was able to attain the position of being the most important Sun Dance woman on the reserve.

The term "manly" as applied to these women does not refer to masculinity of appearance or sexual behavior and in no sense should be taken to mean homosexuality. The term "manly" refers to their aggressiveness and boldness, characteristics considered more appropriate to men. The aggressiveness these women display in sex is only one aspect—and a most important one in this culture—of a generally aggressive personality.

· R E L I G I O N ·

The institutionalized role of women in Piegan religion is a reflection of their social and economic importance. Any woman who fulfills the requirements of unbroken marriage vows may purchase a Sun Dance bundle, but in practice, participation in this or other religious events is limited by social, economic, and personal factors.

Sun Dance bundles were very expensive until recently and only women of wealth or members of wealthy families could undertake to vow a purchase. Further, a woman who vows a Sun Dance takes upon herself the responsibility for the health and well-being of her family. If death or disease strikes any member of her family, it is interpreted to be a result of her broken marriage vows. Many women who are otherwise eligible shrink from the publicity, gossip, and responsibility that attend the position of Sun Dance woman. The average Piegan woman is expected to be shy in public and has no preparation for playing a major role in a religious ceremony. The personality traits necessary for undertaking a Sun Dance are developed largely in girls of well-to-do families and particularly in favored daughters.

Manly-hearted women too are well fitted for participation in religious affairs. They are wealthy and possess the prerequisite personality traits. There were some, known to be unvirtuous, who had the temerity to overlook their pasts in vowing a Sun Dance. We know of only one case in which such a woman was exposed. The aforementioned Widow G. had put up many Sun Dances, although it was common knowledge that she had had many lovers. No one dared to denounce her in public and she continued to purchase bundles unhindered. Once she entered the Sun Lodge with all the good women to take the ordeal of the tongues. The Sun Dance was being put up by the daughter of a former lover, who was a medicine man and chief. When he saw her enter, he stopped the ceremony and said it would not be continued as long as she remained, for she had no right to be there. She left immediately, deeply humiliated. This man died six years later and everyone believed she had caused his death by sorcery. She again began to put up Sun Dances and vowed thirteen of them.

There is an ambivalent attitude toward manly-heartedness, which is a designation both of opprobrium and of distinction. Men are aware of the advantages in being married to a manly-hearted woman; she is a desirable sex partner, a skilled worker, and an economic asset. On the other hand, she refuses to allow her husband mastery of the household, thus exposing him to ridicule. Women consider this unconventional behavior immodest and dread the thought of their own daughters becoming manly-hearted. In another mood, however, they speak with envy and admiration of the courage and skill of manly-hearted women and look upon their deviations as a form of female protest in a man's culture.

We have seen that manly-heartedness is often associated with being a favored child, a chief or favorite wife, a passionate woman, an excellent worker, and a Sun Dance woman. There is a tendency on the part of the natives to view these accomplishments as determinants of manly-heartedness. Although this seems the case, it is difficult to determine the weight that should be attributed to these factors because of the gaps in the data. Any analysis, therefore, can only be suggestive of the problems involved.

There is no one cause for manly-heartedness, nor do all manly-hearted women go through the same stages of development. In some cases a woman will not become manly-hearted until after several marriages, while in others manly-heartedness can be discerned in childhood and adolescence. The latter is particularly true in the cases of favored children, whose background is conducive to the development of the manly-hearted personality.

Favored children, *manipuka*, are placed in situations which other children do not experience, such as having membership in an adult society bought for them and having expensive gifts given away in their names. They have more experience with religious ceremonies, are ceremonially painted on many occasions, and often own religious articles at an early age. This enriched experience predisposes *manipuka* for the career of a medicine woman. Of the six important medicine women on the reserve who are manly-hearted, four are also *manipuka*.

Favored children have more toys, more food to offer playmates, more care and attention from parents and siblings. They are considered as set apart and above others, the effect of which is to make them less shy, more dominating, and give them the bearing of a person of importance. Four of our manly-hearted women were known as leaders in their childhood playgroups. They played boys' games in which they appropriated for themselves the names of great warriors. Such behavior on the part of girls was discouraged by the older women, who characterized them as "girls who acted as if they wanted to run the tribe." Informants believed that a favored child tends to become manly-hearted. Certainly, when a favored daughter becomes the "sit-by" wife of a chief, she is in a position to carry over her childhood attitudes and behavior to her marital status and become a manly-hearted woman. However, only six out of fourteen manly-hearted women had been favored children, indicating that many other factors were at work.

There was a great deal of sex play among children, especially in their tipi games, the native term for which is literally translated as "playing dirty." In every band there were a few girls who were known for their preoccupation with sex. The verbal prohibitions used in discouraging sex play were much stronger for the girls than for the boys. At the same time it was the girls of ten to thirteen who initiated the younger boys into their first sex experiences. This early aggressiveness and sexual activity is significant in view of the fact that in adult life active sexuality is associated with manly-hearted women. Whether the girls who are most active in tipi sex play are the ones apt to become manly-hearted women is an important question that deserves further investigation.

The development of manly-heartedness must also be seen in the light of the discontinuities and conflicts in the lives of many women, who are expected to adapt themselves to changes sometimes brutally extreme. Girls who engaged in active sexuality during the tipi play of childhood and adolescence were, with marriage, thrust into a new status heavy with penalties for unfaithfulness, a change for which they were quite unprepared.[7] In child marriages, which occurred more frequently when the importance of bride price in horses increased, marriage represented an abrupt transition at a tender age. The great age differences between girls and their husbands sometimes led to difficulties in sexual adjustment and represented a reversal of the conditions under which some girls grew up. Before marriage they had sexual relations with boys younger than themselves. The physical differences between their young lovers and their mature husbands, who were usually between the ages of twenty-five and thirty-five, came as a distinct shock to them. One of our manly-hearted women married at the age of nine. She found the sudden break with her childhood friends difficult to bear and often ran away to join her old playmates in their tipi games. Her mother and mother-in-law would call her away and reprimand her, saying, "You are a married woman now, you must stop playing with other boys." When she grew older, she received frequent beatings from her husband but she fought back. She later became known as a manly-hearted woman.

The discontinuities in the lives of women are not limited to the sexual level. With marriage a girl must tan her first skins, make her first clothes, and please her husband in all things, for he has the right to beat her. The beatings a woman receives from her husband are the first ever experienced by her, for parents do not beat their children. In the cases of favored children who become third or lower wives, the adjustments are even more difficult. They are no longer attended but have to attend, they are no longer without responsibilities but have many duties, they no longer go unpunished but are at the mercies of their husbands. Case histories show that manly-heartedness sometimes results from this situation.

Manly-hearted women may be looked upon as a result of the logical working out of Piegan property institutions and of the emphasis placed upon women as sexual objects—factors which give them an important and secure position. However, this is only part of the picture. The Piegan culture is a man's culture, and women who achieve distinction can do so only in terms of men's values, as is seen by the very designation, "manly-hearted" woman. There is a discrepancy between the important economic and religious role played by Piegan women and the established standards of female behavior that laud meekness and docility and require women to relegate themselves to

[7] Ruth Benedict, "Continuities and Discontinuities in Cultural Conditioning," *Psychiatry*, Vol. 1, No. 2 (May, 1938). Dr. Benedict contrasts the discontinuities in conditioning in our culture with the continuities in a number of selected primitive societies. Among the Piegan we find both continuities and discontinuities in the life cycle of women.

the background of Piegan social life. In terms of the cultural norms, the manly-hearted woman is a deviant—a highly endowed woman who takes advantage of the opportunities afforded women in this culture. When women can equal men in their own skills, in personal wealth, in the manipulation of property, in sexual prowess, and in religious participation, they may break away from the verbalized restrictions applied to their sex and become known as manly-hearted women.

Part Three:

RURAL U.S.A.

9

Rural Cross Section[*]

Bell County, on the edge of the Black Waxy in the western part of the Cotton Belt, contains within its borders much of the diversity and color that is Texas. It is characterized by a great variety in topography, types of farming, ethnic groups, and cultural patterns. The county embraces two distinct and contrasting topographical regions, namely, the Black Prairie and the Grand Prairie divisions. The line of separation between these two regions runs approximately north and south near the center of the county. The eastern half of the county, in the Black Prairie Division, is a treeless, level to gently rolling prairie, with rich black sticky soils locally known as "blackwaxy." This land has made the county famous as one of the best cotton counties in Texas. The western half of the county, in the Grand Prairie Division, is rolling to hilly land, with lighter, sandier soils covered with cedar and mesquite grass. Much of the land is rough and stony, and in some places rises to two hundred feet above the surrounding country.

Associated with the striking difference in topography and soils between the eastern and western parts of the county are significant differences in population density, type of farming, levels of living, size of school districts, neighborhood structure, social participation, and the effectiveness of agricultural agencies. This has made for a

[*] This was first published in 1948 in *Scientific Monthly*, Vol. 66, No. 4.

type of local regionalism that is an important aspect of the life of the county.

The diversity of Bell County is in large part a function of its marginal position, which has exposed it to two distinctive influences, that of the Cotton South and the Cattle West. As in the South, cotton has dominated the economy and has made a deep impression on the life and customs of the people. But the plantation system, which was the core of Southern culture, never took root. This, together with the early importance of stock-raising as against cotton-growing, was responsible for the development of cultural characteristics distinct from those of the Deep South. Indeed, King Cotton never reigned alone in Bell County. The tradition of the cowboy has come down from the early days when stock raising was the major occupation, and today every schoolboy knows that the Chisholm Trail ran through the center of the county. Unlike the Deep South, Bell County had no leisure class to romanticize cotton farming, and it could at no time compete with ranching in capturing the imagination of the people as an ideal way of life.[1]

As in the South, there is an extremely high incidence of tenancy; but unlike the South, the county has few sharecroppers. Landlord-tenant relationships are not characterized by the dominance-submission pattern of the Deep South, and tenancy carries much less of the stigma of social inferiority. Levels of living, social participation, and leadership do not closely follow tenure lines. In this respect Bell County resembles the West and Midwest.

The absence of the plantation system, the prevalence of family-sized farms, and the fact that Negroes are not basic to the agricultural economy and are but a small part of the total population make for much less rigidity in social controls and the class structure. The relative recency of the pioneer period, which, because of the late settlement of the eastern portion of the county, lasted until the early 1900's, has had a leveling influence and gives the county some of the characteristic qualities and spirit of the West. The comparatively high standard of living and educational level are also in contrast with the Deep South. Bell County ranks second among thirteen sample Cotton Belt counties in level of living and ranks first in general educational achievement of both farm and nonfarm people.

Although Negro-white relationships are governed by the folkways of the South, the social structure does not revolve around race rela-

---

[1] The people of Bell County generally do not think of themselves as "Southerners" or "Westerners," but as Texans. However, they identify with the South when speaking with "Yankees." It is interesting to note that on the eve of the Civil War the county was about equally divided on the issue of Unionism versus Secession.

tions; and although Negroes are segregated socially and have separate schools, low-income Negroes, Mexicans, and whites may live next door to one another in the towns. Furthermore, Mexican children attend white schools.

The greater ethnic heterogeneity of the population further differentiates Bell County from the Deep South. The Czechs and Germans with their distinctive institutions lend a variety to the social structure similar to that found in the West and Midwest. The presence of a number of Catholic, Czech Moravian, German Lutheran, and German Methodist churches also gives a distinctive quality to the church life of the county.

The position of ethnic minorities in Bell County differs somewhat from both the Deep South and the West. In the Deep South, where the rate of assimilation is exceedingly slow, ethnic groups tend to form clusters of culture islands. In the Midwest and far West, particularly in Oregon, Idaho, and Washington, where settlement came late and was completed in a comparatively short time, where settlers represented a great variety of ethnic backgrounds and spread out in loosely organized open-country nieghborhoods, ethnic differences disappeared rapidly. After a few years, nationality backgrounds became quite unimportant in local life. Bell County can be placed about midway between these two types of ethnic adjustment. The Czechs and Germans of Bell County, unlike those of the Deep South, are becoming assimilated and acculturated at a fairly rapid rate. In this respect they more closely resemble Czechs and Germans in the West and Midwest. Until recently, however, these people formed cultural islands, and they still live in their own communities and have their distinctive churches and social organization.

The concept of the United States as a melting pot of peoples of different nationalities and cultural backgrounds has been applied almost exclusively to urban areas. As a matter of fact, this process has also been going on in rural areas, although more slowly and less perceptibly. Bell County lends itself to a study of this process, and in this survey I shall compare the customs and value systems of the Czech and German farmers with those of the old-line Americans and wherever possible will indicate the changes that have occurred in the process of Americanization.[2]

Two other factors have had a very important influence on the life and people of Bell County. The first factor is the presence of Temple, a large urban center, within the county, and the proximity

[2] Throughout this paper the term "old-line American" is used to refer to third-, fourth-, fifth- (or more) generation individuals of English, Scotch, Irish, or Welsh descent, most of whose parents or grandparents came to Bell County from Southern states.

of the county to large metropolitan centers like Dallas and Fort Worth, a hundred miles to the north, and Austin, less than seventy miles to the south; the second is the excellent means of communication of the county with the outside, including railroads, good highways, buses, an airport at Temple, a radio station, newspapers, telegraph, and telephone. The Gulf, Colorado & Santa Fe and the Missouri-Kansas-Texas railroads run north and south and east and west, respectively, through the county and provide direct contacts with the Pacific Coast to the west, and with the large cities of the East. No town or neighborhood is more than ten or fifteen miles from a railroad, and all railroad stations have Western Union offices. U.S. Highway 81 runs through the county and connects with Waco in the north and Austin in the south.

Farmers in Bell County show a Western disregard of distances. Many think nothing of traveling a hundred miles or more to go on a hunting trip, to attend a football game, or to visit a stock show. The proximity of large urban centers, combined with excellent means of communication, has exposed the rural people to frequent contacts with the Great Society. The townspeople have furthered this trend by making Bell County a cultural center and a meeting place for civic, business, agricultural, and social organizations of the region. The townspeople have also been very active in the support and leadership of farm organizations and thus have been the cultural middlemen between the farmers of Bell County and the outside world. These factors have made for much less provincialism than is characteristic of rural areas in the Deep South.

A further word of introduction is necessary. The social organization of Bell County is in a state of great flux. Rural neighborhoods, schools, and churches are changing; new adjustments and integrations are taking place. These processes are occurring on various levels, between town and country, between ethnic groups, and between different parts of the county. In part, this is a result of the recent trends in agriculture toward greater diversification, and in part it represents a delayed reaction to improvements in the means of communication, greater contacts with the outside, and other developments that have had an accumulative effect over the years. In general, the movement has been away from localism and provincialism toward identification with larger groups over larger areas.

Bell County was selected for study to represent one segment of the Cotton Belt, but it also represents a cross section of a functioning bit of America. Negroes and whites, Mexicans and old-line Americans, townspeople and country people, cotton farmers and ranchers, cedar choppers and charcoal burners, rich and poor—all live together under the common political and administrative rubric of the county.

Although a county study cannot probe as deeply into all facets of life as might a study of a single community, it has the advantage of focusing attention upon the dynamic interrelationships *between* communities, between racial and ethnic groups, between town and country, and between distinctive regions within the county. It is in terms of the interplay of all these factors that the social organization of Bell County is here studied.

In this survey I have attempted to show how the factors of physical environment, history, ethnic composition, and cultural heritage of the farm population have combined to give the rural life and social organization of Bell County its distinctive quality. In the following discussion I shall summarize the role of these factors under three headings: regionalism within the county, the role of cultural factors in farming practices and rural social organizations, and current trends and problems.

Regionalism within the county. The differences in topography and soils between the eastern and western parts of the county have had far-reaching influence on the social and economic life. In the west, the combination of rolling to hilly land, light, sandy soils, and large wooded areas along narrow river valleys and uplands has made the area particularly suited for livestock and small-scale diversified farming. Since pioneer days this has been the dominant pattern of land use. The distribution of these two types of farming depends largely upon the density of cedar: in the more open country in the southwest, we find a mixed grazing of sheep, goats, and cattle, with cedar-chopping as secondary; in the more heavily wooded northwest area, there is small-scale diversified farming based on corn, cotton, and small grains, with cedar-chopping and charcoal-burning important. In both these subareas only a small proportion of the land is in cultivation, and the sparse population, almost exclusively old-line American, lives along the river bottoms where there is a convenient supply of wood and water. Most of the small wild game that remains in Bell County is found here, and hunting, fishing, and trapping are still important economic activities. Except for the small areas of rich bottom land, the western part of the county is unsuited for mechanized farming.

In the northwest, the farms are small and are generally owner-operated, whereas in the grazing area of the southwest, ranches are large and are mostly owned by townspeople and operated by tenants or hired labor. In both these areas, the standard of living is low: housing and sanitary facilities are poor (about 30 per cent of these farmers have no toilet facilities), and few farms have running water or electric lights. Folk practices have persisted, and many farmers still plant by the signs. Here, too, we find the lowest educational standards in the county.

Localism has persisted in this area, particularly in the northwest, where communities have tended to be more stable and local institutions such as the school, the church, and the store have been retained. In the southwestern part, where tenancy is high and where there has been a greater movement of population, communities and local institutions are much weaker. Throughout the western area, however, there are more one-room schoolhouses, fewer school consolidations, and more hamlet-centered communities than in the rest of the county.

It is interesting to note that the farm families of this area, because of their greater reliance upon subsistence agriculture and their lower standard of living, were better able to weather the depression of the thirties. Agricultural agencies have been least effective in this part of the county, particularly among the poorest farmers—the cedar choppers, charcoal burners, and tenants. Here, too, are the fewest Farm Security Agency loans, the least soil-conservation work, and the lowest Agricultural Adjustment Administration payments for good farm practices. The only considerable payment of Agricultural Adjustment Administration money has been for the clearing of cedar and the planting of grasses for sheep- and goat-raising.

In the eastern part of the county two-thirds of all farm families are concentrated on one-third of the land. The gently rolling, treeless prairie, with its rich black soil, is the center of intensive agriculture and cotton production. Over 85 per cent of this land is in cultivation, less than one-third of which is in cotton. During the pioneer period, this part of the county was devoted to stock-raising, but since 1880, when the prairie was settled by the Czechs and Germans, cotton has dominated the economy. From 1900 to 1930, cotton occupied about 80 per cent of the total planted acreage. Only recently has cotton production declined in favor of more diversified farming and a reversion to the early land-use pattern of stock-raising.

The eastern part of the county is characterized by smaller, more town-centered communities, where school consolidation has gone ahead rapidly and local services have declined. The proximity of Temple has contributed to the breakdown of the rural communities and has made for a more urbanized population. The Czech and German communities are concentrated in the east. The standard of living is generally higher in this part of the county.

The role of cultural factors in farming practices and rural social organization. Throughout this article I have tried to show the effects of cultural factors upon types of farming and rural social organization. To this end I have compared the customs and value systems of farmers of Czech and German descent with those of old-line American descent. Before summarizing this material it should be recalled that many of the traits here described as typically Czech and German are found in varying degree among some segments of the old-line American population, especially among the small-scale subsistence farmers who live in the western part of the county.

The farmers of Czech and German descent generally have small farms, which they work intensively and carefully. Johnson grass is rarely seen on their farms, and this has given them the reputation in the county of being excellent farmers. They generally have a greater percentage of their farmland in cultivation and grow more of their own foodstuffs and feed for livestock. It is significant that most of the hammer mills for grinding feed are owned by the Czech and German farmers.

In most Czech and German families there is a greater reliance upon family labor—women and children are expected to work in the fields. Among old-line Americans the tendency is to hire considerable nonfamily labor and to gamble between high costs and high farm prices.

The farmers of Czech and German descent seem to have the strongest attachment to the land and seek security through landownership. Landownership is a more important determinant of status among them than among the old-line Americans. Farm tenancy is lowest among the Czechs and Germans. They also show the lowest percentage of town farmers. Among the old-line Americans the form of tenure is much less important; they seek security for themselves and their children through the operation of larger farms and by taking chances on the cycles of seasons and prices.

Love of the land has made the Czech and German farmers more receptive to government agency programs for the improvement of farm practices. We know that whereas German farmers own or operate only 10 per cent of the farms in the county, they represent 30 per cent of all soil-conservation district co-operators. Also, boys' and girls' 4-H Clubs in preponderantly Czech and German areas are among the best in the county.

The Czech and German communities are among the most cohesive in the county and have the greatest amount of social participation. Social activities center around lodges, beef clubs, insurance and benevolent associations, beer parlors, dance halls, schools, and churches. The church is particularly important as a unifying force in community life. Unlike most old-line American communities, Czech and German communities are not split up along many denominational lines. Furthermore, there are fewer social cleavages in these communities because of the higher incidence of farm ownership, the greater uniformity in size of farms and incomes, and the presence of large extended families.

The picture presented above is necessarily of a generalized nature. It applies most accurately to the older generation and to the conditions in the county that prevailed in the early 1920's. Today many families of German descent are thoroughly acculturated, and acculturation and assimilation are going ahead at a rapid rate among the Czechs and the rest of the Germans. The greater contact with the outside that has resulted from the improvement of roads and means of communication, the consolidation of schools, the greater use of radios and the movies, and the experiences of the young men in the armed services in World War I and II are some of the factors that have incorporated the farmers of Czech and German descent more and more into the main stream of modern American life.

The drive for a higher standard of living seems to be the key to understanding many of the changes that occur in the behavior and value systems of the Czech and German families in the process of Americanization. As the Czech and German families become more acculturated, there is less emphasis upon thrift and self-denial and more money is spent upon labor-saving devices, household conveniences, clothing, and entertainment. The greater cash income necessitated by this higher level of living has made for a trend toward larger farms and bigger operations, more mechanization, and greater reliance upon hired labor. But the great majority of Czech and German farms are too small to support these newly felt needs, and many of the younger generation are leaving the farms or depending more heavily upon off-farm work. A related trend is a greater reliance upon education as a source of security. A high school education is now considered the desirable minimum by most farm families irrespective of nationality backgrounds. These changes have also affected the traditional family division of labor. In the more acculturated Czech and German families the women no longer work in the fields, and they assume a role of greater equality with the men in family and community affairs.

Another significant development is the gradual disappearance of the Czech and German language. Czech is still the first language learned by children in most Czech homes, and it is frequently spoken by adults, but practically all Czechs are bilingual. In contrast, German is rarely spoken, although most adults are still fluent in the language. German is no longer used in church services, whereas Czech frequently is. There is growing pressure from Czech youths to have all services held in English.

Intermarriage is steadily increasing despite the resistance of both Czechs and old-line American parents. In the German communities intermarriage with old-line Americans has gone farther than is the case among the Czechs.

Current trends and problems. The most noticeable trends are the following:

1. Decrease in rural population. The rural population of Bell County has been on the decline since 1930. The war has furthered this process. At present, approximately 60 per cent of the total population of the county is concentrated in three towns—Temple, Belton, and Killeen. This condition will probably persist unless there is an industrial depression with an accompanying back-to-the-farm movement. All evidence points to the fact that a large percentage of the younger people are planning to leave the farm if they can find opportunities elsewhere. The basic reason for this is not dislike of farm life but dissatisfaction with the low standard of living.

2. Shift away from cotton-growing, and related trends. Probably the most significant single change in agriculture in the county in recent years is the marked shift away from cotton-growing. In former years cotton acreage was usually 60–80 per cent of the total acreage. In 1944, a year in which there was no government restriction on cotton-growing, the cotton acreage was less than one-third of the total acreage. It should be noted that the farm labor shortage and the relatively high wages of agricultural workers were contributing factors in the reduction of cotton acreage. Other important and related trends are (a) more diversified farming, (b) the wider use of cover crops for the improvement of soils, and (c) the increase in livestock both on large commercial livestock farms and on family-sized farms.

3. Fewer and larger farms. The number of farms has decreased with the movement of rural population to the towns. Many farms were abandoned during the war because of the excellent opportunities for off-farm employment within the county. Nearby war industries provided a major source of income for about 50 per cent of the farmers.

Since 1930 there has been a steady trend toward larger farm units. In 1940 the average size of farms was 152 acres, an increase of 21 per cent over 1930. One-sixth of all farms, principally stock farms in the western part of the county, were over 1,000 acres. However, in the eastern part of the county most farms are still well below 140 acres, which is considered the minimum size for a well-rounded program of diversified farming. The small, uneconomical size of farms is becoming a serious problem among the Czechs, whose average farm is 80–100 acres.

The trend toward larger farms was first given impetus by the A.A.A. Since the war this development has continued with the consolidation of farms, especially in the southwestern area. However, more mechanization was the most important contributing factor in the increase in size of farms.

4. Mechanization: The trend toward mechanization of farms that began in the 1930's has gone forward despite the war. Since 1940, there has been an increase of approximately five hundred tractors and twenty corn pickers. There are as yet no mechanical cotton pickers, but some of the wealthier farmers, as well as some of the townspeople, expressed a desire for cotton pickers after the war. If the cotton picker is to come into the county at all, it will have to be a machine of small size. Conditions of terrain rule out any large machinery.

5. Decline of rural communities. A large number of rural communities in Bell County are losing their local services, and the rural population is increasingly going to town for shopping, entertainment, and school. This decline has been accelerated by the consolidation and contracting out of schools, the improvement of roads and means of communication, off-farm employment, movement of farm population to the towns, consolidation of farms, high rate of tenancy, and the improvement of town services.

Rural communities are almost always co-terminous with the school district, and the school is one of the most important community institutions. Where the local school is operated, there are generally a greater number of other local services and community life tends to be more active; where the school is contracted out, the community is declining; and where the school has been consolidated, community life is weakest and there are few local services.

Czech and German communities are the most tightly knit in the county and have the most active social life. The breakdown of communities is greatest in the southwest where the land has suffered most from erosion. School consolidation has progressed more rapidly in the east because of the greater proximity of the towns.

Of a total of 61 communities there are 9 trade-centered communities, including Temple and Belton; 5 village-centered communities; 20 hamlet-centered; 21 school-centered; and 6 store-centered communities. Forty-five rural communities have declined so much within the past two decades that they are now open-country neighborhoods that depend entirely upon town services.

The most important current problems are the following:

1. Farm tenancy. In terms of its long-range effects, tenancy is the No. 1 problem of the county. In 1940, 56 per cent of all farm operators were tenants. This percentage has decreased somewhat since the war, but it is still extremely high. Tenancy has existed for so long in the county that it is taken for granted as part of the order of things and generally is neglected as a problem by most government agen-

cies working in the county. Nevertheless, tenancy has been the greatest single obstacle to the spread of improved farm practices. The exploitative use of the land by tenants threatens the very basis of the agricultural economy. This does not mean that tenants are more resistant to culture change than landowners, but rather that the government programs in the county (with the exception of the F.S.A.) were not designed to meet the needs of tenants, who hesitate to improve land not their own. The F.S.A. is the only organization set up to deal with this problem at present. Because of lack of funds it has reached only a very small number of tenants, but as far as it goes, it has been highly successful. What is needed in the postwar period is a greatly expanded F.S.A. program.

2. Soil conservation. Soil conservation is a major aspect of the programs of all the agricultural agencies, such as the Extension Service, Soil Conservation Service, Agricultural Adjustment Administration, and Farm Security Administration. Since 1939 Bell County has been divided into soil-conservation districts. The work up to the present has been more successful in preventing soil erosion than in improving the fertility of the land. The changes have, on the whole, been limited to landowners and better-to-do farmers. There are elaborate postwar plans for continued soil-conservation work, with special emphasis on soil improvement.

3. Need for farmers' organizations and farmers' co-operatives. At present, there is a lack of farmers' organizations in the county. There is no grange or farmers' union; a chapter of the Farm Bureau was organized recently, but the local reaction was a passive one. Many farmers express the need for farm co-operatives, but in the past their efforts to organize co-operatives have met opposition from town merchants.

4. Need for roads and flood control. The need for better farm-to-market roads is felt especially by the farmers in the eastern part of the county, where the sticky black-waxy soils, together with the poor drainage, make dirt roads impassable by car for about five months during the year.

Flood control is badly needed along the Leon River in the western part of the county and along the Little River in the southeastern part. A flood-control project is planned for the postwar period and will probably give employment to a few hundred workers.

5. Need for public-health facilities. Although Temple, Texas, is known as the hospital center of the South, there are inadequate medical facilities in Bell County for the farm population. The shortage of doctors in the small towns and the absence of a county hospital work hardships on the low-income farmers. Some form of health insurance is needed by the farmers in the county.

6. Problem of returning veterans. It is questionable whether any large portion of the 3,500 young men who left the farms for the armed services can be reabsorbed into agriculture in the county. This judgment is based upon the following facts:

a) Despite the exodus of so many young men, farm production has been maintained at approximately prewar levels.

b) The trend toward larger farms and more mechanization has meant a reduction in the amount of necessary farm labor.

c) Many farmers now living and working in towns will, in all probability, return to their farms, thereby limiting opportunities for farming on the part of returned veterans.

d) The present inflated land prices will be a serious drawback to most veterans. Furthermore, most of the best land was bought up by townspeople—doctors, lawyers, and merchants —during the war.

Another aspect of the problem of returning veterans is the question of whether or not they *want* to return to the farms. In the opinion of some informants in the county, a large number of veterans would prefer industrial employment within the county or elsewhere. However, in my survey of thirty-three sample rural communities in the county, I found that 141 out of 466 returned veterans, or about 30 per cent, planned to go back to farming or had already done so. This proportion was higher than anticipated. Of the veterans going back to farming, the highest proportion live in communities in the poorest land areas in the western part of the county, where stock-raising and diversified farming predominate. This regional difference in attitude toward staying on the land was also evident in our study of high school students. Fewer boys from the highly productive black-waxy land areas in the eastern part of the county desire to go into farming.

In the opinion of farm parents interviewed, the only way to ensure the return of the veterans to the farms and to keep the present youth from leaving them is to provide a higher standard of living and more of the conveniences found in towns and cities.

10

Bumper Crops
in the Desert[*]

The farmers of one American county—Franklin County in the state
of Washington—have done an incredible thing. They have succeeded in growing bumper crops of wheat with less than nine inches
of rainfall a year.

Last year these 150 farm families produced two and a half million
bushels of wheat, using a method of dry farming which has enabled
them to conserve each drop of rain and has brought them in a single
life-span from the poverty and hardships of pioneer life to as high a
standard of living as can be found in rural America.

Their accomplishment is no miracle; it is the result of shrewd application of the techniques discovered by the settlers of the semiarid
West in the seventies and eighties of the last century and now practiced in many of the dry areas of the United States, such as the Great
Plains, the Great Basin, and the California Valley. Since the early
1900's it has spread to Canada, South America, Spain, South Africa,
Russia, and China. The development of dry farming has meant that
throughout the world millions of acres of land which only fifty years
ago were thought unsuitable for agriculture now produce food for
the world's needy granaries.

Franklin County, lying between the forks of the Columbia and
Snake rivers, has some of the driest farmland in the United States.
Dry farming is technically defined as growing crops on ten to twenty

* This was first published in 1946 in *Harper's Magazine*.

inches of annual rainfall. In central Texas thirty inches signifies drought; in the cornbelt thirty to fifty inches is the range. Franklin County's bumper crops, grown without irrigation on an average annual rainfall of six to nine inches, have been achieved through a distinctly American combination of large-scale farming and mechanization with family ownership and operation. The one hundred and fifty farmers own and operate 450,000 acres, practically the entire farmland of the county, in farms averaging between 2,000 and 3,000 acres. Some farms are 8,000 acres; a farm of 1,000 acres is small. Every phase of production on these wheat farms is mechanized. A single farmer, with the aid of his machinery, can work 2,000 acres. The investment per farm in machinery ranges from $10,000 to $35,000. Every farm has its own well-equipped machine shop and every farmer is a skilled mechanic.

The original homesteaders in the county—and many of them are still there today, earning gross annual incomes of $20,000 to $40,000 —settled the arid land, having plenty of pioneer spirit but little else that was suited to their new environment. Accustomed to small farms, closely knit villages, and the deep moldboard plow as their essential tool, they had to learn to live on large farms, in isolated homesteads, and to work with the shallow disc plow and new types of cultivators. For the dry winds which came over the mountains used to blow away the precious top soil and, often with it, thousands of acres of seed. Wells had to go down 1,000 to 1,500 feet for water. It was up to the settlers to forge a new way of life or perish; they emerged conquerors of the desert.

Their first innovation was the use of summer fallow. Coming from relatively humid regions where the land customarily yielded one or more crops each year, the settlers found that there was not enough moisture in the soil for such production. Each year, therefore, they planted only one half of their land, allowing the other half to lie idle in order to store up enough water to produce a crop the following year. But just letting the land lie idle was not sufficient; they had to work out a method to preserve the moisture and to prevent the light, sandy soil from blowing away. They developed what is known as stubble mulch dry farming. The stubble (left by the cutting of the wheat at harvest time) is broken up and turned over lightly by a disc plow, preferably while there is plentiful moisture, in order to form clods of sufficient weight to keep the soil down. Thus the stubble, which was formerly burned and turned under with a deep plow, now forms an effective network of vegetation which keeps the soil down and prevents evaporation.

The summer fallow is carefully weeded two or three times. Speed of operation is at a premium, for the weeds must be killed while still

small lest they absorb the precious little moisture. Farmers estimate
that with each weeding they increase the yield by three or four
bushels an acre. The great importance of even small quantities of
moisture for dry farming in this area can be judged by the fact that a
difference of one or two inches of rainfall during the crucial months
may mean the difference between a good crop and a poor one.

As part of the process of learning to dry farm, new tools had to be
invented by the farmers themselves. As far back as 1906, they began
to experiment with crude home-made rod weeders and with shallow
disc plows. The first rod weeders were of the nonrotating or "dead
rod" type, locally called "goosenecked rod slickers" and "go-devils."
These consisted of a sharp blade or rod which went a few inches
under the surface to cut the weeds. They had two serious defects,
both of which increased blowing and reduced moisture. They pul-
verized the light soils and they dragged the weeds, piling them into
heaps and thereby robbing the land of moisture. These early tools
were ineffectual and were described by a farmer as "good man-
killers and good horse-killers but poor weed-killers."

The new rotating weeder, of the type specially developed for
loose, sandy soil, advances over the field, pulling under the ground a
rod which revolves in the opposite direction and tears out the weeds
by the roots. Thrown to the surface, the weeds are killed by the sun;
lumps lifted to the top form a clod mulch, and the soil underneath is
pressed to eliminate air pockets. With a twenty-four-foot hookup of
weeders and a tractor traveling at three miles an hour, the farmer
can cultivate more than eighty acres in a ten-hour day.

The change from "dead rod" weeders to the rotating type represented a major step toward the success of dry farming. It accomplished three important tasks: (1) it effectively killed weeds,
thereby preserving moisture; (2) it brought the weeds near the surface and distributed them evenly over the land, which helped prevent blowing; and (3) it appreciably reduced the sheer physical
labor for man and beast.

At about the same time, the change from deep moldboard plowing
to light discing took place. A few farmers began experimenting with
discing as early as 1906. One old-timer said: "When I first tried
discing in 1906 my neighbors made sport of me. They said I might
just as well be dragging a turkey gobbler backwards by the tail and
letting him scratch."

By 1920 discing and the use of the rotating rod weeder were common practice in the county. However, the final victory over the
desert was not yet won. It had to wait for still greater mechanical
progress, for the conversion from horse power to Diesel caterpillar
tractors.

The shift from horse power to Diesel power was very recent. The first Diesel "cats" came in about 1927–28. Mechanization on a large scale occurred during the depression years and was made possible by the A.A.A. allotments and by other government payments. As late as 1935 some wheat farmers were still using horses. However, it should be emphasized that large-scale wheat farming had been going on long before the coming of tractors. Farms of 5,000 acres were operating in 1905. The use of summer fallow, whereby only one-half of the farmland was in production, and the low yields per acre, made large farms an economic necessity from the very beginning. This type of farming is locally described as "shotgun farming."

The tractor, therefore, did not basically change the type of farming. Nevertheless, it had a number of far-reaching results. First, it made dry farming more effective by supplying the element of speed which is so essential in conserving moisture in the summer fallow. The farmers had long been aware of the importance of speed but could do little about it. They had noticed, for example, that the outer edges of a field, which were disced and weeded first, always gave better yields than the center of the field, which was worked last. With tractors they were able to cover much more ground and could use a day and night shift. Second, the tractor cut down on hired labor and reduced the cost of production by about 35 per cent. Formerly, a farm of 2,000 acres required about one hundred horses and it took two full-time hands to care for them. Keeping the harness in repair was itself a full-time job. With horse power a man could plow only fifteen acres a day. With tractors one man could do sixty acres a day and another sixty acres on the night shift. Third, the tractor meant a great saving of time and gave the farmers much more leisure. Fourth, it meant that farmers could raise cattle on the pasture formerly used by horses. Only after mechanization did wheat farmers begin to raise cattle.

The kind of farming just described takes men of high caliber. The farmers of Franklin County today are the end product of a long weeding-out process which has been going on since this area was first settled. They are the men and women who had the perseverance and ability to stick through the long, trying period of learning to dry farm. Knowing exactly when to do a job and getting it done in the shortest possible time was and still is essential. The delay of a day or two in weeding, discing, seeding, or harvesting may mean the loss of thousands of bushels of wheat.

Unlike the farmers who can rely upon the calendar or upon tradition or the "signs," these wheat farmers had to rely upon themselves. This has made for open-mindedness and for a readiness to accept innovations, particularly time-saving and labor-saving devices. The farmers are experiment-minded and have a definite scientific bent. But they are not book farmers. They couldn't be—because there were no books on dry farming, nor could the U.S. Department of Agriculture help them very much. On the contrary, most of what the Department of Agriculture knows today about this type of farming has been learned from the farmers themselves. Also it is interesting to note that these farmers were practicing shallow plowing long before writers like Edward Faulkner and Louis Bromfield began popularizing it.

Among the wheat farmers in Franklin County one can see the possibility of a rich and colorful rural life: the marvelous control over nature, a high standard of living, family-owned and operated farms, sufficient leisure for the development of cultural interests, and an intelligent and well-informed citizenry. And yet the farmers face problems which threaten to destroy all they have accomplished.

As farms have become larger, farm homes have been increasingly isolated. Because of the great scattering of houses—they are now from three to ten miles apart—there is no rural free delivery and the construction of electric power lines and telephone lines has been delayed. Most of the farms have expensive Delco battery electric plants and only local party telephones. There is almost no community life and there are few opportunities for recreation and diversion. Consolidated schools in the towns are so far away that children must often board away from home while they go to school, particularly high school. Sons and daughters who attend college for four years often do not wish to return to farm life. Many of the farmers who have been wealthier with the bumper wheat crops and high prices of the war years, would like to retire and hand over the management of the farms to their sons, who, in a number of cases, are returned veterans; but they fear that the younger men will not want to return to lead what will seem to them isolated and boring lives. As a result, they are beginning to move to town in the hope that this will keep the family together. It is not difficult to foresee the growth of town farmers, absentee land ownership, and a class of landless farm wagehands.

In this situation—with the technical problems of dry farming solved but the social problems of isolation increasing in complexity —the governmental proposal to bring two irrigation ditches from the Grand Coulee into Franklin County has found attentive listeners. When the wheat farmers were asked to vote last July as to whether or not they would join the Irrigation Project, most of them voted to join. Their decision involved more than a vote for bringing water to dry land. For the coming of Grand Coulee water will bring to Franklin County a diversified crop yield sufficient to support more than thirty times the present population. It meant that they were voting out a type of farming and a way of life which were their peculiar achievement.

All but one hundred and sixty acres of the land of each family will be sold to the U.S. Reclamation Service at an appraised price far below present inflated land values. Franklin County will be transformed from an area of vast wheat fields to a county of truck-farming, dairy-farming, and diversified farming. In another ten or fifteen years, dry farming in Franklin County will be a matter of history—and with it, the basic insecurity of a one-crop system and the isolation which has begun to drive the younger generation away from home. The land which now supports one hundred and fifty farm families will support approximately five thousand, and for the new pioneers there will be community centers, trading and servicing centers, recreation facilities unknown to their hard-bitten forebears.

The prospect of another decade of high wheat prices makes the decision easier, no doubt. Also the wheat farmers know that their victory over the desert has been a life-and-death struggle, endless and costly in human strength. To grow wheat on nine inches of rainfall has been an extraordinary achievement. But few of them would choose to do it just for the fun of it.

Part Four:

PEASANTRY

A: INTRODUCTORY REMARKS

One of the major trends in cultural anthropology during the last years (1940–1970) has been a shift from the study of isolated tribal peoples to the study of peasantry in the economically underdeveloped countries. The village of Tepoztlán in Mexico is especially interesting in this connection because it was one of the first peasant communities to be studied by an American anthropologist. Robert Redfield worked in the village in 1926–27, and in 1930 published *Tepoztlán—A Mexican Village.*[1] Seventeen years later, in 1943, I restudied the village and in 1951 published *Life in a Mexican Village: Tepoztlán Restudied.*[2] In 1956–57 I returned to Tepoztlán to learn what changes had taken place since my earlier work.[*] In all, I have spent approximately three years of field work in the village since 1943. Few peasant communities have been studied more intensively by independent investigators.

I should like to comment briefly on Redfield's attempt to reconcile the differences in our published views on the nature of Tepoztlán and Tepoztecans.[3] He would explain our differences in terms of hidden questions which guided our respective research. He suggests that his question was, "What do these people enjoy?" and my question was, "What do these people suffer from?"[4] While I appreciate the ingenuity of his explanation, I reject it as unsound, and I am inclined to interpret his statement as a gallant effort to defend his early field work.

In view of Redfield's emphasis upon the element of art in the social sciences, I have often wondered why he did not give more attention to the contrast between his own idealized version of peasantry and the sordid descriptions of the novelists. Although Redfield came to recognize the seamy side of peasant life, a careful examination of

---

[1] Chicago: University of Chicago Press.

[2] Urbana: University of Illinois Press.

[*] For a fuller discussion of this and some of the comments that follow, see Essay 2, above.

[3] Robert Redfield, *The Little Community, Viewpoints for the Study of a Human Whole* (Chicago: University of Chicago Press, 1955), pp. 133–36, and *The Primitive World and Its Transformations* (Ithaca: Cornell University Press, 1933), pp. 155–57.

[4] Redfield, *The Little Community . . .* , p. 136.

his last work, *Peasant Society and Culture* (1956), will show that about 90 per cent of the text is devoted to what might be called the positive aspects and only 10 per cent to the negative aspects.

Certainly any well-rounded study of a community should present both what people enjoy and what they suffer from. Redfield's first study of Tepoztlán was primarily a study of the fiesta system, and fiestas were indeed the high point of enjoyment in the life of Tepoztlán. It did not seem necessary for me to repeat this aspect of his work which I checked and found quite accurate. But Redfield's concern with what people enjoy led to errors both of commission and of omission in his report on the village: for example, he pictured Tepoztlán as a village of landowners, whereas, in fact, two-thirds of the villagers were landless when he was there and the village had not yet received its *ejido* grants; and he failed to mention either the high rate of crime or the bloody massacre in the plaza in 1927 which was partially responsible for his leaving the village.

There is, however, a more weighty philosophical issue involved in our differences. It seems to me that concern with what people suffer from is much more important than the study of enjoyment because it lends itself to more productive insight into the human condition, the dynamics of conflict, and the forces for change. A focus upon enjoyment generally leads to a static picture of a society. To stress the enjoyment in peasant life is to argue for its preservation and inadvertently to boost tourism. The romantic view of peasantry still held by a few anthropologists is, at best, a form of escapism from the problems of urban life and, at worst, a kind of inverted snobbism. To stress the problems and suffering of peasantry is to envisage the possibility of fundamental changes in technology, means of communication, and general fund of knowledge, which would alter the very meaning of peasant life as we know it today.

In my opinion, one of the basic differences in our approach has to do with the question of what is a good society. In my own field work, I have a conception of a good society as an ideal type, against which I would measure both the urban life of Chicago and the peasant life of Tepoztlán and find them both wanting, for quite different reasons. The fact that I have stressed some of the dismal aspects of peasant life—the poverty, the high death rate, the physical violence, the frustrations, suspicions, suffering, and the waste of fine human talent—in no sense implies that I personally dislike peasants. On the contrary, some of my best friends are peasants. It is my concern for peasants as human beings that has sensitized me to their problems.

That many of these problems are common to peasant societies in various parts of the world is borne out by my study of Rampur village in north India from October 1952 to June 1953[5] and by my recent work on Puerto Ricans of rural origin.[6] Independent corroboration is given by George Foster, who has shown in an excellent article[7] that a large number of monographs on peasant communities the world over give a picture of the quality of interpersonal relations remarkably congruent with what I described for Tepoztlán.[8] I would like, however, to suggest a modification in Foster's definition of peasant society and, further, to add some other variables to explain what he considers the relatively uniform nature of interpersonal relations in such societies.

Foster, following Kroeber, defines peasant society as a "part-society," that is, "rural peoples living in relation to market towns." [9] I would add the cultivation of the soil as another crucial element of the definition, because it is the man-land relation which orders so much of what is distinctive of peasant life. By Foster's definition, village shoemakers, carpenters, potters, and other artisans who are full-time specialists would have to be classified as peasants, even though they do not engage in agriculture. I find this confusing. By my definition, a north Indian village of sweepers and washermen would not be classified as a peasant community. Similarly, I find it difficult to think of Tzintzuntzan[10] as a peasant community because less than a third of its residents engage in farming.

If I understand Foster correctly, he equates folk society with peasant society. Here again, I believe we must make finer distinctions. I would agree with Redfield's equation of the folk with the primitive or preliterate communities which are not in a symbiotic relation to an urban center, and, indeed, antedate the development of cities.[11] By the same token, peasant communities came into existence only after the rise of cities.

Foster's suggestion that the poor quality of interpersonal relations

[5] Oscar Lewis, *Village Life in Northern India* (Urbana: University of Illinois Press, 1958).

[6] *Six Women: Three Generations in a Puerto Rican Family* (New York: Random House, in process).

[7] "Interpersonal Relations in Peasant Society," *Human Organization,* Vol. 19, No. 4 (Winter, 1960–61), pp. 174–78.

[8] To be sure, the poor quality of interpersonal relations described by Foster occurs in tribal, folk, and urban societies as well.

[9] Foster, *op. cit.* (above, note 7), p. 175.

[10] The community studied by George Foster and reported on in his *Empire's Children: The People of Tzintzuntzan,* Publications of the Institute of Social Anthropology, Smithsonian Institution, No. 6 (Washington, D.C., 1948).

[11] Redfield, *The Primitive World* . . .

in peasant communities is a function of a static economy and low productivity, both of which limit upward mobility, and his further suggestion that these factors become noxious for interpersonal relations with the increase in the size of a community beyond some optimal point, strike me as interesting and important. Still, they offer only a partial explanation, and have the flavor of a crude economic determinism which Foster would be the first to disclaim.

One cannot validly jump from economics and technology to personality and interpersonal relations. Some middle terms or intervening variables are necessary, especially those such as social organization, the nature of the family, and the type of child-rearing. It is this difference in the intervening variables which makes Mexican highland peasant communities so different from the peasantry of north India.* The north Indian peasant seemed to me much less suspicious and withdrawn than the Tepoztecan. And although there was more factionalism in north India than in Tepoztlán, it was better organized and therefore less disruptive to village life. The presence of a clan and caste system in Rampur village gave a cohesive quality to social relations which was in marked contrast to the atomism and nuclear familism of Tepoztlán.

Finally, I would take exception to Foster's evaluation of peasant society as "a successful social device" [12] simply because it has persisted. The success of a social form must also be evaluated in terms of its human costs. Moreover, with the rapid mechanization of agriculture in some of the underdeveloped areas of the world, the disappearance of the traditional peasant community is well under way. It seems to me that anthropologists, particularly those active in applied anthropology, must find ways to ease the strains in peasant communities during this period of transition to new social forms.

* See "Peasant Culture in India and Mexico: A Comparative Analysis," Essay 17, below.

[12] Foster, p. 178.

B: MEXICO

11

Plow Culture and Hoe Culture:

*A Study in Contrasts**

In many parts of Mexico and other Latin American countries, two contrasting types of agriculture representing different historical and technological levels exist side by side. One is the primitive, pre-Hispanic cutting and burning system of hoe culture; the other is the more modern post-Hispanic agriculture which employs plow and oxen. The differences between hoe culture and plow culture are not limited merely to the use of different tools of production. Hoe culture and plow culture represent two distinct systems or culture complexes, each with its associated traits and each with far-reaching social and economic implications. It is the purpose of this paper to examine these two systems as they are found in the village and *municipio* of Tepoztlán, Morelos, Mexico.

Tepoztlán is located about sixty miles south of Mexico City on the escarpment of the Ajusco mountain range at an altitude of about 5,000 feet. It is a village of approximately 3,500 people. The population consists of peasants, artisans, and merchants but the village is primarily agricultural and most of the merchants and artisans are also part-time farmers. Over 90 per cent of the 853 families earn their living by agriculture. The village of Tepoztlán is the *cabecera* or seat of the *municipio* of the same name, which consists of eight villages, all within a radius of less than four miles. The country is rough and forested and the land is poor. Less than 25 per cent of the

* This was first published in June, 1949, in *Rural Sociology*, Vol. 14, No. 2, pp. 116–27.

total land area of the *municipio* is suitable for cultivation, and only a single crop of corn is harvested each year. Some own their agricultural plots or have rights to certain parcels of the public land, which remain with the farmers as long as they continue to work them. Other farmers must till the poor soil of the stony hillsides which belong to the community and are free to anyone who wishes to cut and burn away the bushes every two or three years in order to plant corn and beans. Rapid erosion prevents the poor-land farmer from using the same hillside clearing year after year.

Plow culture and hoe culture, the latter locally known as *tlacolol*,[1] have been known in Tepoztlán since the Spanish Conquest. *Tlacolol* or hoe culture is essentially geared to production for subsistence. Plow culture, on the other hand, is geared to production for the market. Although the latter is in many cases carried on for subsistence purposes, it nevertheless has inherent potentialities for expanded production, depending primarily upon the amount of capital available and the amount of land owned or rented. Hoe culture necessitates a great deal of time and labor but little capital; plow culture needs relatively little time and labor and much capital. In the former there is a dependence almost exclusively upon family labor; in the latter there is a greater dependence upon hired labor. In *tlacolol* the yields per *cuartillo* of seed planted are much greater than in plow culture but the amount of corn planted by each family is relatively low and never reaches the amounts planted by a few of the larger operators in plow agriculture. The differences between the two systems are manifested in a great variety of ways and include differences in the location and type of land used, land tenure, tools of production, work cycles and techniques, production time, yields,

[1] This type of agriculture has been variously referred to in the literature as *milpa* agriculture, fire agriculture, slashing and burning, and cutting and burning. The use of the term "milpa agriculture" applied originally by O. F. Cook in his excellent study of the Maya area ("Milpa Agriculture, A Tropical System," Smithsonian Institute, Annual Report, 1919) has established an unfortunate tradition, for the word *milpa* in Mexico refers to any corn field, whether in hoe culture or plow culture. The term *milpa* may be especially misleading in studying land tenure, for a peasant who speaks of "my milpa" doesn't necessarily mean that he is the owner of the land in question. For a somewhat similar criticism of Cook's use of the term "milpa agriculture," see Felix Webster Mc-Bryde, *Cultural and Historical Geography of Southwest Guatemala*. Smithsonian Institution, Institute of Social Anthropology. Publication No. 4, 1947, pp. 16–17. For a discussion of some of the evolutionary implications of the productive potentials of hoe culture and plow culture, see Fred Cottrell, *Energy and Society* (New York: McGraw Hill Book Company, 1955), especially chap. 7. For a more recent comparative analysis, see Harold C. Conklin, "The Study of Shifting Cultivation," *Current Anthropology*, Vol. 2 (Feb., 1961), pp. 27–61.

costs, effects upon natural resources, and social status in the community. Let us examine some of these items in more detail.

· L O C A T I O N   A N D   T Y P E OF   L A N D   U S E D ·

Plow culture and hoe culture are practiced on different types of land. The land used for plow culture is relatively treeless, level, less rocky than hoe-culture land, and includes the broad valley bottom in the southern part of the *municipio*. The land used in hoe culture is of two types. One is known as *texcal*, which is land covered with volcanic rock and scrub forest, with pockets of rich soil spread thin among the rocks. The other type is known as *cerros* and refers to the mountain slopes with scrub forest and lime rock outcroppings.[2] In both the *texcal* and the *cerros* the use of the plow is ruled out by the nature of the terrain. In *texcal*, for example, the large volcanic rocks are piled on one another in helter-skelter fashion so that it is difficult for a man even to walk.

With few exceptions the land used in plow agriculture is much closer to the village than are the *tlacolol* lands. Farmers who work *tlacolol* lands therefore have to rise at 4 A.M. rather than 7 A.M., must go a distance of two or three hours to reach their fields, and return a few hours later than do the owners of private lands. The building of the road in 1936 through the portion of the *municipio* in which the privately owned lands are located has tended to accentuate this difference between hoe and plow culture. Today, it is not uncommon for some Tepoztecan landowners to take the bus to reach their fields. *Tlacololeros*, however, walk or go by burro and in all probability will continue to do so for many years.

· L A N D   T E N U R E ·

Another difference between hoe culture and plow culture concerns land tenure. Plow culture has until recently been practiced on privately owned land, whereas hoe culture has traditionally been practiced on communally owned land. This sharp distinction has been somewhat blurred since 1930 when Tepoztlán received in restitution

---

[2] Tepoztecans use the word *cerros* to refer both to the spectacular butte-like rock outcroppings and mountains which surround the village and to the steep slopes covered with scrub forest. *Texcal* refers to a strip of land approximately two kilometers wide on the western limits of the *municipio*, covered with a relatively recent volcanic flow which supports a thorny scrub forest with a predominating flora of copal gum, mimosa-like legumes, a tree "sweet potato," and silk cotton trees.

from a neighboring hacienda some *ejido* land, a small portion of which is now used in plow agriculture. At the time of this research approximately 70 per cent of Tepoztecan families worked in plow culture and about 20 per cent in hoe culture. Since plow culture is essentially Spanish and hoe culture essentially native Indian, these figures serve as some indication of the relative importance in the total economy of these two systems. It is apparent therefore that hoe culture is subsidiary to plow culture in terms of the total economy. However, there is some overlapping between the two systems. Some *tlacololeros* may work as day laborers for private landowners. On the other hand, some small landowners may also work *tlacolol* to supplement their meagre income or to allow their privately owned land to rest for a season or two. This latter procedure is resented by many *tlacololeros* who believe that the communal lands should serve the landless. This attitude of *tlacololeros* must be understood in the light of the fact that the communal lands are becoming exhausted and can no longer support the increasing population. It is interesting to note that plow agriculture enjoys a much higher status in the village than does hoe culture. *Tlacolol* has traditionally been looked upon as the last resort of the poor. Most *tlacololeros* are landless and as a group are the poorest in the village.[3] *Tlacololeros* have become conscious of themselves as a distinctive group and have organized as such and now have to be reckoned with politically.

· TOOLS OF PRODUCTION ·

The tools used in *tlacolol* are relatively simple and inexpensive, namely, the hoe (of which there are two types, locally known as the *coa* and the *tlalache*), the ax, and the *machete*. All *tlacololeros* own their own tools. In plow agriculture, on the other hand, the tools of production, primarily the oxen and plow, are much more expensive:

[3] The association of hoe culture and plow culture with different socioeconomic status groups within the peasantry finds a very interesting parallel among the European villagers of the Middle Ages. C. C. Homans, in his study *English Villagers of the Thirteenth Century* (Cambridge, Mass., 1941), writes, "This division of villagers into two main social classes seems to have been common in many parts of Europe under the old peasant social order and to have been determined fundamentally by an economic change. In ancient France, for instance, the two classes were called the *laboureurs* and the *manouvriers*. The laboureurs were the substantial farmers, who had Tenements (holdings) large enough to enable them to keep plow-oxen; the manouvriers were the poorer peasants, who had only their hands with which to work" (p. 73). Again we read, "But what, at last, of the man who was so poor that he was able neither to support plow oxen on his holdings nor to hire them? Perforce he delved up his land with a spade" (p. 80).

only a small percentage of the landowners own their own yoke of oxen and only 52 per cent own their own plows. The inflationary prices in recent years have made it increasingly difficult for Tepoztecans to purchase oxen and plows. Furthermore, the small size of landholdings makes it uneconomical for many to own a yoke of oxen.

· **W O R K   C Y C L E S** ·

Plow culture and hoe culture in Tepoztlán have distinctive work cycles. This is shown in Table 1. It will be seen that the agricultural year begins at different times in each case. The *tlacololeros* begin work soon after the harvest in January and work through the greater part of the dry season when most of the farmers of plow culture are letting their land rest and are busy at other tasks. Most *tlacololeros* are through planting before planting begins in plow culture and many accept work as day laborers and aid with the planting and cultivating in plow culture. However, during late July and early August, the peak labor season for plow agriculture, most *tlacololeros* are busy in their own fields. Similarly, harvest comes at the same time in both systems, despite the fact that in hoe culture the corn is planted about two weeks earlier. At harvest time there is a felt labor shortage in the village and some Tepoztecans have pointed out that the overlapping of work cycles between the two systems makes for a conflict of interests between the *tlacololeros* and private landowners, for the latter are unable to get sufficient hired help. It should be noted in this connection that before the Mexican Revolution of 1910 the local *caciques* in Tepoztlán, on a number of occasions, attempted to prohibit Tepoztecan landless peasants engaged in hoe culture from using the communal lands for planting in order to assure an abundant and cheap labor supply for themselves. Here we find a conflict of group interests which does not fit the usual stereotype of the homogeneity and integration of the folk culture.

The specific production techniques in the growing of corn and the various stages in the work cycles differ considerably between plow culture and hoe culture in Tepoztlán. Generally speaking, the tools and techniques in hoe culture are still known by their *Nahuatl* names, whereas in plow culture Spanish names prevail. Furthermore, we find a greater and more elaborate degree of ritual associated with plow culture than with hoe culture. This again is not what one might have expected in terms of the concept of the folk culture. Also, in *tlacolol*, rotation is practiced by necessity, for the fields cease to produce after the first two years, whereas in plow culture the same field may be planted year after year until the soil fertility is completely exhausted. Another interesting difference is that weeding

TABLE 1

COMPARISON OF WORK CYCLES OF PLOW AND HOE AGRICULTURE—TEPOZTLÁN, 1944.

	Jan.	Feb.	March	April	May	June	July	August	Sept.	Oct.	Nov.	Dec.
PLOW AGRICULTURE	NO WORK IN FIELDS				Clearing land	Plowing, first cultivation & seeding	Second cult.	Third cult.	Visits to field	Weeding	Stripping corn stalks	Harvest. Transport of corn
TLACOLOL AGRICULTURE	Clear land with machete and axe		No work. Brush is left to dry.	Burning brush. Field is left to cool. / Fencing	Seeding		Re-seeding	Weeding with machete or by pulling	Visits to fields to check			Harvest. Transport of corn

in hoe culture is traditionally done by hand with the weeds pulled out roots and all, whereas in plow culture it is more common to cut the weeds with a *machete* and plow them under. An exception to this occurs in the case of preparing a field for bean planting. In this case the weeds are also pulled out by hand.

Perhaps the most striking differences between the two systems are revealed by an analysis of the production time in each (Table 2). An exact analysis of production time is extremely difficult because Tepoztecan peasants keep no records of such things and because a large number of variables have to be considered. The following data, based upon careful observation of all the processes involved as well as upon extended interviews with many Tepoztecans, are therefore presented with an awareness of some shortcomings.

In the first place I found that within each system there is a considerable range in the number of man-days of work that go into clearing, preparing, planting, cultivating, and harvesting a *milpa* or corn field (Tables 3 and 4). The most significant variables found were the nature of the terrain, the quality of the soil, the speed of the oxen and the workers, and the type of seed used. My data show that the total number of man-days of work necessary for the production of one *hectare* of corn in plow agriculture ranges from thirty-five to seventy-eight days, depending upon the variables listed above. If we were to consider forty-five to fifty days as the average, we would be pretty close to the truth.

Production-time estimates in the case of hoe culture are even more complicated because of the existence of two types of terrain used for hoe culture, as indicated earlier. Considering both types, we find that

TABLE 2

COMPARISON OF TIME SPENT IN PRODUCTION OF CORN
IN PLOW AGRICULTURE AND IN HOE CULTURE

Operation	Plow agriculture (plot of one hectare or ten cuartillos)	Hoe culture (texcal) (plot of one hectare or ten cuartillos)
1. Preparation of the land	8	60
2. Planting	2.8	16
3. Cultivation	14	30
4. Harvest	15	12
5. Transport of corn	3	10
6. Shelling of corn	5	15
Total man-days	47.8	143

the range is from 143 days to a little over 180 days. It is a reasonable conclusion that it takes approximately three times as many man-days to produce one *hectare* of corn in *tlacolol* as it does in plow culture in Tepoztlán (Table 2).[4] The single job of weeding by hand takes more time than all three cultivations by plow. The great difference in the total time spent in preparation of the land is also noteworthy. The somewhat longer time period for harvesting and transport is due to the greater distances of the fields used in hoe culture. It should also be noted that fencing the *tlacolol*, which is so time-consuming, has to be repeated every two years or each time a new clearing is made. This is in contrast to the permanent stone fences of the privately owned fields.

In addition to the differences in the actual time spent, there is a corresponding difference in the nature of the work. Tepoztecans who have worked in both types consider work in *tlacolol* infinitely more

[4] Note that the time saved in plow culture as compared to hoe culture is roughly equivalent to the time saved by the change from horse power to tractor power in the production of corn in our own Middle West. This was called to my attention by Edgar Anderson. One might say, therefore, that historically the shift from hoe to plow represents just about the same degree of technological progress as the shift from horse to tractor! However, such a comparison may be misleading since the much greater time taken by hoe culture is as much a function of the differences in terrain and the use of the cutting and burning method as it is of the use of the hoe instead of the plow. On the other hand, it is difficult to separate the single elements, *i.e.*, the hoe and plow, from their respective complexes. As we have seen, hoe culture is intimately associated with the cutting and burning method and this holds true not only for Tepoztlán but for most areas in Latin America where hoe culture is practiced. Whether or not the still earlier digging-stick agriculture of pre-Conquest time was associated exclusively with cutting and burning methods on the steep and rocky slopes is a question difficult to answer. In the case of Tepoztlán we simply do not know whether the level lands now used exclusively for plow culture were used for farming before the Conquest. In the light of data I have obtained from the Mexican archives, it would seem highly probable that the pre-Conquest population of Tepoztlán was greater even than the present-day population. It would hardly seem possible, therefore, that such a large population could be supported only by the hilly and volcanic lands now used for hoe culture. And yet we find the tradition of digging-stick agriculture on the hillsides widespread in other parts of Mexico and in Peru. It may be that in Tepoztlán both the level lands now used for plow culture and the sloping hillsides were used for farming before the Conquest. In that case, the present distribution of hoe culture would have to be explained in terms of plow culture's having pushed the old digging-stick culture out to the margins. Indeed, it may even be that for a time after the Conquest plow culture entirely displaced the old digging-stick–cutting-and-burning method, and that the latter came back slowly, in the form of hoe culture. That hoe culture has had a discontinuous history in the *municipio* is certain; it was forcibly prohibited for a time before the Revolution of 1910.

TABLE 3. ESTIMATE OF TIME SPENT IN PRODUCTION OF CORN IN PLOW AGRICULTURE IN FOUR SAMPLE PLOTS. TEPOZTLÁN, 1944

Operation	Plot I (12 cuartillos)		Plot II (10 cuartillos)		Plot III (10 cuartillos)		Plot IV (10 cuartillos)	
	No. of workers	No. of Man-days	No. of workers	No. of Man-days	No. of workers	No. of Man-days	No. of workers	No. of Man-days
1. *Preparation of the land:*								
Clearing of land (*limpio*)	1	4	1	6	1	3	2	2
Plowing (*barbecho*)	1	6	1	4	1	4	2	2
Total		10		10		7		4
2. *Planting:*								
Plowing (*surcado*)	1	2	1	1.5	1	2	1	1
Seeding (*siembra*)	1	2	1	1.5	1	2	2	2
Total		4		3		4		3
3. *Cultivation:*								
First cultivation (*primer mano*)	2	8	2	4	2	6	2	2
Second cult. (*segundo mano*)	1	4	2	8	1	3	2	2
Third cult. (*cajón, hilling, despacho*)	1	1.5	1	2	1	1	1	1
Weeding (*solada*)	1	3	4	4	1	1	2	2
Total		16.5		18		11		7
4. *Harvest:*								
Stripping corn stalks, picking corn leaves (*zacateo*)	12	12	10	10	1	5	4	4
Tying leaves in bundles (*juntado*)	1	1	1	1	1	1	1	1
Transport (*acarreo*)	1	6	1	6	1	4	6	6
Corn-picking (*pizca*)	4	8	7	7	7	7	4	4
Corn transport (*acarreo mazorca*)	1	3	1	6	1	3	4	4
Corn shelling (*desgranado*)	1	6	1	7	1	3	1	3
Total		36		37		23		22
TOTAL:		66.5 days		68		45 days		36

TABLE 4

ESTIMATED TIME SPENT IN PRODUCTION OF CORN
IN HOE CULTURE. TEPOZTLÁN, 1944

Operation	Texcal type Tlacolol clearing of 10 cuartillos	Cerro type Tlacolol clearing of 7 cuartillos
	No. of Man-days	No. of Man-days
1. *Preparation of Land:*		
Clearing with machete and ax	40	21
Fencing with poles, posts and stones	12	20
Burning	8	1
2. *Planting:*		
Seeding with *caxala*	12	7
Reseeding	4	2
3. *Cultivation:*		
Weeding by hand	30	40
		40 (repair of fence)
4. *Harvesting:*	12	8
Transport of corn	10	15
Shelling corn (15 *cargas*)	15	7
TOTAL NO. OF DAYS	143	161

exhausting than work in plow culture. The *tlacololeros* are in a sense perpetual pioneers making clearings in the forest. Also, weeding by hand is very difficult and leaves welts for days on the hands of the toughest *tlacololeros*. It is said in the village that one can tell a *tlacololero* by his hands.

Another very important difference between the two systems is the difference in time demanded by each. On the whole there is much less time pressure in *tlacolol*. Thus a man can clear his land anytime between January and April. He can work for a few days at clearing, spend a few days doing some other job, and return to clearing. After planting there is also considerable leeway before the time for the first and only weeding. This is not so in plow culture. Although there is considerable leeway in the time of planting, once planting has been done the cultivations must follow soon thereafter at regular intervals, generally every twenty days, or the yields will be cut down appreciably. Furthermore, there is always the need to take advantage of dry days when the oxen can get into the field. The decrease in total production time and the corresponding increase in time pressure which we here see as a consequence of improved technology may be a widespread phenomenon which, I believe, deserves further attention and study.

· Y I E L D S ·

A comparison of the yields from the two types of agriculture reveals that the average corn yields in hoe culture are equal to the best yields in plow culture, and the best yields in hoe culture are about twice the average yields in plow culture. The reasons for this are primarily greater soil fertility in the land used for hoe culture and the different type of corn used. My data show an average corn yield in plow agriculture of about 9.6 *cargas* of shelled corn per hectare or approximately twenty-four bushels per acre. However, an average of this kind is not too meaningful in itself because of the wide range in production depending upon the type of land used. Tepoztecans distinguished three types of land classes, namely, class one, class two, and class three. Class one land will produce an average of 36 bushels of shelled corn per acre, class two land 24 bushels, and class three land 12 bushels. Thus, the range in productivity between the best lands and the poorest lands in plow agriculture is about three times. Only about 5 per cent of plow land is in one; the remainder is equally divided between classes two and three. On this basis I find that approximately twenty bushels per acre is the average yield in plow culture for the village. This is considerably higher than the Mexican national average. In *tlacolol* a normal yield is about 36 bushels per acre; yields of 50 bushels and over are not uncommon.[5]

The larger yields of *tlacolol* make it quite attractive. One might ask, therefore, why more people do not work in *tlacolol*. There are a number of reasons. First, the difficulty of the work and the fact that it has a lower standing in the community discourages many. Furthermore, many men who have worked as day laborers have no corn at harvest time and have to seek cash income regularly to support their families. In other words, even in the case of *tlacolol* which takes so relatively little capital, a man must have sufficient corn to support his family if he is to spend the long periods necessary to clear the scrub forest. However, by far the most important consideration is the limited amount of *tlacolol* lands, a shortage which is being felt more and more as the number of *tlacololeros* has increased.

[5] It should be noted that the above figures are conversions from Tepoztecan data. Tepoztecans think of yields in terms of the number of *cargas* (about 200 liters) of corn per *cuartillo* (2 liters) of seed planted. Similarly, Tepoztecans generally do not think in terms of hectares but rather in terms of the amount of seed needed to plant a given plot.

The *tlacolol* system of cutting and burning by its very nature demands large reserve areas, for it takes about ten years for cleared land to grow back into scrub forest sufficiently to be worth clearing again. If all the villagers were to open *tlacolol* clearings in a single year, there would be practically no possibility of planting again for at least ten years.

The costs in hoe culture in terms of value of man-days of labor are much higher than in plow culture, but little hired labor is used. *Tlacolol* is practical only for people with much time and little capital. It is much too inefficient a system for production for the market on a large scale. There is considerable range in costs even within hoe culture.[6] Most of this range is a function of the difference between the two types of terrain used in hoe culture, that is, the difference between *tlacolol de cerro* and *tlacolol de texcal*. In the former, building fences is a much more time-consuming operation because there is more danger of cattle getting into the fields. Cattle rarely get into the *texcal*.

This brings us to one of the crucial problems in Tepoztlán, namely, the rapid increase of population in the last twenty years with no accompanying increase in resources or improvement in production techniques. On the contrary there has been an increase in the number of *tlacololeros*, which means a return to a more inefficient and primitive type of production in an effort to escape the devastating effects of a money economy during a period of inflation. I have already mentioned the sharp rise in the cost of buying or renting a yoke of oxen as well as the other tools of plow culture. Labor costs have also gone up, and indeed, the wages paid to agricultural day laborers in Tepoztlán are considerably higher than in other parts of the Republic because of the proximity of Tepoztlán to large urban centers. In any case these costs are beyond the capacity of many Tepoztecans, who therefore turn to the more primitive system of *tlacolol*. Although the presence of the communal lands and their availability for hoe culture have helped to ease the shock of the rapid rise in prices and thereby have helped to resolve the immediate problem, the use of communal lands is by no means a satisfactory solution. In fact, it increases the problems to be faced in the future.

Were Tepoztlán a truly primitive culture, with the usual high birth and death rates and a stable and small population, the technique of *tlacolol*, though wasteful and inefficient, might be workable. However, in the face of an ever-increasing population and higher standards of living, the primitive techniques of *tlacolol* seem no longer to be feasible. The necessity of clearing new plots of land

[6] More detailed cost analysis must await later publication.

every few years, the rapid depletion of the land and its forest resources, and the consequent increase in erosion are problems which
will have to be reckoned with sooner or later.

The system of cutting and burning might well be feasible in a pioneer country with relatively limitless areas of uncleared land. However, Tepoztlán with its fixed boundaries presents no such conditions. It is significant in this connection that the most vehement land
disputes with neighboring *municipios* have occurred in those areas
where the boundary line runs through scrub forest used for *tlacolol*
clearings.

In conclusion, and in the light of the above materials on hoe culture and plow culture in Tepoztlán, I should like to consider briefly a
point of theoretical interest concerning the concept of the folk culture and the conceptualization of processes of culture change in
terms of the folk-urban continuum. We have seen that one of the
results of the introduction of plow agriculture in Tepoztlán by the
Spanish conquerors in the sixteenth century was to give the people
an alternative and in some ways more efficient system of farming.
And since the ancient system of agriculture using cutting and burning and the digging stick has persisted in the form of hoe culture, we
find two distinct systems existing side by side. As we have seen,
different families in the same village are therefore occupied in different tasks during the same season, and this makes for a complexity in
village life which does not fit our usual stereotype of the homogeneity of custom in a folk society. Furthermore, the coexistence of hoe
culture and plow culture gives rise to new conflict points within the
total culture of the village because the two systems are not well integrated at all points. This has led to a conflict of interests between the
poor and landless *tlacololeros* who work in hoe culture and the better-to-do peasants who work in plow culture. In other words, the
introduction of plow culture made for a greater heterogeneity in
ways of doing things and also made for a lack of integration. But
since homogeneity and integration are considered two of the important criteria in the definition of the folk culture,[7] we could therefore
say that Tepoztlán has become less folk and more urban. Here, then,
we have a situation where the introduction of folk or rural elements
into a folk culture makes the folk culture more urban. Now, if adding folk and folk gives more urban and adding folk and urban also
gives more urban, then there is something wrong with the logic of
our equation. Obviously city influences are not the sole factors
which make for social change. Folk cultures have been influencing
one another for thousands of years and out of such interaction has

[7] Robert Redfield. "The Folk Society," *The American Journal of Sociology*, Vol.
52 (Jan., 1947), pp. 293–308.

come social change. It does not seem to me that the folk-urban continuum conceptualization adequately provides for this type of widespread situation. Furthermore, these data suggest that in many cases culture change may not be a matter of a folk-urban progression at all but rather a matter of a homogeneity or heterogeneity. This suggests that some of the criteria which have been used to define the folk-urban conceptualization of culture change may be independent variables and can most profitably be used as such.

12

Wealth Differences in a Mexican Village[*]

Anthropologists have long noted the existence of wealth differences in so-called primitive or folk societies and have recognized that there is some relationship between the distribution of wealth and the social structure. However, the absence of quantitative studies of wealth differences has impeded a fuller understanding of the role of wealth and has limited the scope and quality of our analysis of the economics of other societies. In this connection anthropologists might well learn from rural sociologists, who, in their studies of rural groups in our own culture, use quantitative data on property ownership, particularly land, as a starting point in their analysis of rural society. The need for this type of data in anthropological studies has been explicitly recognized in recent years by a number of anthropologists.

I think it is worthwhile to consider briefly why there have been so few quantitative studies of wealth differences. One reason has been the tendency to assume that nonliterate societies are simple and homogeneous and that the study of wealth distribution would not be especially revealing. Another reason is that many anthropologists have frankly not been interested in economics. But even for those anthropologists who have been aware of the need for more precise data on wealth distribution there are serious obstacles of a practical field-work nature. The sheer amount of time and work required for

[*] This was first published in August, 1947, in the *Scientific Monthly*, Vol. 65, No. 2, pp. 127–32.

gathering the necessary economic data—for measuring plots of land, determining land productivity, and obtaining property inventories on hundreds of families—presents a discouraging if not impossible task, especially for the traditional lone anthropologist who goes into the field as a one-man expedition of all the social sciences, eager to get a bit of everything.

It is the purpose of this article to report the results of an effort to study quantitatively the wealth differences in the Mexican village of Tepoztlán and to present a scale devised to measure these differences. *

Our first step in the study of wealth differences was to determine how wealth was defined by the villagers. Invariably, *los ricos,* or "the wealthy," were described as "those who own much land and cattle." Private land ownership (in contrast to *ejido* holdings) was considered the single most important form of wealth. It is the goal of each family to own land; artisans and merchants invest in land when they can. Cattle and oxen rank next in importance as forms of wealth. In all, twelve items were most frequently mentioned by informants as forms of wealth in the village. These were *ejido* plots, privately owned land, team of oxen, plows, cattle, burros, mules, horses, hogs, sewing machines, urban property (i.e., the ownership of more than one house site and house in the village), and plum trees (*S. lutea* or a related species). Of these items we need note here only that they are all means of production and a source of income. The sale of plums, for example, is an important source of income for many families, particularly since the building of the road in 1935.

How are these items of wealth distributed among the 853 families of the village? Let us begin with land. There are three types of land tenure in Tepoztlán. First, there is privately owned land, which can be bought and sold. Second is the *ejido,* which is granted by the national Departamento Agrario to the village and then by the local Ejido Commissioner to an individual family. This land can be held by the family as long as the land is being used. It can be inherited by the succeeding head of the family but cannot be sold. Third is *tlacolol,* which refers to the land on the rocky and wooded mountainsides that form part of the municipal land and which can be cleared and planted by any Tepoztecan. *Tlacolol* is not considered a form of wealth; on the contrary, it has traditionally been viewed as the last resort of the poor.

We found that 311, or 36 per cent, of the 853 families own land. Two hundred sixty-seven families, or 31 per cent, hold *ejido* grants. Of these, 158 families have only *ejido* grants, and 109 own private

* For a description of the village, see the preceding essay.

land in addition. Thus, in a village where the ideal is for each family to own its own plot of land, we find that 64 per cent of the families own no private land and 46 per cent have neither private land nor *ejido* holdings.

The size of privately owned holdings is given in Table 1.

TABLE 1

Size of holding	No. of owners	Percentage
Less than 1 hectare	109	36.2
1–4	97	32.2
5–9	67	22.2
10–14	18	5.9
15–19	4	1.3
20–24	4	1.3
25–29	2	0.66

The striking thing about the land holdings is their extremely small size. This table shows that 90.6 per cent of all private holdings are less than 9 hectares in size, and 68.4 per cent are less than 4 hectares. The largest holding is only about 27 hectares, and there are two such cases in the village. A man with 10 or more hectares is a relatively large landholder. Over 36 per cent are less than 1 hectare. *Ejido* holdings, too, are small—95 per cent are less than 3 hectares in size. When we remember that 384 families own no land at all and have no *ejidos*, the essential land poverty of the villagers is revealed.

Let us now consider the ownership and distribution of cattle. Only 180, or 21 per cent, of all families own cattle. Well over 50 per cent of these own between 1 and 3 cows; about 40 per cent own between 4 and 10 cows. The largest herd, which is owned by the wealthiest man in the village, consists of 70 head.

The distribution of two other items, namely, oxen and plows, also tells us a great deal about the agricultural economy. There are 179 families who own a team of oxen, and 213 families own plows. Thus, of the 469 families who own land or *ejidos* or both, over 63 per cent own no oxen with which to work their land, and 52 per cent own no plow. The families who own oxen therefore do a great deal of custom work, from which they realize a good income.

In order to rank the families according to their wealth, we devised a point scale using one point for every hundred pesos of value. Points were assigned to each of the items in accordance with the approximate sale value or the approximate production value or both. Thus, one hectare (approximately 2.4 acres) of *ejido* land was assigned 3.6 points because the average annual production of one hectare of *ejido* land in Tepoztlán as of June, 1944 had a market value of 360 pesos. On the other hand, one hectare of privately owned land was assigned 7.2 points, which represented both the value of production and the sale value.

We were tempted to assign points for prestige value, as in the case of privately owned versus *ejido* land, but to avoid further complications we decided not to do so.

The items of the scale and the assigned points for each item are given in Table 2.

TABLE 2

1 hectare *ejido*	3.6
1 hectare private land	7.2
1 team of oxen	7.2
1 plow	0.7
1 cow	3.1
1 donkey	1.5
1 mule	3.0
1 horse	2.5
1 hog	1.5
1 sewing machine	3.5
1 urban site & house	7.5
1 plum tree	1.0
1 nonfarm occupation	1.0 for every 100 pesos earned annually

A score was obtained for a given family by adding the points assigned for each item. For example, if a family owned four hectares of land (the minimum size of holding considered necessary by Tepoztecans for a "decent living" for a family of five), one plow, one team of oxen, one horse, one cow, two hogs, two plum trees, and a sewing machine, it would receive a score of 47 points. Since this is a very modest list, even according to Tepoztecan standards, a score of 40 to 50 points may be taken to represent approximately the minimum in property ownership necessary for a self-sufficient farm family. The distribution of scores is presented in Table 3.

The most significant features in this frequency distribution are (1) the extremely wide range of wealth differences from zero to over 400 points, (2) the great majority clustering around the lower end of the scale, indicating widespread poverty (note that 81 per cent of the families have scores below what we have tentatively designated as a minimum for decent subsistence), (3) the 92 families having a zero score, and (4) the manner in which, from the distribution of the scores, the families fall into distinct economic groups. Eighty-one per cent of the families are in the lowest group (point score 0–39); 13.9 per cent are in the middle group (40–99); and 4.4 per cent are in the upper group (100–407.4). The lowest group can be broken down into two subgroups, 0–19 and 20–39, which we shall call I-A

TABLE 3

FREQUENCY DISTRIBUTION OF 853 FAMILIES ON ECONOMIC POINT SCALE

Score	No. of families	Percentage of total	Sub-group	Per-centage of total	Large group	Percentage of total
400–407.4	1	0.11				
220–253.0	3	0.35				
200–219	2	0.23				
190–199	1	0.11	B	1.5		
180–189	1	0.11				
170–179	3	0.35				
160–169	2	0.23			III	4.4
150–159	3	0.35				
140–149	3	0.35				
130–139	5	0.58	A	2.9		
120–129	4	0.46				
110–119	4	0.46				
100–109	6	0.70				
90–99	16	1.87				
80–89	18	2.11				
70–79	17	1.99		13.9	II	13.9
60–69	20	2.34				
50–59	28	3.28				
40–49	20	2.34				
30–39	74	8.67	B	21.6		
20–29	111	13.00				
10–19	206	24.15			I	81.5
1–9	213	24.02	A	59.9		
0	92	10.78				

and I-B, respectively. The middle group will be referred to as Group II, and the upper group as III-A (100–159) and III-B (160 and over).

To test the validity of our groupings, we asked ten informants to name the ten wealthiest families in the village. All those named were in our top group. Another way in which we checked our scale was to present names selected from each of the economic levels of the scale and ask informants to rank them according to their wealth. Again we found a very high correlation.

What are the characteristics of each of these economic groups? First let us consider the families with zero scores. For the most part they are either young married men, most of whom live with their parents, who also have low scores; or they are widows or old men, many of whom live alone. One-third of this group are women, who manage to earn a living by small-scale trade and by doing odd jobs.

Group I-A, which consists of 511 families with scores from zero to

19, contains 97 per cent of the landless people in the village. Three hundred fifty-four, or 70 per cent, of the families in this group have zero score for land. How do these landless people live? Approximately one-third depend upon *tlacolol*, but all depend upon a variety of activities which together provide only a meager income. Thus, many burn charcoal, sell wood, work as peons, are small traders, or have some other part-time occupation. They have some measure of security in that most of them own their houses and house sites or will inherit them. About one-fourth of them plant some corn around their houses and about 40 per cent have some income from plum trees. About one-third have hogs. Less than one-third own a mule, horse, or donkey, which is so essential for work and transportation.

The families in Group II include most of the artisans and merchants as well as better-to-do farmers. The former are the most acculturated group in the village. They are the ones who wear store clothes, who send their children out of Tepoztlán to high school, and who generally have a higher standard of living.

Group III consists of 38 families, all of whom have high scores on land or cattle or both. About one-half of these families have inherited their land from wealthy relatives who before the revolution were *caciques* and dominated the village. The other half have worked their way up to their present position.

One might ask whether there is any relationship between position on this scale and standard of living. Do the wealthiest people have the highest standard of living? This cannot be answered categorically. On the whole, the people in Group III consume more meat, milk, eggs, and bread, and they generally live in better-constructed and better-furnished houses, some of which have running water. However, they are not the ones who go in for modern dress or any ostentatious spending for comforts or luxuries. They are a hardworking people and not a leisure class. One of the distinguishing characteristics of this group is that they generally have hired men all year around, but, with the exception of two men, they work side by side with their peons.

What is the relationship between wealth and the adoption of new habits? The Mexican census of 1940 included three interesting items which provide us with some data on acculturation in relation to standard of living. The questions were: Do you eat bread (as against *tortillas*)? Do you wear shoes (or go barefoot or wear huaraches)? Do you sleep on a bed or a cot (or sleep on the ground or on a *tepexco*—a raised frame upon which the *petate* is placed)?

From a special tabulation of the census of Tepoztlán, we were able to correlate the responses to these questions with the family position on the economic scale. The results are shown in Table 4.

TABLE 4

Group	Percentage who eat bread	Percentage who wear shoes	Percentage who sleep on bed or cot
I-A	23.20	6.46	14.12
I-B	32.30	6.78	23.18
II	50.82	12.06	30.71
III-A	41.55	7.14	21.42
III-B	57.69	5.12	16.66
Tepoztlán as a whole	41.11	7.51	21.22

It is clear that eating bread correlates positively with economic position. Thus 23 per cent of the people in Group I-A as compared with 57 per cent of the people in Group III-B ate bread. Furthermore, we know from our observation that the wealthier people eat bread more often and in greater quantities. The point is that bread is still a luxury item in this village.

Wearing shoes and sleeping in beds do not correlate with wealth, but rather with age. That is, the older people, whether rich or poor, prefer to use huaraches or go barefoot and to sleep on the traditional *petate* or on a raised *tepexco*. We have here a nice example of the factor of selectivity in the adoption of new traits. Families that do not use shoes or beds will often buy sewing machines. For example, whereas only 6 per cent of Group III use shoes, 70 per cent own sewing machines.

It should be noted that a larger percentage of the middle group—Group II—have adopted new traits, even though their economic resources are less than those of Group III.

There remains only for us to discuss the age factor in relation to position on this scale. Table 5 shows the frequency distribution of the age of heads of families by economic categories.

It is apparent that there are no younger people in the upper group

TABLE 5

AGE DISTRIBUTION OF HEADS OF FAMILIES BY ECONOMIC GROUP

Group	Below 29 yrs.	30–49 yrs.	50–69 yrs.	70–99 yrs.	Total
0	31	31	18	12	92
I-A	63	194	132	30	419
I-B	6	88	77	14	185
II	3	46	52	18	119
III-A	0	9	15	1	25
III-B	0	1	11	1	13
TOTAL	103	369	305	76	853

and very few in the middle group. The bulk of the younger people are at the low end of the scale. Conversely, the wealthiest are of an advanced age, mostly between fifty and sixty-nine years of age. Forty-one per cent of the heads of families over age fifty are in Group I; 59 per cent are in Group II; and 74 per cent are in Group III. But while there is a positive correlation between wealth and old age, the converse is not true. The fact that 41 per cent of the older people are in Group I shows that vertical mobility is quite limited. The practice of not dividing up the property until the death of the parents often results in adult married sons with as many as five children being entirely landless and without a house.

Our point scale, although not a refined statistical instrument, has revealed a much wider range and a less equal distribution of wealth than one might anticipate for a community of this type. With this scale we can determine the relative economic status of every family in the village. We are therefore in a position to study such things as leadership, marriage, the *compadre* system, and standard of living in relation to economic status. We believe that if a similar scale were used in studies of other societies, adapted to local conditions as necessary, we should have a much better basis for comparative analysis of the role and distribution of wealth.

13

Family Dynamics
in a Mexican Village[*]

In 1943, as part of my restudy of the village of Tepoztlán[†] I began the systematic collection of data on a number of carefully selected families in an effort to develop an anthropological approach to family studies.[1] It seemed to me that the holistic approach of the an-

[*] This was first published in August, 1959, in Marriage and Family Living, Vol. 21, No. 3, pp. 218–26. I am indebted to my wife, Ruth M. Lewis, for her assistance with the analysis and preparation of the field materials. I am also grateful to Dr. Emanuel K. Schwartz for his reading of the larger manuscript on the Rojas family and for his stimulating suggestions for this paper.

[†] For other discussion of Tepoztlán in this volume, see Essays 2, 5, 11, 12, and 14.

[1] For a discussion of the whole family study approach, see my article "An Anthropological Approach to Family Studies," *American Journal of Sociology*, Vol. 45, No. 5 (March, 1950), pp. 468–75. Since 1950, there has been a growing interest in the possibilities of whole family analysis but very little empirical work has appeared. For examples see Nathan W. Ackerman and Marjorie L. Behrens, "A Study of Family Diagnosis," *American Journal of Psychiatry*, Vol. 26, No. 1 (Jan., 1956), pp. 66–78; Florence Kluckhohn and John P. Spiegel, *Integration and Conflict in Family Behavior*, Report No. 27, Group for the Advancement of Psychiatry, 1953, Topeka, Kans.; J. H. Robb, "Clinical Studies in Marriage and the Family: A Symposium on Method," Part IV, "Experiences with Ordinary Families," *British Journal of Medical Psychiatry*, Vol. 20, No. 1 (Feb., 1957), pp. 1–16; M. K. Opler, *Culture, Psychiatry and Human Values* (Springfield, Ill.: Thomas, 1956); Kaspar D. Naegele, *Hostility and Aggression in Middle Class American Families* (Doctoral dissertation, Harvard University), 1951.

thropologist combined with his traditional emphasis upon studying people in their natural milieu was ideally suited to the intensive studies of families. Two of the objectives of the early phase of this work were to demonstrate the important role of personal and social factors, in addition to cultural ones, in nuclear family life, and to show the wide range of individual personality and family types within a single community. In this paper I will compare the internal structure, psychodynamics, and personality development in two families. I will also attempt to relate the psychodynamics of these two families to the broader social, economic, and political trends in the village and nation, in order to show the differential effects of the Mexican Revolution of 1910–20 upon these families.

The first family is the Rojas family, which consists of seven members—the father Anastasio Rojas (age fifty-four), his wife Soledad Gómez (forty-five), and their five children: Cruz (twenty-six), Lola (twenty-three), Crispin (nineteen), Delfina (sixteen), and Francisca (thirteen). The Martínez family consists of eight members—the father Pedro Martínez (age fifty-nine), his wife Esperanza (fifty-four), their five children, Felipe (twenty-three), Martín (twenty-two), Macrina (seventeen), Ricardo (eighteen), Moisés (thirteen), and a grandson Germán (seven) born out of wedlock to their eldest daughter Conchita. Both families are somewhat larger than the average Tepoztecan family, which has five members. Both are simple biological families living alone on a house site as do over 70 per cent of all Tepoztecan families.

The Rojas family is one of thirty-seven better-to-do landowning families in the upper economic group of the village. Only 4 per cent of the families in the village are in this category. The Martínez family is one of the poorer landless families of the lowest economic group, which consists of about 80 per cent of all families. The two families have contrasting standards of living. The Rojas family are well housed, well fed, and well clothed, according to Tepoztecan standards. They can afford some luxuries and their home contains many modern articles such as beds, chairs, tables, a clock, a flashlight, and a sewing machine. The Martínez family, on the other hand, live close to a bare subsistence level and have a minimum of clothing and house furnishings and none of the luxuries found in the Rojas home. The Martínez family are reduced to a diet of tortillas, chili, and black coffee during several months of the year.

Although the two families are now at different levels on the economic ladder, it is important to remember that at the time when they set up independent households they were both poor. The differential material progress of the two families is all the more striking because the Martínez family has remained poor despite the fact that it has three grown sons, all of whom work hard as farmers, whereas the Rojas family has four daughters, who have been an economic burden, and only one son, who has contributed almost nothing to the family.

Both couples married at approximately the same time, at the very outbreak of the Mexican Revolution. Anastasio's parents belonged to a relatively small, privileged, though not wealthy, middle-peasant group in the village. His wife, Soledad, an only child, came from a somewhat poorer family. The marriage was an arranged one and was celebrated in the church. Anastasio was twenty-two and Soledad only thirteen. For the first seven years, they lived with Anastasio's mother and Anastasio worked his mother's lands.

Both Pedro and his wife Esperanza were from poor, landless lower-class families. Both of their mothers had been abandoned by their husbands very soon after their "free union" marriages, so that neither Pedro nor Esperanza knew their fathers. Both of their mothers worked to support their respective children, who were cared for by relatives and had a difficult childhood. Pedro selected Esperanza as his wife and they were married in the Church about a year after Pedro's mother died.

In terms of village standards, Anastasio had enormous advantages over Pedro from the start. His greater age in relation to his wife, his higher economic status, and his residence with his mother made the traditionally expected male dominance relatively easy for him in the early years of his marriage and gave him a sense of security. Pedro, on the other hand, had to work on distant haciendas and leave his young wife in the care of his mother-in-law for weeks at a time. Although Anastasio received a minimum of economic assistance from his family, even this minimum gave him a great advantage over Pedro. With the help of a well-to-do relative, Anastasio was able to go to the neighboring state of Guerrero on several cattle-buying trips. The profit he made in buying and selling cattle was an important factor in his becoming a landowner.

The Rojas family have had more formal schooling than the Martínez family, and as a whole show a higher degree of literacy. The father and two older daughters have gone through the third grade, the mother through the second grade. However, the mother has forgotten how to read and can barely sign her name. This family is somewhat unusual in that the three younger children are students preparing for professional careers: the daughters are planning to be teachers and the son an agronomist. The father in the Martínez family, though essentially a self-educated man, is much more literate than the father in the Rojas family. His wife, however, never attended school and is illiterate. The eldest daughter was educated to become a teacher but her career was cut short; the rest of the children received only three or four years of schooling. The parents of both families are bilingual, speaking both Spanish and Nahuatl. The Rojas family, like most families in Tepoztlán, is Catholic. The Martínez family is one of the few in Tepoztlán that converted to Protestantism, under pressure of the father, who had been an active Catholic for the first forty years of his life.

Both families are strong, cohesive units and represent relatively close in-groups. Each is held together by traditional bonds of family loyalty and parental authority, by common economic strivings and mutual dependence, by the stability of marriage between the parents, and finally by the absence of other social groupings to which the family might turn in time of need. In the relations between husband and wife and parents and children, the Rojas family more nearly represents new tendencies in the village whereas the Martínez family is an example of an older family pattern.

Closer examination of the Rojas and Martínez families reveals important differences in their internal structure, in the quantity and style of emotional expression, and in the range of personality development. The Rojas family is highly differentiated or segmented in structure, consisting of five clearly delineated interaction units or subgroups. These are: first, husband and wife; second, mother and only son; third, mother and the older daughters; fourth, mother and younger daughter; and fifth, the sisters. The mother plays a crucial role in the communication system, acting as an intermediary between husband and children, and between her son and daughters. Viewed psychologically, she may be seen as a divisive force in the family, separating her husband from his children, her son from her daughters, and the youngest daughter from the older daughters.

In the Martínez family, the internal structure is much more monolithic, with the father at the apex of the pyramid and in direct communication with and in control of all members. Here the role of the

ROJAS FAMILY
(Segmented Type)

MARTINEZ FAMILY
(Monolithic Type)

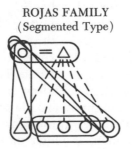

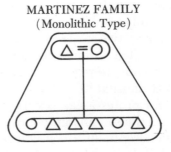

The Internal Structure of Two Families

mother is to carry out Pedro's orders and to support his authority and to contain the latent and manifest resentment of the children toward the father. At times, she also acts as a buffer to protect the children from excessive punishment by the father. In this family, the children are much more united and form a single solidary group, so that generation differences are more clear-cut than in the Rojas family.

The greater segmentation of the Rojas family is a result of its freer, more democratic, generally richer home environment, both in the goods of life and in the variety of alternatives and experiences. Within the limits set by the changing village culture, it has allowed a greater development of individuality and personality differences, a much greater amount of verbalization and expression of emotion, more tensions in interpersonal relations, and more expression of aggression. Like a middle-class family in our own society, it is better able to afford the luxury of internal dissension and to take advantage of the new opportunities which have opened up since the Mexican Revolution.

By contrast, the Martínez family, which suffers from grinding poverty, is more authoritarian. In this family, therefore, there is more repression, less individuality and expressiveness, and less personal freedom. It is as though this family, faced with greater danger, has set up barriers and defenses and is in a constant state of siege, mobilizing all available manpower for common survival.

The greater variety of personality types in the Rojas family as compared to the Martínez family can be demonstrated in many ways. If we apply David Riesman's types, for example, we find that in the Rojas family the father, the eldest daughter, and the son are essentially tradition-directed (with the daughter showing some signs of inner-directedness); the mother, the second daughter, and the youngest daughter are essentially inner-directed; and the third daughter, the one who has brought the greatest changes about in the family, is other-directed. In the Martínez family, the father and eldest daughter are inner-directed and the mother and the rest of the children are tradition-directed or, more accurately, father-directed, since they follow his strong lead.

The parents of the Rojas family, Anastasio and Soledad, form a little subgroup, as I have said. Anastasio customarily addresses himself to his wife when he is at home; his conversation with his children is minimal. He becomes communicative, even affectionate, only when he is drunk. Soledad is more expressive than Anastasio. The parents speak Nahuatl together and Spanish to their children. As Anastasio grew older he became more and more passive in the home, giving his wife an unusual amount of freedom, even though he is still the final authority in all major decisions. His control is based upon Soledad's fear of his temper and occasional outbursts of violence to which she reacts with repressed resentment and an attitude of martyrdom. Soledad plays the role of the good, submissive wife, dutifully bathing and serving her husband, but she manages to dominate him directly and in many ways is the real head of the household. He gives her most of his earnings and rarely demands an accounting. She makes most of the day-to-day decisions for the family, comes and goes as she pleases, has authority to lend or rent out her husband's work animals and tools, and in general takes the initiative in planning for the family.

Anastasio and his wife share common goals: both are working to improve their level of living, to accumulate property, and to educate their younger children. Anastasio, however, places greatest emphasis upon the more traditional investments in land and cattle, whereas Soledad prefers to spend money on modernizing the house and on such items as beds, tableware, and canned food. In doing this, Soledad has the support of the younger children. More serious points of conflict between husband and wife have been money, in-laws, infidelity, and Anastasio's drinking. In the past, he has beaten Soledad cruelly a number of times; once he attempted to choke her with her own braids because of a rumor about her alleged infidelity. Soledad is less forgiving than her husband and harbors hostility towards him, sometimes refusing sexual relations with him for weeks after a quarrel. She often suffers from headaches, and also from *muina,* an illness of anger. Anastasio finds relaxation and escape from his problems in excessive drinking; this he does regularly on Sundays and on fiestas when it does not seriously interfere with his farm work.

The parent-children relationship of the Rojas family in recent years is characterized by an unusual degree of child-orientedness, differentiating it from most Tepoztecan families and giving it a middle-class quality. This is accentuated by the combination of a manipulative mother who desired to live through her children and a relatively permissive father. The Rojas children, as a result, have had an unusually strong position; they have had more freedom, support, opportunities, and power to bring about changes within the family than have most Tepoztecan youth.

The Rojas children are closer to their mother than to their father and are convinced that she is the more interested in their welfare. They interpret Anastasio's withdrawn manner as indifference. Although he loves them and is willing to work hard for them, and although his resistance to expenditures and innovations has been comparatively slight, his children are aware of his essential passivity. In contrast, their mother spends much time with them, discusses village gossip and sometimes family affairs with them, keeps a sharp eye on their activities, scolds or hits them, and takes care of them when they are ill. It is she who recognizes their need for new clothing, for more education, for medical care, and for better food. As the children grew older, Soledad turned to them for support in her conflicts with Anastasio and eventually succeeded in building a barrier between father and children. Soledad uses her intermediary position to her own advantage, rarely refusing a request herself, presenting him in an unfavorable light, and often impressing the children with the fact that she is protecting them from him at risk to herself.

The strong tie between Soledad and her son, Crispin, has created a split in the family and a great deal of resentment on the part of the father and the daughters. Soledad makes no secret of her preference for her son and has taken the role of his protector and benefactor. She often sends her daughters out of the room when she wants to talk to him and she is the only one in whom Crispin confides, although their confidences are necessarily limited by their respect-relationship. Crispin avoids his father, and his relations with his sisters tend to be quarrelsome. Soledad further expresses her favoritism by indulging many of Crispin's whims, serving him special foods, giving him spending money, letting him sleep late, worrying over his poor health, and making his sisters serve him. Soledad justifies herself on the basis of Crispin's history of illness and his being the only one of four sons to survive, but her family and relatives consider her permissiveness excessive. Anastasio is bitterly disappointed in his son, who cannot work hard in the fields, and blames Soledad for "spoiling" the boy.

The women of the family form a large subgroup which in turn is divided into a grouping of the three older girls on the one hand and the mother and youngest daughter on the other. In general, the women in the family are more communicative than the men. They share ideas and even secrets. If one of the girls, for example, plans to go on a pilgrimage or to join the Acción Católica, she first discusses it with the sister closest to her and then with her mother and other sisters. After making a decision, the mother asks the father for permission. Crispin is the last to learn what the rest of the family has been thinking of.

But even among the women there are obstacles to communication. Cruz, the eldest daughter, is withdrawn and inhibited and speaks little to anyone. Lola, the second daughter, is expressive and aggressive like her mother, but as a result she is in conflict with most members of her family and is considered lacking in "respect" by her relatives. Delfina, who is away at school much of the time, confides in her older sisters but is jealous and quarrelsome with her younger sister. Delfina is quite hostile to her mother because of her favoritism toward Crispin and also the youngest daughter, but at the same time she strives for her mother's approval. Actually, Delfina is the only one of the Rojas children who prefers the father to the mother. Francisca, the youngest, is the most erratic in the matter of expressiveness, sometimes talking and singing freely, at other times not speaking to anyone for days. She is most detached from the family, and has friends to whom she is closer than to anyone in the family. She accepts her mother's indulgence of her but shows little signs of reciprocal affection. At age thirteen, she was already looking forward to leaving home and going away to school.

In the Martínez family, Pedro, the father, is an energetic, alert, dominating man who is the primary authority in his home. He demands an unusual amount of obedience, respect, and work, not only from his children but also from his wife. Esperanza, the wife, is a mild, unexpressive, submissive woman who follows the lead of her husband because of tradition, devotion, and fear. The affectional ties between them are deeper than those between the Rojas parents; they have made a more satisfactory sexual adjustment. Esperanza, for example, has never refused sexual relations with her husband, nor does she bear grudges or resentment for long periods. Pedro and Esperanza converse with each other in Nahuatl and form a close unit apart from their children. Pedro, more talkative than his wife, confides in her but rarely asks for or takes her advice. He considers her ignorant, and generally inferior, and when angry tells her so. She complains of his outside activities, neglect of the family, and of his infidelities. They do not quarrel as frequently as the Rojas parents, nor does Pedro become as physically violent as Anastasio, but he is verbally so aggressive that Esperanza occasionally seeks relief in heavy drinking.

Pedro keeps strict control over his family by giving daily instructions, by checking on everyone and everything, by curtailing each person's freedom of movement, of leisure, and of friendships, and also by limiting spending money and by punishing when necessary. Although he usually turns over his and his son's earnings to his wife, he does much of the family spending, even buying clothing for his wife and daughter without consulting them. Unlike Anastasio Rojas, Pedro is communicative and expressive; he has devoted time to his children, training them to work, lecturing them on proper behavior, and personally giving them religious instruction.

Compared to most Tepoztecan men, Pedro carries on an enormous number of activities, many of which are unremunerative. He has participated in local politics since Revolutionary days, has held office three times, has taken a more than usual interest in village and *barrio* affairs, has voluntarily contributed to communal works, was the leader of a group of men who tilled the communal lands, has acted as guide and counselor in legal matters to other peasants, has made frequent trips to other towns and to Mexico City in connection with legal matters and also as a plum merchant, and was a Catholic prayer-leader and *mayordomo* of his *barrio* before his conversion. More recently, as a Seventh Day Adventist, he has successfully converted a number of other village families. Although Pedro was once illiterate, he now reads more than most villagers—the Bible, religious pamphlets, books on the state laws, and now and then a newspaper. His interest in ideas and his adherence to his principles, even in the face of danger, are striking traits. For example, he refused to make charcoal when others in the village were making money that way, because it was denuding the forest and was against village interests.

Pedro's life has been a search for ideals and causes with which to identify: Catholicism, Zapatismo, village politics, education, and most recently Seventh Day Adventism. He tried them all and was disillusioned with all. He had taken their slogans and catchwords literally and had compulsively hoped that each would lead him to a better life and repair the deprivations of his childhood, but in each case he was inevitably disappointed. Perhaps Pedro was not in touch with the reality of the changing times and did not understand the growing money-economy and middle-class values of postrevolutionary Mexico. Anastasio, on the other hand, who was practical, cautious, thrifty, and unconcerned with causes or community projects, was much better adapted to prosper in this period.

Esperanza respects her husband's authoritarian attitude toward their children but she herself tends to be more lenient and protective. Being tradition-oriented, however, she did not approve of advanced education for her eldest daughter and of other of her husband's innovations. She is more interested in the stability of her home and in maintaining present standards of living than in improving them. To this end, she too is interested in controlling the children as much as possible. When her grown sons show signs of rebellion against their father, she persuades them to submit by appealing to their pity and affection for her; to a large extent, she has succeeded in keeping the family together.

The position of the Martínez children, with the exception of the eldest daughter, Conchita, comes close to the ideal pattern of the older generation. Conchita was relieved from the traditional burden of housework and was helped by many sacrifices on the part of the family to study outside the village and to become a schoolteacher. The first of four children to survive, Conchita was her father's favorite, and it occurred to him that through her he could raise the level of the entire family. This was a daring idea for a poor man and he was warned and mocked at by the villagers for being presumptuous. In those years, however, the promise of education was being offered to peasants. Pedro put his entire faith in his daughter, working as a peon for the first time since the Revolution to raise money to educate her. She had taught only a short time when she gave birth to a boy out of wedlock, and returned home. Her failure to have a successful career was a bitter blow to Pedro. Conchita, now married but estranged from her father, still lives in the village; she is secretly visited by her mother and sisters and brothers, who continue affectionate relations with her.

The other Martínez children, in contrast to their older sister, have received a minimum of schooling, have rarely been away from home, and have been given few liberties. Pedro plans to educate his youngest son, who is not strong enough for farm work. Other than to Conchita, no favoritism has been shown by the parents to any of the children and there is no sibling rivalry. However, there is little demonstration of affection in the family, and the children are quiet, withdrawn, and not given to sharing confidences. They have few friends and participate little in village affairs compared to the Rojas children. Although they all look up to their father and believe he is concerned about them, they feel closer to their mother. The older sons sometimes feel that they are being exploited by their father so that he may be free for his other activities. In truth, Pedro treats them as though they were his own arms and legs, allowing them little opportunity for decision-making. He strongly resents any show of independence on their part. The eldest son is most resentful, but he expresses his resentment only by lapsing into long stubborn silence. This son suffers a conflict in roles, for his father does not permit him to carry out the prerogatives and authority of an older brother. However, the son's strong tie to his mother and his fear of the outside world make it impossible for him to leave home as he would like to. The role normally assumed by the eldest daughter went to the younger daughter, not without some resentment on her part, for she had hoped to continue her education. At this point (1948), it looks as though the younger son and the grandson will probably escape Pedro's restrictive hand and will enjoy a fuller life.

· DISCUSSION ·

Our analysis of two authoritarian families from a relatively homogeneous peasant community reveals marked differences in the internal structure, communication patterns, degree of community participation, and the general climate of family life. This suggests that there is wide range of variation in family types in peasant communities, and highlights the need for a typology of families which might be applied cross-culturally. It also suggests that our traditional anthropological characterizations of families as patrilocal, patrilineal, patrifocal, etc., cannot adequately encompass the subtle and complex psychological relationships which form the structure of nuclear family life.

We have seen that both the Rojas and the Martínez families are stable, traditional families well within the village definition of normal. Both are patrilineal and patrilocal and both live within a culture which stresses the inherent rightness of male superiority and dominance. However, here the similarities end. The Martínez family is a simple monolithic structure with the father at the head, in direct control of all family members and responsible for even minor decisions. Here there is a minimum of delegation of power. Family life revolves around the father, family unity is strong, and there is little sibling rivalry. Whatever hostility there is tends to be directed toward the dominating father but is repressed. By contrast, the structure of the Rojas family is much more segmented, and although the father is the ultimate authority, family life revolves around the mother. In this family, there is more friction and expressed aggression in interpersonal relations, hostility is more diffuse, there is more emphasis upon upward mobility, more individuality, and more participation in village affairs on the part of the younger generation.

Our data suggest that the differences in the configurations of these two families are not primarily a function of wealth differences or of class position, for Tepoztlán has no clearly defined social-class differences. Rather, they must be explained primarily in terms of the personality differences between the two sets of spouses, as these have been influenced by their distinctive family backgrounds and life experiences. In each case, we found that a single strong personality has set the tone of family life—in the Rojas family, the mother; in the Martínez family, the father.

How are we to judge the mental health of these two families? By Tepoztecan standards, both are "normal" families, though the more authoritarian Martínez family is much closer to the village ideal. Indeed, in this family we find less role conflict and a better adjustment between husband and wife, parents and children, and siblings.

By contrast, the less authoritarian Rojas family shows more maladjustment, sibling rivalry, and general tension. Part of this may be related to the changing culture and the greater striving for upward mobility of the Rojas family. In any case, the two things which stand out in both families are the great amount of tension that is compatible with family stability in a peasant society, and the tolerance for pathology within the family, so long as family members can manage to carry out their major work roles.

If we compare the individuals of the two families in terms of personal development, variety of experience, and extent and quality of relations outside of the family, we find interesting differences. In the Martínez family, the father and eldest daughter would receive high scores and the mother and children low scores. In the Rojas family, both parents and the older children would receive low scores and the younger children would get high scores. Although the total score of the Rojas family would be somewhat higher than that of the Martínez family, this seems relatively unimportant compared to the distribution of scores within each family. Certainly, from the point of view of a Western-trained clinician, each family reveals problem areas and pathology.

Comparing the two fathers and taking account of Pedro's initial disadvantages, we find that it is Pedro who has shown the greater personal and social development. He relates more easily to others, has more friends outside the family, is more knowledgeable, has a wider range of experience, has considerable prestige in the village despite his poverty, and has been deeply involved in village affairs. However, while Pedro dreamed of a better life for others, his family suffered; it might be said that his personal development has been at the expense of his family. This is closely related to a basic conflict or duality within Pedro—a split between his public and his private personality. On public issues, Pedro has been idealistic, has fought against injustice and oppression and for village interests, and has favored communal village enterprises. But at home he has been authoritarian, demanding, and repressive. Nor has he encouraged his wife and children to participate in village affairs.

Anastasio seems basically more secure and in better touch with reality and does not have Pedro's compulsive need for participation, leadership, and control. By giving his undivided energies to his work as a peasant and by withdrawing from village activities and collective ideals, he has enabled his family to improve its standard of living and forge ahead; they, in effect, have progressed at his expense.

Both families illustrate the generalization about family dynamics recently formulated by John P. Spiegel:

What is functional for one member of the family group may be dys-
functional for the family as a whole. The opposite also holds: What
is functional for the family as a whole may have very harmful effects
on one person. These phenomena take place unwittingly, not only
because of unconscious dynamics within each person, but also because of the operations of the system of relations in which the members of the family are involved.[2]

Of the two mothers, Soledad is clearly the one with the greater
personal and social development, although this has been limited by
village standards and by her own conformity. She is more active
than Esperanza and has a somewhat wider circle of acquaintances.
However, she does not relate as pleasantly to people as does Esperanza, and derives little satisfaction from others. Soledad's motivating
force has been to improve her lot and she has used herself and her
family to this end, rejecting her feminine role and developing traits of
negativism and narcissism. Esperanza, withdrawn from the outside
world and having only limited ability and personality development,
nevertheless has been accepting and supportive within her family.
Without Esperanza, the Martínez family would probably fall apart;
without Soledad, the Rojas family would probably come closer together and live with less friction.

Although the two families described in this paper live in a community which represents a blend of Indian, Colonial-Spanish, and
modern Mexican culture, the reader will undoubtedly be impressed
by the striking similarities between them and nonpeasant families in
our own industrial civilization. In part this may be explained by the
fact that the strong Spanish influence in Mexico is essentially Western European in culture. More specifically, basic similarities include
the predominance of the nuclear family, the patriarchal emphasis,
and Catholicism. However, another part of the explanation may be
that in the intensive study of whole families anywhere in the world,
the universal element, the psychological unity of mankind, comes
through much stronger than it does in descriptions of larger units
such as the community. This is understandable for several reasons.
In whole family studies, we deal much more with real—rather than
with ideal—behavior patterns, and individuals do not get lost in abstract concepts such as culture, role, and status. Moreover, the number of variables in a nuclear family are much fewer than in larger
and more complex systems, thereby limiting the number of possible
family types. In this connection, Smith writes, "The functional pre-
requisites of social systems impose a limited number of possibilities

[2] "The Resolution of Role Conflict Within the Family," *Psychiatry*, Vol. 20
(Feb., 1957), pp. 1–16.

of structuring, and this is particularly true if we begin to examine the sub-systems of such a fundamental nature as domestic groups." [3] He then points to many similarities in "domestic groups" among such dissimilar cultures as Trinidad, Manchester, West Africa, and the southern whites of the U.S.A.

All this suggests that the traditional anthropological emphasis upon cultural differences may be due in part to the unit of study and the methods used. In a description of a total culture pattern, there is an almost inevitable neglect of range of variation in custom and personality which may lead all too readily to overdrawn configurations that play up differences between cultures rather than emphasize human similarities. In other words, the more homogeneous (and I might add, superficial) the picture we get of a single society, the more contrasting will it appear in comparison with other societies. On the other hand, the more we know about the range of behavior within any society, the more readily can we perceive the cross-cultural similarities as well as the basic human similarities.

[3] Raymond T. Smith, *The Negro Family in British Guiana* (London: Routledge and Kegan Paul, 1956), p. 232.

14

Medicine and Politics
in a Mexican Village[*]

Shortly after arriving in the Mexican village of Tepoztlán in 1943, our community research team began to meet with the heads of families in various parts of the settlement to make ourselves known and to explain why we were there. Although our primary objective was to study village life rather than to change it, the villagers took advantage of these introductory occasions to direct attention to their pressing problems. They pointed out that their lands were becoming increasingly sterile, that for lack of water they could raise only a single crop a year, that they needed another school, and that there was no doctor in their village. One dignified, elderly Tepoztecan expressed the general attitude when he said, "Many people have come here to study us, but not one of them has helped us."

At the same time the Mexican Government, through its Department of Health and Welfare, was concerned over the problem of resistance to modern medicine in some of the rural areas. It wanted to know more about the reasons behind the apparent lack of confidence in modern doctors and the difficulties encountered in trying to win the villagers away from native *curanderos*.

Acceding to the wishes of both the villagers and the government, we decided to set up a small medical clinic in Tepoztlán. The villagers had made it clear that if they were to co-operate by satisfying our research aims, they would expect something practical in return.

[*] This was first published in 1955, in Benjamin D. Paul, ed., *Health, Culture, and Community* (New York: Copyright © 1955, Russell Sage Foundation), pp. 403–35.

They had expressed a need for improved medical service, and the clinic appeared to be a good answer to the problem. Federal officials similarly declared themselves more willing to co-operate with us if some of our research work was designed to throw light on problems faced by the government. The Department of Health and Welfare was reluctant to furnish a doctor solely to perform examinations in connection with purely theoretical research on personality development, as we had requested, but readily agreed to send a doctor to treat patients of the proposed medical clinic in Tepoztlán. The Department also became very much interested in our suggestion that, as a method of establishing rapport and winning confidence, the doctor experiment by discussing disease and cure with his patients in terms of native concepts, rather than ignoring these as "unscientific."

The plan to establish a clinic thus appeared to answer expressed needs of both local and government people and to provide a way for us to obtain the active co-operation of both these groups. Arrangements were made to obtain the facilities for the clinic, and a doctor was sent by the Mexican Health and Welfare Department. The clinic was only one part of a broader program of services made available to the villagers at their behest. In addition, two agronomists and four social workers were brought in to serve the villagers. Little or no opposition was encountered to their work and to the research itself.

During the first week, in early February, the clinic had eleven patients, and after about two months this number increased to thirty-five. Then abruptly, in April, patients stopped coming and the clinic came to a complete standstill. What lay behind the failure of the clinic? Why should attendance cease so suddenly and completely in the face of an expressed need by both the government and the villagers? To find the answers, we must understand the social structure and the people of Tepoztlán: their resources, hopes, fears, and attitudes toward authority. Because the medical service program was only one part of our team's activities and because the parts became linked in devious ways, it is also essential to explain the psychological phase of our research and the response it engendered.

• TEPOZTLÁN AND ITS PEOPLE •

Tepoztlán is fifteen miles from Cuernavaca, the capital of the state of Morelos, and sixty miles south of Mexico City.* Since 1936 it has been connected by a paved road to the highway running between Mexico City and Cuernavaca and has a daily bus service. Tepoztlán is

* For further description of Tepoztlán, see "Plow Culture and Hoe Culture—A Study in Contrasts," Essay 11, above.

located just above the malaria area and is considered one of the most healthful spots in the state of Morelos, with one of its lowest death rates. However, this is a relative matter. The average rate of infant mortality for the period 1930 to 1940 was 102.3 (deaths per 1,000 live births), and the general mortality rate for the same period was 20.2 (deaths per 1,000 inhabitants).

Both Spanish and Nahuatl, the native Indian language, are spoken in the village. About half of the people are bilingual; the other half speak only Spanish. More than 40 per cent of the adults are illiterate. There are two schools in the village, attended by more than 500 children.

The village is divided into seven *barrios*, each with its patron saint, internal religious organization, festivals, and a plot of land worked collectively by the men of the *barrio* to provide for the upkeep of the chapel. There is considerable *esprit de corps* among *barrio* members, who act as a co-operative unit on some occasions. The *barrio* is a more meaningful unit to many villagers than the official governmental divisions of the village into political wards. In addition to the seven *barrio* chapels, there is also a large central village church with a resident Catholic priest.

The village has changed in important ways since the Revolution. These changes may be summarized as follows: a rapid increase in population; some improvement in modern health services, threatening the position of the *curanderos;* a rise in the standard of living and in the aspiration level of the people; a decrease in the number of peon and landless families (formerly these constituted the bulk of the families); the growth of a greater variety and specialization of occupations; a decrease in the use of Nahuatl and a corresponding spread in the use of Spanish; a rise in literacy and the beginnings of newspaper reading.

In sharp contrast to the rapid changes which have occurred in other aspects of life, there has been no comparable improvement in the agricultural techniques and capacities of the village. This has given rise to a dilemma: on the one hand, there are a rapidly increasing population and a higher aspiration level; on the other hand, there are a growing sterility of the land, decreasing yields, and progressive difficulty in satisfying newly felt needs.

· SETTING UP THE CLINIC ·

Once we had decided to set up a medical clinic, we began to plan its organization. At first we considered the idea of setting up a temporary clinic to last only for the duration of the assignment of the doctor provided by the Department of Health and Welfare. Later, how-

ever, at the suggestion of the Department, we decided to establish
the clinic as a village co-operative. The co-operative form of organization was being encouraged by the federal government at that time,
on the assumption that it was in accord with native tradition. We also
believed that a co-operative would be more useful in that the doctor
might be kept on by the village itself long after we had left and the
doctor's original assignment had expired. Moreover, we viewed this
enterprise as an experiment in setting up a democratic institution in
a village in which the tradition of democracy was practically absent,
and as a test of the readiness and ability of the Tepoztecans for such
an organization.

The plan for the co-operative was fully explained to the local authorities in Tepoztlán, especially to the mayor of the municipality,
and it seemed to meet with his interest and approval. When a doctor
was finally obtained from the Department of Health and Welfare,
the mayor was asked to call a meeting of the entire community to
introduce the doctor and to discuss plans for the co-operative. He
promised to call such a meeting but never did. The members of our
mission thereupon visited many of the families in each *barrio*, and a
meeting of the villagers was arranged. A Tepoztecan band was hired
to create a fiesta atmosphere, for we had already learned that practically the only occasion that will bring Tepoztecans together is a
fiesta. More than 160 Tepoztecans attended the meeting. This was a
good turnout for the village, considering their general lack of confidence. The organization of the co-operative was discussed, and
many Tepoztecans participated in the discussion.

It was decided to charge a membership fee of one peso, and 25
centavos a month thereafter. In addition, members were to pay one
peso to consult the doctor, and this fee would include free medicines. The money collected was to form a fund for the purchase of
medicines and other supplies and for paying the rent of the doctor's
office. The ultimate objective was for the co-operative to be self-
supporting, even to the extent of paying for a doctor if it had to. It
was hoped that the six-month period for which the doctor was assigned by the Department of Health and Welfare would give the
co-operative the opportunity to accumulate the necessary funds to
carry on independently.

It was believed by the staff and borne out by the consensus of the
first meeting that the *barrio* provided the most logical basis upon
which a co-operative organization could be built because it was the
primary co-operative unit in the social organization of the village.
Fiestas were traditionally organized on a *barrio* basis, and in recent
years participation in sports events has been on a similar basis. Thus,
the few co-operative activities in the village were *barrio* activities.

Furthermore, the *barrio* chose its own ceremonial officials in a fairly democratic fashion, whereas the village officials, though nominally elected, were in practice chosen by the governor of the state of Morelos. In organizing the co-operative on a *barrio* basis, we were therefore attempting to tie it to a geographical and social unit which still retained some of its indigenous co-operative traditions.

At the mass meeting a central village committee of seven members was elected, one from each *barrio*, and provisions were made for the election of *barrio* committees consisting of three persons each. These local committees were to be charged with recruiting members in their *barrios* and with popularizing the co-operative. The meeting ended on a hopeful note, and the central committee promised to get right to work organizing the *barrio* committees. But at the first scheduled meeting of the central committee, only three members appeared, and this was symptomatic of what was to follow. After three weeks, only three of the seven *barrio* committees had been organized.

In the meantime, the doctor furnished by the Department of Health and Welfare arrived in Tepoztlán. A room in a house on the central plaza was obtained as an office. Essential equipment and medicines were purchased out of the first funds collected by the co-operative. Although no nurse was available, the social worker attached to the community research project assumed some of the nursing duties and accompanied the doctor on home visits. In addition to his clinic duties, the doctor worked in a research capacity with another part of the program, but he remained on call at all times for clinical services.

In line with our intention that the clinic serve a research function as well as provide medical services, it was planned that before the usual physical examination of each patient, the doctor should fill out forms that called for the following kinds of information: an account of the history and causes of the diseases from the patient's point of view, whether the patient visited the *curandero*, the diagnosis and therapy of the *curandero*, the fees paid, and so on. The doctor was expected to utilize this information wherever possible in establishing rapport with the patient. Furthermore, we hoped that in this way it would be possible systematically to obtain important data on native concepts of disease and therapy, and by comparing the diagnosis of the patient and the *curandero* with that of the doctor, to understand better the rationale behind native concepts.

Since funds from the co-operative came in slowly, the facilities of the clinic were never quite adequate. In addition, the first doctor furnished by the Department of Health and Welfare was a young unmarried man whose previous experience was limited and had been confined to urban areas. Neither by training nor temperament was he particularly well fitted for the sensitive and demanding task of treating the people of a rural Mexican village. After a month, he was replaced by an older doctor with more experience.

However, our initial difficulties in getting a suitable physician and adequate equipment did not appear to trouble the prospective clients of the clinic. During the first week, as already indicated, the doctor had eleven patients, and subsequently the figure slowly increased to thirty-five. Then, quite suddenly, patients ceased to come altogether. To all intents and purposes, the clinic was a failure.

It would be tempting at this point to attribute the demise of the clinic to the inadequacies of its doctors and physical facilities and to look no further to find reasons for its downfall. But such an explanation would be partial at best. In the first place, the drop in attendance was abrupt and complete, not the gradual falling off one might expect to result from cumulative dissatisfactions. Second, as we shall see, there are good reasons for believing that much the same thing would have happened even if the service had been excellent and the physical facilities exemplary. Although we cannot discount completely the effect of dissatisfaction over the quality of the clinical service, it will become apparent that other forces at work in Tepoztlán exerted greater influence. To discern the nature of these forces, we must look to the general climate of the village, particularly the medical and political climate.

• THE MEDICAL CLIMATE OF TEPOZTLÁN •

The trial clinic on the central plaza of Tepoztlán was not introduced into a medical vacuum. On the contrary, it found itself within a milieu of well-established medical beliefs and theories of disease and within a network of traditional practitioners whose curative techniques reflected these beliefs and theories.

There are three kinds of health practitioners in Tepoztlán—*curanderos, mágicos,* and "el doctor." *Curanderos* are the most numerous and are primarily women. They are visited most frequently and charge small fees of twenty-five or fifty centavos. There are two *mágicos,* men who may use the herb remedies of the women but also resort to spiritualism and magic and are feared for their great power. Their fees are higher, ranging between one and ten pesos. The *curanderos* and *mágicos* are, of course, Tepoztecans. However, "el doctor" is an outsider who has taken up residence in the village. He poses as a doctor but has no professional training. He charges fees as high as one hundred pesos. *Curanderos* are sometimes paid in corn or other produce. This is one of the very few remnants of the old barter economy and indicates how closely the *curandero* system and the native economy were integrated. With the increasing dominance of a money economy, there is now more cash available, and some families visit the doctors in Cuernavaca.

There was no resident doctor in 1943, but the villagers had had some previous experience with doctors and modern medicine. Two young Mexican doctors had spent six months each in the village in fulfillment of their training requirements for the doctor's degree. Public health teams had visited the village frequently since 1936 to administer injections against infectious diseases; some Tepoztecans had visited the federal Public Health Station in nearby Cuernavaca; and a few of the local midwives had received some instruction from public health nurses.

For the majority of people, however, indigenous folk medicine as practiced by *curanderos* is still the dominant form of medicine. Thus, the traditional remedies for "evil eye" and "fright" involve a combination of folk beliefs, ancient herbal lore, and Catholic practice. A child is believed to be the victim of the evil eye if he comes home crying and very much disturbed. An egg is broken into a glass: if a long eye-shaped spot appears on the yolk, the person responsible for putting the eye upon the child is a man; if the spot is round, it is a woman. The child's clothes are changed and he is "cleansed" with a soiled kerchief or shirt if the guilty person was male, and with an apron or shawl if a female. Some children are cured by being cleansed on their foreheads, with the tongue making the form of a cross.

"Fright" is an illness which leaves children sad and pale; it is cured by women who can "lay the shadow" that afflicts them. These *curanderos* keep a supply of powdered cedar, palm, and blessed laurel which they throw on the forehead, breast, wrists, palms of the hand, nape of the neck, and into the nostrils of the sick child. While this is being done, the woman prays the Credo, and at the end holds the child's head and cries out that the shadow should withdraw and that the child no longer need be frightened. Some cure fright by having the priest read the gospel over the child in the presence of the child's godparent of the same sex.

The most celebrated healer in Tepoztlán is one Rosalino Vargas, known as Don Rosas. He is also believed to be a powerful sorcerer and is feared by many of the villagers. Some people claim to have seen him riding through the village at midnight wearing a long black cape, with sparks issuing from his eyes and mouth. Don Rosas, who often uses the fear he inspires to his own advantage, has several enemies, at least three of whom have made attempts to murder him in recent years. Don Rosas is wealthy and has a flourishing practice. He has seven female assistants; there is much gossip to the effect that these women are his paramours and sleep with him in turn, one for each day in the week. Don Rosas' loyal clientele insist that the seven women help him treat the sick and perform a series of mysterious devotions which he practices nearly every night.

The technique employed by Don Rosas on his patients contains an interesting combination of Catholic, pagan, and possibly African elements. He does not deal directly with a patient but gets information concerning the nature of the illness through an assistant who questions the patient. After the conference the patient is taken to a room which resembles a chapel in that it has an altar and images of saints. The patient is seated on a chair close to a heavy curtain behind which sits Don Rosas. The visitor is given an image of a saint to hold while the *curandero* prays and goes into a trance. When he is "as if dead" an assistant wafts incense smoke toward him and he begins to speak, as though from a deep sleep, telling what illness the patient is suffering from. Whether or not a cure is possible, is determined by a glass of water which has been placed among the images near the incense burner. If the water turns white, there is hope for a cure; if black, there is none.

If a remedy is possible, Don Rosas then points out the necessary steps to protect the individual and his family from the enemy who is provoking the symptoms. The patient must drink a sweet-sour tasting liquid, prepared by Don Rosas and stirred with a metal cross. The patient then pays two pesos for the cure but first must cleanse himself with the bills in the parts of his body which give him pain, and leave the money on the altar. Before leaving, the patient is given additional medicines to take each night and is generally advised to cleanse himself with very hot herb applications. More medicine is given as needed without charge and the patient is advised that the medicine must never be placed on the ground since it would lose its potency. Some patients need several consultations, all of which are conducted in the same manner, before they feel well again.

Although he does not hold any official municipal position, Don Rosas is a tremendous power in Tepoztlán because of his prestige and renown as a curer. There is little doubt that the introduction of a medical clinic in the center of his own community did not escape his watchful eye. Nor did it escape the notice of others in positions of power who did hold office. Although the medical aspects of the clinic were of paramount concern to local health practitioners, its organizational aspects attracted the watchfulness of local political officials.

• THE POLITICAL CLIMATE
OF TEPOZTLÁN •

The village of Tepoztlán is the largest of eight villages that comprise the municipality of Tepoztlán. It is the seat of the municipal government and as such is the administrative and political center of the municipality. The municipality of Tepoztlán is one of twenty-seven *municipios* in the state of Morelos. It is governed by the state constitution, which provides for "free *municipios*," local governments elected by popular vote.

The municipal government consists of the following officers: mayor, syndic, comptroller, secretary, treasurer, police chief, subpolice chief, justice of the peace, his secretary, and a porter. In addition, there are eight councilmen, each representing one of the wards of the village. The four major officials—mayor, syndic, comptroller, and justice of the peace—are elected by popular vote for a two-year period. The other officials are appointed by the mayor in agreement with the syndic and comptroller.

The duties of the major officials are determined by state law. Their manner of functioning depends upon their personalities. A meek mayor will serve only as a figurehead and allow the syndic and secretary to run the government. An aggressive mayor may take over the functions of the other officials. As executive officer, the mayor is the official representative of Tepoztlán in dealings with the outside. His signature is necessary for most correspondence and official acts. He sets the fines for infractions of the law; in addition, villagers often bring their private difficulties and family quarrels to him.

By far the greatest number of tasks falls to the secretary. He is generally the most literate of the officials. He opens and closes the government offices six days a week, signs all correspondence, attends all public functions, maintains the records of the *municipio*, advises the other officers of the state law, keeps the mayor informed of all complaints, and attends to all complaints and requests for certifications.

According to the law of the State of Morelos, Tepoztlán is supposed to be a free and autonomous political and administrative unit. In practice, however, the *municipio* appears more as an administrative dependency of the state governor. It is he who makes most of the *municipio's* major decisions, and decides local conflicts. There are no well-organized political parties in Tepoztlán; rather, there are a number of loosely organized factions. This makes it necessary for every candidate for political office to play politics skillfully to obtain sufficient support from the unorganized electorate. Any recent incident or situation in the public eye is enlisted to further one's political fortunes. Municipal elections command much public attention and are bitterly fought.

When the medical clinic was established early in 1944, local politicians were looking ahead to the municipal elections in November. The mayor especially was worried about his position, since he had been temporarily jailed a short time before by the state governor for practicing nepotism. The comptroller, who had been appointed mayor *pro tem,* was most reluctant to relinquish this office when the mayor was released and ready to resume his post. Two councilmen with their eye on higher office had formed an "Education Committee" to espouse the construction of a new school and were hostile to the newly appointed principal of the existing school.

It was into this atmosphere of political intrigue and jockeying for power that the clinic happened to be introduced. It intruded directly or indirectly into the sphere of interest of important and influential figures in Tepoztlán—Don Rosas, the mayor, the comptroller, the Education Committee, the school principal, and others. Since none of these could claim credit for introducing this new public service and since its presence distracted the people from the coming elections and served as a reminder of how little the local officials did for the village, the clinic became the object of their attack. Each in his own way examined our project as a whole to find something that presented a vulnerable front for attack. They found it in the testing program.

• THE ATTACK ON THE TESTING PROGRAM •

When we arrived in Tepoztlán, we brought official letters to the principal of the school from the Minister of Education and the Director of Education in Cuernavaca—letters which recommended our project and asked for all necessary co-operation. We met with the principal and school staff to explain the purpose of the testing program and to describe briefly each of the tests. We also explained that each child to be tested would first be examined, fully clothed, by our doctors to determine the existence of any physical defects that might affect the psychological responses. The teachers and principal all expressed interest in the program and willingness to co-operate.

Among other things, the testing program included administration of the Rorschach test. We arranged to have four women of our staff give the various tests daily in the mornings. Since each selected child had to be tested four times, we were careful to space the tests so that no child was tested more than once a day. All of these tests were individual and had to be administered privately. There were no classrooms available for our use, so we had to do the best we could out of doors. The principal set up four tables for us in the courtyard of the school. The spot was by no means secluded, since six of the classrooms had windows and doors which faced it. At the open end of the court were a number of banana trees, behind which were the toilets. Thus, the court was seldom without passersby, and we were rarely alone.

For four months our investigation in the school and in the rest of the village proceeded smoothly, with many manifestations of good will and co-operation on the part of the villagers. Then, quite unexpectedly, in April, the principal of the school put an abrupt stop to all the testing, claiming that a small group of men and women had accused our workers of asking the children immoral questions and had threatened to stone them if they did not leave the village at once. The municipal authorities, without consulting us, had begun an "investigation" of these rumors and were calling witnesses and questioning them in such a way as to create more suspicion and to spread the gossip throughout the village.

The accusations were specifically as follows: that the testers were showing indecent pictures to the children; that the testers were taking the children off alone to the banana grove for the purpose of undressing them; that the doctor was undressing the girls for physical examinations.

This turn of affairs was a serious threat to the entire project. We set to work at once to investigate. We visited the principal of the school and went over each test in detail with him and with his staff. They all declared that the tests were in no way objectionable and that the accusations were unfounded. The principal explained that a mother had come to the school to tell him that her husband had forbidden her children to return to school because he thought they were losing too much time as a result of the testing program. The principal had asked her to send her children back and he promised to end the testing. In checking the chronology of events, we learned that the principal had ordered the testing program stopped two days before the mother appeared at the school.

The principal went on to say that a few days after he was visited by the mother, a committee of twelve men and women came to the school to protest against the "immoral" tests which we were giving their children. The leaders of this group were members of the Education Committee, bitter enemies of the school, who had been attacking the principal ever since he had arrived in Tepoztlán. After visiting the school, the Committee went to the town hall, where they persuaded the mayor to institute an investigation.

We spoke with the two councilmen who were the leaders of the

Committee and showed them the tests. They agreed that they were not immoral but stated that this was no proof that our workers were not asking other questions not included in the tests. They said they were of the opinion that the tests were too complicated and too advanced for so backward a people and were bound to be misinterpreted by them. This device of citing the ignorance of the people as a reason for rejecting innovations was frequently used by the conservatives in the village. We urged them to put a stop to the mayor's "investigation," but they refused. A talk with the mayor was equally unsuccessful. He was continuing the investigation with enthusiasm, evidently impelled by motives of his own. He turned a deaf ear to our explanations and was noncommittal during the interview. The municipal secretary, one of the few Tepoztecan women to hold this post, was a religious fanatic and was much disliked in the village. She had a great deal of influence over the mayor and was conducting the investigation for him.

That evening we were visited by a man who introduced himself as "Antonio López, a Christian, and a friend of the Tepoztecans." He had a marked military manner, clicked his heels, and spoke with a German accent. He said he was a friend of one of the leaders of the Education Committee and wished to warn us that he did not like the work we were doing in Tepoztlán. He said that, although it was true that for the present Mexico and the United States were friendly, he was of the opinion that the situation would not last long and that the people were suspicious of our motives. In the course of our conversation, he also lamented the fact that education was no longer in the hands of the Church but said that, too, might be changed in the future. We later learned that this man was part German and had been educated in Germany. He was a Synarchist and four years before had been ordered out of Tepoztlán by the state governor because he was behaving like a Nazi agent.

Synarchism is a well-organized political movement, the Mexican brand of Fascism. Although it has received the support of and worked closely with Nazi and Falangist elements since its inception, it is nevertheless a grass-roots movement with a large peasant base. In 1943 the strength of the Synarchist membership was estimated at well over a million. Tepoztlán was marginal to the regions of Synarchist concentration, but nearby towns had suffered from Synarchist-inspired uprisings in protest against the government program of conscription.

We appealed to a state senator who was a native of Tepoztlán and who happened to be living in the village at the time. He offered to help us, and we arranged to go to the state governor with him the following morning. The governor was not in Cuernavaca, and we had to speak to his aide. We told him our story, and he was satisfied with our explanations. He wrote a strong letter addressed to the mayor of Tepoztlán, stating that our study was a Mexican government project and had the full approval of the governor of Morelos. He added that the accusations against us were unfounded, and ordered the cessation of the investigation. He also asked the authorities to detain Antonio López and to bring him to Cuernavaca for questioning. We were encouraged by the co-operation and friendliness of the governor's aide and thought that the whole matter would soon be cleared up.

We returned to Tepoztlán and presented the letter of the governor's aide to the municipal secretary, since the mayor himself was not in, as usual. Her response was that the investigation would continue, that López was not in the village (although we had seen him), that in her opinion López was a friend of the Tepoztecans, and that nothing should be done to molest him.

We learned that day of the manner in which the village investigation was being conducted. The head of one of the local families working with us received a peremptory order from the mayor to present himself at the town hall within a half-hour. He was asked to tell what immoral questions the project social worker who lived in his house was asking. This man's daughter, aged thirteen, was taken into a room by the woman secretary and was asked, "Is it not true that the workers are asking you bad questions?" When the girl denied this, the secretary told her not to be ashamed and to speak to her as a woman. She said, "Is it not true that the doctor undressed you? What bad things did you talk about in the banana grove?" With such procedures, the secretary succeeded in aggravating the situation and in arousing more people against our work.

With the co-operation of the state senator, we arranged a hearing at the town hall with the two councilmen for the following day. When we arrived, we found the room filled with people—about twenty-five women in addition to the two men. We knew that it was impossible to have a calm hearing with these women and suspected another maneuver on the part of the local secretary and the mayor. However, we had to proceed. We took the names of all the women present and found that not one of them had a child who had been tested by us. We then read the questions of our tests, and one of our workers made a moving speech, which seemed to calm the women. However, the secretary brought in a surprise witness, a girl of twelve, whom she had succeeded in intimidating. The child was frightened, tense, and on the verge of tears. She stated that we had asked her the questions we had been accused of asking (she repeated those mentioned above), and her words once more aroused the women in the audience. We produced the test of this particular child and wanted to read her responses, but the secretary shouted that no one wanted to hear the immoral answers and that we would read only the good things and leave out the bad. The women began to shout and some began to cry.

The mayor then arose and said that it was clear that we were not wanted in the village and that under no circumstances should we continue with our work. We answered that this group was only a tiny minority of the village and did not represent the true village opinion. We asked the mayor to call a meeting of the entire village so that we could demonstrate the sentiment of the people; he agreed to call a larger meeting for the following Sunday. As the meeting began to break up, the secretary asked to see the Rorschach cards which we had shown earlier to the women without comment from them. The secretary said she had seen things in the cards which proved her point and that she would like to show them to those present. She thereupon began to point out the sexual organs and phallic symbols which she "saw" in almost every one of the ten amorphous designs—this, in spite of the fact that there were men present. It is interesting to note that claiming to see sexual objects in the cards occurred very rarely in the 125 Rorschachs given to children and adults in Tepoztlán. By her actions, the secretary unconsciously revealed her own personality and helped to explain her behavior. This demonstration naturally agitated the women further.

We left this meeting with a feeling that things were going from bad to worse. However, we were later visited by a group of Tepoztecans who said that they were very much ashamed of the way these people were behaving and said that the same thing happened time and again whenever an attempt was made to improve the village. We decided to see the governor, but again he was inaccessible, and we proceeded to Mexico City to advise Dr. Manuel Gamio, director of the Inter-American Indian Institute and sponsor of our project. Dr. Gamio pointed out that cultural missions in the past had run into similar or more serious difficulties in the villages. Dr. Gamio and the senator thereupon conferred with high government officials who gave us a letter to the governor of Morelos, and we set out for Cuernavaca to see him.

Our interview with the governor was both a surprise and a disappointment. At first he said that he had never heard of our project. We made the necessary explanations and told him of our recent difficulties. He thereupon said that the United States owed Mexico a great debt because of our imperialistic history and that Americans should be more "loyal" to Mexicans than vice versa. Americans do not understand Mexicans and cannot get along with them. In connection with Antonio López, he observed that Nazi doctrine, "because of its belief in order and authority," had a much greater appeal to the peasants than did our American democracy. We left the meeting with the realization that we could expect nothing from the governor. However he said he wanted to send his aide to the planned meeting on Sunday.

Upon our return to Tepoztlán we were again visited by the group of friendly Tepoztecans. They came to advise us against attending the Sunday meeting and suggested that the proper procedure would be to have the governor call the two councilmen to Cuernavaca for a talk and a cooling-off period, charging them with defamation of honor. We agreed with them but said we did not want to use such methods. Furthermore, it was too late for us to prevent the meeting. The group then offered to bring about two hundred men and women to the meeting to support us. At their suggestion, we agreed to accompany them to the governor's aide before the meeting in order to present him with their point of view.

This man, probably advised by the governor, spoke to us in a very different manner during this second visit. He declared before our committee of Tepoztecans that he had never heard of our project or of the Inter-American Indian Institute and scolded us for not informing his office of our mission. We reminded him that we had presented the governor with a letter from Dr. Gamio and had received an acknowledgment of the same, and that we had been accompanied at the time by the senator, who also introduced us. The governor's aide flatly denied all we said and asked his clerk to look up the letters in the file. I reminded him that we had a letter written by him on our behalf addressed to the mayor of Tepoztlán. The clerk said that the letters were not in the file but that she would look again.

Encouraged by this, the governor's aide continued to berate us and said that in all probability we did not know how to get along with Mexican peasants. He said that as technicians we probably were not sufficiently *simpático* and that we should have known that our tests and ink blots were bound to suggest sexual and immoral symbols to rustic people. The clerk had by this time found the letters in question, and the governor's aide changed his tone a bit. However, his performance had a depressing effect on our Tepoztecan friends, who had believed that we had the strong support of the government, and the situation was quite embarrassing. The governor's aide said he would attend the Sunday meeting and would settle the entire matter for us. Although the governor's aide, the senator, and the school principal all promised to speak in our favor and defend our work on Sunday, we were by this time skeptical of promises and awaited the meeting with curiosity but with little hope.

The Sunday meeting drew only about a hundred persons, in spite of the fact that the mayor and his assistants visited every home in the village to persuade the residents to be present against us. Of the hundred, the majority were friendly to our project. However, the same twenty-five women and the two hostile councilmen grouped themselves about the speakers and were the only ones of the assembly who could make themselves heard. There were very few other women present because, as we were told later, no decent woman would attend such a meeting. The rest of the village had the impression that only those who were against us were supposed to come.

All three speakers, the governor's aide, the senator, and the school principal, made ingratiating speeches full of demagogic promises and without a word in our defense. The governor's aide said he was proud of these mothers who defended their children with such zeal and that he would see that the testing program would not continue. He urged the people to be patient, as we were winding up our work and would soon leave the village. The senator avoided the subject of our project entirely, while the principal sought to gain the good will of the village by stating that as soon as he heard we were doing indecent things he stopped the testing immediately for, above all, he was eager to guard the children entrusted to his care. Our friends, who had gathered there to speak for us, thought that it was useless to do so in view of the attitude of the main speakers, so not a good word was put in except by ourselves.

Shortly after the meeting, we were visited by a delegation from the organization of the poor-land farmers, who had supported us throughout our difficulties, and by a delegation of those who worked the communal lands. They spoke with great feeling and said that we were the objects of a political intrigue. They said that the women did not represent more than a small minority and that they were widows or spinsters, because no man would permit his wife to behave in so scandalous a manner. They asked us to stay on and continue our work in Tepoztlán, and they believed that the whole thing would blow over in a few weeks and that no one would molest us. They offered to circulate a petition and get six hundred signatures to convince us that we should continue our beneficial work. We agreed and asked them to address it to Dr. Gamio and the Institute. In a few days, they brought us about two hundred names, saying that they could not get any more because the mayor had heard of what they were doing and began to threaten the people who signed.

As a result of this affair, our entire testing program was temporarily suspended. Our research staff continued to interview informants and devoted themselves to writing up their backlog of material. Little by little, however, we increased our activities and succeeded in giving more tests in the homes. When assignments of our research workers ended and they had to leave the village, they were given warm send-offs by their Tepoztecan friends, departing for their homes elsewhere in Mexico loaded with gifts and with invitations to return.

· **WHAT LAY BEHIND THE ATTACK** ·

What lay behind the attack on the testing program? The mayor, the secretary, the school principal, the two councilmen on the Education Committee, and others who openly denounced the program justified their opposition on the grounds that the tests were immoral. Some of those who opposed the program may sincerely have believed this, but there is ample reason to believe that other reasons were of equal or greater importance. We have already seen that there were a number of highly influential people in Tepoztlán who saw in the clinic a threat to their own position and that there were others who saw the presence of active outsiders as an opportunity to advance their own political interests.

In the former category the outstanding person was Don Rosas, Tepoztlán's most eminent *curandero*. In spite of the power and prestige he enjoys, Don Rosas cannot help seeing the gradual and inexorable advance of modern medicine into rural Mexico as a threat to his position. Opening the clinic in the central plaza of Tepoztlán placed his enemy on his front doorstep; the very first patients to visit the clinic were those whose ailments had not responded to treatment by the *curanderos*. Although Don Rosas himself did not play an active part in the various meetings where the hostility of the villagers to the program was expressed, he was an active influence behind the scenes. Not only did he agitate the mayor, the secretary, and others, but he was directly responsible for the rumor that indecent pictures were being shown.

When the clinic was first established, it was immediately seen by Don Rosas as a threat, and one to be eliminated by any means. But he was too clever to risk an open attack on a venture that was patently humanitarian and had already received the support of a substantial number of villagers. Casting around for the best strategy, he hit upon the testing program as the logical target. The purposes of psychological testing were difficult for many villagers to grasp. Moreover, the pictures shown on one of the tests were highly ambiguous in form and subject to all sorts of interpretations. Don Rosas made a trip to Mexico City and there purchased a set of pornographic pictures. Upon his return he showed these pictures around the village, telling the parents, "*These* are the pictures they are showing your children! *This* is what they call science!"

Don Rosas was not the only influential figure in Tepoztlán who saw the clinic as a threat. Its inception was a danger signal to the mayor, and through him to the state senator and state governor, all of whom had already been alerted to the disruptive potentialities of the research team by a previous incident.

We had been in Tepoztlán one month, when a committee of poor-land farmers appealed to us to aid them in a boundary dispute with a neighboring village. The communal land was involved and if the dispute was lost, two hundred families might face destitution. In spite of the fact that communal land was in question, neither the mayor nor the senator was doing anything about the case. The poor-land farmers claimed that these two officials were acting on the orders of, or out of fear of, the state governor, who they said had an interest in a large cement factory which obtained its fuel from the forests located on the disputed land. The committee had come to us because we happened to have an attorney on our staff. We explained that we could not help them officially or appear in court for them, but that our lawyer could advise them privately, as a friend. We made this decision because many of the families involved had been co-operating with us in our study of family life. Also, we felt that the dispute was a real threat to a large group of Tepoztecans and to the entire village. An investigation convinced us that their claims were just, and we felt obligated to do what we could. The word got around, and apparently the state governor and the senator, as well as the mayor, interpreted our decision as strengthening the hand of political forces opposed to the established powers.

When the clinic was set up, people began to say that the project members were doing more for their welfare than their own mayor was doing. This was ample grounds for mobilizing the opposition of the mayor, already made wary by the communal land incident. Don Rosas would have had little difficulty in persuading the mayor to direct the power of his office against the program. Perceiving the service activities of the project as a threat to their interests, Don Rosas, the mayor, and the governor instigated or supported feeling against the project.

Another group of influential figures decided to capitalize on this resentment, once aroused, to further their own political fortunes. Municipal elections were to be held in a few months. In addition to the mayor, who hoped to exploit public indignation over "immorality" to gain reelection, one of the two councilmen who headed the Education Committee was hoping to become mayor and promoted resentment for similar reasons. These two men became the spear-head of the attack on the project.

The opposition of the school principal was related to the activities of the Education Committee. The principal, newly appointed to Tepoztlán, was being opposed at every turn by the Education Committee. This group charged the principal with being immoral and a Communist, because he allowed special dances to be given in the school for the purpose of raising funds. The Committee had opposed innovations in the school and was engaging in obstructive activities. Our presence provided further grounds for fighting the school.

The eagerness of the principal in stopping the testing program without consulting us or investigating the charges could have been attributed to his fear of the Education Committee. However, he had ordered our workers out of the school before a single complaint had been made. One of the teachers told us that the principal, in an effort to ingratiate himself with the Education Committee and represent himself as a defender of morality, went to them with accusations against us, which they eagerly took up and carried further, since they had been looking for some grounds for attacking our project. Arranging the visit of the mothers to the school and the town hall was their way of carrying out plans to persuade the mayor to conduct an investigation and to arouse the village.

The actions of the Education Committee were also tied to Antonio López, the Synarchist organizer. He had succeeded, years before, in converting the two councilmen who headed the Education Committee. At one time these men had openly proclaimed themselves as Synarchists, but recently had ceased doing so although they still were intimates of López. These men had branded our group "an imperialist mission," and their anti-U.S. sentiments provided further incentive for their opposition to us.

In brief, our well-intentioned efforts to win the co-operation of the villagers by helping them solve some of their problems were interpreted by several local figures as a personal threat.

By advising the poor-land farmers we unwittingly were helping the faction out of power; by establishing the clinic we were implicitly reproaching the "do-nothings" in power. The testing program, whose purposes were only vaguely comprehended and only indirectly beneficial to the people, provided a vulnerable target, and it was here that hostility aroused by the introduction of the medical clinic could be played out.

The strategy was effective. The loudly expressed indignation of the officials and a small but vocal group of villagers succeeded in intimidating the rest of the people for a period of time. The clinic languished and we made no attempt to reestablish it. The testing program was stopped in the school but continued quietly in the homes; in the six months that followed, the research program was carried out without further disturbance.

• CO-OPERATIVES, INDIVIDUALISM, AND POLITICS •

We have already seen that inadequacies in the facilities of the clinic had little bearing on its failure. In fact, one might speculate that the clinic would have aroused even greater opposition had it been medically more effective. If so humble an example of modern medicine could provoke disruptive antagonism, a well-equipped clinic, better able to meet the needs of the villagers, might have posed an even greater threat to those in power.

It is also possible that less opposition would have been aroused had we not decided to organize the clinic on a co-operative basis. We have already given the rationale for deciding on the co-operative type of organization. Had we known then what we found out later, we would have reconsidered our decision. However, the very fact that we acted as we did set into motion events that gave us additional insights into the culture of Tepoztlán.

The Mexican Revolution had far-reaching effects on Tepoztlán. It succeeded in breaking down the rigid social class distinctions which once existed in the village and imbued the people with a consciousness of their rights as individuals. The strong individualism of Tepoztecans manifests itself in their social and economic institutions. The biological family is the more or less self-sufficient and independent economic unit. Social relations between families and even close relatives are formal and distant. Land is owned individually, and even the communal lands are worked individually. Work exchange is uncommon; wage labor prevails in intra-village relations. Occasions upon which either men or women co-operate in their daily tasks are few. Before the Spanish conquest more than four hundred years ago, there existed a system of co-operative labor called *cuatequitl* which was used for the building of village public works, but it was never a purely voluntary organization and has now almost completely disintegrated.

Practically the only occasions upon which the Tepoztecans have shown either a willingness or capacity to work together has been in planning their fiestas and in resisting threats to their communal lands. But even in regard to the latter, there is growing disunity. In the land dispute previously described, only those individuals whose interests were directly affected took measures to protect themselves.

Another reason the co-operative form was not appropriate to

Tepoztlán relates to the great complexity of social, economic, political, and religious cleavages among the villagers. There are landless peons and wealthy farmers; literate and sophisticated merchants of the central plaza and illiterate and primitive farmers of the outlying *barrios;* the sons of the families that dominated Tepoztlán prior to the Revolution and the very Zapatistas who overthrew them; the fanatic believers in the old Catholic religion as practiced in Tepoztlán, with its elements of paganism, and a Protestant sect which has succeeded in winning almost an entire *barrio* as adherents; sympathizers of Synarchism on the one hand and sympathizers of the left-wing labor movement on the other. In addition to all this, within many families there are differences between the younger and older generations which reflect the rapid changes taking place in the village.

Implications

Our experience in Tepoztlán suggests a number of more general problems concerning the comprehensiveness of village research and improvement programs, the type of doctors suitable for work in rural areas, the role of local organizational patterns, and the significance of the local balance of power.

• COMBINED PROGRAMS •

From the standpoint of our research aims, it seemed desirable to provide the services of a medical clinic to gain good will and co-operation. Conversely, the psychological-testing program seemed warranted, quite apart from its value as a social science research tool, as one means of understanding the people's attitudes and behavior in order to have a better basis for predicting the outcome of health and betterment programs. Thus, a combination of research and service programs held out the promise of better results than could be expected from either activity alone. At the same time, each was capable—as it turned out—of arousing overt or covert opposition which could be directed against the other. It might be argued that a limitation of activity in the village would expose a smaller flank for attack. The merits and handicaps of mixing research and service are difficult to assess apart from the particular situation. Even in a specific case, as in Tepoztlán, the fact that one course of action encountered trouble does not necessarily imply that an opposite course would have been more successful.

A more positive stand can be taken on the issue of whether a medical care program would thrive better if it were introduced by itself or if it were made part of a more comprehensive improvement program. Although it is possible that a more general approach might threaten more interests and thus incite a more general counterattack, it is also clear that even a very limited program of modern medical care such as was attempted in Tepoztlán would have great difficulty sustaining itself so long as the villagers remain as poor as they are. Even the modest fee of one peso charged by the co-operative proved too much for many. Financial means is not the whole answer, but it is a necessary element in the totality of factors affecting the success or failure of a medical service clinic. The spread of modern medicine hinges, among other things, on increasing the income of the villagers and is related to the larger problem of raising the standard of living by increasing purchasing power. This in turn requires an action program wider than health improvement by itself.

• INTRODUCING MODERN MEDICINE IN RURAL MEXICO •

Despite their high degree of acculturation, the majority of Tepoztecans are not ready to give up their *curanderos*. However, they are ready to consider the doctor an alternative, especially in cases of chronic or serious illnesses. This was clearly shown by the fact already mentioned that the doctor's first patients were persons who suffered from chronic illnesses which apparently had not responded to the treatment of the *curanderos*. Because of this circumstance the doctor begins with a handicap. Unable to produce miraculous cures in these far-gone cases, he loses prestige.

There is a great lack of confidence in doctors, partly because so many of them display an attitude of superiority toward native concepts of disease and often ridicule native beliefs and practices. Indeed, the Tepoztecans, as well as the doctors, are keenly aware of their different conceptual worlds. This is undoubtedly a serious obstacle to the spreading of modern medical practice, and unless the gap between these two distinct levels of explanation is bridged, progress will be very slow.

A few examples from Tepoztlán will help to make this clear. According to Tepoztecans, there are "hot" and "cold" diseases, just as there are "hot" and "cold" foods.[1] A mother who is convinced that her child is suffering from a hot disease brought on by the adultery of her husband, knows that the child needs a cold medicine. If she

[1] Rheumatism, tuberculosis, and earache are examples of cold diseases. Dysentery, sore throat, and swellings and irritations of the gums, the tongue, and the lips are examples of hot diseases. For a general discussion of the hot-cold classification in Mexico, see Richard L. Currier, "The Hot-Cold Syndrome and Symbolic Balance in Mexican and Spanish-American Folk Medicine," *Ethnology*, Vol. 5 (July, 1966), pp. 251–63.

goes to a *curandero,* she tells him that the child is suffering from a
hot disease, but if she goes to a doctor she says nothing. If the doctor's medicine does not improve the child, the mother attributes it to
the fact that the doctor did not understand the nature of the illness
and gave the child a hot medicine instead of a cold medicine.

On the other hand, if the *curandero* does not effect a cure, her
explanation is of a different kind. She now believes that the heat of
the disease was so great that there was no medicine cold enough to
counteract it; her faith in the *curandero* and distrust of the doctor
continue. In the case of the illnesses supposedly caused by humors
or spirits of the air, most Tepoztecans are reluctant to visit a doctor
because of their conviction that doctors do not understand either the
cause or the cure of such diseases.

Governed by their own interpretation of illness, people in the village approach modern doctors with distrust, realizing that they do
not fully understand certain classes of illness, such as those due to
evil humors or those related to the hot-cold distinction. It is, therefore, important for the doctor to become familiar with the native
concepts and to utilize them as a psychological means of gaining
confidence. The job of establishing rapport and gaining confidence
under these conditions is no easy one. It demands a doctor who has
the zeal and spirit of a missionary and some understanding of the
relativity of cultural values.

Aside from factors of personality and of understanding local beliefs, the ability of a doctor to gain confidence and prestige depends
upon his technical skill in making accurate diagnoses and effecting
cures. Although it is unfair to generalize about the quality of Mexican rural doctors as a whole, our impression from personal experience is that they are poorly trained and equipped and show little
enthusiasm for work in the villages. Considering the conditions
under which rural doctors must live and work in Mexico, it is probable that this phenomenon is more widespread. There is little incentive for the superior doctor to leave the city and go to rural areas. At
best, few are willing to undergo the hardships of rural life with its
isolation and lack of comforts and diversions; in addition, salaries
are low, opportunities for advancement are few, and there is little
permanency of assignment. As a result of these conditions, rural doctors are frequently recruited from those of inferior abilities and this
in turn makes it more difficult to win over the Indian villager to
modern medicine.

· LOCAL ORGANIZATIONAL PATTERNS ·

Any attempt to revive or establish a "democratic" institution, such as a co-operative in a community that has lived for years under an authoritarian system, must take cognizance of the profound effect of this conditioning to authority upon the psychology of the people. The lack of personal initiative and village spirit found in Tepoztlán may be attributed to this conditioning. Our experience made it clear that chances for success would have been better if we had operated according to current organizational practices. Had the doctors been brought in to set up a private clinic rather than a co-operative, there might have been less difficulty. Previous attempts to set up co-operatives in other activities had met with similar or more drastic difficulties. In 1930 Tepoztlán organized a Forestry Co-operative for the production and sale of charcoal. It lasted only a few years, for the village divided into hostile political factions. The officers of the co-operative were suspected of stealing funds, the president was murdered, and the co-operative dissolved. A more recent co-operative to run the bus line between Tepoztlán and Cuernavaca also is rent by dissension and violence.

The results in Tepoztlán lead to the conclusion that the introduction of modern medicine should not be attempted through the mechanism of co-operatives in regions where a long-standing co-operative tradition is lacking. The more general lesson is that programs, to be practical, are not to be devised according to an ideal organizational model, however much this model may appeal to program planners, but must take account of the organizational pattern familiar to the people of the particular community.

· ENTRENCHED POWER ·

Those who enter a community to engage in an action program must recognize the implications of the fact that they are not entering a power vacuum. In every human community there exists a network of relations between individuals. It is to the interest of many of these individuals to maintain this system of relationships. Any group of outsiders moving into a community will be seen by some as potentially disruptive, even if they plan no action. If they do plan action, whatever positive measures they undertake, no matter how benign, will be perceived by some community members as a threat to their own status and interests.

It is tempting to attribute the antagonism of these people and their obstructive activities to the fact that they are wicked people, opposing common good because of selfish motives. Even if this were so, the frequency of such obstruction makes it reasonable to anticipate its occurrence and to be able to cope with it realistically.

It may appear to some that the downfall of the clinic in Tepoztlán can be attributed simply and directly to the personal antagonism of Don Rosas. Already worried that his power and position of privilege would be undermined if modern medicine got a foothold in the village, he immediately viewed the clinic as a competitor and resorted to unscrupulous methods to bring about its downfall. This is undoubtedly true, but can the clinic's downfall be simply attributed to the personal villainy of one man?

Don Rosas' actions were motivated by the fact that he belonged to a profession that was being slowly crowded out by newer and more modern techniques. There is no reason to believe that any of the other *curanderos* in the village felt differently about the clinic. But since Don Rosas was more powerful than the others, he was in a better position to do something about his antagonism. Rather than an evil individual, Don Rosas can be taken as a symbol of the traditional practitioner everywhere who is being deprived of his status and importance by the advance of modern medicine.

But aside from the threat to traditional medicine, we have seen that Don Rosas was not alone in opposing the clinic. In fact, virtually every established political figure in Tepoztlán—the mayor, the school principal, the councilmen, the secretary, and others—had or found reasons for sabotaging the clinic. If we are to attribute personal villainy to Don Rosas, we must do the same for the whole of Tepoztlán officialdom. And we must also include the governor and senator of the State of Morelos. Rather than conclude that this just happened to be a particularly corrupt regime and expect the next one to be different, it would seem more rational to consider this state of affairs as something inherent in the culture of Tepoztlán and, in fact, of many communities.

Instead of explaining the attack on the medical clinic in Tepoztlán as the unscrupulous work of a fortuitous aggregation of villains, it would be more realistic to regard it as a special case of a general response to the introduction of any new enterprise into an established community. Whenever the activities of an outside group—health team, research project, or any enterprise affecting the pattern of interpersonal relations within a community—are perceived by those in power as threatening their position, they will attempt directly or indirectly to undermine the efforts of that group.

· CONCLUSIONS ·

Compared with carefully planned, government-sponsored health and medical programs in underdeveloped areas, our small-scale endeavor which grew out of the needs of a research project was clearly a minor, almost amateur, effort. Nevertheless, this case study highlights a number of principles and problems to be found in most attempts to introduce modern medicine into so-called backward areas of the world.

This case throws light upon the dynamic forces at work in a peasant community which, on the surface, appears simple and static. It shows quite clearly that the success or failure of a medical program depends on many cultural factors besides the competence of doctors and the quality of services. The major obstacles encountered in the Tepoztlán case were these: readiness to distrust innovations and a generalized lack of interest in changing local ways of doing things; inadequacy of economic resources, even the one-peso fee being too high for many villagers; lack of rapport between doctors and patients, resting on the doctors' ignorance of native illness concepts and an attitude of superiority; continued faith of the villagers in their local *curanderos;* finally, and perhaps most important, readiness of local interest groups, headed by the leading *curandero,* to view the medical co-operative as a threat to their power.

C: INDIA

· INTRODUCTION ·

This study grew out of a larger pilot research project in village Rampur,[1] sponsored by the Programme Evaluation Organization of the Planning Commission. The field research was carried on by the writer over a period of seven months from November, 1952 to May, 1953, with the assistance of Indian students.[2] The research methods used in this study were those of the current anthropological and sociological repertory and included participant-observers, interviews, the use of schedules and questionnaires, autobiographies, case studies, and the use of village records and census data.

The broad objectives of the research project were: (1) to demonstrate the relevancy of an intimate understanding of village life and organization for the work of the evaluation officers as well as for the multipurpose Village Workers; (2) to obtain significant baseline data in a village within a community project area prior to the start of the action program, so that some measure of control can be had in the study of the impact of the community-development program upon the culture and economy of the village; (3) to develop some research papers which would reflect modern fieldwork techniques of cultural anthropology and sociology and could thereby serve as research models for the evaluation officers; and (4) finally, it was hoped that we might develop some relatively simple but reliable methods for the study of social organization, leadership, and value systems-methods which might be applied on a broader scale by the evaluation officers.

Primarily for reasons of convenience of access to New Delhi, a village in the Community Development Project of Delhi State was selected for this intensive study. After a brief review of some of the characteristics of the one hundred villages within the community projects area we realized that there were at least fifteen variables which would seem to be significant for a cultural study of a community. These variables included such items as location in the relatively

[1] This name is fictitious.

[2] I am grateful to the following students who participated in the research: R. N. Bansal, Harvant Singh Dhillon, Inder Paul Singh Monga, Venu Ramdas and Rajpal Singh Rathee.

unhealthy lowland area along the Jumna River as over against location in the higher and drier area known as the Bhangar; population
size; the number of separate castes and the occupational distribution
within a single village; the relative degree of isolation due to differences in communication facilities; the incidence of disease; the presence or absence of a school in the village; the degree of influence of
the Arya Samaj movement; the incidence of tenancy; the extent of
irrigation; the proportion of communal lands to privately held lands,
and finally the extent to which government programs had been active in the village in past years.

It was apparent that no single village could possibly give us a
sample of the total range of diversity found in the project area, much
less that of North India as a whole. On the other hand, almost any
village would serve our purposes so long as we knew what the village was typical of and what it was not typical of.[3] We therefore
decided to select a village that would be about in the middle of the
population range of the one hundred villages in the project area,
and would have a good representation of castes and occupations.

Our major objective during the first few weeks of the research was
to establish and solidify our rapport with the villagers. Accordingly,
the first week was devoted to informal talks with villagers in which
we discussed village problems, the felt needs for improvements, the
kinds of improvements they thought most feasible, both on an individual family basis and on a village basis, the history of past efforts
at improvement by the government, the attitudes of the villagers towards the Community Projects Administration, and their knowledge
of the Five Year Plan. Most of these sessions were group sessions, as
much by necessity as design, since we found it almost impossible to
hold a private interview without neighbors and relatives dropping
in. This situation must be kept in mind by any student from the West
who takes privacy for granted and whose research methods, such as
polling, depend upon individual opinions and responses. Only after
two months of work in the village did we feel that we could insist
upon private interviews, when necessary, especially in connection
with taking life histories of villagers. During some of the interviews I
used an interpreter who was also an expert in shorthand. He recorded the interview verbatim, thereby providing greater accuracy

[3] It must be remembered that the community study method is not primarily a
matter of studying the community. Rather, it uses the community as a natural
setting for the study of human behavior and the interconnections between
social and psychological acts and processes. It is assumed that communities give
us some cell-like minimal duplication of the basic cultural and structural whole,
especially in a peasant country like India.

and objectivity of the interview situation as well as capturing some of the flavor of the local idiom.

Our next step was to gather a sufficient amount of basic demographic economic and social data which would serve as a background for the analysis of any specific problem. Much of these data was recorded on a household and family basis and an accumulative dossier was built up for each household. Each family and household was assigned a number which thereafter was used to identify the family. In addition alphabetical lists of both sexes were drawn up, caste-wise, with the corresponding family and housesite number after each name. In this way we were able to identify all individuals in the village in respect of caste and family membership.

To avoid unnecessary annoyance to the villagers, as many data as possible were obtained from village *patvari* records. Later, as our rapport improved, a house-to-house village census was taken which covered the following items: name, sex, age, *gotra,* and caste of each family member; marital status, age at the time of betrothal, age at time of celebration of the *gona;* village of birth; occupation; employment outside of the village; pensions; educational experience and literacy; leadership position in terms of membership in official *panchayat* organization. In the case of agriculturists we obtained data on land ownership; size of cultivation units; fragmentation in terms of number of separate plots; land self-cultivated; land rented in; land rented out; land mortgaged in; land mortgaged out; ownership of oxen, bullock carts, and agricultural machinery.

With the aid of the above data a socioeconomic point scale was developed by which each household was ranked according to the score it received, on five separate indices: housing, land ownership, income from outside employment, highest grade completed by family members, and literacy. In addition a total socioeconomic score was obtained by each family. With the aid of this point scale we were able to select a highly representative sample of thirty households which represented all the major socioeconomic variables in the village. These thirty families now became the subjects of special intensive studies of felt needs in housing, in health, in education. In addition, other special studies were undertaken, such as an analysis of the village *patvari* records, intercaste relations and the breakdown of the *jajmani* system, a comparison of the old caste *panchayat* and the new statutory *panchayat,* a study of the ceremonial cycle and the life cycle, and finally a brief study of the religious and ethical concepts of the villagers.

15

Group Dynamics:

*A Study of Factions Within Castes**

Most discussions of Indian village social organization have emphasized the importance of caste, kinship, intervillage networks, and occasional alliances between castes which have been called factions or parties. In our study of Rampur we discovered still another dimension of the social structure, and one which has received insufficient attention in the past: namely, the existence of small cohesive groups within castes which are the locus of power and decision-making and contribute to the compartmentalized and segmented nature of village social organization. The study of these small groups takes us to the very heart of village life. It provides us with the key to the communications channels of the society and also reflects many of the values of the people. Let us, then, systematically examine the nature of these small groups, their number, size, age, composition, economic and social characteristics, internal structure and leadership, the processes by which they are formed, and, finally, some of the practical implications of these findings for community development programs in India.

After intensive study in Rampur, we found twelve small groups locally known as *dhars*. The word *dhar* literally means the upper part of the body and the use of this term for groups of people carries out the idea of physical unity, that is, members of the same *dhar* are

* This was published in 1958 in my book, *Village Life in Northern India* (Urbana: University of Illinois Press). Earlier versions were published in India in 1954.

all of one body. The *Hindustani Dictionary* of J. T. Platts (1925) defines *dhar* as "bodies" but adds that in North India the common meaning is "parties." In Rampur, however, the word "parties" refers to larger political groupings and to more temporary alliances than is denoted by the term *dhar*. I have therefore translated *dhar* as "faction," for this seems to me the nearest equivalent in English for the sense in which the villagers themselves use the term. However, it must be emphasized at the outset that the term "faction" as here used does not denote only opposition or hostile relations between groups, nor is discord or dissension necessarily the predominant quality in interfaction relations. The small groups which we have delineated are held together primarily by co-operative economic, social, and ceremonial relations. Dhillon has put it well in his recent comparative analysis of a similar phenomenon in the South Indian village of Haripura. He writes: "While hostility towards other groups is a common attribute of factions and new factions are often formed as a result of quarrels and disputes, this is seldom the only or even the major force which holds factions together." [1]

Although most villagers in Rampur are perfectly aware of the existence of these factions both in their own and in other castes, it is not an easy task to delineate them, because of the complexity of interfaction relations and the reluctance of villagers to talk with outsiders about the intimate details of village life. The factions are generally referred to by the names of their leaders or in some instances by the nickname of a lineage, that is, when the faction and the lineage are synonymous. For example, many years ago a number of Jat families who were expelled by a village *panchayat* decree sought refuge in a village called Dhamar. Later, when they returned to Rampur, they became known as the Dhamariyas and now all belong to a single faction.

As indicated above, the factions follow caste lines. However, factions from different castes may and do form alliances or blocs, which in effect are factions on a different level from those discussed here.

The distribution of factions by caste is as follows: six among the seventy-eight Jat families; one among the fifteen Brahman families; two among the twenty-one Camar families; two among the ten Bhangi families; and one among the seven Kumhar families. Of these, the Jat factions are by far the most powerful and dominate the political life of the village. Because of the small number and economic dependence of most of the lower castes, they do not have the strength to act as independent factions. As a matter of fact, the

[1] See Harvant Dhillon, *Leadership and Groups in a South Indian Village* (New Delhi, 1955), p. 30. Whether or not we define the term *dhar* as "faction" does not materially alter the analysis.

Camar factions are relatively recent and their emergence is closely related to the increase in jobs outside the village and the gradual breakdown of the old *jajmani* system. It is noteworthy that both the Jats and the lower castes are split among themselves. However, the Brahmans form a more or less cohesive group, although they are in many ways subservient to Jat interests. In short, we can think of the factions in the village in terms of three sets, Jats, Brahmans, and Harijans (lower castes).

The functions of factions differ somewhat by caste. All factions operate as more or less cohesive units on ceremonial occasions, particularly births, betrothals, and marriages; in court litigations; in the operation of the traditional caste *panchayats;* and in recent years in district board, state, and national elections.[2] Moreover, all of the factions have one or more of their own hookah-smoking groups which serve as social centers where there is daily face-to-face contact. Jat factions have a few special functions. They act as units in co-operative economic undertakings such as money-lending and the renting of land, and also in quarrels over land, especially village communal lands.

For a faction to operate successfully over an extended period of time it must meet three conditions: (1) It must be sufficiently cohesive to act as a unit. (2) It must be large enough to act as a self-sufficient ceremonial group, for example, it must be able to summon an impressive number of relatives for a marriage party. (3) It must have sufficient economic resources to be independent of other groups. This means that it must have some well-to-do families that can rent out land or act as money-lenders for its poorer members. It must also have sufficient resources to fight expensive and lengthy court cases. If we examine our twelve factions in terms of these criteria it at once becomes apparent that the Jats come much closer to approaching these conditions than the non-Jats and are therefore stronger and truer factions. Four of the six non-Jat factions cannot meet the economic criteria and therefore can hardly be considered as independent factions of the same order as the Jats.

In interfaction relations members of friendly groups will share most of the functions we have described above for each faction, except that it is done on a lesser scale and the relationship is much less stable than within a single faction. For example, on ceremonial occasions it is expected that all the members of a single faction will be invited, including the women. But in relations between friendly factions it is obligatory to invite only one male representative from each

[2] Prior to 1947 and Independence the franchise for district board elections was based on possession of property. This meant a practical exclusion of all non-Jats from the voters' list in Rampur.

of the lineages of the faction. Thus, if there are four married brothers living in separate households only one need be invited, although more may be. However, their wives are generally not invited and this cutting out of the women is one of the major differences between intrafaction and interfaction relations. Similarly, there is much less informal visiting among the women of separate though friendly factions than among women of the same faction.

Members of hostile factions will not attend each other's ceremonial celebrations, will not visit each other's homes, and as a rule will not smoke the hookah together, except at the home of a member of a neutral faction. In *panchayat* meetings the representatives of hostile factions can be counted upon to marshal vicious gossip about rivals. However, direct attack in public is rare. Instead, indirection is developed to a fine art. It is to be noted that members of hostile factions generally do not cease talking to one another, and are polite. This allows for the possibility of improving relations or at least joining up temporarily with one hostile group to fight another. Factions which enjoy the reputation of being relatively neutral and of having friendly relations with all groups are the most influential in the village.

There are some occasions, though these are relatively few and far between, when members of different factions come together despite their differences and unite for some common action. The major occasions are funerals, the building of village wells, the cleaning of the village pond (twice in the past forty years), the repair of subcanals for irrigation, and certain holidays such as Holi and Tij. Moreover, there is a tradition of presenting an appearance of unity to the outside. For example, if two men of hostile factions have married daughters living in the same village, whenever one of the men visits that village he must visit the daughter of the hostile faction and pay the customary one rupee to symbolize the fact that she, like his own daughter, is a daughter of the village.

· S P A T I A L   D I S T R I B U T I O N   W I T H I N   T H E   V I L L A G E ·

The distribution pattern of the houses of the various faction members is shown in Map 1.

It can be seen that the houses of C are clustered together and form a single neighborhood. This is also true of E, all of whose houses are on a single street. The houses of D form two separate neighborhoods; those of B are on three separate streets and can be said to form three adjoining neighborhoods. However, the houses of A and F are scattered all over the village, with the scattering greatest in F,

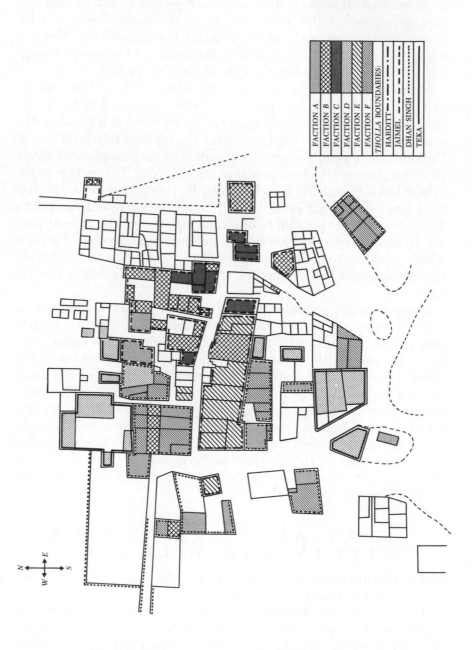

MAP 1. *Distribution of house sites by Jat factions, Rampur, 1953.*

the least cohesive of all the factions. It is interesting to note that *C* and *E*, geographically the most compact, are also the two most cohesive factions in the village. This will be discussed in detail later.

· NUMERICAL STRENGTH ·

The size of factions in terms of numbers and families, total population, and total number of adult males is shown in Table 1.

We see that there are four large factions and two small ones. The largest, *B*, is three times the size of the smallest, *C*. There is also considerable range in average size of family within each faction. *D* has the largest families with an average of 10.7 members per family, followed by *A* and *E*. *B*, *F*, and *C* have the smallest, with *C* showing 7.1 as the average size.

TABLE 1

POPULATION CHARACTERISTICS OF JAT FACTIONS, RAMPUR, 1953

Faction	Total Number of Families	Total Number of Family Members	Average Size of Family	Number of Adult Males
B	21	166	7.9	49
A	14	121	8.6	32
D	14	141	10.7	37
F	13	93	7.1	28
E	9	77	8.0	17
C	7	50	7.1	14

The larger families in *D* reflect the stability of the joint family in this group. Seven out of fourteen families in D have from ten to nineteen members and seven out of fourteen families in A have from ten to eighteen members.

There appears to be no relationship between the influence of factions and their size. *F*, which is the least influential, has thirteen families, whereas *D*, the most influential, has fourteen. There appears to be an inverse relationship between size and cohesiveness, that is, the smaller factions are the most cohesive. However, there are other factors involved which will be discussed later.

· FACTIONS AND KINSHIP ·

The role of kinship in the composition of factions is extremely important. Informants questioned about the membership of their particular faction tend to equate their faction with their kinship group, even when they are aware that the two may not entirely coincide.

This is particularly true when kin belong to separate but friendly factions. There is a strong reticence, however, about volunteering the information that close kin belong to hostile factions. But when the question is put directly, the fact will be admitted. There is not a single case of brothers belonging to separate factions, and there is only one case of first and second cousins, and only four cases (out of fourteen) of third cousins.

Of the six Jat factions, one consists of members of a single lineage, another consists of members of two lineages, each of a different clan, three consist of three lineages, again representing more than one clan, and one consists of four lineages representing two clans. (See Table 2.)

TABLE 2

DISTRIBUTION OF JAT LINEAGES AND CLANS
BY FACTION, RAMPUR, 1953

Faction	Number of Families	Number of Lineages	Number of Clans
C	7	1	1
E	9	2	2
A	14	3	2
D	14	4	2
B	21	3	2
F	13	3	1

It is clear that the lineage and the faction are not synonymous. However, they seem to have been so about a hundred years ago when only two factions existed, each a lineage of a single clan. At present, however, members of as many as four lineages are joined together in a single faction because of common interests. The present composition of factions therefore represents different historic levels of faction development. Apparently new factions developed when members of new clans came into the village. This will be discussed later.

· **F A C T I O N S   A N D   P A N A S** ·

There are three factions in each *pana*: A, F, and D in Dhan Singh, and B, C, and E in Harditt. (See Chart 1.)

It can be seen that in each *pana* two of the factions are hostile to each other and one is neutral. The hostile factions within each *pana* combine with one of the groups in the opposite *pana* so that each hostile faction is hostile to two groups (one in each *pana*) and friendly to a third. This pattern is in accord with the well-known

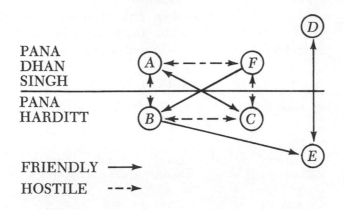

PANA
DHAN
SINGH

PANA
HARDITT

FRIENDLY ⟶
HOSTILE ---►

CHART 1. *Sociogram showing inter- and intra-*pana *faction relations, Rampur, 1953.*

Indian proverb which says, "The enemy of your enemy is your friend."

The hostility between factions of the same *pana* is generally more bitter than between factions of opposite *panas,* for it represents a violation of the ideal pattern whereby relatives are supposed to get along. But by the same token the closer kinship bonds between factions of the same *pana* imply a greater potential for some future rapprochement. The traditional obligations to family members on ceremonial occasions act as a constant pull for unity.

· FACTIONS AND THOLLAS ·

Each *pana* is divided into two subgroups known as *thollas.* The number of factions within the *thollas* increases progressively as we go from the smallest to the largest *tholla.* Teka *tholla,* the smallest, has one faction; Harditt *tholla* has two, Jaimel *tholla* has three, and Dhan Singh *tholla* has four. In terms of the *tholla* composition of factions, we find that three factions consist of families from one *tholla* each and three consist of families from two *thollas.*

· ECONOMIC AND SOCIAL CHARACTERISTICS ·

The factions show significant differences in a number of important economic and social characteristics. The study of these differences has been greatly facilitated by our earlier determination of the relative socioeconomic position of all families in the village with the aid of various point scales. We can establish the ranking of the Jat factions by adding up the total number of points obtained on all of the scores by the families in each faction and dividing by the number of families per faction. The ranking is shown in Table 3.

TABLE 3

RANK ORDER OF JAT FACTIONS ON SOCIOECONOMIC INDEXES, RAMPUR, 1953

Faction	Total Socio-economic Score	Housing	Land Owned	Land Cultivated	Outside Income	Highest Grade Completed
A	1	1	6	6	1	2
D	2	2	1	1	5	5
C	3	3	2	2	6	1
E	4	4	3	3	4	4
B	5	6	4	4	2	3
F	6	5	5	5	3	6

Beginning with the total socioeconomic scores, we see that A, D, and C rank highest and E, B, and F lowest. The correlation between the total scores and the separate scores is very high in housing and quite high in most of the other indexes, with only a few exceptions. In short, A, D, and C are clearly the wealthiest groups. It is noteworthy, however, that the basis of the faction socioeconomic strength differs considerably. A, which ranks first on total score, ranks sixth or last on land owned and land cultivated. But it ranks first in outside income and second in education. This negative correlation is significant and reflects a widespread trend whereby the smaller landowners seek outside employment and rely more heavily upon the education of their children. The converse of this proposition is shown strikingly in the case of D.

A more detailed examination of the landownership picture reveals that D, C, and E own the most land per family, and B, F, and A the least. The total land of each faction and the average per family are given in Table 4.

It can be noted that the rank order of factions for land owned and land cultivated per family is almost identical. In A, which ranks lowest, six out of fourteen families do not cultivate land, whereas in D, C, and E all but one family (in E) are cultivators.

In comparing Tables 4 and 5 we are struck by the inverse relationship between landholding and amount of outside income on a faction basis. We have no specific information which would fully explain why the families in A have so much higher incomes than those in D. However, we know that the educational level of A is consider-

TABLE 4

DISTRIBUTION OF LANDOWNERSHIP BY FACTION, RAMPUR, 1953

Faction	Number of Families	Land Owned (acres)	Average per Family (acres)
D	14	181.47	12.96
C	7	86.04	12.29
E	9	87.29	9.69
B	21	173.33	8.25
F	13	102.27	7.86
A	14	85.42	6.10

ably higher than that of D. Moreover, we have seen that the bulk of the noncultivating Jat families are in A, and five out of six of these families have outside income.

Perhaps the most dramatic evidence for the socioeconomic basis of the factions emerges from a study of the renting and mortgaging of land. In five of the six factions, not a single individual rents land out to other factions. D, the only exception, has a surplus of land and rents out to B and E as well as to Brahmans and Camars. However, in principle no faction will rent out land outside of its own faction if there is anyone within the faction who needs land. In the case of mortgaging, faction solidarity is even more striking, for there has not been a single case in the last five years of land mortgaged outside of one's own faction. This is all the more significant in the face of the demand and competition for land.

TABLE 5

AVERAGE MONTHLY OUTSIDE INCOME BY JAT FACTION, RAMPUR, 1953

Faction	Number of Families	Number of Employed Families	Income (rupees)	Average Income per Employed Family
A	14	9	1843	205
B	21	10	1781	178
E	9	4	602	150
F	13	9	940	104
C	7	2	195	98
D	14	8	716	89

Turning from a comparison of the factions to a consideration of the wealth distribution within the factions, we find that each faction tends to reflect a cross section of the wealth distribution pattern of the village. Each has at least one well-to-do family which acts as money-lender and has sufficient land to rent out to poorer members of the faction. Each faction also has one or more strong and dynamic figures who tend to keep the faction united. An analysis of the socioeconomic position of the families within each faction shows that five out of the six factions have one member in the highest group or Group III. *D* and *A* both have a preponderance of Group II families. *B*, which has the largest percentage of poor (Group I) families, is also the least cohesive of all the factions.

· COHESIVENESS ·

The varying degree of cohesiveness of the factions appears to be a function of the size of the group, geographical compactness, closeness of kinship ties, the degree of economic self-sufficiency, the past history of factionalism, and the age of the group. When all these factors are considered together we find that the factions fall into three groups: *C* and *E* the most cohesive, *A* and *D* less so, and *B* and *F* the least cohesive. Now let us examine each group in more detail, beginning with the most cohesive and ending with the least cohesive.

Faction *C*—seven families—is united by close kinship bonds. Its members are of a single lineage of Dabas clan and are descendants of a common great-great-grandfather. The houses of *C* form a compact neighborhood. This faction in its present form is about thirty-five years old. However, none of the present members or their ancestors, for a period of 125 years, have belonged to a separate or opposing faction. At no time has there been a quarrel among the present members. The sense of unity and distinctness of this faction is reflected by the popular saying of the villagers that this group, known as Dhamariyas, forms an independent village within a village, or a fifth village within the four-village unit. *C* has a tradition of strong and popular leaders known for their aggressiveness. This has tended to isolate this faction from the rest of the village, thereby strengthening its internal cohesiveness. The members of *C* never rent land to or from the members of other groups nor do they take loans from any of the factions within the village. They prefer to deal with moneylenders in other villages to maintain their independence in their own village.

Faction *E*—nine families—consists of members of two lineages which, though not closely related (one is of Dabas clan and the other of Dahya clan), have been together in a single faction for many years. The age of the present faction composition is twelve years. However, the present members have acted as a unit for the past thirty-five years, during the earlier years of which they were part of a larger faction. Still earlier, there was some conflict between some of the families of the same lineage. The houses of *E* form a single cluster and are on one street. Because the group is small it tends to act as one large family. The members sit and smoke together often and consult with each other even on small matters. They constitute a single hookah group. Unlike C, the leaders of E have a reputation for being quiet and humble men who are secure in their wealth and exert a great deal of influence by their relative neutrality. They are closely tied with D, from which they rent land.

Faction A—fourteen families—consists of three lineages, two of which are closely related (both are Kharab clan), one with eleven families and one with two. The third (Dabas clan), consisting of only one family, is unrelated. The heads of nine of the eleven families have the same grandfather and constitute the core of the faction. The houses of A are scattered all over the village and there are two separate hookah groups. The present members or their ancestors have been in a single faction for over one hundred years. During this time there has been some splintering off of some families and this has hurt the reputation of the group. However, the history of factions indicates that during crisis periods the families that had left the faction reunited with it. Because of this, A is considered tricky and unpredictable. Like C, A has a tradition of aggressive leadership and is relatively isolated from the rest of the factions.

Faction D—fourteen families—is made up of four lineages. Three of these, consisting of twelve families of Dabas clan, are closely related. The fourth, consisting of two families of Kharab clan, is unrelated. The houses of D form two separate neighborhoods and have two hookah groups. The members of D are proud of the fact that no one from the three core lineages belongs to other factions. Between thirty-five and fifty years ago, some of the present members or their predecessors belonged to opposing factions, but they never fought court cases against one another. The leaders of D are also proud that their group represents the oldest genealogical lineage in this and three other surrounding villages. The members of D, along with those of A and C, can also boast of being direct descendants of some of the most popular and traditional leaders of the village.

Faction B—twenty-one families—consists of three lineages, two of which, made up of families of Dabas clan, are closely related, whereas the third, consisting of seven families of Deswal clan, is unrelated and belongs to a different *tholla*. The houses of B are somewhat scattered and constitute three adjoining neighborhoods. One of the elements of strength of B is that both headmen of the village belong to this faction. In fact, this means that most of the official contacts from the outside are established through members of this faction.

Faction F—thirteen families—consists of three closely related lineages of Kharab clan. The houses are widely scattered, as in A. This is the youngest of the factions. It was formed about four years ago and some of its members joined only two years ago. All of the members formerly belonged to A. Moreover, they did not all split as a unit but left one or two at a time, more because of their hostile relations within A than because of any great pull of F; that is, they were pushed out rather than pulled in. Most of the families who recently left A are poor and may therefore be tempted to rejoin their relatives in A.

In summary, the factors which make for greater cohesiveness are the small size of the group, the compact residence pattern within one neighborhood and few hookah groups, the internal structural homogeneity of lineage and clan membership, economic self-sufficiency, a long history of internal peace and unity, and strong leadership.

· INTERNAL STRUCTURE AND LEADERSHIP ·

The internal structure of each of the six Jat factions shows many interesting differences. This structure is represented graphically in Chart 2.

The first thing to note is the rather large number of men who are considered spokesmen or leaders—twenty for seventy-eight families —indicating the tendency to spread leadership roles. The greatest spread is in D, the smallest in F. The large squares within the circles represent primary leaders, the smaller squares, secondary leaders. It will be seen that five of the six groups recognize more than a single man as leader. In A, D, C, and E any one of the leaders may speak for the group as a whole and in critical situations may make independent decisions, although the practice of delegating authority to individuals is frowned upon and the leaders themselves are not in the habit of making independent decisions. In C the major leader is an aggressive and dominating figure and in his absence there is no able spokesman for the group. In B and F the leaders are much more dependent upon constant consultation with other members of their respective factions because these factions are much less cohesive than the other four. The four more cohesive groups are conscious of this weakness of B and F and will sometimes deride them on this score.

In A, D, and B there is a division of labor among the leaders. The older men act as ceremonial leaders, the younger and more educated men as representatives of the group on secular committees. In E the two leaders are of about equal age and play interchangeable roles.

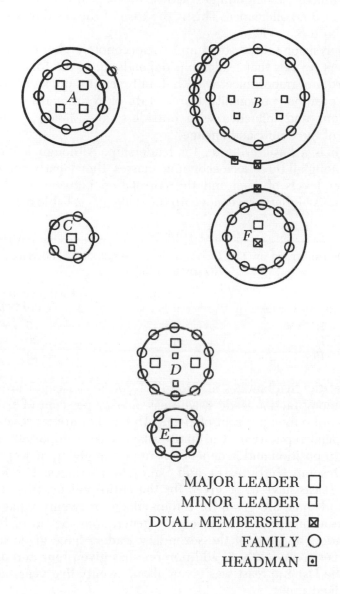

MAJOR LEADER □
MINOR LEADER ▫
DUAL MEMBERSHIP ⊠
FAMILY ○
HEADMAN ▣

CHART 2. Internal structure and leadership of Jat factions, Rampur, 1953.

It will be seen that *A, F,* and *B* are shown in Chart 2 with outer circles. This is intended to indicate that there are families in each of these factions which show the beginnings of dual loyalties. *B* has the largest number of such families. However, only in *F* is there a clear-cut case of dual allegiance. This is the case of the headman who belongs to both *B* and *F.*

An analysis of the personal and socioeconomic characteristics of Jat leaders reveals that leadership depends upon the following factors in order of importance: wealth, family reputation, age and genealogical position, personality traits, state of retirement, education, connections and influence with outsiders, and, finally, numerical strength of the family and lineage.

Wealth is a basic criterion for leadership. Although leaders are found among all three socioeconomic classes, they clearly come from the upper levels of each and the correlation between wealth and leadership is highest as we move up the scale. (See Table 6.)

TABLE 6

DISTRIBUTION OF JAT LEADERS BY SOCIOECONOMIC POSITION,
RAMPUR, 1953

Socioeconomic Group	Number of Leaders	Total Number of Families in Village
III	4	5
II	14	30
I*b*	1	43

Four of the five families in Group III (or 80 per cent) are represented among faction leaders, whereas only 47 per cent of Group II families and only 2 per cent of Group I*b* families are represented.

The social reputation of a family plays a very important role in leadership position and is dependent upon the giving of Kaj (death feast), Desotan (birth feast), and elaborate marriages. The Kaj and Desotan feasts have to be given for the entire village, including all castes, and some are given for a four-village or twenty-village unit. These occasions are remembered for generations. Seven of the primary leaders and one of the secondary leaders have given at least one Kaj ceremony each; in addition one has given four and another three. The last Kaj feast was given about twenty-five years ago but is still talked about.

Family reputation is also judged in terms of the charity given to the Gaushala (charitable organization for the support of cows) and to schools. In the recent campaign for funds to build the Kanjhawla secondary school, twelve of the fifteen families that contributed over a hundred *rupees* each were from among Rampur's leaders. Families that have held official positions as revenue officials, or headmen or who have been money-lenders are also popular. Among the things which hurt family reputation are the mortgaging out of land, sexual misdemeanors, and being jailed. However, families which have the reputation of being aggressive and fighters are feared and may become leaders.

Age is another clear-cut criterion of leadership. (See Table 7.)

TABLE 7

Age Distribution of Jat Leaders, Rampur, 1953

	Age Group	Number of Leaders	Total
Over 50	57–65	8	12
	51–56	4	
Below 50	40–50	6	6
Below 40	30–40	0	2
	20–30	2	
Below 20		0	0

Only one primary or major faction leader is below the age of fifty; eight of the twelve leaders over fifty are between fifty-seven and sixty-five years of age. However, of these only two leaders, those of *E* and *F*, are the sole representatives of their groups. The remaining six are essentially ceremonial leaders and are leaders by virtue of the respect for their seniority of age and genealogical position in the lineage. They are relatively inactive and delegate their powers to younger secondary leaders, particularly in activities which require education, such as membership on the school committees and official *panchayats*. The four leaders still in their early fifties are all active leaders and spokesmen for their factions. Only the leader of *B* consults with his faction members on matters relating to *E*.

All leaders below fifty are secondary leaders. They act as advisers and carry out the activities delegated to them by the primary leader. The presence of two leaders in their twenties points to a new trend and shows the great value placed upon education.

A fundamental requisite for leadership in this village is humility, self-abnegation, and hospitality, especially within the in-group. The importance given to these values is reflected in everyday life by the use of conventional expressions and behavior, such as respectful kinship terminology, the kneeling of women before older people to ask for blessings, and the use of phrases such as "Come and sit in my humble home," or "Please partake of our poor food." In answering inquiries concerning the ownership of land or houses, they will always say, "This is your land." Similarly, in replying to questions about the relationship of family members they say, "This is your son," or "This is your daughter." Leaders never refer to themselves as such, and make a point of attributing leadership qualities to the others who are present.

Other traits which are highly valued include unquestioning loyalty to the group, the keeping of promises, and speaking ability, especially at *panchayats*. Aggressiveness is valued if it is expressed against an out-group in defense of the in-group. However, as we have seen, the most influential leaders are the nonaggressive men.

The next important factor for leadership is the need to have sufficient time at one's disposal to devote to the various activities which leaders must carry on, particularly in attending *panchayats*, in fighting court cases, in collecting contributions for various causes, in arranging marriages, and in other ceremonial activities. Thus traditionally most leaders have been retired or semiretired men. Eight of Rampur's leaders are fully retired and five are semiretired, doing agricultural work. All of the eight leaders are primary leaders. Another group of five leaders are middle-aged men with jobs. Still another group of leaders is emerging from among the young, educated men in the village who are unemployed. Although there are still only two in this group, one a primary leader, the other a secondary leader, this is a trend that will probably increase.

Of the twenty leaders, eleven, or over 50 per cent, have some school education, four are literate but with no formal schooling, and five are illiterate. All five illiterate leaders are in their late fifties and with one exception are ceremonial leaders only. The four literate but uneducated leaders are secondary leaders. Of the eleven educated leaders, five are secondary leaders but all are in their forties. Thus we see that education is an important factor in achieving primary leadership, though once jobs are obtained the role becomes that of secondary leader.

Families with good connections on the outside either through marriage into important families or through personal friendships with officials or other important people enhance their leadership position in the village. These connections are utilized by the leaders to help the members of their respective factions in the marriage of sons, in getting jobs, and in court cases.

We now come to the final factor in leadership—family size and the size of the lineage. We find a significant correlation between leadership and family size. Seventeen out of the twenty families of Rampur's leaders have the largest families in their respective factions. Moreover the families of the primary leaders are generally larger than those of secondary leaders. There are only four families among the Jats which are as large as the leaders' families but do not have a leadership role. In the case of the three leaders with small families we find that they have the support of very large lineages.

In summary, we see that in the traditional pattern of leadership the older men were both the ceremonial and *panchayat* leaders. With the coming of education and outside employment, however, middle-aged educated people are being given opportunities by the older people to represent them in official *panchayats*, school committees, and deputations outside the village. Moreover, youth leadership, particularly of the educated unemployed, is developing and represents a threat to the traditional values of the villagers.

· I N T E R F A C T I O N   R E L A T I O N S ·

A study of the present-day behavior and the history of relationships between members of the various factions in the village enables us to distinguish three broad types of relationships: positive or friendly, negative or hostile, and neutral. The strength and quality of each of these relations differ considerably. Moreover, the positive relations can further be classified into four orders of preference which reflect differences in the quality of the relationship. Preference can be defined in terms of the intensity of the relationship and the number of people who interact in any two groups. For example, when two groups have primary reciprocal preferences it signifies that more members from each group have active friendly relations with one another than with members of any other groups. As the order of preference between any two groups decreases, the intensity of the relationship decreases and fewer people interact.

To facilitate an analysis of these varied relationships, we have constructed a sociogram indicating the relationships between the factions by various symbols. It should be noted that most groups give or have preferences, and are the objects of preferences by others. We will begin our analysis with the major Jat factions and then go on to examine the relations between the Jats and non-Jats.

Chart 3 shows three major sets of factions among the Jats consisting of two groups each, namely, A and C, B and F, and D and E. The first two sets have hostile relations, as indicated by the fact that no lines connect them. However, neutral set D-E is more closely related to B and F than to A and C. If we examine each order of preference between the groups, the relationship pattern will become clear. Only two of the three sets have a primary reciprocal relationship, that is, A and C, and D and E. F owes its primary relationship to B, and B in turn to E.

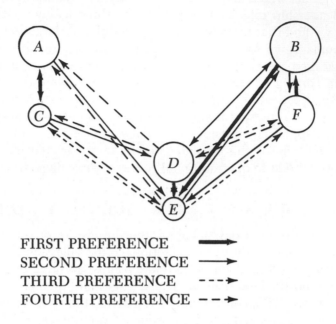

FIRST PREFERENCE

SECOND PREFERENCE

THIRD PREFERENCE

FOURTH PREFERENCE

CHART 3. Sociogram showing all preferences in interfaction relations among Jats.

In tracing the secondary preferences we see that the lines are essentially from both sets of hostile factions to the neutral ones, *D* and *E*. However, the ties between sets *B-F* and *D-E* are obviously much stronger than the ties between sets *A-C* and *D-E*, for in the latter case *D* and *E* receive secondary preferences but do not reciprocate. The third preferences show that *A* and *C* are now receiving some support from *D* and *E*, and *F* is showing some support toward *D*. However, it is not until we come to the fourth or weakest preferences that *F* receives allegiance from *D* and *E*. It is clear that *F* is in the weakest position in its relationship to *D* and *E*, followed only by *C*.

In an attempt to quantify the relative influence of each group in relation to the others, we can examine the number of arrows of various orders of preferences directed toward each group. The influence of a faction can be seen from the number and types of preferences which it receives from other groups. (See Table 8.)

From this point of view we see that *E* is the most influential group since two factions representing about 50 per cent of the Jat families

TABLE 8

INTERFACTION RELATIONS SHOWING NUMBER AND TYPES OF
PREFERENCES RECEIVED BY EACH JAT FACTION, RAMPUR, 1953

Faction	First Preference	Second Preference	Third Preference	Fourth Preference	Total Number of Preferences Received
E	2	2	1	—	5
D	1	2	2	—	5
B	1	2	—	—	3
A	1	—	2	—	3
C	1	—	1	1	3
F	—	1	—	2	3

owe primary allegiance to it. Moreover, two other factions give it
secondary preference and the third gives it tertiary preference. It
can be seen that *D* ranks second in influence. It receives preference
from all groups, one primary, two secondary, and two tertiary. *B*
ranks third, receiving one primary and two secondary. *A* and *C* come
next, both receiving one primary each, *A* receiving two tertiary preferences and *C* one tertiary and one quaternary preference. *F* is by
far the most isolated group, receiving no first preference, only one
secondary, and two fourth preferences.

In order to illustrate the meaning and content of interfaction relations and convey something of their flavor and complexity, we will
present the relations of a single faction, *E*, with each of the other
factions.

• RELATIONSHIPS OF FACTION E •

The closest ties of *E* are with members of *D*. *E* invites the members
of *D* to attend all important ceremonies, including the birth of a son,
the ceremonial first bath of the mother after birth, the ceremony
symbolizing the purification of the mother ten days after the birth,
and all the various ceremonies involved in marriage, beginning with
the betrothal and ending with the receiving of the marriage party.
The close unity between the two factions is most clearly reflected in
the practice by the members of both factions of extending a *chulah
neota*, whereby one entire family is fed for a day. *E* and *D* have had
these close relations for at least thirty-five years and have supported
each other in numerous court cases and other quarrels. There is not a
single case in which they have opposed one another. However, in
two cases *D* remained neutral while *E* opposed *B*.

The relationship of *E* to *B* is weaker than to *D*, primarily because

E has differentiated relations with some of the lineages in *B*.[3] The members of *E* have consistently been on intimate terms with a Dabas lineage of seven families in *B*, with whom they exchange the traditional ceremonial invitations and visit frequently. With another Deswal lineage of seven families of *B* who are of the same *tholla* as *E*, the members of *E* continue their ceremonial relations despite one serious court case between them about fifty years ago. They also smoke together frequently at each other's hookah groups, which are just across the street from one another. With a third lineage of seven families in *B* the members of *E* have severed all ceremonial relations, though they do not abuse each other and will sometimes smoke together at the hookah group of some of the other families in *B*. There have been three serious court cases between the members of *E* and these seven families of *B*.

In the first case, which occurred about 1898, the headman who belonged to *E* was implicated as an accomplice in a murder case. A Jat of *E* killed his wife by tying her in a room with smoking cow dung. With the help of the headman of his own faction he then attempted to cremate her and thereby cover up any evidence of murder. The story goes that while the dead body was being taken to the cremation ground with the help of the headman, some members of *B*, with the help of *C*, stopped the cremation, called the police, and arranged for an autopsy. The case went to court, the man was convicted, and the headman lost his post, which was taken over by a member of *B*. The second case involved a quarrel over irrigation rights. It went to court and lasted for several years. *E* finally won. The third case occurred in 1947 when the headman took possession of a house vacated by Muslims who had left the village. The headman claimed that he took the house in place of payment of a debt owed by the Muslims. The members of *E*, with the help of *A*, took the case to court on the ground that the property of a non-Jat belonged to the village and so could not be sold to a private individual. *B* won the case, which was then taken up by *A* and *C* without the help of *E*.

As we have indicated earlier, *E* also had a serious court case in about 1908 with the Deswal lineage of *B* over the inheritance of land. An adopted member of *E*, who came to the village with his brother, died issueless and two hundred *bighas* of his land were claimed by the families of *B*. The case went to court and dragged on for many years. *B* finally won. However, a Dabas *panchayat* was called and *B* returned one hundred *bighas* to assuage *E*.

[3] It should be noted that until 1946, for a period of eight years, the present members of *B* and *E*, along with half the members of *D*, were the members of a single large faction.

The relationship between E and A, which we have designated as the third preference of E, is considerably weaker than those described earlier. Seven of the nine families of E visit very rarely and only occasionally smoke hookah together with the members of A; the women have no ceremonial relations with one another except for one ceremony of the exhibition of the dowry at marriage. However, the seven families of E still send the traditional invitation to marriage ceremonies to one male member of each of several families in A. Two families of E are close neighbors of one of the leading lineages of A. They visit each other's houses, smoke together, will act as host for each other's guests, and invite each other, including the women, to all ceremonies.

E has fought a number of cases against A in recent years, as well as many years ago. The last case occurred about fifteen years ago, when E supported members of D and E against A, and in another case when A remained neutral while B was fighting E. This mutual neutrality tended to reduce the earlier hostility. Finally, in 1947 E and A united together, in the Muslim house case mentioned earlier, against the headman's lineage within B. But when B won the case, E dropped out and refused to renew it as desired by A because of the pressure of the Deswal lineage of B.

The relationship between E and C is rather complicated. Here we find a combination of hostile and friendly relations which on the whole tend to cancel each other and thereby make for a neutral quality. Indeed, most of the fourth preference relationships approximate neutrality. None of the families of E and C invite one another to traditional ceremonies, nor do they have any economic relations at present. Two of the families of E who smoke at the hookah group of A have developed quite friendly relations with it. Only rarely do members of E and C smoke at each other's hookah groups. Because of their aggressive nature, the leaders of C sometimes attempt to establish their superiority over E, boasting that they have helped them in the past.

The undercurrent of hostility between these two factions is expressed by their attitudes toward each other. Members of C boast that they have given loans to E to help them marry their daughters as well as to help them in a court case. They also sometimes remind listeners that about twenty years ago C saved members of E from a beating by members of B who were outraged because of allegations of illicit sexual relations between a married man of E and a woman of B. Similarly, they boast of having helped members of E redirect the flow of water in one of the subcanals which had been forcibly blocked off by inhabitants of the adjoining village of Rasulpur, who knew that members of E were too weak to oppose them. On the other hand members of *C* also boast of having successfully fought a case against *E* about sixty years ago, which cost *E* its *lambardari*.

For its part, the members of *E* are also quite critical of members of *C*, claiming that they are aggressive, boastful, and deceitful. However, the attitudes of *E* toward *C* are much milder than those of *B* and *F* toward *C*.

The relations of *E* to *F* are similar to those of *E* to *C*, for *F*, like *C*, is a very isolated group. Except for occasional visiting and smoking together, there are no ceremonial, economic, or political relations between the two. The fact that the leader of *F* is a close friend of the headman's lineage of *B*, which is hostile to *E*, does not improve the relationship between *F* and *E*. However, this potentially hostile influence is partially canceled by the fact that *F* also has friendly relations with the Deswal lineage of *B*, which in turn has close relations with *E*.

There have been neither quarrels nor collaboration between *E* and *F* in the four years since *F* has emerged as a faction. It is significant, however, that the two groups do not use abusive language against each other, thereby making for a kind of stable neutrality.

It is interesting to note that in terms of sociogram analysis the preference of *E* for *F* is fourth while that of *F* for *E* is second. This indicates how much more isolated *F* is than *E* in relationship to the other factions.

· JAT AND NON-JAT FACTION RELATIONS ·

The non-Jats in the village are split into a number of factions along caste lines and within castes. The number and strength of these factions are shown in Table 9.

It will be seen that the average size of family of most of the non-Jats is much smaller than that of the Jats, in some cases less than half

TABLE 9

POPULATION CHARACTERISTICS OF NON-JAT FACTIONS, RAMPUR, 1953

Caste	Faction	Total Number of Families	Total Number of Family Members	Average Size of Family	Number of Adult Males
Camar	*a*	16	81	5.06	16
Camar	*b*	5	26	5.2	6
Brahman		15	110	7.33	23
Bhangi	*a*	5	30	6	5
Bhangi	*b*	5	22	4.4	6
Kumhar		7	39	5.57	10

as large. Camar *b* and the two Bhangi factions are so weak in total
numbers and in adult males that they are quite ineffective as
independent factions from both a social and an economic point of
view. But they think of themselves as separate factions. On the
whole the non-Jats depend much more heavily upon intervillage relations for their ceremonial life than do the Jats. Moreover, all except the Camars are still occupationally dependent upon the Jats.

In terms of our socioeconomic scale the Brahmans are clearly at
the top and the Bhangis at the bottom of the ladder. The Brahmans
are twice as well off as the Camars and the Camars twice as well off
as the Bhangis. (See Table 10.)

TABLE 10

AVERAGE SOCIOECONOMIC SCORE PER FAMILY OF
NON-JAT FACTIONS, RAMPUR, 1953

Caste	Average Socioeconomic Score
Brahman	9.53
Camar *b*	4.66
Camar *a*	4.17
Kumhar	2.18
Bhangi *a*	2.46
Bhangi *b*	1.50

A comparison of the distribution of Jats and non-Jats shows that
approximately 41 per cent were in the lowest group, I*a*, 56 per cent
in I*b*, 1 per cent in II, and 0 per cent in the top group, III.

In examining the distribution pattern of wealth within each faction we find that only among the Brahmans is there a single family
with sufficient wealth to keep the group united. Moreover, twelve out
of the fifteen Brahman families are in the upper-lower group whereas
most of the non-Jats are in the lower-lower. However, the Camars
rank next to the Brahmans in their distribution in the upper-lower or
Group I*b*. This reflects the tendency toward upward mobility of the
Camar group in the village, resulting primarily from the large number of jobs they have had outside the village. Since 1943 they have
attained complete occupational independence from the Jats and this
has increased the tension between the Camars and the Jats. Only
the Camars and the Brahmans feel strong enough to take an independent stand on some issues in their relations with the Jats.

The pattern of leadership within the non-Jats follows the older
traditional lines in which the older members are the spokesmen of the
various groups. Only among the Camars is education beginning to
enter as a new factor in leadership.

• INTERFACTION RELATIONS
AMONG THE NON-JATS •

The split within the Camar group dates back to the twenties, when the families in Camar *b* were accused by the other Camars in the village of betraying the Harijan struggle against the payment of the house tax to the Jats. Later in the thirties the split was intensified when the Camars of a neighboring village, aided by Camar *b*, abducted a relative of the leader of Camar *a*. The Camars of Rampur held a *panchayat* to persuade the members of Camar *b* to return the girl. When this failed, a *panchayat* of a few hundred villagers was called. Again no agreement was arrived at. The case finally went to court and three of the five members of Camar *b* were arrested. They were released with the help of the Jat headman who posted a bond for them. The case was finally won by Camar *a*, but it resulted in the emergence of two clear-cut factions among Camars, not only in Rampur but also in most of the villages of the area. Since the watchman of the village is from Camar *b*, the group feels more closely tied to the Jats, especially to *D* and *F*, than to their fellow Camars.

The split within the Bhangis took place about thirty-five years ago over the question of the inheritance of leadership after the death of the Bhangi leader. The son of the dead leader was challenged in his assumption of leadership by a Bhangi of a different lineage who was much older and claimed to be a "brother" of the dead leader. However, since the mother of this man had two husbands, one of whom was not of this village, some of the Bhangis claimed that the man's father was not of their clan and had no rights to ceremonial or secular leadership. As a result of this quarrel a split developed, after which they stopped attending each other's marriage ceremonies. In 1944, while most of the adult males from Bhangi *a* were away in military service, the members of Bhangi *b* constructed a wall encroaching upon the house sites of *a* and thereby took possession of the trees. The case was reported to the police by Jat *A*. Again the headman of Jat *B* sided with Bhangi *b* while Jat *A* sided with Bhangi *a*, but the latter lost out.

The Brahmans, consisting of two lineages, are united within the village and attend each other's ceremonies. They have very close relations with Jat *D*, whose land they hold as occupancy tenants. Unlike other non-Jat factions, they have been acting as an independent unit for many years, both because of their economic independence as occupancy tenants and because of the mutual dependence of Brahmans and Jats upon one another on ceremonial occasions.[4] The

4 It should be noted that although Brahmans in the village of Rampur have not

houses of the Brahmans are found in two groups, one a compact unit on the outskirts of the village and the other a unit inside the village. The two groups visit each other frequently.

The Kumhars, who live together in a compact unit, are the descendants of families who have lived for hundreds of years in this village. The Kumhars are all related to one another and are generally consulted on village-wide matters by Jats, with whom they still maintain their traditional occupational relations.

In Chart 4 we see that each of the Camar groups gives its allegiance to separate Jat factions which are hostile to each other and also to two factions which are neutral. The relationship between Camar *a* and Jat *D* has been quite friendly for many years. This was expressed in 1932 during an Arya Samaj (a Hindu religious reform movement) conference in the village when one family from *D*, alone among all the Jats in the village, acceded to the Arya Samaj request to take water with the Camars. Similarly, in the 1943 quarrel between Jats and non-Jats one of the lineages of Jat *D* supported the Camars. Again, only a few years ago one of the Jats of *D* gave one hundred rupees to a Camar *a* family to help them marry their daughter. In 1949, during a quarrel of Camars with one of the leaders of Jat *B* over the ownership of land, *D* was inclined toward the Camars, though it did not support them as openly and actively as did Jat factions *A* and *E*.

The friendship between Camar *a* and Jat *A* is based upon their common hostility toward Jat factions *B* and *F*. During the 1949 quarrel between the Camars and Jat *B*, the members of Jat *A*, along with *F*, supported the Camars in their court fight. It should also be noted that during the boycott of Camars by Jats in 1943, one of the leading families of Jat *A* gave milk to the Camars, for which it was fined by the Jat *panchayat*. *A* also gave some support to the Camars in a house-tax case of 1938, which will be described later.

The friendship between Camar *b* and Jat factions *B* and *F* developed in 1935 as a result of Jat *B*'s aid to Camar *b* during its quarrels with Camar *a*. The friendship was strengthened in 1947 when the headmen of Jat *B* were instrumental in getting a man from Camar *b* appointed as village watchman.

One Bhangi faction owes its preference to Jat *A* and the other to *D*. Although Bhangi *b* has no hostile relations with any of the Jat factions, Bhangi *a* is hostile to Jat factions *B* and *F*, the very groups to which Camar *b* is most closely attached. This has the effect of weakening the unity of Bhangis and Camars. On the other hand, Bhangi

---

been acting as priests for many years they still rank quite high socially and are invited to various ceremonies as a token of respect.

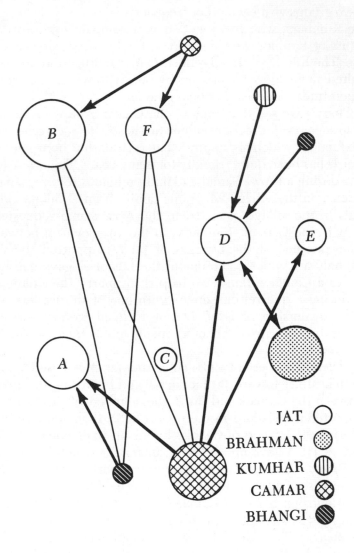

CHART 4. *Sociogram of village factions showing primary and hostile relations of non-Jats to Jats.*

a and Camar *a* have close relations and their loyalties and hostilities with respect to the Jats follow similar patterns. Both of these Harijan factions accuse Bhangi *b* and Camar *b* of betraying Harijan unity and being dominated by the Jats.

The Camars appear to be the only low-caste group in the village who have attempted to take an independent stand against the traditions of Jat domination and to champion the cause of the Harijans in this and the surrounding villages. Four factors have combined to make this possible: (1) increased occupational independence, (2) the refusal of the Jats to employ Camars as agricultural laborers on the traditional grain-share basis because of the high price of grain, (3) the increased educational opportunity for the Harijans, and (4) the encouragement and support received from the Congress, and, much earlier, the Arya Samaj.

These trends began at least as early as the First World War when some Camars found outside employment. After the war, when the Camars faced unemployment, they found that the Jats had begun to do agricultural labor themselves because of the high price of grain, and no longer wanted them as field hands. Of course a contributing factor was the increased population among the Jats.

There is a growing sense of Harijan solidarity despite the existence of splits among them. This solidarity has been encouraged by the special consideration given to the Harijans in education and in employment opportunities. These special privileges have increased the hostility of the Jats, who somewhat ironically demand equal treatment and opportunity for Jats on the ground that some of them are just as poor as Harijans.

The interfaction relations of both Jats and non-Jats extend across village lines. There is a group of about twenty-five villages which are the most actively connected in this faction network. In intervillage relations the faction picture is considerably simplified, since as a rule there are only two major factions per caste in each village. In all but one of the past eight district board elections which we have studied, there were never more than two candidates, each backed by a faction, from the constituency.

· THE PROCESS OF FACTION FORMATION ·

To understand better the process of the formation, splitting, and reformation of factions, we must examine the history of factions in the village. This history can be divided into five periods which reveal four separate stages in faction development. These stages are presented graphically in Chart 5.

In Stage 1 we find two hostile factions along *pana* lines. In Stage 2 there are still only two major factions along *pana* lines but some of the membership shifts back and forth. It should be noted that Stage 2 sometimes reverts back to Stage 1 since there is always the pull of kinship bonds. In Stage 3 a new faction develops, drawing members from each of the two earlier factions, and all three are hostile to one another. In Stage 4 the present stage is reached. Here we see the pattern described earlier whereby each *pana* has three factions, two of which are hostile to each other and the third neutral, with the strongest friendly relations across *pana* lines. Now let us turn to an examination of the outline of events in each of the historical periods we have delineated. It will be helpful to the reader to refer back to Chart 5 as the discussion develops.

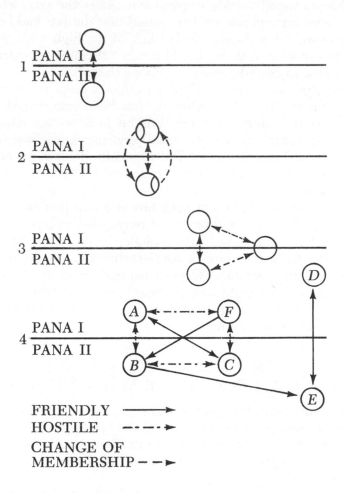

CHART 5. *Stages in the development of Jat factions, 1800–1953.*

· FIRST PERIOD ·

The earliest horizons in social organization that can be reconstructed
with the aid of informants date back to a period about 120 to 150
years ago when the ancestors of the present-day members of Teka
tholla (faction *D*) invited in their sisters' sons who were naturally
not of the same clan as the Dabas (Kharabs), and gave them a part
of their nine hundred *bighas* of land. During this period the Kharabs
and members of Teka *tholla* constituted one *pana* (which we shall
call *pana* I) and one faction. Ancestors of present-day Jaimel and
Harditt formed another faction and *pana* (which we shall call *pana*
II). Thus we see that in this first stage the faction and *pana* were
synonymous.

· SECOND PERIOD, 1835–90 ·

About twenty years before the Mutiny of 1857 the Dabas members
of Teka *tholla* quarreled with their *bhanjas* or sisters' sons, who were
trying to grab more and more land, and joined the Dabas of the opposite faction against the Kharabs. However, the Dabas had been
seriously weakened somewhat earlier when one of their own *panchayats* had expelled a strong group of Dabas families who were accused of murdering the person who had brought in the Kharabs.[5]
After these families were expelled, the Kharabs took possession of
the greater part of Teka *tholla* land and drove most of the remaining
Dabas out of the village. A few years before the Mutiny of 1857 a
large multivillage Dabas *panchayat* was called and it was decided to
bring the Dabas back to Rampur. Most of the Dabas regained their
land, but the lineage of Teka *tholla* which had originally invited the
Kharabs could not get their land. Again, a Dabas *panchayat* was
called and a tax of eight *annas* per family was assessed to raise funds
to fight the case in court against the Kharabs. The case continued for
four years and the Dabas finally won the decision. However, the
leader of the victorious family was poisoned on the very day of the
court decision and the court documents which he carried were
stolen by the Kharabs. The Mutiny of 1857 occurred in the same
month, and with the ensuing confusion in the years that followed the
case could not be pursued and the Kharabs remained in possession of
the land thereafter.

During the four years that the above case was in the courts there
were other violent struggles between the Kharabs and Dabas fac-

---

[5] Most informants claim that the Kharabs killed this man but managed to cast
suspicion on the Dabas.

tions in the village; the most serious involved the abduction by one of the Kharabs of a Dabas girl from a neighboring village.[6] This led to physical violence in which fifteen men were wounded and a Kharab killed. Some Dabas were arrested but were freed with the breakdown of law and order during the period of the mutiny.

Still another quarrel during this period takes us back to the Teka lineage. When this lineage returned to the village they invited in another group of *bhanjas* locally remembered as "Bhupenwallias," who, following the example of the Kharabs and with their help, took away most of Teka *tholla* land. A Dabas multivillage *panchayat* was again called, funds were raised, the case was successfully fought in the courts, and the "Bhupenwallias" were ousted from the village.

· THIRD PERIOD, 1890–1915 ·

In the beginning of the third period we find that Teka *tholla* left their Dabas brethren and allies and realigned themselves with the Kharabs. However, after some years a split developed within Teka *tholla* and one important lineage headed by a strong and popular leader left the group and joined the opposing faction. A number of events combined to bring about this realignment. In 1890 a serious quarrel arose over land boundaries between the Brahmans and the Dhamariya group of Jats which led to the death of one Brahman and the infliction of critical injuries on another four. When the case went to court the Brahmans were supported by the Kharabs as well as by Teka *tholla*, the latter because it felt responsible for the Brahmans, having brought them to the village, the former because of their enmity to the Dhamariyas, who had killed one of their members. The case went through a few courts and the Dhamariyas were finally freed.[7] This common action of the Kharabs with Teka *tholla* brought them together.

The next shift in group membership involved a split within one *pana* which occurred as a result of the headman case described earlier, whereby a family in Harditt *tholla* lost its headman to Jaimel *tholla* as a result of the efforts of Jaimel. This family left its lineage and joined the Teka-Harditt group of *pana* I.

About five years later a difference within Teka *tholla* developed over an issue of land inheritance. One of the family heads in Teka *tholla* gave half of the land of his issueless deceased brother to the

---

[6] The family which suffered this dishonor is locally referred to as Muc-kate, or "Those who lost their mustaches," that is, their honor.

[7] Because the leaders of a nearby five-village unit helped the Dhamariyas in this case, they have remained close friends and have been supporting each other's candidates in elections.

sons of his paternal cross-cousin, whose wife he had married. After his death his sons were induced by members of the opposite *pana* (II) to take the case to court. However, the case was dropped and Teka *tholla* split, half of the members aligning themselves with the opposite *pana*.

Still another change of membership across *pana* lines occurred in about 1900 when a member of Jaimel lineage was murdered by someone of another lineage of Jaimel, leading the first lineage to join the opposite *pana*.

Thus at the end of this period there were still only two major factions in the village. One faction, primarily of *pana* Dhan Singh (*pana* I), consisted of the following: all of the Kharabs, one-half of Teka families, one lineage of Jaimel, and one family of Harditt. The second faction, primarily of Jaimel, consisted of the rest of the families. There was hostility between these two factions and they fought a bitter court case against one another during the preparation of one of the village men's houses in 1910.

• FOURTH PERIOD, 1915–39 •

During the fourth period a new faction developed, drawing its members partly from each of the two former factions. This third group, hostile to the other two, was formed when the Teka families who were divided, half in *pana* I and half in *pana* II, joined together and took along with them some members from each of the two earlier groups, thus forming a heterogeneous unit. The three groups now became a triangle of hostility and fought famous court cases against one another, most of which have been mentioned earlier in our discussion of interfaction relations.

It should be noted that these twenty-four years were a transition period during which the bases for new patterns of leadership and factionalism were prepared as a result of the many economic and educational changes which followed World War I. These new forces led to considerable shifting about of faction membership and finally resulted in the emergence of our present-day factions.

• FIFTH PERIOD, 1939–53 •

During the fifth period the Kharab faction of *pana* I split in two, forming the present-day factions *A* and *F,* and the mixed faction split three ways into the present-day factions *D, B,* and *E.* The third group remained stable and is our faction *C.* The specific causes for these splits have already been discussed. However, from a broader point of view the increase in numbers of factions can be seen as the result of forces which had been growing in the third period but which received their expression later. This will be discussed on the following pages.

· C O N C L U S I O N S ·

By way of conclusion let us attempt some answers to two sets of questions which have implications for both theoretical and practical purposes. First, what are the causes of factions? How stable are they? Under what conditions do they develop or break down? Second, what does the study of factions reveal about the nature of village social organization, leadership patterns, and value systems? What are the implications of these data for practical programs of rural reconstruction?

It is clear from our data that factions are an old, ingrained pattern in village life and need to be considered as a basic aspect of traditional village social organization along with castes, *thollas, panas,* clans, lineages, and other groupings. Moreover, in view of a common misconception, it is important to note that they are not political groupings, or temporary alliances of individuals to fight court cases, although some of them do take on political functions and become involved in power politics. Rather, they are primarily kinship groupings which carry on important social, economic, and ceremonial functions in addition to their factional struggles against one another. It is these positive functions which account for the remarkable stability of these groups over the years. When changes in faction membership do occur it is the family and sometimes the large extended family which shifts allegiance from one faction to another, rather than individuals.

Viewed broadly, one of the fundamental causes of factions is the insecurity of village life with its scarcity of land and limited resources. More specifically, we have found that new factions developed as a result of (1) quarrels over the inheritance of land, (2) quarrels over the adoption of sons (the presence of an only son in a family makes a potentially charged situation because of the threat from the *hakikis,* or inheritance claimants), (3) quarrels over housesites and irrigation rights, (4) quarrels over sexual offenses, (5) murders, and finally (6) quarrels between the castes. The villagers sum this all up by a popular saying that both factions and quarrels revolve around wealth, women, and land.

The sharp increase in the number of factions since 1939 seems to be related to the gradual accumulation and culmination of forces which had been at work in the previous fifty years. Chief among these forces were the rapid rise in population, the gradual weakening of the joint family, increased vertical economic mobility, with some families going up and others down, and increased education. Whereas earlier quarrels had led to minor shiftings of members from one faction to another, quarrels in this later period, when families were larger and had increased sources of income, led to the splitting off of larger units which were strong enough both socially and economically to form independent factions.

However, in the long run these same forces which have led to the mushrooming of factions may bring about the elimination of factions based on kinship. This trend can already be sensed, although only faintly, in Rampur, where we find increasing instances of members of one joint family joining up with opposite factions. Moreover, education is beginning to provide a new basis for unity between individuals on a nonkinship level. For example, the children of opposing village factions who have been to a higher school together are developing bonds which in the future may affect faction alignments. The elimination of poverty and ignorance, the raising of living standards, the continued increase in education, and the gradual incorporation of the peasants into the mainstream of national life may in the future weaken or eliminate factions based on kinship.

Our findings in Rampur suggest that the community in the sense of a cohesive and united village community or in the sense of the American neighborhood, village, or trading center community hardly exists. Caste and kinship still form the core of village social organization and this splits the village into separate communities which have their close affiliations across village lines. As we have seen earlier, there are occasions when the village acts as a unit. However, these are relatively infrequent and with the weakening of the old and traditional *jajmani* system the segmentation within the village is all the more striking, nor has it been replaced by any new uniting forms of social organization.

However, the weakness of the village community is partially compensated for by the strength of intervillage networks. The persistence of these traditional large-scale intervillage networks for ceremonial and *panchayat* purposes provides a natural grouping of villages and ready-made channels of communication which might be effectively utilized by the Community Projects Administration in its organization of village circles and in other aspects of its work. Moreover, the fact that the village in northern India is not a self-sufficient isolate for social and economic purposes suggests that the process of diffusion of new knowledge and practices may occur in India at a more rapid rate than in other countries where the village is a highly isolated, integrated, and cohesive unit. For example, our study of innovations in agriculture over the past thirty years showed that new seeds and practices came in from villages which formed part of the *panchayat* and kinship network.

The kinship basis of village social organization, whereby an individual's primary loyalties are to his own family and lineage, shows the difficulties ahead in building a modern secular democratic system based upon voting and the delegation of authority to selected individuals to represent large masses of people. The theoretical assumption behind the democratic system based on voting is that the individual is an independent, thinking being capable of making his own decisions and ready to do so. However, in a kinship-organized society such as village Rampur, it is the large extended family which is the basic unit for most decision-making. At best, voting becomes an extended family process which violates the spirit of individuality inherent in the Western electoral system.

Leadership in Rampur is limited to faction leadership and is primarily of a protective and defensive nature in which each faction or combination of factions defends its family interests. The leader is essentially a spokesman for a family or a group of related families and has little authority to make independent decisions or to exercise power over the group.

Village-wide leadership does not yet exist and the idea of positive constructive leadership in the public interest is only now gradually beginning to emerge, particularly in connection with the establishment of village schools. As yet there are no village heroes or outstanding citizens who are popular for their contribution to village welfare as a whole.

The outstanding characteristics of Jat leaders are the possession of wealth, good family background, a reputation for being charitable and giving elaborate feasts, advanced age, education, influence with townspeople, free time to pursue the interests of the group, humility, hospitality, trustworthiness, speaking ability, and the support of a large extended family.

The fact that leadership is spread out rather than concentrated is a great advantage to the village-level worker. Since one out of every four or five heads of families holds some leadership position, the village-level worker is bound to come into contact with leaders even in a random sampling of co-operators.

Other important and perhaps distinctive aspects of leadership patterns include the following:

1. The effort to minimize rank and status differences within the castes. For example, it was difficult to find out who the leaders were by direct questioning. A typical response to the question "Who are the leaders?" was "Every Jat is a leader." This playing down of individual differences is one of the crucial values in this culture.

2. The reluctance to delegate authority or leadership functions to any single individual over a period of time without provision for frequent consultation with his faction members in decision-making. This is one of the main reasons for the lack of popularity of the new official *panchayat* which is based upon elections. Since the three official *panchayat* members from Rampur represent only three of the twelve factions, the villagers do not consider this body as truly representative of their interests. Consequently, the old traditional caste and village *panchayats* enjoy much more prestige and authority than the official *panchayat*. When village-wide public issues, such as land consolidation and the building of a school, arose in the past few years, they were entrusted to the caste *panchayat* rather than to the official *panchayat*, which has already become a court for personal litigations.

3. The almost complete absence of youth leadership. That age is still very important can be seen from the fact that most leaders are over forty. However, youth leadership is slowly beginning to emerge with increased education. Younger educated men who live in the village are acting as representatives in school and *panchayat* matters, and are coming forward in village discussions of public issues.

4. Women have no direct role in leadership. They do not attend *panchayats*.

The implications of our findings for community development work are many-faceted. The existence of factions, the persistence of kinship loyalties, the absence of village-wide leadership, and the limited identification with larger groups—all present some hurdles for community development. It is essential that all those connected with village work understand the complexity of village social organization so that they can utilize that organization most effectively in the attainment of their goals. If those sponsoring community development work desire to encourage the breakdown of factions and the development of village-wide and nation-wide loyalties, the first step must be to become aware of the existing factions, their nature and dynamics. To ignore these factions or, just as bad, to admit that they exist and then forget about them will simply help to perpetuate rather than eliminate them. It is only in action programs around common goals that factionalism can be reduced and perhaps eventually eliminated.

However, it must be emphasized that the small groups which we have called factions have their positive aspects for community development work: (1) They provide ready-made communication channels to the people. If a village-level worker reaches even a single leader in each faction, his message is sure to reach all the families of the village. (2) They provide ready-made co-operative groups for community projects, and thereby obviate the greater amount of work that would be necessary in a less organized and more individualistic type of society. (3) The organization of leadership on a faction basis provides for a much closer representation of the people than is possible in that more sophisticated and monolithic type of political democracy of some modern Western nations which is based on delegated authority. In view of this, it may be desirable to build upon the present faction organization and sense of wider community loyalties rather than to destroy the traditional organization.

Our data underline the well-known dangers of working only or primarily through the official headmen of a village. If one followed this approach in the case of Rampur he would find it difficult to reach all the villagers, and even worse, he might offend and estrange a large portion of them. As we have seen earlier, both of the official headmen happen to belong to a single Jat faction, B, which along with F is hostile to A and C. Our own field research experience illustrates what might readily happen to an action program. We first established contact with the villagers through the aid of a native of the village who happened to be an agricultural government officer. His family belonged to B so our early contacts were with the members of that faction, including the two headmen. We worked in the village for over six weeks before we could break out of this small circle without offending our friends who, it seems, consciously or unconsciously were keeping us away from the group toward which they were hostile. Our contacts slowly spread from members of B to F, D, and E, but it was not until we systematically set out to study the social organization of the village that we realized the importance of A and C, which comprise over 30 per cent of all the Jat families. Moreover, the leaders of these groups knew we were working in the village but did not approach us. And when on a few occasions we asked the official headmen to call the villagers together, they avoided contacting members of C and A.

In terms of the interfaction relationships in this village, it is clear that D and E would be the crucial ones for village-level workers to work through since most of the communication between the villagers becomes channelized through these two relatively neutral and very influential groups.

Knowledge of the social organization of the village might also enable one to channel the hostility between groups in positive and constructive directions by encouraging their competition toward village-wide goals. The possibilities of this approach received dramatic confirmation in an experimental meeting called by our staff for the purpose of checking, in a relatively controlled situation, the findings of our study. If our findings were accurate, we might expect that a meeting of all the faction leaders would result in the expression of aggression between the hostile groups. A meeting was called and each of the members of the field staff kept careful notes on the content and sequence of all that transpired. Less than half an hour after the meeting began, the factional groupings became glaringly apparent, with open attacks one against another. The purpose of the meeting had been explained in terms of asking the leaders to decide upon some priority among the things they would like to do themselves to improve their village, as part of their participation in the community development scheme. After much discussion and some controversy, the leaders agreed that the most urgent need of the village which might feasibly be met with the aid of the Community Projects Administration was the cleaning of the village pond. However, they emphasized that although they were willing to contribute labor they could not pay a single *pie*. Indeed, they sounded as if they were doing a favor to the community projects by agreeing to do something for their own village. Finally, one of the more aggressive and sophisticated faction leaders stood up and said that some money could be collected if it were done on a group basis and that his group would contribute one hundred *rupees* more than any other group in the village. This started the ball rolling, and soon the leader of an opposing faction stood up and said that his group would also contribute.

Another incident which occurred a few days later showed the importance of understanding the faction relations across village lines. The project executive officer came into the village accompanied by a friend who was the principal of a nearby secondary school and an outstanding leader of one of the two factions active in this area on an intervillage level. He asked the headmen to call the villagers together, and a few of the leaders and villagers of B, F, D, and E were called. Interviews with members of A and C later revealed that they suspected the neutrality and motives of the project officer because he traveled in the company of an opposite faction leader. Moreover, the absence of representatives from opposing factions in the village made the meeting dull, and the officer left feeling that these villagers were apathetic. Two days later he returned to the village, this time calling together the leaders of all factions. The villagers showed considerably more enthusiasm and arrangements were made to begin work on the pond.

It should be emphasized that both the theoretical and the practical findings of this study would be considerably enhanced by additional comparative studies of village social organization in other parts of India. Studies of social organization are particularly crucial for any evaluation effort which attempts to understand the effects of the community development program upon the culture and psychology of the people.

In the past few years a great deal has been written and spoken about the meaning and goals of the community development program and its crucial importance for the future of India. Throughout this discussion two dominant themes have appeared—one economic, the other psychological. On the economic side the stress has been upon the goals of improved technology, increased production, and a higher standard of living. On the psychological side the goals have been stated in terms of enhancing the spiritual values of the villagers, developing initiative and respect for the dignity of labor, and changing the total world outlook.

Between these two levels of description or analysis, the economic and the psychological or spiritual, there has been a gaping abyss which many have been trying to bridge by the simple statement that economics and psychology are related. In some quarters it has been assumed that economic development would almost automatically change the psychology of the people. Indeed, I have heard speakers state categorically that it is difficult to measure progress toward the spiritual goals since they are imponderables, but that the clearest evidence of change in individual psychology is increased production. Such thinking agrees neither with the findings of modern social science nor with the philosophical traditions of India.

Our study suggests that a crucially important middle term in the economic-psychological equation needs to receive more attention and can help to resolve the dilemma created by the above dichotomy. This term is social organization. The middle ground of social organization is the framework within which the economic and psychological factors operate and interact and must be clearly understood. On the village level the so-called imponderables or psychological factors can be studied most effectively in terms of what happens to the social organization (the family structure, the caste system, the class system, factions), voluntary local organizations, and local government. Certainly, for sponsors of community development programs this sociological approach would seem to be more practical than the approach of individual psychology which, if applied scientifically, would mean the administration of psychological tests to villagers to determine whether their mentality has been changed by the program.

The relative emphasis upon economics and psychology rather than sociology in India is probably a passing phase. The very term "social organization" still seems to carry abstract and negative connotations to administrators. In part this is due to the inherent difficulties in studying social relations, which are subtle and complex and have to be inferred from behavior rather than studied directly. Economics seems much more practical and concrete, and psychology, too, has a stronger ideological basis in traditional Indian culture because of the Hindu philosophical emphasis upon introspection and salvation through individual effort and self-improvement rather than through planned changes in the very structure of the society.

It is through the integration of all three disciplines—economics, sociology-anthropology, and psychology—that the social scientists can make their most effective contribution both to the study of society and to action programs.

16

Caste and the *Jajmani* System in a North Indian Village[*]

Although there is a great deal of literature about the caste system of India, very little attention has been paid to its economic aspects.[1] Most books and articles on caste have concerned themselves with the problems of its historical origin and development, with the rules and sanctions governing endogamy, food taboos, ritual purity, caste-ranking, and the more dramatic injustices of untouchability. It is common in works about caste for the author to list the castes of a particular region with some account of the traditional occupation of each; but it is a curious fact that the author generally avoids what might logically seem to be a next step—an analysis of how these groups interact with one another in the production and exchange of goods and services. William H. Wiser, in a book called *The Hindu Jajmani System*,[2] was the first to describe in detail how such goods

[*] Appeared originally as an article written in 1956 in collaboration with Victor Barnouw, *Scientific Monthly*, Vol. 83, pp. 66–81.

[1] A caste is an endogamous social unit, membership in which is determined by birth; it is often associated with a particular occupation and with restrictions about the acceptance of food and water from other caste groups. Castes tend to be ranked, with the Brahmans being traditionally assigned the highest status and "untouchable" castes like the Bhangi (sweeper) the lowest.

[2] Lucknow, India: Lucknow Publishing House, 1936. There have been a few other works dealing with the relationship between caste and economics, notably S. S. Nehru's *Caste and Credit in the Rural Area* (Calcutta: Longmans, Green, 1932). Kumar Goshal has emphasized the economic basis for the caste system in the following words: "Hindu reformers failed to make any headway against

and services are exchanged in a rural Indian village. It is greatly to Wiser's credit that he was able to characterize *jajmani* relations *as a system*. Some knowledge of this system is crucial for an understanding of the economic aspects of caste in rural India.

Under this system each caste group within a village is expected to give certain standardized services to the families of other castes. A Khati (carpenter) repairs tools, for example, a Nai (barber) cuts hair; but they do not necessarily perform these services for everyone. Each man works for a particular family or group of families with which he has hereditary ties. His father worked for the same families before him, and his son will continue to work for them, the occupation or service being determined by caste. The family or family head served by an individual is known as his *jajman*,[3] while the man who performs service is known as the *jajman's kamin* or *kam karne-wala* (literally, worker). These are the terms used in northwestern India; in other parts of India where the system prevails other terms may be used.

---

the caste system because it was rooted in the economy of India, and only a change in that economy could bring about a change in the social structure. The economic system was stabilized at a low level, based upon more or less self-sufficient village communities which combined agriculture and handicrafts. Production was on a small scale, and for consumption rather than exchange. Everything moved in narrow, well-worn grooves fixed by custom. It was a pre-capitalist economic system, whose static quality could have been altered only by an expanding dynamic market for exchange of commodities. As long as this was lacking, the social relationships of the people could not possibly be altered." (Kumar Goshal, *The People of India* [New York: Sheridan House, 1944], p. 59.) O. C. Cox was also aware of the importance of economic factors, as the following quotation shows: "The caste structure is fundamentally a labor structure, a system of interrelated services originating in specialized groups and traditionalized in a religious matrix." Cox quotes Pramathanath Bannerjea as follows: "The chief economic significance of the system is that it fixes absolutely the supply of any kind of labor. The scope given for the play of competition thus becomes limited, and consequently the law of demand and supply is rendered inoperative or oppressive in its operation. When any change takes place in the economic world, labor is unable to adjust itself. . . . Wages and prices have very often to be regulated by custom or some artificial means." (O. C. Cox, *Caste, Class, and Race* [New York, 1948], pp. 62, 67.) An awareness of the relationship between caste and economy, however, seems to be missing in even such a standard book as J. H. Hutton's *Caste in India* (London: Oxford University Press), in the revised edition of which (1951) there is no reference to the *jajmani* system or to Wiser's work.

[3] Webster's Dictionary (1950) defines *jajman* as "a person by whom a Brahman is hired to perform religious services; hence, a patron; client." The word derives from the Sanskrit *yajamana*, the present participle of *yaj*, to sacrifice. The term ultimately came to be used for anyone standing in the relationship of employer.

It is a characteristic of this system to operate without much exchange of money. For it is not an open-market economy, and the ties between *jajman* and *kamin* are not like those of employer and employee in a capitalistic system. The *jajman* compensates his *kamins* for their work through periodic payments in cash or grain, made throughout the year on a daily, monthly, or biyearly basis. *Kamins* may also receive benefits such as free food, clothing, and residence site, the use of certain tools and raw materials, etc. To Wiser these concessions represent the strength of the system and are more important than the monetary payments.[4] Despite the increased use of money in recent years, the peasants nowadays tend to prefer grain payments to cash, since grain prices have risen so enormously in the past decade.[5]

When Wiser wrote his book he did not know how general or widespread this system might be, although he referred to some passages in the works of other writers which suggested that it had a wide range of diffusion. This conclusion is supported by more recent studies, which give evidence for much the same kind of system in eastern Uttar Pradesh,[6] parts of Malabar and Cochin,[7] Mysore District,[8] Tanjore,[9] Hyderabad,[10] Gujarat,[11] and the Punjab.[12] Regional differences of course appear.

A major function of the *jajmani* system is to assure a stable labor supply for the dominant agricultural caste in a particular region by limiting the mobility of the lower castes, especially those who assist in agricultural work. If a *kamin* leaves the village, he must get someone to take his place—usually a member of the same joint family.

[4] Wiser, 1936: pp. 6–11.

[5] See E. Eames, "Some Aspects of Urban Migration from a Village in North Central India," *Eastern Anthropologist*, Vol. 8 (1954), p. 19.

[6] M. Opler and R. D. Singh, "The Division of Labor in an Indian Village," in C. S. Coon (ed.), *A Reader in General Anthropology* (New York, 1948), pp. 464–96; N. S. Reddy, "Functional Relations of Lohars in a North Indian Village," *Eastern Anthropologist*, Vol. 8 (1955), p. 129.

[7] E. J. Miller, "Village Structure in North Kerala," *Economic Weekly* (Bombay, Feb. 9, 1952), pp. 159–64.

[8] M. N. Srinivas, "The Social System of a Mysore Village," in M. Marriott (ed.), *Village India; Studies in the Little Community* (Menasha, Wis.: American Anthropological Association, 1955), pp. 1–35; A. R. Beals, "Interplay Among Factors of Change in a Mysore Village," *ibid.*, pp. 78–101.

[9] E. K. Gough, "The Social Structure of a Tanjore Village," *ibid.*, pp. 36–52.

[10] S. C. Dube, *Indian Village* (Ithaca: Cornell University Press, 1955).

[11] Gittel Steed, lecture notes, hectographed.

[12] M. L. Darling, *Wisdom and Waste in the Punjab Village* (London: Oxford University Press, 1934).

This does not usually involve sale, and the *jajman* is not likely to object, so long as the position is filled. But such transfers are rare.[13] The *kamins* have valued rights and advantages which make them hesitate to move. We get a picture of this from the autobiography of a sweeper:

> . . . my father's family have been serving a certain number of houses for the last few hundred years, from generation to generation. It was an unwritten law that if my family wanted to move out of the town to go somewhere else, they would have to find someone else in their place. In this matter the high castes have no choice as to who would work for them. If my people wanted to sell the work of the street in which they were working they could do so to another family of our own caste. The sale was only effected on condition that in that particular area no others of our community had any claim, and also that the people who bought it were satisfied that our family had been working there for at least two generations; the price would be fixed according to the income of the area. . . . But sales of this nature very rarely take place, as it means losing one's birthright and the family reputation. Also, this is the only means of livelihood open to us, and the richer the landlord we serve, the more prestige and honor we have. . . .[14]

Moreover, the community may put pressure on an individual to make him stay. Nehru cites the case of a village which instituted legal proceedings in a criminal court, seeking to insure that the village Lohar (blacksmith) not migrate to another community, as he had threatened to do,[15] and Wiser describes the efforts of the people of Karimpur to keep a restless Dhobi (washerman) within the village.[16] Even if a *jajman* should be dissatisfied with his *kamin's* work, he would find it hard to replace him.

> It is not easy for an agriculturist to remove a family attached to his household and secure the services of another. For example, A, a barber, is attached to the family of B, an agriculturist. If for any reason B is greatly dissatisfied with the services of A and wants those of another, he cannot abruptly dismiss A. His difficulty will not be in dismissing him, but in finding a substitute. Each of these castes has its own inter-village council. Occupational castes have a developed trade unionism. . . . No one else would be willing to act as a substitute, for fear of being penalized by the caste *panchayat*. It may

[13] Eames, p. 21; Reddy, p. 135. According to M. Singh, in his book *The Depressed Classes* (Bombay: Hind Kitabs, 1947), *Bhangis* (sweepers) can sell their *jajmani* rights for as much as two hundred *rupees*.

[14] Hazari, *An Indian Outcaste* (London: Bannisdale Press, 1951), pp. 12–13.

[15] Nehru, p. 27.

[16] Wiser, p. 123.

even be difficult for a number of families to join together and import a family belonging to that occupational caste from a different village. First, under these conditions of tension, an outside family would not come for fear of social pressure and ultimate ostracism for such an action. And if they do come, the caste fellows already in the village would make things very difficult, even unbearable, for them.[17]

Not every village has a full complement of specialists. In a survey of fifty-four villages in the mid-Gangetic valley S. S. Nehru found that no single caste occurred in all the villages surveyed. Camars (leatherworkers) were found in only 64 per cent of the villages; Ahirs (herders) in 60 per cent; Brahmans, Nais, Lohars, and Telis (oilworkers) in 40 per cent; Dhobis and Kurmis (weavers) in 36 per cent; Kumhars (potters) in 30 per cent; and Baniyas (merchants) in 16 per cent.[18] Nehru gives various reasons for the unexpectedly low figures of these caste groups. The Nai (barber), for instance, is a journeyman who goes from door to door and village to village. "No client needs him more than once a week and less than once a month. Also, the various festivals and ceremonies when his services are in urgent demand do not figure all too frequently in the village calendar. Hence alone or through a relation, one Nai can minister to the needs of more than one village; if the figures are an index, more than two villages." [19] The Dhobi (washerman), on the other hand, has a small representation because he serves primarily upper-caste or upper-class patrons. The womenfolk of most lower-class families do the family wash. According to Singh, one seldom finds more than three Dhobi families in a village, and often only one, catering to a group of villages. Singh also says that the Bhangis (sweepers) are as sparsely scattered as the Dhobis, with their largest concentration in the towns.[20] Nehru explains that a single Baniya (merchant) can finance operations in villages within a radius of ten to twenty miles or more; hence one need not expect to find Baniyas in every village.[21] The supply and demand factor suggests that there must be some mobility, despite the localizing function of the *jajmani* system.

Jajmani rights, however, which link one to certain families, may be regarded as a form of property passing from father to son. Like land property, it is equally apportioned among brothers when they separate.[22] Certain problems eventuate from this: "When a Lohar

[17] Dube, p. 60.
[18] Nehru, pp. 23–29.
[19] Nehru, pp. 24–25.
[20] Singh, pp. 93, 95.
[21] Nehru, pp. 26–27.
[22] Reddy, p. 133.

family multiplies and divides the work, each share comes to compass the work of fewer agriculturists unless they also multiply at the same rate. Of course when the latter multiply faster, the Lohars become responsible to a greater number of agricultural families, even though the extent of work may remain the same." [23] The apportionment of *jajmani* rights may prove to be very unequal, as Reddy has shown. From a table giving the number of *jajmans* served by ten Lohar families in Senapur, it appears that one Lohar family serves only seven *jajman* families, while another serves thirty-seven. [24] The rewards in grain and other benefits are of course proportionate. The *jajmani* system, then, provides some security in assuring one a position in society, but also gives rise to economic insecurity for some of the *kamins*.

In his pioneer work Wiser summed up what seemed to him to be the advantages and disadvantages of the *jajmani* system in relation to the nation, the village community, the caste group, and the individual. On the whole, he emphasized the integrating and security-giving aspects of the system and described how it provided "peace and contentment" for the villagers. [25] Yet at other times, as we shall see, Wiser emphasized its attendant injustices. How the *jajmani* system affects the villagers who live by it, and what the future of the system may be in a developing money economy, are subjects that will be discussed toward the end of this chapter. First we will describe how the *jajmani* system functions at present in Rampur.

· THE JAJMANI SYSTEM IN RAMPUR ·

In Wiser's terms the Jats are the principal *jajmans* for the other caste groups in Rampur. [26] According to the traditional mode of ranking, the Brahmans are superior to the Jats. The Brahmans do have the dominant position in Wiser's village of Karimpur, where they are the landowners and number forty-one families in a population of 754. [27] But in Rampur the Brahmans are occupancy tenants of the Jats and are subservient to them.

The caste groups of Rampur have traditionally been related to one

[23] Reddy, p. 130.

[24] Reddy, p. 133.

[25] Wiser, p. 187.

[26] Rampur is twenty-seven miles off the main Delhi-Fazilka road, with which it is connected by a cart track. The village can also be reached from the Delhi-Ferozpur railway line. Gheora and Nangloi, the two nearest railway stations, are at a distance of a few miles from the village.

[27] Wiser, p. 19.

another through the mutual obligations of the *jajmani* system, the rules of which have been codified. Table 1 is an extract from the *wajib-ul'-arz*, the customary law of Rampur, which specifies the kinds of work to be done by the different caste groups and the rates of compensation. The provisions of the *wajib-ul'-arz* have legal effect, for British legislation continued to support these customary rules under civil law.[28]

TABLE 1

RULES OF SERVICE, RAMPUR

Caste	Type of Service	Rights Earned Through Service
Khati (carpenter)	To repair agricultural tools.	One *maund* of grain per year along with *ori* rights (2½ *sirs* of grain twice a year at each sowing season).
Lohar (blacksmith)	As above.	As above.
Kumhar (potter)	To supply earthenware vessels and to render services of light nature at weddings.	Grain to the value of the vessels. Additional grain at the son's or daughter's marriage, according to status and capacity.
Hajjam or Nai (barber)	To shave and cut hair; to attend to guests on their arrival and to render other services of light nature at weddings.	At each harvest as much grain as the man can lift by himself. Additional grain at the son's or daughter's marriage, according to status and capacity.
Khakrul or Bhangi (sweeper)	To prepare cow-dung cakes; to gather sweepings, to remove dead mules and donkeys; to collect cots for extraordinary needs, and to render services at weddings.	Meals and *rabri* twice a day; at each harvest as much grain as the man can lift by himself and also at the son's or daughter's marriage, according to status and capacity.
Camar (leather-worker)	If a man assists in agriculture and gives all kinds of light services	he gets one-twentieth of the produce.
	If he does *begar* (compulsory labor), renders ordinary service, and removes dead cattle	he gets one-fourth of the produce and the skins of dead cattle.

[28] Wiser, pp. 14–15.

It may be noted in this table that various rights and duties are specified in connection with weddings. Marriages are the high points in the social life of a village and represent a great expenditure of wealth by the families concerned. All the castes, or most of them, are brought into some connection with a wedding, in which the importance of the family and the village is demonstrated, and in which a *jajman's* ties with his *kamins* may be strengthened. The same is true, to a lesser extent, of funerals and other *rites de passage,* as well as of village festivals. The service ties of the various caste groups are indicated in Table 2.[29]

TABLE 2

JAJMANI RELATIONSHIPS AMONG DIFFERENT CASTES, RAMPUR

Number	Caste	Serves	Is Served by
1	Brahman	2, 3, 4, 5, 6, 7, 8, 9, 10	3, 4, 6, 7, 8, 10, 11, 12
2	Jat		1, 3, 4, 6, 7, 8, 10, 11, 12
3	Baniya	all	1, 4, 8, 10, 11, 12
4	Nai	1, 2, 3, 5, 6, 7, 8, 9, 10	1, 3, 8, 10, 11, 12
5	Chipi	1, 4, 10	1, 3, 4, 8, 10, 11, 12
6	Khati	1, 2, 3, 4	1, 3, 4, 8, 10, 11, 12
7	Lohar	1, 2, 3, 4	1, 3, 4, 8, 10, 11, 12
8	Kumhar	all	1, 4, 10, 11, 12
9	Jhinvar	cash relationships	cash relationships
10	Dhobi	all	1, 3, 4, 8, 11, 12
11	Camar	1, 2, 3, 4, 5, 6, 7, 8, 9, 10	8, 12
12	Bhangi	all	8, 10

Thirty or forty years ago a Khati at Rampur worked for his *jajman* all the year round. His work consisted in making plows and repairing them in the fields, making plow yokes, three-legged stools, legs for string cots, and various farming implements. The wood was supplied by his *jajman.*[30]

The traditional payments for this work are specified in Table 1 but informants gave a somewhat different itemization as follows:

1. Forty-five *sirs* of grain from the wheat crop (in the dry season).

2. As much wheat fodder as one person can carry (in the dry season).

3. As much *jovar* fodder as one person can carry (in the rainy season).

4. One or two *maunds* of green fodder (gram or peas).

[29] S. Misra gives a list of payments at marriage and sacred-thread ceremonies to different "village servants" in a village in U.P.: "Earnings of Village Servants in U. P.," *Eastern Anthropologist,* Vol. 5 (1952), p. 98.

[30] For a fuller list of items made by village carpenters, see Wiser, pp. 35–36.

A common form of payment, as specified in items 2 and 3 above and in the barber's list of rights in Table 1, is the provision that a man may take home from the crop as much grain as he can carry by himself. This is, of course, an elastic amount. A generation ago the village Lohar carried such a heavy load that he vomited blood on reaching home, and died instantly.

In addition to the grain payments received from each *jajman*, a Khati also gets payment in cash or kind for noncustomary services such as the making of wheels, planks, handles of milling stones, etc. Daily meals are provided while the Khati is working at wedding preparations for a *jajman*'s family, cutting the wood for fuel, etc., and he is feasted at the wedding itself and given one *rupee* thereafter. Interservice relationships exist between the Khati and Nai, Dhobi, and Kumhar families. Each of the Khati families acts as *jajman* toward one Camar and one Bhangi family, which provide services for them and work at their weddings, when both families are feasted.

While *jajmani* services are still exchanged, cash payments for carpentry are increasing and *jajmani* ties have weakened. The Khatis have fewer *jajmans* than formerly. They seldom repair plows in the fields nowadays, and they are slow in completing jobs required by their *jajmani* obligations. The *jajmans* find that if they want to get work done on time, it is better to pay something in cash as well.

The famine of 1944–45 damaged the *jajmani* relationships between the Khatis and the Jats. Since grain was scarce, the Jats decided to reduce the customary dues. The village *panchayat* accordingly announced that the grain payments would be half the traditional amount that year. The Rampur Khatis and Lohars did not agree to these conditions and said that they would not work for their *jajmans* if they insisted on such terms. Six Jat families then broke off *jajmani* relationships with the Khatis and now do their own work, or else get it done by cash payments. Three of the Jat families have taken up carpentry. One of these families is dependent upon it as a full-time profession, while the other two are on a near-professional basis. The full-time Jat carpenter learned his trade while he was employed at the civil ordnance depot at the Delhi cantonment. The others learned the trade by themselves.

Only two of the four Khati families at Rampur now carry on the traditional trade. Two Khatis are teachers; one of these supplements his income by prescribing medicines. The trade of carpentry has seen some reverses in recent years. Bullock carts formerly had wooden wheels, which used to last for a year or two, and thus provided the Khati with a dependable source of income. But now iron wheels have taken their place. Out of thirty-three bullock carts now at Rampur, thirty-one have iron wheels. Plankmaking has also declined; people from Rampur now prefer to have their wood cut in Delhi by a buzz saw. The two Khati carpenters at Rampur are in debt. One of them has two employed sons who help to ease his burden; the other Khati has some part-time work as a mason and also sells milk, but he is still in debt. The decline of the carpenter's importance in this village may be seen from the fact that whereas Rampur's 1,100 inhabitants are served by two or three underemployed carpenters, Wiser's village of Karimpur, with 754 inhabitants, had eight carpenter families whom Wiser described as being "constantly occupied."[31]

The single Lohar in Rampur is also in debt. He formerly made and repaired his *jajman*'s agricultural implements (axes, knives, and chopping tools) and during the harvest sharpened their sickles daily. In return his *jajmans* paid him according to the schedule given in Table 1. The sale of tools was a supplementary source of income.[32]

Technological change is not responsible for the Rampur Lohar's poverty. He does not have the money to buy tools and equipment. His difficulties seem to stem largely from having too large a family; he married twice and had three children (all daughters) by his first wife and seven children (four sons, three daughters) by the second. The marriages of his daughters put him in debt. The efforts of this man to support himself and his family show the difficulties of making ends meet in a village like Rampur. In order to pay off his debts, the Lohar decided to make some extra money by plying a horse-*tonga* (two-wheeled passenger cart) between Mundka and Rampur. So he borrowed three hundred *rupees* at 15 per cent interest and bought a *tonga*. But then the Lohar fell sick and had to sell the *tonga* again for 150 *rupees* in order to pay for his treatment. Harassed by his creditors, the Lohar left the village after handing over the charge of his *jajmans* to a Lohar from a neighboring village. A year later, when he returned to Rampur, the Lohar found it hard to get his *jajmans* back. He had also lost some of his land in the meantime, and

---

[31] Wiser, p. 40.

[32] Reddy gives some details about the Lohar's work and payments in eastern Uttar Pradesh (p. 136). The work includes carpentry, which in Rampur would be done by the carpenter. "The carpentry that is needed in the construction of houses, major repairs of mechanical chaff-cutter and sugar-cane press and making of carts are outside the Jajmani system. Small repairs in the house or minor adjustments of the chaff-cutter and sugar-cane press are generally done by one's own Lohar *Parjan*. If the work takes less than an hour, the Lohar does not get any payment. If such work, however, extends over a few hours, he gets a nominal payment in grain that is sufficient for one meal. If the work outside the Jajmani system takes a whole day or more, he gets fixed wages."

the income from supplementary sources had been insignificant. His debts are still mounting, for the Lohar has to support his wife, four sons, two daughters, and two daughters-in-law. His oldest son, who is sixteen years old, helps him in his work, but there are no other earning members in the family.

The "mixed" nature of the *jajmani* system at Rampur is illustrated in the cases of the Chipi and Dhobi. Two generations ago there were no tailors in Rampur, but a Chipi from Gheora came from time to time to stitch clothes. Then the villagers urged him to move in and stay. He did so, and his descendants (two families) still carry on the trade. The Chipis charge fixed rates in cash or kind for their work when dealing with Jat, Baniya, Khati, Lohar, or Jhinvar (water carrier) families. However, in the case of the Nais and Dhobis they stitch clothes free of charge in return for the latters' services. For services at weddings the Chipis receive from 15 to 30 *rupees*. They are supplied with earthenware by a Kumhar, who receives so much grain per vessel; a Dhobi washes their clothes without charge; a Bhangi does all their sweeping in exchange for one *capati* (wheat cake) a day with leftover food and an occasional present of old clothes. These families are feasted and given money at Chipi weddings—5 *rupees* for the Kumhar and 1 each for the Dhobi and Bhangi. A Camar is given 1 *rupee* at the weddings at which he assists, but there have never been interservice relationships between the Chipis and Camars.

There are four Dhobi families in the village, but two of the family heads have turned to other occupations—agricultural labor in one case and work in an ordnance plant in the other. The two remaining Dhobi families have twenty-one *jajmans* in Rampur between them and from ten to fifteen in a neighboring village. They receive from ten to twenty *sirs* of grain from each *jajman*. They also have interservice relationships with Nai, Chipi, and Kumhar families, while some Bhangis do their sweeping at the *capati*-per-day rate. Formerly the Dhobis depended completely upon their local *jajmans* for a living, but nowadays they have customers in Delhi as well.[33]

Both social and technological changes have affected the position of the Nais, or barbers, in Rampur. The Nais used to cut the hair, toenails and fingernails of their *jajmans*, while their wives shampooed the women's hair. On harvest days the Nai at Rampur shaved his *jajmans* in the fields and received one sheaf from each one. After the harvest the Nai was invited to take a load of as many sheaves as he

[33] For a good account of a Dhobi's work in a South Indian village, written at the end of the nineteenth century, see T. B. Pandian, *Indian Village Folk* (London, 1898), pp. 23 ff.

could carry, or else he was given from twenty *sirs* to one *maund* of grain. The Nai also served as marriage go-between. A barber was often commissioned by a girl's parents to find a suitable match for the daughter. When the barber had found a boy with the right qualifications, he was sent to the youth's home along with a Brahman to offer *tika*, the ceremonial placing of a forehead mark. The Nai received *neg jog* from the boy's parents, a gift consisting of fifteen *rupees* in cash and a double cotton sheet, while the Brahman received nine *rupees* and a single sheet. It was the Nai who arranged the match; the Brahman's role was secondary. The Nai was thus a man of importance in the village. According to Wiser, the Nai and his wife were among the few people at Karimpur who devoted all of their time to their *jajmans*. They had no time for farming.[34]

In recent years the Nai's position at Rampur has changed for the worse. About twenty-five years ago a Jat *panchayat* at Bawana ruled that a Nai would thenceforth receive only six *rupees* as *neg jog*. The Bawana Nais refused to accept this ruling. The Jats then decided to dispense with Nais as go-betweens and to arrange their daughters' marriages themselves. In protest the Nais stopped shaving and cutting their *jajmans*' hair, hoping that this would lead the Jats to resume the old system. Instead, it led some of the Jats to buy razors and to shave themselves, so that when the barbers took up their trade again, they found that they had lost some of their *jajmans*.

Meanwhile changes in women's hair styles have adversely affected the Nain, or barber's wife. Formerly hair was set above the head; the barber's wife, who was expert in setting it after a shampoo, received 1 *sir* of grain for dressing it. The present hair style is simpler; any woman can now arrange her own. Thus she is apt to shampoo and dress it herself and seldom calls in a Nain.

One of the three Nais from Rampur is now working as a barber in Delhi; the second is a teacher, and the third a truck driver in Delhi. But they all come back to Rampur on Sundays and give shaves and haircuts to their remaining *jajmans*.

Another group affected by recent *panchayat* rulings is the Kumhars (potters), of whom there are seven families at Rampur. Except for one family whose head man is working in Delhi, each of the Kumhar families has a fixed number of *jajmans* to whom it supplies

[34] "Shaving under the arms weekly, finger-nail cutting weekly, and toe-nail cutting fortnightly, are added to the tonsorial duties of the barber. Ordinarily hair is cut monthly except when his clients have their heads shaved for religious purposes or through choice. . . . At the time of a wedding he not only shaves the men in his own *jajman*'s household, but he also shaves the guests from other villages—relatives of his *jajmans*." Wiser, pp. 38–39.

clay vessels in exchange for specified amounts of grain.[35] The *jajman* must take earthenware from his own Kumhar and from none other. No other Kumhar would supply such vessels in any case, unless the *jajman*'s own Kumhar lacked them. The Kumhars keep donkeys which are needed for hauling clay from the river banks. These donkeys are lent out to *jajmans* when needed. This adds to the grain supplied by the latter—from twenty *sirs* to one *maund* of grain plus one bundle of dry fodder. A bundle of green fodder is also given from the *kharif* crop. Still more grain may be obtained from weaving, a supplementary trade engaged in by Kumhars. There are also, of course, opportunities at weddings, when *jajmans* require many clay vessels for their guests, and when the Kumhars are feasted. On these occasions they receive about two and a half *rupees* and about five and a quarter *sirs* of grain.

A commodity much needed by the Kumhars—and by all the other villagers as well—is cow dung. Since there are only thirty-seven trees in the whole village (each privately owned and having a fixed monetary value), wood cannot be used for burning, and cow dung is the only available fuel. Everyone needs it for that purpose, but the Kumhars need more than others, for they must have plenty of fuel to fire their pottery. Firing takes place about seven times a year, and enough cow dung must be acquired each time. The competitive scramble for cow dung among the villagers has deprived the fields of manure for fertilizer. Faced with this problem, the village *panchayat* passed a ruling three years ago prohibiting its collection and imposing a fine of five *rupees* upon anyone who violated the rule. Much clandestine collecting no doubt takes place, but the Kumhars have now been compelled to buy much of their fuel. For each firing about nine *rupees*' worth of cow-dung cakes must be obtained. All the Kumhars are now heavily in debt and can hardly afford the extra costs. One Kumhar owes a debt of over five hundred *rupees* but cannot pay a single *pie* toward either the principal or interest.

The handling of cow dung is traditionally the Bhangi's job. There are ten Bhangi (sweeper) families in Rampur, about half of which have found employment in Delhi or elsewhere. The remaining families still work for their *jajmans*. Bhangis used to receive a *capati* a day from the latter and from twenty *sirs* to one *maund* of grain at harvest time. They were feasted at weddings and received one *rupee*

[35] "The Kumhar makes for village use, large round-bellied water jars, various types of jars used for milking, boiling, churning, etc., lids for water and milk jars, funnel-shaped tobacco pipe bowls, saucers which are used for the mustard oil lights, saucers for serving liquid foods at weddings, cups without handles, jars for storing grain, smaller jars for preserving spices and chutneys, feeding jars for cattle, and various other types of clay vessels." Wiser, pp. 45–46.

in cash, together with the leftovers of the meal. For playing drums on the occasion of the birth of a son to a *jajman*, the Bhangis were given some *gur* and wheat; while at a Bhangi wedding the *jajman* of the family presented a *rupee* and from two and a half to five *sirs* of grain. These obligations are no longer adhered to with regularity. Only a few *jajmans* give grain annually nowadays. Some do so if the Bhangi helps with the harvest, but the payment is small. One Bhangi who had sixteen Jat families as *jajmans* helped nine of the families at harvest time. Three families gave him only five *sirs* of grain; the other six gave from fifteen to twenty *sirs*. The women in most of the Jat and Brahman families at Rampur now handle cow dung and make cow-dung cakes themselves. However, the Bhangis are still indispensable as sweepers and removers of refuse from the home. So the *jajmani* relationship persists, although at a low rate of return for the Bhangis.

All the Bhangis at Rampur are heavily in debt and owe money to the Jats. In the past they used to borrow money from their *jajmans*, either interest-free or at very low rates, but now they must pay from 12 to 18 per cent a year. Moreover, it is not easy to get loans. If a Bhangi approaches one of the Jats for this purpose, he may be told sarcastically to seek help from the Congress Party or from one of the politicians the Bhangi voted for on election day.

It is not surprising that the Bhangis have become hostile toward the Jats, as have the Camars, who will be discussed below. This hostility has been fanned by some restrictive measures which have cut down the Bhangis' sources of income. The Bhangis formerly kept poultry. But the Jats were annoyed when the chickens made tracks over their freshly made cow-dung cakes, and they expressed their displeasure by manhandling some of the Bhangis. No chickens are kept nowadays. The Bhangis also used to keep pigs. But the pigs, like the chickens, were apt to stray and spoil somebody's crops. The Jats told the Bhangis that the pigs would not be allowed to drink at the village pond. Fines were imposed if pigs were found drinking there. The Bhangis therefore had to sell their pigs or else take them away to relatives in other villages. The loss of chickens and pigs meant a loss of supplementary income—not a small matter to people so deeply in debt.[36]

The greatest break with the *jajmani* system at Rampur has come from the Camars, traditionally the leatherworkers of India. They formerly removed their *jajmans'* dead cattle, repaired their shoes and

[36] According to Mukerjee, however, some low-caste groups have deliberately abandoned the raising of pigs and poultry in order to raise their status. See R. Mukerjee *et al.*, "Intercaste Tensions" (University of Lucknow, mimeographed, 1951), p. 14.

other leather objects, and helped them in agricultural work. George Briggs, writing as long ago as 1920, affirmed that the special role of the Camar in India's rural villages was doomed:

> With the rise of the large-scale tanning industry in certain large centers, the village tanner's enterprise is being reduced to smaller dimensions. There is little likelihood that the rural industry will survive. In this connection it is interesting to note that during the decade ending in 1911 there was a very marked decrease (36.9 per cent) in the number engaged in tanning, currying, dressing, and dyeing leather. At the same time the Chamar population increased. Furthermore one of the results of the war has been a very great advance in large-scale tanning. The demand for village tanned leather is gradually being reduced to that of water-buckets and thongs. The former will be supplied more and more from chrome tanned leather, which is not a rural product at all, and finally, cheaper fabrics made from vegetable fibres will supplant leather for irrigation purposes. Slowly factory tanned leather will supplant village tanned leather in the village shoe-making industry.[37]

However, leatherworking is only one of the Camar's traditional tasks. Ibbetson has described some of their duties in the Karnal tract, not far from Rampur: "The Chamars are the coolies of the tract. They cut grass, carry wood, put up tents, carry bundles, act as watchmen and the like for officials; and this work is shared by all the Chamars in the village. They also plaster the houses with mud when needed. They take the skins of all the animals which die in the village except those which die on Saturday or Sunday, or the first which dies of cattle plague. They generally give one pair of boots per ox and two pairs per buffalo skin so taken to the owner." [38]

Table 3 gives some of the traditional obligations and payments for the Camars at Rampur.

Camars were formerly required to perform *begar,* including compulsory service for government officials who visited the village. In general, their position has always been a very low one, but recently they have been making efforts to raise their status, and have discontinued some of their traditional *jajmani* obligations and services. They have developed mutual feelings of hostility toward the Jats in consequence. During the past twenty years or so the Camars seem to have been losing some of the sense of inferiority associated with

[37] G. Briggs, *The Chamars* (London: Oxford University Press, 1920), p. 227. The increasing use of Persian wells has cut down on the demand for leather buckets.

[38] D. C. J. Ibbetson, *Report on the Revision of Settlement of the Panipat Tahsil and Karnal Parganah of the Karnal District, 1872–1880* (Allahabad: Pioneer Press, 1883), pp. 116–17.

TABLE 3

SERVICES RENDERED AND PAYMENTS RECEIVED BY CAMARS, RAMPUR

Occasion	*Service Rendered*	*Payment Received*
Boy's marriage	1. Felling trees, cutting wood for fuel. 2. Providing a watch at the house after the wedding party has left. 3. Accompanying the wedding party; attending to the bullocks at the bride's home.	1. Meals given when cutting wood. 2. One *rupee* at departure of the wedding party. 3. One *rupee* at departure of the wedding party from the bride's home. 4. One *rupee* and some grain (usually 5 to 10 *sirs* of wheat).
Girl's marriage	1. Cutting wood for fuel. 2. Assistance in reception of wedding party. 3. Feeding their bullocks. 4. Keeping watch where party camps. 5. Making repairs in the house.	1. Meals given to the whole family four times during the three-day stay. 2. One *rupee* at wedding party's departure. 3. One *rupee*, wheat (usually 5 to 10 *sirs*), and clothes after the wedding.
Ordinary service	1. Work without payment for officials (*begar*). 2. Repairs of *jajman*'s shoes. 3. Work in extraordinary situations (illness or death, etc.). 4. Help in harvesting. 5. Removal of dead cattle.	1. Meals on days of work for *jajman*. 2. One *sir* of grain at harvest time. 3. Grain left over on the threshing floor. 4. Animal carcasses taken. 5. One-fortieth of the grain produced (minimum 2 to 5 *maunds*).
Extraordinary service	1. Full-time work in harvesting *rabi* crop. 2. Full-time work in harvesting *kharif* crops.	1. One-twentieth of the produce. 2. One-tenth of the produce if 100 *maunds* or over: more if the *kharif* crop is less. 3. Meals given on workdays.

their low-caste status and untouchability. This has partly been due to the efforts of organizations like the Arya Samaj, the Congress Party, and some of the other political parties in India. The Arya Samaj, a Hindu religious reform movement, has long campaigned against caste restrictions in this area, apparently with some effect. At an Arya Samaj conference in Rampur in 1910 some non-Brahman groups, principally the Jats, were persuaded to wear the sacred thread, formerly reserved for the use of Brahmans. The Jats were urged not to feast Brahmans on ceremonial occasions, for this custom merely developed greediness in the latter caste. Besides, the speakers pointed out, village Brahmans are mostly illiterate, being Brahmans only by birth, and have no real knowledge of the Vedas. In 1933 a second Arya Samaj conference was held at Rampur, this time directed against untouchability. The speakers told the Camars in the audience that unpaid *begar* service had no legal basis and that they should refuse to perform it. The speakers promised the Camars assistance if they got into trouble for refusing *begar* service. As a result, the Camars stopped rendering *begar*.

The Camars who carried away the dead animals of their *jajmans* used to eat the flesh of these animals. When previous attempts had been made to remove untouchability, the Jats had objected on the grounds that the Camars ate carrion. At the 1933 conference the Arya Samaj speakers exhorted the Camars to give up eating the flesh of dead animals and to keep themselves and their homes clean, so that untouchability could be removed. The Camars took a vow to do so. Most of the Jats at the conference then drank water at the hands of the Camars. These Jats were subsequently boycotted by the Brahmans for this violation of caste rules.

Despite this gesture on the part of some of the Jats, tensions developed between the Jats and the Camars which had been manifest before the 1933 conference. In 1926 the Camars refused to pay the traditional house tax (*kudhi-tarif*) of two *rupees* per year to the Jats. The Camars of the few surrounding villages raised 450 *rupees,* a tremendous sum at that time, and took the case to the court. However, the other non-Jats of the village, still dependent upon the Jats as their *kamins,* did not support the Camars. All the Jat factions united in opposing the Camars. The case dragged on for two years, and the Jats finally won. However, the Camars still refused to pay the tax, and a court decree was obtained by the Jats for the auction of the Camars' property. Both the *lambardars* of the village and other Jats, led by the court-appointed officer, went to the house of the leader of the Camars and forcibly confiscated some brass vessels, *ghi,* and cotton, all of which were taken to a Jat's house where they were held until the tax was paid.

A few years later the Camars and Jats fought another court case. This time the Camars brought criminal proceedings against some Jats who had beaten them for carrying meat in their pots. Then, in 1938, the house-tax question came up again. During the preceding ten years the Jats had failed to collect the house tax, which they now demanded in a lump sum. When the Camars pleaded inability to pay, the taxes during this ten-year period were forgiven. But the

Camars went on to pay taxes from 1938 to 1947. There were three other court cases between the Camars and Jats from 1930 to 1947. In one case the Jats asked the Camars to assign a man each day to keep a day watch to guard Jat harvests against animals and thieves. When the Camars refused, the Jats took the case to court. A compromise was reached in which the Camars agreed to a night watch rather than a day watch. The Camars interpreted this as a victory and they became more aggressive, severing all their occupational and ceremonial relations with the Jats including the burial of dead animals. After about six months, however, they resumed the removal of dead animals and maintained this service until the time of Independence. During World War II many Camars from Rampur were employed in a nearby ordnance depot and in other military jobs, which gave them an opportunity to take an independent stand.

With the coming of Independence, the position of the Camars was strengthened both legally and ideologically. Now the Jats could no longer enforce the provisions of the *wajib-ul'-arz*, which specified the traditional village duties. The Camars stopped payment of the house tax and the handling of dead animals. However, with the more limited opportunities for employment after the war the Camars once again became dependent upon the Jats. This put them in a difficult position vis-à-vis the Jats, because they had openly opposed the latter in the *panchayat* and had supported the Congress Party candidate who was opposed by most of the Jats.[39]

Giving up the practice of removing dead animals was a gradual process. For a while the Camars removed only those dead animals which had died a lingering death from foul-smelling body wounds. The Jats disposed of other carcasses by burial. This violated provisions laid down in the *wajib-ul'-arz*. Previously, when a Jat had buried a dead bullock, the Camars had reported the matter to the police, who then had the carcass dug up and turned over to them. If the skin were decomposed, the Jat was made to pay the cost of the skin to his Camar.

The burial of animals by the Jats, however, was not without precedent. A mass burial of animals used to take place at *akta* ceremonies, when there was a cattle epidemic. On these occasions a curer was brought to the village, and all the livestock was brought together in one place. The curer performed some ritual actions and burned incense near the animals, all of which were driven beneath a sacred stick. Ganges water was sprinkled about in all the houses. No outsiders were admitted into the village on this day, nor could any of

[39] For a similar dilemma, see "The Changing Status of a Depressed Caste," based on reports by Bernard S. Cohn, in *Village India* (above, note 8), pp. 68 ff.

the villagers leave. Various taboos prevailed: no iron utensils were used, flour was not milled, *capatis* were not cooked, and houses remained unswept. The ceremony began on a Saturday and lasted until Sunday evening. At these times the Jats used to seek the Camars' permission to kill and bury the cattle, but this permission was readily granted, for the Camars also wanted the epidemic to end. Gradually, however, the Jats began to perpetuate the practice of burying dead cattle.

In 1934–35 the Camars temporarily gave up removing dead animals, partly owing to objections raised by a doctor, who claimed that they were skinned too near the villagers' homes. Two years later, when a different place was set aside for the skinning, the removal of dead animals was resumed rather half-heartedly by the Camars. In 1947, on the eve of Indian independence, the Camars at Rampur gave up the practice altogether and have not resumed it since.

After the 1933 Arya Samaj conference, when the Camars gave up rendering *begar* service, the Jats began to cut down on the amounts of grain given them, claiming that the stipulations in the *wajib-ul'-arz* had been violated by the Camars. Some of the latter say that this was a mere excuse on the part of the Jats. The main factor, according to them, was the increased price of grain.

Another factor must have been the increasing fragmentation of land. When landholdings were large and could not be managed without outside help, the traditional assistance of the Camars was sought and welcomed by the Jats; but as landholdings became smaller and families larger, and as pressure on the land brought about further fragmentation, the assistance of the Camars became less crucial. This was, of course, a gradual process; it did not happen overnight.[40]

Technological changes have also had their effect. A mechanical iron cane crusher has now supplanted the old wooden type of crusher and obviated the large work crew that managed the old machine. Chaff-cutting machines have supplanted the old tools used for that purpose. The Jat landowners are now less dependent upon the Camars in these areas.

Camar ties to their *jajmans* have also weakened. Gradually they have given up repairing the latter's shoes, one of their traditional

[40] Some aspects of the conflict between the Jats and Camars at Rampur have been dealt with in Essay 15, "Group Dynamics in a North Indian Village: A Study in Factions." A discussion of land tenure, population pressures, and related economic problems appears in my article, "Aspects of Land Tenure and Economics in a North Indian Village," *Economic Development and Cultural Change*, Vol. 6 (1956), pp. 279–302.

jajmani obligations, and as we have seen, they have been trying to raise their socio-religious status by following higher-caste practices and giving up the consumption of dead animal flesh.

The opportunity to enter schools is a new channel to higher status. None of the older Camars at Rampur can read or write, but 85 per cent of their boys aged six to fifteen are attending school. In Kanjhawla High School the untouchables and higher-caste boys eat together, while in the local school young Camars and Jats sit side by side. Since 1949 a Camar has been elected to the newly constituted four-village council.

During World War II new kinds of employment were made available to the Camars, and some went to Delhi to work. Although there has been a postwar contraction of employment, four of the twenty-one Camar families at Rampur have found employment outside the village. Two work as agricultural laborers for one or two months a year at daily wages. Some work as occasional day laborers. Three Camar families do weaving, four have taken up a guava garden on a contract basis, and four have started vegetable growing. Some raise cattle to supplement their income. Only two Camars in the village are shoemakers.

One of the Camars was asked why the other Camars did not also make shoes to supplement their income. He answered that capital is needed to buy cured hides, which cost from fifty to sixty *rupees.* Even if they somehow managed to buy a hide, they would have to sell shoes on credit and in most cases receive only grain in return. The problem of getting funds for another hide would remain as before. The informant was questioned as follows:

Q. "How did you manage it before?"

A. "We used to remove the dead cattle and tan the hides ourselves."

Q. "Couldn't that system be revived?"

A. "Most of us don't want to skin leather any more."

Q. "But couldn't you find just one man who would agree to do it for the others?"

A. "Well . . . that's a good idea. But all the other villagers would have to agree."

As it is, under the present system all the hides at Rampur are going to waste, buried in the earth year after year. If cured hides cost from 50 to 60 *rupees,* this represents an enormous loss to the villagers.

It is not only low-caste groups which have abandoned their *jajmani* obligations at Rampur. The Brahmans have also done so. They formerly used to officiate at marriages and other ceremonies at the homes of their *jajmans,* at which times they received from twenty *sirs* to two *maunds* of grain and fodder. Every day during the cane-crushing season a farmer would set aside from one and a half to two *sirs* of *gur* for his Brahman. Brahmans had traditional roles to play at festivals such as Kanagat and Makar Sankrant, at which they were feasted, and also in the event of a Kaj, a celebration in honor of the dead. The Arya Samaj, as has been noted, has expressed opposition to the feasting of Brahmans, and the Jats have been influenced by this point of view. Partly for this reason—perhaps also for the sake of economy—they have stopped feasting Brahmans. A Kaj has not been given for several years, and at festival times the Brahmans are seldom fed. (Cows or young girls are sometimes fed instead.) The Rampur Brahmans, for their part, claim to regard the acceptance of food and charity as demeaning and prefer not to receive it. The Brahmans no longer settle marriage agreements, cook food at weddings, or carry on priestly functions. Four of the Rampur Brahmans are now cultivators, although only two make this their sole means of support. One of the Brahmans is a tailor, another sells silk.

There is one Baniya (merchant) family in the village which owns a shop. According to Wiser, the Vaisyas, who are absent in Karimpur, do not form an essential part of the Hindu *jajmani* system. This grouping would include the Baniya. Wiser quotes Sir Henry Maine to the effect that "the grain dealer (Vaisya) is never a hereditary trader incorporated with the village group." [41] The villagers at Rampur, however, speak of the Baniya as if he took part in the *jajmani* system. He has *jajmani*-type relationships, at least, with the Brahman families in Rampur and is served by Nais, Dhobis, Kumhars, Camars, and Bhangis. Besides selling grain and other commodities the Baniya enters certain records in an account book for the benefit of some Rampur families. The gift of money (*neota*) presented at a wedding is recorded in this book, for double that sum must be paid back when there is a marriage in the donor's household. The Baniya receives two *rupees* for this service. He also keeps records without charge of loans made by one man to another. The Baniya was formerly paid for weighing grain, but most people weigh it themselves nowadays, and he has lost this source of income. According to Ibbetson, the Baniyas in the Karnal tract give a ball of *gur* on the day after Holi and some parched rice or sweets on Divali to the proprietors "in recognition of the subordinate position which they occupy in the village." [42]

To sum up the present situation of the *jajmani* system: The system is still functioning in Rampur, a village close to Delhi, the nation's

[41] Wiser, p. 143.
[42] Ibbetson, p. 118.

capital. Despite modern improvements, technological changes, India's five-year plans, the influence of reformist movements and political ideologies, the system is not yet dead. However, changes are taking place. The Camars have stopped fulfilling some of their *jajmani* obligations toward the Jats, who have reciprocated in turn. There are also indications of tension between the Jats and the Bhangis, although the latter continue to serve their *jajmans*. The Brahmans have lost their priestly functions. The Dhobis, who formerly depended completely upon their local *jajmans,* now have customers in Delhi as well. The Khatis and the Lohars are abandoning their traditional trades. The Nais have lost their roles as marriage go-betweens as well as some of their opportunities as barbers. Some of their former *jajmans* shave themselves; their wives shampoo their own hair.

Most of the lower-caste villagers—and many of the Jats—are in debt. Some have been led to change their occupations and have gone to Delhi to look for work. Technological changes and the increasing land fragmentation have reduced the need for help in agriculture among the Jat families. Meanwhile, the Arya Samaj and some of the political parties have preached, with some effect, against caste restrictions. All these factors have led to a loosening of *jajmani* ties and obligations.

· DISCUSSION ·

In a chapter in which he weighed the advantages and disadvantages of the *jajmani* system, Wiser drew an essentially benevolent picture of how it provided "peace and contentment" for the villagers.[43] The account by Opler and Singh has a similar emphasis: "Not only does everyone have some place within the Hindu system, but it is significant that every group, from the Brahman to the Chamar caste, has been somehow integrated into the social and ceremonial round of the community and has been given some opportunity to feel indispensable and proud." [44]

[43] Wiser, p. 187.

[44] Opler and Singh, p. 496. The institution of caste has, of course, been lauded and attacked by various writers both in India and in the West. H. Maine described it as "the most disastrous and blighting of all institutions," and R. Tagore called it "a gigantic system of cold-blooded repression." (Quoted in *Indian Caste Customs,* by L. S. S. O'Malley [Cambridge, England: Cambridge University Press, 1932], p. vii.) But Abbé Dubois, who was often critical of Indian customs, referred to caste as "the happiest effort of Hindu legislation." (J. A. Dubois, *Hindu Manners, Customs, and Ceremonies,* trans. H. K. Beauchamp [Oxford, Clarendon Press, 1947], p. 28.) Gandhi expressed both points of view at different times. "Historically speaking," he once averred, "caste may be regarded as man's experiment or social adjustment in the laboratory of

Our picture of Rampur, however, leads to a quite different assessment, for it seems evident that the relationship between *jajman* and *kamin* lends itself to the exploitation of the latter. Landownership is the basis of power in Rampur. All the village land, including the house sites, is owned by the Jats; the other castes are thus living there more or less at the sufferance of the Jats. It was this crucial relationship to the land, with the attendant power of eviction, which made it possible for the Jats to exact *begar* service from the Camars in the past, and still enables them to dominate the other caste groups. Moreover, some of the latter, like the Bhangis, are deeply in debt to their *jajmans*. This gives the Jats an additional hold over their *kamins*.

This exploitative situation can be shown to exist in other areas where the *jajmani* system is found. Writing of a village near Lucknow, Majumdar and his colleagues observe that the higher-caste people always try to humiliate the lower castes. "The Thakurs dictate the most ruthless terms to the Chamars who take their fields as share croppers." [45] Reddy notes that a Lohar receives much less for his work from his Thakur *jajmans* than he gets from other castes.[46] Even Wiser, despite his favorable assessment, saw the harsh realities of the power relationship.

> The leaders of our village are so sure of their power that they make no effort to display it. The casual visitor finds little to distinguish them from other farmers. . . . And yet when one of them appears among men of serving caste, the latter express respect and fear in every guarded word and gesture. The serving ones have learned that as long as their subservience is unquestioned, the hand which directs them rests lightly. But let there be any move toward independence or even indifference among them, and the paternal touch becomes a strangle-hold. . . . in every detail of life have the leaders bound the villagers to themselves. Their favour may bring about a man's prosperity and their disfavour may cause him to fall, or may make life so unbearable for him that he will leave the village.[47]

Indian society. If we can prove it to be a success, it can be offered to the world as a leaven and as the best remedy against heartless competition and social disintegration born of avarice and greed." (*Selections from Gandhi*, ed. N. K. Bose [Ahmedabad: Navajivan Publishing House, 1938], p. 232.) But Gandhi also wrote, "Caste has nothing to do with religion. It is harmful both to spiritual and national growth." (*Ibid.*, p. 234.)

[45] D. N. Majumdar *et al.*, "Intercaste relations in Gohanakallan, a Village near Lucknow," *Eastern Anthropologist*, Vol. 7 (1955), p. 211.

[46] Reddy, p. 137. Reddy also mentions that Lohars get beaten by their *jajmans* for delinquencies in their obligations, pp. 139–40.

[47] C. V. Wiser and W. H. Wiser, *Behind Mud Walls* (New York: Agricultural Mission, 1951), pp. 18–19. See also Cohn, p. 61 (above, note 39).

It is also evident from Wiser's data that the upper castes receive much more than the lower castes do in goods and services,[48] and this is borne out by Misra's list of payments.[49]

That the ownership of land, including house sites, is the crucial factor, appears in other areas as well. "In the old days," writes Darling of the Punjab, "village servants were in complete subjection to their 'masters,' and this is still largely the case in the feudal north and west. There the fear of ejection from the village is a yoke which keeps the head bowed, and only those who own their own house and courtyard dare assert themselves." [50] An informant told Gittel Steed: "You have seen the whole Bakrana, every house probably. Have you seen any house that can be called a good house? This is because everyone is frightened of being driven out at any time. No one wants to build a good house here." [51] "That the *zamindar* [landowner] is all-powerful in such places need hardly be stressed," writes Mohinder Singh. "The threat of demolishing a man's dwelling or ejecting him therefrom are powerful weapons in his hand for extorting *begar*. Till recently the cultivators did not have any rights in their house sites." [52] Miriam Young presents a striking passage in relation to *begar:* "The Jats said [to the Camars] 'You'll do no more forced labor for us? Very well, then you shall no longer have any rights or privileges in this village.' They were not allowed to graze their cattle on common land, not allowed to bring in fuel from the fields or the jungle. If they got out of their own quarters into neighboring fields or jungle it was by stealth. Access to wells which they had regarded as their own was denied them, debts of long standing were suddenly foreclosed, land which they were renting was seized from them, individuals were beaten and their property looted." [53]

While the landowners are generally of higher caste in Indian villages, it is their position as landowners, rather than caste membership *per se*, which gives them status and power. In Karimpur, where the Brahmans are the landowners, the traditional caste hierarchy prevails. But in Rampur the Jats own the land and the Brahmans are subservient to them. Majumdar and his colleagues present a similar picture in their description of the village near Lucknow: "The respect which the Brahmins enjoy is merely conventional; in daily life, how-

[48] Wiser, *The Hindu Jajmani System*, pp. 70–71.

[49] Misra, p. 98.

[50] Darling, p. 272.

[51] Steed, lecture notes.

[52] Singh, p. 35 (above, note 13).

[53] Miriam Young, *Seen and Heard in a Punjab Village* (London: Student Christian Movement Press, 1931), p. 152.

ever, the Brahmins are treated on an equal footing with the other castes. . . . The Thakurs are the most influential group of people in the village because they are economically better off. They own most of the agricultural land in the village. They are the landlords who give employment to the other caste-people. The various other castes serve the Thakurs as their dependents." [54] Opler and Singh also report that in Madhopur the Brahmans, "in spite of their top position in the orthodox social scale, are not influential. The reason is that they are economically dependent on others." [55] In Madhopur it is the Thakurs who own the land, over 82 per cent of it, and it is they who form the dominant caste, as in the study just cited. In another village described by Opler and Singh a lower-caste Ahir is headman of the village and leader of the village *panchayat*. He owns 50 acres—"the only villager who has actual ownership of any substantial portion of village land." [56] In an early work by Russell and Hira Lal an area is discussed where Kunbis have higher than usual status. "The only reasonable explanation of this rise in status appears to be that the Kunbi has taken possession of the land and has obtained the rank which from time immemorial belongs to the hereditary cultivator as a member and citizen of the village community." [57]

Since the passing of *zamindari* abolition bills, the key power of landowners may have been curtailed in certain areas. Majumdar and his colleagues, for example, report that in the village they studied near Lucknow, where *zamindari* abolition has taken place, Camars now refuse to perform *begar,* while the barbers refuse to draw water for the Thakurs and will not wash their utensils or remove their leaf plates any more.[58] However, the occurrence of *begar* since Independence has been noted in some areas—by Gittel Steed, for example,[59] and by Shridhar Misra.[60]

[54] Majumdar *et al.,* p. 193.

[55] M. E. Opler and R. D. Singh, "Two Villages of Eastern Uttar Pradesh," *American Anthropologist,* Vol. 54 (1952), p. 180.

[56] *Ibid.,* p. 187.

[57] R. V. Russell and R. B. Hira Lal, *The Tribes and Castes of the Central Provinces of India* (London, 1916), Vol. 4, p. 22.

[58] Majumdar *et al.,* pp. 191–92.

[59] Steed, lecture notes.

[60] Shridhar Misra, "Caste Survey in Two Modal Villages with Stereotyped Discriminations," in "Intercaste Tensions" (above, note 36), p. 58. In a rural survey conducted by Misra, eleven out of forty persons examined on the subject of *begar* admitted that they had to do *begar* at the instance of *zamindars.* Such *begar* usually takes the form of plowing without payment once a year. For some striking descriptions of *begar* during the period of British rule, see G. Emerson, *Voiceless India* (New York, 1944), pp. 28, 173.

A qualification may be suggested, that while a landowner may have both tenants and *kamins*, the two groups need not be identical. He may have *kamins* who are not his tenants. This point is made by Opler and Singh, who also note that when there are disputes between Thakurs, tenants align themselves with their landlords.[61] Perhaps a more crucial consideration, however, is that the Thakurs in Senapur, like the Jats in Rampur, form a caste group which may (despite factional cleavages and differences in wealth) join ranks in solidarity against the lower castes in crucial issues. All the Jat factions in Rampur, for example, united in opposing the Camars over the house-tax matter.

The lower castes, theoretically at least, have a potential retaliatory weapon in the boycott, or withdrawal of their services. Thus, when the Nais of Rampur were informed of a decision of the Jats to reduce the *neg jog* paid at weddings, they stopped shaving and cutting their *jajmans'* hair in protest. But the sequel is instructive: The Jats retaliated by buying razors and shaving themselves. This shows that such protests may prove self-defeating. It also indicates that the *jajmani* system may be disrupted by action of either the *jajmans* or the *kamins*, or by the cumulative effect of both.

As the *jajmani* system declines, a great deal of tension is bound to develop between the landed and the landless, between the upper and lower castes, particularly since the system's decline is concomitant with a great increase in population and a decrease in the size of landholdings. Although the dominant position of the Jats is not yet in jeopardy in Rampur, their influence over the lower castes has been much reduced, and the demands of the lower castes have increased. It would therefore seem that the *jajmani* system contains some explosive potentialities and that, as the system continues to weaken, we may expect to see a heightening of the conflict between the dominant and subordinate castes in villages like Rampur.

Meanwhile, despite the weakening of the *jajmani* system and the inroads of a money economy in Rampur, the social aspects of the caste system have changed very little. The rules of endogamy are not questioned.[62] In spite of the influence of the Arya Samaj, the traditional caste rules governing interdining and the taking of water still prevail. The Jats will not share their hookahs with Camars or sit on

[61] Opler and Singh, "The Division of Labor," p. 495.

[62] Caste endogamy is still the rule even in large cities, as was shown in a study by N. P. Gist, "Caste Differentials in South India," *American Sociological Review*, Vol. 19 (1954), p. 138. "Out of some two thousand married Hindu household heads who supplied information," writes Gist, "only nine stated that they and their wives belong to different castes." These surveys were made in Mysore and Bangalore.

the same string cots with them.[63] When community project speakers address the people of Rampur in would-be democratic assemblages, the Camars remain on the outskirts of the crowd. Patterns of hierarchy and social distance persist, and the psychology of caste still permeates interpersonal relationships.

In some ways caste identifications have even strengthened in Rampur. Among the Jats the emphasis on caste loyalty may represent a defensive reaction to the weakening of the *jajmani* system, while among the Camars it signifies a united stand against the higher-caste landowners. A similar point, on a broader scale, has been made by Srinivas, who discusses the ways in which the modern political system, including universal adult franchise, has strengthened caste.

> The principle of caste is so firmly entrenched in our political and social life that everyone including the leaders have accepted tacitly the principle that, in the provincial cabinets at any rate, each major caste should have a minister. (And this principle has travelled from our provincial capitals back to our village *panchayats*—nowadays the latter give representation on the *panchayat* to each caste including Harijans.) In the first popular cabinet in Mysore State, headed by Shri K. C. Reedy, not only were the ministers chosen on a caste basis, but each had a secretary from his own sub-sub-sub-caste. And today in Mysore this principle is followed not only in every appointment, but also in the allotment of seats in schools and colleges. . . . voting is on a caste basis, and voters do not understand that it is immoral to demand that the elected minister help his caste-folk and village-folk. . . . no explanation of provincial politics in any part of India is possible without reference to caste. . . . In general, it may be said that the last hundred years have seen a great increase in caste solidarity and the concomitant decrease of a sense of interdependence between the different castes living in a region.[64]

While this may perhaps be overstating the case, it is a necessary corrective to the more widely held assumption that caste is crumbling rapidly. The decline of the *jajmani* system then will not necessarily be followed by an automatic or speedy disintegration of the caste system. Instead, caste may continue to take on new functions and manifestations.

[63] Cohn, p. 61 (above, note 39).

[64] M. N. Srinivas, "Castes: Can They Exist in India of Tomorrow?" *Economic Weekly* (Bombay, Oct. 15, 1955), pp. 1231–32. For some other discussions of the new functions of castes, see D. R. Gadgil, *Poona: A Socio-Economic Survey* (Poona: Gokhale Institute, 1952), Part 2, p. 187; B. Ryan, *Caste in Modern Ceylon* (New Brunswick, N.J.: Rutgers University Press, 1953), p. 321; Kingsley Davis, *The Population of India and Pakistan* (Princeton, N.J.: Princeton University Press, 1951), p. 175.

17

Peasant Culture in India and Mexico:

*A Comparative Analysis**

In this chapter I want to compare, briefly but systematically, some of the similarities and differences between the North Indian village of Rampur and the Mexican village of Tepoztlán. The major purpose of this comparison is to contribute toward our general understanding of peasantry. It is recognized that there are similarities among peasants all over the world, even in the most different historical and cultural settings. On the other hand, it is also true that the cultural setting and the general nature of the larger society of which peasantry is a part must undoubtedly influence the forms of peasant life and the very nature of the people.

Since most discussions of peasantry have emphasized the common elements, I have chosen in this chapter to elaborate more fully upon the differences in order to illustrate the wide range of cultural forms possible under the rubric of peasant society and thereby indicate the need for a typology of peasantry. At the same time, I recognize the crucial importance, especially for theoretical purposes, of discerning and documenting the similarity within diversity. Moreover, I suspect that this similarity will probably be greater in the field of values, a field only touched upon in this essay.[1]

* This was first published in 1955, in McKim Marriott, ed., *Village India* (Chicago: Copyright © 1955, University of Chicago Press), pp. 145–70.

[1] I am grateful to Robert Redfield for his kind and stimulating discussion of this and other points. His paper "The Peasant's View of the Good Life" (mimeographed version of a lecture delivered at the University of Chicago, May 14,

Two additional and secondary aspects of this chapter, bearing primarily upon methodological considerations, may now be mentioned. This study represents one of the relatively few examples of first-hand comparative field research by the same investigator in peasant society in different parts of the world. It seems to me that this kind of research enables one to make more detailed and refined comparisons than is generally possible by the traditional library methods, since the investigator carries with him a common frame of reference, similar methods of work, and a similar sense of problem. From a more personal point of view this kind of research pays double dividends. Not only did it provide me with first-hand knowledge of a new culture but it also sharpened and somewhat altered my earlier understanding of Tepoztlán and of Mexico.

Second, this essay raises the question of the degree to which a single village, selected more or less at random in terms of our problem, can tell us something about the nation of which it is a part. It is my own belief that almost any village in a predominantly agricultural nation reflects some distinctive aspects of the nation, its culture, and its problems. It is my hope that this essay will convey to the reader some feeling for the differences not only between Rampur and Tepoztlán but also between India and Mexico.

At the outset, I would like to point to a few difficulties in making comparisons between the two villages. In dealing with two villages in distant and contrasting culture areas of the world the question arises whether the village is a meaningful and proper unit for comparison, especially since the Indian village differs so markedly in its structure and functions from the Mexican village. Despite these differences, I believe that the two villages are sufficiently similar, isolable, and well-defined units for comparative study. However, to acknowledge that the village is an isolable unit does not mean that we should treat it as an isolate. To do so could lead only to a limited understanding. Neither Tepoztlán nor Rampur is an isolated entity. Each, in its own distinctive way, is part of a larger socio-cultural system, a larger whole—the region and the nation—through which it must be understood.[2]

1954) is a pioneer effort toward getting at some of the common elements in peasant value systems. [See Essay 1, above.]

[2] The discussion of this point in my study of Tepoztlán applies with double force to the study of peasant villages in India: "anthropological studies in Mexico . . . have been characterized by what might be called an ideological localism whereby each little community is treated as self-sufficient and isolated. Undoubtedly, this is a carry-over from an older anthropological tradition which was concerned with salvaging cultural data from rapidly disappearing primitive peoples. While such an approach might still have some justification in dealing

Comparison between a Mexican and an Indian village presents problems over and above those encountered in comparing villages within a single country or a single great tradition. Items which exist in one and not in the other are simply not comparable. For example, Tepoztlán has no caste system, and Rampur has no *compadre* system. In Tepoztlán the *municipio* is the landholding unit (for communal lands); in Rampur the village is the landholding unit. How are we to weight the influence of such items on the total culture pattern of the community? Both the caste system and the *compadre* system are cohesive forces in social life, but can we equate them? The answer is probably "No," but the matter of weighting is not so easy.

The difference in size of communities may also be important. Tepoztlán is over three times as large as Rampur, and it may be that some of the matters to be discussed are related to size of population. Then there is the difference in topography and climate. Tepoztlán is in a hilly, mountainous area, while Rampur is on a level, almost treeless plain. However, this difference reflects national differences and to this extent our choice may inadvertently have been advantageous. We generally think of Mexico as a mountainous country and of India in terms of its vast plains.

In regard to climate, both are relatively dry areas. But the average annual rainfall in Tepoztlán is approximately sixty inches, whereas that of Rampur is less than thirty. This difference is less important than it seems, because in both cases the rains come within the four-month rainy season, and there is practically no rain for seven or eight months of the year. Both communities feel the greatest need is for more water for irrigation.

Finally, there is the difference in the intensity with which each community was studied. I spent about two and a half years in five separate visits in Tepoztlán.* I spent only seven months in Rampur

with an isolated tribe in the jungles of New Guinea, it has little justification in studies of modern Mexico.

"In studying communities in Mexico [or India] it is important that the anthropologist become a student not merely of the single community but of the region and the nation as well. The anthropologist must be sufficiently versed in the more important historical, geographical, economic, and cultural characteristics of the region and nation to be able to place his community in relation to each of them, and to indicate just what the community is representative of in the larger scene . . . the anthropologist must know what is unique to his community and what it shares with broader areas, what is new and what is old, what is primitive and what is modern." Oscar Lewis, *Life in a Mexican Village: Tepoztlán Restudied* (Urbana, Ill.: University of Illinois Press, 1951), pp. xx, xxi.

* Since this was written I have spent another two years in the village.

and only a portion of this on a full-time basis, relying much more heavily upon my Indian research assistants. In short, I know Tepoztlán much better than Rampur, and what follows is subject to this limitation.

· T E P O Z T L Á N   A N D R A M P U R   C O M P A R E D ·

Tepoztlán is a Catholic village of about 3,500 people, fifteen miles from Cuernavaca, the state capital, and sixty miles south of Mexico City. It is an ancient highland village which has been continuously inhabited since the Archaic period, or for at least two thousand years. Two languages are spoken in Tepoztlán: Spanish and the indigenous Nahuatl. About half the population is bilingual, the other half speaks only Spanish.

Rampur is a Hindu village of 1,100 people, about fifteen miles from New Delhi, the national capital. It is only two miles from a major highway which runs to Delhi. It is an old village which was conquered about 750 years ago by the Jats, an ethnic group which is now the dominant caste in the village. The language spoken is a local dialect of Hindi mixed with a sprinkling of Punjabi. Only a few people speak English.

Both villages may be designated as peasant societies in the sense that both are old and stable populations with a great love of the land, both depend upon agriculture, both are integrated into larger political units such as the state and the nation and are subject to their laws, both exist side by side with cities and have been exposed to urban influences for long periods of time, and both have borrowed from other rural areas as well as from urban centers but have managed to integrate the new traits into a relatively stable culture pattern. Moreover, both communities exist by a relatively primitive technology and depend upon hoe culture as well as plow and oxen in agriculture; both produce primarily for subsistence but also participate in a money economy and use barter; both are relatively poor, have a high incidence of illiteracy, a high birth rate and a high death rate; and, finally, both communities have lived under foreign domination for long periods in their history and have developed that peculiar combination of dependence on and hostility toward government which is so characteristic of colonial peoples.

• SETTLEMENT PATTERN •

So much for the broad similarities. Now let us examine some differences. One of the first things that impressed me about Rampur and other Indian villages, as compared to Tepoztlán, was the village settlement pattern (or rather the absence of pattern), the greater density of population, the greater crowding, the housing shortage, the shortage of space for animals, and, in general, an atmosphere of much greater poverty.

Unlike Tepoztlán (and other Mexican highland villages), with its relatively well-ordered grid pattern of streets at right angles, its plaza and market place, its *palacio*, or government building, and its central church, Rampur has no orderly arrangement of streets, many of which are narrow dead-end alleys, no village center, no government or public building for the village as a whole.[3]

In Tepoztlán the houses are spread out, and most house sites have their own patio, corral, and orchard; in Rampur the houses are crowded together, and, unlike Tepoztlán, which has many vacant houses, there was not a single available house for our field workers in Rampur.

Another thing which stood out in Rampur because of its contrast with Tepoztlán was the much greater separation of the sexes. The preferred arrangement for family living is to have two residences, one for the women and children, another for the men and the cattle. There are also two *caupals*, or men's houses, one for each division of the village, which are used for male smoking groups and other social gatherings.

• LAND AND ECONOMY •

I have said that agriculture is important in both villages. But here the similarity ends. In Rampur agriculture is much more intensive than in Tepoztlán. Of the 784 acres of Rampur, 721, or well over 90 per cent of the total area, is under cultivation, as compared with only 15 per cent in Tepoztlán. Moreover, Tepoztlán depends almost

---

[3] That some of the elements here described may apply to India as a whole is suggested by the description by Spate, who writes of the settlement pattern as follows: "There is in general very little that looks like a 'plan,' other than that dictated by such site factors as alignment along bluffs or levees, grouping around a fort or a tank; but within the seemingly chaotic agglomeration there is, as a rule, a strong internal differentiation, that of the separate quarters for various castes." O. H. K. Spate, *India and Pakistan: A General and Regional Geography* (London: Methuen, 1954), p. 172.

entirely on a single crop, corn, with beans and squash of minor importance, whereas Rampur has a diversity of crops which include, in order of importance, wheat, millets (*juar* and *bajra*), gram, sugar cane, and hemp. Unlike Tepoztlán, which has no irrigation and produces only one crop a year, Rampur grows two crops a year on about one-fifth of its lands which are under canal and well irrigation.

The apparently greater agricultural resources of Rampur are tempered by serious limiting factors. Rampur has practically no grazing lands and no forest resources. This makes for a crucial fuel shortage so that the valuable cow dung has to be used for fuel instead of fertilizer, and the cattle have to be stall-fed rather than pastured. By contrast, Tepoztlán has very rich forest resources (almost 50 per cent of the total area), and these provide ample firewood and charcoal both for domestic consumption and for sale.

Still other differences in the village economy need to be mentioned. In Tepoztlán over 90 per cent of the 853 families engage directly in agriculture as cultivators, and until recently even the shopkeepers and artisans would close shop to plant corn when the rains came. In Rampur only 53 per cent of the 150 families engage directly in agriculture, that is, are cultivators, and most of these belong to a single caste, the Jats.

The importance of this difference goes beyond the matter of the relative proportion in the community of what in the United States would be called the "farm" and "nonfarm" populations. It is related to a fundamental difference in the social and economic structure of the two villages. In Tepoztlán the family is much more of a self-sufficient unit, free to engage in a variety of activities and occupations, and it cherishes this self-sufficiency and independence from others. In Rampur the specialization of occupations along caste lines makes for a greater dependence of the villagers upon each other. But it is a dependence organized along hierarchical lines, institutionalized in the traditional, semifeudal *jajmani* system of reciprocal obligations in economic and ceremonial affairs among the various castes. In the past the potential contradictions between the interests of the farm and nonfarm populations in the village were held in check by the power of the landholders and by the lack of alternatives for the untouchables and other low-caste people. Now that the system is weakening, primarily because of the increased opportunities for employment in munitions factories, the nonfarm population in the village is beginning to take on aspects of a rural proletariat with its own special problems and its own sense of growing power.

If, on the basis of other studies, one could generalize these differences on a national level, it would be possible to say that in India there is a much greater landless rural proletariat than in Mexico and that this may well have important implications in the respective political developments in the two countries. And I might add that the Five Year Plans of the government of India, with their emphasis upon increased agricultural production, have relatively little to offer to the rural nonagricultural portions of the population.

Returning again to the agricultural economy, we find that in both villages there are privately owned and communally owned lands. The communal lands of Tepoztlán are truly communal in the sense that any member of the *municipio* of Tepoztlán has equal rights to their use. However, the communal lands of Rampur are held by the Jats on a share basis, and the rights of the Jat families in the communal, or *samilat,* lands are proportionate to the size of their holdings of private land.

In Tepoztlán about 80 per cent of all the land is communally held either as municipal lands or, since the Mexican Revolution, as *ejidal* (common) lands. In Rampur about 7 per cent of the lands are communally owned, and most of these consist of the village house sites, the village pond, roads, and some uncultivable areas. Traditionally, the communal lands in North India were intended to serve as pasture and woodland. In both Rampur and Tepoztlán the communal lands have been a source of constant strife, but for different reasons. In the former it was between families within the village who attempted to appropriate communal lands for themselves. In the latter it was between villages, concerning the rights of villages to the communal lands. It is important to note that in both cases the communal lands are not subject to taxation. In the case of Tepoztlán this means that about 80 per cent of its total area is tax-free.

Population pressure on the land is considerable in both communities. But whereas Tepoztlán has 1.5 acres of cultivable land per capita, Rampur has only .75 of an acre. The advantage for Tepoztlán is even greater than is indicated by these figures, for, whereas Rampur has practically no other land, Tepoztlán has an additional eight acres per capita of forest and grazing lands, and about 10 per cent of this area can be used for growing corn by the primitive method of cutting and burning the forest to make temporary clearings.

In Tepoztlán only about 36 per cent of the families had private landholdings, as compared to 52 per cent of the families in Rampur.[4]

---

[4] Again the difference is somewhat offset because almost 20 per cent of Tepoztecan families have *ejido* holdings. During the course of the Spanish Conquest and domination of Mexico, from 1519 to 1810, Tepoztlán lost a portion of its best lands, which were converted into sugar plantations. After the Mexican Revolution of 1910–20 and as part of the national *ejido* program, Tepoztlán recovered many of its lost lands, and these were divided among the landless villagers into small holdings.

Whereas the landless families of Tepoztlán have access to the rich resources of the communal lands, the landless of Rampur have to depend primarily upon nonagricultural occupations. It may be noted that in both communities hoe culture is looked down upon as a last resort of the poor. In Rampur about fifteen low-caste families raise vegetables as a part-time occupation on land rented from the Jats. Some Jat families have also taken to raising vegetables.

The size of private landholdings shows fundamental similarities in both communities. Holdings are very small. In both cases 50 per cent of the holdings are less than five acres, 70 per cent are less than ten acres, and 90 per cent are less than twenty acres. The range in size of holdings is also remarkably similar: from less than a half acre, of which there are many, to fifty acres, of which there is one in each community. It is noteworthy that in both Tepoztlán and Rampur the peasants independently suggested the same figure of about ten acres as a desirable minimum-sized holding for a "decent" standard of living for a family of five. This figure is apparently based upon the acreage that can be worked economically with a single team of oxen.

As might be expected, there is a striking difference between the two communities in regard to the respective role of livestock in the economy and the attitude toward livestock. In India there is an ancient cattle complex, and most people are vegetarians. In Mexico domesticated cattle are relatively recent, dating back to the Spanish Conquest. The cattle industry was never very important and never became well integrated with the economy. In Tepoztlán there is relatively little livestock, and most of it is of poor quality. Investment in cattle is viewed as precarious. By contrast, the little village of Rampur supports a remarkably large number of livestock and this with practically no grazing resources. Whereas 85 per cent of the cultivators in plow agriculture own at least one ox in Rampur, only 45 per cent own oxen in Tepoztlán.

• SOCIAL ORGANIZATION •

It is in the field of social organization that we find the most remarkable differences between these two peasant societies. Indeed, they seem like separate worlds, and I might add that by comparison with Rampur, Tepoztlán in retrospect seems much less complicated and much more familiar, very Western-like, and almost North American. Undoubtedly one of the reasons for this is the fact that the Spanish Conquest left its indelible mark on Mexican culture. Spain, for all its cultural idiosyncrasies in sixteenth-century Europe, was part of the Western European culture pattern.

The distinctive aspects of the social organization of Rampur as compared to Tepoztlán can be discussed in terms of (1) the more pervasive role of kinship, (2) the presence of a caste system, (3) the existence of multiple factions based on kinship, and (4) the differences in the role of the village as a community.

1. *The role of kinship.* In Rampur kinship plays a major role in the ordering of human relations and is the basis of most social and political groupings such as the *thollas* and *panas*, the clans, the smoking groups, the factions, the castes, the *panchayats*, and the intervillage networks. The extended family is strong and forms a basic unit for individual identification. The caste system acts as an integrating and cohesive factor in village life, primarily within the castes and to some extent between castes. Caste members are bound by kinship, by common traditions, interests, and social interaction. The castes in turn are bound by economic interdependence resulting from the specialization of occupations, and this is formalized by the *jajmani* system of reciprocal obligations.

In Tepoztlán kinship is a much less pervasive force: the nuclear family predominates, the extended family is weak (the elaborate *compadre* system seems designed to make up for this), and social relations and social solidarity are organized on religious, political, and other nonkinship bases. The independence and individualism of the nuclear or biological family in Tepoztlán make for an atomistic quality in social relations. And while these discrete family units are organized into larger units such as the *barrio,* the village, and the *municipio*, these organizational forms are relatively impersonal and do not impinge so directly upon the lives of the individuals as does the extended family, the faction, and the caste in Rampur. In Rampur the extended family, the faction, and the caste are the units which demand one's loyalties and channelize most of one's life-activities. But by the same token they provide the individual with a much greater degree of psychological security than is present in Tepoztlán, and this in turn affects the quality of community life.

The role of kinship organization on the political level is also markedly different in the two villages. In Tepoztlán the connection between the village and the state and federal government is in terms of elected officials who vote as members of their *demarcación*, an arbitrary division of the village for secular purposes. The officials do not represent kinship units or even the *barrios*. But in Rampur the political organization and the kinship organization are more closely intertwined. Each of the two headmen of the village represents a *pana*, which is essentially a kinship unit consisting of related patrilineages.

Rampur, like other villages in North India, is fundamentally a part of a larger intervillage network based upon kinship ties. Other villagers are very often relatives, and entire villages are classified by the kinship terminology as mother's brother villages, grandfather villages, grandmother villages, etc. As we have seen, Rampur is a member of a four-village unit known as a *caugama* and of a twenty-village unit known as a *bisagama*. These are known as Dabas villages, that is, they are descended from a common ancestor, Dabas. These twenty-village units in turn are members of larger intervillage networks which culminate in a 360-village unit, whose inhabitants' ancestors were all related in the distant past. The four- and twenty-village units are still active in this area, although less so than in the past. Within them there is a traditional division of labor for ceremonial and *panchayat* purposes, and each village performs special functions at *panchayat* meetings.

2. *The caste system.* In Rampur the caste system organizes life in terms of hierarchical principles and plays up the status differences between groups. The Jats are by tradition agriculturalists and own all the land of the village, including the house sites, that is, the land upon which the houses of the other castes are built. In a sense, then, the other castes, even the Brahmans, are in the village at the sufferance of the Jats. The village is officially known as a Jat village, and clearly the Jats dominate village life. Even the formal organization of the village into two *panas,* each with its headman, is solely in terms of the Jats. The lower castes tend to live on the outskirts of the village and are not part of this formal organization despite the fact that some of the lower-caste families are ancient inhabitants.

In Tepoztlán there is no caste system, and the society is much more democratically organized. No one group dominates the life of the village. Each family, whether rich or poor, owns its house site and house, has recognized status, and can proudly say, "This is my village." The quality of interpersonal relations among Tepoztecans is comparable with what exists within the single caste of Jats, that is, status differences are played down at least on a verbal level, and wealthy individuals are careful not to "pull rank."

In Rampur the caste system divides the village and weakens the sense of village solidarity. The caste generally represents a distinct ethnic group with its own history, traditions, and identifications, and each caste lives in more or less separate quarters of the village. There are separate wells for the Harijans, or untouchables; dining and smoking between higher and lower castes are still taboo; low-caste persons (this does not include Baniya, Khati, or Nai) will not sit together on the same *carpai,* or cot, with a Jat or Brahman; and when government officials come to the village and call meetings to explain the new Community Development Projects, the Harijans may attend, but they stay off to one side in the audience and "know their place." In a sense, then, each caste, or at least those with larger representation in the village, forms a separate little community. The social structure of the village therefore has somewhat the quality of our urban communities with their variety of ethnic and minority groups and a high degree of division of labor.

In Tepoztlán the population and the tradition are much more homogeneous, and there is nothing comparable to the divisive effects of the caste system. Perhaps the nearest approximation to segmentation in the village results from the organization of separate *barrios*, each with its own chapel, patron saint, and *esprit de corps*. The *barrios*, like the castes, can be thought of as subcommunities within the village. This was truer thirty years ago, when *barrio* localism in Tepoztlán was stronger than it is today. But of course the *barrio* and the caste are very different in nature. The *barrio* is primarily a religious and social unit rather than a kinship unit. It does not control marriage, and there is no tradition of *barrio* members' having a common origin. And while the physical limits of the *barrios* have remained remarkably stable over the past few hundred years, *barrio* membership is changeable, and one can belong to two *barrios* at the same time, provided the *barrio* house-site tax is paid. Moreover, the *barrio* organization is strictly within the village and is unified on a village-wide basis by the central village church.[5] But the castes cut across villages and have their cross-village organizations.

The caste system in Rampur is undergoing changes and in some ways may even be said to be breaking down. The proximity to Delhi, the Gandhian movement against untouchability, the preaching of the Arya Samaj, and increased off-farm employment opportunities as a result of the past two world wars have all had some effect.

Perhaps the greatest change in the caste system has occurred in relation to the occupational structure, that is, caste and occupation are now less synonymous than formerly. Some of the Jat families no longer cultivate their land, and their children have become school-teachers or have taken miscellaneous jobs in Delhi. The Brahmans no longer carry on their priestly functions. Most of them are occu-

[5] It seems clear that Catholicism and the Church, embracing the principle of hierarchy and centralization, play a much more decisive role in the formal organization of Tepoztlán and other Mexican villages than does Hinduism in Rampur and other North Indian villages. That the Mexican pattern applies over even wider areas is shown by Redfield and Tax, who write of Mesoamerican Indian society as follows: "The community consists of a village, a group of hamlets or a rural region, but in any case its residents look toward a common civic and religious center, where is housed the image of a saint that is patron to them all. The community tends to be endogamous." Robert Redfield and Sol Tax, "General Characteristics of Present Day Mesoamerican Indian Society," in Sol Tax (ed.), *Heritage of Conquest* (Glencoe, Ill.: Free Press, 1953), p. 31.

pancy tenants of the Jats, but only four are cultivators; one family sells milk, another does tailoring, and the remainder are employed in jobs outside the village. Though the Camars are leather workers by caste, only two are now shoemakers, and they no longer skin the dead cattle. The substitution of Persian wheels for the earlier system of drawing water with leather buckets threw some of the Camars out of work; three families are weavers, four rent land from the Jats for vegetable gardening, four are employed outside the village, and the remainder earn a living in the village by combining part-time agricultural labor with cattle raising. Of all the castes, the Bhangis, or sweepers, seem to have shown the least change in occupation.

There have been other changes. Children of all castes now attend the village school, and there is no discrimination or segregation in the seating arrangements. And since 1949 a Camar has been elected to the new four-village council. However, despite all these trends the caste system is still very strong in the village.

3. *Factions*. In both villages there are factions, but their structure, functions, and role in village life differ greatly. As we have shown in Chapter 4, factions in Rampur are an old, ingrained pattern in village life and must be considered as a basic structural aspect of traditional village organization, along with lineages, castes, *thollas*, *panas*, and other groupings. The factions in Rampur are small and relatively cohesive groups of varied lineage and clan composition which act as units in social, economic, and ceremonial undertakings. The quarrels between factions center around wealth, women, and land.

In Tepoztlán factions are political groupings rather than kinship groupings and reflect diverse social and economic interests. The factions are fewer in number, only two as a rule, and are larger and more loosely organized. Faction membership is less stable and faction loyalty more tenuous. In Tepoztlán, unlike Rampur, brothers may be members of hostile and opposed factions. In Rampur, first, second, and even third cousins are generally members of the same faction.

One of the major cleavages in Tepoztlán was between the *Bolsheviki* and the *Centrales*. These groups became clearly delineated in the early twenties when two socialistically oriented Tepoztecans from Mexico City, who were members of the Confederación Regional de Obreros Mexicanos, returned to the village to organize the peasants in defense of the communal lands against the sons of the ex-*caciques* (political bosses) who controlled the local government and allegedly were exploiting the forest resources of the *municipio* in their own interests. The *Bolsheviki* had their greatest strength in the smaller and poorer *barrios* of the upper part of the village, while the

Centrales were strongest in the larger central *barrios*. To some extent this grouping corresponded to class distinctions, since, in the days before the Mexican Revolution of 1910–20, most of the *caciques* and well-to-do merchants lived in the center of the village.

In contrast to the predominantly private familial objectives of factions in Rampur, the objectives of the factions in Tepoztlán were broadly social and political. The aim was to dominate the local government and to appeal to the voters in terms of broad public issues. In the twenties the slogan was "Conserve the Communal Forests," and in the thirties the new organization known as the *Fraternales* had the slogan "Union, Justice and Civilization."

Since the middle thirties the factional groupings have more and more become political groupings which align themselves for or against the government in power. The establishment by Tepoztecans of two competing bus lines from Tepoztlán to Cuernavaca has led to bitter quarrels and violence and has again split the village into hostile groupings.

4. *The village as a community.* The comparative consideration of the question, "Is the village a community?" is more complex than it seems, for there are numerous dimensions of "community," such as the ecological, physical, social, economic, political, religious, and psychological. To what extent do the physical limits of the village define the limits for these dimensions? Or to what extent do these aspects of community spill over into other villages so that the community might better be defined in terms of units larger than the single village? As we might expect, not all aspects of community have the same spatial distribution, so that a village may be a clearly self-contained unit for some purposes and not for others.

There is yet another aspect of the problem, namely, what is the quality of social relations, of mutual interdependence of persons or social groups within each village? We must be ready to deal with the possibility that although Village A does not define the physical area of social, economic, and other relations as clearly as does Village B, the quality of such relations in A or subgroups within it may be so much more cohesive that we are justified in saying that there is more community within A (as well as the villages into which this spills over) than there is in B. With these observations in mind, let us first consider those aspects of community which Rampur and Tepoztlán share and then go on to consider some of the more important differences.

Both Tepoztlán and Rampur are corporate bodies which enjoy legal status and can take suits to law courts. Both are units of taxation for the respective revenue departments. In both cases the greater part of the social, economic, and religious activities takes place within the village. The village is home and there is relatively little out-migration, but more in Tepoztlán than in Rampur. Of Tepoztlán it can be said that most villagers are born there, live and work there, and die there. This cannot be said of Rampur, for the married women were not born there, and the daughters of the village will not die there. Yet the very designation "daughter of the village" speaks eloquently for the sense of village consciousness.

In both villages, despite the existence of schisms and factions, there are occasions when the villagers act together as a unit for some common goal such as the building of a road or a school, drainage of a pond, or the defense of the village against attack from the outside. In the case of Tepoztlán the defense of the village last occurred in the twenties, when it was attacked by the *Cristeros*.[6] In the case of Rampur one must go back almost a hundred years for a comparable occasion.

One of the important differences between our two villages is related to the contrast in settlement pattern between highland Mexico and the Indo-Gangetic plain. The Mexican pattern is that of relatively self-contained nuclear groupings or pockets of a small number of villages centrally located within *municipios*, so that the density of population decreases almost to zero as one moves from the center or seat of the community to the periphery. In North India, on the other hand, there is an almost even and continuous scattering of large numbers of villages, so that no distinct pattern of groupings emerges. Thus in Mexico the physical groupings of villages practically define and encompass the social and political groupings, whereas in India the physical pattern gives much less of a clue, and one must trace out the specific kinship and other alignments which organize villages into units. This contrast between the centripetal settlement pattern of Mexican villages and the amorphous pattern of India applies also to the internal settlement pattern of the villages, so that the Mexican village stands out more clearly as a centrally organized unit.

From an economic point of view, the village of Rampur is a more clearly isolable and self-contained community than the village of Tepoztlán. Village boundaries are clearly fixed and contain within them the land resources upon which the villagers depend for their livelihood. In Tepoztlán the larger *municipio* is the functional resource unit. Village boundaries are ill-defined and are essentially moral boundaries, whereas the municipal boundaries are clearly demarcated. It is within the bounds of the *municipio* that the everyday world of the Tepoztecan exists. Here the farmers work the commu-

---

[6] The *Cristeros* movement was a counterrevolutionary rebellion organized and supported by the Church against the Mexican government.

nal lands, cut and burn communal forests, graze their cattle, and hunt for medicinal herbs.

From the point of view of village government Tepoztlán stands out as a more clearly organized and centralized community. When I first studied Tepoztlán, local government seemed very weak indeed, but by comparison with Rampur and North India in general it now seems extremely well developed, what with elected village presidents, councils, judges, the collection of taxes for public works, police powers, and the obligations of villagers to give twelve days a year for co-operative village works. The traditional local government in Rampur is much more informal and consists of caste *panchayats* which cut across village lines. Only recently has the government established a new statutory local *panchayat* with taxation powers, which, however, has not been effective so far.

Village-wide leadership in Tepoztlán is formally expressed by the local government. In Rampur it does not yet exist, and the idea of positive constructive leadership in the public interest is only now beginning, particularly in connection with the establishment of public schools. As yet there are no village heroes or outstanding citizens who are popular for their contribution to village welfare as a whole.

In Rampur leadership is limited to faction leadership and is primarily of a protective and defensive nature in which each faction or combination of factions defends its family interests. The "leader" is essentially a spokesman for a family or a group of related families and has little authority to make independent decisions or to exercise power over the group.

In Tepoztlán there is more verbalization about village community spirit. Candidates for political office always speak in terms of "*mi pueblo*" and promise to improve their village. The fact that officials may in fact do very little and may even steal public funds is another matter. But at least the sense of village identification and loyalty exists as a potential ideological force. Village solidarity is also reflected, albeit in a negative sense, by Tepoztecan characterizations of the surrounding villages of the *municipio* as "assassins," "dullheads," "primitive," and "backward." Moreover, the bogeyman used to frighten children is often a man from a neighboring village. In Rampur there were no comparable designations of neighboring villages, most of which contain related lineages.

The difference in the role of the village as a community can also be appreciated if we examine marriage in both cases. In Tepoztlán over 90 per cent of the marriages take place within the village, and, lest this be thought a function of the larger size of the village, we can point out that 42 per cent of the marriages were within the same *barrio* within the village. The single important rule in marriage is not to marry close relatives, and this generally means eliminating first, second, and third cousins.

In Rampur the question of whom one can marry is much more complicated. Marriage is controlled by a combination of factors, namely, caste endogamy, village exogamy, limited territorial exogamy, and clan exogamy. As a result of all these regulations fathers or go-betweens must go long distances to find eligible mates for their daughters, and for months before the marriage season they scour the countryside for husbands.

Our study of Rampur showed that the 266 married women living in the village came from about two hundred separate villages at distances of up to forty miles. We found also that the average distance between spouses' villages varied considerably by caste, with the lower castes, who are less numerous, having to go much longer distances. If we now examine the other side of the picture, that is, the daughters who married out of the village, we find that over 220 daughters of Rampur married out into about two hundred villages. Thus, this relatively small village of 150 households becomes the locus of affinal kinship ties with over four hundred other villages. This makes for a kind of rural cosmopolitanism which is in sharpest contrast to the village isolationism in Mexico.

• THE PEOPLE •

Finally we come to a brief comparison of the people in both villages. I have noted elsewhere that Tepoztecans are a reserved, constricted people who tend to view other human beings as dangerous and the world in general as hostile. Children are required to be obedient, quiet, and unobtrusive, and parents play upon children's fears to maintain control. There is a certain pervading air of tension and fearfulness among Tepoztecans; the individual and the small biological family seem to stand alone against the world.

Despite the much smaller size of Rampur, one has the impression that there are more people there. One rarely sees a solitary figure: children play in groups, men talk and smoke in groups, women go to the well or collect cow dung in groups, and a visitor is always surrounded and followed about by crowds of people. The low value placed upon privacy in Rampur is in marked contrast with Tepoztlán, where privacy is so valued that one gets the feeling of an apartment-house psychology in this ancient village.

Faces are different in the two villages. In Tepoztlán, outside the home, faces are generally unsmiling, unrevealing masks. In Rampur faces seem more secure. Children are more open-faced and laughing, old men are bland and peaceful, young men restless but unrebellious, women straight and proud. Here too there is individual reserve and formalized behavior, but it does not seem to mask so much of an undercurrent of hostility and fear as in Tepoztlán.

The women of Rampur work even harder than the women of Tepoztlán, but they appear less drab and bemeaned. They seem strong, bold, gay, and sharp-tongued. Their skirts and head scarves are brilliantly colored and spangled with rhinestones and mirrors. Heavy silver jewelry on their ankles, wrists, and necks seems to validate their worth as women. Even with their faces modestly covered, the women of Rampur seem more independent than Tepoztecan women and have less of a martyr complex.[7]

It must be remembered that these observations on the people of Rampur are highly impressionistic and deserve more careful study.

· CONCLUSIONS ·

I believe that our comparative data from these two villages demonstrate the wide range of culture that can exist in peasant societies. When I went to India I expected to find many similarities between Indian and Mexican peasant communities, this despite my earlier critique of the folk-society concept. I did find similarities, but on the whole I was more impressed by the differences. The similarities are greatest in material culture, level of technology, and economics, and the differences are greatest in social organization, value systems, and personality. In terms of raising the standard of living the problems seem much the same, for the bulk of the population in both villages is poor, illiterate, landless, and lives so close to the survival margin that it cannot afford to experiment with new things and ideas.

[7] David G. Mandelbaum, in his article "The World and the World View of the Kota" in *Village India,* has suggested that some of our findings on Rampur are not only local or regional but reflect a basic Indic quality and are found in most villages in India. Among these traits he mentions ranked groupings, concern with pollution, the wide contractual and informal relations with other villagers and other groups, a reluctance to delegate authority to leaders, and a jealous guarding of traditional functions by each village (p. 251). Mandelbaum also raises the interesting question of how to explain the greater psychological security of the villagers of Rampur as compared to Tepoztlán, especially in the face of the reported quarrels and factional disputes in Rampur. He writes, "Can it be that the quarrels, the status competition, the defensive machinations, add up to a world which is generally more rewarding than another which may be as well endowed physically but not as well provided with societal extensions of the self? In [Rampur] . . . the individual sees himself as always identified with a large range of people, as part of a main. In Tepoztlán the individual evidently more often sees himself as an island, or perhaps as part of an archipelago" (p. 252).

However, the poverty of the Indian people seems so much greater and the agrarian problems so overwhelming and complex as to defy any easy solution even on the theoretical level.

In making comparisons between Mexico and India, we must remember that they are in different stages of evolution in terms of nationhood. Mexico has had its political independence for almost 150 years and has lived through the great Revolution of 1910–20, while India has only recently gained its freedom and has not had the equivalent of the Mexican agrarian revolution. These broad differences are reflected in many ways in our two villages.

In stressing the range of variation possible under the rubric of peasant society, I do not intend to suggest that the concept "peasant society" is not meaningful or useful as a classification for comparative research. However, it is not sufficiently predictive in regard to cultural content and structure to take the place of knowledge of concrete reality situations, especially in planning programs of culture change. For both applied and theoretical anthropology we need typologies of peasantry for the major culture areas of the world, such as Latin America, India, and Africa. Moreover, within each area we need more refined subclassifications. Only after such studies are available will we be in a position to formulate broad generalizations about the dynamics of peasant culture as a whole. The difficulties encountered in this paper suggest that a typology of peasant societies for Mexico or Latin American would hardly serve for North India. However, once we had adequate typologies for both areas, meaningful comparisons could more readily be made.

One of the most striking findings in our study of Rampur, especially when compared with the report of Beals[8] on a South Indian village, is the remarkable stability of local village life and institutions, despite the proximity of Rampur to Delhi and the many urban influences to which it has been subject, such as Arya Samaj, the Congress and other political movements, and increased opportunities for education and jobs. The stability is particularly evident in the agricultural economy. The Jats still love the land; in the last fifty years there have been only two families who sold their land and left the village. The land-tenure system continues as of old, with the Jats still in control. The caste system still remains strong and dominates the thinking of the villagers, despite the many reformist movements and the coming of independence. But the *jajmani* system has weakened, and this has increased intercaste tensions, particularly in the case of the Camars.

Rampur and Tepoztlán face many common problems. In both vil-

[8] Alan Robin Beals, "Change in the Leadership of a Mysore Village," *Economic Weekly*, Vol. 5 (Bombay, 1953), pp. 487–92.

lages population has increased rapidly in the last thirty years, means of communication have been improved, there is greater dependence upon a cash economy, education is increasingly valued, and the general aspiration level of the people is going up. But there have been no comparable changes in agricultural production.

We have seen that both villages are meaningful units for comparative study. However, our analysis has shown the complexities involved in evaluating the extent to which each village is a community. From some points of view it would seem that Tepoztlán is more of an organized and centralized village community, that is, in terms of the internal settlement pattern, the greater ethnic homogeneity of the population, the formal organization of village government with elected and paid village officials, the religious organization with a central church, the village market and plaza, and the absence of multiple intervillage networks based on kinship.

From the point of view of ecology Rampur is a more clearly defined and self-contained community than Tepoztlán. Moreover, if we define community in terms of the degree and intensity of interaction and interdependence of people, then we might conclude that, despite the divisive effects of castes and multiple factions within castes, there is more community within Rampur than within Tepoztlán. Villagers in Rampur seem psychologically more secure and relate better to each other. There is a greater readiness to engage in co-operative activities within kinship and caste. The villager spends a greater proportion of his time in some group activity, in smoking groups, in the extended family, in co-operative economic undertakings, and in the caste councils. There is more frequent visiting and more sociability. It is tempting to view the greater verbalization about village identification and solidarity in Tepoztlán as a psychological compensation for the actual atomistic nature of social relations. And by the same token the absence of such verbalization in Rampur may reflect the greater cohesiveness of social relations.

Our data on social organization from North India call attention to aspects of village organization, both in its internal and in its external relations, which either have been neglected or have not been given sufficient weight in earlier considerations of peasantry and in the formulations of models for the peasant society. It will be recalled that in Redfield's model the peasant society is intermediate between the folk society and civilization. It differs from the folk society in that it has developed economic and political relations with the city, but in its relations with other villages it still retains a good deal of the folk quality of isolation and "looking in." [9]

[9] Robert Redfield, *The Primitive World and Its Transformations* (Ithaca: Cornell University Press, 1953), p. 33.

This formulation applies better to Tepoztlán and other Mexican villages than to Rampur and other North Indian villages. It does not adequately provide for situations like Rampur, where the village is part of multiple intervillage networks and where a single village is related by affinal and lineage ties with over four hundred other villages, thereby making for a kind of rural cosmopolitanism.

The widespread affinal and lineage relationships of Rampur find their closest parallel in reports of tribal societies rather than of peasant societies. And indeed there is a tribal flavor in the Jat social organization which recalls the description by Evans-Pritchard of the Nuer, a people of the Anglo-Egyptian Sudan numbering over 200,-000 and consisting of many tribes, some of which have populations of over 40,000. In both cases we find patrilineal clans, maximal and minimal lineages, the dominance of a single lineage within villages, and local exogamy.[10] Evans-Pritchard writes:

> . . . Nuer people see themselves as a unique community and their culture as a unique culture. . . . All Nuer live in a continuous stretch of country. There are no isolated sections. However, their feeling of community goes deeper than recognition of cultural identity. Between Nuer, wherever they hail from, and though they be strangers to one another, friendly relations are at once established when they meet outside their country, for a Nuer is never a foreigner to another as he is to a Dinka or Shilluk.[11]
>
> Their members, individuals and families, move often and freely. . . . Wherever they go they are easily incorporated into the new community through one or more kinship links . . . Nuer frequently visit all the villages in their neighborhood, and in all of them they have kinsfolk . . . the different local communities of a whole tribe could be presented on a single genealogical chart. Given unlimited time and patience, the entire population of Nuerland could be so presented. *There are no closed communities.*[12]

The contrast is striking between this and the picture of small localized hamlets of the mountainous areas of the Philippines[13] in which groups in the next valley are fair game for head-hunting.

Our data suggest that it may be helpful to re-examine a good deal of the literature on the social structure of folk and peasant societies in terms of our well-known and traditional concepts of endogamy and

[10] E. E. Evans-Pritchard, *The Nuer* (Oxford: Clarendon Press, 1947), pp. 123–24, and *Kinship and Marriage among the Nuer* (Oxford: Clarendon Press, 1951), pp. 1–48.

[11] Evans-Pritchard, *The Nuer*, p. 123.

[12] Evans-Pritchard, *Kinship and Marriage*, p. 29.

[13] R. F. Barton, "Ifugao Economics," *University of California Publications in American Archaeology and Ethnology*, Vol. 15, No. 5, pp. 385–446.

exogamy, but from a somewhat different point of view than in the past. I believe most discussions of exogamy and endogamy have been in terms of rules applying to some unit, generally a clan or lineage within a local community. But when the entire local group is exogamous or endogamous very important consequences follow—indeed so important that it might be useful to add endogamy and exogamy as crucial universal variables in our models of the folk society and peasant society. Moreover, these two variables seem to be quite independent of some of the other variables, such as size and homogeneity. The world-view of a small, homogeneous, and endogamous village or local group will necessarily be more "isolationist" and "inward-looking" than that of a small, homogeneous, but exogamous village or local group. Furthermore, the difference between exogamy and endogamy sets up processes which in themselves accentuate localism or play it down. When half the total adult population (i.e., the women of the patrilocal exogamous village) goes out of the village generation after generation, and new women from other villages come in, there is the basis for a type of intervillage relation which differs considerably from that of endogamous villages or communities. In the former case there is a natural development of a "one-world" concept in terms of a region whose limits are determined by kinship bonds. Also, in the case of exogamic villages the children are reared by parents from different villages, so that in a sense village differences are bred out over the generations. Murdock has recently demonstrated this last point with American Indian data.

The difference between the "inward-looking" and the "outward-looking" peasant village is of course a relative matter. All tribal and peasant societies have some relations with the outside. It might therefore be more profitable to compare the nature, occasions, and quality of these relations. In the case of Tepoztlán and Rampur the differences are striking. In the former, trade is the primary bond between Tepoztlán and the outlying villages, with religious pilgrimages ranking second, and kinship ties a very low third. By contrast, in Rampur intervillage relations result primarily from affinal and consanguinal ties, with religious pilgrimages ranking a low second, and trade a very low third. The type of impersonality in intervillage relations based on trade, reported by Redfield for Guatemala[14] and applicable also to Tepoztlán, would be unthinkable in the case of North Indian villages where relations are more intimate and personal because they are primarily familial and not trade relations.

While the distinction between relatively inward-looking and outward looking communities may be one of the differentiating charac-

[14] Robert Redfield, "Primitive Merchants of Guatemala," *Quarterly Journal of Inter-American Affairs,* 1 (Washington, D.C., 1939), p. 53.

teristics between a tribal society and a peasant society, the distinction also has meaning both *within* the tribal level and *within* the peasant level. It may be argued that kinship ties, no matter how far-flung, still represent an inward-looking orientation. We believe, however, that there is a significant social and psychological difference between relations confined within a small area and to relatively few people and relations which, though still based on kinship, are spread out over vast areas and encompass thousands of people who are personally unknown, yet are potentially accessible and part of the in-group.

A typology of peasant societies must also include as a variable the role of kinship, that is, the extent to which the society is organized on a kinship basis. Where the kinship basis is pervasive, as in Rampur, we can say that the society is more primitive or tribal. As Kroeber writes: "It is generally accepted that among primitive peoples society is structured primarily on the basis of kinship and in more civilized nations largely in terms of economic and political factors. The function of kinship is relatively less in higher civilization, and may be absolutely less. But kinship considerations always persist." [15]

On the basis of our comparative findings and in line with the generally accepted position as stated by Kroeber, we might go on to classify modern nations with predominantly peasant populations in terms of the role of kinship in the social organization of village life and intervillage relations. If our findings for Tepoztlán and Rampur could be generalized for Mexico and India as nations, and this is an empirical question, then we would have to conclude that, insofar as the role of kinship is concerned, India is much more "primitive" than Mexico and represents a different stage of socio-cultural evolution.[16] However, in terms of other variables, such as the ethnic composition of the population, we have seen that Tepoztlán is more homogeneous than Rampur. Similarly, the communal land system of Tepoztlán seems to be more primitive than that of Rampur.

One conclusion to be drawn from these facts is that separate institutions or aspects of culture develop at different rates, within limits, in accord with particular historical circumstance. It is this factor

[15] Alfred L. Kroeber, "The Societies of Primitive Man," in *The Nature of Culture* (Chicago: University of Chicago Press, 1952), p. 219.

[16] The manifold implications of such a finding cannot be treated here. However, this finding suggests that the introduction of a modern Western democratic process, based upon voting, elections, and the spirit of individuality implicit in this system, is more foreign to contemporary Indian culture than to contemporary Mexican culture. Perhaps this is what Gandhi had in mind when he suggested many years ago that India would have to work out forms of representation which would be more in keeping with India's special tradition.

which creates serious difficulties in the construction of holistic societal or cultural typologies which are not historically and regionally defined. This would also help explain how Tepoztlán and Rampur can be so similar in terms of economics and so different in terms of social organization.

Part Five:

URBAN STUDIES

18

Urbanization without Breakdown:

A Case Study[*]

This is a preliminary work report on a research project on urbanization in Mexico City. The research is an outgrowth and continuation of my earlier work in the village of Tepoztlán. In brief, we attempted to learn what happened to individuals and families from the village of Tepoztlán who had gone to live in Mexico City.[†]

Before presenting some of the findings, I should like to indicate how our work is related to other studies in the same field. In the first place, it should be noted that there have been very few studies of the socio-psychological aspects of urbanization in Mexico or other Latin American countries. Urban sociology in Mexico has lagged behind developments in some of the other social sciences. The data most nearly comparable to ours are to be found in the rural-urban migration studies done by rural sociologists in the United States. These studies have been primarily concerned with the causes, the rate and direction, and the amount of migration, factors of selectivity, and occupational accommodation.

To the extent to which they have dealt with the adjustment of migrants in the city, the findings have on the whole highlighted the

[*] This article first appeared in 1952, in *Scientific Monthly*, Vol. 75, No. 1, pp. 31–41.

[†] I am grateful to the Graduate Research Board of the University of Illinois for financial assistance on this project. The field research in Mexico City was carried out in the summer of 1951 with the aid of a group of students from the University of Illinois.

negative aspects, such as personal maladjustment, breakdown of family life, decline of religion, and increase of delinquency. The total picture has been one of disorganization, sometimes referred to as culture shock incident upon city living. One common theoretical explanation of these findings has been in terms of the change from the primary group environment, which is generally characterized as warm, personal, moral, and intimate, to a secondary group environment, which is described as cold, impersonal, mechanistic, non-moral, and unfriendly.[1]

The preliminary findings of the present study of urbanization in Mexico City indicate quite different trends and suggest the possibility of urbanization without breakdown. They also suggest that some of the hitherto unquestioned sociological generalizations about urbanization may be culture-bound and in need of re-examination in the light of comparative studies of urbanization in other areas.[2] Some of our generalizations about the differences between rural and urban life also need to be re-examined. It should be recalled that direct studies of the urbanization process itself are difficult, and most studies have been indirect and inferential. Sociological generalizations about the differences between rural and urban society have been based largely on comparative statistical data on the incidence

---

[1] The tendency to view the city as the source of all evil and to idealize rural life has been corrected somewhat by the work of rural sociologists in recent years. We are no longer certain that rural society *per se* is nearly as Rousseauan and anxiety-free as we once thought. Studies by Mangus and his colleagues suggest just as high an incidence of psychosomatic illness among the farm population of portions of Ohio as in urban areas (see A. R. Mangus and John R. Seeley, *Mental Health Needs in a Rural and Semirural Area of Ohio*, Mimeographed Bulletin No. 1951. Columbus: Ohio State University [January, 1947]). Moreover, a study by Goldhamer and Marshall suggests that there has been no increase in the psychoses (and, by inference, also in the neuroses) over the past hundred years in the state of Massachusetts, a state that has undergone considerable industrial development during this period (see Herbert Goldhamer and Andrew W. Marshall, *The Frequency of Mental Disease: Long-Term Trends and Present Status*. The RAND Corporation [July, 1949]).

[2] Theodore Caplow's excellent article on "The Social Ecology of Guatemala City" (*Social Forces*, Vol. 28, p. 113 [Dec., 1949]) suggests the provincialism of earlier sociological ideas about the nature of the city. Caplow writes, "The literature of urban geography and urban sociology has a tendency to project as universals those characteristics of urbanism with which European and American students are most familiar. . . . There was until recently a tendency to ascribe to all cities characteristics which now appear to be specific to Chicago . . ." (p. 132). Caplow raises the question whether "much of the anarchic and unstable character attributed by many authorities to urban life in general is not merely a particular aspect of the urban history of the United States and Western Europe since the Renaissance" (p. 133).

of crime in rural and urban areas, on birth, fertility, and death rates, size of family, educational opportunities, and social participation. As Ralph Beals has recently pointed out, "Sociologists paid much more attention to urbanism than to urbanization." [3] Moreover, we know very little about the psychological aspects of urbanization as it affects specific individuals and families.

Perhaps one of the difficulties in this field has been the inadequate methodology. There is not, to my knowledge, a single study that has followed up migrants from a rural community which had first been the subject of intensive analysis on the social, economic, political, and psychological levels. An adequate research design for the study of the socio-psychological aspects of urbanization would require a project consisting of three phases: a well-rounded study of a rural or peasant community, including intensive family and psychological studies; locating families from this community who have gone to live in the city, an intensive study of these families in the city.

The present research has attempted to conform to this design. The first phase was completed some time ago with a study of the village of Tepoztlán. The second and third phases were begun in the summer of 1951 in Mexico City.

The specific objectives of the research were conceived as follows: (1) to study the process of urbanization directly by analyzing the changes in customs, attitudes, and value systems of Tepoztecan individuals and families who had gone to live in Mexico City, (2) to compare family life and interpersonal relations of selected urban families of Tepoztecan origin with those of the rural community from which they had migrated, and (3) to relate our findings to the more general theoretical findings and problems in the field of culture change.

The study was planned on two levels. First, we wanted to do a broad survey of all Tepoztecan families in Mexico City and obtain data for each family on such items as date of and reasons for leaving the village, size of family, kinship composition of the household, the extent of bilingualism (Spanish and the native Indian language, Nahuatl), the general level of living, the religious life, the *compadre* system, curing practices, and the life cycle. For most of these items we had rather full data on the village of Tepoztlán; these data could therefore be used as a base line from which to analyze the nature and direction of change.

Second, we planned to do intensive studies of a few selected families representative of the different lengths of residence in the city and of different socioeconomic levels. Other variables that might be-

[3] "Urbanism, Urbanization, Acculturation," *American Anthropology,* Vol. 53, No. 1 (Jan.–March, 1951), p. 5.

come significant in the course of the study were also to be taken into consideration.

We located one hundred Tepoztecan families in Mexico City and interviewed each family at least once. Sixty-nine families were interviewed twice, and ten of these were interviewed ten times. The quantitative data in this paper are based on the sixty-nine families for which we had the fullest data. The major factor in our inability to gather more information on the remainder of the families was lack of time. On the basis of the data obtained in the one interview with each of the thirty-one remaining families, it appears probable that our total picture would not have been appreciably changed. The fact that the sixty-nine families were distributed in many different sections of the city and that they represented distinct socioeconomic levels further insures against an inadvertently loaded sample.

Some of the city families were located with the help of our informants in Tepoztlán, many of whom had friends and relatives in the city. But most of the families were located with the aid of officers of the now-defunct Colonia Tepozteca, an organization of Tepoztecans in Mexico City, which kept a list of the names and addresses of Tepoztecans living in the city. We have reason to believe that the one hundred families we located represent approximately 90 per cent of all Tepoztecans living in the city.

It should be noted that field work in the city is in many ways more difficult, more costly, and more time-consuming than in the village. The Tepoztecan families were scattered in twenty-two different *colonias,* or neighborhoods, extending from one end of the city to the other. Much time was lost in traveling to and from the homes, in making appointments for interviews (only one of the families had a telephone), and in establishing rapport. Often we would spend an entire morning calling on two or three families, only to find people out or otherwise unavailable. Moreover, we did not have the advantage of working through community leaders, of becoming familiar and accepted figures in the community, or of utilizing neighbors— and village gossip—as sources of information.

The earliest contacts between Mexico City and Tepoztlán probably resulted from trade. A small number of Tepoztecan merchants regularly sold their products (mainly hog plums and corn) in the Merced, Lagunilla, and Tacubaya markets. Consequently, some of the earliest migrants of whom we have record, settled near these markets, and to this day there are small concentrations of Tepoztecan families around the markets.

Our study revealed that the Tepoztecan families now living in Mexico City came in three distinct periods of migration. The first was prior to the Mexican Revolution of 1910; the second was during

the Revolution, from about 1910 to 1920; the third since 1920. The
motives for migration and the number and quality of migrants, as
well as their social composition, show interesting differences for
each of these periods.

During the first period only young men left, their primary motives
being to get a higher education and to seek better employment opportunities. These early migrants were generally poor young men
related to the best families in the village. We located fifteen individuals who left during this period. In general these early migrants
made good, economically speaking. Some became professionals and
have achieved important positions in the city. Many became the intellectuals who later formed the core of the Colonia Tepozteca,
which was to play such an important part in community affairs.

The second period was one of forced migration, when hundreds of
Tepoztecans left the village, generally as family units, to escape the
ravages of the civil war. The earliest ones to leave during this period
were the *cacique* families who fled before the threat of the Zapatista
revolutionaries. Later, when the village became a battleground for
opposing forces, people from all social levels fled. It is estimated that
by 1918 there were approximately a thousand Tepoztecans in the
city, and, according to our informants, approximately seven hundred
attended one of the early meetings preceding the formation of the
Colonia Tepozteca. Most of these migrants returned to the village
after peace was established. Many of those who remained were the
conservative, wealthier families who had been ruined by the Revolution. About 65 per cent of the families we studied came to the city
during this period.

The striking thing about migration during the third period is the
relatively small number of migrants. Only 25 per cent of our families
came during 1920–50. We find a wider variety of motives for migration than formerly, but the two most important seem to be improved
educational and economic opportunities. During the later twenties
and early thirties, however, a number of men left because of the intense political strife which flared up in the village. Again we find
that the young men predominated in the exodus, but now there were
also young women, who came either to attend school or to serve as
domestics. In all cases during this period, the migrants came to live
with relatives or *compadres*. There was apparently a sharp increase
in the number of migrants to the city toward the latter part of this
period, particularly after the road was built in 1936.

The number of Tepoztecans in Mexico City is not an accurate index of the total migration from the village. This was established by
a study of all the cases that have left the village since 1943. Of
seventy-four cases that left, only forty-one went to live in Mexico

City; the remainder went to other villages and towns. Of the forty-one in Mexico City, there were twenty-three single males, sixteen single females, and one married couple. Over 90 per cent were from two large *barrios* in the center of the village.

Tepoztecans in the city live in three types of housing: the *vecindad*, the apartment house, and the separate, privately owned dwelling. The *vecindad* represents some of the poorest housing conditions in the city. It consists of a series of one-story dwellings arranged around a courtyard. Often there is a communal water fountain in the center and one or two toilets for a settlement of twenty-five families. In a few cases there is piped water in each apartment. One of our families lived in a *vecindad* of 150 families—practically a small community in itself. The rentals varied from twenty-five to sixty-five pesos ($3–$8) a month. Forty-four per cent of Tepoztecan families live in *vecindades*. The dwellings are generally small, usually consisting of two rooms.

The apartment house provides much more privacy and represents a distinctly higher standard of living. Sixteen per cent of the families lived in apartment houses, at rentals ranging from 65 to 300 pesos a month. Professionals and skilled laborers live here—typical Mexican lower-middle-class families. The apartments are better constructed than the *vecindades* and have more and larger rooms.

Privately owned homes were dwellings for 28 per cent of the families. There was a wide range in the styles, size, and property value of these houses. Some were one- or two-room wooden shacks built on tiny lots on the outskirts of the city; others were modern eight- or ten-room buildings, with enclosed private gardens and patios, located in a thriving middle-class neighborhood. Home ownership is therefore not a good index of wealth or class position.

The average size of Tepoztecan households in the city was somewhat larger than in the village—5.8 as compared to about 5 (Table 1).

The composition of the household shows about the same pattern as in the village except that there is a slightly higher percentage of extended families living in the city (Table 2). In contrast to

TABLE 1

NUMBER OF PERSONS PER HOUSE SITE,
TEPOZTLÁN AND MEXICO CITY

No. of Persons per House Site	Percentage of House Sites, Tepoztlán	Percentage of House Sites, Mexico City
1–5	44.2	41
6–10	52.5	53
11 and over	3.3	6

TABLE 2

KINSHIP COMPOSITION BY HOUSEHOLDS—TEPOZTLÁN, 1943,
AND MEXICO CITY, 1951

Type	Families in Mexico City (69) (Percentage of all Families)	Families in Tepoztlán (662) (Percentage of all Families)
Simple biological family	66.6	70
Biological family with married children and grandchildren	17.2	13.5
Married siblings with their children	2.9	2.1
Persons living alone	0	6.7
Unrelated families living together	0	.7
Miscellaneous	13.3	7.5

Tepoztlán there were no cases of persons living alone or of unrelated families living together. There is probably greater economic pressure for families to live together in the city than in the country. In Tepoztlán, if young couples do not get along well with the in-laws and wish to live alone, they can almost always find someone who has an empty house that can be used rent-free. The same is true of old people and widows, who manage to eke out a living with garden produce and by raising chickens or pigs.

We found very little evidence of family disorganization in the city. There were no cases of abandoned mothers and children among our sixty-nine families studied, nor was there a history of separation or divorce in more than a few families. Families remain strong; in fact, there is some evidence that family cohesiveness increases in the city in the face of the difficulties of city life. In Tepoztlán the extended family shows solidarity only in times of crisis or emergency. Although there is more freedom for young people in the city, the authority of parents shows little sign of weakening, and the phenomenon of rebellion against parental authority hardly exists. Nor are the second-generation children ashamed of their parents. Perhaps this can be explained by the general cultural emphasis upon respect for age, authority, and parenthood. Similarly, we found no sharp generation cleavage in values and general outlook on life.

As might be expected, the general standard of living of Tepoztecan families in Mexico City shows upward movement as compared with Tepoztlán. Thus, 78 per cent of our city families had radios as compared to about 1 per cent in the village; 83 per cent had clocks as compared to about 20 per cent in the village; 54 per cent had sewing machines as compared to 25 per cent in Tepoztlán; 41 per cent reported buying a newspaper with some regularity as compared to 6 per cent in Tepoztlán; 3 of our 69 families owned cars in the city, but there were no car owners at the time of our Tepoztlán study. In the city all slept in beds; in the village only 19 per cent slept in beds in 1940. However, there seemed to be more crowding in the city, especially among the poor families. In some *vecindades,* there were 10 people living in one room and sharing two beds. A similar situation holds in regard to toilet facilities. All Tepoztecan families in the city had some toilet facilities, but we found some *vecindades* where 15 families shared a single toilet, and others where there was a semi-enclosed toilet in the kitchen. From the point of view of hygiene, it is doubtful whether this was an improvement over the orchards of Tepoztlán.

The diet of the city families is similar to that of the village except that there is greater variety, depending upon income. The city dwellers all enjoy Tepoztecan cooking and continue to make *mole* on festive occasions. They strongly prefer Tepoztecan *tortillas,* and many continue to prepare beans with *epazote,* as in Tepoztlán. About 80 per cent of the families continue to use the *metate* and *meclapil,* especially for preparing fiesta meals. A few buy corn and make *tortillas* at home; a larger number buy mill-ground corn, or *masa;* a still larger number buy ready-made *tortillas.*

The Tepoztecan custom of having household pets continues in the city. Fifty-four per cent of the families owned a pet—dogs, cats, or pigeons, and 24 per cent owned either chickens or pigs or both. Most of these families lived in privately owned homes.

The religious life of Tepoztecans in Mexico City appears to be at least as vigorous as in Tepoztlán. Again, the evidence does not support the findings of rural sociologists in this country to the effect that there is a decline in church attendance and religious practices when farm people move to the city. In our study it is not so much a matter of becoming more or less religious, but rather of a change in the content and form of religious expression. Specifically, it is a matter of becoming more Catholic and less Indian.

In general, the city Tepoztecans follow the Roman Catholic tradition more closely. The village belief that El Tepozteco is the son of Mary is no longer held and is regarded as backward and superstitious. Tepoztecans in the city tend to send their children more regularly to Sunday School to learn doctrine, to take first communion, and to attend mass. Confession is as unpopular among city Tepoztecans as in the village, but probably occurs more often.

Mexico City, as the center of the Catholic Church in Mexico, has better organized and better staffed associations, which carry on intensive programs of indoctrination. In many *vecindades* we found religious shrines, usually containing a statue of the Virgin of Guadalupe, and all residents are expected to honor the patron saint of the *vecindad,* to lift the hat in passing, to cross themselves, or to partake in the collective prayers organized by some enterprising member of the *vecindad.* That social control is strong can be seen from this statement by an informant: "If one does not salute the Virgin, the janitor and all the old women of the *vecindad* begin to call one a heretic and throw dirty looks."

Such shrines are also found in some of the factories in which our informants worked. A few of our Tepoztecans who are bus drivers tell of the requirement to carry images of San Cristobal, the patron saint of their union. They also tell of religious pilgrimages organized by the unions. One Tepoztecan explained that he had never bothered about the Virgin of Guadalupe when he was in Tepoztlán, but since working in the city has gone on two union pilgrimages. This same informant, who as a child in the village had received no training in doctrine classes, had no first communion, and rarely was obliged to attend mass, now attends mass frequently, consults a priest about his economic and domestic problems, and, thanks to the perseverance of Acción Católica, regularly sends his four children to Sunday School.

Another example of the increased identification with the church is the fact that several of our city informants draped their doors with black crepe to mourn the death of a Catholic bishop. In Tepoztlán it is doubtful whether the death of the Pope himself would lead to such action.

There are some differences in church organization in the city which affect participation of Tepoztecans. Unlike the village church, the churches in Mexico City have no *barrio mayordomos.* In the village many of the tasks connected with the care of images and the church are assigned to members of the community or to the specific *barrio;* in the city, these tasks are carried out by paid church personnel. Since many of these jobs were the work of men in the village, the net result is that in the city the men play much smaller roles in the religious life. Another difference is that the Tepoztecans in the city contribute less money to the church than in the village.

The system of *compadrazgo* continues to function among Tepoztecans in the city. Each Tepoztecan interviewed in Mexico City had *compadres,* godparents, and godchildren. With one or two exceptions the changes that *compadrazgo* has undergone represent an adaptation to urban life rather than a breakdown or even a weakening of the system.

A major change in *compadrazgo* in the city is the disappearance of several types of godparents known in the village—namely, the godfather of *miscotón,* godfather of the ribbon, godfather of *evangelio,* godfather of the scapulary, godfather of the Child Jesus. There is also much less use of the godfather of confirmation and the godfather of communion. The *compadrazgo* system is largely limited to the godparents of baptism and of marriage, thereby resembling the original Catholic practice as introduced by the early Spaniards and as practiced to this day in Spain.

The decline in the role of the godfather of baptism is another important change. In the city he is no longer consulted in the selection of the godparent of confirmation in the cases where this occurs. Moreover, in the city there is no *sacamisa,* thereby eliminating the role of the godparent of baptism in this ritual. The absence of the *sacamisa* is probably due to the unwillingness of the mothers to remain at home for forty days after the birth of the child, as is required in Tepoztlán. Another adaptation to city life is the delayed baptism. In Tepoztlán babies are baptized as soon as possible, often when only a few days old, almost always before three months. In Mexico City baptisms in our families did not occur for twelve to eighteen months and sometimes not for several years. This delay may be attributed in part to the lower death rate among infants born in the city and to a lessened anxiety about infant health.

Another interesting change in the city is the increased frequency with which relatives are selected as godparents. In Tepoztlán it is unusual to find relatives who are *compadres.* Most Tepoztecans consider this undesirable, for it conflicts with the basic notion of respect and social distance that should exist between *compadres.* In the city, where Tepoztecans find themselves without friends, they turn to relatives for godparents. Family ties are thereby reinforced by the ties of *compadrazgo.* But this changes the character of the *compadrazgo* relationship from a formal and ceremonial relationship to a more informal and personal one. The mode of address among *compadres* in the village is always of "Vd.–Vd." In the city it is frequently merely a continuation of the form of address used prior to becoming *compadres.* Thus, in the city we find *compadres* addressing each other as "*tu–tu,*" "*Vd.–tu,*" and "*Vd.–Vd.*" The "*tu–tu*" is used between brothers or sisters who have become *compadres.* The "*Vd.–tu*" is used when an uncle and nephew become *compadres.* In rural Spain I found the *compadre* system to be practically identical with the urban forms in Mexico.

Still another change in the system in the city is the custom whereby a man or woman will offer to be a godparent before the child is born. In the village one always waits to be asked in a formal manner. Since it might be taken as an insult to turn down an offer of godparentage, the net effect is to reduce parental control in the matter of selection. The obligations of godparents to godchildren and of *compadres* to one another are more clearly and specifically defined in the village than in the city. In the city there is much more familiarity between *compadres,* and a *compadre* may ask for almost any kind of favor.

Many Tepoztecan families in the city still use herbs for cooking and curing. In almost all the privately owned homes and in some of the *vecindades* common herbs such as *yerba buena, santa maria,* and *manzanilla* are grown in gardens and flowerpots. Herbs are used to cure colds, headaches, stomach ache, toothache, and so on, much the way they are in Tepoztlán; however, city families tend to rely more upon patent medicines than do village families. Illnesses such as evil eye, *los aires,* and *muina* ("illness of anger"), for which there are no patent medicines, necessarily are cured by native herbs. In these cases it is not uncommon for city people to return to the village to be cured. It should also be noted that, when other illnesses do not respond to patent medicines or to medical treatment, the sick person may be taken to the village for rediagnosis and cure. One informant told of suffering a partial paralysis of the face and of being treated unsuccessfully by several doctors. Finally, a visitor from Tepoztlán diagnosed it as an attack of *los aires,* whereupon the patient went to the village and was promptly cured by means of appropriate herbs placed in a bag suspended around his neck. The daughter of another informant was stricken with poliomyelitis and despite hospital treatment remained paralyzed. Her father, in desperation, took her to Tepoztlán, where she was given a series of sweat baths in a *temazcal.* This treatment, according to her parent, brought about considerable improvement. Sometimes, in the hope that the local *curanderos* will "understand" the illness better, an incurably ill person may be taken from the city to the village, only to die there. Thus, not only do country people go to the city seeking cures, but the same process works the other way around.

In considering stability or change in the way of life of Tepoztecans in Mexico City, it is important to realize that the ties between the city families and their relatives in the village remain strong and enduring. Almost all the city families studied visit the village at least once a year on the occasion of the *Carnaval.* Many go much more often, to celebrate their own Saint's Day, to attend their *barrio* fiesta, a funeral, or the inauguration of a new bridge or school, to act as godparent for some child, or to celebrate a wedding anniversary, or the Day of the Dead. The ties with the village do not seem to weaken with increase in years away from it. On the contrary, some of the most ardent and nostalgic villagers are those who have been away from it the longest. Many old people expressed a desire to return to the village to die. Some men, who have been living in the city for thirty years, still think of themselves as Tepoztecans first and Mexicans second. Fifty-six per cent of the families studied owned a house in the village, and 30 per cent owned their private *milpas*.

The proximity to Tepoztlán, and the bus line which now runs to the village, facilitate visiting. The young people enjoy spending a weekend or a Sunday in their village. There is also some visiting from Tepoztlán to friends and relatives in the city.

In the past few years Tepoztecans in the city have organized a soccer team and play against the village team. The organization of a team in the city means that Tepoztecans from distant *colonias* must get together; however, their cohesiveness with their village is much greater than with Tepoztecans in the city. The Colonia Tepozteca has not been functioning for many years, having broken up because of factionalism within the organization.

In summary, this study provides further evidence that urbanization is not a simple, unitary, universally similar process, but that it assumes different forms and meanings, depending upon the prevailing historic, economic, social, and cultural conditions. Generalizations concerning urbanization must take these conditions into consideration. From my study of Tepoztecans living in Mexico City, I find that peasants in Mexico adapt to city life with far greater ease than do American farm families. There is little evidence of disorganization and breakdown,[4] of culture conflict, or of irreconcilable differences between generations; many of the trends and characteristics found among these urbanized Tepoztecans are in direct opposition to those that occur among urbanized farm families in the United States. Family life remains strong in Mexico City. Family cohesiveness and extended family ties increase in the city, fewer cases of separation and divorce occur, no cases of abandoned mothers and children, no cases of persons living alone or of unrelated families living together. Household composition is similar to village patterns except that more extended families live together in the city. There is a general rise in the standard of living in the city, but dietary patterns do

[4] There is the possibility of other kinds of disorganization which might be manifested on a "deeper" level. In this connection it will be interesting to compare the findings on the Rorschachs given to the Tepoztecan families living in the city with the findings on the Rorschachs from the village of Tepoztlán. It should also be noted that our findings for Tepoztecan families in Mexico City do not mean that there is no "disorganization" in Mexico City as a whole. A comparison of the statistical indices on crime, delinquency, and divorce, between urban and rural populations in Mexico, shows a much higher incidence for urban areas (see José E. Iturriaga. *La Estructura Social y Cultural de México*. Fondo de Cultura Económica, México [1951]).

not change greatly. Religious life in the city becomes more Catholic and disciplined; however, men play a smaller religious role and contribute less money to the church in the city. The system of *compadrazgo* has undergone important changes, but remains strong. Although there is a greater reliance upon doctors and patent medicines to cure illness, city Tepoztecans still use village herbal cures and in cases of severe illness sometimes return to the village to be cured. Village ties remain strong, with much visiting back and forth.

In considering possible explanations for the above findings, the following factors would seem to be most relevant: (1) Mexico City has been an important political, economic, and religious center for Tepoztecans since pre-Hispanic times. The contact with an urban, albeit Indian, culture was an old pattern, and has continued throughout recent history. (2) Mexico City is much more homogeneous than most large urban centers in the United States, both in terms of the predominance of Catholicism and of the cultural backgrounds of its people. Neither Mexico City nor Mexico as a whole has had much immigration from other parts of the world. The population of Mexico City therefore has very close ties with the rural hinterlands. (3) Mexico City is essentially conservative in tradition. In Mexico most of the revolutions have begun in the country. The city has been the refuge for the well-to-do rural families whose local positions were threatened. (4) Mexico City is not as highly industrialized as many American cities and does not present the same conditions of life. (5) Mexican farmers live in well-organized villages that are more like cities and towns than like the open-country settlement pattern of American farmers. (6) Finally, Tepoztlán is close to Mexico City, not only geographically but also culturally. The similarities between the value systems of working-class and lower-middle-class families in Mexico City and those of Tepoztecans are probably much greater than those between, let us say, families from the hill country of Arkansas and working- and middle-class families from St. Louis or Detroit.

In conclusion, it must be emphasized that this study is still in its preliminary stage, and the findings are therefore tentative. The primary purpose has been to indicate a research design which might yield valid and reliable data for the understanding of the urbanization process.

It may be that Tepoztlán was not the best possible choice for this kind of study because of its proximity to Mexico City. It may also be that Tepoztlán is a special case from other points of view. Certainly we need other studies. We should have follow-up studies of migrants to the city from George Foster's Tarascan village of Tzintzuntzan, from Robert Redfield's and Villa Rojas' Maya village of Chan Kom, from Julio de la Fuente's Zapotecan village of Yalalag, to determine to what extent the findings agree with those from Tepoztlán. It would also be important to have comparative studies of migrants to Mexico City, not from ancient and stable communities like Tepoztlán, but from plantation areas populated by poor and landless farm laborers.

19

The Culture of the *Vecindad* in Mexico City:

*Two Case Studies**

The recent shift in anthropology from the study of tribal peoples to the study of peasants, and, as in the case of this paper, to urban dwellers, lends a potentially new and practical significance to the findings of anthropologists. It also calls for a re-evaluation of the relationship between the anthropologist and the people he studies, most of whom are desperately poor. Although poverty is quite familiar to anthropologists, they have often taken it for granted in their studies of preliterate societies because it seemed a natural and integral part of the whole way of life, intimately related to the poor technology and poor resources or both. In fact, many anthropologists have taken it upon themselves to defend and perpetuate this way of life against the inroads of civilization. But poverty in modern nations is a very different matter. It suggests class antagonism, social problems, and the need for change; and often it is so interpreted by the subjects of the study.

In Mexico City most of the poor live in slumlike housing settlements known as *vecindades*. Usually, *vecindades* consist of one or more rows of single story dwellings with one or two rooms, facing a common patio or courtyard. The dwellings are constructed of cement, brick or adobe, and form a well-defined unit with some of the

* This was first published in 1958, in *Actas del XXXIII Congreso Internacional de Americanistas*, San Jose (July 20–27), pp. 387–402. My first brief discussion of the culture of poverty concept appeared in this article but has been eliminated in the present version to avoid reduplication.

characteristics of a small community. The size and type of *vecindades* vary enormously. Some consist of only a few dwellings, others of a few hundred. Some are found in the commercial heart of the city, in sixteenth- and seventeenth-century two- and three-story Spanish-Colonial buildings which have become rundown, while others, on the outskirts of the city, consist of wooden shacks or *jacales* and look like semi-tropical Hoovervilles which were so common in the United States during the Depression.

In this paper I will describe and compare my preliminary findings on two *vecindades* in Mexico City, which I studied during 1956–57, in order to illustrate the variations as well as some of the common factors of *vecindad* life. The first *vecindad* I have called the Casa Grande, the second the Panaderos *vecindad*.

The Casa Grande stands between the Street of the Barbers and the Street of the Tinsmiths, only a short distance from the Thieves' Market. This is a giant *vecindad* which houses over 700 people. Spread out over an entire square block, the Casa Grande is a little world of its own, enclosed by high, cement walls on the north and south, and by rows of shops which face the streets on the other two sides. These shops, food stores, a dry cleaner, a glazier, a carpenter, a beauty parlor, together with the neighborhood market and public baths, supply the basic needs of the *vecindad,* so that many of the tenants, particularly those who come from rural areas, seldom leave the immediate neighborhood and are almost strangers to the rest of Mexico City. This section of the city was once the home of the underworld, and even today people fear to walk here late at night. But most of the criminal element has moved away and the majority of the residents are poor tradesmen, artisans, and workers.

Two narrow, inconspicuous entrances, each with a high gate open during the day but locked every night at ten o'clock, lead into the *vecindad* on the east and west sides. Anyone coming or going after hours must ring for the janitor and pay to have the gate opened. The *vecindad* is protected by its two patron saints, the Virgin of Guadalupe and the Virgin of Zapopan, whose statues stand in glass cases, one at each entrance. Offerings of flowers and candles surround the images and on their skirts are fastened small shiny medals, each a testimonial of a miracle performed for someone in the *vecindad*. Few residents pass the Virgins without some gesture of recognition, be it only a glance or a hurried sign of the Cross.

Within the *vecindad* stretch four long, cement-paved patios, or courtyards, about fifteen feet wide. These are formed by wide rectangular cement buildings divided into 157 one-room apartments, each with a barn-red door, which open onto the patios at regular intervals of about twelve feet. In the daytime, rough wooden ladders stand beside most of the doors, leading to low flat roofs over the kitchen portion of each apartment. These roofs serve many uses and are crowded with lines of laundry, chicken coops, dove cotes, pots of flowers or medicinal herbs, tanks of gas for cooking, and an occasional TV antenna.

Just inside the door of each apartment is a small kitchen that serves as a passageway into the sleeping room. To the left of the door is a washtub and a small toilet enclosed by a half-shutter swinging door. To the right, is a stove, a table and chairs and perhaps a cabinet. In kitchens with more elaborate equipment there is usually no room for a table, in which case it is kept in the bedroom. In some apartments, the bedroom too has become jammed with beds, matching bureau and dressing table, a wardrobe, sewing machine, TV set, and other furniture, forcing the tenants to build a *tapanco,* or balcony, for extra sleeping space, which they reach by ladder.

The Casa Grande is a melting pot of Mexico. Its residents have come from as many as twenty-four of the thirty-two states and territories of the Mexican nation. About a third of the heads of households were born in small villages, a third in provincial towns or cities and another third in Mexico City. The central states of Guanajuato, Jalisco, Mexico, Hidalgo, Michoacan, and Puebla account for most of the residents, but some are from as far south as Oaxaca, Yucatan and Chiapas, and others from the northern states of Chihuahua and Sinaloa. The process of fusion of regional cultural elements which goes on in the *vecindad* makes for the development of a new composite which is lower-class urban culture. It also leads to the development among *vecindad* tenants of a much greater sophistication and awareness of Mexican regional differences than exists among the more provincial rural dwellers.

Residence in the *vecindad* is quite stable. About 10 per cent of the residents have been in the city ten years or less; 59 per cent, eleven to twenty-five years; and 31 per cent, over twenty-five years. Seventy-seven per cent of the heads of households have lived there six to twenty-one years and 56 per cent more than eleven years. The median length of residence was twelve years. This stability of residence is due to the low fixed rentals in the *vecindad* and the shortage of medium-priced housing in the city. Some families of higher income are waiting to move to better quarters, but the majority are contented, indeed proud, of living in the Casa Grande.

About 72 per cent of our sample of 71 households in the *vecindad* were occupied by the simple biological or nuclear family and 28 per cent by some form of extended family. Of a total of 158 married people living in the 71 households, 91 were women and 67 were men. In other words, twenty-four married women were living without a husband, either as heads of households or with some relative. Nine women were widowed and the remaining 15 were either separated, divorced or deserted. Twenty per cent of all marriages were of the common-law type with most of them in the lower income group; and in twenty per cent of all households in the *vecindad* there was at least one woman who had been deserted.

Partly because of the stability of residence, the *vecindad* has taken on some of the characteristics usually associated with a small community. About a third of the households were related by blood ties, and about a fourth by marriage and *compadrazgo*. Although the majority of related families had relatives in only one other household, there were several that had blood relatives in three, four, and even seven different households. Forty-six of the households were related through females as compared to only 15 through males. For example, there were 16 sister-sister relationships, and 11 daughter-mother relationships, as compared with only 6 brother-brother, one father-daughter, and no father-son relationships. This suggests that the extended family ties were quite strong in the *vecindad,* particularly among women. It is apparent that the mother provides the most solid and stable nucleus for family life.

The closeness and crowding of the households and the sharing of a common patio by many families makes for much interaction within the *vecindad* and reinforces the sense of community. Women chat as they hang up clothes, do household tasks outside their doors, or queue up for water. Children play here because it is safer than in the streets. In the afternoons, gangs of older boys often take over a patio to play a rough game of soccer and adolescent girls go in twos and threes on errands for their mothers. The young people attend the same schools, belong to the Casa Grande gang, and form loyalties and lifelong friendships. On Sunday nights there is usually an outdoor dance in one of the patios, organized by the youth and attended by people of all ages.

Most adults have a few friends whom they visit and from whom they borrow. Groups of neighbors may buy a lottery ticket co-operatively, organize raffles and *tandas,* or informal mutual savings and credit plans, in an effort at self-help. They also participate in religious pilgrimages and together celebrate the festival of the *vecindad* patron saints, the Christmas *Posadas* and a few other holidays. But these group efforts are occasional; for the most part adults "mind their own business" and try to maintain family privacy. Most doors are kept shut and it is customary to knock and wait for permission to enter when visiting. Some people visit only relatives or *compadres* and have actually entered few of the apartments. It is not common to invite friends or neighbors to eat, except on formal occasions such as birthday or religious celebrations. Although some neighborly help occurs, especially during emergencies, it is kept at a minimum. Quarrels between families over the mischief of children, street fights between gangs, and personal feuds between boys in the Casa Grande, are not uncommon.

The people of the Casa Grande earn their living in a large miscellany of occupations which practically defies classification. The Census of 1950 listed seventy-two occupations for this single *vecindad*. The largest occupational groups were shoemakers, petty tradesmen, salaried workers, chauffeurs, seamstresses, and mechanics. About a third of our household sample had at least one member whose full-time or part-time occupation was carried on at home. Some women take in washing or do dressmaking, some men are shoemakers, hat cleaners, or sellers of fruit or candy. Many men, however, go outside of the *vecindad* to work as chauffeurs, as factory workers, as peddlers, etc. The one single occupation that is most numerous is shoemaking, most of which is contracted from small manufacturers in the neighborhood. Each shoemaker usually confines himself to a specialty, the making of heels, for example, or the sewing of shoe linings. This trade is more or less typical of the small-scale home industry still found in many large cities in Mexico.

Although the living standards of the Casa Grande are low they are by no means the lowest to be found in Mexico City. Monthly incomes per capita per household range from 23 to 500 pesos, and can be classified into four groups.[1] (See Table 2.) Twenty-seven per cent of the households showed less than 100 pesos per capita income, 41 per cent showed between 101–200 pesos; 22 per cent between 201–300 pesos, and 10 per cent between 301–500 pesos.

In an effort to delineate the range of levels of living in the *vecindad,* a material culture inventory consisting of thirty-four items was constructed and applied in each of our sample households. Eleven items were then selected as luxury items which might be diagnostic of standard of living: radio, gas stove, wristwatch, the use of knives and forks in eating, sewing machine, aluminum pots, electric blender, television, washing machine, automobile, and refrigerator. We found that 79 per cent had radios, 55 per cent gas stoves, 54 per cent wristwatches, 49 per cent used knives and forks (spoons were quite common but most eating was done with *tortilla* and hands), 46 per cent had sewing machines, 41 per cent aluminum pots, 22 per cent electric blenders (informants referred to the traditional stone mortar and pestle as the Mexican blender), 21 per cent television sets, 10 per cent washing machines, 6 per

---

[1] The rate of exchange was 12.50 Mexican pesos for one U.S. dollar.

cent automobiles, and 4 per cent refrigerators. The increase in the standard of living was notable in the five years since I first began to study this *vecindad*. Radios had become so common that they no longer served as diagnostic items for wealth. The distribution of the eleven luxury items in the *vecindad* is shown in the following table.

TABLE 1

DISTRIBUTION OF LUXURY ITEMS IN THE CASA GRANDE
Vecindad, MEXICO CITY, 1956

Item	Number	Per Cent of Total Households
Radio	56	79
Gas Stove	39	55
Wristwatch	38	54
Knives and forks	35	49
Sewing Machine	33	46
Aluminum Pots	29	41
Blender	16	22
Television Set	15	21
Washing Machine	7	10
Automobile	4	6
Refrigerator	3	4
TOTAL	275	

We found that gas stoves, television sets, the use of knives and forks for eating, and wristwatches, were the most diagnostic items for general level of living and income level. The relationship between the possession of luxury items and income per capita is seen in Table 2.

While some households did not own a single luxury item, others owned nine of the eleven items. Although there is considerable overlapping in the number of luxury items owned by the different income groups the average number of items goes up steadily from 2 for the lower-income group to 5.57 for the upper group. However, the average number of items per household in the upper middle and upper groups is about the same, that is, 5.53 and 5.57 items, respectively. The relationship between luxury items and income levels is much more striking for the lower group, the lower-middle group and the upper-middle group.

Television ownership was concentrated in the two upper-income groups which had ten of the fifteen sets. There were no sets in the lowest group. One-third of the families that were three months delinquent in rent owned TV sets. TV is widely appreciated as a medium of entertainment and education in the *vecindad* by owners and

TABLE 2

DISTRIBUTION OF LUXURY ITEMS BY HOUSEHOLDS AND INCOME GROUPINGS IN THE CASA GRANDE

Vecindad, Mexico, D. F., 1956

Monthly Income per Cap. (Pesos)	Households No.	%	Average Number of Items per Family	Television Set No.	%	Gas Stove No.	%	Blender No.	%	Wrist-Watch No.	%	Silverware No.	%	Alum. Pots No.	%
Upper Group $301–500	7	10%	5.57	3	43%	6	86%	3	43%	5	72%	7	100%	4	57%
Upper Middle Group $201–300	15	22%	5.53	7	47%	12	80%	6	40%	10	67%	10	67%	9	60%
Lower Middle Group $101–200	27	41%	4.21	5	18%	18	67%	6	22%	18	67%	14	52%	12	44%
Lower Group $100 or Less	18	27%	2.00	0	0%	3	17%	1	5%	5	28%	4	22%	4	22%
TOTAL	67		4.06	15		39		16		38		35		29	

nonowners alike. Among the wealthier families TV is maintained exclusively for the use of the family, except for occasional invited
guests. The poorer families, however, charge a fee of twenty-five or
thirty centavos to the children of the *vecindad* and several lower-
income families who have bought their television set on time hope to
pay for the machine in this way.

The gas stove is even more indicative of socioeconomic levels than
the television set. Thirty-six of the thirty-nine gas stoves are found in
the three upper groups. Most of the lower group uses a kerosene
stove or charcoal. Two families of the middle-income group who
have television still use kerosene and eight families with kerosene
still use charcoal.

From a statistical point of view the use of tableware for eating
would seem to be the single most diagnostic trait for socioeconomic
levels. Whereas 100 per cent of all the upper-group households had
tableware, only 22 per cent of the lowest-income group had it.

There seems to be little positive relationship between the time
spent in the city and membership in the higher-economic groups.
However, whereas only 14 per cent of the members of the upper
group were born in rural areas, 41 per cent of the lower group were
born in rural areas.

There is a wide range of level of education in our *vecindad* sample, varying from twelve adults who have never attended school to
one woman who attended for eleven years. The average number of
years of school attendance among the 198 adults of our sample is
surprisingly low at 4.7 years. Those born in Mexico City have a
somewhat higher level of education (4.9) than those born in other
urban centers (4.0) and in rural areas (3.0). Education also shows a
positive correlation with income: those in the upper-income group
of the sample have approximately one year more schooling than
those in the upper-middle group, and about a year and a half more
than the lower-middle and lower groups.

The children of the *vecindad* show a substantial educational advantage over their parents. Among the children of school age, there
are none who have never been to school and none who are illiterate.
Furthermore, the younger generation, many of whom were still
attending school at the time of this study, already had significantly
more schooling than their parents. Children of people born in rural
areas have thus far, an average of 5.7 years of schooling, or 2.7 more
than their parents. The children of those from urban areas other
than Mexico City, have an average of 6.4 years or 2.4 more than their
parents. Children of Mexico City-born parents show the least difference with an average of 6.1 years or 1.2 more than their parents.
Among city-born children, females have a higher average school at-

tendance, in contrast to the parental group in which males had the advantage.

Let us now turn briefly to a description of our second case, the Panaderos *vecindad*. The Panaderos *vecindad*, huddled between two brick buildings on a bare lot a few blocks from the Casa Grande, is one of the poorest housing settlements in Mexico City. Unprotected from the street by a wall or a closed entranceway, the row of miserable one-room connected dwellings and their makeshift additions, built along the left side and across the back of the lot, are exposed to the gaze of the passersby. Also in full view, for the use of the residents, is a large cement water trough where the women wash their dishes and laundry and bathe their children, and two broken-down toilets curtained by pieces of torn burlap and flushed by pails of water. The bare earth of the thirty-foot-wide lot is dotted with rocks and stones and forked poles that hold up the clothes lines stretched crisscross between the two neighboring buildings. Here and there, a hole dug by the children or an unexpected sewer opening, haphazardly covered by a rock, makes walking precarious.

Five of the twelve dwellings have sheds or lean-tos constructed by setting up two poles and extending the kitchen roofs made of scraps of tarpaper, tin and corrugated metal, held down by stones and piled high with firewood and odds and ends. The sheds were built primarily to provide a dry, shady place to work for the artisans who live there. Two of them make tin pails, another makes toys from scrap metal and the fourth makes miniature water bottles and repairs bicycles. Piles of equipment, tin sheets, bundles of waste steel strips, wire, nails and tools, kept on old tables and benches, clutter up the space under the sheds.

The other men of this *vecindad* work at various jobs; three in shoe factories, one in a belt factory and one selling newspapers. Because their earnings are small and much of it is spent on drink, every one of the wives and many of the children work to add to their income. Some of the younger women work in shops, others as ambulant pedlars, but most prefer to work at home, doing piecework, making sweets or cooked food to sell in the street nearby, dealing in old clothes, and taking in washing and ironing. The clothes lines are almost always hung with the laundry of others, providing a multicolored curtain behind which life in the *vecindad* can be conducted with a bit more sense of privacy.

The heads of families of the Panaderos *vecindad* come from six of the central states of Mexico, Guanajuato, Querétaro, Mexico, Hidalgo, Aguascalientes, and Morelos. Four were born in small rural villages, seven in urban centers outside of Mexico City, and ten in Mexico City Only three couples came to the *vecindad* already married, having lived in other parts of the city previously. As in the case of the Casa Grande, most of the immigrants were brought to the city by their parents or came themselves at an early age. The time spent in the city by those from other areas ranges from twelve to forty-nine years. The average time in Mexico City is 26.2 years. This is greater than the average for the other *vecindad*. This suggests that the greater persistence of rural traits in the smaller *vecindad* is not a function of the recency of arrival from the country. As we shall see, it is a function of poverty and lower-class membership.

The Panaderos *vecindad* is a more cohesive community than the Casa Grande. Nine of the twelve households are related by kinship ties, and constitute three extended families. One mother has a married daughter in the *vecindad;* another mother has a married son and a married daughter; and a third has two married sons and one married daughter. All the families of the *vecindad* are related by *compadrazgo*. However, it is difficult to maintain the traditional formal respect relations between *compadres* in these crowded quarters; quarrels among the children of the *vecindad* often lead to quarrels among *compadres*. Visiting and borrowing are very frequent among the *vecindad* inhabitants who drift easily in and out of each other's rooms. There is little privacy and everyone knows each other's business. However, in some ways there is less organization here than in the Casa Grande. The Panaderos *vecindad* has no protecting patron saint, no gang of boys and girls (perhaps because it is so small), and no weekly dance.

The biological or nuclear family is the predominant type in the *vecindad*. Six of the thirteen families found in the twelve households are of the simple biological type consisting of husband, wife and children. Three apartments are occupied by widowed or abandoned women living with their grown children, and two apartments are occupied by men who have separated from their wives. In only one apartment is there a real extended family consisting of a man and his wife and their married daughter and grandchildren.

There are a total of thirteen marriages, in five of which the partners have ceased to live together. Six of the thirteen (46 per cent) were common-law marriages, five were married by both civil and church authorities, one by the church exclusively and one by civil law alone. The high proportion of 46 per cent common-law union contrasts sharply with the much lower rate of 20 per cent in the Casa Grande.

The average number of years of school attendance of the twenty-five individuals who have completed their education is 2.1 years per person, as compared to 4.7 in the Casa Grande. Moreover, the upper limit of schooling here was only five years as compared with eleven years in the larger *vecindad*. Probably the most striking contrast between the two *vecindades* is the much higher rate of illiteracy; 40 per cent as compared with 8 per cent in the Casa Grande. Within each *vecindad* the highest rate of illiteracy is found among those from rural backgrounds. However, while only 17 per cent of the city-born were illiterate in the Casa Grande, 42 per cent were illiterate in the Panaderos *vecindad*. Also, the younger city-born generation of the Casa Grande had a definite educational advantage over its parents, which was not the case in the Panaderos *vecindad*. This suggests a much greater emphasis placed upon education in the Casa Grande families and is undoubtedly related to the higher income, higher standard of living and in general to the operation of middle-class values as opposed to lower-class values.

The much greater poverty of the Panaderos *vecindad* is revealed in the lower income per capita and in the absence of most of the luxury items found in the Casa Grande, as seen in Table 3.

The income ranged from twenty-eight pesos per capita per month to 280 pesos. There was no household that could be classified in the upper-income group of the Casa Grande. In Panaderos we found only seventeen luxury items (an average of 1.42 per household) while the Casa Grande had a total of 275 items (an average of 4.06 per household). As in the case of the Casa Grande, most of the houses had radios so that even here radios were not diagnostic of level of living. The complete absence of knives and forks and gas stoves is especially diagnostic of the low standard of living and of lower-class membership. The Panaderos families live at more or less the same level as the group of lower-income families of the Casa Grande.

Another interesting difference between the two *vecindades* can be seen by comparing the relationship between income levels and education in each. In the Casa Grande we find a small positive relationship, that is, as we go from the lower to the higher income groups the educational level rises from an average of 4.7 years to 6.1 years. In the Panaderos *vecindad* there is no such positive relation, again indicating that education is not viewed as a means of upward mobility.

As a final point of comparison between the two *vecindades* we will examine briefly the celebration of the Day of the Dead. Although most families in both *vecindades* celebrated the occasion, there was a sharp difference in beliefs. In the Panaderos *vecindad* ten of the eleven families studied believed in the coming of the dead. In the Casa Grande only 34 per cent said they believed, 29 per cent were doubtful and 37 per cent said they did not believe. The offerings and celebration were much more elaborate in the Panaderos *vecindad*.

TABLE 3

RELATIONSHIP OF MONTHLY INCOME PER CAPITA AND MATERIAL CULTURE ITEMS
IN THE PANADEROS *Vecindad*, MEXICO, D. F., 1956

Monthly Income per Cap. (Pesos)	No. of Households No.	%	Average Number of Items per Household	Television Set No.	%	Gas Stove No.	Blender No.	Wrist-Watch No.	Silverware No.	Alum. Pots No.
Upper Group $301–500	0	0	0	0	0	0	0	0	0	0
Upper Middle Group $201–300	2	17%	2	1	100%	0	0	1	0	0
Lower Middle Group $101–200	5	41.5%	1.8	0	0	0	0	1	0	1
Lower Group $100 or Less	5	41.5%	.8	0	0	0	0	0	0	0
TOTAL	12		Aver. = 1.42	1		0	0	2	0	1

Here 4 families used charcoal and incense, 8 left an offering of food, 9 left flowers, and 10 left a glass of water and a candle. By contrast, in the Casa Grande a much smaller per cent used charcoal and incense and the percentage of the families that left a food offering was only about half that of Panaderos. The distribution by households is shown in the following chart.

	CASA GRANDE		PANADEROS	
Items	*No.*	*Per Cent*	*No.*	*Per Cent*
Charcoal	8	19	4	36
Offerings	16	39	8	72
Flowers	29	71	9	81
Water	32	79	10	91
Candle	39	95	10	71

There appears to be a regular and predictable order of elimination of items as one moves from the group of believers to nonbelievers. The order of elimination is, first, charcoal, incense, then flowers, water, and candles, respectively. Thus, if an informant used charcoal it is certain that she used all the other items.

· CONCLUSIONS ·

Our preliminary findings suggest that the lower-class residents of Mexico City show much less of the personal anonymity and isolation of the individual which has been described as characteristic of residents of large cities in the United States. The *vecindad* and the neighborhood break up the city into small communities which act as cohesive and personalizing factors. People spend most of their lives within a single neighborhood or *colonia* and even when there are frequent changes of residence it is usually within a restricted geographical area. Most marriages also occur within the neighborhood or *colonia*. Moreover, the extended family ties are strong, especially in times of emergency. We found that a large number of kin, living and dead, were recognized and remembered. (For similar results see Firth, 1956.) *Compadrazgo* is also a cohesive factor and much stronger in the smaller *vecindad*.

In spite of the Mexican cult of *machismo* and the over-all cultural emphasis upon male superiority and dominance, we found a tendency toward matricentered families in which the mother plays a crucial role in parent-child relations even after the children are married. One of the factors responsible for this situation may be the frequency with which men abandon their wives, and the existence of a *casa chica* pattern in which the men spend relatively little time with their children. Perhaps just as important is the demoralizing effect on men who have difficulty in fulfilling their expected roles as the economic mainstay and head of the family in a culture where unemployment, irregularity of jobs, and low wages are chronic conditions.

The *vecindad* acts as a shock absorber for the rural migrants to the city because of the similarity between its culture and that of rural communities. Indeed, we found no sharp differences in family structure, diet, dress and belief systems of the *vecindad* tenants, according to their rural-urban origins. The use of herbs for curing, the raising of animals, the belief in sorcery, spiritualism, the celebration of the Day of the Dead, political apathy and cynicism about government seemed just as common among persons who have been in the city for over thirty years as among more recent arrivals. One might well call these people urban peasantry.[2]

Various socioeconomic levels must be distinguished within the lower class in Mexico City. It may be useful to develop a typology along the lines of Lloyd Warner, distinguishing between the lower-lower, middle-lower, and upper-lower, in terms which are meaningful for the Mexican milieu. In such a scheme our smaller *vecindad* would probably fall into the lower-lower and middle-lower, while the Casa Grande shows all lower levels with the beginnings of a lower-middle class. The Panaderos *vecindad* shows a much higher incidence of extended family ties, of *compadrazgo*, of illiteracy, of working women, and of common-law marriages. The income level is much lower, as is the average number of luxury items. Some of the diagnostic items for an intra-class and inter-class typology would seem to be attitudes toward education and upward mobility, attitudes toward cleanliness, income, types of clothing (for example, a coat and a tie would seem to be diagnostic of middle-class membership), the use of knives and forks for eating, the gas stove, etc. It is interesting to note that the *vecindad* residents of peasant background who come from small landowning families showed more middle-class aspirations in their desire for a higher standard of living and education for their children than did city-born residents of the lower income group.

[2] Eliot Freidson in a review of Hoggart's book on the lower-class English suggests this term. He writes: "The view that he gives us of a kind of urban peasantry—concrete and personal in thought, indifferent, skeptical, suspicious, and even hostile toward the nation outside the neighborhood . . ." *American Journal of Sociology* (July, 1958), p. 98.

20

The Possessions
of the Poor[*]

We all recognize poverty when we are confronted with it, but it is
not easy to define the condition in objective terms. Income itself is
not an entirely adequate measure because it does not tell us how people actually live. We come closer to describing what poverty is when
we define it as the inability to satisfy one's material wants or needs.
It occurred to me that it might be interesting and useful to study the
material possessions of poverty-stricken people as a concrete expression of the lives they lead. In the hope of finding new insights into
the nature of poverty, I undertook a systematic examination of the
possessions of a group of poor families living in a Mexico City slum
tenement.

In many respects such a survey is analogous to an archaeological
examination of the material remains of a civilization. From an analysis of material objects the archaeologist can learn much about a people's history, achievements, cultural influences, values and ways of
life and can make important generalizations about the society. Similarly, a quantitative analysis of the material possessions of a living society should tell us many things, including information that might
escape notice in a direct study of the people themselves. In the case
of a living people we have the advantage of being able to supplement
the story told by the material objects by questioning the people about
their possessions.

[*] This was first published in October, 1969, in *Scientific American*, pp. 114–24.

The inquiry opens up a mine of interesting questions. What proportions of their income do poor people spend on furniture, on clothing, on religious objects, on luxury items, on medicines? How much of what they buy is new? How much is secondhand? To what extent do they depend on gifts or hand-me-downs? (Welfare contributions did not enter into the picture in my study, as there was no public welfare system in Mexico City.) How do families in poverty finance their purchases? Where do they do their shopping? How wide are their choices? What is the physical condition of their possessions? How long do they manage to hold on to them? I was able to obtain rather detailed information on all these matters.

The scene of my study was a small *vecindad,* one of the poorest in Mexico City, that housed fourteen families totaling eighty-three people (an average of about six persons per family). The tenement consisted of a row of fourteen windowless one-room apartments built of adobe brick and covered with a cement roof that joined them all together. Each apartment had a small entranceway with a makeshift roof of tar paper or metal and a door so low that one had to stoop to enter. These entrances also served as kitchens. A walk of rough stone slabs laid by the tenants to combat the mud ran parallel to the row of apartments and was cluttered with laundry tubs, pails, chamber pots and articles set out to dry in the sun. Firewood, covered with old gunnysacks or pieces of cardboard, was stored on the roof. Some of the tenants, who plied their trade at home, had built flimsy sheds as workshops against the front of their apartment; the sheds were used to store piles of materials and tools. In the yard was a large cement water trough that served all the tenants for washing dishes and laundry and for bathing children. Toward the back of the yard there were two common toilets, dilapidated adobe structures curtained with pieces of torn burlap.

Clotheslines strung on forked poles crisscrossed the yard, and the ground was strewn with rocks and pitted with holes dug by the children. In the daytime the yard was filled with half-naked babies and ragged youngsters playing in the dirt.

The impression of extreme poverty given by the *vecindad* was amply substantiated by my inventory of the possessions of the fourteen households. The total value of all their belongings (based on a detailed estimate of the cost or value of each item) was about $4,730 in U.S. dollars, or an average of about $338 per household. There was considerable variation among the households: the amount ranged from $119 for the poorest household to $937 for the "wealthiest." Twelve of the fourteen households owned less than $480 worth of goods.

For purposes of analysis I classified the family possessions into thirteen categories: furniture and furnishings (including radios and television sets), personal clothing, bedclothes, household equipment, kitchen equipment, household decorations, jewelry and other items of personal adornment, religious objects, toys (including bicycles), medicines, animals, plants, and the tools and materials of those householders who carried on trades at home. I shall first mention some general findings and then discuss the categories in more detail.

Not surprisingly, my inquiry showed that substantial proportions of the people's possessions had been bought secondhand; this was true, for example, of about 35 per cent of all the furniture and 13 per cent of the personal clothing owned by the fourteen households. Less than 15 per cent of all their goods had been purchased in shops; most of their possessions (60 per cent) had been bought in open street markets. The tenants' shopping area was narrowly circumscribed: 66 per cent of all their purchased possessions had been bought either within the tenement itself or within the neighborhood, and about a fifth of the purchases had been made in markets in nearby neighborhoods. Thus about 85 per cent of the purchases were made within a radius of less than a mile from the tenement. Of the remaining purchases 8.9 per cent were made in distant neighborhoods of Mexico City and 5.6 per cent were made outside the city. Although the tenement was within a few minutes' walk of Mexico City's downtown shopping center, comparatively few of the tenants' possessions had been bought there or in more distant places. (Indeed, apart from occasional religious excursions to pilgrimage centers, most of the families had traveled very little, either within the city or outside it.)

The tenants' principal possession was furniture, accounting for about a third of all their expenditures on material goods. At the time of my inventory each family had among its furnishings at least one bed, a mattress, a table, a shelf for an altar and a set of shelves for dishes. They considered these items to be the minimal essentials, although most of the families had lived without some or all of them in the past.

The fourteen households owned a total of twenty-three beds for their eighty-three members, so that in most of the households some members (usually the older sons) had to sleep on straw mats or rags on the floor. Of the twenty-three beds, seven had been bought new, thirteen secondhand and three had been received as gifts. The new beds ranged in price from $4.40 to $12.

The bed or beds usually took up most of the space in the one-room apartment. During the day the bed was used for sitting, for work, for sorting laundry and for many other purposes, including a play area

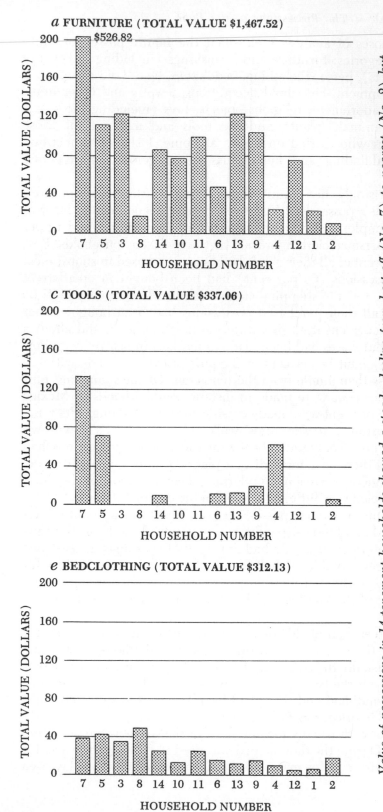

a FURNITURE (TOTAL VALUE $1,467.52)

$526.82

c TOOLS (TOTAL VALUE $337.06)

e BEDCLOTHING (TOTAL VALUE $312.13)

TOTAL VALUE (DOLLARS)

HOUSEHOLD NUMBER

Value of possessions in 14 tenement households showed a steady decline from best-off (No. 7) to poorest (No. 2) but varied greatly from family to family. Furniture (a) was the most valuable possession and personal clothing (b) the next. With a total valuation of more than $2,800, the two were worth more than all other possessions combined. More than 90 per cent of the best-off family's investment in furniture, however, was in a $480 television set, and nearly half of the value of all the toys (i) owned by the families that had children was represented by the $64 bicycle in household

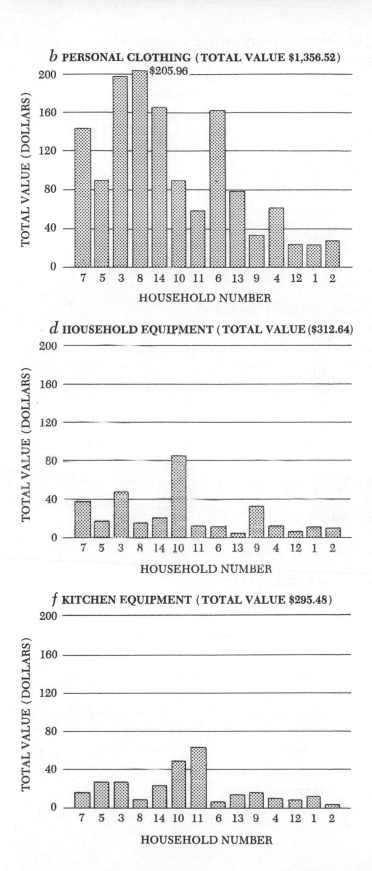

b PERSONAL CLOTHING (TOTAL VALUE $1,356.52)

$205.96

TOTAL VALUE (DOLLARS)

HOUSEHOLD NUMBER

7 5 3 8 14 10 11 6 13 9 4 12 1 2

d HOUSEHOLD EQUIPMENT (TOTAL VALUE ($312.64)

TOTAL VALUE (DOLLARS)

HOUSEHOLD NUMBER

7 5 3 8 14 10 11 6 13 9 4 12 1 2

f KITCHEN EQUIPMENT (TOTAL VALUE $295.48)

TOTAL VALUE (DOLLARS)

HOUSEHOLD NUMBER

7 5 3 8 14 10 11 6 13 9 4 12 1 2

No. 5. Unevenness in the decline from best-off to poorest in household equipment (d) is because households No. 3, No. 10 and No. 9 had sewing machines. Not only clocks but also wristwatches were found in four of the seven better-off households, but the seven poorer ones had no clocks at all. All, however, had electric light and an electric iron. Only one had no chairs, only two had no wardrobe for clothes and only three had no radio.

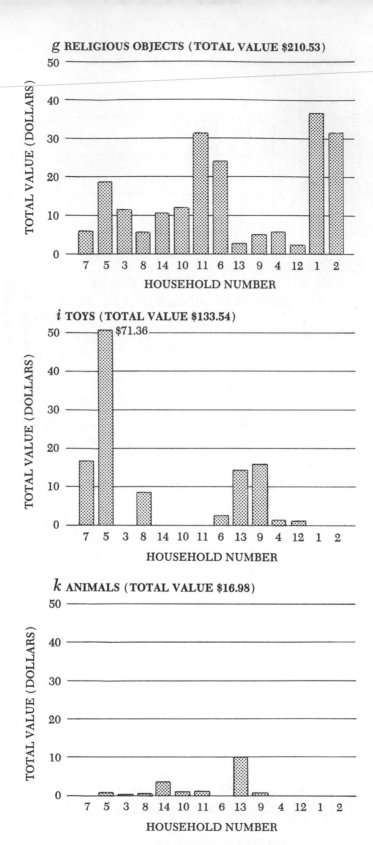

g RELIGIOUS OBJECTS (TOTAL VALUE $210.53)

i TOYS (TOTAL VALUE $133.54)

k ANIMALS (TOTAL VALUE $16.98)

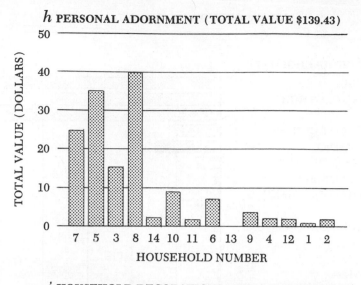

h PERSONAL ADORNMENT (TOTAL VALUE $139.43)

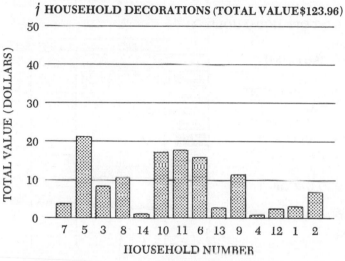

j HOUSEHOLD DECORATIONS (TOTAL VALUE $123.96)

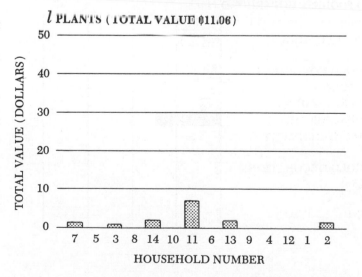

l PLANTS (TOTAL VALUE $11.06)

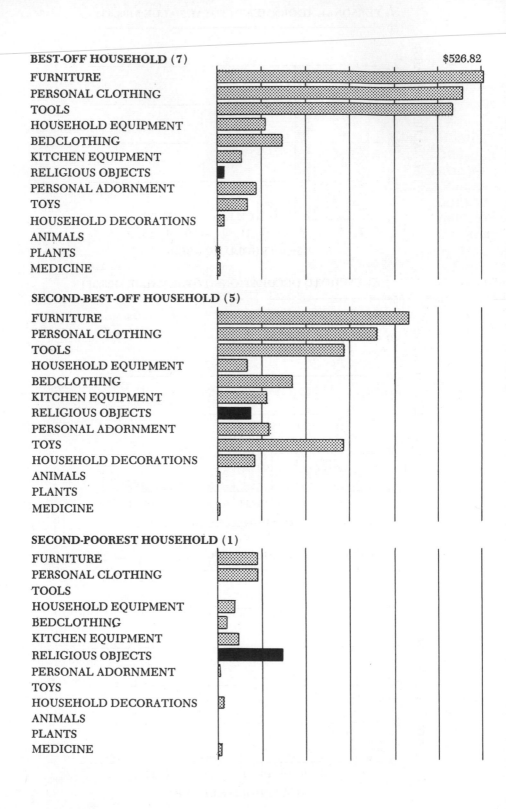

BEST-OFF HOUSEHOLD (7) $526.82
FURNITURE
PERSONAL CLOTHING
TOOLS
HOUSEHOLD EQUIPMENT
BEDCLOTHING
KITCHEN EQUIPMENT
RELIGIOUS OBJECTS
PERSONAL ADORNMENT
TOYS
HOUSEHOLD DECORATIONS
ANIMALS
PLANTS
MEDICINE

SECOND-BEST-OFF HOUSEHOLD (5)
FURNITURE
PERSONAL CLOTHING
TOOLS
HOUSEHOLD EQUIPMENT
BEDCLOTHING
KITCHEN EQUIPMENT
RELIGIOUS OBJECTS
PERSONAL ADORNMENT
TOYS
HOUSEHOLD DECORATIONS
ANIMALS
PLANTS
MEDICINE

SECOND-POOREST HOUSEHOLD (1)
FURNITURE
PERSONAL CLOTHING
TOOLS
HOUSEHOLD EQUIPMENT
BEDCLOTHING
KITCHEN EQUIPMENT
RELIGIOUS OBJECTS
PERSONAL ADORNMENT
TOYS
HOUSEHOLD DECORATIONS
ANIMALS
PLANTS
MEDICINE

POOREST HOUSEHOLD (2)

FURNITURE
PERSONAL CLOTHING
TOOLS
HOUSEHOLD EQUIPMENT
BEDCLOTHING
KITCHEN EQUIPMENT
RELIGIOUS OBJECTS
PERSONAL ADORNMENT
TOYS
HOUSEHOLD DECORATIONS
ANIMALS
PLANTS
MEDICINE

```
0     25     50     75     100     125     150
```

TOTAL VALUES (DOLLARS)

Sharp contrast in value between the possessions of the two best-off and the two poorest households, although it was predictable, had one surprising element. All the possessions in the two poorest households were worth less than half the value of those in No. 5, the second-best-off household, and those in No. 7 were worth nearly twice as much as those in No. 5. The value of holy pictures and other religious objects in either of the poorest households, however, far outstripped the value of such objects in the best-off: combined, they constituted 33 per cent of the total value of such objects in all 14 households in the tenement.

for the children. In families in which a night worker had to sleep during the day, he slept on one side of the bed while the other members of the family sat, worked or played on the other side.

The average length of ownership of a bed among these families was only four years eight months, not because the beds wore out rapidly but because for one reason or another—prolonged illness, family separations, death or economic emergency—the families occasionally had to pawn or sell their furniture to raise money for food and other necessities. The instability of bed ownership was only one instance of the brief and uncertain possession of furniture items among these families. The mean time of possession for all the pieces of furniture in the tenement was only four and a half years, although a majority of the families had lived there for more than fifteen years. The brevity of possession was frequently due to the inability of the families to meet the installment payments on furniture bought on credit.

The poverty of the possessions is perhaps most vividly illustrated by the mattresses on which the people slept. Most of the mattresses were of cheap quality and stuffed with lumpy cotton or straw; only four families had invested relatively heavily (from $22 to $44) in better-quality mattresses with springs. The condition of many of the mattresses was incredibly bad because of hard wear and lack of any protective covering. They were almost all stained, torn and infested with bedbugs and fleas. Of the twenty-six mattresses in the *vecindad*, fourteen had been bought new, two were gifts and ten had been bought secondhand, their poor condition notwithstanding. In spite of the low price of the used mattresses (ranging from 56 cents to $2.40) the total amount invested in mattresses ($178) was higher than the amount invested in beds ($132). The average duration of mattress ownership was three years eight months.

Each household had at least one shelf for votive candles dedicated to the saints, even if it was only a small board hung with string from nails on the wall. The altar was often loaded with a clutter of non-religious objects: needles, thread, razors and other things that had to be kept out of reach of children. On holy days it was cleared and decorated with colored tissue paper.

Kitchen shelves were also found in every household, although many of the families had at one time been unable to afford them and had had to keep tableware and food on the floor. The shelves were inexpensive, none costing more than $1.20. The majority of them had been bought secondhand, received as gifts or built by members of the household.

The fifth essential article, a table, was also owned by every family. Some of the better-off families had two or three tables and had managed to paint or varnish them or cover them with oilcloth. The majority of the tables were cheap unpainted wood ones; the most expensive cost $5.20, and three-fourths of them were valued at $1.20 or less. None had been bought in a store; most had been acquired at street markets or from relatives or acquaintances.

In addition to the five indispensable articles of furniture, nearly all the families considered three others to be necessary for a decent standard of living. One of them was a chair. Only one household had no chairs at all; the adults there sat on the bed and the children on the floor. One family had eight chairs; another, seven; most had at least two. The chairs made the single small room of the apartment very crowded indeed. In the tenement as a whole, however, there were only fifty-two chairs for the eighty-three residents; at mealtimes many had to sit on the bed, on a low stool or on the floor. Like the other furniture, all the chairs were inexpensive; none had cost more than $2.

A wardrobe for clothing also was regarded as a necessity, since none of the apartments had a closet. Twelve of the fourteen households had a wardrobe; in the other two clothes were hung on nails or kept in boxes. A wardrobe represented a relatively large investment, and the families considered it to be a prestige item. It was often a wedding gift from the husband to the wife.

Most of the wardrobes had been bought new, at an average cost of $16.80, and they were generally the longest-held article of furniture in the apartment. Some had been there for as many as fifteen years. In all but a few instances the wardrobe was in poor condition—battered and with the door mirrors either cracked or missing. Only one family had been able to afford to replace its broken mirrors.

Every family considered a radio essential, and at the time of my study eleven of the fourteen households had one. One family had two radios. The radio was usually the family's most expensive piece of furniture. More money ($414) had been invested in radios than in any other item except for two television sets. Most of the radios had been bought new on credit, at prices ranging from $20 to $74. Because of the precariousness of the tenants' financial situation, the radio tended to be only a briefly held possession; its ownership averaged less than three years. Frequently the radio had to be given up because the family could not meet installment payments on it or could not afford to have it repaired when it broke down. Many radios were pawned, usually in a clandestine pawnshop that charged 20 per cent interest per month on the loan. After losing the radio most families would buy another as soon as circumstances permitted.

Only one of the families was able to buy and hold on to a television set. This family, financially the best-off in the tenement, was managing to keep up the payments on a set costing a little more than $480—an amount greater than the combined value of all the family's other material possessions and greater than the total personal property of twelve of the other tenants. A second family had a television set when I began my study, but it pawned and lost the set before I had completed the investigation. The family bought another set later, committing itself to paying $24 a month for several years; it would be a most extraordinary achievement if the family succeeded in maintaining the payments. Needless to say, everyone in the tenement, particularly the young people, would like to have a television set, but few other families have attempted to buy one.

Some of the families in better economic circumstances had extra items of furniture such as glass-fronted dish cabinets and, in one case, three armchairs. These articles apparently were esteemed by their owners more for prestige value than for utility; in the one-room apartment they were impractical and they crowded the small space to a point of extreme inconvenience. The owner of the armchairs was a young shoemaker who was trying hard to raise his standard of living. He had bought a television set and the first and only gas stove ever used in the *vecindad,* but he had lost both by pawning one and not meeting the time payments on the other.

In nearly all cases furniture items (such as new mattresses, wardrobes and radios) that cost more than a few dollars were bought on credit. The public markets or itinerant salesmen from whom they were bought did not require a down payment, but for the privilege of paying in installments the buyer had to pay twice as much as the cash price of the article. The tenants were aware of this, but their cash resources were so small that they could obtain these articles only by buying them on credit. The weekly installments were usually low, averaging 80 cents, and often extended over more than a year for a single article.

The purchases of secondhand furniture were usually made from relatives or friends, most often within the same tenement. Since eleven of the fourteen households were closely related, there was considerable opportunity for intrafamily commerce, usually at bargain prices.

Kitchen equipment in the fourteen households was generally restricted to inexpensive items. The largest total investment in this category by any family was $42.63, and the aggregate for the fourteen households was $230.36. None of the apartments had a refrigerator. The principal item of kitchen equipment was usually a stove. Eleven apartments had kerosene or petroleum stoves; in the other three cooking was done on a brazier or an earthenware plate over a charcoal hearth on the floor. The cooking vessels were generally inexpensive *ollas* or *cazuelas* (narrow-mouthed or wide-mouthed vessels of clay). Only two families had aluminum pots and only five had copper kettles. Twelve owned frying pans.

Every family had a few spoons that were used for cooking and for eating soup. There were few other eating utensils; only two families owned forks and only seven had table knives. Solid foods were usually eaten with the fingers, often with the aid of a tortilla to wrap or scoop up the food. The eating plates were most commonly "tin" ones (costing from 8 to 16 cents); one family had a six-piece place setting of china, which it had owned for fourteen years. Because glassware was a favorite gift item in the community, particularly on Mother's Day, the households had more glasses than traditional Mexican clay cups. One family owned seventy-six glasses. Some families also had

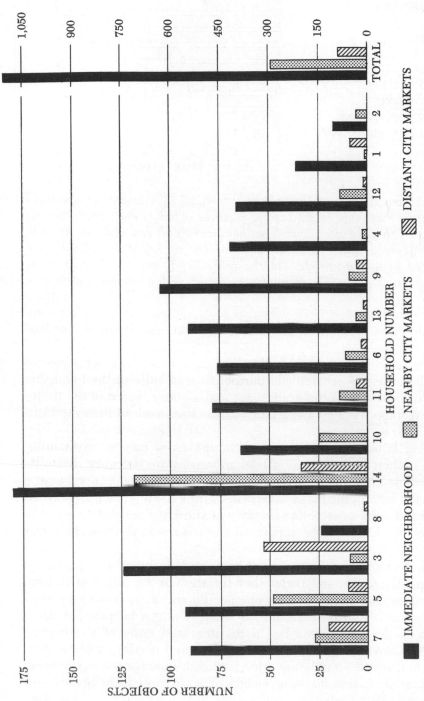

Buying habits of the tenement families were analyzed by finding out where some 1,600 objects had been bought. In every case, buying in the immediate neighborhood and within the tenement itself outweighed purchases at nearby or more distant city markets. In part this reflects buying from itinerant peddlers who visited the tenement regularly. Two households contained more than four objects obtained outside Mexico City; some had come from as far away as Guadalajara, Acapulco and the state of Chiapas.

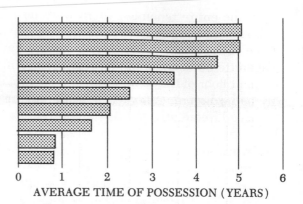

RELIGIOUS OBJECTS
TOOLS
FURNITURE
HOUSEHOLD DECORATIONS
KITCHEN EQUIPMENT
HOUSEHOLD EQUIPMENT
BEDCLOTHING
PERSONAL CLOTHING
PERSONAL ADORNMENT

0   1   2   3   4   5   6

AVERAGE TIME OF POSSESSION (YEARS)

Average length of time that objects remained in a tenement household was at its maximum in the case of pictures of saints and other religious items, which were often considered heirlooms. This was also true of tools, which were a source of livelihood for the tenement households that engaged in manufacturing. On the other hand, items that were easily pawned, such as jewelry, or quickly worn out, such as clothing, were soon let go.

serving trays and other "luxury" items that had been received as gifts.

Almost 90 per cent of the kitchen equipment had been bought new because it was relatively inexpensive. In spite of the breakable nature of much of it this equipment had a better record of durability (the average was two and a half years) than many of the other articles in our inventories.

Other household equipment, although more meager in quantity than kitchen utensils, was placed in a separate category of study. Household equipment for all the families totaled $294 in value and ranked fourth in the list of categories. Three sewing machines owned by three families accounted for about a third of this total. One of the sewing machines had been pawned three times in three years to pay debts.

All the women in the community sewed; many of them mended and made clothes and bedclothes for the family, much of it from flour sacks. All owned at least one needle and most owned a pair of scissors, although on occasion the scissors might be pawned. Only seven of the households had a thimble, and none of the women owned a sewing basket for storing thread and needles. They usually bought thread in small quantities, sufficient only for the job at hand. Each family had at least one electric iron, in most cases bought secondhand. Two better-off families had ironing boards; in the other households the women ironed on the table.

In the entire tenement there were no wastebaskets and only two ashtrays, although most of the men and many of the women smoked. Nine of the fourteen households had no garbage can for the kitchen. Cigarette butts and all other trash were simply thrown on the dirt or cement floor of the room and were eventually swept out. Every family had a broom, generally a crude handmade affair that had to be replaced frequently because of constant use.

Two water taps in the yard were the only source of water for the apartment and every family required several buckets or containers for fetching water. The fourteen households had a total of forty-three pails. They also owned a total of twenty-one tubs, some of them quite large, for laundering and for bathing. Fewer than half of the families owned dishpans; only four had a washstand. Toothbrushes were a luxury; in only three families did each person have a toothbrush of his own. Among the more unusual items were three douche bags, a syringe and three eyecups.

Awareness of time and of schedules was increasing among the slum dwellers, and most of the families felt the need of a clock—for feeding babies, giving medicine, getting children off to school on time or listening to favorite radio programs. Still, only half of the families, and only the better-to-do ones, owned a clock. The others kept track of the time either by their radio or by asking their clock-owning neighbors.

All the apartments had electric light. Three households owned gasoline or kerosene lanterns for use in their workshop at night. One household owned an electric heater; for all the others the only source of heat on cold nights was the cooking stove.

As they did in other respects, the families of the tenement varied considerably in the poverty of their household equipment. The better-to-do families not only owned more items in this category (165 articles for the upper seven families compared with 104 for the lower seven) but also had a wider range of objects. One family (the second-poorest) owned no washtub, no clothespins, no scissors or thimble, no storage receptacles, no dishpan, no floor brush, no clothesbrush, no toothbrush and of course no sewing machine or clock. In the tenement as a whole the length of possession of household equipment was very brief, averaging only two years.

Bedclothes, the fifth most costly material goods in the community, accounted for a value of $279.99, or 6.8 per cent of the total. This relatively high figure was due mainly to the expensiveness of blankets and quilts; the number of items was actually quite small. No family had more than thirty articles of bedclothing, including sheets, pillows, pillowcases, blankets and quilts. The best-off family owned a silk bedspread. Much of the bedclothing had been bought new, mainly on credit, but a large proportion was homemade. The women of the *vecindad*, even in the better-off families, usually made their sheets from flour sacks. Four sacks made an average-sized sheet. The length of possession of bedclothing averaged only 1.7 years. This was partly because of wear and partly because even bedclothes sometimes had to be sold to meet more urgent needs.

I shall merely summarize briefly here the inventory of the other five categories of general household goods: decorative objects, religious objects, animals, plants and medicines. The principal investment in decoration was expended on photographs of family members. There was an average of more than seven photographs per apartment. They were usually framed and often in color and represented a total cost of $82.38. Most of the apartments were also adorned with pictures of saints and with colorful calendars, usually religious ones that had been obtained free. A few households had different types of pictures, painted vases, china figurines of animals and other items.

The investment in religious objects by these impoverished families was remarkably large. A total of 147 pictures of Catholic saints and Biblical scenes, an average of more than ten pictures per household, hung on the walls of the tenement apartments. There were also flowered vases, candles, small religious figures and a variety of other religious objects displayed on the altars. In the tenement as a whole the total investment in religious objects was $210.53. About half had been bought by the residents themselves and half had come as gifts.

The emphasis on religious objects was greatest among the poorest families. The family that ranked lowest in total investment in material possessions actually stood highest in the value of its religious objects. This family and the next-poorest had spent almost as much on religious articles as on furniture. If we include the religious gifts they received, their religious possessions represented nearly twice the total value of their furniture. Nearly all the religious objects in the fourteen households had been bought new and were kept for an average of 5.07 years, longer than possessions in any other category.

The investment in the other categories of general household belongings—animals, plants and medicines—was so small that it calls for little comment. The tenement residents loved animals; almost every family had a cat or dog (partly as protection against rats and thieves) and some tenants also kept chickens, pigeons and other birds. Their total cash investment, however, was only $15.94 for animals and $10.20 for plants. The fourteen families' entire investment in the medicines on their shelves amounted to $7.76.

In the category of personal possessions, clothing was of course the major item. Clothing ranked second to furniture among the thirteen property categories, and it accounted for 27.4 per cent of the tenants' total investment in material goods. The fourteen families had spent a total of $1,127.36 on the clothing they owned at the time of the inventory. About 87 per cent of their purchased clothing had been bought new (usually for cash but a third of it on credit); the rest had been obtained secondhand. A substantial proportion of their total of clothing possessions were gifts and clothing made at home.

The families differed markedly in their expenditures for clothes. The poorest families bought very little, relying mainly on gifts from relatives. One family, for example, had spent only $3.92 for clothing and had received $20.72 worth as gifts. The largest outlay for clothing by any family was $192.64. This family ranked near the bottom in furniture possessions. Generally those families that invested heavily in clothing tended to spend little on furniture.

In every household the women supplemented the clothing purchases and gifts with clothing they made themselves, often out of flour sacks or scraps. Most of this home manufacture was for the women and children. For example, the mother in the family with the largest number of children (eight) had produced forty-two articles, including fifteen items for her youngest baby, eleven dresses, nine slips and seven shirts.

The clothing of all fourteen families was limited to a few basic items. Every woman owned at least a dress and a pair of shoes, usually only one pair, so that much of the time she went barefoot. The adult women had an average of fewer than four dresses apiece; the young girls averaged six apiece. Nearly all the women had a *rebozo*, the traditional Mexican shawl, and most of them also owned a sweater, two or more slips (often homemade), underpants (an average of about three pairs per woman) and brassieres. About half of the women had skirt-and-blouse outfits; none wore slacks. There were only fifteen pairs of stockings in the entire community; these belonged mainly to teen-age girls. One woman and five girls had coats, one woman had a bathrobe and one owned a pocketbook. Handkerchiefs were rare; among the eighty-three residents in the tenement the only people who had this item were two men and two young girls.

The children and men of the community were better shod than the women. The basic wardrobe of the men consisted of shoes, undershorts (often homemade), a pair of pants, one or more shirts and a jacket or coat against the cold. There were only two suits in the community, belonging to two boys who had worn them at their confirmation. A number of men had no socks or undershirts. No male in the tenement owned a necktie. A few men had working overalls, several had a cap or a straw hat and one owned a bathing suit.

The clothing of this community, generally of poor quality and subjected to frequent wear, had a short lifetime. The average length of possession for all items of clothing was only 9.9 months. Sometimes clothes were sold before they wore out because of a financial crisis. In one instance the man of the household sold much of the family's wardrobe during a prolonged drinking spree, leaving his wife with only a single torn dress.

In the category of personal adornment the list of articles is brief. The entire investment in this category was $126.32, more than half of which was accounted for by five wristwatches owned by comparatively well-off families. Religious medals, finger rings and cheap earrings, also owned mainly by less poor families, constituted the rest of the articles in this category. Women's jewelry was extremely scarce. Not a single woman had a necklace, a bracelet or a brooch. In any case, the possession of such items in this community was ephemeral—averaging only 9.8 months—because of the ready convertibility of jewelry into cash.

Toys were even scarcer than jewelry among these families. Of the total investment of $121.62 in toys, more than half was represented by two bicycles. One had been bought new on installments and was rented out part of the time; the other was a secondhand bicycle without tires. There were also three tricycles in the community, two of them secondhand. Only half of the families in the tenement were able to invest in any toys for their children.

Finally, there were a few households that owned material goods in a special category: tools and materials for manufacturing in the home. In total value this category ranked third, after furniture and personal clothing. Three artisans who worked at home accounted for most of the investment: a shoemaker and two household heads who made and sold toy water bottles. The shoemaker had a stock of soles, heels, nails and various other things required for shoe repairing. Having little capital, he could maintain only a small supply of materials and had to replenish it every few days. Most of the materials and tools had been bought used. All three artisans had held on to their tools for a comparatively long time (an average of 5.05 years), since the tools constituted the family's means of livelihood and could not be sold or pawned as casually as other household goods.

It is surely significant that two of the three households that had managed to scrape up enough capital to make a substantial investment in income-producing tools and materials were also the most affluent families in the tenement in terms of their total accumulation of material possessions. The best-off family owned $134.38 worth of tools, whereas two of the three poorest families in the tenement had no tools whatever.

What conclusions, if any, can one draw from the inventory of the possessions of these fourteen slum families? For one thing, I was struck by the truly remarkable differences within this group of families, all of whom might seem to a casual observer to be living at the same level of poverty. Moreover, the differences in the value of their possessions were greater than differences in their income. If we compare the possessions of the three "wealthiest" families [*Families 7, 5 and 3 in the tables on pages 444 and 447*] with those of the three poorest families [*Families 12, 1 and 2*], we see that the top three owned a total of $1,754.46 worth of purchased goods, whereas the bottom three owned a total of $250.55—only a seventh as much. The largest differential was in the families' relative investment in furniture and clothing: $1,093.92 for the top three against only $149.49 for the bottom three. There were similar differences in expenditures for luxury items such as jewelry ($71.97 against $2.38) and toys ($88.58 against $13.68).

The only category in which the poorer families had spent more than the better-off was that of religious objects. The difference in amount was small ($23.45 by the poorer families compared with $21.78 by the better-off), but in its proportion to the families' total investment in material goods the contrast was great. Whereas the better-off families had invested only slightly more than 1 per cent of their money in religious items, the poorer families had invested nearly 14 per cent. Furthermore, religious objects also predominated in the gifts the poorer families had received; such objects represented nearly half of all gifts received, whereas religious objects accounted for less than 15 per cent of the gifts in the better-off families.

The fact that the tenement dwellers had held on to religious objects longer than most of their other possessions attests to the crucial role of religion in the lives of the poor. It appears also that religious objects may be the only things they own long enough to establish a real identification with. Yet even these are held for a fairly brief period, an average of about five years. The brevity of possession, and the singular absence of heirlooms passed down from generation to generation, suggest that the life of the very poor is weak in tradition and is oriented almost exclusively to day-to-day concerns.

It might be supposed that for lack of funds people in poverty are driven to making their own goods such as clothing or furniture. I found, however, that the better-off families in the tenement were the most productive in this sense because only they owned sewing machines or work tools and could afford to buy the materials. These families produced five times as much clothing (in value) as the poorer families did. By the same token they were also able to buy more of their goods new. Whereas about 25 per cent of all purchases by the three poorest families were secondhand, only about 7 per cent of those by the three best-off families were secondhand. The contrast was greatest in furniture purchases. The poorer families bought three-quarters of their furniture secondhand; the better-off families bought three-quarters of theirs new.

The study of possessions, while confirming some previous findings about the poor, raises questions about others. For instance, there has been reason to believe that the mobility of poor people is highly restricted, that they rarely venture out of their immediate neighborhood. The analysis of the fourteen families' possessions, however, showed that the objects came from forty-three different markets or localities, some of them at considerable distances from Mexico City. Eight of the families owned objects that came from fourteen marketplaces outside the capital. One family had possessions that were bought in twenty-eight marketplaces, eleven of which were in distant cities, one as far away as Chiapas. It therefore appears that at least some of the Mexican urban poor may move about more widely than has been supposed.

Part Six:

SELECTIONS FROM LIFE HISTORIES

21

A Thursday with Manuel[*]

"Get up, *vieja*, and see what you can heat me up for breakfast. Come on, get going. Look at her! She looks half dead."

"Eh? Eh?" she says, opening her eyes.

"Didn't I tell you last night I was going to Carrera to sell shirts and I have to get up at seven?"

"Yes, but . . ."

"Oh, *carajo!* Are you going to begin with your buts! On your feet."

My wife, María, got out of bed reluctantly and groped in the dark for the electric-light bulb hanging from the ceiling. She stumbled over Carmela and Carlota, two seventeen-year-old girls who were asleep on a mattress on the floor. These girls were in need of a home and were staying with us. María turned on the light and went into the kitchen to struggle with the kerosene stove. Lolita, our three-year-old daughter who slept in the bed with us, had become uncovered and I pulled the blanket up over her. I resisted leaving the warm bed, but I knew that the good locations in the market get taken early and I wanted a place right on the corner. That's where you can really sell. So I got up and went straight to the laundry tub next to the toilet in the kitchen.

"*Jijo! vieja*, this water is cold! Say, did you count the shirts last night?"

"Yes, a hundred and forty-five."

[*] This essay was first published in July-August, 1966, in the *New Left Review* (London), pp. 3–21.

"Well, not bad. I bought them for ten *pesos* apiece and I'll sell them at twelve and thirteen. If sales are good, maybe I'll take in sixty or seventy *pesos*."

"With luck, maybe a hundred, *viejo*."

"Sure, sure, nothing to it. Pass me the towel, *vieja*. Are you going to have to turn the house upside down to find a towel? *Carajo!*" My wife went on emptying all the drawers in the dresser, until she finally found the damned towel and tossed it to me. She served my coffee in a glass and as I gulped it down, I put my arm around her waist. "Have yourself a cup of coffee, *vieja*."

A little smile came to her lips, then a yawn. "I'm very sleepy," she said.

"You lazy old devil. As soon as I am gone you can go back to sleep. Till one o'clock if you want—you and Carmela and Carlota. What a bunch! Let's go! Open both doors, *vieja*. I can't get through with these boxes."

With two steps, María crossed the little kitchen that separated the bedroom from the front door and opened it wide. "Wait, *viejo*, let me help you as far as the street."

And so, once more I set out to face my destiny. Buy and sell, sell and buy, every day, at the public markets of Mexico City. It isn't often that I get up this early to earn our daily bread, but I am a real hustler on Thursday because that's the day of the races at the *Hipódromo* and I need money to play the horses.

María and I got through the front gate of our *vecindad* and waited on the corner for a cab to take me to the Carrera market.

"There goes one! Whistle, *viejo*, whistle."

The driver heard me and pulled over to the curb. "What do you say, pal? Do me a favor and take me to Carrera?" He didn't say a word but looked pointedly down at my boxes. I caught on and explained. "They're shirts, pal. The boxes aren't heavy and I'll give you something extra."

"It's a deal, brother. Let's go."

I lifted the boxes into the back seats and turned to say good-bye to my wife.

"Listen," she said. "What about money for dinner? Don't act dumb, wise guy."

"I have just enough for the cab fare. Better meet me and we'll grab a *taco* at the market. I'll have money by then, *vieja*. Go on in now, you're shaking with cold."

"*Jijos!* it's a cold morning, isn't it, pal?" I said to the driver as we started off.

"Yes! You'd never think it was summertime. Say, you guys clean up at the Carrera market, don't you? Looks like a lot of people go there to buy."

"Don't you believe it, pal. Things are lousy, otherwise I wouldn't be selling in these markets. I work the Tepito market, but they won't let us sell these shirts in the used goods section."

"Why, are they new ones?"

"No, they are laundry shirts, the ones the customers send to be washed and never claim."

"Then why don't they let you sell them in Tepito?"

"Just because of the whim of the damned administrator of that section. But it is not really his fault. We ourselves are to blame. We're a bunch of suckers."

The driver smiled. "How right you are. Look at us cab drivers! We pass a stop light . . . fifty smackers! If they grab you without a license, fifty slugs. And gasoline, even though it is 'ours,' eighty *centavos* a liter. *Chingao,* we were better off when the *gringos* and the English had our oil! And now that the government has nationalized electricity too, wait and see what those bastards are going to pull on us. And there's no stealing it now . . . you're robbing the nation! Before that, *chingao,* when the electric company caught you stealing the juice, all they did was take away your wire and that was it."

"We vendors get screwed too! We have to belong to the second-hand dealers' union, have a permit from the Social Welfare Department, a card from Police Headquarters, a permit from the Ministry of Health . . . just to buy and sell second-hand goods! Bah!"

"You don't say!"

"By God, yes, And that's not the end of it. You can't sell new clothing, or new or repaired shoes, or washed and rerepaired clothing, and you can't hawk your merchandise or they slap a fine on you. If you don't wear your denim jacket uniform, a fine. If they catch you taking up more than one meter of space, a fine."

"Whew! So what can you sell?"

"Pal, I don't know what they want. Our asses, I guess."

"Well, here we are. Where do you want me to stop?"

"Just drop me right here on the corner, please. How much do I owe you, pal?"

"Let's call it five *pesos,* brother. Good luck, man, *adios.*"

"Well, now to set up shop," I thought to myself as my eyes tried to pick out the cops on duty in this market. I untied the boxes, laid out newspapers, put an old bedspread on top and this way I had my space reserved. Buses, packed with people, stopped at the corner to let them off. Delivery trucks came and went, up and down the busy street. The owner of the *tortillería* right in front of my spot already had his corn mill going. A man threw a long rope up into the branches of a tree to stretch his "awning," a piece of cloth to protect his goods from the sun. Further off, an elderly lady was patting *tortillas* ready to be filled with beans and put on the fire. Some vendors came over, sizing me up with their eyes, trying to make up their minds whether they would settle down next to me or not. Finally, they began to spread out their merchandise.

"Oh, oh, the law!" Here come the cops, one short fat guy and the other tall and skinny, with glasses, walking in step, looking over their shoulders at my fellow vendors.

I said to my neighbor, "Young man, won't you keep an eye on my boxes? I have to go purify myself with the authorities."

"Sure, sure, of course. Go ahead."

Walking sideways so I could watch my boxes, I went over to talk to the two birds.

"Chief . . ." He turns around. "Good morning," I said with a smile. "You know, I am taking up a spot over there."

"Where?" asked the cop turning to see the place.

"Over there, right on the corner. I'm selling shirts."

"All right. So what?"

"No, nothing," I said shrugging my shoulders, "I just wanted to know how much."

"Up to you. It's the corner, don't forget."

I'm screwed! "Yes, it's the corner. But we'll figure it according to how it goes, eh?"

"Nothing doing, my boy. The time to spill the tears is when you're laying out the corpse. So cough up."

"All right. I'll give you five. Okay?"

He raised his hands up to his eyes, adjusting his glasses and said, "Right now."

"I haven't got it now, chief. But after my first sale, I'll dance for you. I'll fork over or you can kick me out of the market. Good enough?"

"Okay, go on, but if you try to sneak away on me, better not show up here again because there won't be a place for you!"

I went back to my spot and I began to put the shirts out on the bedspread.

"One, two, three, four . . ." Then I began to shout at the top of my lungs. "Sale on shirts, what do you say, *marchanta*? Pick it up, lady. Look them over . . . feel them. Shirts . . . twelve and thirteen *pesos* apiece. We have MacGregor, Medalla, American Van Heusen, English labels . . . we've got all makes. Step right over close, *marchantita*. Have no fear . . . they don't bite, they're dead."

"Do you have size fifteen?"

"Why, certainly, *marchante* . . . about fifty of them. Here's one for thirteen *pesos,* but just look at the quality! Measure it, boss. Go ahead, take hold of it."

"But I was just on my way to the baths," he said with a rural accent.

"That doesn't matter. We sell cheap here, whether you've bathed or not."

I picked out four and gave them to his wife. When he made a movement with his hand, I could tell I had a sale.

"*Marchante* . . . ," she started to say.

"No, no, don't even try to make me an offer. That is the bottom price. Really, lady, that is the least I'll take."

"All right," he said; "then just wrap them up for us in a piece of paper."

"Sorry, boss, I'm going to have to owe you the piece of paper. I don't take enough out of the business for that."

By now the people began to crowd around my spot.

"What sizes do you have, *marchante?*"

"All sizes, lady, even for little elephants. Pickmeup, pickmeup . . . the bargains go first . . . first come, first served . . . the rest are out of luck . . . get them while they last . . ."

Then, when I was selling at my hottest, a car parks right in front of me and a guy about my height and build gets out. He touches me on the shoulder and says, "Say, buddy, you know what? You are going to have to move away from here."

"Really? Would you just mind telling me why?"

"Because this is my spot on Thursday."

"Your spot? You don't say? Just show me the bill of sale." While I talked, I took off my windbreaker as I was getting overheated with all the activity. Then I rolled up my sleeves.

"So you are not going to move?"

"No, brother of mine, I got here before you did." And my customers bore me out. One lady said: "How do you like that? Not only is he a lazy pup, but he starts barking."

A man who was also buying from me said: "No, don't let him get away with it, young fellow. This is a public market and anybody who wants to can sell, whoever comes first." My rival backed down and walked away. Another customer said: "He probably went for the cops."

I just listened to the discussion and kept on quoting prices and showing the merchandise. I expected bad news and stretched my neck and turned my head to see where it was coming from. It took about ten minutes. From the opposite corner I saw the man coming with a cop and the collector of the market.

"That's him," says this guy pointing me out. But I had a ten *peso* bill all ready folded in my hand. I stood right next to the cop and let him feel it. Zas! in a flash he had it in his fingers. Man, what practice! So, I turned to my rival and said, "Who is this? Your uncle, jerk? *Ay, ay, ay,* look at the fairy boy hiding behind the policeman."

He made a vulgar gesture at me. But the cop had already noticed that I had slipped him ten instead of five, and winking at the collector, said: "No, brother, there's no call for you to be getting riled. The spots go to whoever gets there first. After all, God gives to everyone. Get up earlier next Thursday."

Having "legally" won that battle, I went on with my selling. The hours flew by and more and more people gathered around my spot. I really had a mob.

I kept thinking of that damned old woman of mine who didn't show up to help me keep an eye on things. It was one o'clock and I watched every bus that passed to see if María got off. I really needed a drink and something to eat. Just as I was going to do something about it, a bus stopped and I saw my old woman get off. Here she came with her wobbly steps. Only nineteen and she walks like a duck, poor little thing.

I said to myself: "Well, finally!" She had Lolita with her, filthy as usual. Poor little girl, so pretty and then they go and bring her to me all dirty.

She said: "*Viejo,* I brought you these dresses you had left over from the other lot. Maybe you can sell them here, don't you think?"

"Well, what do you know! *Chingao!* And what made you think of it right now, anyway?"

"Oh, stop . . . ! I just thought maybe you could sell them."

"You did fine. Just put them down there. Listen, *vieja,* there is one thing I would like to know . . . What is the big idea, please? Look, sales are very good, I guess I must have over five hundred *pesos* sold and here you come in your sloppy rags, man! People are going to say I don't make enough to buy you anything better. Have a heart, dammit!"

"Look at him! If you want to know, I was doing my housework."

"Yes, yes, you've always got an explanation, but man I don't think it could take you over fifteen minutes to fix yourself . . . to clean yourself up . . . please, man! Are you hungry yet?"

"Me, yes, *papá,*" said Lolita. "I want my coffee."

"What? Haven't you had your breakfast yet, daughter?"

"No, but . . ." began María.

"Well, I'll be damned, *vieja.* How can you keep the little girl without breakfast until this hour? Well, what's the use. Here . . . here's money. See what you can go and buy."

"All right, What shall I get?"

"Wow! That's what I'm telling you! How do I know?"

"All right. Do you want roast pork?"

"Okay, fine. The man in the butcher shop over there makes very very delicious roast pork."

"How much shall I buy?"

"Well, buy . . . how much for three? . . . half a kilo, no?"

"No, *viejo*, that's much too much."

"Okay, take money and buy as much as you want."

Now the customers began to fall off on account of the heat. A woman who had been standing to one side, watching me for quite a long while, finally came over and said: "Say, aren't you Manuel, the 'Chink'? The one they call the 'Chink' over in the Tepito market?"

"Well, I'll be blessed! Blondie . . . sure! How many years is it since I've seen you? Must be four or so, isn't it? How goes it with you, Blondie?"

"Bad. Things are bad, very bad. I haven't even crossed myself for my first sale today. Lord, I don't know what we are going to do. For one thing, nobody has money . . . nobody wants to spend, especially not on bracelets and the kind of little stuff I sell. For another, there are those lousy bastards, if you'll pardon me for the expression, from the Police Department. If you try to sell in a market where you are not authorized, they come around and clean you out. Like the other day. Imagine, there I was in *Colonia* Two Hundred and One . . . They built the new market and now they don't allow any more sidewalk selling."

"Sure, Blondie, but what can we do? That's the way things go. But you'll sell. The sun comes out for everybody, sooner or later."

"Here comes your old woman, I'm going to go sit down. I don't want her getting jealous."

Blondie went and sat down at her spot again. My wife came over and said: "Look, *viejo*, this roast pork is very good, not like the ordinary kind."

"Yes, *vieja*. How much does a kilo cost?"

"It didn't say, so first I asked for a hundred grams."

"Stop it, *vieja*. What do you mean, a hundred grams? Are we dogs or what? A hundred grams of *carnitas* for three people?"

"Look, everybody has his own system of buying. Why do you have to mix in women's business?"

"Okay . . . that's what I get for butting in. So how much did you buy?"

"Eight *pesos*' worth."

"Why, you old bitch, now you did buy a lot. Never mind, we'll invite Blondie to have a *taco* with us. She used to buy all kinds of stuff and now look at how she goes around. She's even wearing *huaraches* instead of shoes. And she used to make very good money, that woman."

"Mmm . . . yes, you can see she is in a bad way. I'll bring you a bottle of lemonade."

"Look, *vieja,* there's a fresh lemonade stand right over there across the street. Better buy that."

So she and Lolita went to buy the drinks and I continued selling. There were just a few customers at that hour. I watched my wife cross the street. The lemonade stand was set up in a shoe-repair shop and the shoemaker himself stopped working on the shoes to serve the drinks. I thought: "I'll bet that bastard handles all those filthy shoes and then in the morning he squeezes out the fruit with the same hands and that's what he sells. Better a bottled drink." And so when my old woman showed up with the lemonade, I said to her: "Listen, *vieja,* you know . . ." and I told her what I had been thinking.

"*Ay,* Manuelito," she says. "What a pig you are! Cut it out, will you? What do we do now? We can't throw it away."

"Okay, if you want to drink, go ahead. What else did you buy?"

"Well, I bought chilis and tomatoes and onions to make Mexican sauce. Shall I buy one of those little thirty-*centavo* clay mortars to grind it in?"

"Buy it, *vieja.*"

So, off she ran to get the clay dish. It was about one-thirty and I began to feel the itch . . . the horses. I pulled out the *Racing Form* I had bought the night before and began to study the selections. Well, like always, the same as with all us horse players who think we know something about it, I saw a double in the second race that looked very good . . . one and six. I said to myself: "There are the numbers in this race, all right. I'll play it, once or twice. It pays seventy-five *pesos* . . . so for an investment of forty it makes a hundred and fifty. I have to take the plunge and see if I win something. But what am I going to say to my old woman? She gets mad if I go there."

Right then my old woman came back and so I put away the *Racing Form* fast. I said to her: "Listen, *vieja,* there's not much business now any more, so I think what we'll do is just have our *tacos* and go. Go on, make the *tacos.*" The little girl had already begun to get busy.

"Lolita, stop handling the meat. Leave it alone. María, can't you see her hands are dirty? Give her one . . . go on, she's hungry. But you didn't get avocados, you dope."

"*Ay!* that's right, *viejo.* I forgot them but I am going to make Mexican sauce."

"Forget the Mexican sauce. We'll eat them just like this."

The truth of the matter was that I was in a hurry to finish and get to the track. The food tasted very good. The little girl was moving her jaws from side to side chewing her *taco*. I tossed down the last *taco* and said: "I'm going to close up shop." I began to throw the shirts into the box any which way, without arranging them.

"Count them," María says to me.

"Why count them? We can count them tonight at home. If they gypped me, they gypped me. If they swiped two or three . . . so what? Counting them won't help."

"*Ay, viejo*. I get it. I know where you are going. Today is Thursday."

"Okay. So what? What do you care? I'll go anyway. Do I have to ask for your permission, or what?"

"*Ay, viejo*. You really don't understand, and that's the truth."

"Oh, *chingao!* Now you are going to give me the business. OK, so I am going to go to the races, so what?"

"All right. The money is all yours. You work and you earn it, so it's up to you whether you go or don't go. But . . . well, all I hope is that you win."

"What? You hope I win? That sounds a little forced, *vieja*. I wish you were really saying it from the heart."

Finally, I got the shirts into the box, all thrown together. We crossed the street and stopped a taxi. "To the Street of the Tin smiths, please, pal."

We got into the taxi and my old woman says, "Listen, *viejo*, give me money for another pair of slippers, eh?"

"Ah, you lousy old nag, you've got those other shoes at home."

"Yes, but I don't like them, they are too tight on me."

"Ah, *cabr.* . . . Well, OK. Here. Buy yourself a twenty-two *peso* pair. Don't be buying that junk like you did the other day."

While we were riding in the taxi, I was holding Lolita on my lap. She kept talking and talking to me right along and who knows what she was telling me in her baby talk. I just kept saying: "Sure, my daughter, of course," and so on.

The cab was going very fast, but to me it seemed slow. We finally pulled up at the Casa Grande. I got out with my boxes, my kid, and my wife and we went straight to our room. My big box had gotten considerably lighter and I was able to carry one in each hand.

When we opened the door, the smell hit me . . . you know, of unmade beds . . . of a house that hasn't been swept yet or the dishes washed or anything. So I said: "Look here, *vieja*, instead of going around criticizing me for my vices, why the hell haven't you fixed the house yet? Where are those two bitches who are supposed to help out?" I was giving those crazy sluts a home so they could take care of Lolita and clean the house while María worked as a waitress. They were thrown out of their own homes for acting like little whores so I took pity on them. But I did get mad when they acted like little pigs.

"Who would believe that the house would still be in a mess at this hour? I've told you a hundred times, María. Look at that . . . the diapers there in the sink . . . in the sink next to the dishes we eat out of. *Carajo!* Can't you forget your old habits, María? Are we going to live like pigs the rest of our lives? Now do you know why I go to the track? What the hell do I want money for, anyway? Why should I buy things? For what? To throw pearls before swine? Why should I be sacrificing myself for you? I'd be a jerk tossing things into a bottomless hole. No, *vieja*, as long as you keep on like this, I am going to have to go to the track."

"Oh! Didn't I tell you that I slept late?"

"Yes, *vieja*, I know. But you are not clean, the house is not clean, not even the baby is clean. Why should anybody feel like coming back to a house like this. I'm going." So I turned around, very angry, slammed the door and left.

I went out through the gate and waited for a cab. Finally one came along and I signaled to him. I just opened the door, got in, and said: "To the *Hipódromo de las Américas*, please." I acted very serious because if I spoke to him like a regular and called him "pal," he'd make an excuse not to drive me way out there. He made a face, all right, but he agreed. So I said to him: "Take the quickest route, pal —don't go through downtown. You know how things are nowadays, we have to scratch for the *centavos*, pal. It's rough, very rough."

"You can say that again. Are you going to the track to play?"

"Nah . . . who plays! What do you think I am, a sucker? No, I have a friend who owes me some money, see, and if I don't go to the track and grab him there, I never will. The bastard is never around."

"I have heard that nobody wins there," he says, "I think the races are fixed, right?"

"Well, I guess they are, but you know how it is. Sometimes I don't know what to think. There is always one smart guy and a lot of jerks so there have got to be fixes in gambling. That's the way it is all the time, and I realize it, I know it, but in spite of it, there I go anyway. Once a jerk, always a jerk. But then I look at it this way . . . the jockey risks his life when he rides. Two or three kids have been killed already there in the *Hipódromo*. Now, if you are going to ride a horse and you know that you are risking your life . . . if you were to know positively which horse was going to win, why, man, wouldn't you put a thousand *pesos* on that horse? Let's suppose you double your money . . . that's two thousand. And if you keep doing that in one sure race after another, *carajo*, no jockey would have to ride more than six months. The thing is, it's a lottery there. Look, when you go to the *Hipódromo*, pal, take my advice and don't pay attention to any so-and-so there who tries to tip you off. Nobody knows anything about anything there. The day you go . . . pick what you like but don't listen to anybody."

"Not me, pal," he said. "I have all I can do to scrape together enough for beans these days. Look how the government has loused us up now with all the new cabs they gave permits to. Yesterday I made . . . how much do you think I made yesterday? Seventeen *pesos!*"

"What! Starting in the morning?"

"Yes, from the morning. So help me God! Look, I have a little girl who is sick and I haven't been able to make enough to buy her medicine. Yesterday I felt like pocketing the proceeds and not turning it over to the boss. But how could I, if that's what I live off? No, brother, there's no living here in Mexico any more."

After that we were quiet for a while, each sunk in his own thoughts. We entered the new viaduct in the middle of Ejército Nacional and were able to drive faster. Finally we arrived at the race track. I paid the driver six *pesos* and a few *centavos* and we said good-bye.

"So long, buddy. Let's see when we stop being suckers."

With that he pulled out. I paid my admission and went running in. The people were already lined up to buy tickets for the daily double. The race was about due to start and it looked like I wouldn't get to any of the five windows in time because of the lines. So I went over to a man near the head of a line and said, "Please, be a good fellow and buy me two and six, what do you say?"

"I can't, I got too many."

So I kept on going from one to another until I found somebody who was willing and he bought them for me.

"They're off!" Six got off to a good start and kept moving until he took the lead, then came seven and eight and two in fifth place. Come on six! Nobody'll catch that bastard now! I began to feel myself getting excited. There I was in the middle of the crowd stretching my neck to see, until I finally climbed up a pipe. Six kept coming, six kept coming! He held the lead all down the straightway and was five lengths ahead at the turn. They can't catch him now . . . I hope! And where is two? At that moment two began to gain ground. He was right next to the rail and coming up fast, in fourth place. Then he moved up into third and started fighting for second slot. There he was neck and neck. Six passed by, keeping his lead.

Come on two, come on two! That bastard of a two didn't come in, damn it! Well, so I lost twenty *pesos. Jijos,* there's no luck for an honest man. Well, what can we do? So, I figured I'd go down and see about the next race.

On the way I felt like going to the toilet so I went down a few steps past the bar and went in, but the two spots were taken. Goddam, what are those guys doing that is taking them so long? Son-of-a-bitch! Meanwhile there was another fellow waiting there, gritting his teeth. Some more customers came in and we all had to wait, keeping our eyes on the two pairs of feet under the toilet doors. One wore broken-down shoes, without heels or laces, a worker, the other wore shiny, good-quality shoes and nice woollen trousers, the kind heavy betters wear. But rich or poor, both pairs of feet were planted firmly on the floor, with no sign that either was ready to come out.

So I say to the other guy, "Hmmm, I thought that here at the race track everything is done on the run!"

"Yes, but there are some constipated bastards who don't understand that."

And so we joked until we had our turn. I didn't wash my hands when I left because I thought the dirt might bring me luck.

Outside, I met the Saracen, a friend from the marketplace.

"*Ay,* Manuel, you bum, so you're here again!"

"Well, what can we do, brother? Here we are inside . . . we're caught, eh?"

"Which horse looks good to you in this race?"

"Look, brother, according to the *Racing Form* only three and four can win."

"No," says the Saracen; "it can only be six and four. Your horse, Tornado, is a miler."

"Yes, but he has good form. Now, look here, this whole section is for Tornado, the applause is for Tornado, the press is for Tornado, and my calculations from the *Racing Form* also point to Tornado. I'm going to put mine on three. I'll see you later." And I went to look for my friends. I saw Beto and Miguel, the owner of the café my wife works in, sitting near the bar and I went over to them.

"How goes it? Just winning *peso* bills, eh?"

"No, man, don't ask! I was telling my *compadre* Miguel here, 'Let's buy six-eight.' But no, my *compadre* went and got eight-six and it was six-eight that won. He lost a hundred and seventy-five *pesos.* We could have had it won, but no, he didn't like it."

Miguel says, "Which one do you pick, Manuel?"

"Well, Tornado."

"Go on, you're crazy, man! How can it be Tornado, he's a miler."

"Okay, Maestro, but still I like him. And I like him so much you are going to watch me place a hundred grams of paper bills on him right now."

We heard the *ta ta ta* of the bugle and the horses were led out to the track. They filed by and when I saw that damned Tornado, I didn't like him any more. No, the lousy horse was too fat and he seemed to limp on his front leg. No, I better not put it on three. So there I go and pum, I put my money on another horse. "Five minutes left to buy your tickets." The announcement is made in Spanish and English. The horses were already lined up behind the barrier. There was a lot of activity there, right? The caretakers were holding the horses by the reins and getting them into position. Number two was resisting and Beto said, "*Ay, carajo*, Miguel, that horse must have been injected. Look at how lively he is. He has spirit. I'm going to lay mine on two."

And Beto ran to the window for all he was worth, because the race was about to start. Everything was ready and *pus!* they were off. That's when I get gooseflesh. There goes my horse up front. He passed number five and pulled ahead of a few more. And I said: "There's a bit of a chance! There's a bit of a chance! Saint Bastard, don't let me down."

There he came and he pulled ahead, alone, all down the straightway and around the curve. Then the horses behind began to close in on him. Pum, pum, pum. Will they let him go on? Then number four caught up, then another horse. And that famous Tornado was coming up behind all of them, but now that they had reached the long, straight stretch, he really began to move. He lifted his little legs so that it seemed they didn't even touch the ground. And when I least expected it, there goes that lousy Tornado right into first place. Number three won the race!

Ay, what fury! My guts twisted into knots. At five to one it would have paid off sixty-four *pesos* per ticket. I had to go and change my mind! *Adios,* my fifty *pesos,* good-bye!

"You see, Beto? There you are! Didn't three win?"

"Well, I'll be a son of a . . . you were right! Why didn't you bet on him?"

"No, man, shut up! Stop rubbing it in."

"Well, now you know that around here you shouldn't pay attention to others. You were all for three, you should have stuck to three."

"Sure, Beto, but experience always arrives too late for fools. Don't ask!"

Well, the fourth race was coming up, in the first *quiniela* of the afternoon.

"Which one looks good, Miguel?"

"Well, this one."

"No," says Beto, "this one."

I studied the *Racing Form*. Seven looked like a cinch to me and I thought, "No, you son of a . . . here there is nothing better than two-seven." I got up quietly and said, "I'm going to the toilet."

I went to the twenty-*peso* window and bought three tickets for two-seven.

They're off! Neither two nor seven made it. Some other bastards won and paid off a thousand or so *pesos* for the *quiniela*. It left me cold. That's the way, time after time, the races went for me. And not to drag out the story, I left the track with barely enough for bus fare. We all walked sadly down the avenue of tears.

Beto said: "But we'll go again, won't we? 'Let's go to the races,' we'll say, and then again we'll leave feeling like fools, kicking the tickets on the ground to see if we come across a good one."

"Sure, sure," I say; "but why did you have to nag me into changing my opinion of number three!"

"Who was going to believe . . . what was a miler doing in that race? You see? it's because those guys do whatever they want around here."

There we went, without any money. It is strange . . . I don't know what goes on inside me . . . but though I didn't have a *centavo*, I felt a great inner tranquility. I always feel that way when I leave the *Hipódromo*.

I got on the bus alone because I still blamed the others for making me change from number three. And along comes the Saracen with his friends.

"How did it go?"

"What a dumb question . . . the way it always goes with us, brother."

"No, man, I had good luck . . . I won!"

"Oh, yes? I hope you get rich this year, you sap."

"No, really, I won straight, God's truth. I won in the sixth and in the last."

"Oh! That's nice."

I had no more to say so I grabbed a seat near the window and tried to sleep. It was about six-thirty and was getting dark outside. I must have slept because I was almost home when the Saracen shook me.

"Get going, lazy. I'll be seeing you, brother. Tomorrow we'll have to hustle so we can play on Saturday, eh? You have to get out and get more money."

"Sure, brother. They take away our lousy money, but not our passion, right?"

"Right you are! But who's complaining?"

And there goes the bum, pushing through the crowded bus, grabbing and pinching the girls, the old rascal, until he made his way to the door and jumped out while the bus was still moving.

A few blocks later, I too jumped off before the bus came to a stop. With my hands in my pockets and bowed down by the weight of my debts and the fact that I had been had, I walked through the busy streets until I came to Carolina's café. Her husband, Gilberto, was there and he nodded to me, sympathetically.

"So they did you in, eh?" he said.

"Oh, so you know."

"Dammit, Manuel, just think, last night I had a dream about a friend of mine in the shop whose address is the very same number of the horse that won the last *quiniela,* the one that pays off a thousand pesos."

"You don't say! *Qué barbaridad!* And why didn't you send someone to tell me? You could have at least sent your daughter at lunchtime."

"But you didn't come!"

"Ah, yes, that's right. I went to Carrera to sell and from there I went to the races . . . and now I come here to rest. Come on, Carolina, aren't you going to serve me supper?"

"Do you have any money?"

"Ho, are you going to start putting the screws on me? You know that I never have money when I come from the *Hipódromo.*"

"Yes, you tramp, but you never learn."

She brought me the day's special . . . fried meat with green chili sauce, noodle soup and rice. I ate it all, with Gilberto keeping me company.

"Are you going again on Saturday?"

"I don't know, Gilberto. I have no *centavos* but I'll see how I make out. I still have those shirts of Chucho's. What a day, don't ask, man! I sold about five hundred shirts and I still come out losing a hundred *pesos* of Chucho's money. Well, it doesn't matter, because the money I lost I'll take out of my earnings. But I'm screwed anyway because I take my profit even before I sell, so it's all spent. But after all, Chucho has gouged me two out of three times, too, so how can he yell because of a hundred *pesos?*"

"Okay, so what? Where are you going tomorrow?"

"I was thinking of going to Toluca to sell, but now I think I won't do anything. I'll just go to the market to see what I can pick up. And what about your job?"

"Pretty good. But what do you think of this? My brother was re-elected to be treasurer of his union."

"Ah, the lucky bastard! Then he'll be surrounded with nothing but money, eh?"

"What a development! He wanted to sacrifice himself for the workers and he said he would be treasurer only once, but he got to love it. Naturally, it's easier to grab *centavos* from suckers than to break your back working. The company gives him all the time he needs for the union, so the officers don't have to go to work."

"Mm, he has it soft. *Ay*, Gilberto, life is such a bitch! But sometimes I think I go along with it. You won't believe me, but sometimes I get to thinking. Like now, I don't have a *centavo*, right? But I believe it is an incentive to me, because tomorrow I get up, full of faith, and I go out to get some. I get up with this thought, 'I must get some money. I must,' and in that way I get active. But when I have a thousand *pesos* in my pocket, right away I think, 'Why should I get up? What do I want more money for?' "

"No, Manuel, no. That's bad, because a man without ambition isn't a man; he is nothing. A man can allow himself all things, but not to lose his ambition. I don't understand you. *Carajo!* I've seen bigger dopes than you who have money."

"But they have an incentive. What incentive do I have? That my kid is little and that I have to work for her future?"

"No, no, no. Not that, Manuel. I never wanted to have a lot of money because then the children act like buzzards, even wanting you to die sooner so that you can leave them the *centavos*. I've seen many cases like that."

"There are times when I say: 'Now I'm going to save,' and I begin to pile up some *centavos*—not much, because I never had much, right?—but let's say about five hundred *pesos*. Then, if I have to take out fifty *pesos, jijo*, how it hurts! As though I were in the middle class or something."

"Yes, Manuel, I know what you're driving at. I have a friend in the middle class, one of the men in the printing shop, and is he a stingy bastard! Once we all went out to get drunk and this time the other guys got together and agreed to make him pay. Because, God's truth, whenever we were together he never spent five *centavos*. Well, this time he had to pay a bill of fifty *pesos*. You won't believe it but, by God, I swear that when he got out of there he leaned on a lamppost and cried and cried because we made him pay. I have another friend who also lives well. He has a refrigerator, a console, a television set, his wife dresses well and he does too. But that type fills me with pity."

"But why, Gilberto? If he has what others don't have, why should you pity him?"

"No, of course, if you base it on material goods, sure he is worth more than we are, but I pity him because that guy lives to work. He doesn't live to live. He doesn't live to give himself pleasure. The day the devil takes him, is he going to put the television set in his coffin or will he use the refrigerator to preserve himself?"

"Well, Gilberto, I think the same way. When we leave this world, it's worse to go crying: 'Ay, what a pretty house I must leave behind. All the scrounging I did to buy it and now I am going into a hole in the ground! I have so much money in the bank and I can't tell that bastard Death to wait another ten years to take me.' Really, you are right. There are times when I feel compassion for those fellows."

"Well, yes, but they have the advantage of spending a nice old age, don't they? All they have to do is take money out of the bank. They don't have to go begging for a handout. If they like a woman, they can have her; if they want wine, they can drink it. And in the end? Hell, I suppose. Who knows? No one has returned from hell to tell me it's there, or from heaven. So I say, all we have is our own hide and if one is not good to oneself, no one else will be."

"Yes, the satisfactions we don't get for ourselves, no one else will die to get for us. Maybe I'm a fool, but I have stopped running after money; I prefer to enjoy myself."

"In certain ways, it is better to live your way, Manuel. The big industrialists and those who are out to make big money are always planning, they're always thinking. There are types who even think of what they will do five years from now. What devils assure us that we will live five more years? No one guarantees that, do they?"

"Right, right. So what? Are you going to play the horses on Saturday?"

"I think not, Manuel. Right now I have a hex on me. Lately, I haven't seen a horse of mine come in."

"Let's go, man! Let's go, even if we bet only five *pesos*. I don't have money either. Let's see how we make out."

"Okay, let's see how we do."

I don't know how long we spoke but by that time a few regular customers were there, eating supper. Most of the clientele of the café dressed the same way I did, in a pair of ordinary pants and a work shirt open at the collar. Very rarely did someone come in dressed in a suit. At about eleven o'clock, one of this type, a fellow named the "Duck," walked in. The Duck was a real member of the middle class.

"Manuelito, how are you? Good evening."

"Good evening, *Pato,* how goes it?"

"How is it at Tepito?"

"Things are a bit tough, brother, a bit tough. There's not much selling. I don't know what we're going to do."

"I suppose you went to the races today. Did you lose?"

"You know by now, brother. In that place even the PRI can't win." [1]

"So why do you keep going?"

"Well, I like it, that's why. We each keep our own tastes until we die."

I don't know how we came to the subject of class, but before I knew it we were all wrapped up in a discussion of it. He was trying to belittle my class, see? He said we go around dirty and unpresentable, whereas he had five or six suits.

"No, *Pato*," I said. "You're not so well off, with that bank-clerk's salary of yours. You can't show off with me because you wear a suit and fine shoes, and I'll tell you why. Because for you, your suit, your white shirt, your tie, your polished shoes, are nothing more than miserable work tools. Just try to go to work in the bank dressed the way I am! You'll see that you dress this way not because you want to but because you are forced to. Man, you have no reason to look down at the poor. Clothing is nothing more than a disguise."

"Yes, but Manuel, it is a question of training. Take you, for example. You are the type who can earn a lot of *pesos*, but what good does it do you?"

"Okay, but it's the way I like it, isn't it? It may be bad management on my part but you can't say that every poor man is poor because he is a dope. I get up when I please and I do what I please. You hold down two jobs and, brother, you're a slave."

"Yes, but what security do you have?"

"Just the security of doing things in my own way, that's all."

We went on talking until they began to close up the café. Not realizing it was so late, I borrowed money from Carolina and ran out to get a cab, which took me to the café where my wife worked.

There were Miguel, my wife's boss, and Beto, and another friend, all working on crossword puzzles. María was still busy so we men started a game of dominoes. By the time the metal shutters were pulled down, I had lost fifteen *pesos*.

María and I went out to look for a taxi. It's true I was broke, but it was hard to get a bus at that hour and, besides, I preferred to take a taxi. It made me feel good. María and I sat back. I was silent all the way home. I was tired from all the navigating I had done. María

[1] *The Partido Revolucionario Institucional,* the major political party in Mexico, whose candidates always win.

chattered about her problems with the boss's wife and about the little envies of the other waitresses.

Once more we arrived at the famous Casa Grande on the Street of the Tinsmiths. I paid the taxi driver his *pesos* and kicked the front gate of the *vecindad* . . . three strong kicks.

"That's right, *viejo*, so the janitor will jump out of bed. You know how slow he is. Give it to him again!"

"Damned old bastard! Why can't he get up more quickly!"

I kicked again and again, until the *portero* came out rubbing his eyes and smelling of the bed. He unlocked the lock, opened the gate, put out his hand for his twenty *centavos* and we went into the courtyard. All the *patios* were quiet and very dark because there was no moon.

So I said to my old woman, "Stick close to me, *vieja*, because there is a lousy devil that hangs around the bathhouse."

"Shut up, *sangrón!* What prayers will you say to God when the devil appears someday? Watch what you say."

"Why, I already have that old devil running errands for me. You'll see, I hope the old bastard comes out."

"Shut up, Manuel, please. What a man you are! One day God will appear and will punish you."

"Well, let Him! Then I'll ask Him to tell me which horse will win on Saturday. They ruined me today."

"See! There you have it! But you keep going. *Ay, viejo,* I have to urinate. I don't think I can wait till we get to the house."

"Listen, *vieja*, stop being a nuisance. I suppose you're going to pull down your pants here, eh? Keep walking. Our courtyard is close by."

"No, I can't hold it in any more. Wait."

"I'm fed up with you. You are the most inopportune person there is. Hurry, woman, I hear someone coming."

Well, María squatted right there and did what she had to do. The dogs at the corner of the *patio* began to bark, the sons-of-bitches.

"Some day I'm going to poison those bastards," I said.

"Be careful, *viejo*, because that one will bite you."

"If he bites me, I'll turn him inside out the way I did to a dog in Tijuana."

"*Ay*, you just like to talk. How could you turn him inside out?"

"Yes, *vieja*. Just think, he opened his snout like this to bite me and I stuck my hand way in until I reached his tail. I grabbed it and gave a pull as the bastard turned inside out."

"In God's name, what a liar you are! Go on and open the door."

I opened it slowly. "I'm going to see what those two crazy sluts are doing in there."

But no, everything was quiet. I turned on the light in the kitchen. The supper plates and cups were on the table and the sink; leftover beans and chili sauce were in a pot.

"Look, *vieja,* do you see why I tell you not to leave dirty dishes in the sink? Look at all the cockroaches crawling around underneath!"

"I'll put salt on them"; and María took the salt shaker and shook it under the sink.

I turned on the light in the bedroom. Carmela and Carlota were fast asleep on the floor and did not stir. We moved Lolita over to one side of our bed and María kicked off her shoes and lay down next to her. I lay down too, grabbing a copy of the *Reader's Digest* from the wood crate next to the bed.

"Are you going to read now, old boy? You look tired."

"Not tired, old girl, just bored. I'm bored with knocking around all day . . . I don't know what I'm really looking for. I'm fed up with living like this. Look at you, for instance. Aren't you going to undress? Tomorrow you'll iron your dress on the run or wear it with wrinkles."

So María took off her dress and got under the covers. I took off my pants and shirt and jacket and got into bed in my underwear. I read a little more and my eyes began to close.

I thought of the two girls lying on the floor. What a sad life for them, just dragging around, looking for favors. They must really be stupid because the way they are going about it, they can barely get enough to eat. So how could I throw them out into the street like dogs? After all, I too have felt all alone in the world at times. And I know how bitter it is to cry one's own tears alone.

Can that saying be true, that we pay for everything we do? I want to mend my ways, I want to behave the way I should, but the thing is that María is driving me out of my mind. She doesn't understand me and just will not change. If it rains or thunders or flashes lightning, she is always the same. That woman will live at least a hundred years!

"Move over, *vieja.* Look, you left me with only a little space here. Every day all I get is half an inch. Move over, *vieja. Carajo!* You look half-dead."

María didn't answer. She was asleep.

22

Visit to a Holy Shrine[*]

"We won't be going to Chalma to see Our Lord this year, shorty." My wife Paula looked at me, disappointed. "Oh, come now, don't look so sad. It's only because I'm broke."

"*Ay*, don't say that, old man, after I went and packed the clothes and blankets in the corn sacks."

"I'm afraid that's the way it is, pugnose. I have just enough for the fare to Santiago and we can't go like beggars, especially with the kids. You and I could get by, but what about them?"

"*Ay*, well, I guess that's that. Children of the poor have to get used to everything. But tell me, do you have so little faith in the Lord?"

"The problem is not lack of faith but lack of money. Would you believe it, that cheap crumb of a boss wouldn't lend me twenty lousy *pesos*. But what can you expect from an evangelist? Some day he'll get a taste of his own medicine."

"An evangelist?"

"Yes, one of those hallelujahs—the ones who don't believe in the saints."

"Oh, naturally. Never mind, old man. Why don't we go anyway? You can take the napkins your brother brought us and sell them when we get to Chalma. They'd pay you a *peso* apiece, wouldn't they?"

"Old girl, you just hit the bull's-eye!" And I got up from the bed

[*] This essay first appeared in October, 1962, in *Holiday Magazine*, Vol. 32, No. 4, pp. 52–62.

and went over and put my arms around my wife and kissed her on those plump cheeks of hers. "All right, you win. Let's go in the name of God and see what happens."

Then, when we were leaving the house for the Santiago-Tianguistengo bus terminal, my brother and my wife's *mamá* and stepfather and sister all latched onto us and came along. "Now we're done for," I thought to myself, but I didn't say anything to my wife because I could see the worry like a shadow over her face. When she made a little gesture meaning "What are we going to do?" I just smiled at her.

We walked along Manuel Doblado Street and turned into Anillo de Circunvalación until we reached San Pablo. It embarrassed me to be carrying a sack over my shoulder, but, because there were so many peddlers on the streets, I hoped that no one would take notice of us. My wife looked like one of those camp followers during the Revolution, laden with bundles and with the baby wrapped in her shawl at her breast.

And our little dog Grasshopper! My wife insisted on taking him along and I was angry at her stubbornness.

Finally, we came to where we take the bus for Santiago. Whew! What a crowd! There were so many people waiting to take the bus that I thought we wouldn't get out that night. "Get in line, get in line! I'm going to see if there isn't some way of moving up closer," I said. But there was no way, since I didn't know anyone in the line. Well, it couldn't be helped, and we spent hours in the damned line, sleepy and worried, moving ahead slowly, inch by inch.

Paula asked me to buy a straw mat to sleep on in Chalma.

"What are you talking about? With what stinking money? It's worse now because there are more of us. Did you bring along the beans and coffee?"

"Yes, Manuel. The grocery-shop lady trusted me with a can of milk for the baby and a dozen eggs, which I boiled. We're not as bad off as you think." And we both laughed.

"OK, stop pushing, you son-of-a-bitch," I said to the fellow behind us.

"Blessed Mother Mary," said the little old woman in front of us. "Even going to see our Holy Lord of Chalma doesn't shut their dirty mouths."

"Stinking old busybody," I thought to myself, and I gave her a dirty look.

"Get at the end of the line! Get at the end!" we shouted at some people who were sneaking up in front. Finally, after a lot of bad temper and pushing and pulling, it came our turn to get in the bus.

"OK now, old girl, hop on. Hurry up, get in and save us some

seats. Quick, you dope!" My wife was on the steps of the bus, looking around for little Mariquita and shouting, "My little girl! Where
is my little girl?"

"Here she is! I have her," yelled my sister-in-law Dalila.

I was already in the bus, having been pushed in by the others. I
had to bury my elbows in the guy in back of me so he would stop
shoving, though he himself was being pushed. I shouted to Dalila to
hand me Mariquita through the window. "Through here, Dalila.
Look at her, look at her, the stupid idiot. Here, I said. Did my
brother get on? And your mother and everybody?"

"Yes, we're all in and we've got seats," my mother-in-law yelled
from the rear of the bus.

"Fine! We're off to Santiago-Tianguistengo!"

Not long after the bus pulled out, I got angry with my wife. How
could she expect me *not* to get mad when she told me a half-hour too
late that the guy selling candy pinched her behind as she stepped
into the bus? She didn't tell me then, when I could have beat him up!
No, she told me when he was no longer around. It was enough to get
anyone mad, wasn't it?

"Forgive me, old man. Why don't you sing me a song? Yes?" she
asked. "Sing *Rayando el Sol.* You do that one real nice."

"Hmmmm. Well, all right." And so, with my knees pressed up
against the seat in front of me, and with my little Mariquita on my
lap, I began to sing, with my wife's loving eyes on me.

> *"Qué chulos ojos los que tiene esa mujer,*
> *Bonitos modos que tiene para querer.*
> *Que por ahí dicen, que a mí me robó el placer.*
> *Ay! Qué esperanzas, que la deje de querer."*

> *What beautiful eyes that woman has,*
> *What pretty ways to make love.*
> *They say she stole my joy.*
> *Ah! What hope is there*
> *That I can stop loving her.*

"Cross yourself, old man, and cross our little girl, because we're
passing the Dolores cemetery. And entrust yourself to the blessed
souls of purgatory to free us all from evil." Paula turned around and
made a sign to her *mamá* and sister and they promptly moved their
lips in silent prayer.

"Come on, now," I said to Paula. "Don't tell me you think our Lord
of Chalma is going to forsake us. The thing is, when your number is
up, it's up, and that is all there is to it. You aren't afraid, are you? Or
are you?"

"No, it's not on my account. It's that the children are so little and they did tell us that two of these buses full of people smashed up. You never know what life holds in store. Say, old man, Grasshopper keeps turning around and around. You don't suppose he wants to make, do you?"

"You see? You see?" I said. "You had to bring him along, no matter what. So now *you* hold him out the window so he can go."

"Ay, Manuel, what if he gets a chill?"

"It'll be worse if he messes on your shawl. It'll get on the baby, besides. Go on, stick him out, right now, do you hear?" And she held him out of the window by the scruff of his neck. "Ha ha, ha! I'm laughing because this is the first dog I ever saw relieving himself in mid-air."

My wife laughed, too, and pulled in the dog. Then she turned around and her expression changed. "Damn glutton. The hell! That mutt of a brother of yours is wolfing the eggs. Look at him!"

"Ha, ha, ha! Let him. I don't think he had anything to eat."

"Well, all right, but I hope he leaves some for the way. You know how hungry it makes a person." I reprimanded her for making a fuss over a few lousy eggs and she hung her head and shut up. I turned my face to the window and looked out.

It was dark outside but I could see the trees and the hills rush by in the blackness. The hills took on shapes of immense animals asleep and waiting for something. The trees, dumb and silent to our ears, were conversing among themselves as they danced in the wind. They took advantage of the wind to shake off the dust on their leaves, as though they knew it made them look bad.

Down below, far away, lights blinked in and out, as though they were old and sick. They went off and on, the way a dying person opens and closes his mouth. The purring of the bus, the soft murmur of the passengers gradually blurred my foolish imaginings and I fell asleep.

"Manuel, Manuel. We're in Santiago, old man. We've arrived."

"What, what? I fell asleep. How did we get here so fast?"

"So fast? You lazy bum, you slept all the way."

I jumped up and yelled to my brother to hurry off and keep an eye on our sacks of clothing. "We don't want to be left naked," I shouted, "if some so-and-so helps himself to our stuff."

"God forbid, Manuel, in this cold weather," said my sister-in-law.

My legs were numb and I was trying to stand on them. "Damned uncomfortable buses!" I called to my mother-in-law through the window, "Please hand me my coat. It's there at the top of the sack. The little girl is asleep and I want to cover her. And you, pugnose, pull a blanket over you so the baby will be covered, and put down that stinking dog!"

"Oh, no, old man, it's awfully cold and he is shivering. My poor little Grasshopper!"

"Put him down, I tell you. With all I'm going through here, a damned dog can suffer a little too." We were all shivering, so I said, "What do you say to a cup of coffee, mother-in-law? Let's all of us have some hot coffee." And we all went over to a little food stand at the side of the road.

The woman was very attentive. "What would you like to have? Pork with greens? Chitlings in green chili sauce? Rice? Macaroni? Beans?"

"Do you have any turkey?" I asked, and my wife and the others turned to look at me in surprise.

"No, sir, it's all gone," the woman answered.

"Well, in that case, just serve us coffee. Too bad there's no turkey." And we all laughed. But when I saw Paula look at the trays of food, trying not to let me notice, it wasn't funny any more. I began to think about selling some napkins when an old acquaintance of mine, Victor, stopped with his wife at the same stand. He greeted me with an embrace and I introduced everyone. "And these are my children," I said.

"Two already? Say, aren't you going fast? Don't you think you and your wife are working too hard?" asked my indiscreet friend. Everybody smiled sly little smiles—everybody except my mother-in-law. When I invited Victor and his wife to have something to eat, Paula just opened her eyes wide. Sure, I remembered that we didn't have enough money, but what could I do?

We sat there on the bench made of a board laid across a couple of boxes, talking and talking. Finally, Victor stood up to say good-bye, and asked the woman, "What do I owe?"

"What do you mean, brother, I invited you," I protested, but very weakly.

I could see the coffee get stuck in Paula's throat.

But Victor insisted on paying. "Look, Manuel, you can treat me to a drink in Chalma, OK?"

"OK, Victor—and thanks, brother." I said good-bye, not without assuring him that he would have his drink as soon as we got to Chalma, God willing.

"Were you relieved when he paid, old girl? Me, too, but I felt ashamed. I was miserable for not having been able to come out strongly with the words, 'I'm paying.'"

Paula understood. She said, "Well, let's go and look for some place where we can lie down and get a couple of hours' sleep. It's about one o'clock in the morning now and we don't have to start walking until three."

"Look, Manuel," my father-in-law said, "there is room over there, in the archway of the town hall. Shall we go?"

"Let's go," I said. We picked up our sacks and crossed the little square of Santiago-Tianguistengo, leaving behind the food stands that were going full blast because of the large number of pilgrims arriving in the buses. Those who were not eating were stretched out asleep, snoring or sitting on their bundles, drowsing, all sons-of-bitches around, and that's the truth. Two of them, stinking drunk, got into a fight. They were really getting on everybody's nerves when a couple of soldiers arrived and, with a good crack in the ribs with the butts of their rifles, they quieted down. And then the soldiers dragged them off bodily to the jail.

I noticed that the bundle of clothing lying next to my wife was actually a man under his blanket, so I tried to wake her. "Old girl, shorty, better come over to this side." But she was sound asleep, so I pulled her over and got in between her and the sleeping man. Yes, I didn't want the devil to rise in him during the night and have that son-of-a-bitch think that Paula was his old woman lying there next to him.

When the town-hall clock struck three, I woke up everyone in my party, as well as some other people who had asked me to let them come along with us as it was their first pilgrimage. "Up, up, everybody. On your feet, all you lazy people. It's time to get going."

One by one they got up. My father-in-law was still asleep, snoring and making noises. Dalila said, in disgust, "Dirty pig, low-life, this animal is smelling up the place." Little Mariquita, out of sorts, began to cry, and my wife sat down and wrapped the baby in a blanket and then arranged her shawl so that she could hold her close in it. My father-in-law finally got up and began to put the blankets back into the sacks. My brother jumped up and down to get the numbness out of his legs. "Aren't we going to have coffee?" he said, his face all innocence.

"Go to hell, you jerk. Didn't you have some just a little while ago?"

"I didn't really want any," he answered, "I was just saying I did."

Everyone bustled about, getting things in order, and then we were all ready to begin the nine-hour trek to Ocuila. The procession got moving, with me and a man who had a flashlight showing the way. There we were, walking through the darkness out in the open country, feeling the fresh cold air in our nostrils and lungs. The air seemed to enter more freely than the used-up air of Mexico City. It was nice to smell the damp earth and to see the tiny lights of the processions in the far distance, ascending the first of the little hills that rose up out of the plain.

"Let's go, let's go," we kept saying to those who were lagging behind. "Here we come," they would answer. The mothers would say to their children, "Now, don't get too far away from me. A wolf or a coyote might be waiting for you." Paula was behind me, carrying the baby and trying to keep up with my pace. Grasshopper raced back and forth, barking with happiness in his puppy voice, his little tail straight up, slashing the air as he ran.

Then, all of a sudden, we noticed that the man with the lamp, who had been leading us, had disappeared. We called and looked around but he was gone, as though he had fallen over a cliff. Then the old women began saying he must have been a witch who had led us astray, and the mothers called for their children and prayed the Magnificat. They were afraid the witch would carry off the little ones to suck their blood. Paula looked as scared as the others. We formed a circle and put all the children in the center. An old lady, who looked like a witch herself, took out a pair of scissors and, holding them in the form of a cross, walked around the circle to keep away the evil spirit.

I didn't know the road, so I told everyone to stay where they were until dawn. It was very cold, so we men built a big fire in the center of the circle and everyone sat down to wait. Finally we heard the first call of the linnet, and then another, farther away, answering. Standing out against the horizon, the fuzzy silhouettes began to take on clear outlines. The sun was coming out and the cold, too, was taking shape, in the form of mist or a veil which was unwillingly being drawn aside by the king star.

With the first rays of light, our fears left us and we started to walk again. Up a hill and then down onto the plain, our procession pushed ahead like industrious ants. We felt good as we sweated under the steady exercise and ate up the distance with our feet. Our walking raised a fine dust that seemed to purify our bodies and flooded our souls with a glorious faith.

I remember we came to a group of huts where they were frying pork, and we could smell the chili freshly crushed in the stone mortars and the *tortillas* toasting on the griddles. People were sitting along the side of the road eating or drinking hot black coffee. I saw my wife inhale the odor of the pork as hard as she could, three times, and three times she smelled hot coffee. She took a good look at the chili sauce and then walked on at my side. No, this time we couldn't allow ourselves the luxury of sitting down to eat. Our route had to be straight ahead. We were broke.

How high the sun was, and how exhausting it is to be in the country! It is a different sun from the one in the city. "Are you tired, pugnose? Yes, you are tired now, old girl, but don't sit down. That makes it worse. Your bones get chilled and you'll be less able to go on. Shall I help you with the baby for a while? No? All right, then your good health will give you strength."

The road wound on and on, one moment stretching out before us, the next going down, down into mother earth. We passed a little old man who seemed barely able to walk. "Courage, brothers, courage," he said, to help us on our way. That made me pull myself up straighter, inspired by his example. Could his faith have been stronger than mine? No! Compared to him, we younger ones were the day dawning. He was the setting sun, poor old fellow.

"Manuel, old boy, I want to go to the toilet. Where can I go?" It was Paula.

"Ha, ha! You dope! With the whole mountain available, you look for a place. Right here, anywhere. Just let me make a little house for you with my coat."

With the sun up high and me holding my sack over my rear end by now, we finally saw the domes of the little Church of Our Lord of Ocuila. I swear we couldn't go another step. We were all ready for a rest. My sister-in-law went ahead to buy the miraculous salve for us to smear on our tired, dusty, swollen feet.

We came to the house at which we ask for lodging every year. They gave us two reed mats and we all lay down except my old lady, who went to heat up the beans and *tortillas* we had brought along.

"Old boy, can you give me five *pesos* to buy something?"

"Yes, old girl. Here, take them, but don't start cooking. You're too tired."

My mother-in-law got up, borrowed a pot, asked permission to use an edge of the fire and put up coffee. I took a little nap. I was pretty hungry but it took time to prepare the meal. I woke up when they called me. My wife handed me a plate with fried steak, sliced hard-boiled egg, beans nice and crispy, well fried in pure pork lard, a chili sauce and fragrant, steaming coffee. That's what I saw when I opened my eyes. A spread fit for a king, followed by the sleep of the just!

The next day we walked to the legendary, incredible *ahuehuete* tree, halfway between Ocuila and Chalma. It was five o'clock in the morning when we set out and went onward in the name of God to have breakfast at the famous tree. We left the village behind us and joined the hundreds of pilgrims, a real river of humanity, raising a cloud of dust. Some walked with light footsteps, some were slow or dragging their feet, others were clutching their middles as though they were ill. There were vendors of all kinds on both sides of the road, selling *enchiladas,* drinks made of lemon and sage, white *zapote* fruit picked unripe. Horses and donkeys were coming and going, loaded with suitcases or men and women.

It was all downhill from Ocuila, so we were soon at the half-moon formed by the curve in the road. At the bend we saw the great *ahuehuete* tree, which stands out among its companion trees the way a mighty athlete stands out among a bunch of skinny, knock-kneed people. It is so big it would take ten men to encircle it, and a little river of healing water flows out from under it. Here pilgrims bathe and hang votive offerings in the branches, and those who come for the first time are supposed to dance under the tree. This tree is the nicest thing about going to Chalma.

We went down the side of the hill, not using the path but clambering down the stones to get there quicker. We called out greetings to some people we knew who were standing next to the trunk of the tree. We began to see a lot of familiar faces, people who lived in our neighborhood.

"Come on over here," shouted Dalila from a place where we could prepare breakfast. My brother and I went to collect firewood while my mother-in-law and her husband looked for three stones for the hearth. Paula washed the pots, plates and spoons in the river. Her skirt was up and her legs apart as she squatted there. I whistled to her and made a sign and she understood me, closing her legs and pulling down her skirt.

"Say, old girl, even though I'm left without a stinking *centavo*, go bring some roast pork. I can't resist any longer. God will look out for us." And she went and bought it. She came hurrying back, saying, "Look, Manuel, hurry, come on and see the two *gringos* dancing at the *ahuehuete* tree. There's a *gringa* dancing too."

"Yes? How do you like that? But take a look at what they are carrying—a knapsack, boots, hatchet, hunting knife, binoculars, mountain-climbing ropes and a first aid kit. Wow! Those people know how to live, old girl. Don't you get a kick out of them coming all this way to see the Lord and dancing just like anybody else, without feeling any embarrassment?"

"Yes, Manuel, but they must know that if you don't dance here the trip is useless. The Lord doesn't take you into account unless you fulfill this requirement." Then she said, "Say, I wonder what they will leave on the tree as a souvenir. I am going to cut Mariquita's hair to leave it here."

"Go jump in the lake, you crazy old bat! Why don't you leave your own hair? None of that stuff, now! Come on, let's get a move on and finish eating before the hot sun catches up with us."

And so we started walking again, carrying our sacks and once more losing ourselves in the river of people on the final lap of the journey. "Hey, you jerk, pull your horse over that way," I shouted at a man who nearly knocked down Paula and the baby. "What are you, a mule? Can't you see?"

"Why don't you take an airplane if you're so sensitive, you animal?" he said, driving his horse on with a crack against the rump, leaving me standing there, chewing my rage.

That last stretch was a lucky one for me. My wife didn't want me to pick up the rag that was sticking out of the mud, but when I washed it off it turned out to be a pure wool coat. A mule driver gave me fifty *pesos* for it. And then there was the flashlight lost by a man who was walking ahead of us. They paid me twenty *pesos* for it. "We should always have it this tough," I said to Paula, with seventy *pesos* in my pocket now. Even the sack I was carrying began to get lighter.

Walking, walking and more walking, in the exhausting heat. I wonder how those mule drivers do it. They make five round trips a day between Ocuila and Chalma. Back and forth behind their animals without showing signs of fatigue!

"The thing is, they breathe pure air and don't have bad habits like us," I explained to my wife. "They go to sleep when the sun sets and they get up before it comes out, and besides, instead of drinking soda, they drink *pulque,* which is just one step away from being meat."

Between the puffing up the hills and wondering whether we were going to make it or not, the distance separating us from our goal grew shorter and shorter. Everybody was sweating, young and old, those carrying and those being carried. Faces had no shine on them, because of the dust; eyelashes looked like the dusty eaves of long-abandoned houses. But eyes were shining and hearts were bursting with happiness and flooded with faith in the All-Powerful who would cure us of sickness of the body or the spirit.

We passed by the mill, jabbed our heels into a little cobbled rise, listened to the chirrup of the locusts as we walked, jumping to the right or left to move out of the way of a donkey, leaping over a little brook, whistling to Grasshopper, who was constantly getting tangled up under the horses' hooves. Finally, we came to the first little houses on the outskirts of Chalma—the fences, avocado patches, tangerine and banana groves. We were getting close; soon we would see the roadside crosses. The sun never let up its suffocating heat, but there was our goal right ahead.

Blessed be Thy name, O Lord, and blessed Thy mercy. We arrived safely. We were in Chalma.

23

"In New York You Get Swallowed by a Horse"*

We had been talking of this and that when I asked him, "Have you ever been in New York, Hector?"

"Yes, yes, I've been to New York."

"And what did you think of life there?"

"New York! I want no part of it! Man, do you know what it's like? You get up in a rush, have breakfast in a rush, get to work in a rush, go home in a rush, even shit in a rush. That's life in New York! Not for me! Never again! Not unless I was crazy.

"Look, I'll explain. The way things are in New York, you'll get nothing there. But nothing! It's different in Puerto Rico. Here, if you're hungry, you come to me and say, 'Man, I'm broke, I've had nothing to eat.' And I'd say, 'Ay, Bendito! Poor thing!' And I'd give you some food. No matter what, you wouldn't have to go to bed hungry. Here in Puerto Rico you can make out. But in New York, if you don't have a nickel, or twenty cents, you're worthless, and that's for sure. You don't count. You get swallowed by a horse!

"Don't mention New York to me, man! I suffered too much there. I had to sleep in the street, in alleys and doorways. When that happened, I went two or three days without a bite of food. If I approached anyone and told him I hadn't eaten, he'd just say, 'Get out of here!' If you ask for food in New York that's all the answer you get; you won't find a soul who'll give you a nickel or a bit of bread or

* This essay was first published in November, 1964, in *Commentary*, pp. 69–73.

a plate of rice. No 'Ay, Bendito' there, muchacho. There you have to look out for yourself. If you're one of those teenager bums, the kind who goes around asking for hand-outs, New York will make a man out of you. Because if you don't work, you starve.

"What made me decide to go to New York? Nothing special, really. I had problems with my family, so I left home and went to work for a couple of weeks until I saved enough to pay my fare. When I got there, I went to my uncle's on a Hundred Thirty-eighth Street, in the Bronx. And you know? I was broke because I had to pay ten dollars' taxi fare from the airport. Ten dollars! All I had left was seventy-five cents.

"So you know what happens? Your uncle, being a relative, gives you room and board for a week while you look for a job. You're still jobless by the end of the week? Well, muchacho, you haven't got a chance. Because, right off, your uncle kicks you out. Now, suppose you did find a job. Your uncle may decide to let you stay on with him. That'll be twelve dollars at least. Twelve dollars for three meals a day and a room to keep your clothes in. And don't think he'll allow his wife to do your washing. Oh, no! You'll have to take it to the laundry. You'll have to pay all your other expenses too . . . beer, everything! Your life isn't worth a plugged nickel there. Just like the song says, 'La vida no vale na'.'

"That's not the worst of it, either. Let me tell you, boy, New York's a madhouse. You can live twenty years in the same building without ever getting acquainted with your next-door neighbor. Twenty years! My friends here say, 'Oh, New York! It's so pretty, so wonderful, the best!' But if you stop to look at the city, what is it? Nothing but big, big buildings. Just walls and windows.

"Then I explain to my friends about New York in winter. Closed doors, closed windows, no people. If you do see people, you just see them walking. Walking, walking, all the time. You can't stop to talk to them because you are rushing off to work. Besides, you'll freeze. When I wanted to go out I had to put on a coat and an overcoat, woolen underwear, wool pants, three pairs of woolen socks. I'd go out bundled up in all those clothes and, man, my legs would shake with cold. Comes winter, people in New York put their milk bottles on the window sills and don't need a refrigerator at all. Spit outdoors and it turns to ice before it hits the ground!

"In New York, you freeze in the winter and bake in summer. My little girl had one cold after another, fevers, all kinds of illnesses there. Here, blessed be God, she hasn't had so much as a running nose since we returned. How can anyone compare New York with Puerto Rico, with the sun and the pretty flowers and things we have here?

"Sure, some guys have good luck in New York and like it there. Some even make a lot of money. Suppose you want to get rich. First thing you do is begin to sell narcotics or get into the numbers racket. Gambling in New York can make you a profit of ninety cents to the dollar. If you manage to sell drugs for a whole year without getting caught by the police, you'll make eight, twelve thousand dollars for sure. On the other hand, if the cops catch you, you get ten years in Atlanta Federal Penitentiary. So, tell me, which would you rather have?

"We honest people, who don't know how to get mixed up in a racket, just have to work. But it takes some doing to get a job. To find a job in New York you have to really take yourself in hand. To get from where you live to the street, you have to go down a lot of steps because the houses are four or five stories high. You go down those stairs and if you don't want to get lost—like I did that first time—you stop in front of the door and take a good look at your building and at the one across the way. So you will remember, see? It's easy to get lost there. I've cried like a baby in those New York streets where you can get lost worse than in a jungle. There'll be a lot of people around you, but what do the sons of bitches do when you ask for help? They'll realize you're a rookie and they'll say, 'Go that way,' and it'll be the wrong way so you'll get more lost and the hell with you.

"Here in San Juan you can go up to anybody and say, 'Pardon me, where is Cristo Street?' or Tanca Street or·any street you want to find and whoever you ask stops and listens. If you happen to ask someone in a car that's going your way he'll say, 'Hop in, I'll take you there.' But not in New York!

"Well, so you're looking for a job and you start walking. Man, how long, how long are the streets of New York! You can walk and walk and never get to the end of them. While you walk you keep your eyes peeled for places where they might hire someone. You go into a shop. 'Do you need a man to work here?' In some places they tell you 'No.' In other places they say, 'I don't speak Spanish.' You just walk on and on and on. One time, you know what happened to me? I went to this place and they had a *latino* there, the son of a bitch. I knew he was a *latino*, so I went and talked to him in Spanish. I said, '*Muchacho,* you know, I'm down and out. I'm broke, see, and I'm looking for a job.'

"This son of a great whore answered in English, 'Wat you min? I no spik Spanish.' I'm telling you, it's the Puerto Ricans themselves who'll be your worst enemies in New York.

"So you keep on walking until you finally land a job. At least that's the way I got mine, at a brassière factory. I was hired as shipping clerk for forty dollars a week. I had ambition, you know, that thing that makes a man want to earn more, and I paid attention and learned my job and was promoted to another department and another and another. Five years I worked there. The most I ever earned was seventy-five dollars a week and I had to work hard for it. Because in New York you have to work, really work, see?

"Here in Puerto Rico you have more freedom. You can stand on a street corner, in a park—you can even stand in front of the Governor's Palace all day long and nobody asks you to move on or interferes with you in any way. Not in New York. That's not allowed there.

"When you land a job they give you a form to fill out. You look at it and think, 'What's this all about?' You have to fill it out, see? So you read it, if you can read English. If you can't, you're out of luck. They ask you your name, where were you born, are you single or do you have a couple of children and a wife to support. Two children plus a wife makes three, right? That's four people to support counting you, because you support yourself, too. You start with a salary of forty-two dollars. If you have four people to support, they won't deduct a cent, not one single cent, from your pay check. But if you mark that bit of paper with a circle around the word 'Single,' then you're done for.

"Out of forty-two dollars, all you'll get your hands on is thirty-two. Out of those thirty-two, you'll pay ten dollars for a room, if you're lucky. And you won't have it to yourself . . . you'll be sharing it with the rats. You can't expect a nice room for ten dollars a week. Then there's the laundry, and breakfast, lunch, and dinner. How much will be left after you pay all that? Just figure it out.

"By that time, you'll be wanting to get back to Puerto Rico, but you haven't been able to save a cent to pay your fare. So you write, '*Mami*, things are bad here and I want to go back. Send me money for my fare.'

"Suppose when you filled in that little paper you said you had a family to support. The police come around to investigate, to see if you told the truth. If it turns out you're single, man! you have to return every cent they were supposed to deduct. All the tax money. If not, you'll land in jail. So, which would you choose? No, man! *Deja eso*. Leave New York alone. You can't live there. You just can't live. You get swallowed by a horse!

"I got sick shortly after I had started working. *Ave María!* I was in the hospital two months and felt so bad that every night I thought I wouldn't live to see the next morning. My girl friend rushed over to see me the minute she heard I was in the hospital. She came every day for a whole month in every kind of weather: rain, thunder, lightning, freezing cold. If it rained fire she would still have come. We were not really sweethearts or engaged at that time, but we went out together and liked each other and all.

"When I went back to work I kept thinking, 'They'll fire me, they'll fire me, for sure. I'm new here, just arrived from Puerto Rico and I was out so long . . .' At the factory, I didn't speak to anybody. I just sort of sneaked in and looked at the time cards. When I saw mine was still there, oh, man! hope stirred in me. Hope, that beautiful thing. You know what I mean? After seeing my card, I went to work.

"The man from the office came in and I tried to explain, 'Oh, sir, I'm sorry . . . you know . . . I was . . .'

" 'Never mind, man! We had a call from the hospital letting us know you were sick. Social Security called, too, to tell us you were hospitalized. So never mind. Just get to work.'

"When it was time to go home, what happened? They asked me to go to the office. Oh, my God! My heart leaped into my throat. I thought, 'Now they're going to fire me.'

"I go to the office and they tell me, 'You've worked here for such and such a length of time and, let's see . . .' Then they start bringing out papers and more papers . . . man! I was sweating. Then that man grabs a paper and gives me an envelope. I didn't open it. I swear, I didn't dare open it. I just thought, 'I'm fired.' I put it in my pocket and walked out. I got home and was taking off my shirt and shoes when my sweetheart walks in. 'Oh, baby, look here. I'm afraid they've fired me. Get that envelope in my shirt pocket and open it. I'd rather you saw it first.'

"She opened the envelope. 'Look here, Hector. It's a check!'

" 'A check? You must be going blind, girl.' Then I looked, and what do I see? Man! I couldn't believe my eyes! A check for two hundred forty-five dollars! Payment for three or four weeks of illness plus per diem or something, I don't know. Two hundred forty-five dollars! That's when I really started sweating and my legs began to tremble all over.

"Next day, when I got to work, one of my friends calls me, 'Hector, come here.' Then he gives me another envelope with forty-five dollars that had been collected among the other workers. There were nine hundred workers in that company. After that I really threw myself into my work. What with the two hundred and forty-five and the money my friends collected and the work I did that week, I was able to tell my sweetheart, 'Look, baby, you know what? I don't want a fancy wedding. This money is enough for us to get married on.' So we did. We got married. And that woman has turned out to be straight as a shot. What a woman! She still looks at me like on the first day. She's with me all the way. She adores me, you know. She loves me completely.

"My wife and I both had to work. I was paid on Friday and she on Saturday and by the time Friday came around again we didn't have any money. Not one cent. I had to pay ninety-six dollars rent for a tiny apartment. The bedroom barely had room for a bed and a crib. The front room was even smaller. For ninety-six dollars!

"In New York if you owe a month's rent, the landlady sends you a bit of paper. Suppose you're two months behind in your rent, you haven't been able to land a job and you spend your time walking like crazy looking for work because you have your wife and child to take care of, and all sorts of debts. You know what'll happen to you? One evening after walking the streets like a madman, you get home and you find your furniture piled up on the sidewalk in the rain, the snow, the heat, in no matter what weather, because the sheriff came with a court order. It won't make any difference that your wife or child is sick, or that you've tried hard to look for a job and it isn't your fault you haven't found one. That's New York for you.

"You have to watch out how you go at things, see? And you need luck in New York, especially to choose a woman and to get married, because there a woman can get away with anything. Suppose you get married. Then one day you come home from work. You've had a hard day. You got out of bed in a hurry, had breakfast in a hurry, went to work in a hurry, and hurried home, tired, worn out. And what do you find? There's your wife in bed with another man. You rush out to get the cops so they can see what's going on. Then, what happens? She wins! Even if you screw your soul working all day long to provide for her needs, she'll win all the same. If you slap her, she'll go and call the cops. Slap a woman! Don't dream of it! You get six months in jail, see? Not just a fine—jail! If you kill the man, you'll fry for it. That kind of thing isn't allowed there. No, sir!

"New York is a crazy place. Suppose you have children. You take off your belt and whack them a couple of times. If you do it in front of a cop, you get six months. And if you should leave a bruise, *muchacho!* you're really out of luck. That's why things are so screwed up in New York. That's why there's so much evil, so many criminals, so many gangs. How could it be otherwise? A place where you can't even beat your own wife and children!

"In New York a dog is worth more than a man. Yes, sir, only three things are valued there, dogs, women, and children! As long as you're a minor, you can kill, belong to a gang, steal, or raise hell. No matter what you do, you won't fry, see? Of course, if you're a woman you can get away with anything as long as you live. But if you're a man and over twenty-one and you so much as pick up a stone and aim it at a dog, it means six months in jail. If you hit the dog, it's worse. You can't even defend yourself. Women and dogs can attack you any time and you lose the case, no matter what. Know why? It's the law. That's the way it's written, man. And if you never heard of that law, you're sunk. After you're twenty-one you're an adult and know what you are doing, see? A dog can't talk, so he wins, but *you* get eaten by a horse.

"It was because of a woman that I left New York and returned to Puerto Rico. One day I went to work. It was a Monday and when I got there I found about twelve badly made brassières at my place. The girl claimed I was the one who had sewn them. I told her, 'Damn it to hell, you're a liar! You might have noticed that I work a two-needle machine and these were made with a single needle. You were the one who made them!' But women can get away with anything there. They can call a man an imbecile, a fool and anything else they please. She called me all those names. Man! She'd better have kept her mouth shut because I just grabbed that bundle and was going to crack her skull with it when the foreman came up and said, 'Hector, what are you doing? She's a *woman*. Stop that! Don't go looking for trouble.'

"I said, 'Give me my money because I'm leaving. Quick, right now.'

"So he takes me to the office. The boss says, 'Think it over, Hector. You've worked with us several years. You've made a lot of friends who are very fond of you. Yet you want to leave over a little thing like this?'

"Then I said, 'This isn't all. How about that raise you promised me? I've never seen it. And on top of everything else that idiot calls me a fool in front of everyone. I'm quitting. If I stay I'll be in trouble for sure, because next time I'll really break her head. I don't want to argue any more. Make arrangements so I can get my money and leave.'

"I worked the rest of that day and on Tuesday I took a plane to Puerto Rico. Now I'm thankful to that woman. I am infinitely thankful to her. If it hadn't been for her, I'd still be stuck there."

All this time, Hector and I had been talking in the restaurant where he worked. The bartender had been listening to our conversation while he washed the glasses and cleaned up. It was late and the place was completely deserted except for us and another man who worked in the kitchen. When Hector stopped speaking, the bartender leaned over the bar and, looking straight at Hector, said in a booming voice, "New York, the best in the world!"

Hector and I turned around in surprise.

"Yes, sir. The best in the world. Whoever hasn't lived in New York, hasn't lived. In New York, there's money to burn. When I arrived I bought a bakery for a thousand dollars and after nine months, I sold it for seven thousand. New York is good, son, if you can't be happy in New York, you can't be happy anywhere. It's the best in the world."

24

Reminiscences of
an Aging Puerto Rican[*]

I'm a self-made man, a taxi driver, and a driver deals with all classes: the rich, the middle class, the poor. I may not know how to express myself well, but I've learned plenty about life. You might say I'm a graduate of worldology. Listen, I could even write a book. It would be a bad book because my spelling is poor, but I could write one.

If you want to know what mankind is really like you must seek the truth among the simple and humble people. You will never find it among the rich and greedy. All you find there is hypocrisy. Why should I be a hypocrite? I have no reason to refuse to talk about my life, and since it cost me nothing I give it freely.

I'm an old man and I thank God I've reached my sixtieth birthday. This last part of my life is the best of all. It's the descent, the passive, restful part. I'm not so worried about life any more. I have no money and no ambition, and I feel at peace. My business used to rob me of time, and now that I've lost it I have time for everything. I'm really better off than a millionaire. How can a millionaire be happy when he's always thinking of his interest, his capital, his debts? No! His is a desperate life; mine is a pensive one. I have my daily bread. Between Social Security and my lottery agency I earn enough to get along. I've had diabetes for fifteen years and I'm too sick to work, so my woman Delia runs things. Now I'm just a decorative figure in my house. What a turn of events!

* This essay is published here for the first time. It is part of a larger volume now in preparation.

When I recall my youth, the voice of my conscience makes me weep. I was so irresponsible, so crude and brutal. I lived only for physical pleasure.

We Albas have strong passions. I must have inherited my appetite for life, and especially for sex, from my *papá*. He had eighteen children with my mother, and a mistress and children on the side, to which he didn't mind admitting. Here and there he also had his "stolen loves," as songwriter Felipe Rodriguez would say.

I have a violent temper, just like *papá's*. He used to punish me almost every day for fighting with some other boy. He didn't want me to fight, but I had to. If someone abused me, I had to defend myself. Sometimes I'd get two beatings, one from the boy I was fighting and one from *papá*.

I also have my sentimental side, which I get from my *mamá*. She was a very quiet, mild woman. I wasn't always so good, and when *papá* would hit me *mamá* would jump between us, preferring to get hit herself. Both of my parents were very good to me, but *mamá* is the one I love most.

When I was small, I learned what it was for a man to go off with another woman. It was the custom in those days. My *papá* had begun with his mistress Francisca before I was born. She lived on a part of our farm, in a house that he had built for her. She originally came from Morovis with a man they called Vicente Youtía. Germán Pescador took her away from Vicente Youtía, and she had two children with him. Then *papá* took her away from Germán and she had José and Carmen with him. That's the Latin in our blood.

I used to play with José, Francisca's son, who was a year older than I. Later, when I was married and so was he, he came to work with me, like a brother, to help me out in the business. He wanted our last name; but according to the law, all my father's legitimate sons had to sign an agreement. I was willing to do it, but José had to consult with my other brothers, and the time just dragged on and on. He let me know how much he resented not having our name. When we Puerto Ricans are called "bastards," we don't like it. It hurts us. It really hurts! I'm a legitimate child, but if they call any Puerto Ricans bastards it wounds me. So I have to feel sorry for my half-brother.

Francisca had quite a few arguments with *mamá*, who would grab her by the hair and *Ave María!* Then *papá* and his woman had a quarrel and she went off to another town. *Papá* followed her and abandoned us for a few years.

When a home is broken, as ours was broken, what can one be expected to say? A man has strong emotions: he suffers; he feels. I resented my father for what he did, but not so much for myself. I felt it more because it harmed my mother. She didn't know how to reason well, and she suffered very much while *papá* was away. I didn't miss him because I lived comfortably. My brother Ramón was like a father to us all. He bought a house in town, where he worked, and we went there to live, and what was left of the farm was put into the hands of a sharecropper who used to harvest the fruits and bring them to us.

Then there was a miracle. It was a Saturday and *mamá* was ironing in the dining room. We had electricity at the time, but she was using a little charcoal iron. She heard a traveling salesman out in the street yelling, "Prayers and *novenas* for sale!" and she went out on the balcony to talk to him. "How much are the prayers?" she asked.

"Ten cents apiece," he said.

"Give me one for the Virgin of Everlasting Mercy and one for *el Niño de Atocha*," *mamá* said, and paid him twenty cents.

At night *mamá* always used to say the Rosary of the Virgin, with all of us gathered around. That's a custom we've forgotten! But that night, before reciting the Rosary, *mamá* told my sister Aida to kneel beside her and together they recited the two prayers she had bought. I don't know what *mamá* asked the saints for in return for the prayers, because she prayed silently. I only know that five days later, at three o'clock in the morning, we heard a knock on the kitchen window and a man's voice calling *mamá*'s name: *"María! María!"*

"Who is it?" *mamá* called out.

"It's me, Roberto, your husband. I come for forgiveness. Open up!"

Mamá opened the kitchen door and *papá* came in. He threw his arms around her and fell to his knees, crying, "I'll never abandon you again!" And he never did.

When you're young, you do what others do. My father and lots of other married men went out with women, and when I got married, I did the same. I didn't realize how wrong I was or how much my wife Ramona suffered. Ordinarily Ramona was a peaceful woman, but one day she found a woman's handkerchief in my coat pocket and went into a rage. She threw me out! When her father heard about it, he scolded her. He said, "Your husband is a man, and men go out. Women stay home!"

I should have gone back to my wife, but I didn't. I didn't hate her, but I didn't love her either; I was just indifferent. I never even sent her a *peso* for herself and our two daughters. Her father had money, so I let him take care of them. What a husband I was!

Years later, when I was living with Delia, I saw my wife again. Her father had lost all his money and she was poor, but I had come up in the world. My taxicab business was prosperous and I was president of the municipal assembly. I was a man of power and influence. One day I was going to visit my brother in the hospital and I saw my two daughters running down the hall toward me. *"Papi, papi, mami's* very sick!" they cried.

Ramona had double pneumonia and was near death. The people in the hospital, who thought I was married to Delia, didn't know Ramona was my wife, so they didn't give her any special treatment. She was just another poor sick woman to them. I was ashamed when I saw her lying in the women's ward. She looked so thin and pale. My brother was in a private room, which I got for him, but my wife was put to bed wearing the clothes she wore when she came in, and there was no linen on her bed.

I told the head nurse that Ramona was my wife and got her moved to a private room. While they were preparing her I went out and bought her three nightgowns—one pink, one yellow, and one blue—and some sheets and pillow cases for her bed. When she was brought to her room, the bed was already made up and the nightgowns were laid out on it. I was afraid she would throw them at me if she saw me, so I watched her from the hall where I couldn't be seen.

Ramona was weak and sat on the bed. She looked at the nightgowns and asked the nurse who bought them. *"Don* Paco Alba," the nurse said. Ramona smiled and picked up the blue nightgown and held it to her. "Paco, Paco, Paco!" she said and began to cry. I felt as if someone had stabbed me in my heart. Only then did I realize how much my wife loved me and how much I had hurt her. That night she died.

I was born ignorant, and it was in my ignorance that I did so much harm in the world. I knew only the animal part of myself and I became a slave to its demands. I thought of no one else.

The church couldn't save me from my sins because it wanted to keep me in my place. It didn't want me to learn the truth about God because an ignorant man is easier to control.

Now that I know the truth, I'm a different man. I know that I am not all animal. There is a part of God in me, as there is in every human being. It is the spiritual part of my nature and it tells me how to resist my selfish physical desires. As long as I listen to that Divine Voice inside me, I know I can never harm anyone again. You see, I don't care about myself now; I care about you and the other fellow.

Human life is a part of all life, and I believe it exists forever—in the little birds, in the forests, in the atmosphere. We are a part of nature, and we react according to the way nature reacts. We have our sad moments, our disastrous moments—our cyclones and hurricanes; then comes the fair weather, and whatever was carried away by the storm is made over again. Our life is a continuous struggle between good and evil, right and wrong. We have times of peace and joy, but also times of suffering and restlessness, when men are made. I've learned to savor my unpleasant experiences because one can't achieve manhood unless it is forged in pain.

I'm a Spiritist now and I try to help people. When they come to me with their problems, I seek help from the spirits of the dead that inhabit the cosmos. Someday, when my earthly days are over, my soul will join those spirits, and whatever wisdom I have gained in this life will be passed on to those who remain on earth. I want my soul to be a helpful one, so I'm trying to lead a good life while I'm here.

When I was in my teens an ideal was born in me. I was working out in the cane fields and some workers came marching by, carrying a flag. "Rise up! You're not getting paid a fair wage!" they shouted. The plantation owners tried to stop them, and that's when the bullets started flying. I found myself on the side of the marchers, throwing rocks at the men with guns. In that one split second I had learned what democracy was all about: it means that a man has a right to profit from his sweat. I decided to spend my life fighting for that right.

If I had had an opportunity to study when I was young, I probably would have become a lawyer, like Perry Mason. But I would have defended the poor, never the rich. Instead of being a lawyer, I went into politics. First I was a Socialist. In Puerto Rico the Socialists weren't radical, like the Communists; they stood for a better way of life and the rights of all men, and their program was very much like Muñoz Marín's today.

Muñoz used to be a Socialist, too. All the liberals were. The only other major party in those days was the Republican Party, and that was conservative. Only the rich people, the *blanquitos*, were Republicans.

In 1936 the Socialists thought they could win the election by forming an alliance with the Republicans. What a mistake that was! They won the election, but they had to give in to the Republicans and the Coalition Government they formed was a dismal affair. That's when I stopped being a Socialist.

I've been a Popular ever since Muñoz formed the party in 1940. He called it the party of Bread, Land, and Liberty, and the straw hat of the worker became its symbol. All the old liberals gathered around him. I remember him making speeches that year, and I thought to myself, "I'm for any man who wants to improve our way of life, and that's what this man is trying to do." He won that election, thank God!

Puerto Rico has a good government now. Anyone who can't see how much progress we've made since 1940 must be blind! I remember when the rich were the lords of the world. They were the ones who gave out the jobs, and the poor had to work for whatever they chose to pay. A taxi driver got a ticket for almost anything in those days, and when I got one I couldn't go right to a judge and defend myself. First I had to go to a *blanquito* and ask him for a pass; then I could go in to see the judge and if I was lucky he might reduce my fine from twenty-five *pesos* to five. And for that I had to go back and thank the *blanquito!*

My father lost his land to the rich sugar-mill owners. They would advance him the money to plant cane in his fields, but when the crops came in they would offer my father next to nothing for them. He always wound up in debt to them and little by little he had to sell them his land. Our farm really belonged to my mother, who had inherited it from her father, so she had to sign each piece away. I remember how she used to cry.

The poor may be quiet, but they have feelings. They needed someone to speak up for them, and that's what Muñoz Marín did. Today the poor have influence; they matter. Before 1940 people were starving to death in Puerto Rico. Now there's bread for everybody who's willing to work for it, and if a man goes hungry it's because he's lazy. There are plenty of jobs. Even the servants in the homes of the *blanquitos* get a good salary. And if they aren't treated decently, they can quit and go on relief. No wonder the rich hate Muñoz!

Today a poor man can go where he pleases, even to the best hotels. A poor boy goes to school with a *peseta* in his pocket; he rides in a free bus and eats a good lunch in the school dining room. When I was a boy I had neither the *peseta*, the bus, nor the lunch. If that isn't progress, tell me what is.

Mine is the path of improving and improving, not for myself but for mankind. In 1944 I was elected president of our municipal assembly, and I may not have been the smartest politician, but I was sincere. I have a loud voice and I could win people over. I wasn't like some politicians who only look out for their own interests. I had my share of fights with that kind, but I usually got their support because they could see that I wanted nothing for myself. I had no "sweet potatoes" of my own. I was for the people. I was in office for four years and mine was a good administration because I got everyone to work together. When the poor were sick, we saw that they got medicine; and when they needed a school, we managed to build one.

A politician has to be practical. I remember when Muñoz wanted Puerto Rico to be independent. Now he says that was an error of his youth. Those who still want independence are angry with him, but they don't understand him. He's an intelligent man. He knows that without the United States to protect us we'd be eaten up by Cuba.

If you really love people and want to get help for them, you have to be diplomatic. Muñoz understands that. He's getting help from the Americans, but without giving up anything of our own in return. We Puerto Ricans run our own affairs, but we're allied with the strongest country in the world. We're better off than if we had listened to Albizu Campos, who was willing to shed blood for independence. What did he care about the people! If he loved them so much, why did he arm little children with sticks and send them out into the streets against soldiers with rifles? Muñoz could never do a thing like that. He says, "Let's get Puerto Ricans to the point where they can live without going hungry."

We're moving uphill, but we have a long way to go. We still have our problems and we need time to solve them. Most of our capital comes from the United States, and I know the Americans aren't investing their money in us because they love us. But Puerto Rican investors are afraid to risk their money in their own country. Someday that will change.

At times it looks as if man's ignorance will win out, but it never really does. Goodness always marches ahead. Someday we Puerto Ricans will be strong and proud. I may not live to see it, but someday my children will be as good as any American.

GLOSSARY
of Spanish Terms

baberos—bib

barrio—village subdivision with its own chapel and patron saint

cabecera—seat of the *municipio,* or county

caciques—an elite who controlled the local government; local political bosses

cerros—refers to the spectacular buttelike rock outcroppings which surround the village; also, the steep slopes covered with scrub forest

colonias—subdivision of the city consisting of many neighborhoods

compadrazgo—A fictive type of kinship in which kinlike ties are established between a child (the *ahijado* or *ahijada*) and a man and woman (the *padrino* or *madrina*) who are godparents. In turn, a special respect relationship—*compadrazgo*—is established between the true parents and the godparents. This relationship involves a variety of social and economic aspects. The more *compadres* one has, the wider the circle of persons who can be counted on for favors. The godparenthood system was introduced to Latin America by the Spaniards as an integral part of Catholicism.

compadre—godfather of one's child or the father of one's godchild

comuneros—men who work the communally owned lands of the *municipio,* or county

cuartillo—local measure for corn, equal to two liters

cuatequitl—traditional form of collective labor

curanderos—native healers

chaleco—waistcoat or vest

chinchol—trade name for a spray which kills bugs, applied to a potent alcoholic drink

chirimiteros—flute players

diarrhea—"cold" disease

ejidatarios—those who hold *ejido* parcels

ejido—Land granted by the nation to the municipality or village and distributed by the elected *ejido* authorities to some peasants. The *ejido* lands are worked by the individual families and are passed on by inheritance. They cannot be sold.

epazote—native Aztec herb; one of the most commonly used herbs in Mexican cooking

evangelio—gospel

hectárea—2.471 acres

huehuechiques—men who perform traditional ritual in Nahuatl at some of the fiestas

huaraches—Mexican leather sandals

jacales—the poorest houses, which are made of corn stalks or Mexican bamboo, with thatched roof and earthen floor

ladino—Spanish-speaking, racially mixed persons

los aires—bad air; air or winds that bring illness because of evil spirits

macetero—container for flower pots

mecapal—Aztec tumpline worn around the forehead to support a load carried on the back

mestizo—person of mixed Indian and Spanish ancestry

milpa—corn field

miscotón—sweater used to establish a ritual relationship of god parenthood

mole—an Aztec sauce made with chili, chocolate and tomatoes; commonly served with turkey or chicken

muina—illness of anger

municipio—municipality consisting of a large central village and surrounding hamlets, very much like a county

novenas—acts of devotion, such as prayers, masses, etc., carried out by a person over a period of nine consecutive days

petate—a straw mat for sleeping

playera—lightweight jacket

portavianda—*fiambrera* basket, box or aluminum container for carrying food

pulque—a mildly alcoholic drink made from the fermented juice of the maguey plant, a variety of the century plant

rebozo—the traditional Mexican shawl, with a variety of uses, e.g., to keep warm, to cover the head in church, to hold a baby

sacamisa—the first mass attended by a mother forty days after the birth of her child

santo—saint

temazcal—Aztec sweat-bath hut

texcal—a strip of land, approximately two kilometers wide, on the western limits of the *municipio,* covered with a relatively recent volcanic flow which supports a thorny scrub forest with a pre-dominating flora of copal gum, mimosalike legumes, a tree "sweet potato" and silk-cotton trees

tlacolol—hoe culture

trasteros—a set of shelves for dishes

tú—the informal Spanish form of the pronoun "you," used when addressing people to whom one is close, or who are younger or in an inferior position

V., V*d.* (*usted*)—in Spanish the formal form of the pronoun "you." It indicates the social standing of one individual in relation to another and is also used to show respect for position or age.

vecindad—a type of urban settlement consisting of a series of one- or two-story dwellings or apartments arranged around an inner courtyard

Zapatistas—followers of Zapata, the folk hero and leader during the Mexican Revolution

GLOSSARY
of Hindi Terms

ākta—ceremony at mass cattle burial during epidemic
begār—obligatory labor without pay
Bhangi—the sweeper caste
bīgha—about one-fifth of an acre
Brahman—the highest of the four main caste divisions among the
   Hindus
capātī—a thin wheat cake of unleavened flour
gona—consummation of marriage
gotras—nonlocalized patrilineal clans
gur—a crude brown sugar which includes molasses
Harijan—low-caste untouchable
Jat—the largest cultivating caste in northwestern India
Kamīn—worker; menial servant
Kumhar—the potter caste
lambardārī—the office of headman of a *panā* responsible for government revenue
maund—a unit of weight containing 40 *sīrs*
neg job—presents made on a festive occasion, as in the conclusion of
   marriage arrangements
ori—sowing season
panā—subdivision of a village
panchayat—a body of arbitrators—usually five—assembled for the
   purpose of settling petty disputes among people; generally caste
   or village council

patvāri—village accountant, land recorder

rabri—thickened milk; a preparation made of churned curds and flour

sīr—a weight of about two pounds

thollā—subdivision of a *panā*

tonga—two-wheeled passenger cart

Publications of
Oscar Lewis

Books:

* *The Effects of White Contact Upon Blackfoot Culture. Monographs of the American Ethnological Society, New York.* J. J. Augustin, New York. Vol. 5, 1942, 73 pp. Reprinted by University of Washington Press, 1966.

On the Edge of the Black Waxy: A Cultural Survey of Bell County, Texas. Washington University Studies—New Series, Social and Philosophical Sciences, No. 7. St. Louis, 1948, 110 pp.

Life in a Mexican Village: Tepoztlán Restudied. Urbana, Ill.: University of Illinois Press, 1951, 500 pp.

Village Life in Northern India. Urbana, Ill.: University of Illinois Press, 1958, 384 pp.

Five Families: Mexican Case Studies in the Culture of Poverty. New York: Basic Books, 1959, 351 pp.

The Children of Sánchez. New York: Random House, 1961, 499 pp.

Tepoztlán, Village in Mexico. New York: Holt, Rinehart and Winston, 1960, 104 pp.

Pedro Martínez, A Mexican Peasant and his Family. New York: Random House, 1964, 500 pp.

La Vida: A Puerto Rican Family in the Culture of Poverty—San Juan and New York. New York: Random House, 1966, 669 pp.

A Study of Slum Culture: Backgrounds for La Vida. New York: Random House, 1968, 240 pp.

A Death in the Sánchez Family. New York: Random House, 1969, 119 pp.

* Indicates articles that appear in this volume.

Articles:

* "Manly-Hearted Women among the North Piegan," *American Anthropologist*, n.s. April-June, 1941, Vol. 3, No. 2, pp. 173–87.

"Social and Economic Changes in a Mexican Village: Tepoztlán 1926–44," *América Indígena*, Vol. 4, No. 4, October, 1944, pp. 281–314.

Oscar Lewis and Ernest E. Maes. "Base para una Nueva Definición Práctica del Indio," *América Indígena*, Vol. 5, No. 2, April, 1945, pp. 107–18.

* "Wealth Differences in a Mexican Village," *Scientific Monthly*, Vol. 65, No. 2 (August, 1947), pp. 127–32.

* "Bumper Crops in the Desert," *Harper's Magazine*, Vol. 193, No. 1159, December, 1946, pp. 525–28.

* "Rural Cross Section," *Scientific Monthly*, Vol. 66, No. 4 (April, 1948).

* "Plow Culture and Hoe Culture: A Study in Contrasts," *Rural Sociology*, Vol. 14, No. 2 (June, 1949), pp. 116–27.

"Aspects of Land Tenure and Economics in a Mexican Village," *Middle American Research Records*, Vol. 1, No. 13 (May, 1949), pp. 195–209.

"Husbands and Wives in a Mexican Village: A Study in Role Conflict," *American Anthropologist*, Vol. 51, No. 4 (October-December, 1949), pp. 602–10.

* "An Anthropological Approach to Family Studies," *American Journal of Sociology*, Vol. 55, No. 5 (March, 1950), pp. 468–75.

"The Effects of Technological Progress on Mental Health among Rural Populations," *América Indígena*, October, 1952, pp. 299–307.

"Dynamics of Culture Patterns—Summary," in J. E. Hulett, Jr., and Ross Stagner (eds.), *Problems in Social Psychology: An Interdisciplinary Inquiry*, Urbana, Ill.: University of Illinois Press, pp. 222–27.

* "Urbanization without Breakdown: A Case Study," *Scientific Monthly*, Vol. 75, No. 1 (1952), pp. 31–41.

* "Controls and Experiments in Anthropological Field Work," in *Anthropology Today* (prepared under the chairmanship of A. L. Kroeber), The University of Chicago Press, Chicago, 1953, pp. 452–75.

* "Tepoztlán Restudied: A Critique of the Folk-Urban Conceptualization of Social Change," *Rural Sociology*, Vol. 18, No. 2 (June, 1953), pp. 121–36.

"Concepts of Health and Disease in a North Indian Village," Program Evaluation Organization, *National Planning Commission*. New Delhi: Government of India, 1953, 41 pp.

"A Preliminary Guide to the Use of Village Patwari Records," Program Evaluation Organization, *National Planning Commission*. New Delhi: Government of India, 1953, 38 pp.

"Group Dynamics in an Indian Village: A Study of Factions," in *The Economic Weekly of Bombay*, Vol. 6 (1954), pp. 423–25, 445–51, 477–82, 501–06.

* "Group Dynamics in a North Indian Village," *Planning Commission*. New Delhi: Government of India, 1954, 48 pp.

Discussion of Otto Klineberg's "How Far Can the Society and Culture of a People Be Gauged Through Their Personality Characteristics?" pp. 35–39, in Francis L. K. Hsu (ed.), *Aspects of Culture and Personality*. New York: Abelard-Schuman, 1954.

Discussion of G. K. Yocorzynski's "The Nature of Man," pp. 183–84, in Francis L. K. Hsu (ed.), *Aspects of Culture and Personality*. New York: Abelard-Schuman, 1954.

* "Peasant Culture in India and Mexico: A Comparative Analysis," in McKim Marriott (ed.), *Village India*. Chicago: University of Chicago Press, 1955, pp. 145–70.

"La Cultura Campesina en la India y en México," *Ciencias Sociales*, Union Panamericana, Washington, D.C., Vol. 6, No. 34 (August, 1955), pp. 194–218.

* "Comparisons in Cultural Anthropology," in *Yearbook of Anthropology—1955*, William L. Thomas, Jr. (ed.) with the assistance of Jean S. Stewart, Wenner-Gren Foundation for Anthropological Research, Inc. New York, 1955, pp. 259–92.

* "Medicine and Politics in a Mexican Village," in Benjamin D. Paul (ed.), *Health, Culture, and Community*, Russell Sage Foundation, New York, 1955, pp. 403–35.

Oscar and Ruth Lewis. "A Day in the Life of a Mexican Peasant Family," *Marriage and Family Living*, Meyer Nimkoff (ed.), Vol. 18, No. 1 (February, 1956), pp. 3–13.

"The Festival Cycle in a North Indian Jat Village," *Proceedings of the American Philosophical Society*, Vol. 100, No. 3 (June, 1956), pp. 168–96.

* Oscar Lewis and Victor Barnouw. "Caste and the *Jajmani* System in a North Indian Village," *Scientific Monthly*, Vol. 83, No. 2 (August, 1956), pp. 66–81.

"Urbanización sin Desorganización: Las Familias Tepoztecas en la Ciudad de México," *América Indígena*, Vol. 17, No. 3 (1957), pp. 231–46.

"México desde 1940," *Investigación Económica*, Universidad Nacional Autónoma de México, D.F., Vol. 18, No. 70 (1958), pp. 185–256.

* "The Culture of the *Vecindad* in Mexico City: Two Case Studies," *Actas de XXXIII Congreso Internacional de Americanistas*, San José (July 20–27, 1958), pp. 387–402.

"La Cultura de Vecindad en la Ciudad de México," *Ciencias Políticas y Sociales*, México, D.F., Vol. 5, No. 17 (July-September, 1959), pp. 349–64.

* "Family Dynamics in a Mexican Village," *Marriage and Family Living*, Vol. 21, No. 3 (August, 1959), pp. 218–26.

"The Culture of Poverty in Mexico City: Two Case Studies," *The Economic Weekly of Bombay*, Special Number, June, 1960, pp. 965–72.

"Dinámica Familiar Comparada en un pueblo Mexicano," *Tlatoani*, Escuela Nacional de Antropología e Historia, Agosto, 1960, pp. 7–14.

"Some of My Best Friends Are Peasants," *Human Organization*, Vol. 19, No. 4 (Winter, 1960–61), pp. 179–80.

"Mexico Since Cárdenas," in *Social Change in Latin America Today*. New York: Vintage Books, 1961, pp. 285–345.

"Manuel in the Thieves' Market," *Harper's Magazine*, June, 1961, pp. 66–76.

"Preliminary Guide for the Study of Village Culture in Northern India," in *Journal of Pakistan Academy for Village Development*; Special Issue, *Rural Social Research*, July, 1962, pp. 26–47.

* "Visit to a Holy Shrine," in *Holiday Magazine*, Vol. 32, No. 4 (October, 1962), pp. 52–62.

"The Culture of Poverty," in John J. TePaske and Sydney Nettleton Fisher (eds.), *Explosive Forces in Latin America* (Publications of the Graduate Institute for World Affairs of the Ohio State University, No. 2). Columbus, Ohio: Ohio State University Press, 1964, pp. 149–73.

"The Tender Violence of Pedro Martínez," *Harper's Magazine*, Vol. 228, No. 1365, February, 1964, pp. 54–60.

"After the Revolution," *The Reporter*, April 19, 1964, pp. 34–36.

* "In New York You Get Swallowed by a Horse," *Commentary*, Vol. 38, No. 5, November, 1964, pp. 69–73.

"Mother and Son in a Puerto Rican Slum," *Harper's Magazine*, Vol. 231, No. 1387, December, 1965, pp. 71–84.

* "Further Observations on the Folk-Urban Continuum and Urbanization with Special Reference to Mexico City," in Philip M. Hauser and Leo F. Schnore (eds.), *The Study of Urbanization*. New York: John Wiley, 1965, pp. 491–503.

"Portrait of Gabriel: A Puerto Rican Family in San Juan and New York," *Harper's Magazine*, Vol. 232, No. 1388, January, 1966, pp. 54–59.

* "A Thursday with Manuel," *New Left Review* (London), July-August, 1966, pp. 3–21.

"I'm Proud to be Poor," *Commentary*, Vol. 42, No. 2, August, 1966, pp. 44–47.

* "The Culture of Poverty," *Scientific American*, Vol. 215, No. 4 (October, 1966), pp. 19–25.

"Even the Saints Cry," *Trans-action*, Vol. 4, No. 1 (November, 1966), pp. 18–23.

"La Cultura de la pobreza," *Mundo Nuevo*, No. 5 (November, 1966), pp. 36–42.

A *Redbook* Dialogue: Robert Kennedy and Oscar Lewis, September, 1967, pp. 73–106.

Current Anthropology, CA Book Review of *The Children of Sánchez, Pedro Martínez* and *La Vida*, Vol. 8, No. 5 (December, 1967), pp. 480–500.

"Ghetto Education" (A Special Supplement. Dialogue: Robert F. Kennedy, Kenneth B. Clark, Oscar Lewis, Neil V. Sullivan, Robert M. Hutchins, Harry S. Ashmore), *Center Magazine*, Vol. I, No. 7 (November, 1968), pp. 46–60.

"Love in El Barrio," *New York Magazine*, December 9, 1968, pp. 33–46.

"The Culture of Poverty," *Man in Adaptation: The Cultural Present*, essays, Yehudi A. Cohen (ed.). Chicago: Aldine Press, 1968, pp. 406–14.

"A Puerto Rican Boy," *Culture Change, Mental Health, and Poverty*, essays, Joseph C. Finney (ed.). Lexington: University of Kentucky Press, 1939, pp. 149–72.

"La Esmeralda," *The Critic*, Vol. 27, No. 5, April-May, 1969, pp. 12–23.

Book Review of *Culture and Poverty*, Charles A. Valentine, *Caribbean Review*, Vol. 1, No. 1, Spring, 1969, pp. 5–6.

"CA Book Review of *Culture and Poverty: Critique and Counter Proposals*, by Charles A. Valentine," *Current Anthropology*, April-June, 1969, Vol. 10, No. 2–3, pp. 189–92.

"One Can Suffer Anywhere," *Harper's Magazine*, Vol. 238, No. 1428, May, 1969, pp. 54–60.

"Portrait," from *The Children of Sánchez*, in *Breakthrough* by Robert E. Yarber. Menlo Park, California: Cummings Publishing Co., 1969, pp. 100–04.

"The Death of Dolores," *Trans-action*, Vol. 6, No. 7, May, 1969, pp. 10–19.

"A Death in the Sánchez Family," A Special Supplement: *The New York Review of Books*, Part I in Vol. 13, No. 4, September 11, 1969, pp. 31–37; Part II in Vol. 13, No. 5, September 25, 1969, pp. 34–38.

* "The Possessions of the Poor," *Scientific American*, Vol. 221, No. 4, October, 1969, pp. 114–24.

Index

ABOUT THE AUTHOR

OSCAR LEWIS was born in New York City in 1914 and grew up on a small farm in upstate New York. He received his Ph.D. in anthropology from Columbia University in 1940; he taught at Brooklyn College and Washington University and has been a professor of anthropology at the University of Illinois since 1948. He has also been the recipient of various distinguished fellowships and grants.

From his first visit to Mexico in 1943, Mexican peasants and city dwellers have been among his major interests. His book *Life in a Mexican Village: Tepoztlán Restudied* initiated a whole new trend in independent restudies in anthropology. In addition to *A Death in the Sánchez Family,* his other studies of Mexican life include *Five Families, Pedro Martínez* and *The Children of Sánchez.* He is also the author of *La Vida: A Puerto Rican Family in the Culture of Poverty—San Juan and New York,* which received the National Book Award. A further study of Puerto Rican culture, *Six Women,* will be published in 1971.

Professor Lewis is now in Cuba on a research program to study family and community life.